SOCIAL WELFARE: VALUES, MEANS, and ENDS

Donald S. Howard

UNIVERSITY OF CALIFORNIA, LOS ANGELES

SOCIAL WELFARE: VALUES, MEANS, and ENDS

RANDOM
HOUSE
New York

To
B. N. H.
without whose continuing support
and invaluable help
this book would not have been finished

Acknowledgments

Writers quite commonly admit their indebtedness to named and nameless others who, directly or indirectly, have influenced their lives and thinking. But, when one writes specifically about values, human interdependence, and well-being, he becomes particularly aware of the degree to which he and his work are social products. I therefore gladly acknowledge, to the "wonderful world," filled with a lot of wonderful people, my debt for the enriching life experiences out of which this book has grown. To my parents, I am grateful for a childhood home in which values were of central importance, not only in parental teaching, but in living. To our present family I am deeply indebted for the continuing opportunities to enjoy "the good" in family living and in other dimensions of life. However, I regret that I succumbed for so long to "writers' neglect," a malady commonly admitted by authors, and hope that this book is, for them, at least some compensation for other values temporarily foregone.

The University of California, Los Angeles, has provided an almost perfect setting for thought and writing without which the book would not have been possible. Like any teacher, I am under heavy obligation to students, who usually are the first to have inflicted upon them the "new ideas" of their instructors, but whose responsiveness and questions over the years contribute greatly to the refinement of those ideas.

The superlative service of the University's Stenographic Bureau and, more particularly, the always efficient and gracious help of Miss Ellen G. Cole, Mrs. Beatrice Gould, and Mrs. Ivy Tunick has been invaluable. Similarly excellent service has been rendered by several secretaries, but especially by Mrs. Betty Gunderson, who prepared the earliest drafts, and Miss Carol Hansen, who worked on the later ones. Also to be acknowledged are the services of several teaching and research assistants who have rendered yeoman service in libraries and files. Most noteworthy in this respect is Mr. Johnny A. Watkins, a genial, persistent, and efficient resource finder.

Colleagues, of course, always contribute to the development and refinement of one's thinking, and mine are no exception. Special thanks are due, though, to Professors Maurice F. Connery and Jerome Cohen, who have reviewed some of the chapters and have contributed to their improvement. Other friends who have reviewed manuscript material include Professor Abraham Kaplan of the University of Michigan and Dr. Ewan Clague, former Commissioner of Labor Statistics. To all I am deeply grateful and hope that my ability to benefit from their wisdom is sufficient to warrant their painstaking work and generous assistance. Former colleagues who have been helpful in idea-sharpening include Professors Karl de Schweinitz, Mary E. Duren, and Martin B. Loeb.

To Dean Charles I. Schottland, his colleagues, and students of the Florence Heller Graduate School for Advanced Studies in Social Welfare, Brandeis University, are also due some special thanks for the opportunity, while on leave from my own university, to sense their interest in, and criticism of, many ideas now presented—in improved form, hopefully—in this book.

To Random House, Inc., and, more specifically, Mr. Theodore Caris, Senior Editor of the College Department, I am particularly grateful for the promise seen in my handiwork and for the exceedingly helpful comments of unnamed "readers." Invaluable and deeply appreciated help has been given by Mrs. Leonore C. Hauck, Managing Editor of the College Department, and by Mr. Henry Bretzfield, copy editor. Their perceptive insight, sympathetic understanding, sense of proportion, and eagle-eyed but gentle correction leave me deeply in their debt and, for readers, have greatly shortened, straightened, and smoothed the path that lies ahead.

Many more observers and writers than those quoted in the text have contributed to the thought developed there. While I am grateful to them all, I am especially thankful to the writers quoted—and to their publishers—for the arrangements under which their publications could be quoted here.

Los Angeles, California   DONALD S. HOWARD
January 1968

Contents

SOCIAL WELFARE: VALUES, MEANS, and ENDS

Introduction

"**W**elfare" and "social welfare" are highly controversial subjects. Related concepts such as "welfare state," relief, philanthropy, and charity also evoke widely differing sentiments and reactions. Charity, for example, is extolled in religious circles as a major virtue. Yet in the United States, Great Britain, and other countries one often encounters among intended beneficiaries the reaction "I want none of your charity."

Similarly, in some quarters "the welfare state" is defended as staunchly as, in other quarters, it is bitterly condemned. Countries like India and Burma boast that their constitutions declare them to be welfare states. Other countries such as Sweden and Great Britain —which, by most prevailing definitions, would be regarded as welfare states—are tending, however, to play down this designation. Welfare leaders in Sweden have explained that the welfare state label had seemed to alienate opinion in countries such as the United States. Consequently, they are stressing, rather, the extent to which Swedish welfare programs are "help for self-help." In Britain one hears increasingly of the "Welfare Society," a term intended to convey the idea that not only the state but all elements of a society should be expected to serve the nation's well-being.

Among recent moves to break identification with the word "welfare" are those made in 1967 in New York when state and local departments of welfare, or social welfare, changed their names to departments of social service. In Los Angeles, at about the same time, the Bureau of Public Assistance, which had been part of the anachronistically named County Department of Charities, was reconstituted as an independent Department of Public Social Services. At the federal level, the Welfare Administration within the Department of Health, Education, and Welfare was abolished and superseded by a new Rehabilitation Services Administration.

This abandonment of terminology that was believed to have seriously inimical connotations is reminiscent of moves made a generation ago to rechristen old almshouses and "county homes," calling them instead "welfare homes." Although a rose by any other name may smell as sweet, it takes some doing to transform another flower —though labeling it a rose—into one. Yet, changes in labels can help to hasten the changes they symbolize.

Not long ago in the United States a committee made up of professional and lay leaders in the social welfare field was planning the program for a state conference. A layman, prefacing his suggestion with the remark that it was possible that he knew only "all the wrong people," proposed that the theme of the conference be "Is Social Welfare Un-American?" It was contended that it is the "American Way" to reward most liberally those who achieve most, whereas welfare services seem to do just the opposite. Social workers on the committee, convinced of the fundamental importance of social welfare to dignity, freedom, and democracy (which they thought included the concept "to each according to his need"), were utterly nonplused by their associate's suggestion and quickly rejected it. To them, social welfare seemed the very essence of democracy and one of its finest fruits; to the layman and the circles he represented it seemed to be un-American.

Social workers and other welfare personnel are not alone in their appraisal of welfare services; this is suggested by what Columbia University philosopher Charles Frankel told a Canadian audience when he was with the U. S. Department of State. "Welfare is an appealing ideal, a much celebrated one these days," he said. "It represents, indeed, the special contribution of our era to the history of human social ideals." [1]

Nevertheless, when Senator Abraham Ribicoff was serving in the Cabinet of President John F. Kennedy, he said about the governmental sector of the welfare field, "Public welfare probably never will be popular. As a governor, a congressman, and now as Secretary of the Department of Health, Education, and Welfare, I know the frustration and resentment with which legislators and administrators meet their welfare bills." [2]

Similarly conflicting viewpoints appear in religious injunctions over the ages "to do good," and in the present-day contempt for the "do-gooder."

Social workers and social work students are often perplexed at the ambivalence with which they are viewed. "Wanting to help people" seems to them to be the very quintessence of idealism. Yet they frequently encounter the sort of reaction illustrated by the wife of a social work student when she asked, "When we wives get together and some gals say that their husbands are studying law or medicine, why do the others 'oh' and 'ah'? But when I say that my husband is studying social work, why is there always that *dull thud?*"

The low prestige of personnel in the welfare field has been frequently noted; but there is no loss of prestige in visits to orphanages, hospitals, youth camps, and various welfare agencies by royalty, heads of governments, and other prestigious personages. In fact, they feel they are enhancing their public image by appearing to be genuinely concerned about people. Charity balls also seem to have a magic power: to transform otherwise unconscionable ostentation and social waste into something that is socially defensible, however small the proportion of the total proceeds that ever gets to a charity.

When a one-time Minister of War in Britain was driven out of the government in disgrace in the 1960's because of a sex scandal, he began a new life as a volunteer at Toynbee Hall. The widespread publicity accorded even in the United States to this service in "the mother of the social settlements" treated it as a sort of modern penance. A prominent member of a nationally eminent family in this country was arrested for speeding and then, in lieu of being fined or sent to jail, was "sentenced" to render a stipulated number of hours of service to mentally retarded children.

This ambivalence explains in part why social welfare work is a hazardous occupation. What social workers and other welfare personnel experience in their more discouraging moments recalls the fate of Prometheus, who suffered many afflictions because he gave men fire, which had previously been available only to the gods. In their more optimistic moments, however, social workers hope that their role will be seen in the light of the meaning of Prometheus' name: "forethought." Psychologist Gordon W. Allport once observed:

It is a defect in social service . . . that it lacks self-confidence. . . . In a society where competitiveness and aggressiveness reap conspicuous rewards . . . the ideals of cooperation, to which social service is committed, represent a minority point of view.[3]

Others have commented upon this matter. For example, when Abraham Ribicoff was Secretary of the U. S. Department of Health, Education, and Welfare, and when federal aid to education and health insurance were particularly live issues, he complained, "The friends of these measures . . . avoid professing openly and proudly that they are in favor of promoting the general welfare, as if this were somehow an unwise or shameful thing to do." [4]

In the introduction to his book *Language in Thought and Action*, S. I. Hayakawa discusses the different meanings that different people associate with certain words.[5] To persons familiar with the welfare field it is hardly surprising that to illustrate differences in word meanings and in the feelings they evoke he selected examples such as "relief" and "unemployment insurance."

Controversy characterizes most aspects of social life: Are the advantages of minimum wage and other labor laws more than offset by their disadvantages? Are new "gains" for Negroes or other disadvantaged groups more than offset by the frequent "backlashes" against them? Does a nation's foreign policy promote its security or jeopardize it? However, because of the penchant of social workers and others intimately involved in the social welfare field for consensus and mutual agreement, controversy is probably more unpalatable to them than it is to those in other fields who engage in public discussion.

Nor is controversy about welfare a recent phenomenon. Indeed, the very emphasis placed by religious leaders throughout history upon man's responsibility to his needy fellow-man suggests a certain pervasive reluctance, on the part of men generally, to respond to other men's needs. Even the controversies in the United States in the 1960's about the so-called welfare messes (such as those in Louisiana, Mississippi, New York, and California) and the major differences over foreign aid are highly reminiscent of similar public debates in other decades, even in other centuries and in other countries. The "welfare messes" of the 1960's have much in common with those of the 1940's, which were described in a professional journal at the time in a series entitled "Public Assistance Returns to Page One." [6] But when "public assistance" is off page one, it does not stay off long. The mid- and late 1960's were certainly no exception to this generalization. In hearings held over the country by a senate committee investigating the War on Poverty, highly placed and responsible observers were calling the nation's welfare program bankrupt and archaic. And an almost unprecedented spate of blistering books appeared around and after the mid-1960's (among them, Joseph P. Lyford's *The Airtight Cage*, Edgar May's *The Wasted Americans*, Joseph P. Ritz's *The Despised Poor*, Charles E. Silberman's *Crisis in Black and White*, Gilbert Y. Steiner's *Social Insecurity: The Politics of Welfare*, William Stringfellow's *Dissenter in a Great Society*, and *The Law of the Poor* by Jacobus ten

Broek and others). These books excoriated both governmental and voluntary welfare services. However, unlike earlier critics who attacked welfare services as "coddling" and "weakening" beneficiaries and who demanded retrenchment of the offending services, the new critics were demanding different and, by their standards, more humane programs.

Welfare issues have long been a page-one subject, not only in the United States but in other countries as well. In this connection, our imagination can produce headlines about long-past historical events.

For example:

" 'Great Debate' Begun: Is Man His Brother's Keeper?" (Bible Lands, n.d.)

"Amos Attacks Privileged Classes for 'Oppressing the Poor' " (Bible Lands, *circa* 750 B.C.).

"Subsidies for Poor Instituted to Thwart Social Reform: Plato and Aristotle Disagree on Issues—Plato Advocates 'Prevention'; Aristotle, Higher Relief Standards" (Athens, fourth century B.C.).

"Relief Offices and Hospitals Ease Rigors of Chandragupta Reign" (India, *circa* 300 B.C.).

"Caesar Gives Free Land to Veterans Threatening His Regime" (Rome, *circa* 35 B.C.).

"Increase of Relief-Giving by Monasteries Deemed Threat to Parish Relief" (Europe, *circa* A.D. 600).

"Begging Prohibited to Relieve Labor Shortage Resulting from Black Plague: Employers Chalk Up Notable Victory" (England, 1394).

"New War on Poverty—Begging Prohibited Despite Charges of Undermining Christian Virtue of Charity" (Ypres, *circa* 1525).

"Henry VIII Takes Over Monasteries, Secularizes Relief-Giving: Church-State Issue Sharpened" (England, 1531).

"Revolutionaries Transfer Relief Responsibilities from Religious Bodies to Cities" (Paris, 1789).

But these are only scattered events and seem hardly even to anticipate the nineteenth century, when headlines became bigger— and more frequent.

Past controversies and the pendulumlike swings in welfare policy—from punishment to "treatment" of poor persons; from township to county responsibility then back to township jurisdiction; from county to state and back again to county responsibility; from voluntary to governmental responsibilities only to return to more emphasis upon voluntary action; from state to national responsibility and then back to state—all these suggest that the problems were never sufficiently analyzed to permit "real" solutions. However, since "new occasions teach new duties," it is also possible that even a perfect answer on one day might not be even a good answer on the next. Thus, controversy is heightened—and continues.

In passing we might observe that defenders and critics of welfare policies seldom defend or attack them *in toto*. Even the most rigorous attackers are likely to specify that "of course" no one should be allowed to starve, or that "naturally" they are in favor of "appropriate" help to the "genuinely" needy, the "really worthy," and the like. Similarly, critics may affirm (as did Senator Barry M. Goldwater, in his unsuccessful bid for the Presidency of the United States in 1964) that "real needs" should of course be met, but by private agencies, not government.

Ambivalence about social welfare shows itself in many ways. For example, in the United States at about the time of the 1964 presidential election the Harris Survey asked a sample of voters about their attitudes toward the Welfare State. Of those canvassed, 74 percent (but only 62 percent of the Republicans) thought that "Government must be used to protect the weak"; 68 percent (54 percent of the Republicans) believed that "Government must see that no one is without food, clothing or shelter." However, 64 percent (but 82 percent of the Republicans) thought that "Welfare and relief make people lazy." [7] Whether this 64 percent thought that inherited wealth, generous parents, quickly gained riches, too-low pay, inability to find work, or other factors also might "make people lazy" was not reported.

About two months after this survey was made, a Gallup Poll asked a cross-section sample including rich and poor persons, "What are your over-all feelings about welfare and relief programs?" Of the total, 43 percent responded "Favorable," while 45 percent reported "Mixed feelings." However, only 6 percent favored doing away with these programs. [8]

But even a single individual may, at different times, show this same ambivalence. For instance, Arthur Foster, a World Council of Churches official engaged in work with refugees, once declared, "Anyone has to be mad to get into this business . . . and loony to want to get out of it once he's in it." [9] Even those who, in principle, ardently favor "help for the needy" may react sharply when their tax bills arrive or United Fund pledges fall due. As generous as they are at some times, men are not generous at all times.

Social welfare not only is a controversial subject but also is so widely pervasive that almost no member of any modern community can avoid some involvement with it. Taxpayers support governmental welfare services; consumers pay prices that have been inflated to cover costs of welfare services to employees, corporation gifts to philanthropy, and taxes paid by business or industry for governmental welfare services at home and abroad; millions contribute voluntarily (and some under considerable duress) to United Funds and Community Chests; national, state, and local legislators shape governmental welfare policy; lay and professional persons, as members of advisory boards and consultants, guide the destinies of governmental and voluntary agencies; administrative and professional personnel in both governmental and voluntary agencies are responsible for delivering welfare services to intended beneficiaries. Finally, there are those who are supposed to be beneficiaries of welfare services. All of these groups, in current sociological parlance, are members of "the social welfare system." Because of the broad scope of this system, this book is addressed to a wide audience.

The primary focus of our analysis will be "value." What, in selected welfare services, is considered "good"? What is to be valued, and by whom, and by what criteria? What is considered "bad," or to be disvalued, and by what standards? Are there differences in values that are attached to different aspects of welfare services by, say, taxpayers, legislators, social workers, or the intended beneficiaries? Why, for example, is charity, which church leaders regard as a virtue, so often disvalued by intended beneficiaries who "want none of it" and by welfare agencies, which publicly insist that they are not "charities"? In short, what aspects of social welfare services seem good (or bad) to whom and under what circumstances? What do contributors get for their money? Are their contributions "something for nothing," as is commonly charged? Is this money—as severer critics often allege—"money down a rathole"?

In tackling questions like these, we will be assuming with Clyde Kluckhohn that "A value is a conception, explicit or implicit, distinctive of an individual or characteristic of a group, of the desirable which influences the selection from available modes, means and ends of action." [10] In this analysis we shall be concerned with values—and with their opposites, disvalues (which Ralph Linton speaks of as "negative values")—that are inherent both in some of the ends served by welfare programs (food, clothing, housing, and other "goods" provided) and in various means (self-help, intrafamilial cooperation, mutual aid, and outside "help") by which the ends are gained.

Thus, the term "value" will not refer to what Professor Abraham Kaplan calls "the standards or principles of worth, what makes something have value." Rather, we will be concerned with the "worthy things themselves," which Kaplan refers to as "valuables." [11] In so doing we are somewhat less judicious, perhaps, than Robert A. Dahl and Charles Lindblom in their *Politics, Economics and Welfare.* To avoid "philosophical battle" (explanation, defense, justification, and so on), they often eschewed the term "values" and spoke instead of "goals." [12]

In our own attempt to avoid "philosophical battle" no attempt will be made to "prove" that certain specific values or goals are superior to others. This is the task of philosophers and moralists. We shall attempt, rather, to demonstrate in human terms the outcomes of pursuing specific values in particular ways and to point up some effects that may not always be apparent and therefore not taken into account by those who pursue these values. This approach will be useful, we hope, to those who share Professor Frankel's view that values may serve "as guides in the formation of hypotheses for the solution of definite problems. And in relation to their capacity to perform this function, they can be accepted, dismissed, corrected, modified or expanded." [13] We hope also that the discussion may be of use to those who judge values (as Professor Kaplan puts it) "by the fruit, not the seed." [14]

From their vantage point in the School of Engineering, colleagues of mine at the University of California once wrote, "The gathering of data on an engineering system is the slow process of replacing prejudices with facts." [15] Whether any facts about social welfare systems presented here will replace any prejudices I do not know. I hope, though, that some of these facts will be of use in evaluating social welfare services. For I believe that, as Alfred Jules Ayer wrote many years ago, in "disputes about questions of value . . . the dispute is not really about a question of value, but about a question of fact." Accordingly, I concur with him further that agreement on values can be won only if there is agreement "about the nature of the empirical facts." [16] In a similar spirit, Professor Ralph Barton Perry, while at Harvard, once wrote, "Moral knowledge possesses the same general characteristics, and is subject to the same discipline, as all knowledge. It is true or false according to the evidence." [17]

If, therefore, this book contributes to knowledge and a broader consensus about values related to social welfare services, it will have served a major purpose. However, the present discussion is not intended as a comprehensive analysis of the relevance of values to welfare services. That would require several volumes. Here, the focus is rather upon a way of looking at welfare services, upon a few selected ends and means, and upon how these appear to be furthered or thwarted by particular welfare policies and services.

To take values as the center of attention is not today as novel as when this enterprise was first begun. For example, Robert C. Weaver, first Secretary of the U. S. Department of Housing and Urban Development, used this approach in *The Urban Complex: Human Values in Urban Life*. Even the Federal Bureau of Public Roads entitled its 1966 report *Highways and Human Values*. An earlier and widely influential book employing values as tools of analysis was Professor Howard S. Becker's *Through Values to Social Interpretation*.

That values should increasingly be taken as the lenses through which social phenomena are scrutinized is not surprising because they are of pivotal importance not only to social institutions and social systems but also to individuals, groups, and communities—and, in fact, to the world.

As is well known, Erik Erikson has strongly emphasized the importance of one's sense of identity. In this, values play a part because, as he wrote, identity is a "sense of coincidence between inner resources, traditional values, and opportunities for action." [18] Or, as Saul Ginsburg puts it in an article, "Values and the Psychiatrist": "Values represent our orientation to society and our attitude toward human welfare. In the last analysis adjustment is the name for the process of living up to a set of values." [19]

So central are values to social organization that Kingsley Davis has defined a community or a society as a group "adhering to the same ultimate set of values and pursuing the same set of common ends." [20] In terms of the world, according to Kenneth S. Carlston, "If there is to be a more stable world organization, one essential requirement will be to develop into a social system characterized by a conscious coordination of action to attain valued goals." [21]

Thus, values may be thought of as at least one ingredient in the cement that holds together the world, societies, and even individuals. Conversely, too great ambivalence with respect to values, or pursuit of antithetical values or goals, may destroy an individual, a social institution—or the world. In this connection, one text on social problems, *Problems of American Society*, by John F. Cuber and Robert A. Harper, has as its subtitle, *Values in Conflict*. The connection between values and problems was picked up by the consultant who was invited by the Secretary General of the United Nations to assist in the reappraisal of that body's social services. He observed that the label "social problem" might be applied to "human situations to which a community attaches a negative valuation, and to which it tends to react by deliberate measures of some sort." [22]

Values (or, if one prefers, goals) will be discussed in relative terms, because what may be regarded as "good" by or for one person or group may not be so regarded by or for others. Or, what may be considered of value for any one individual or group under certain circumstances may not be so regarded under different circumstances. We agree with Kaplan that "Every value judgment is *contextual:* it must specify, at least tacitly, for whom and under what conditions there would be intrinsic value." [23] On this point, Professor Harold H. Titus has written: "Values . . . are products of the interaction between two variables—a person and an environmental situation. . . . A value is a relationship between a person and an environmental situation which evokes an appreciative response." [24]

Relativism in this sense is not a "free-floating" relativism that shrugs off all value judgments with a cynical "It all depends." It is true that "it all depends," but we believe that "all" depends upon, and is relative to, the specific groups, the time, and the particular circumstances to which one applies some concept of value.

We shall have occasion to note that men and societies do not always act in accord with values they purport to hold. "All God's chillun what talks 'bout heav'n ain't goin' there." "Do as I say, not as I do." We shall sometimes distinguish therefore between "declared" and "operational" values to differentiate between what men claim to value and what seems to govern their actions. In Max Lerner's monumental *America as a Civilization,* he distinguishes between "what Americans believe they believe" and "what animates them and what their main energy drives actually are." [25] The distinction is critical to an analysis of welfare services—as to other analyses also. This was, of course, a major point in Gunnar Myrdal's classic, *An American Dilemma,* which contrasted America's treatment of Negroes with the "American Creed."

We will also mention "degrees of value," because "too much" of even a good thing may no longer be "good." One dose can cure, but too many can kill.

We shall also refer to conflicts among values. Valued life may sometimes be sacrificed for "liberty," and "liberty" sometimes forfeited for "order." Such conflicts, moreover, often involve sacrifices by some persons in the interest of others. Soldiers who lay down their lives in defense of "freedom" do so for the freedom of others—including people in countries other than their own and even generations still unborn.[26]

We will also refer from time to time to the pluralistic or multidimensional nature of values. This is exemplified on a small scale in the familiar triads: "life, liberty, and the pursuit of happiness"—"liberty, equality, and fraternity"—or the "health, wealth, and happiness" of fairy tales. However useful such simple enumerations may be as slogans, the range of values to which individuals—to say nothing of societies—aspire in real life is usually much broader and is likely to be expressed in much more specific terms. When we refer to this aspect of values, we will borrow from T. V. Smith the term "multidimensionality." [27]

The multidimensionality of values provides a framework within which one (or a society) may evaluate the relevance of any specific value in any particular situation. Even a value that in principle might usually be regarded as good and only good and that continually may, under certain circumstances, have consequences that, when appraised in the light of other values in one's (or a society's) total system of values, may lead to reevaluation of the original value. Again in the words of Kaplan, "A particular value judgment made in a certain context is grounded in facts established with the help of values which are not problematic in that same context." [28]

We shall employ the term "social welfare" to denote a state of social well-being. As such we see social welfare as falling within the broader concept of "the general welfare" familiar to all Americans. Our opinion as to how these two realms of well-being are related will be presented later, as will our notion of the nature of "social welfare services."

The term "social worker" will be reserved for persons having the professional education prescribed in any country for such workers. Others serving in social welfare agencies will be called "welfare workers," "welfare personnel," and the like. By "social work" we will mean the service rendered by professional social workers. We do not assume that social workers are employed only in social welfare services, but recognize that they may engage in private practice or be employed in industry, in physicians' offices, or under other auspices.

The readership envisaged for this volume, as already noted, is a broad one. Although behavioral and social scientists as such were not specifically mentioned as among those for whom it is intended, we hope nevertheless that analysis of welfare services in the light of values inherent in them may, because of the centricity of values in psychological and social theory, facilitate linkages between these disciplines and the social welfare field.

Readers familiar with the work of behavioral scientists who have dipped into the welfare field for evidence to support or illustrate some concept or theory will find my approach quite different. Whereas others have begun with concepts and even comprehensive systems of thought but have dealt with only bits and pieces of the welfare field relevant to their purposes, I have probed in some detail a set of interrelated welfare problems and then, when possible, have drawn upon social science knowledge and theory to explain them. But, when this was not possible and a *lacuna* in knowledge (or a presumed one) was encountered, I have offered some surmises and hypotheses of my own. These, as a result of what other observers and researchers may do, may some day be either promoted to the status of knowledge or demoted to that of unwarranted supposition.

In view of my interest in relating phenomena in the social welfare field to a wide range of human experiences in other fields, in different countries, and in earlier times—and also in view of limits upon my own competence and resources—I have often had to rely upon what specialists in these wider fields will undoubtedly consider far less satisfactory than primary sources would have been. To avoid distractions for readers not interested in more detail than is included in the text about cited sources, these are placed at the end of each chapter. But, for readers wishing to pursue these and other sources particularly relevant to the specific points discussed, numerous references (well over a thousand, in fact) have been included. Many of these represent viewpoints quite different from those in the text. Inasmuch as the references at the end of each chapter are related to specific topics, the Bibliography is very general in nature and is organized along more traditional lines than those underlying organization of the text.

Throughout the discussion, I will try to suggest criteria for identifying and defining what might usefully be classed as social welfare services and for distinguishing these from other social institutions. In this connection, it has been somewhat irreverently suggested that this book be entitled "What the Hell Is Social Welfare?"

Concern with defining the field stems from the conviction that many controversies over social welfare are attributable to vastly different interpretations as to what it does and does not encompass. Bitter attacks in one quarter may be upon issues that in other quarters are not even regarded as relevant. Much of the ambivalence about welfare is undoubtedly due to ambiguity in what it denotes.

Also, if generalizations are not to be very broad, the phenomena to which they relate must be reasonably homogeneous. It is much easier to generalize about five members of a basketball team, for example, than about four basketball players and, say, one giraffe.

But, even after excluding the "giraffes" from some interpretations of social welfare services, the problem still remains of further differentiation among, and generalizations about, subgroups of services that (although possessing much in common) still need to be distinguished from one another. Failure to do this would be like generalizing about water, milk, whiskey, sulphuric acid, or cyanide brew only in terms of their liquidity.

Problems arising from lack of exact distinctions between services designed to meet human needs are not, unfortunately, limited to the United States. For example, Professor Richard M. Titmuss, writing of the situation in Great Britain, has observed, "No consistent principle seems to obtain in the definition of what is a 'social service.' . . . When so much confusion exists . . . it is difficult to know precisely what it is that the critics are criticizing." [29]

The social welfare field is not alone, of course, in finding it difficult to define social phenomena with which it is concerned. Similar difficulties confront physicians in defining health; psychiatrists, in defining mental health; lawyers, in defining justice; political scientists, in defining, say, a nation.

I am under no illusion that definitions developed in this book will necessarily commend themselves to others. Nevertheless, I hope that they may contribute to a recognition of the need for precision in thinking, and arguing, about welfare services. I agree with Sidney Hook that "Definitions are adequate or inadequate, not true or false like . . . primary statements of observation. . . . They are justified or controlled by the consequences of their use." [30]

As I discuss various ways of thinking about welfare services, I shall attempt to show what are (differentially for contributors, policy makers, administrators, intended beneficiaries, or other members of the welfare system) at least some of "the consequences of [the] use" of particular patterns of thought.

To the extent possible, I shall attempt a world view of social welfare services and will frequently compare relevant services—and values—in other countries with those in the United States. However, because I am more familiar with my own country, I will discuss many points largely in terms of experience here. Because of the lack of an adequate adjective to describe phenomena pertaining to the United States, I shall, parochial as this may be, use the word "American," even though the term properly applies also to other countries of the Americas.

When I refer to my experience in China, I will be referring to the Nationalist China of 1945–1946. At that time I served there with the United Nations Relief and Rehabilitation Administration (UNRRA). Through the opportunity to observe widely different social structures and value systems I learned a great deal about social welfare in the United States.

My stance in this undertaking is that of a friendly critic—or of a skeptical friend—of the field of social welfare, a field in which I have been engaged throughout my professional career. However, ardent supporters of the field may regard this discussion as more critical than friendly, while welfare's more severe critics are likely to regard it as more friendly than skeptical.

This book, unfortunately, will not be a "neat" one. Nice, precise distinctions among values and disvalues, good policies and bad, will be in short supply. Nor will categorization of different types of social institutions be neat and clean. This is not because I shy away from neatness, but because I attempt to describe as accurately as possible a wide range of human experiences and complex social phenomena that are themselves inordinately complex, are often riddled with contradictions and ambiguities, and are themselves not neat. The word "calculus" will be employed frequently and will mean the difficult process of weighing a variety of factors—many of which will be conflicting and even antithetical—in analyzing or evaluating a phenomenon.

Great disservice has been done in the past by attempts to oversimplify phenomena in the welfare field and to make half-truths appear as "truth." As a result, probably no field can better appreciate Alfred North Whitehead's observation that "what plays the devil in human affairs is mistaking a half-truth for a whole truth." [31] But documented knowledge on many aspects of social welfare is at best exceedingly limited and, at worst, nonexistent. To reduce dangers of overstatement and of oversimplification, therefore, I shall often present diametrically opposite views of, and conjectures about, some of the phenomena discussed. Not infrequently I will advance certain presumptions as to how apparently irreconcilable views might conceivably be reconciled. These will not, however, be presented as "answers" to current dilemmas, but only as conjecture or as plausible hypotheses. Given the time and resources, interested researchers may test some of these empirically and can either transform them into new knowledge or dissolve them into error.

Because of the present state of knowledge in the field, and not because of timidity on my part, the language I use is guarded and many observations are advanced tentatively. If so brilliant a genius as Benjamin Franklin could, as he once said, eliminate from his vocabulary such words as "certainly" and "undoubtedly," and could settle for such terms as "I conceive," "I apprehend," and "I imagine," surely far lesser men can be similarly indulged.

Thus, I make no pretense that this is a "definitive work." Rather, it is an "exploratory" endeavor. In assuming the risks of this undertaking I find reassurance in the knowledge that others too have faced—and even survived—similar hazards. Particularly reassuring to me is what Arthur E. Sutherland wrote about the immensely broad and complex subjects of law and justice:

After so many centuries, I do not expect to delimit the just and the unjust. . . . But the recurrent search is worth while even if all that results is consciousness that terms in common use are undefinable. If one has to use vague words, it is better to do so knowingly and to recognize what has made it necessary.[32]

:: Notes and References

1. Charles Frankel, "The Moral Framework of the Idea of Welfare," in John S. Morgan, ed., *Welfare and Wisdom* (Toronto: University of Toronto Press, 1966), p. 147.
2. Abraham Ribicoff, "Politics and Social Workers," *Social Work,* 7 (April 1962), 3.
3. Gordon W. Allport, "The Limits of Social Service," in James E. Russell, ed., *National Policies for Education, Health and Social Services* (New York: Doubleday, 1955), pp. 210–211.
4. Abraham Ribicoff, "To Promote the General Welfare," *The New York Times Magazine,* July 9, 1961, p. 9.
5. S. I. Hayakawa, "A Semantic Parable," *Language in Thought and Action* (New York: Harcourt, Brace & World, 1941), pp. 1–7.
6. Donald S. Howard, "Public Assistance Returns to Page One," *The Compass,* 29 (April 1948), 47–54; 29 (July 1948), 114–120. For more recent treatment of the same theme see Samuel Mencher's "Newburgh: The Recurrent Crisis of Public Assistance," *Social Work,* 7 (January 1962), 3–11, and his "Perspectives in Recent Welfare Legislation, Fore and Aft," *Social Work,* 8 (July 1963), 59–65. Also see Elizabeth Wickenden, "The Recurrent Crises of Public Welfare—Asset or Handicap?" *Public Welfare,* XXI (October 1963), 171–174, 224.
7. Louis Harris, "Most Oppose Growth of a Welfare State," The Harris Survey, *Los Angeles Times,* October 5, 1964.
8. George Gallup, "Public Backs Tighter Relief Rules," Gallup Poll, *Los Angeles Times,* January 24, 1965.
9. Quoted by Robert Kee in *Refugee World* (London: Oxford University Press, 1961), p. 73.
10. Clyde Kluckhohn, "Values and Value-Orientations in the Theory of Action," in Talcott Parsons and Edward A. Shils, eds., *Toward a General Theory of Action* (Cambridge: Harvard University Press, 1959), p. 395. This book includes many other useful discussions of values and value orientations, notably that of the editors (with James Olds) in "Systems of Value Orientation," pp. 159–189.
11. Abraham Kaplan, *The Conduct of Inquiry* (San Francisco: Chandler, 1964), p. 370.
12. Robert A. Dahl and Charles Lindblom, *Politics, Economics and Welfare* (New York: Harper & Row, 1953), p. 26. Ralph H. Turner makes the same distinction between values and goals in *The Social Context of Ambition* (San Francisco: Chandler, 1964), p. 269.

13. Frankel, "The Transformation of Welfare," in John S. Morgan, ed., *Welfare and Wisdom, op. cit.,* p. 166.

14. Abraham Kaplan, *American Ethics and Public Policy* (New York: Oxford University Press, 1963), p. 23.

15. Allen B. Rosenstein and J. Morley English, *Design as a Basis for a Unified Engineering Curriculum* (Los Angeles: School of Engineering, University of California, *ca.* 1960), p. 18. (Mimeographed.)

16. Alfred Jules Ayer, *Language, Truth and Logic,* rev. ed. (London: Gollancz, 1947), pp. 110–111. See also Frank H. Knight, "Fact and Value in Social Science," in Ruth Anshen, ed., *Science and Man* (New York: Harcourt, Brace & World, 1942) and in the author's *Freedom and Reform: Essays in Economics and Social Philosophy* (New York: Harper & Row, 1947), pp. 225–245.

17. Ralph Barton Perry, *Realms of Value: A Critique of Human Civilization* (Cambridge: Harvard University Press, 1954), p. 122.

18. Erik Erikson, *Children,* 7 (March–April 1960), 46.

19. Saul Ginsburg, "Values and the Psychiatrist," *American Journal of Orthopsychiatry,* 20 (July 1950), 478. See also Charlotte Buhler, *Values in Psychotherapy* (New York: Free Press, 1962).

20. Kingsley Davis, *Human Society* (New York: Macmillan, 1949), p. 143.

21. Kenneth S. Carlston, *Law and Organization in World Society* (Urbana: University of Illinois Press, 1962), p. 96.

22. Eugen Pusic, *Reappraisal of the United Nations Social Service Programme* (New York: United Nations, Economic and Social Council, 1965), p. 20.

23. Kaplan, *The Conduct of Inquiry, op. cit.,* p. 390.

24. Harold H. Titus, *Ethics for Today* (New York: American Book, 1947), p. 226. An ardent appeal to apply to ethical decisions the principles inherent in the contextual and situational approaches may be found in Joseph Fletcher (Professor of Christian Ethics at Episcopal Theological School and President of Association of Professors of Social Ethics), *Situation Ethics: The New Morality* (Philadelphia: Westminster Press, 1966). To appreciate the method he proposes for arriving at ethical decisions, one need not necessarily accept his particular religious orientation or his idea of a single criterion for judging what is "good." For a critique of Fletcher's position, see Paul Ramsey, *Deeds and Rules in Christian Ethics* (New York: Scribner, 1967).

25. Max Lerner, *America as a Civilization: Life and Thought in the United States Today* (New York: Simon and Schuster, 1957), p. 689.

26. In terms of the United States alone there are many analyses of conflicting values. Most notable, perhaps, is Lee Coleman's "What Is American? A Study of Alleged American Traits," *Social Forces,* XIX (May 1941), 492–499. With respect to Japan, conflicts were symbolized, of course, in the title of Ruth Benedict's *The Chrysanthemum and the Sword.*

As for Canada, *Values in Conflict,* papers presented at the 32nd Couchiching Conference under the auspices of the Canadian Institute on Public Affairs (Toronto: University of Toronto Press, 1963) is of special interest. The intergenerational aspect of value conflicts is strongly emphasized by a French participant, Bertrand de Jouvenel, Président-Directeur Général de la Société d'Etudes de Documentation Economiques Industrielles et

Sociales, in "Personal Freedom and Social Responsibility," pp. 21–27.

Value conflicts confronted by more specialized groups such as social workers are analyzed in *Values in Social Work: A Re-Examination* (New York: National Association of Social Workers, 1967). Of special relevance is Charles G. Chakerian, "Variations in Values," pp. 36–50. Value conflicts that jeopardize health and impede development of medical care are tellingly portrayed by George James, M.D., "The Ailing Poor," in R. M. MacIver, ed., *The Assault on Poverty* (New York: Harper & Row, 1965), pp. 49–58.

In 1961, when poverty was beginning to be widely discussed, but before President Lyndon B. Johnson declared unconditional war upon it, Dr. Leonard J. Duhl of the National Institute of Mental Health presented a provocative paper "Are We Mentally Prepared for the Elimination of Poverty?" While this is not specifically cast in terms of value conflicts, Dr. Duhl's repeated emphasis upon the need to "change," "rearrange," and "re-evaluate" current values clearly suggests at least competition if not conflict among them. See *The Social Welfare Forum, 1961*, Proceedings of the National Conference on Social Welfare (New York: Columbia University Press, 1961), pp. 100–113.

27. T. V. Smith, "Solve, Resolve, and Absolve," *The Social Welfare Forum, 1955*, Official Proceedings, National Conference of Social Work (New York: Columbia University Press, 1955), p. 3.

28. Kaplan, *The Conduct of Inquiry, op. cit.,* p. 390.

29. Richard M. Titmuss, *Essays on "The Welfare State"* (New Haven: Yale University Press, 1959), pp. 40, 41, 54.

30. Sidney Hook, *The Quest for Being, and Other Studies in Naturalism and Humanism* (New York: St. Martin's Press, 1961), p. 51.

31. Quoted by Lucien Price in *Dialogues of Alfred North Whitehead* (Boston: Little, Brown, 1954), p. 276.

32. Arthur E. Sutherland, *The Law and One Man Among Many* (Madison: University of Wisconsin Press, 1956), p. 65.

I
VALUES
and
PERSONAL
EXPERIENCE

The teaching of values is often said to be the job of the home, school, and church. Although socialization processes appear in many ways to be quite hit-or-miss affairs, they have a power that from one value orientation might be viewed as highly efficient, but from another might be regarded as frightening or even ruthless.

Cultures, including their characteristic value orientations, are born of experience. As the experiences of human groups differ from those of other groups, their cultures, including their values, also tend to differ. As Robert M. MacIver, Emeritus Professor of Columbia University, has put it, "The values and standards of a people inevitably are related to the conditions they have experienced." [1] Conversely, as cultures differ, so do the experiences of individuals within them. Within cultures, there may be subcultures and "ways of life" within which people whose experience differs from that of others in the broader culture develop somewhat different value orientations and different ways of living. Of special relevance to the welfare field in the United States are Arthur B. Shostak and William Gomberg's *Blue-Collar World*, Kenneth B. Clark's *Dark Ghetto*, William F. Whyte's *Street Corner Society,* Walter B. Miller's "subculture of delinquency," Oscar Lewis' "culture of poverty," and Catherine S. Chilman's "subcultures of poverty."

Notwithstanding the tendency of cultures and subcultures to provide participants with common experiences, individuals tend to test against their own idiosyncratic experience what is learned in the home, school, church, and the broader society. Thus individual experience serves as a device for validating what is learned just as it is a determinant of what one is able to learn. Perhaps it was this phenomenon, perceived even in his day, that led Cicero to observe, "That fits a man best which is most his own."

RELATIONSHIP OF EXPERIENCE TO LEARNING

It is profoundly difficult even to conceive of something that is in no wise related to one's own experience. The problem is illustrated by the sweet young thing to whom an atomic scientist was attempting to explain the unprecedented power and demonic destructiveness of the newest atomic bomb. After listening incredulously, she responded, "Gee, that stuff's *dynamite,* isn't it?"

Many years ago a missionary in Africa encountered the same difficulty when he attempted to interpret the meaning of "cold" to tropical children who had never been cold and hardly knew what it was to be even chilly. He was carried away by recollections of Michigan winters, went on to describe snow, and finally ended with a description of ice that became so hard that one could *walk* across a river! After recess the missionary was chagrined to find that his success in communicating the meaning of cold had been somewhat less than spectacular. For, while the children had been at play, a fellow missionary heard one youngster say to another, "Oh, you lie like a missionary!"

With respect to learning about values, Charles Frankel has observed, "If men are going to negotiate their disagreements over values rationally, they have to appeal to evidence that is equally available to all." [2]

PERSONAL AND CULTURAL DETERMINANTS
OF VALUES

"Never having tasted liberty," Herodotus quotes a Greek as saying to a Persian, "you cannot tell whether it be sweet or no." [3]

In more recent and broader terms an American anthropologist, referring to difficulties encountered by North Americans in their relationships with Latin Americans, declared:

The "American dream" of equal opportunity for everyone, of peace, prosperity, and happiness for all, does not have the same appeal everywhere. For a great many Latin Americans these goals have never been highly valued. Indeed, for many they are completely outside the range of their experience.[4]

Because of the interrelationships between a man's experience and what he learns to value, a "lesser" good, experienced and at least directly known for what it is, may well supplant "greater" goods not similarly known at first hand. A man who has never tasted caviar cannot know whether or not he prefers it to hot dogs.

Thus, a person's own knowledge and experience (including what he thinks the future holds for him) directly affect his conceptions of value and good. Whether a man thinks that something is or is not good depends largely upon what he thinks *is*. One of the world's richest men, J. Paul Getty, is quoted as saying, "No man's opinions are better than his information." Men who, in their respective worlds, do not share the same news can hardly be expected to share the same views. As men's perceptions differ, so do their responses to what is perceived. When a hard-of-hearing father was attempting to allay the fears of a young son during a violent thunderstorm, the boy retorted, "Dad, if you could hear as good as me, you'd be as scared as me."

During the Depression, I had a revealing experience. After a tasty, hot dinner with fellow residents at the University of Chicago Settlement, I went to meet with our club for unemployed Polish women. This was before public relief was well organized and the women were desperate. There was tension in the air. They had all sorts of dramatic ideas, including one to tear down the gates of the nearby meat-packing plant where they had previously been employed. After repeated questions as to what this or that proposal would really accomplish, the group became somewhat less aggressive. Then, by way of explaining their earlier angry frustration, the president of the club turned to me and said, "Mr. Howard, if you think we have empty heads, perhaps we get them from our empty stomachs."

That night I saw that a settlement resident could be *in* a community—but not necessarily *of* it. That extraordinary observer Paul Jacobs, who lived the life of an "unemployed" worker just to get a view of unemployment and poverty from as close to the inside as possible, makes the same point. Although in his actor role he could directly experience "the life of the poor," he knew that at any minute a ten-cent phone call could lift him out of it. Similarly, John Howard Griffin could boldly simulate being colored, as described in *Black Like Me*, but when he chose, he could allow the dye to fade.

One's experience includes his exposure to other persons. One hears repeatedly of people who say the first they knew they were poor was "when somebody told me" or of people who did not know until they were told that they were living in a slum. In South America dissatisfaction with living in *favelas* is said to arise from the disdain of those who do not live in them. Obviously, the experience of a man living in a slum where people do not know it is a slum (or do not know that they are poor) and are not disdained by others is quite different from the experience of those who know about their living conditions and are aware that better conditions exist.

To families that are comfortably situated, "keeping children out of school" may seem to be a flagrant flaunting of community values. But what are the comfortably situated to say to the poverty-stricken mother in Washington, D.C., who said she kept her children home so that when they were hungry she could "comfort them"?

On the same note, advantaged families know little of such momentous decisions as spending for electricity public assistance allowances for food, in themselves inadequate, so that lights can be left on all night to reduce the chance that the children will be bitten by rats.

São Paulo's "child of the dark" has written, "Hunger acts as a judge. . . . Only those who have gone hungry know the value of food. . . . Hunger is also a teacher. . . . It's necessary to know hunger to know how to describe it." [5]

Phenomena like these lead to the observation, "If you have to ask, you'll never know." It was this thought that led that passionate humanist, Lincoln Steffens, to contend that no judge should ever be allowed to pass judgment on an offense that he had never been tempted to commit.

Whether one values a particular way of life such as democracy or communism depends in large part upon what he senses as (or has been induced to believe are) the realities of human nature and the human condition. If one assumes that human personality has certain attributes and that social conditions are of a particular character, one might project from such a base the hypothesis that democracy is a good thing. However, if one has a distorted view of human nature (distorted, that is, from the view of the democrat) and a quite different picture (from that of the democrat) of existing social conditions, he might quite understandably project from this base a value wholly antithetical to democracy. Or, if one believes that some of the views underlying democratic ideology are correct and some of those underlying communist interpretations are correct, a still different sort of value might, by triangulation, be reached. The situation is depicted in Chart 1 on page 26.

The possibilities of distortion that are suggested here were described by Lewis Mumford just before the United States entered World War II:

During the last century, certain mathematicians proved that a whole system of geometry could be constructed on different axioms than Euclid used. . . .

The fascists have brought about a similar change in politics. . . . Not merely do the fascist dictators deny the ethical postulates of society; they have created a system with a reverse set of values.[6]

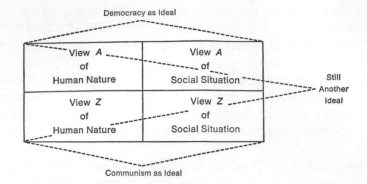

Thus, whether men's differing perceptions of the same "realities" are inaccurate or whether they allow their perceptions to be distorted by others, the net result is much the same. Moreover, the relevant "realities" include not only those of the here and now, but also those likely to obtain in the future. "Reality," for anyone, includes not only what *is*, but also what he thinks inevitably or probably *will be*. The importance of this fact to concepts of value is implicit in Sidney Hook's view that "Ideals or values . . . are hypotheses about the foreseen consequences of striving or acting in a given way. They are true or false if the actual consequences which ensue agree or disagree with the foreseen consequences." [7]

Within the social welfare field, these interrelationships between values and experience are of consummate importance. For, as we will see later (Chapter II), welfare agencies work constantly with persons who, for one reason or another (discrimination, poor education, physical handicap, low income, and the like), have not found through existing social arrangements opportunity to savor the satisfactions enjoyed by others more favorably situated (satisfactions such as employment, regular wages, health services, stable family life, schooling, status, success, and so on). Nor do the prospects for the future of many disadvantaged persons give much real hope of ever enjoying these satisfactions.

CULTURES AS TEACHERS: ERRATIC OR EFFECTIVE?

But what is even more serious is that groups that are kept out of the mainstream of life by forces not of their own choosing tend to find refuge in little eddies of subcultures of their own. Then, when the larger community finds the behavior of these "foreigners" distasteful, if not obnoxious (because of failure to conform to at least the predominant values), it tends to punish them rather than look at and remedy the faulty socializing processes and social structures that caused the deviant conduct.

When testifying before a California state legislative committee especially concerned with the numbers of illegitimate Negro children receiving public aid in 1961, the writer pointed out that, although "no man is an island," discriminatory practices do often keep certain groups "offshore"—isolated from the mainland of socializing forces. These forces cannot therefore reach those confined to slum ghettos, relegated to second-rate schools, barred from all but the lowest-paid jobs, unwelcome in churches other than their own. If, as a result, behavior patterns evolve that deviate from community norms, these must be attributed to social forces as much as to those who deviate.

"The walls of the ghetto," says the National Urban League Report for 1966, "are held in place by those on the outside, not by those within."

Dominant groups cannot avoid, shun, isolate, and discriminate against minority groups and then expect them to be like themselves. The dilemma is dramatically illustrated by James Baldwin, who, in *The Fire Next Time*, tells of walking toward the public library in midtown New York City one day only to be accosted by a policeman, who asked why he did not remain among his own kind in Harlem. One can hardly expect another to absorb the "good things" of a society if he is denied access to them or is humiliated when he does pursue them. From this point of view, then, cultures may be regarded as quite erratic teachers.

Despite widespread belief that disadvantaged persons fail to "get the word" about the nature of the values of their society, recent research reveals increasingly the effectiveness of a culture in transmitting its ideals even to persons in circumstances where their realization is highly problematic. For example, Lola M. Irelan and Arthur Besner of the federal Welfare Administration, speaking of the values of "the poor," say, "Essentially, they seek and value the same things as other Americans." [8]

Even among the mothers in the poor families she studied in Harlem, Joan Gordon found that "There is no evidence that these women reject or are ignorant of the central values of American culture." The children, too, she says, "have learned their cultural lesson very well. School and getting an education are GOOD." [9]

Catherine S. Chilman, also of the Welfare Administration, after an extensive review of research concerning not merely "the poor," but "the very poor," put the matter thus:

It could hardly be said that the very poor are satisfied with their poverty situation. . . . The very poor ascribe, at least in aspirations, to the middle-class way. Like most other parents they want their children to "have a good education"; they want better jobs for themselves and even better ones for their sons and daughters. They too aspire to homes of their own and the material comforts of our society. Good physical and mental health is also a goal. . . . Like other human beings, they, too, want the security and warmth of a stable, satisfying marriage and family life.[10]

However, the same society that communicates effectively the nature of approved goals seems not to have communicated with equal effectiveness the knowledge as to how these goals can be attained. Study after study that shows the degree to which disadvantaged groups share the values of the larger society also reveals these failures. Catherine Chilman, quoted above, adds, "They [the very poor] have little knowledge as to how such aspirations may be fulfilled." With respect to poor mothers in Harlem, Joan Gordon reports, "A significant proportion are unable to implement these values." [11] Moreover, resources and opportunities essential to such implementation are often denied to those who are disadvantaged. It is almost as if within an "affluent society" a Tantalusian sector had been set up, where the values of the society are effectively held before the eyes of individuals and groups, like the fruit over the head of Tantalus. But, although effective in presenting these values, the society is far less effective in assuring the means for attaining them.

Winifred Bell, after her broad study of Aid to Dependent Children, suggests that the tension between the pull of societal values and their unattainability could hardly have been better created if done so purposely:

Social scientists might speculate that one of the more effective methods available to an affluent nation to ensure continued dependency from one generation to another was to isolate the poor, close the door to opportunity, weaken fragile parental ties, all the time exposing poor families to a materialistic and opportunistic value system.[12]

It is not surprising that observers who have studied those relegated to Tantalusia often find them conscious of their isolation and powerlessness and therefore either bitter or apathetic and resigned.

In *The Pattern of Dependent Poverty in California*, Earl Raab and Hugh Folk describe poor persons as living in a "Trap Ghetto." They discuss not only the erratic but also the effective aspects of the culture surrounding this ghetto, which they differentiate from the older immigrant ghettos of the past:

The Trap Ghetto is . . . distinguished from the traditional ghettos by its "closed circle" character . . . formed by low economic status, low educational status, low levels of employment opportunity and limited social contact. . . .

It is a common misconception that the aspirations of those in the ghetto are uniformly low. . . . A sharp distinction must be made between levels of aspiration, and levels of hopefulness; between what people want, and what they think they can get.

The Trap Ghetto, *being* a trap, is encircled by . . . hopelessness, which becomes part of the vicious circle. . . .

. . . Since the basic aspirations of the ghetto-dwellers are, by and large, the same as those of the rest of society, they are fully conscious of having been cut off. . . . The Trap is bitter. It . . . breeds a sense of alienation.[13]

Societies that take pride in how effectively their cultures inculcate values, but are unconcerned about the erratic way in which "the good things of life" become available, face an additional problem. Its nature has been described by Robert K. Merton, who points out that a man constantly thwarted by the social structure goes beyond the fox in the fable. The man does not merely dismiss unreachable grapes as sour; he tells himself that it is not grapes he wants after all. Such transpositions of value appear in descriptions of a number of subcultures and ways of life, such as those of the Negro, of poverty, of "street-corner society," and of delinquency.

However effective a culture may be in securing (even in unlikely quarters) acceptance of a society's values, if the society is erratic in providing access to these values, it invites the thwarted to develop escape routes. These may lead into fairly structured life styles within which different value systems arise. These systems then develop a logic of their own and, as they become more firmly established, become increasingly impervious to influences of the larger society.

The picture of the world of poor persons in the United States, vividly portrayed by Ben H. Bagdikian, points up the problem:

There is a culture of poverty that perpetuates itself inside its own geography behind a border that separates the despairing from the hopeful. It provides an enclave for refugees from the world of success . . . duchies of deprivation. . . . From the outside, the inhabitants seem hostile and irrational. But from within, the culture is sensible and inevi-

table. . . . Middle-class assumptions of common sense and social responsibility often make no sense to the poor. What is prudent for the
well-fed may be irresponsible for the poor. . . . For the poor the future
is demonstrably treacherous. Self-denial brings them not the reward of
evenly distributed joy but the punishment of permanent loss.[14]

Readers familiar with Oscar Lewis' classics, such as *The Children of Sanchez,* probably find quite understandable some of the reactions of his memorable characters to their experiences. These experiences also give substance to the previously quoted view of Sidney
Hook, that values are "hypotheses about the foreseen consequences
of striving or acting in a given way." To save, but to have one's savings repeatedly wiped out by having to buy medicine for a sick relative or friend; to work, but repeatedly to be bilked out of one's earnings; to marry and have a family, but to be unable to meet one's
responsibilities; to abide by the law, but to find oneself falsely arrested and brutally treated by police over and over again—all these
experiences understandably affect attitudes toward thrift, monogamous marriage, the discipline of work, and the dignity of law and
order. Roger Starr, writing in *The Living End: The City and Its
Critics,* is more specific: "What strikes observers of the poor as the
'rejection of middle-class standards' . . . reflects their sense that if
the world in which they are living has done so poorly by them, it
cannot reasonably be expected to do better." [15]

Both Bagdikian's and Lewis' observations have profound implications for social welfare not only in the United States but in other
countries also. For whether it is because of faulty socialization, the
lessons of bitter experience, thwarted aspirations, or alienation, one
of the realities of life is that many persons served by welfare agencies come to hold firmly and persistently—*as long as the constellations of their circumstances remain virtually unchanged*—what
seem to them to be values but are disfavored by society.

Although this phenomenon may be included in what social scientists term "anomie," it is not the normlessness that anomie usually
implies. For the central problem is not that individuals and groups
have no norms, but that—because of their peculiar life experiences
—they live by norms upon which the larger society frowns. To make
this distinction clear, and for want of a better word, I shall use the
term "dysnomie" to designate apparent attachment to values
strongly disfavored by society. The term "anomie" will be reserved
for the stricter sense of normlessness, the lack of identification with
any standard of value. In terms of the world—and not just of Mex-

ico, with which he has been conspicuously identified—anthropologist Oscar Lewis points up what we would term the dysnomic effects of what he calls the culture of poverty:

Poverty in modern nations is not only a state of economic deprivation, of disorganization, or of the absence of something. It is also *something positive* [emphasis added] in the sense that it has a structure, a rationale, and defense mechanisms without which the poor could hardly carry on. In short, it is a way of life, remarkably stable and persistent, passed down from generation to generation along family lines. The culture of poverty has its own modalities and distinctive social and psychological consequences for its members. It is a dynamic factor which affects participation in the larger national culture and becomes a subculture of its own.[16]

Unbelievable as it may seem to persons accustomed to "the American way of life," there are some people who live in squalor, by indifferent effort, and on uncertain income who seem to like it that way—or to think that they do. The writer learned this lesson the hard way very early in his professional career when he tried vigorously (though perhaps not wisely or skillfully) to get an old man to give up living—with his horse—in an officially condemned one-room shack on a city lot; there was no water, no sewer. To enhance the intimacy of these arrangements, one wall of the room was only about three feet high; as a result, the horse could reach over it and well into the room. For the old man, this was *life*. He was not without values. He tenaciously adhered to his way of life and its alleged freedom, notwithstanding (but in part because of) the precariousness of the living he eked out with his housemate and wagon.

This phenomenon has been encountered over and over again—in slum areas, deteriorated areas marked for urban renewal, among displaced persons in miserable camps in Europe, and among American Indians whose unpromising reservations still seemed preferable to the dubious promise of a better life elsewhere. A not uncommon phenomenon has just been reported from Caracas, where some slum dwellers who had moved into low-rent apartments had abandoned them as too confining—and returned to the slums.

An important variant of this problem may be found in those persons (and in those nations) who appear to aspire to socially approved end values, but do not value also the restraint, self-control, effort, or other means essential to realization of the presumptively desired ends. These groups sometimes seem to want gravy, as the larger societies define it, but are often unable or unwilling to collect the necessary ingredients or to learn how to blend them. Parents may claim that they want education for their children but be unwilling to forego the earnings that the youngsters would receive if they went to work. Serious pursuit of values requires also pursuit of inherently antecedent values. The progress men desire often requires changes they detest or cannot effect; goals to which they aspire may be attainable only upon conditions they abhor or cannot meet.

What a community condemns as "careless love" may in fact be "careful" love—if one has no job, no promise of one, and no money with which to support a wife or child. What those in more settled and rewarding ways of living may condemn as "carefree living and avoidance of disciplined routine" may be only a wholly human response to menial jobs, low pay, irregular work. In fact, efforts directed by a community at ameliorating some living conditions it finds objectionable are often viewed as unwonted intrusion. Here the problem is not normlessness but—things being what they are—devotion to a way of life which, *under the circumstances*, has an appeal all its own. From this point of view, social processes that permit disadvantaged persons to adapt to a society with which they cannot otherwise cope are "effective," even though they may be regarded as highly "ineffective" in terms of making the values of that society more widely accessible.

While a larger society may condemn a subculture, that same society, whimsically, may be largely responsible for its development because of either ineffective socialization or denial of opportunity, which denial, in turn, fosters frustration and transpositions of value. These results, even though a society may pretend to deplore them, may nevertheless "effectively" serve a functional purpose for its dominant elements because they help to keep disadvantaged groups "in their place," reduce competition for the supply of the "good things" of the society, and lessen pressure for inclusion in privileged circles.

The interrelatedness of values and experience strongly suggests that if value orientations and behavior patterns based upon them are to be improved in the way a society desires, consideration must be given to the *whole constellation of operative factors and not to only one or a few. Unless a new constellation of factors* in toto *gives promise of equal or greater satisfaction than a preexisting constellation, little gain can be expected.* This is an instance in which the multidimensionality of values must be taken into account.

One specific "benefit" cannot often upset the balance among values found in other dimensions of life. Thus, water piped into the homes of a village in India may give purer water, but the women of the village may not use it because they consider their open well not only a source of water but also a source of information and gossip; it is, in fact, a social center. Until a replacement of these values is found, the piped water may remain unused. We see this phenomenon in highly developed countries where a single benefit—such as an apartment in a public housing unit in the United States or a flat in a "new town" in Great Britain—cannot offset advantages enjoyed in former neighborhoods: informal relationships with neighbors, familiar gathering places, and opportunities for small moneymaking enterprises.

If, as sometimes happens, a young girl is shunned by her peers —including other girls—unless she too is sexually promiscuous, efforts to convince her of the "error of her ways" may have hard sledding. When the choice is sex with companionship versus "respectability" in isolation from one's usual companions, "virtue" is not always triumphant. In terms of the world, John Scott's *Democracy Is Not Enough* is a sobering reminder that what he calls "the Hungry World" may not be able both to be democratic and to develop the programs needed to keep it from remaining hungry.

However, it is not impossible for one single value regarded as consummately important to sanctify a whole complex of disvalues. For example, outsiders may criticize an African state for overthrowing pseudodemocratic, white colonial rulers, only to replace them with a black dictator. Yet, the high preference for being governed by "one of their own" may make even the dictatorship seem to be a price worth paying to get the white man "off their backs." This phenomenon is not without its hazards. To recognize this, one has only to recall the recent past when superficial observers thought Hitlerism, fascism, and Maoism must be all right because they opposed communism, ran the trains on time, and waged campaigns against flies and rats.

How one very important "good" is allowed to outweigh many lesser ones is amusingly depicted by Andrew Carnegie. He tells of a judge who could not understand why a slave had run away when, as he testified, he had had enough to eat, had had good clothes, and had lived in a "pretty little cabin." Seeing the judge's unresolved perplexity, the runaway replied, "Well, Judge, I lef de situation down dar open. You kin go rite down and git it." [17]

On the other hand, both nations and individuals may forego a variety of attainable values if, to get them, they must give up even one value they believe to be consummately important. One aspect of this theme is the tenacity with which individuals, groups, and nations hang on to their own sense of independence and do so to such a degree they forego aid (and other "good" things for which it might be used) that they could have if they chose to claim it. As we shall see in Chapter VII, many economically needy persons in the United States, Britain, and France eschew public aid that would label them as "dependent," rob them of their sense of "independence," and bring down upon themselves the social stigma attached to "dependency."

Looking at this problem in broad perspective, John Kenneth Galbraith, economist and former United States Ambassador to India, in 1964 urged that United States foreign aid be granted without "strings." American aid, he contended, "would lose its value if it were subordinated to day-to-day politics—U.N. votes, . . . toeing the line on alliances. Such demands would mean that the price of our help was the one thing even more precious to the new countries than economic development—their national independence." [18]

It was quite a shock to Americans attending a World Council of Churches meeting in Geneva in 1966 to recognize that representatives from the "Southern World" (South America, Africa, and Asia) branded both the United States and the U.S.S.R. as dominating powers. Because they saw in both this same fault, they went no further to ascertain other ways in which one might be distinguished from the other.

Realization of some exceptionally important value may open up whole new realms of value. When I returned to India for the first time after it had attained independence, I was very much surprised at the new emphasis upon social welfare programs and at the variety of social measures that were being developed. Upon asking the reason for this upsurge in interest, since the problems being attacked had been there all the time, I was told repeatedly that, as long as the cause of independence had been uppermost in people's minds, this so absorbed their time and energies, and those of their leaders, that they had little strength left for subsidiary "goods." Glen Leet, Executive Director of the Community Development Foundation, received the same sort of reply in even more recently born African nations. Preoccupation with getting the colonial powers "off their backs," he was told, had diverted attention from the more mundane task of promoting development of their own communities.

In terms of the individual this same mechanism might possibly prove useful. As individuals are given a greater sense of power and more control over their own affairs, they too may be able to divert to more constructive purposes energies wasted in fruitless frustration bucking insuperable odds.

Over the world, and over time, the one good that has led more than any other to pursuit of further "goods" is probably education. In retrospect, it is interesting to note how correct were the predictions of those who contended that neither Negro slaves in the South (where it was a criminal offense to teach them to read or write) nor "colonials" in Africa would long remain content with their lot if they were educated. However, whether education, as its opponents claimed, "spoiled" those to whom it was made available or whether, as others thought, it "liberated" and equipped them to pursue additional "goods" are issues to be decided only in relation to value orientations.

Thus, the social task is usually to modify not one factor alone but whole constellations of values. This is one practical implication of the previously mentioned multidimensionality of values. It is therefore unfortunate that different welfare services tend to be highly particular in nature and to serve quite specific purposes. To change for their beneficiaries but a single aspect of interrelated value patterns and living arrangements, but to leave others untouched, is often like trying to alter the course of an iceberg by blowing upon its shoulder while subsurface currents carry it inexorably in another direction.

CULTURES AS TEACHERS: HIGHLY EFFICIENT OR FRIGHTENING?

We have observed that social forces may operate quite unevenly. Depending upon one's values, they may appear erratic in that they do not assure to all equal opportunity or they may appear quite effective in that they keep "the poor," Negroes, or others "in their place." One may look further, though, at socializing forces and, depending upon his values, think them either highly efficient or downright frightening. This is most evident in historical perspective but is apparent even in contemporary societies.

The awesome power of a culture may be seen, for example, in ancient Carthage. There, as Gilbert and Colette Charles-Picard record, "The priests . . . were . . . responsible for the persistence of customs which filled even the ancients with horror . . . customs such as human sacrifice, and especially the holocaust of very young children." [19] That an entire people can be persuaded, generation after generation, to accept practices that mean the death of fellow humans—including perhaps their own kin or even themselves (as in Mayan culture)—underlines what some would regard as a frightening aspect of culture, but which the "Establishment" of the day must have thought "highly efficient."

From India, too, the same phenomenon has been reported in connection with the brutal practice of suttee (brutal from the outsider's viewpoint and now from India's viewpoint too): throwing living widows upon the funeral pyres of their husbands. This practice, now outlawed, was defended on the grounds that the Indian woman's life revolved so largely around that of her husband that, when he was dead, virtually no role remained for her if she stayed alive. In fact, records show that even after the social sanctions supporting this apparently cruel practice had been relaxed and widows were no longer required to be burned alive, some would tear themselves away from the restraining hands of relatives and throw themselves into the flames. These widows, unhappily, were not the last to hold "better dead than role-less." This, apparently, is the belief of many suicides even in our own day.

But even a Westerner need not go so far back into history or so far abroad to be awed by the power of a culture. Witness a peace-loving people that, despite their usual value preferences, can be whipped into a frenzy of fear and hate, go to war, and permit their sons to be shot, wounded, gassed, seared by flamethrowers, or beheaded. The average citizen would probably see this as the efficiency of a culture. To the pacifist it might appear frightening.

We may note less dramatically the influences that lead Negroes, Spanish-Americans, and members of other minority groups to accept the majority's view of their "inferiority" and of "keeping them in their place." Even the great American Negro leader Whitney M. Young, Jr., tells of his misgivings when on an airplane in Africa he noted that the pilot and copilot were Negro. He mentioned this at the International Conference of Social Work in 1966 to illustrate how even he could be "brainwashed" to the point of even temporarily questioning the competence of a pilot of his own race.

To many who are disadvantaged there is perhaps no sadder aspect of a culture than that which brings poverty-stricken families, unemployed workers, handicapped persons, and others to look upon themselves as the majority looks upon them—and as that majority wants them to look upon themselves. To majorities, of course, this bespeaks the efficiency of their culture, but to those who are, or side with, the victims of this efficiency it can indeed be frightening.

For any number of disadvantaged persons the world around, Bobby Burns' famous prayer might well be adapted to read:

O gie us the power,
The giftie gie us
To see ourselves as we really are,
Not merely as others see us.

Were such a prayer to be answered, though, the plans of many an Establishment would be upset.

The power of a culture makes it easy automatically to view as "right" whatever happens to become incorporated into law. It takes considerable insight and courage to make the distinction that President John F. Kennedy made when, in referring to segregation in the South, he observed, "It may be the law, but it isn't right."

EFFECT OF EXPERIENCE ON ASPIRATION

Personal experience and the social forces shaping it affect not only men's values but even more fundamentally, perhaps, their aspirations—the force essential to pursue that which they value. Whatever the ends to be sought, aspiration is consummately important in evoking human effort. Without it the chase never even begins.

Writing about New York's human "derelicts" who frequent flophouses, one observer has said, "They have found security in the only place where it is unchallengeable—at the bottom of the heap where no man can fall. 'The Bowery Man' cannot . . . be disappointed because he has no hope." [20] Or, as a railroad president once observed, "Blessed are they that expect nothing, for that's what they get." [21]

The importance of aspiration to even so basic a concept as freedom is illustrated by the fact that Professor Herbert J. Muller, in his *Freedom in the Ancient World*, approvingly quotes Christian Boy's definition of freedom: "A person is free to the extent that he has the capacity, the opportunity, and the *incentive* to give expression to what is in him and to develop his potentialities." [22] [Emphasis added.]

Experience and the Act of Aspiring

Individuals and groups with high aspirations and bright future prospects may easily overlook circumstances that not only thwart aspiration but also make men lethargic, resigned, and hopeless. This not only happens in broad areas in which fatalism is more common than hope, but also happens, even within generally dynamic societies, when individuals and subgroups are denied access to those experiences that make their societies dynamic. Although the very act of aspiring may appear to be a highly individual and personal matter, it is to a great extent socially conditioned. Indeed, aspiration may in many respects be seen as a social product.

Aspiration that in many quarters may be assumed to be so natural to man that it can be taken for granted as a fact of life is, however, a very tender plant. Nurturing it requires support from its environment. In fact, it is not too much to say that its genesis is as much in society as in the breast of man. In the parlance of the race track one might even say that aspiration is "out of man, by society."

Just how fragile a plant is aspiration is well shown by James N. Morgan and his coauthors in *Income and Welfare in the United States*. Here they trace what might be termed the natural history of "expectations." They identify stages in the life of families at which, for example, earlier parental expectations for their children are lowered as certain realities in their experience are recognized.[23]

In view of the extreme importance of aspiration to human achievement, one might think that by now science would have discovered what, under varying combinations of circumstances, best evokes this highly valued force; what "makes men tick"; what makes Sammy—or Shankarlal or Suzuki-chan—run. The literature on class differences in aspirations and values is extensive.[24] Nevertheless, theories about how men are best motivated range from one extreme to the other.

On the one hand it is assumed that it is deprivation that drives men onward. This view has a distinctly class odor to it, however. When large corporations want to spur their executives on to greater effort, they do not reduce their salaries and tell them, "Now, to avoid being hungry, get in there and push production!" Yet, as will be shown in Chapter VI, this is exactly what more privileged groups keep saying to disadvantaged persons. The spur of hunger and deprivation is somehow considered necessary at only one end of the social spectrum. At the other end, reliance is placed rather upon "incentive" pay—high salaries, bonuses, stock options, liberal pension plans. Seldom does it seem to occur to observers that what is good for corporation executives might be good for disadvantaged persons, too.

Among those who have taken this view is A. Delafield Smith, who was long legal counsel of the U. S. Social Security Board. "Life," he once wrote, "is not driven by its necessities. It is lured by its hopes. . . . Individuals typically . . . have steadily sought higher levels of living. This has not resulted from compulsion but from aspiration—not from what lies behind but from what lies ahead." [25]

Although there have been many studies of motivation, these still tend, unfortunately, to be of exceedingly limited scope. They have not yet proved very useful in helping us to understand why one man exerts great effort to "get ahead" and to keep his family together, whereas another in apparently similar circumstances folds up. Yet some relevant observations have been made.

One of these, which not only antedates modern research but goes back some 3,000 years, was made by the author of the book of Proverbs: "Hope deferred maketh the heart sick." Subsequent human experience strongly suggests further that a heart thus sickened "stayeth the hand"; that hope too often deferred may breed lethargy, hopelessness, and resignation; that hope too long deferred may itself die. Its death may be either sudden or lingering.

Hope that suffered a lingering death is apparent in the life of Manuel, who, in Oscar Lewis' monumental *The Children of Sanchez,* is shown to have hoped, time and again, to save a little money. But, every time he had set aside some small amount, some relative or friend fell ill, so that Manuel had to exhaust his little nest egg to buy medicine. This went on so many times that, by simple and understandable logic, Manuel concluded that it was his savings that brought on the illnesses. Consequently, to avert them, he discontinued his efforts to save.

Even affluent societies that urge their members to "save for a rainy day" have yet to come up with any very helpful advice about what to do when it rains every day. It was doubtless harsh experience that led to the slight alteration of the punctuation in a familiar sentence, making it read, "There is a divinity that shapes our ends rough, hew them how we will."

So much is said these days about the "revolution of rising expectations" throughout the world (in the United States, notably among Negroes) that it is easy to overlook the equally relevant fact of the devolution of thwarted expectations. Perhaps this accounts for the fact that widespread race riots in the United States in the later 1960's were not in the South (where Negroes could hardly expect really significant advances) but in the North, where things were allegedly better, and where more was being promised but was slow in being actualized.

Many observers have noted general tendencies toward resignation and fatalism in underdeveloped and other deprived areas. Acquiescent acceptance of deprivation as being "in the order of things," or even as an expression of divine will, may be seen in the *mai pen rai* ("it hardly matters") of Thailand; the *bopen nyan* ("it does not matter") of Buddhist Laos; the *Bhagya* of India; the *kismet* of the Middle East; the "it is God's will" of the English-speaking Christian world.

Westerners, fortunate enough to live in a milieu that justifies their perennial optimism, may be surprised to learn that in vast areas of the world this optimism they feel is so unusual that they are considered "peculiar"—a word quoted by Professor Lawrence H. Fuchs in the title of his book *"Those Peculiar Americans": The Peace Corps and the American Character.*

In Sierra Leone the Mende are reported by George H. T. Kimble to have a saying, "If God dishes your rice in a basket, you should not wish to eat soup." Kimble interprets this to mean that "if you are a poor man, you should not aspire to be rich. . . . Only the more well-to-do can regularly afford the palm oil, meat and other ingredients that go into the local 'chop,' or soup." [26]

How any one God or gods—over time—may have felt about being considered responsible for the human condition is not given to many men to know. However, when Homer essayed to speak for his gods, he strongly implied that they thought that mundane men somewhat overestimated their divinities' responsibility. For Homer, purporting to speak for his divinities, wrote:

> *How falsely men accuse us Gods as authors of their ill*
> *When by the bane their own bad lives instill*
> *They suffer all the miseries of their states—*
> *Past our inflictions and beyond their fates.*[27]

São Paulo's "child of the dark" put the issue poignantly when she wrote of a day in her life, "If I had soap I'd wash the clothes. I'm really not negligent. . . . For those who aren't going to heaven, it doesn't help to look up. It's the same with us who don't like the favela, but are obliged to live in one. . . . It doesn't help to look up." [28]

It should be noted, however, that after her book, which was originally written on scraps of wastepaper, won some success, this "child of the dark" did "look up."

One aspect of fatalism that is often overlooked is its contagiousness and the infectiousness of the environment that fosters it. In many areas of the world one can see once eager persons who had gone there from other countries to help their more disadvantaged fellow world-citizens, but who themselves became infected by, and succumbed to, the very lethargy and apathy they had gone to help overcome. Even the contagiousness of the apathy or environment of a subgroup within a single nation can take its toll. Harvard research psychiatrist Robert Coles, for example, speaks of once dutiful teachers who, upon being assigned to teach in poverty-stricken areas, themselves become indifferent. Conversely, there are indications that, even though much in their lives remains unchanged, exposure to more privileged groups (as through the busing of ghetto children to superior schools) actually leads disadvantaged persons to modify their aspirations. "Higher things" too can be contagious—if one can only get exposed to them.

Although poverty and lethargy, deprivation and fatalism appear interrelated, it is difficult to say which causes which. Nevertheless there are many suggestions that psychological factors enter into the resultant vicious circles as much as do other components such as poverty, ill health, and illiteracy. But the extent to which apathy is due to circumstance and the extent to which circumstance is due to apathy are not known. The trick is to distinguish, as did Homer, men's inevitable "inflictions" and "fates" from "the bane their own bad lives instill."

However, fatalism and resignation, especially in the face of overwhelming adversity and catastrophe, may serve important social functions—preservation of social order, stability, and "peace of mind," for example—even if these thwart "progress." Opinions will differ on whether this reflects efficient or frightening cultures. One observer who, upon visiting an Arab refugee camp, saw these two aspects of apathy wrote, "At its best, the resignation of the Arab is saintly. At its worst, it is a stultifying fatalism that becomes an excuse for doing nothing to fight evil or alleviate suffering." [29] Here again, depending upon one's system of values, one might wish to reverse the position of "best" and "worst" in this quotation.

That quietism and even fatalism are not unalterable is strongly suggested (as in the case of "the child of the dark") in those areas of the world where economic development and social progress have overtaken the preexisting apathy and stagnation. For example, there is Louis J. Walinsky's report of the ten-year (1951–1961) effect of the economic development program in Burma, which had long been regarded as a country not much interested in social progress and not particularly devoted to individual enterprise. But, in his appraisal Walinsky observes:

The impact of the program went deep to the core of the culture. . . .

Industrialization, urbanization and technology brought a changing tempo and a new emphasis on energy and drive, on skill, on management, on accounting for time and costs, on the necessity and dignity of work, on the need for social discipline and responsibility.[30]

Burma's apparent choice may not be a lasting one. However, if Burma should lose its interest in development, it can at least do so with the knowledge of what it was like.

The importance of this phenomenon was once expressed by P. C. J. Van Loon of The Netherlands, who is himself an international authority on community development in many countries: "One cannot expect people to be interested in raising the productivity of their own efforts if conditions in the local community do not improve. There is a close connection between improving the conditions in which people are living and their belief in progress." [31]

We should perhaps note in passing that the *shikata ga nai* ("it can't be helped") of Japan was long blamed for that country's apparent lack of interest in social and economic progress. More recent times and Japan's resurgence as a vigorous and enterprising nation have shown, however, that "it" can, indeed, often be helped.

But if individuals or societies have not experienced and see no prospect of experiencing particular values, it is difficult to evoke interest in them. This difficulty applies not only to their own pursuit of these "goods," but also even to their ability to accept assistance in attaining them. The Dutch authority just quoted put the issue this way, "Some people are too poor to be helped. Malnutrition, disease and a perpetual preoccupation with bare survival may so demoralize people that they can no longer cooperate." [32]

Writing many years ago, Earl Koos, reporting on troubled families in the United States, observed the extent to which these families —in the face of their difficulties—seemed to become apathetic and unconcerned.[33]

A preeminent American leader, calling for support for better opportunities for Negroes in the Seething Sixties, put the depth of the need in these terms:

Since the Negro citizen is not innately superior to other human beings, it follows logically that generations of suppression, exploitation, segregation, and discrimination have left their mark. Individual behavior patterns often indicate hostility, suspicion, aggression, withdrawal, resignation, defeatism, and exaggerated deference.[34]

With respect to Spanish-Americans in the Southwest, Robert G. Hayden has reported, "Continued discrimination has encouraged a certain fatalism about their position in Southwestern society, to the point of inducing in them some Anglo beliefs about the inferiority of Latins." [35] This reference to "inferiority" obviously recalls what was said earlier about the efficient or frightening aspects of culture.

Thus, expectation and hope do not spring spontaneously and full-blown from the breast of individual man. They are largely social products. To rise, a man must both stand up and be allowed to stand up. Hope can be "deferred" and aspiration thwarted as much by social structures and climate as by an individual's incapacity or failure. In either case the devolution of aspiration is likely to follow the same course to deterioration: As one is unsuccessful, he tends to feel ineffectual, then powerless, then useless, and then helpless. When the taproot of his enterprising ability is cut, he is likely to become unaspiring. "Why take all that guff when it doesn't get you anyplace anyway?"

If, as is commonly said, "Not failure but low aim is crime," there is far more delinquency in this world than ever shows up on police blotters. However, if, as we suggest, what people are allowed to experience and to do also contributes to lack of aspiration and low aim, then there are many—including whole societies—who must be considered accessories to this "crime."

In retrospect, it is surprising that not until about the 1960's in the United States—and, more particularly, after President Johnson's declaration of War on Poverty—did social policy take any real notice of the need for helping people of low aspiration to raise their sights. It was perhaps James B. Conant, former president of Harvard, who, through his studies of high school dropouts and the resulting high unemployment among young persons (which he characterized as "social dynamite"), first pinpointed the problem of low aspiration and roused widespread public concern about it.[36] But once social interest was awakened, extensive and costly remedial measures to mitigate the problem revealed a society that was willing to see itself as at least partly responsible for the lack of aspiration and opportunity that many of its members were suffering. One must wonder, though, if these responsibilities accepted by a society in the 1960's were not also, in the 1950's, 1940's, and 1930's, social responsibilities on which the society defaulted.

Emphasis upon community development in underdeveloped countries around the world also reflects social responsibility for fostering individual aspirations and hope.

Experience and Levels of Aspirations

Just as the very act of aspiring appears to be related to one's experience and to the social support given to it, so also do the changing levels of man's aspirations appear to be related to experience. In fact, what we have just discussed as the relativity of aspiring—the tendency of men who have the least (or have been denied the most) to have few wants—is one of the bitterest ironies of life.

From North Africa, an observer reports that the worldly wisdom that prevails there suggests, "You will always have enough because you . . . [do not need too much]; it is not necessary to use a hatchet . . . to open an egg." [37] The "security" reflected in views like these is amusingly depicted by cartoonist Chon Day in *The Saturday Evening Post* when he has one youngster say to another, "What I like about first grade is that they can't put you back." [38] The man who thinks he "has arrived" *has*—and at what is perhaps for him the end of the road. Conversely, "Civilization itself," Professor Muller reminds us, is what Whitehead once called it: "a program of discontent." Muller then recalls that Lord Raglan once observed that "The most civilized people are those who regard as necessities the largest number of luxuries," and who, Muller adds significantly, "therefore lay themselves open to more discontent." [39]

The stultifying modesty of some men's wants is, like not wanting at all, a leg chain slowing social advance. To persons interested in social progress, modesty of aspiration is a tragedy second in importance only to want of aspiration. On the other hand, those wishing to keep the advantages they have may be pleased if others do not clamor for a larger share of them. But, modesty of aspiration has an additional degree of social usefulness in that it helps to preserve social order and stability. When only two or three men seek the Presidency, there is confusion enough. If everybody wanted to be President, confusion would be hopelessly compounded. The question, then, comes back to one of relativities: how much modesty in aspiring for how much order and stability? But, whether for better or worse, the levels of men's aspirations tend to be modest. Workmen are more likely to want to be foremen and foremen to be superintendents than either are likely to aspire to be president of the corporation.

Although standards of "modesty" in relation to aspirations—like standards of other types of modesty—differ from observer to observer, it is noteworthy that when Charles Lebeaux and his associates applied to a section of Detroit's "inner city" Hadley Cantril's techniques for measuring people's conceptions of a good life, they found these conceptions (at least as they would probably appear to middle-class Americans) quite modest. A Negro woman is quoted as saying that, for her, an "improved standard of living" would mean "that my husband and I go back together and the kids all in school and he's got a nice job. That . . . I could feed them properly all the time. That would be it." [40]

Hadley Cantril himself reports that when he and his associates asked French and Italian workers in 1955–1956 "what their salaries *were now* and what they felt their salaries *should be* in order to provide for their needs and wants, the discrepancy between the two figures turns out to be appreciable but not fanciful." [41] The mean salaries *desired* by the French and Italian workers were, respectively, 49 percent and 120 percent higher than the mean salaries they were receiving. An Italian worker who had to leave his home town to find a job is quoted as saying, "I don't want anything from charity but all I ask for is a steady job. . . . My greatest aspiration is to go back and live with my wife and children." A French tool- and die-maker said, "No worker expects [to get rich]. . . . A worker wants enough money after a good hard week's work to let him go to the movies and take the missus, too. We want to live like human beings, without being short." [42]

Just as standards of modesty differ from one observer to another, so do standards of opulence. A striking and widely publicized example first appeared in a report of the Rosenberg Foundation. This report told of a Negro youth who was urged to emulate a Negro man who had become successful. "Yeah man," the youth replied, "but that cat was born with a silver spoon in his mouth. . . . For one thing that cat had a father; for another, his father taught him a trade." [43] Conversely, Indian maharajas, whose principalities were incorporated into the state of India, have bemoaned the scale of living they can maintain through their government-supplied "purses." One complained of the "agony" of his existence in his palace with "only" 100 servants. In his opinion, "the guillotine of the French Revolution would have been more merciful."

Bernard Berelson and Gary A. Steiner, after reporting Charles Morris' findings about "ways of life" preferred by college students in several countries, observe, "Such values typically stay close to home." Elsewhere, they have reported, "Typically, a class aspires to and struggles for mobility only to the next higher rank(s)." [44]

Many, many studies of the aspirations of all kinds of persons in many different countries reveal this same general tendency toward modesty of aspiration. This was true in the study of both Japanese and American students who were asked what each would do if he were given a million dollars. It was also true in a study made by a team of psychologists and psychiatrists in the United States, who asked each of a sample of "well-adjusted" housewives what she would do if given $5 million. A report made by Rena Corman on this study contrasts these "contented wives" (who constituted the "backbone of their society") with the discontents of the Tom Paines, Garibaldis, Freuds, Clara Bartons and other malcontents who shook the "Establishments" of their day but are now regarded as having advanced social progress.[45]

In Britain, Eric Deakins, in analyzing why so many workingmen fail to support the Labour Party despite its intent to put "working class interests in the forefront of its political programme," mentions, among other things, that "There is still some truth in the assertion that no one is as conservative as the working class man." [46]

Failure to recognize the frequently modest nature of the aspirations of disadvantaged persons has led to wide acceptance of what is probably a misconception. This has, however, undoubtedly worked to the advantage of otherwise disadvantaged people the world over. This probable misconception is that deprived people, out of their distress, are likely to rise up in revolution. They are therefore accorded advantages they might not otherwise have been given.

Unfortunately, we do not know definitively what degrees of deprivation invite what degrees of hostile reaction. Perhaps some day we may be able to speak with some assurance of a calculus of resentment and revolt as we may also arrive, in time, at a calculus of aspiration. In the meantime, the analyses of others suggest (as does my own experience) that the most disadvantaged groups are not the instigators of revolt and revolution. Having worked among unemployed persons in Chicago before public relief became generally available and among people in China who were actually starving, I know that woefully deprived groups just do not have the energy or strength for violence. Consequently I find quite plausible the views of such scholars as Harvard historian Crane Brinton who, in *The Anatomy of Revolution*, stresses the revolutionary roles, not of those who are down-and-out, miserable, and starving, but of persons higher in the socioeconomic scale who, however, are not included among the most privileged groups.[47] Harold D. Lasswell, in *Poli-*

tics: Who Gets What, When, How, expresses a similar view. He writes, "Deprivations, alone, are insufficient to produce revolutionary upheavals. Social revolutions occur when new indulgences have been made possible by the growth of new social formations as an incident of technical development. Only the new self-confidence of success gives strength for resentment against deprivation." [48] In the previously cited *The Politics of Despair,* in which Hadley Cantril analyzes why French and Italian voters who are not communists sometimes vote for the communist party, he makes much the same point.

Thus, it might be said that revolution is fomented less by the historic "let them eat cake" taunt flung at breadless people than by the more modern "let's have another piece of pie." It was this point, perhaps, that President Lyndon B. Johnson meant to emphasize when, during his campaign for reelection in 1964, he recalled that President Franklin D. Roosevelt had once said, "It is an unfortunate human failing that a full pocketbook often groans more loudly than an empty stomach." [49] This is not to suggest that masses of poor and hungry people may not be factors in revolutions. They are factors, but more as examples of the failure of a regime than as fomenters of its overthrow, more as instruments to be used by others than as instigators themselves.

Men's aspirations, as already suggested, tend to be modest, and, ironically, the more deprived men are, the more modest their aspirations tend to be. But as some gain is made, more is desired. As this is attained, still more is sought.

The mechanism at work was illustrated by our son when he was a boy. After a swim, he and I were returning home for dinner. He asked whether he could have a piece of candy when we got home. I said, "No, not before dinner." "May I have a cookie?" he asked. Again I said, "No." Then he asked, "A cracker?" I said "Yes." "*Two* crackers?" he countered. Although the words were those of a little boy, the reaction was a broadly human one. Men frustrated at one point and then again at another tend to press their advantage once they find a point that does yield.

This mechanism is related to what has been termed the "virtuous" circle and the "agglutination" of values. The principle underlying these concepts is exemplified in a touching way by work done by the Community Development Foundation in Greece. Just after managing to get food into a mountain village so that children could have energy enough to go to school, there came a new appeal—for shoes.

These were required for walking to the school over the cold mountain trails, but were never really missed as long as the children lacked energy to wander very far from home.

Escalation of aspiration is well illustrated by Guy Hunter, who in discussing the principle in *The New Societies of Tropical Africa* quotes from D. H. Lawrence's *Wages:*

> The wages of work is cash.
> The wages of cash is want more cash.
> The wages of want more cash is vicious competition.[50]

The potency of this mechanism may be seen clearly in the career of Andrew Carnegie. Admirers, carried away by his later successes, may not recall that while making up the monthly payroll for the railroad for which he worked, he came across the division manager's $125. "I wondered," he reminisces, "what he did with it all. I was then getting thirty-five." [51] But Carnegie—like others who win small gains—was quick to learn.

Douglas Jay quotes Britain's labor leader, Ernest Bevin, as saying about pay increases, "A rise is all right—till you get used to it." [52]

In President Johnson's inaugural address in 1965 he reminded his hearers that "in abundance" men sometimes forget what they learned "in hardship." He might have said with equal truth that, in abundance, men learn things of which, in hardship, they never even dreamed. Men learn quickly, however, and achievement, money, and other acquisitions are master teachers.

Perhaps it was insight into this phenomenon that led the Biblical writer who said that "hope deferred maketh the heart sick" to add immediately thereafter, "but when the desire cometh, it is a tree of life."

In more general and scientific terms, Berelson and Steiner have written:

Strong claims for improvement in the standard of living come more from strata above the bottom than from those at the bottom itself (the *lumpenproletariat*).

Those who have advanced even a little begin to appreciate what advancement can mean to them, and thus they press harder for it; they begin to have the energy to do so; they begin to win time to do so from the very battle for existence waged at the bottom; they begin to see what education and literacy can do for them; they begin to develop broader horizons and to grow some leaders of their own. Once the process of improvement gets under way and becomes visible, even the lowest groups are more and more drawn into action.

    . . . The appetite grows by what it feeds on.[53]

Despite the drag of past experience upon men's aspirations, gradual—and not so gradual—escalation can be seen all over the world. In the United States in the sixties the ever-rising expectations of Negroes were among the more dramatic phenomena of this kind. Demands by Negroes, and by white persons on behalf of Negroes, moved swiftly from elimination of discriminatory bars on employment to free access to public transportation and public facilities, to free access to places of public accommodation, to integrated schools, to private housing, and to the right to register and vote. Each hard-won victory extended the perimeters of the struggle as the horizons of expectation gradually widened—and widened even to more directorships of corporations.

In these respects progress was only following the pattern of change and reform that has gone on through history.

"Two crackers?"

The foregoing shows why battles for social justice—like the current War on Poverty—are battles with no promise of a "V-Day." The point, rather, is: Reform should improve conditions, whatever additional improvements may have to be made later. Although the War on Poverty may not liquidate poverty, one can hope that it will help to make tomorrow's poverty as different from today's as today's is different from yesterday's.

Underdeveloped areas of the world are also undergoing dramatic change. Progress that seemed hardly possible a generation ago is now being made because progress is being made elsewhere, because outside aid is available to facilitate it, and because new scientific and social inventions make it possible. But, as progress is made, goals are constantly advanced. The "revolution of rising expectations" of itself leads to the evolution of ever-new expectations. Peggy and Pierre Streit, reporting from the Middle East, observe, "The Iranian peasant admits that he lives better than he did ten years ago. Now, however, that he and the more articulate members of the new middle class have more bread in their stomachs and sugar in their tea, now that some of the pressures for the essentials of life have been relieved, the scope of their demands has shifted and grown." [54]

Escalation of aspiration is a phenomenon that is observable not only in a single generation but—perhaps even more dramatically—

from generation to generation. Commenting upon this broader dimension, but also underlining the relative modesty of the aspirations of deprived people, J. R. Schwendeman observes:

The demands of most peasant people are minimal, from the American point of view. [They] . . . ask simply for food, a new plowshare, common medicines, and a book or two. . . . They want clothing to keep them warm in winter and sufficient income to meet the incidental—though often heavy—expenses of ceremonial occasions. But each generation . . . wants more than the preceding generation.* [55]

Any individual's (or nation's) aspirations are, of course, affected by one's reference group. As others with whom one compares himself enjoy particular "goods," the more he is likely to want them for himself. In this respect, levels of aspiration—like the previously discussed act of aspiring—tend to be social products. Study of the "social context of ambition" of high school students in Los Angeles led University of California Professor Ralph H. Turner to conclude, "The average level of the neighborhood probably has about as much effect as the level of individual family background in determining how high the child's ambition will be." [56]

A fascinating analysis of how changes of reference groups have affected expectations of different social classes in England may be found in W. G. Runciman's *Relative Deprivation and Social Justice.*[57] In broader terms one can see in the experience of Japan the effect of a change in reference groups. Having attained a high degree of economic development after World War II, Japan is no longer satisfied with having "the highest level of living in Asia," but is now comparing itself with other highly industrialized nations.

In both current and historical terms levels of aspiration tend to change in relation to men's changing experiences and milieus. It is often this that is at issue when welfare services are criticized on grounds that they "spoil" or "weaken" persons they serve; that "the more 'welfare' people get, the more they want." While the possibility of "creating dependency" may indeed be real, the larger reality is probably not one of weakening people but of awakening them, of whetting their aspirations. Having gotten ahold of one cracker, they want another.

In a paper presented to social workers in Athens, Britain's

* A typographical error in an early draft of this manuscript—made probably by a typist who disliked greedy, grasping people—modified the first sentence in this quotation to read, "The demands of most pleasant people are minimal." Typists, like writers, have their preferences.

Dame Eileen Younghusband, one of the great social workers of the world, puts the issue boldly:

Social work belongs wherever it has the ability to contribute to man's awakening. This you may . . . rightly feel is a very beautiful thought. . . . But . . . we are playing with fire whenever we help people to become more alive . . . for this venture brings not peace but a sword.[58]

Worldly wisdom constantly reminds us that "nothing succeeds like success." However, the truth implicit in this aphorism might be stated, "No one more than the successful wants more success." This determination to "get ahead" might generally be regarded as a "good thing." Or it might be deprecated by those who are already ahead and resent being overtaken by others. However, like other good things, it too (as noted in Chapter III) may be carried too far.

Before leaving this problem of the calculus of aspiration, a further word should be said about aspirations that are intergenerational in character: the aspirations of men who want for their children "goods" that they themselves do not and never expect to enjoy. Whether one looks at the *favelas* of South America, at Harlem or other depressed areas in North America, at Africa or Asia, one repeatedly encounters evidence that fathers do not want their sons to have to accept what they have had to accept. Parents want their children to wrest from the future more than they have been able to wrest from the past.

From a welter of examples from all over the world may be selected that of a 1965 conference on "the Bedouin problem" in the Middle East. Bedouins at the conference proved unresponsive to suggestions that they give up their nomadic life. To them, "sedentary" lives seemed unthinkable. However, they were eager to have education and other advantages for their children, so that when they grew up, they could live "settled" lives.

The capacity of one "good" to whet the appetite for another and the power of one achievement to spur one on to another have long been tremendous forces favoring social advance. But they can quickly transform underdeveloped areas into what others may consider overdemanding ones. Whether the world can keep pace with the escalation of expectations only time will tell. If the present "revolution of rising expectations" has proved to be a challenge, the next stage—when earlier expectations will have been realized and new ones developed—may well be a "revolution of rising demands" and is likely to be still more challenging.

Despite all the explosive potential within it, aspiration is yet a fragile plant. In the breast of the Ifugao farmer, in that of the Pakistani camel driver, in that of the unemployed university graduate in New Delhi, in the *favelas*, in the "trap ghettos" in the United States —this tender plant will surely wither without the sunlight of effective opportunity. For, as we have suggested, even the act of aspiring is socially conditioned, and levels of aspiration are also as much the products of society as of individuals. Low aspiration must be seen not only in terms of an individual's need to "raise his sights," but also in terms of a society's need to remove structural and institutional obstacles that block the individual's view and impede progress toward his goals.

Not all human beings find themselves in an environment where they get a favorable response to even simple entreaties. Although the answer to the question "a cracker?" may be "yes," the answer to "two crackers?" may be "no." This has regrettably been the case where creative and stimulating Headstart projects for seriously disadvantaged youngsters have succeeded in arousing and encouraging interest in schooling. However, according to a number of recent studies, when it came time for these same youngsters to go on with their schooling, the poor neighborhood schools in some areas proved inadequate to quench the thirst that the earlier programs had created. The same may be said of many basic education and training programs for adults (sometimes called training for training) that have fallen far short of effectively preparing men for either work or better work-oriented training.

In future chapters we will have occasion to mention again this phenomenon of heroic efforts that are made to overcome particular problems only to encounter others for which no corrective provision has been made. The difficulty is often that "a boy is sent to do a man's work." More formally this has been called "tokenism." Welfare services, unfortunately, often prove to be "boys" when "men"— frequently *big* men—are required.

Aspiring and failing to aspire are relative matters. Even communities that condemn subgroups for their lack of aspiration may themselves be lacking ardor for "goods" to which they might well aspire. Before community "pots" call subgroup "kettles" black because they think these should be more aspiring, they should consider the possible inadequacies of their own aspirations. For example, Adolf A. Berle, Jr., has criticized communities for not pursuing "transcendental" values. Among these he included "truth" and "beauty," which, if pursued, could solve many other community problems. Of beauty, for example, he says:

If a pent-up demand that cities shall be beautiful as well as profitable were ever unloosed, the economic effect would be explosive. No one would then say there was not enough work to be done.

. . . Demand powered by the value of beauty alone would virtually end unemployment for years to come.[59]

Although Berle does not go on to say so, perhaps such an abolition of unemployment and the creation of real opportunities for previously disadvantaged and apparently "unaspiring" groups might show that they actually did aspire to "good" things, but had simply found them inaccessible.

1. R. M. MacIver, "The Responsibility Is Ours," in R. M. MacIver, ed., *Assault on Poverty* (New York: Harper & Row, 1965), p. 5. See also Otto von Mering, *A Grammar of Values* (Pittsburgh: University of Pittsburgh Press, 1961), especially pp. 64–71.

2. Charles Frankel, *The Case for Modern Man* (Boston: Beacon Press, 1959), p. 67.

3. Herbert J. Muller, *The Loom of History* (New York: Harper & Row, 1958), p. 9.

4. Allan R. Holmberg, "Changing Community Attitudes and Values in Peru: A Case Study in Guided Change," in Richard N. Adams, ed., *Social Change in Latin America Today* (New York: Harper & Row, 1960), p. 63. For a related observation with respect to another part of the world, see F. M. Esfandiary, "Middle East Paradox—The 'Beggar Rich,'" *The New York Times Magazine*, November 3, 1963, p. 83.

5. Carolina Maria de Jesus, *Child of the Dark*, David St. Clair, tr. (New York: Dutton, 1962), pp. 61, 62, 38, 37.

6. Lewis Mumford, *Faith for Living* (New York: Harcourt, Brace & World, 1940), p. 182.

7. Sidney Hook, *Reason, Social Myths and Democracy* (New York: Humanities Press, 1950), p. 29.

8. Lola M. Irelan and Arthur Besner, "Low-Income Outlook on Life," in Lola M. Irelan, ed., *Low-Income Life Styles* (Washington, D.C.: Government Printing Office, 1966), p. 5.

9. Joan Gordon, *The Poor of Harlem* (New York: Office of the Mayor, Interdepartmental Neighborhood Service Center, 1965), p. 132, 161.

10. Catherine S. Chilman, *Growing Up Poor* (Washington, D.C.: Government Printing Office, 1966), p. 25.

11. *Ibid.*, p. 25, and Gordon, *op. cit.*, p. 161. On this same point see Martin Deutsch, "The Disadvantaged Child and the Learning Process," in Louis A. Ferman *et al.*, eds., *Poverty in America: A Book of Readings* (Ann Arbor: University of Michigan Press, 1965), p. 358.

12. Winifred Bell, *Aid to Dependent Children* (New York: Columbia University Press, 1965), p. 58.

13. Earl Raab and Hugh Folk, *The Pattern of Dependent Poverty in California* (Sacramento: Welfare Study Commission, 1963), pp. 46, 48, 49. For a useful synthesis of views on various subcultures, see S. M. Miller and Martin Rein in Howard S. Becker, ed., *Social Problems: A Modern Approach* (New York: Wiley, 1966), pp. 488–493.

14. Ben H. Bagdikian, *In the Midst of Plenty: The Poor in America* (Boston: Beacon Press, 1964), p. 56.
15. Roger Starr, *The Living End: The City and Its Critics* (New York: Coward-McCann, 1966), p. 44.
16. Oscar Lewis, *The Children of Sanchez: Autobiography of a Mexican Family* (New York: Random House, 1961), pp. 347, 338.
17. John C. Van Dyke, ed., *Autobiography of Andrew Carnegie* (Boston: Houghton Mifflin, 1920), p. 331.
18. John Kenneth Galbraith, "Galbraith Defends AID," Letters to The Times, *The New York Times*, January 12, 1964.
19. Gilbert and Colette Charles-Picard, *Daily Life in Carthage at the Time of Hannibal* (London: G. Allen, 1961), p. 81. For a description of human sacrifices in Mexico, see J. Eric S. Thompson, *The Rise and Fall of Maya Civilization* (Norman: University of Oklahoma Press, 1954), p. 248.
20. Elmer Bendiner, " 'Immovable Obstacle' in the Way of a New Bowery," *The New York Times Magazine*, January 21, 1962, p. 22.
21. Quoted by Alphaeus Thomas Mason in *Brandeis: A Free Man's Life* (New York: Viking, 1946), p. 195.
22. Quoted by Herbert J. Muller in *Freedom in the Ancient World* (New York: Harper & Row, 1961), p. xiii.
23. James N. Morgan, Martin H. David, Wilbur J. Cohen, and Harvey E. Brazer, *Income and Welfare in the United States* (New York: McGraw-Hill, 1962). See especially Chapter 26, "Parents' Aspirations for Educating Their Children," pp. 387–400, and Chapter 27, "Some Implications for the Demand for Education," pp. 401–404. See also Chapter 28, "Plans for Sending Children to College," pp. 405–414, and Chapter 30, "Planning for the Future and the Family's Finances," pp. 427–436.
24. The following references cover differences in both the "act of aspiring" and "levels of aspirations," which, in our own discussion, have been treated separately. Of special importance is Robert K. Merton, "Social Structure and Anomie," *American Sociological Review*, 3 (October 1938), 672–682, and his *Social Theory and Social Structure* (New York: Free Press, 1957). A number of important papers have been brought together under the heading, "Working Class: Old and New," in Arthur B. Shostak and William Gomberg, eds., *Blue-Collar World* (Englewood Cliffs, N.J.: Prentice-Hall, 1964), pp. 2–57. See also Martin Deutsch, *et al., The Disadvantaged Child* (New York: Basic Books, 1967); Salvador Minuchin, Braulio Montalvo, *et al., Families of the Slums* (New York: Basic Books, 1967); Frank Riessman, *The Culturally Deprived Child* (New York: Harper & Row, 1962); Ephraim H. Mizruchi, *Success and Opportunity: Class Values and Anomie in American Life* (New York: Free Press, 1964); Richard A. Cloward and Lloyd E. Ohlin, *Delinquency and Opportunity* (New York: Free Press, 1960).

Useful materials more widely dispersed include Robert R. Bell, "Lower Class Negro Mothers' Aspirations for Their Children," *Social Forces*, 43 (May 1965), 493–500; Richard A. Cloward, "Illegitimate Means, Anomie, and Deviant Behavior," *American Sociological Review*, 24 (April 1959), 164–176; Allison Davis, "The Motivation of the Underprivileged Worker," in William F. Whyte, ed., *Industry and Society* (New York: McGraw-Hill,

1946), pp. 84–106; Robert Dubin, "Industrial Workers' Worlds: A Study of the 'Central Life Interest' of Industrial Workers," *Social Problems*, 3 (January 1956), 131–142; La Mar J. Empey, "Social Class and Occupational Aspirations: A Comparison of Absolute and Relative Measurement," *American Sociological Review*, 21 (December 1956), 703–709; Rosalind Gould, "Some Sociological Determinants of Goal Strivings," *Journal of Social Psychology*, 13 (May 1941), 461–473; Elizabeth Herzog, "Some Assumptions About the Poor," *Social Service Review*, 37 (December 1963), 389–402; Herbert H. Hyman, "The Value Systems of Different Classes: A Social Psychological Contribution to the Analysis of Stratification," in Reinhard Bendix and Seymour M. Lipset, eds., *Class, Status and Power* (New York: Free Press, 1966), pp. 488–499; Alex Inkeles, "Industrial Man: The Relation of Status to Experience, Perception, and Value," *The American Journal of Sociology*, LXVI (July 1960), 1–31; Suzanne Keller and Marisa Zavalloni, "Ambition and Social Class: A Respecification," *Social Forces*, 43 (October 1964), 58–71; Dorothy L. Meier and Wendell Bell, "Anomia and Differential Access to the Achievement of Life Goals," *American Sociological Review*, 24 (April 1959), 189–202; Gerald D. Bell, "Processes in the Formation of Adolescents' Aspirations," *Social Forces*, 42 (December 1963), 179–186; Hyman Rodman, "The Lower-Class Value Stretch," *Social Forces*, 42 (December 1963), 205–215; William H. Sewell, Archie O. Haller, and Murray A. Straus, "Social Status and Educational and Occupational Aspiration," *American Sociological Review*, 22 (February 1957), 67–73; Elliot Studt, "The Delinquent and Community Values," *Social Work*, 1 (October 1956), 26–31; William Foote Whyte, "Corner Boys: A Study of Clique Behavior," *The American Journal of Sociology*, XLVI (March 1941), 647–664.

25. A. Delafield Smith, *The Right to Life* (Chapel Hill: University of North Carolina Press, 1955), pp. 20–21.

26. George H. T. Kimble, "Words to the Wise—From Africa," *The New York Times Magazine*, January 28, 1962, p. 51.

27. Homer, *The Odyssey*, Book I, lines 50–54.

28. Jesus, *op. cit.*, p. 50.

29. Elizabeth Hamilton, quoted by Gertrude Samuels in *The New York Times Book Review*, March 23, 1958, p. 32, in a review of *Put Off Thy Shoes: A Journey Through Palestine* (New York: Scribner, 1958).

30. Louis J. Walinsky, *Economic Development in Burma, 1951–1960* (New York: Twentieth Century Fund, 1962), p. 368.

31. P. C. J. Van Loon, "The Role of Voluntary Action," in J. A. Ponsionen, ed., *Social Welfare Policy Contributions to Methodology*, Second Collection (The Hague: Mouton, 1962), p. 169.

32. *Ibid.*

33. Earl L. Loos, *Families in Trouble* (New York: King's Crown Press, 1946). Also relevant, but unfortunately also dated, is Lee R. Steiner's *Where Do People Take Their Troubles?* (Boston: Houghton Mifflin, 1945). Relevant to the international scene is Lawrence H. Fuchs' *"Those Peculiar Americans": The Peace Corps and the American Character* (New York: Meredith Press, 1967), pp. 70, 81, *i.a.*

34. Whitney M. Young, Jr., "Racial Discrimination," in Nathan E. Cohen, ed.,

Social Work and Social Problems (New York: National Association of Social Workers, 1964), p. 357.

35. Robert G. Hayden, "Spanish-Americans of the Southwest: Life Style Patterns and Their Implications," *Welfare in Review*, 4 (April 1966), 19.

36. James B. Conant, *Slums and Suburbs* (New York: McGraw-Hill, 1961). See also *Social Dynamite* (Washington, D.C.: National Committee for Children and Youth, 1961), especially pp. 26–42.

37. Guido Rosa, *North Africa Speaks* (New York: John Day, 1946), p. 59.

38. Chon Day, *The Saturday Evening Post*, June 10, 1961, p. 73.

39. Herbert J. Muller, *Issues of Freedom: Paradoxes and Promises* (New York: Harper & Row, 1960), p. 50.

40. Charles Lebeaux and Eleanor Wolf, "515": *A Study of a Low-Income Negro Area*, Part II, *Studies in Change and Renewal in an Urban Community* (Detroit: Wayne State University, 1965), p. 71.

41. Hadley Cantril, *The Politics of Despair* (New York: Collier Books, 1962), p. 67.

42. *Ibid.*, pp. 62–63, 51.

43. *Annual Report, 1960* (San Francisco: The Rosenberg Foundation, 1960), p. 2.

44. Bernard Berelson and Gary A. Steiner, *Human Behavior: An Inventory of Scientific Findings* (New York: Harcourt, Brace & World, 1964), p. 561.

45. Rena Corman, "Close-up of the 'Normal' Wife," *The New York Times Magazine*, September 8, 1963, pp. 52, 54, 60, 69. For an illuminating account of what young people in Japan would do if given a very large sum of money, see Jean Stoetzel, *Without the Chrysanthemum and the Sword: A Study of the Attitudes of Youth in Post-War Japan* (New York: Columbia University Press, 1955).

46. Eric Deakins, *A Faith to Fight For* (London: Gollancz, 1964), p. 43. See also Eric A. Nordlinger, *The Working-Class Tories* (Berkeley and Los Angeles: University of California Press, 1967).

47. Crane Brinton, *The Anatomy of Revolution*, rev. ed. (New York: Random House, 1952). An interesting development of the thesis that wars are caused by "have" rather than "have-not" nations may be found in Ernest W. Lefever, *Ethics and United States Foreign Policy* (Cleveland and New York: World Publishing, 1957), pp. 113–114 *i.a.*

48. Harold D. Lasswell, *Politics: Who Gets What, When, How* (Cleveland and New York: World Publishing, 1958), p. 170. See also Norman Birnbaum, "Great Britain: The Reactive Revolt," and Robert Waelder, "Protest and Revolution against Western Societies," in Morton A. Kaplan, ed., *The Revolution in World Politics* (New York: Wiley, 1962), pp. 31–68, 3–27, respectively; W. G. Runciman, *Relative Deprivation and Social Justice: A Study of Attitudes to Social Inequality in Twentieth Century England* (Berkeley and Los Angeles: University of California Press, 1966); and Barrington Moore, Jr., *Social Origins of Dictatorships and Democracy: Lord and Peasant in the Making of the Modern World* (Boston: Beacon Press, 1966), especially pp. 413–483.

49. Lyndon B. Johnson, *My Hope for America* (New York: Random House, 1964), p. 41. The quoted excerpt is from a speech given by President Roosevelt in Brooklyn, New York. It is reported by *The New York Times*,

November 2, 1940. For a very similar view, from Britain, see Runciman, *Relative Deprivation and Social Justice, op. cit.*, pp. 64–65, 89 *i.a.*

50. D. H. Lawrence, *Wages,* quoted by Guy Hunter in *The New Societies of Tropical Africa: A Selective Study* (London: Oxford University Press, 1962), p. 341.

51. John C. Van Dyke, ed., *op. cit.*, pp. 54–55, 73.

52. Douglas Jay, *Socialism in the New Society* (London: Longmans, Green, 1962), p. 387.

53. Berelson and Steiner, *op. cit.*, pp. 464–465.

54. Peggy and Pierre Streit, "In Iran, a New Group Challenges Us," *The New York Times Magazine,* July 23, 1961, p. 11.

55. Quoted in Irwin T. Sanders, ed., *Societies Around the World* (New York: Dryden Press, 1953), Vol. II, Introduction, p. 3.

56. Ralph H. Turner, *The Social Context of Ambition: A Study of High School Seniors in Los Angeles* (San Francisco: Chandler, 1964), p. 65. See also Alan T. Wilson, "Residential Segregation of Social Classes and Aspiration of High School Boys," *American Sociological Review,* 24 (December 1959), 836–845.

57. Runciman, *op. cit.*

58. Eileen Younghusband, "The Philosophy of Social Work," *Social Work and Social Change* (London: G. Allen, 1964), p. 105.

59. Adolf A. Berle, Jr., "The Transcendental Margin," *SCAA Viewpoint,* 9 (New York: State Communities Aid Association of New York, Fall 1962) 7.

II
VALUES WITH SPECIAL RELEVANCE for SOCIAL WELFARE SERVICES

D isparities in the degree to which individuals, families, groups, communities, and even nations do not, or cannot, enjoy certain social values lead to the establishment of social welfare services. These may therefore be described as social instrumentalities designed to make it possible for different groups—ranging from individuals to nations—to attain specific kinds of values or "goods."

This view of welfare services as positively facilitating the attainment of "goods" or key values is not so different, as might be supposed, from the more traditional view that they are designed to meet "needs" or, as is often said, "basic human needs." For, the very concept of "need" assumes a lack of something "good," something thought to have "value." "Need" for food or shelter, for example, presupposes that food and shelter are "good things."

Of interrelationships between values and needs Abraham Kaplan holds that "the ground of values consists, with suitable and important qualifications, in the satisfaction of human wants, needs, desires, interests, and the like." [1] In accord with this view, rights also are related to value because societies tend to give individuals rights to those "goods" that are regarded as preeminently important, such as life, liberty, due process, and so forth.

Because others have preponderantly stressed the roles of welfare services in "meeting human needs," my emphasis will remain upon their roles in making possible the realization of a wide range of values. Professor Leonard C. Marsh of the University of British Columbia in Canada, also views welfare services as implementing values, which he describes as religious, ethical, and humanitarian.[2] World-wide interest in values and social welfare is reflected in the fact that the International Association of Schools of Social Work selected for its 1968 congress in Helsinki the theme "Values and Social Work Education."

Notwithstanding what was said in Chapter I about the relation of values to human experience, analysis of the "goods" and values that social welfare services in many parts of the world seek to further reveals a great similarity in their aims. Such an analysis obviously involves two variables: first, what one chooses to regard as a social welfare service, whose objectives he then analyzes; second, the terms in which one elects to identify the social values served. Examples of the types of services I regard as welfare services whose objectives have been analyzed in value terms appear in Appendix I. How I define the values fostered by what I believe to be social welfare services is discussed below. Other observers, making different assumptions with respect to either the nature of welfare services or their objectives, might arrive at quite different interpretations.

We will consider here two kinds of values: end values, and valuations that are placed upon different means for the attainment of these valued ends.

VALUED ENDS SERVED BY SOCIAL WELFARE SERVICES

"End values" whose attainment is fostered by social welfare services not only in the United States but also in other countries include:

Life and health	Home management
Sense of dignity, worth, and purpose	Education and training
Aspiration to achieve	Employment
Freedom to make choices	Legal protection
Role and status	Group and community participation
Food	Leisure and opportunity for its use
Housing	Aesthetic enjoyment
Clothing	Religion
Family relationships	Promise of decent burial

These, which will be called "key" values, are not the only end values promoted by social welfare services. But when reference is made to end values, it is these (or at least some of them) that are meant. Although these are termed "end" values, in order to distinguish them from values seen in particular kinds of means to the attainment of various "goods," these "end" values may, of course, also be means to other ends. Thus, food may be regarded as a good for its own sake, but it is also a means to health, life, and other "goods." Freedom to make choices may be a "good" in and of itself, but it is more realistically seen as a necessary condition to choices of "goods" (schooling, employment, pursuit of happiness, housing, keeping or giving up one's baby, group participation, voting, and so on) and to avoidance of want, fear, pain, and the like.

To be sure, welfare services are not the only social institutions that further our key values. Other institutions—familial, economic, educational, health, religious—governmental or nongovernmental —also promote these key "goods."

When the above key values are referred to in the parlance of welfare services they are often qualified. For example: "constructive" or "congenial" family relationships; clothing required for "decency and health"; food "adequate for health and growth"; housing that is "safe and sanitary." And so on. But in the interest of brevity, the key values will be denoted here without such qualifications.

Values cannot be viewed as disparate and discrete "goods," of course. One might be in perfect health—but in prison; a bountiful turkey dinner might look quite good as food—but might be a prisoner's last meal before going to the electric chair. Thus, what was said about the multidimensionality of values must be kept in mind in relation to those discussed here.

If "promise of a decent burial" seems out of place in a listing of this kind, one should reflect upon the historic fear, in Western societies, of being buried in the "potter's field" or in a "pauper's grave." In the United States this problem is much less serious today than in the past because legislation permits public assistance or other agencies to authorize comparatively generous amounts for the burial of needy persons. Even in ancient Athens and Rome poor persons pooled their resources so that, at death, appropriate burial rites might be conducted.

Fear of not having a proper funeral or a decent burial is by no means characteristic of the West alone. In Asia poor families will further impoverish themselves to provide a "proper" funeral for a deceased relative. In China I have seen old farming couples who, though scrounging and skimping through life, had behind their hovels cypress coffins ready for the day of use. In fact, one might even add to the key values "dying in dignity": A German charitable organization makes a specialty of picking up persons—as in India— who are dying in the streets and of moving them into prepared hostels where they can "die as human beings."

No pretense is made here that each and every one of our key values would everywhere and under all circumstances be furthered by social welfare services, or that every possible value in which there is indeed a high degree of social interest will be found in the list, or that each is similarly valued. Among these values some are more critical than others. At different times and under different circumstances some may be accorded quite different orders of priority.

Universality of Key Values

To American eyes these key values may have a peculiarly "American look." However, there is much evidence, in both literature and direct experience, that to British eyes they would have a "British look," to Yugoslavian eyes a "Yugoslavian look," to Japanese eyes a "Japanese look," and to the United Nations a "universal look." This "international look" is apparent in, say, the United Nations Universal Declaration of Human Rights. If one takes just this single document and limits himself to identifying in it *specific* references employing terms identical or synonymous with those in which our key values have been identified, he can see that those things that the United Nations believes "all men everywhere" should have include: dignity, worth, equality of rights, better standards of life, larger freedom (Preamble); life, liberty, security of person (Article 3); family (Article 16); social security, free development of personality (Article 22); work, existence worthy of human dignity (Article 23); rest, leisure, holidays (Article 24); health, food, clothing, housing, medical care, necessary social services (Article 25); education (with at least elementary education to be compulsory and free) for the full development of the human personality, for the strengthening of respect for human rights and fundamental freedoms, and for understanding, tolerance, and friendship among all nations and racial or religious groups, and for peace (Article 26); participation in the cultural life of one's community and enjoyment of the arts (Article 27). Article 29 reads in part, "Everyone has duties to the community in which alone the free and full development of his personality is possible."

The Universal Declaration of Human Rights, it is important to recall, was unanimously adopted in 1948 with the support of representatives of both "the West" and the so-called communist bloc, whose values are sometimes thought to differ markedly. Since this action was taken before many subsequently created nations had come into being, it is noteworthy that at least some of them (West Germany, Libya, Cameroun, and Madagascar, among others) have endorsed in their constitutions the principles embodied in the declaration.

It must be remembered that values reflected in the declaration are "declared" values. Nations differ widely as to which are made operational and to what extent. But this need not detract from the apparent consensus upon what is widely regarded as "good" in life.

The universality of these values is further supported by the striking correspondence between the rights incorporated in the United Nations Declaration and those embodied in the earlier "Statement of Essential Human Rights," which was composed in 1946 by a committee appointed by the American Law Institute. Of the broadly representative nature of this committee, selected with a particular view to making its findings widely representative of the world's cultures, the statement reports: "The cultures or countries represented, besides the United States, are the Arabic, British, Canadian, Chinese, pre-Nazi German, Italian, Indian, Latin American, Polish, Soviet Russian, and Spanish." [3]

Because people of any country identify so closely with values they hear espoused, they find it easy to think of them as exclusively their own and to forget both their origin and their universality. When Henry Steele Commager discussed the "explosive principles" in the American Declaration of Independence, he pointed out—as must have been sobering to chauvinists—that "Americans did not invent these heady doctrines." [4] In fact, Max Lerner's *America as a Civilization* traces to Europe so many of the roots of the civilization that some critics have questioned the propriety of calling it "American."

When students who speak of some allegedly characteristic American value are asked to look at it more closely to determine where it was "manufactured" or where it was "processed" and "packaged for wider consumption," they are often quite surprised to see that some that they most closely identify with individual initiative and enterprise (often thought of as quite characteristic "American" values) are stamped "Made in Manchester" or "Made in Paris," or come from Geneva, Sinai, Judea, Capernaum, Alexandria, ancient Greece or Rome. Students, typically, are surprised to see that elements of "the Protestant ethic" that are closely related to welfare concerns (to be discussed in later chapters) have deep roots in ancient Jewish culture, in France, and even in Spain, which were relatively unaffected by the Protestant Reformation.

The universality of certain values was once stressed by United States Secretary of State Dean Rusk when reporters asked him if foreign aid programs were not unwarrantedly exporting "American" values to countries that did not necessarily cherish them. Rusk answered:

The kind of world that fits our own tradition . . . is a part of the great human tradition.

. . . When we talk to people . . . in different parts of the world, we don't really have to spend much time arguing with them about what we're after. We're after the most elementary opportunities for a decent life and they understand that. . . . We don't debate about purposes. These purposes are in the nature of man. We've articulated them in one way, they've articulated them in others. . . .

. . . We do not have a monopoly on these central ideas that we talk about here in our American society.[5]

Or, as Professor Stuart Gerry Brown of Syracuse University puts it in his *Memo for Overseas Americans:* "What is at once most touching and most practical about the American dream is precisely that it is not simply American and need not remain a dream."[6]

When Professor Hajime Nakamura completed for UNESCO his truly monumental report, *The Ways of Thinking of Eastern Peoples,* which included, incidentally, "ways of thinking" about values, Tetsuro Watsuji wrote in the Foreword on behalf of the Japanese National Commission for UNESCO:

When the external shell of the manifold and diversified languages of the human race are eliminated, the internal, essential and universally human thought common to all mankind appears and man is able to understand his fellowman. . . . When we . . . penetrate into the inner recesses of the substance of . . . cultures we find the universally common human element which makes us understand each others' aspirations and spiritual values.

After more than 600 pages of text Professor Nakamura himself says, "The inevitable conclusion is that *there are no features of the ways of thinking exclusively shared by the East Asians as a whole.*"[7]

Although different countries may all value certain discrete "goods," the extent to which these are implemented (or, in Rusk's terminology, are "articulated") and are accessible to the general population may differ widely from country to country. Also, priorities accorded from place to place and from time to time will vary.

To say that the key values presented here may be widely accepted in a variety of societies is not, of course, to say that they would necessarily be interpreted similarly in those societies. Ways in which particular values may be interpreted and the forms they take in different cultures and subcultures may vary. Status, for example, may be measured in one culture by how much wealth a man has, but in another by how much he gives away. Or, in a so-called subculture of delinquency in the United States, status may depend on how much a young man can "dish out" and "take" in a fight conducted with bicycle chains.

To suggest that particular values have a significance that transcends national boundaries or, as suggested in Chapter I, transcends even the various subcultures within any one society is to risk overstatement. Writing of the United States, Professor Suzanne Keller maintains that differences of opinion concerning "the value consensus existing among the different social classes" present "an important and controversial issue." She then reviews a wide range of studies, some of which "argue that there is a consensus," while others "argue that there is no such consensus and that lower class values differ from and are even opposed to middle-class or general societal values." Professor Keller then adds, "Still others have argued that both are true. . . . Lower class values, it is claimed, are specialized versions of general or standard societal values adapted to the particular context of lower class life." Her own conclusion, after her broad survey, is that "There *are* special values created and maintained in lower-class milieus that differ from the values held by the members of the higher classes and encouraged in the society at large. These include traditionalism, authoritarianism, ethnocentrism, anti-intellectualism, person rather than object orientation, and love of power."

However, Professor Keller also finds that "There are other values which have a resonance in the general culture even though they may receive a particular class-bound emphasis here. These are familism, respectability, a love of excitement and break in routine, a concern with money and security." [8]

When the Watts area of Los Angeles erupted in racial violence in 1965, speculation about the nature of the values of Negroes in that ghetto ran rife. However, careful subsequent study by University of California colleagues led one of the chief researchers to conclude, "Although the revolt was violent in nature, it was not a revolution which challenged the fundamental value system. On the contrary, it was an effort to have the existing value system implemented more adequately." [9] Another colleague who in addition to Watts studied other racial and poverty ghettos in the region became convinced that the people who live in them had substantially the same motivations and values held by more advantaged groups. [10] According to the National Urban League, "If we were to look beneath the abstractions, we could arrive at a true consensus among Americans about goals each man pursues: a good job; a comfortable home in a safe, pleasant neighborhood; a wife who does not have to work to support the family; children who will be able to get a good education. *The basic fact we are dealing with is that these goals are out of reach for a large part of our population."* [11]

Studies of values held or not held in different subcultures or societies have been defined in many terms—but never, as far as I can ascertain, in terms of what I have been calling key values. It is therefore impossible to say positively that the presumed universality of these values even within the United States would indeed be supported by research. At least, I know of no substantial evidence that would contraindicate this presumption, particularly if allowance is made, as previously suggested, for differences in interpretation concerning which statuses, which varieties and quantities of food and clothing, what kinds of houses, and so on are valued in particular subcultures or societies.

The basic and elemental nature of values served by welfare programs undoubtedly contributes to such universality as can be claimed for them. For, as Ralph Linton has suggested, "If universal values exist, they must be . . . those which stand in closest relation to the individual needs, and social imperatives shared by the whole of mankind." [12]

Furthermore, even if among certain social classes within a society particular values—such as the traditionalism and authoritarianism mentioned by Professor Keller—might be appraised somewhat differently than in the larger society, the degree of consensus on such values as are held in common—as the familism, respectability, and security also mentioned by Professor Keller—would appear to offer a possible basis for collaboration toward broader common goals.

To the problem of the presumed universality of certain values there is yet another dimension: Privileged groups may think that values that are just right for them are "too good" for less advantaged persons. Power groups in a society may covet for themselves a variety of "goods" that they are not, however, willing to share with others. Conversely, advantaged groups may seek to perpetuate, through welfare services for disadvantaged groups, values they themselves have abandoned.

When a national social work leader in the United States opened a conference on poverty in 1964, he exclaimed with apparent relief that here—*at last*—was *one* social ill that everyone was against. If that were really true, poverty as currently defined could be quickly abolished. This is difficult to accomplish, however, because there are too many who profit from poverty. Privileged groups want a pool of labor for menial services; employers want to exploit low-paid workers; slumlords profit handsomely from exorbitant rents for illegally substandard dwellings; merchants rake in large profits from high carrying charges and the frequent repossession and resale of merchandise. Even in the twentieth century one can still say of poverty what Margaret James says of it in England in earlier times, "Though poverty was generally assumed to be an individual crime, it was also . . . a public convenience." [13] Ernest S. Turner in *Roads to Ruin: The Shocking History of Social Reform* provides a fascinating account, in historical perspective, of what Margaret James would call the "public convenience" of "climbing boys" to clean (and be smothered in) chimneys, of mantraps that could maim or kill poachers on lordly estates, and of many other social "evils" England "reformed."

MEANS TO THE ATTAINMENT OF VALUED ENDS

Ends are of course inseparable from the means to their attainment. Ideally, both should accord with one's system of values. One may rejoice with Jean Valjean that he did at last get hold of some bread, but deplore the stealing. Interrelationships between ends and means have plagued philosophers and moralists for a long, long time. *Does the end justify the means?* However difficult it may be to answer this question, it is easy to see that means can sweeten or curdle ends. A man may highly "enjoy" the modest inheritance left to him, but grieve deeply the premature death of his father who bequeathed it. A young graduate may relish the degree newly conferred upon him, but forever regret the price paid by his wife who worked to "put him through" school but later became estranged because of the disparity in their interests.

If men often seem to give insufficient attention to means, perhaps it is because of too ready acceptance of the idea that "there are many ways (none more efficient than others?) to skin a cat." Or, it may be said, "All roads lead to Rome." From this they infer that any road is as good as another, whereas one may run through mountains and along precipitous cliffs while another runs along a safer seaside; one road may be infested by brigands, while another may run through a peaceful countryside; one may be paved and the other may be only a long slough.

Another problem is that persons sometimes become so attached to particular means that they do nothing to remedy a particular situation if they cannot see how to do it in *their* way. President Franklin Roosevelt's widow once explained that as a problem-solver her husband differed markedly both from his predecessor in the White House and from Winston Churchill. She said that he faced problems with a "no-holds-barred" attitude, a willingness to try anything that gave promise of success—Hoover and Churchill, on the other hand, were more likely not to act at all if their predispositions as to means did not seem feasible.

During the 1960 Presidential campaign in the United States, John F. Kennedy said it was "nonsense" to argue (as did his opponent) that they agreed on goals but differed only as to means. "The goal is meaningless," said Kennedy, if one "refuses to take the only road that will reach it." [14] Whether any given road is indeed the "only" one would, of course, be subject to debate. Nevertheless, the inseparability of ends and means seems clear.

Problems seem inevitable when particular means, either specific ones or broader constellations (such as "communism" or "socialism" or "capitalism") come to be valued—as Robert Theobald says—for their own sakes rather than as ways of access to other end values. Thus, preoccupation with particular means often distracts attention from important ends. Within a single country such as the United States, certain groups keep advocating more and more "freedom" without being specific about freedom from what, for what, and for whom—or about how it relates to the similar interests of others. At the other extreme are advocates of more and more governmental intervention to assure some objective, but who give little thought to effects this may have upon other "goods" desired. Eric Deakins complained about this when, in discussing a conference of the British Labour Party, he mourned, "The whole talk is of means [such as nationalization of industry] without regard to the ends which are to be achieved by them." [15] Consequently, we are here concerned with focusing attention upon the degree to which values inhere in means as well as in ends. This is highly relevant to social welfare problems because even admittedly and presumably effective action has often been eschewed because it could not be effected in ways meeting public approval. Conversely, welfare services may become so preoccupied with specific means that they fail to achieve desired ends at all or attain them only at the price of other (and possibly more highly) valued ends.

Accordingly, we shall be concerned with the nature of different means to attainment of various values, but will recognize that, under some or even most circumstances, means that might normally be "preferred" may not necessarily be the optimal ones under other circumstances.

Different nations and subcultures within a nation will pattern differently their overall institutional arrangements for furthering their values—giving rise to "British," "Russian," and "Indian" institutions, and, within societies, to different subcultures and life styles. In fact, Ralph Linton suggests that "Two societies which share the same basic conceptual value may fail to recognize the fact because of their different ways of implementing it." [16] However, within countries and subcultures whose institutional complexes and patterns of living vary markedly, there are specific means for value attainment that prevail widely. Among these means are self-help, intrafamilial cooperation, mutual aid, and gratuitous help.

Values attached to gratuitous help under varying circumstances will be explored in later chapters. We will also be devoting considerable attention later to self-help and mutual aid. But, although we later allude to intrafamilial cooperation, it is not discussed in detail (to do so would require a book in itself). We will therefore be assuming that families universally, though differentially, serve as socializing institutions ("carriers of the culture"), serve as preeminently important sources of love, affection, and emotional support for their members and as important sources of material support and other key values.

Intrafamilial Cooperation

What families do in all these respects is, of course, supplemented by other social institutions. Many social institutions (schools, churches, and advertising businesses among others) share with families their responsibilities for socialization, sometimes "working with" and sometimes "working against" what families try to do or are expected to do.

Families are typically expected to provide material support for their members. The situation throughout the world is exceedingly varied, however, and even within any given country it is in a state of flux. Within the United States, for example, the historic responsibilities of family members for one another's support are constantly changing. Brothers and sisters and grandchildren and grandparents, who used to be held legally responsible for one another before any could qualify for public aid, are nowadays much less frequently held responsible. Even adult children are now less frequently expected than formerly to support their aged parents in lieu of public relief. Thus, it could truthfully be said in many places early in the twentieth century, "The state sticketh closer than a brother." It could be said with equal truth after midcentury, "The state sticketh closer even than a son."

In world terms an almost universal phenomenon is the gradual shrinking of the previously typical "joint" or "extended" families, thus substantially altering the degree to which family members provide for one another various goods and services.

One exceedingly important variable in the degree to which families are trusted as "carriers of the culture" appears in times of rapid social change or when social change for particular groups is especially desired. Revolutionary societies, particularly during the early stages of revolutions (as in the U.S.S.R. and Maoist China) tend to distrust families as too conservative and to by-pass them with devices for the socialization of children. Even in the United States, when the cultural deprivation of many children was belatedly recognized, various programs, such as Headstart, did not wait for the cultural enrichment of families but concentrated upon this for children. In fact, numerous social programs must be seen as votes of public "*dis*confidence" in at least certain types of families.

We are not entering here into the merits of these tendencies. We are only noting the realities in contemporary life and will be assuming that families are still exceedingly important and valued sources of love, affection, and emotional support; important and valued but by no means exclusive socializing influences; and, differentially in different areas, important sources of material support, especially for young children, whatever may be the changing family roles vis-à-vis the support of older persons.

Gratuitous Help

A fourth important means by which men gain access to a wide variety of valued ends is what we shall term "gratuitous help." By this we mean help given to a man by someone other than himself or a member of his family (however "family" may be defined in his culture) and not given on a mutual-aid basis. Thus, we would exclude from our definition of gratuitous help the help a man might be to himself if he bought himself a loaf of bread, the help he might be to his wife if he bought her a new coat, and the help a mother might give to a daughter getting dressed for nursery school. Excluded also from our definition is the help young couples might give one another on a mutual-aid basis by baby-sitting each others' youngsters, and the help members of a car pool might give to one another as each takes his turn in driving the others to work. Similarly, services that members of an Israeli kibbutz render to one another would not, by our definition, be regarded as gratuitous help.

Values that are differentially attached—over the world—to self-help, intrafamilial cooperation, mutual aid, and gratuitous help vary, of course, not only in accordance with differences in cultures, but also with time and circumstance even within a single culture.

Not many students of the social welfare field, unfortunately, have attempted to differentiate among different kinds of "helping." One notable exception, though, is Dora Peyser, who writes from extensive experience in Germany and Australia. In her *The Strong and the Weak*, she provocatively distinguishes various kinds of help, but does not distinguish, as we have, between gratuitous help and "family help" or "mutual aid." This is unfortunate because, if our own analysis is correct, these different kinds of help are quite differently evaluated.

MECHANISMS THROUGH WHICH MEANS OPERATE

Despite the values differentially placed upon self-help and other means to value attainment, it is hardly expected that, in contemporary societies, a man should himself grow his own food and fibers. Nor is it expected that families and mutual-aid groups should hew their own timbers and build their own houses, weave their own cloth and make their own clothes, read only what they themselves had written or enjoy only pictures they themselves had painted. Societies have invented many kinds of mechanisms through which the various means to value attainment operate. Moreover, quite different valuations are placed upon particular social institutions, even though they may provide a medium through which even valued means can be employed. For example, one might greatly admire the devoted cooperation of a family in a concentration camp where parents and children heroically scrounge for and share their meager food, yet might detest the institution within which this devotion was demonstrated.

Although mention might properly be made of numerous types of mechanisms through which different means may be transformed into valued ends, we shall here mention only three, which will be called marketlike transactions, social utilities, and services preponderantly offering gratuitous help.

Marketlike Transactions

By the term "marketlike transactions" is meant any transaction in which the medium of exchange for either goods or services is money—"cash on the barrelhead"—or, in areas where barter is the usual means of exchange, the trading of goods and services. We do not limit these marketlike transactions to those occurring in "the marketplace," as this is usually defined, because money (or goods for barter), which for our purposes is regarded as the essential ingredient of marketlike transactions—and the indispensable link between the individual and that which he wants—is the necessary quid pro quo characterizing many transactions outside of the marketplace as traditionally conceived. Thus, we will include in our marketlike transactions purchases of food, clothing, and other necessities sold in stores; rent paid for housing, public or private; services for which fees are paid to lawyers, doctors, and other professional persons, including social workers in private practice; bus and other transportation (public or private) for which fares must be paid; insurance programs under which benefits are available only in return for premiums paid or paid on one's behalf by one's employer (thus including both classical social insurance and private insurance, whether commercial or "nonprofit" such as Blue Cross and Blue Shield). Included also in this concept are any other transactions in which receipt of goods, services, or privileges is directly conditioned upon specific payment of money, whether the enterprise in question is a private or governmental enterprise (such as a toll road or a publicly owned water, gas, or electricity distribution system) whose charges are roughly equivalent to the economic cost of the benefit provided.

For all the high value accorded to markets all over the world, this value and the value seen in marketlike transactions are not—unfortunately for observers who like their values all neatly packaged—without limits. For those without money, a market may be only a mockery. Moreover, a society may place so high a value upon some things or regard others as so dangerous that it prohibits traffic in them. Accordingly, the buying and selling of human beings (slavery, "white slavery," and "black-market babies"), sex (prostitution), justice, narcotics, dangerous drugs, and the like may be proscribed or limited—however lucrative the trade in them might be and however eager purchasers might be to buy. Also, complex societies have found it impossible to provide on only a marketlike basis a wide array of desired amenities such as public health services, education, parks, and highways.

Social Utilities

By the term "social utilities" we mean services provided by either governmental or nongovernmental bodies for the general public (or for stipulated subgroups thereof*) either free or at nominal cost, but without specific payment, without any test of economic need or other qualification other than capacity to utilize the service. Services we would class as social utilities include, in addition to free education (or education provided for purely nominal fees and highly subsidized by other sources), such things as libraries, art museums, parks and playgrounds, zoos, highways (other than self-financing toll roads), sidewalks, public health, police and fire department services, American Coast Guard and mountain rescue-team searches for lost persons, universal pensions and family allowances involving no tests of income, the British National Health Service, Norway's Health Security Service, the provision gratis of Seeing-Eye Dogs to blind persons.

A touching tribute is paid to the universal availability of social utilities by Dick Gregory, internationally known entertainer, who recalls the Depression, when his family was "on relief." Having suffered many indignities and humiliations because of his family's economic situation, he recalls even in adulthood how surprised and pleased he had been as a child when, upon returning to his community, he found that a house was on fire and that firemen began to fight it without even asking about the financial status or the race (which happened to be Negro) of its owners.

However, the nature of an institution, in and of itself, is not sufficient to assure equitable and decent service. For, one of the bitterest humiliations recalled by Gregory many years later (and described in Chapter VII) was the cruelly humiliating treatment by his teacher in school, which is also a social utility. Lest such brutal treatment be thought to have faded into history along with the Great Depression, it is noteworthy that one of the chief laments of representatives of a Clients' Advisory Committee working with one of

---

* Thus, free education might be limited to children who are educable and meet prescribed age limits.

New York City's Welfare Centers in 1966 was that schoolteachers giving children free lunch tickets called them up before the class to receive them.[17] In a school district near my own home, free tickets for school lunches are of a different color from purchased tickets, thus identifying their bearers. Social institutions whose nature is wholly acceptable do not necessarily render similarly acceptable services.

Nevertheless, we will assume here that attending a public school—like walking on a sidewalk, or borrowing a book from a library, or taking advantage of any other social utility—tends to be generally viewed as a quite "customary" matter and seldom in inimical terms. Depending upon one's sociopolitical orientation he might condemn a social utility as "socialistic" or "communistic" (as ultra-conservatives in both Britain and the United States have regarded free governmental schools, which, they aver, should be given up in favor of private enterprise). But as these facilities now exist, there is little tendency to view inimically one's reliance upon them. It is true that some elites may prefer, for reasons of prestige, to send their children to private rather than public schools or to have their own libraries rather than to patronize public libraries. However, doing these things is seen as an allegedly "plus factor" in their favor and by no means places under a cloud the use that others make of social utilities.

Elements in our definition of social utilities involve, obviously, various relativities. When are prices "purely nominal" and when should something be regarded as "highly subsidized"? But, as we shall see in later chapters, other kinds of distinctions are often similarly difficult to draw. Also in later chapters we will consider values placed upon marketlike transactions and social utilities, but particularly in relation to evaluations of other mechanisms.

Services Characterized by Gratuitous Help

A third type of mechanism for the attainment of valued ends by individuals, families, communities, and even nations is that represented by a wide variety of organizations that characteristically offer gratuitous help other than that provided through mechanisms already defined. The term "gratuitous," as employed here, is used in its basic sense of "freely bestowed," but without its sometimes inimical connotation, as in "a gratuitous insult." As noted already, we exclude from our concept of gratuitous help self-help, help given by family members to one another, and mutual aid. However, gratuitously offered help, as we define it, might foster any of these other kinds of help.

Although social utilities, as here conceived, offer their services freely to one and all, without qualification other than capacity to utilize the service in question, we exclude these from our concept of gratuitously helping services. We do not construe as gratuitous help the service of a highway crew repairing a roadway or keeping a road open, or the help a teacher gives students in a public school. From the viewpoint of the marketplace we would exclude from our definition of gratuitous help that which a clerk gives a customer in selecting a suit or that which a store or radio station gives to a family if, in some advertiser's gigantic giveaway program, it gave the family presenting the most poignant need a refrigerator, clothes dryer, and the like. If a policeman in the course of his duties helped an old lady across the street, we would regard this as part of his role within a social utility. But if over and above the call of duty he dug into his own pocket to buy food for a stranded family, we would regard this as gratuitous help. Similarly, if a customer, being "helped" by a salesman to select a purchase (part of a marketlike transaction), were suddenly to have a heart attack and the clerk rushed him to a hospital, this would fall within our definition of gratuitous help.

Gratuitously helping services are of wide variety. On the one hand, there are philanthropic foundations that pride themselves upon identifying future national and world leaders and giving them generous resources for advanced education, international travel, or "think time" better to prepare themselves for leadership roles.

Then, there is a wide range of services commonly known as social welfare services (like those enumerated in Appendix I), which gratuitously offer family service, child welfare service, protective service, adoption service, and many others, including financial aid to individuals and families who do not have enough money to supply themselves with the requirements that those who offer the aid think they should have. It is with gratuitously helping services of these kinds that we shall be preponderantly concerned. To distinguish them from other gratuitous services, they are defined as organized aids gratuitously offered by social groups to enable persons who otherwise could not do so to enjoy particular values regarded by these social groups (1) to be essential to the fundamental human functioning, constructive family living, or basic group participation of those to whom they are offered, and (2) to be essential also to the well-being both of those offering the aid and of larger communities of which they are a part.

When we say "organized aids," we exclude person-to-person help and intrafamilial cooperation. The form of "organization" may vary from a small voluntary agency to a state, national, or international organization—private, governmental or intergovernmental. The aids may run from material resources and support and direct service to broad action directed at changing environments or social institutions that impede the attainment of key values. Reference to services "gratuitously offered" is not intended to exclude services that are provided for only part pay or for nominal fees, but would exclude services for which fees represent substantially the full cost of the service.

"Social groups" that provide services may range from a tightly knit religious group (or any other body of associated individuals) to the citizenry of an entire state or nation—or, for that matter, of the world (as would be the case with social welfare services provided by the United Nations). Members of groups offering a service may voluntarily contribute to what is provided, may solicit contributions from others, or may be required (through taxes or assessments) to make their contributions.

The last part of the definition just given is included as a corrective for the sometimes exuberant claims that social welfare services are designed to "help people realize their full potential." Analysis of social welfare services, at least as they are conceived of here, suggests that they typically stop very much short of helping individuals to reach their "full potential." Family service agencies, for example, are likely to terminate their relationships with clients once family members have been helped to get along fairly amicably together. They do not continue service until families are always exuberantly ecstatic over one another. There are, however, important exceptions: situations in which one's "full potential" (as in the case of a brain-damaged child or of a terribly mangled man in need of rehabilitation) is little more than what, for less disadvantaged persons, would be only "fundamental human functioning."

One small way in which the more modest aims of social welfare services are reflected in our key values is in the wording of "freedom to make choices." We have deliberately eschewed "freedom of choice" lest this suggest that welfare agencies might necessarily help a beneficiary in Los Angeles to choose a Swiss or New York surgeon or a beneficiary anywhere to choose a Rolls-Royce instead of bus transportation. Even in the absence of such wide-open choices, inestimable good is often served by presenting even one alternative when persons think they have none whatsoever—even the alternative of a bus ride when a man thinks he has no choice but to walk to pick up his surplus commodities or to go to a free clinic. A girl often thinks very differently about relinquishing or keeping her illegitimate baby when she is permitted to do either and is not forced to do one or the other.

What is defined as "fundamental human functioning," "constructive family living," and "basic group participation"—and what is regarded as "essential"—will, of course, vary from country to country, from time to time, and even from social group to social group within any one society.

One other phrase in the definition deserves attention. When we spoke of offering to persons otherwise unable to enjoy them the opportunity to realize certain values, we did not distinguish between persons who sought these values but (without help) were unable to achieve them, and, on the other hand, persons who were "unable to enjoy them" because they did not regard them as valuable. The latter, too (as noted later), are a concern of social welfare services.

The definition we have given will seem much too limited to observers who want to include among "welfare services" some (such as social insurance programs) that we have characterized as marketlike transactions or others (such as universal pensions, Canadian or British family allowances, or the British, Swedish, and other health services) that we classify as social utilities. However, the differences in, and different values placed upon, *the bases upon which the services of various institutions are delivered* seem of sufficient significance to make them the grounds for categorizing and distinguishing among institutions. In other words, we will be concerned not so much with *what* institutions do (which is usually the basis for classifying social institutions) and how this is valued, but with values placed upon the terms upon which institutions do them.

Similarly, differences in values attached even to different types of gratuitous help suggest the usefulness of treating differentially, say, the giving of an art museum or library to a community and, on the other hand, "giving food to the needy."

To facilitate analysis in these terms, we will be thinking of social welfare services as defined earlier.* Other observers may well

* To those who are familiar with social welfare literature, the concepts presented here will inevitably raise questions as to whether the position taken favors the "residual" or the "institutional" view of social welfare services. This issue is discussed later and we choose, at the moment, to say only that either the institutional or residual interpretation depends upon (1) what body of services one selects as those about which to generalize (all basketball players? all giraffes? some of both?), and upon (2) how one characterizes

prefer broader definitions not limited to gratuitously helping services or, if so limited, not restricted to the range of gratuitously helping services we have specified. For such observers, welfare services, as we have defined them, would be only a subcategory (or even a sub-subcategory) of services more broadly defined.

Whether narrowly or broadly defined, welfare services—like other mechanisms by which men attain "the good things of life"—may be valued quite differently within different societies and even within a single society, depending upon time and circumstance, upon possible alternatives, and upon whether one is providing a service or benefiting by it.

DIFFERING EVALUATIONS OF THE ENDS AND MEANS OF WELFARE SERVICES

One of the fundamental dilemmas and bitterest ironies confronting the welfare field—or probably any field—is that specific end values or valued means to the attainment of valued ends may not be valued (at the moment of offer, at least) also by those to whom they are proffered.

Paul G. Hoffman once put the issue succinctly with respect to international aid. In a review of criticisms of the aid programs of industrialized countries, he quoted a Latin peasant who had complained, "You scratch us where it doesn't itch." Roland L. Warren, when he was with the State Charities Aid Association of New York, also stated the issue neatly in an article entitled "How to Interest People in What They Don't Want to Know." And a veteran social worker, Alice Overton, carried the issue further in a paper in *Social Casework* (July 1953), "Serving Families Who 'Don't Want Help.'"

Social welfare services all over the world are constantly doing exactly these things. The man who has been so buffeted by adversity that he has become comfortably "overdependent" may be encouraged by a welfare service to become self-supporting; a family service agency may stand fully prepared to help a family that is deleteriously squabbling. Yet neither the man nor the family may be "itching" for help. From California, Martin Wolins once reported, "A number of factors act as barriers to the use of existing welfare serv-

---

other social institutions to which welfare services may be "residual" or among which they may properly be seen as fellow institutions. Since, in our view, an all-important basis for categorizing and classifying institutions is the value or preference societies place upon them and upon the terms on which their services are rendered, we prefer to defer until later any further characterization of welfare services.

ices. First, many persons . . . are unaware that they have problems (the person with incipient tuberculosis or psychosis or with a minor mental or personality difficulty may not know that he has a problem)." [18] From Britain, Ilys Booker, speaking of both Sicily and London, reports, "In both situations the attitudes of the groups toward agencies which are set up to assist can often be apathetic or even hostile." [19]

Although this phenomenon is not limited to the welfare field, it leads welfare personnel all over the world to say that often the greatest problem they encounter is to get individuals, groups, and communities to recognize as problems what welfare personnel see as problems. It can be very frustrating to be ready to scratch but to have no itching backs within reach. One's greatest need is often to be able to sense a need of which he is unaware. All this is frustrating enough, but if one sees human development more broadly as meaning a constant *growth* of interests, the problem assumes even greater dimension. Melvin Rader, for one, contends, "It is important not merely to fulfill interests but to get more interests to fulfill: to pass from a narrower to a wider range of interests and to fulfill this wider range. . . . The good . . . is *the cultivation and fulfillment of positive interests*." [20]

THE CONCEPT OF VALUE PROPAGATION

Whether one looks at these issues from so broad a perspective or from the more limited one of seeing people who one thinks have problems but do not recognize them, there arises the possible necessity for what we shall call "value propagation." Every kind of institution engages in value propagation—homes, schools, churches, and many others, including of course advertising agencies. An amusing aspect of advertising is that the consumers of advertised products are required (through the prices they are charged) to pay for the appeals to other hoped-for purchasers.

Not all value propagation is consciously done. Social institutions, social change, and everyday human experiences, whether or not they are designed to do so, affect people's value systems (as suggested in Chapter I) by either giving rise to new values or eroding old ones. Changing patterns of family living—whether consciously or unconsciously adopted—readily give rise to new values.

Problems Posed by "Hands-Off" Policies Regarding Values

Notwithstanding the impossibility of remaining neutral amid the various human forces that consciously or unconsciously are working to further one value or another—even at the expense of others—there are many humane persons who are reticent, as they say, to "tamper with" the values of others. These individuals often do not realize that even though *they* may not want to "tamper with" others' values, other individuals (or forces) propagating values seldom sign any truce in the continual struggle to capture men's attention and support. Thus not "to tamper" is only to relinquish the field to the tamperers.

On this subject, one social work educator in the United States, Kenneth W. Kindelsperger, wrote in 1962, "Some social workers, highly influenced . . . by an extreme psychiatric orientation, have almost felt that their role in helping people was to maintain an antiseptic neutrality [toward values]." [21] He then said that, to him, this idea was "sheer nonsense" and went on to illustrate how in adoption cases and other services social workers did invoke value judgments.

In this connection it is important to recall that deviant behavior, such as that of juvenile delinquents, does not result only from environmental forces that "happen to" constitute the milieu within which young persons grow up. Delinquent gangs sometimes actually *recruit* members—propagate what the larger society would regard as *dis*values. One notorious gang in the United States makes a point of identifying nonsucceeding young men (or youths shunned by others because of physical deformities or disfiguring facial scars) and then *offers* them acceptance and fellowship. The first advances may be quite tentative: "Why struggle with school? You probably won't make the grade anyway." The final winning over, then, may come through an offer of the gang leader himself to have the new recruit as his own roommate.

Such acceptance as contrasted with avoidance by others tends to draw a young man into a way of living quite different from that which he previously pursued. Neutrality in propagating values may, therefore, play into the hands of those propagating what a community might regard as *dis*values.

On this point of learning deviant behavior, Professor Howard S. Becker writes, "Before engaging in the activity on a more or less regular basis, the person has no notion of the pleasures to be derived from it; he learns these in the course of interaction with more experienced deviants." [22]

Moreover, to the extent that it is true that men's values are largely affected by their past and current experience, to attempt to remain neutral on questions of value is either currently (or retroactively) to confirm the "goodness" of that experience. Thus, a hands-off policy vis-à-vis values may only reenforce values that (as noted in Chapter I) have been inculcated—even to a person's own hurt. For example, when Dr. Julius Nyerere was president of newly independent Tanganyika, he declared before its legislative body, "Our independence is no longer [a question] of demanding but of planning. And the planning is really a question of decolonization. . . . But . . . one of the most difficult things to decolonize is going to be the minds of some Honorable Members here." [23] Under circumstances such as this, not to tamper with values is to condone or even sanction past (or present) injustice, deprivation, or exploitation that even the nontamperer may have thought wrong.

A second group that resists value propagation is that which views it as undemocratic or as "cultural imperialism"—whether in international terms or between social classes within a single society. This school believes that in an open and pluralistic society people should be free to choose what values they want. According to this view, disadvantaged groups feel their inferiority and already suffer enough without adding insult to injury by telling them their values are all wrong.

This view overlooks the reality that few other propagators of values are similarly eschewing the promotion of *their* values. So, to withdraw from the fray is again to yield the advantage to others. Moreover, perhaps discovery and experience of values that a larger society has found to be "good" may outweigh not only the "insults" apparently paid to previously held value systems, but may also compensate for, if not overcome, the antecedent injury caused by the disadvantages encountered. There is still a lot of scope for pluralism over and above a base of social well-being as construed by a society.

Nevertheless, that there is some substance to the fear of "cultural imperialism" and its counterpart, the creation of "cultural colonials," has been suggested by Charles E. Silberman, who writes, with respect to Negroes, "They do not acculturate because they regard doing the things implied by that term as treason to their race— as 'going along with Mr. Charlie's program.' " [24]

Followers of the hands-off school may well have found momentary comfort in the title of an article, "The Poor Don't Want to Be Middle-Class," written for *The New York Times Magazine* by Harvard research psychiatrist Robert Coles. The article reveals, however, that the poor persons who are quoted reiterated time and again that what they wanted was jobs, money, homes, schooling, medical care, better choices for their children—all values that some might think have a middle-class ring to them but that in reality have much wider appeal.[25] What seems clearer in this article is that poor persons want many of the "good things" enjoyed by the middle class, but that they do not want to be pushed, shoved, and forced into the middle class—a problem to which we soon turn.

A common misconception that frequently militates against recognition that certain groups might want to change their ways of living has been the misapprehension, by privileged groups, of the degree of "happiness" among unprivileged groups. Whether these misinterpretations arc born of misperceptions or of guilt at not sharing more of one's advantages would be difficult to say. Nevertheless, the fact of misinterpretation seems undeniable. One effective guard against such misreadings would be to offer, in accord with concepts of value propagation presented here, opportunities for disadvantaged persons and communities to choose effectively the kind of "happiness" they want. This would at least avoid the travesty of falsely attributing contentment and happiness to individuals who, in effect, have had no real choices.

Value Propagation by Coercion

Another group that has difficulty with the concept of value propagation (and there are many social workers in it) is the one that dismisses the whole question by saying, "One must not impose his own values upon others." Or, as more class-conscious persons sometimes say, "We must not impose middle-class values upon lower-class people." In this, they would be correct. *Imposition* of values is not desirable, but this position is wrong in that those who take it tend to leave the whole matter there.

The old saying "You can lead a horse to water, but you cannot make him drink" is often taken as an excuse for not leading the horse to water. It seldom occurs to those who use this as a glib excuse for not leading horses that it might be a good idea for a horse to be near water—so that *when he needs a drink* he can get to it. And get to it easily. If he were separated from water by a fence, he might conceivably die of thirst—or rip his hide on the barbed wire—when he did decide he needed a drink.

Horace, nearly 2,000 years ago, stated the problem a little too strongly perhaps when he said, "Who helps a man against his will, does the same as murder him." Welfare workers would probably agree, though, that—if it could indeed be done—a man helped "against his will," would not be helped much.

From a more recent historical perspective, it is interesting to contemplate what might have been the course, and fate, of the British "Welfare State" if the then young Winston Churchill, in the early 1900's, had not resisted some of the proposals of Sidney and Beatrice Webb. Notwithstanding their solid scholarship, creativity, and hatred of the Poor Law, their zeal for reform led them to propose some measures that included strong sanctions. Such were included, for instance, in proposals to induce unemployed men to work and in measures to induce mothers to care for their children properly. Although Churchill, as youthful president of the Board of Trade, was strongly influenced by the Webbs, he rejected the coercive features of their proposals.[26] The widely acclaimed "National Minimum" advocated by the Webbs was, indeed, in many respects a minimum below which no one was to be *allowed* to fall. Although, as noted later, there are still some who speak in similar terms of "Welfare State" measures, a more general view is that a welfare state should seek to establish a floor below which no one *need* fall.

In both England and the United States in the late nineteenth and early twentieth centuries, the Charity Organization Societies certainly were not above heavy duress to secure behaviors demanded of their beneficiaries. Although Octavia Hill had quite a different view of herself, an American welfare leader of the day significantly dubbed her "an iron scepter twined with roses." [27]

Today's welfare workers, recognizing the difficulties of helping a man "against his will," would be likely to agree, however, that part of their job is what Graham Taylor once said about his settlement, Chicago Commons, "We sought only to inspire its members with an aspiration for something a little better and higher than what had satisfied them." [28] This statement really underestimates Taylor's role, however, because few ever did more than he not only to "inspire" but also to change social conditions so that newly roused aspirations could be more readily achieved.

Despite widespread questions of the effectiveness or propriety of promoting values (or at least value-conforming behavior) through coercion, one can see attempts still being made through duress, law, the Russian *druzhina* and the like, just as one can see in historical perspective "the Book or the sword," Calvin's vigilantes in Geneva, and Savonarola's "ragamuffins" in Florence.

That this danger is not avoided in the social welfare field is shown in some detail in Chapter VI. It is relevant here, however, to note that Samuel Mencher has written, "We must be constantly on guard that merely because some citizens are dependent for economic support on the community's treasury, they must *perforce* [emphasis added] accept the community's prescription for their way of life. It would be better to be part of a society that gives the same freedom to its dependent members . . . than rely on the good will of a society willing to intervene in the lives of those of its members whose economic and social failures make them amenable to social control." [29]

The welfare field more generally would probably regard compulsion as the least effective of available methods of value propagation. Personnel in the field have struggled too long in trying to help individuals and groups to new levels of aspiration and value attainment to give much credence to the phrases in the cowboy song popularized on TV in the 1960's, "Don't try to understand 'em, just rope, and throw, and brand 'em."

In the study of character development in "Prairie City," Robert J. Havighurst of the University of Chicago, Robert F. Peck of the University of Texas, and their associates found that even authoritarianism—to say nothing of coercion—was ineffective as a means for value propagation. Peck has reported:

In school, church or scout work it is fatal to the development of mature character to enjoin behavior solely on the weight of authority, or because "it says so here." . . . *Even if tradition is right,* to teach children to obey simply *because* it is tradition, or an "authority," is to cripple their capacity to become truly mature and intelligently self-governing in their moral behavior.

Somewhat earlier Peck had reported, "It is a matter of record that the 'punishment' theory of crime prevention simply does not work; and it worked no better with Prairie City children." [30]

A number of years ago Kurt Lewin wrote along similar lines:

Feeling threatened, he [i.e., an individual who is made a subject of re-education against his will] reacts with hostility. This threat is felt all the more keenly if the individual is not voluntarily exposing himself to re-education. . . .

. . . If the individual complies merely from fear of punishment rather than through the dictates of his free will and conscience, the new set of values he is expected to accept does not assume in him the position of a super-ego, and his re-education therefore remains unrealized.[31]

But, "imposition" of values and compulsion are not the only ways to consider. Values may also be propagated through purchase and persuasion.

Value Propagation Through Purchase

Value propagation through "buying" people's allegiance to certain values (or behavior in conformity with them) is of course common and, at least in short runs, often effective. In the United States this device is commonly employed in federal grants to states, which can receive these funds only upon the condition that certain standards are observed (nondiscrimination in employment or in public schools, decent treatment of public assistance recipients, and so on). In federal-state relations, however, even those states whose adherence to certain standards is to be "bought" at least have a voice in the legislative process that sets the standards. Gifts with "strings" attached may also be regarded as ways of influencing behavior through purchase.

These devices, especially in the short haul, can prove quite efficient. However, if one is interested in seeing that those whose devotion is "bought" really internalize the values in question and make them truly their own, purchase alone may not do the job. If only purchase is relied upon, then one must always worry about someone who might offer a higher price for some other allegiance.

Skepticism about "purchase" of loyalty to particular values is evident in the contempt in which the "rice Christian" was held in the Far East and that was accorded to the "soup, flop and salvation" of "mission" services to homeless men in the United States.

Paul R. Abrecht of the World Council of Churches has reported that in 1960 a young Christian member of the parliament in Nigeria engaged in a public debate on the question of bribing voters—the bribery consisting of small sums of money or free drinks and food during an election campaign. The debate apparently roused strong feelings until, according to Abrecht, "A Nigerian churchman restored perspective to the discussion by recalling that the Church itself had once won converts in Nigeria by offering schooling, food, and clothing to the children. 'Was this bribery?' he asked." [32]

Even in his day Seneca saw that "To reproach a man at the very moment that you are doing him a service is madness; it is to mix insult with your favours. . . . Even if there be some subject upon which you wish to warn your friend, choose some other time of doing so." [33]

Granting the power of the profit motive (although, as we shall see in later chapters, it is not given much recognition in some social welfare programs), it is hardly surprising that various experiments are being made actually to pay youths in delinquency areas to "conform" to law-abiding standards. Nor is it surprising that mothers in very disadvantaged families might actually be paid, say, twenty-five cents a day for each child they manage to get washed, cleanly dressed, and off to school. On a wider scale, the promise held out to Southeast Asia for massive help with their social and economic development may also be viewed in the context of attempts "to purchase" valued peace.

But, if allegiance to a specific value can, indeed, be bought—or for that matter imposed—for a time, the value may so commend itself that it comes to be embraced for its own sake. Thus, whether or not compulsion or purchase is involved, persuasion—or experience—must be looked to for effective, long-range value propagation.

Value Propagation Through Persuasion

Although compulsion and purchase may have roles to play in value propagation, at least in short runs, the best long-range hope of winning acceptance of new values lies in persuasion. In relation to any particular value, persuasion—as we see it—has three components: education about the value, helping people directly to experience it, and then, hopefully, their internalization of the value—embracing it and making it their own. Hereafter, when we speak of value propagation, the term will be assumed to include these three elements.

To Kurt Lewin, this method would probably have seemed consonant with what he has presented as a "re-educative process." This, he says, "affects the individual in three ways. It changes his *cognitive structure.* . . . It modifies his *valences and values.* . . . And it affects *motoric action*, involving the degree of the individual's control over his physical and social movements." [34]

Support for value propagation as we have defined it, and as distinguished especially from coercion, may be found in the previ-

ously mentioned study of character development in "Prairie City."
According to Peck:

The *only* method that works in favor of mature, dependable character is
first to give people—whether children or adults—reason to feel an *incentive* to behave ethically; and then to guide them intelligently, pa-
tiently, and with growing freedom to make and test their own decisions.
This way works; *none* of the other methods of child rearing, or of reformation, breeds more than unthinking, rigid compliance at best—and
many methods breed savagely hostile revenge behavior.[35]

Education about values: To teach about values is not to impose them upon others but to expose others to them. Of the role of
the social caseworker in this regard, Werner Boehm once wrote: "As
an agent of society, he . . . helps the client become aware of
norms which, as appropriate, the worker helps him to incorporate
into his behavior." [36]

On this same point Henry Maas has written that although caseworkers "guard against their imposing their own value judgments
upon the client . . . caseworkers may help the client to see as
clearly as possible and to modify apparently obstructing attitudes,
feelings, and objective realities in his problem situation." [37]

Of another kind of social action—community development—
T. R. Batten, a world authority on the subject, has written:

. . . Community development . . . is intended directly to affect the
lives of many hundreds of thousands of ordinary folk, and it depends for
its success on their willing and active cooperation.

"In contrast to the past," stated the Indian Community Projects Administration, "the servants of Government must approach the villager as
a friend—one who wants to and will help the villager learn how to make
decisions and achieve for himself and his family a better way of life.
He must not go to preach but to . . . create a desire to learn."

"He must be able to stimulate and create desires," stated the Pakistan Village-Aid Administration. "He should be able to engender a . . .
hope for the future . . . and a missionary zeal to do something about
it." [38]

In this connection the relationship of community development
to antecedent education programs is interesting. Of this Harold Wilson in 1953 wrote in *The War on World Poverty,* by which he meant
of course a global War on Poverty and not the more recent civil war
started by President Johnson in the United States:

This movement was first known as "mass education" but is coming more correctly to be known as "community development." The term as defined at the Colonial Service Summer Conference . . . in 1948:

"A movement designed to promote better living for the whole community . . . on the initiative of the community, but, if this initiative is not forthcoming spontaneously, by the use of techniques for arousing and stimulating it in order to secure its active and enthusiastic response to the movement." [39]

Teaching about values may include such information as what in a given situation *can* be changed; what is (at least for the moment) unalterable; what effects a given course of action can be expected to have in the short run and in the long run; what needs to be done now in order to realize some value in the future; what is required in order to receive social approbation and rewards now; and what is required now for what is likely to be the situation in the future. These are not topics to be taken lightly or questions to be left unasked, if one is interested in fostering social change.

Employing a somewhat surprising word, Professor Warren C. Haggstrom of the University of California has said that a community development specialist entering a marginal neighborhood must be "unrealistic." He then explains this in terms of perceiving people "as they can be." Haggstrom then adds:

Noting what is possible, the organizer projects this possibility and moves people to accept it and to seek to realize it. . . . People are moved to accept the new world of which they catch a glimpse because it appears to be attainable in practice and intrinsically superior to the world in which they have been living.[40]

Experience of value: Hearing and thinking about values is only the first step. To be effectual in human lives they need to be experienced.

A perceptive student, in commenting upon how much sermonizing was done to poor persons in the United States without giving them real opportunities to act upon the sermons, once pointed out how deeply embedded this penchant is in human history. In support of his claim, he cited from the New Testament (Luke 11:5): "The blind receive their sight, and the lame walk, the lepers are cleansed, and the deaf hear and the dead are raised up, and the poor have good tidings preached to them."

What has been said already about the relationship of experience to values and to aspiration (Chapter I) is of course relevant here. In fact, although another may teach, it is doubtful whether one can really learn about values unless he experiences them. U. S. Supreme Court Justice Felix Frankfurter used to say that he counted more on "man's ability to learn than to be taught." [41] And a large proportion of the human race probably would side with Winston Churchill when he said he liked to learn but did not like it as well *to be taught*.[42]

In support of concepts about "learning through doing" there is, of course, a vast literature. For our purposes here, however, we will note only that Dr. Seaman Knapp, who developed America's eminently successful and world-famous agricultural extension service, based this service upon the premise "What a man hears, he may doubt; what he sees, he possibly may doubt; but what he does for himself, he cannot doubt." [43]

The plethora of recorded evaluations of the importance of personal experience to social change makes selection difficult. However, M. A. M. Dickie, in writing about rural community development in the "Crofting Counties" of Scotland, has observed, "Defeatism and apathy must be overcome and there is no better way of doing this than when people see their life improved through their own efforts." [44]

What we have here termed value propagation has had a degree of acceptance in the international welfare field. This is suggested by the fact that one of the commissions, meeting at the time of the XIth International Conference of Social Work in Brazil, included in its report to the conference the following:

Neutralism toward values due perhaps to pseudo-scientific cultural relativity, i.e., the view that what a Community—at any one time—may regard as 'good' is necessarily good for that community, is a most serious obstacle. Community development and community organization are necessarily concerned with educating people about, with helping them to experience, and with helping them to achieve such values as life, health, education and training, income-producing activity and service, etc., in preference to such alternatives as unnecessary death, preventable disease, illiteracy and lack of training, unnecessary unemployment and underemployment, etc.[45]

One reason I like the term value "propagation" is that its root, *propago*, means a slip for transplanting and thus suggests that an idea that is planted in a man's mind is then transplanted into experience, so that he can directly sense the worth of what had previously been only described as worthy. In fact, to raise expectations and then not help men to experience them can be a cruel mockery. For example, when David Caplovitz writes about the way merchants exploit low-income customers who have few resources and little credit, he says, "It is possible that (in the absence of effective alternatives to their present shopping habits) educational efforts will only increase their discomfort. . . . this knowledge would only make visible to them the horns of their dilemma." [46]

One cringes at the thought of a young Negro school dropout who might at last be convinced to give up important values in his current way of life and to make sacrifices essential to secure training for employment (and the satisfactions that he is led to anticipate in useful work and regular wages), only to discover after all his investment that his color still bars him from enjoying these satisfactions. In many respects, it may be true that "experience is the best teacher." In terms of *really learning* values it may well be that experience is the *only* teacher.

The importance of helping persons to experience values positively is highlighted by what Gordon W. Allport says about fostering understanding and dislodging prejudice. Among the "positive principles" he has suggested for overcoming prejudice is the following: "Action is ordinarily better than mere information. Programs do well therefore to involve the individual in some project. . . . When he *does* something, he *becomes* something." [47]

In a chapter in *The Politics of Despair*, "The Nature of Our Reality World," Hadley Cantril speaks of the necessity for constant revisions of one's "reality world." These revisions, he goes on to say, "seem to come about only insofar as we sense the inadequacies of our assumptions as a result of action which we ourselves take or as we learn by sharing the experience of others." [48]

Social welfare personnel clearly see that if individuals and communities are to experience the advantages of certain values over others, the "field settings" of those to whom they are appealing must be sufficiently modified to provide genuine opportunity for that experience. This is what leads social welfare leaders and organizations to espouse and engage in social change, social action, and social reform—to help create real-life situations in which the values that are advocated can be directly experienced in valued ways.

Writing of middle- and lower-class ways of child-rearing, Catherine S. Chilman observes:

In our technically advanced society the middle-class way brings far greater social and economic rewards than do poverty group patterns. Since most of the poor, like the rest of our citizens, seem to want these rewards, it appears to be defensible for members of the service professions to work with the poor to help them change their life styles so that they have a better chance of joining the "haves" in our generally affluent society. Working with parents and children to break entrenched poverty patterns is quite different from imposing a middle-class value system on a captive client group.[49]

Even the mention of a "captive group" calls vividly to mind one of the most poignant of human documents, *Democracy's Scrap Heap,* which is Pansy Schmidt's story of rehabilitating seriously regressed patients in the "back-ward" of a mental hospital. Here was value propagation of a high order indeed—and against tremendous and what had long seemed insuperable odds.[50]

Before leaving this question of the importance of experience to learning new values, let us note the degree to which various social programs are often delayed because it is felt that the intended beneficiaries would not want them. Much action has been thwarted by presuppositions that persons mired in poverty, those caught in the toils of delinquency, or those in a particular racial group all have "their own set of values" and would not respond to values that the larger community favors. Evidence (like that already cited) suggests, however, that societal values do indeed have appeal for subgroups even when they cannot or do not live by them. Moreover (see Chapter I), people may modify their goals and expectations when circumstances so change that it seems possible to obtain "goods" that they previously thought hopelessly out of reach.

One important test of the degree to which persons and groups do indeed share societal values would be to open up genuine opportunities to enjoy them and then see their response. It is highly probable that education, persuasion—to say nothing of coercion—would be much less necessary to win respect for certain values than is commonly supposed. Commenting on Negroes' alleged preference for living in preponderantly Negro communities, Kenneth B. Clark observes, "No one will ever, in fact, know whether Negro culture *does* bind its members together until Negroes have the freedom to live anywhere." [51]

Early in the twentieth century in the United States there was great concern because so little was known about the number of blind or mentally retarded persons (then called mental defectives) in the country. Repeated "censuses" brought to light some information, which, however, later proved to be very incomplete. But as special schools or other services became available for these groups and there was thus some point to revealing blindness or mental defects, greater numbers of these disabled persons were reported. In connection with leprosy the same phenomenon has been observed. As long as there was no known cure and lepers were being sent away from their communities, there was reluctance to report even those known to have the disease. However, with the development of treatment within the community and with some promise of success, lepers who had previously been lost to view either came forward or were brought forward by their families. Phenomena of this kind suggest the hypothesis that in the absence of some promising remedy for a need, it is virtually impossible to get a very reliable picture of the extent of that need.

It is very likely that persons now thought to "prefer" values differing from those of the overall community would quickly reveal their devotion to the community values if they were given real opportunity to realize them. Certainly, if a beginning were made in this direction, one could then see the actual scope of the remaining need for value propagation of any kind.

Closely related to problems arising from uncertainty as to whether those to whom a service is offered will value it is the problem posed by people who appear not to know what they do want. "Let sleeping dogs lie," say those who shy away from value propagation on these grounds.

There is a common saying, "What you don't know won't hurt you." This is only a half-truth. What one may not know may not hurt his *feelings*—but may kill him. Many a man has been blown to bits by a gun "he didn't know was loaded." Not knowing what one is missing may indeed protect one's sensibilities—so that his face is thus "saved"—but through this sort of ignorance some potential "good" may be lost and some evil utterly destroy him.

Because welfare agencies are constantly confronted by persons who "don't know what they want," it is relevant to recall the sage observation once made by Professor Frank H. Knight of the University of Chicago:

In all the folk-lore to which human thinking has given rise, perhaps the most false and misleading single item is the common notion that men "know what they want." . . . The principal thing that men actually want is to find out what they do really want; and the bulk of what they want, or think they want, is wanted because they think that in some sense they "ought" to do so, that it is "right." They want to be "in the right." [52]

It is exactly these "wants" that value propagation as defined here can help to fulfill.

Embracement (internalization) of value: There is no better way—perhaps even no *other* way—to propagate American values, say, than to give persons who do not now share them a real stake in American life, a chance through experience to learn what others through *their* experience have already learned. Then, when they have experienced these values, the hope is that persons who may at first have tasted them only gingerly will come to relish them and become devoted consumers. One cannot be kept "outside" and be expected to regard as values what only "insiders" have come to sense as values. But once one has experienced the worth of the major values of his society, the expectation is that he will not lightly give up this enjoyment. Dorothy Lee writes:

We experience value when we find meaning in our life, when we feel good, when we act not out of calculating choice and not for extraneous purpose, but rather because this is the only way that we, as ourselves, deeply want to act. I believe that value can be experienced only when *relatedness with the surroundings* [emphasis added] is immediate and in a sense active.[53]

But, it must be recalled (Chapter I) that values tend to be multidimensional in character, and it cannot be expected that any one value—even if directly experienced—can necessarily offset a whole constellation of values around which one's life is built. For example, to return to our Negro dropout: If he enjoys, in his unemployment and unrelatedness to school, the inestimable advantages of acceptance by, and association with, his peers, it is unlikely that even a job and sense of achievement (if, after his training, he is indeed lucky enough to find them) will be of much satisfaction to him unless he experiences also the joys of acceptance and association. If his fellow workers avoid him because of his color, isolate him, and refuse to associate with him, it is improbable that the job alone will prove much of a satisfaction. This is why value propagation in any one quarter often requires changes to permit realization of values in other quarters, too.

The problem of attempting to effectuate realization of one value but without achieving other "goods," too, was poignantly illustrated by university students who went into a Southern state to give special help to Negro students. There they found that schools were "integrated," but that Negro students were required to sit so that the teacher's back was toward them. Then, when one did offer to recite, the teacher would ask, "If you want to talk, why don't you go to school with your own kind?" Of some 200 Negro students who had begun the school year in one of these "integrated" schools, all but eighty had dropped out by Christmas.

Extensive, difficult, and challenging though the task may be, welfare agencies often stand ready to offer access to values that those to whom they are proffered may not value. Agencies must therefore be prepared to awaken interest in these values. Only thus can they hope to help reduce the number who might otherwise suffer what Robert Frost wrote about an old, homeless, and dying farmhand, who had "nothing to look forward to with hope, nothing to look back upon with pride." [54] Or, it might be said that welfare personnel share the concern expressed by Professor Kaspar Naegele of the University of British Columbia for what he termed "much unlived life." [55]

:: Notes
and
References

1. Abraham Kaplan, *The Conduct of Inquiry* (San Francisco: Chandler, 1964), p. 389. The currently accepted classic on the "needs" that are commonly met by social welfare services is Charlotte Towle, *Common Human Needs* (New York: National Association of Social Workers, 1957). In broader perspective, Michael Graham, *Human Needs* (London: Crescent Press, 1951) clearly illustrates the interrelatedness of needs and values.

2. Leonard C. Marsh, "Social Welfare and the Social Sciences," in William G. Dixon, ed., *Social Welfare and the Preservation of Human Values* (Vancouver: Dent, 1957), pp. 32–42, especially pp. 39–41.

3. Committee appointed by the American Law Institute, "Statement of Essential Human Rights," *The Annals*, 243 (January 1946), p. 18. For extended analyses of John R. Ellingston's "The Right to Work" and of C. Wilfred Jenks' "The Five Economic and Social Rights" (education, work, conditions of work, food and housing, and social security), see pp. 27–39 and pp. 40–46, respectively.

   Of preeminent importance on the subject of the universality of values is Ralph Linton, "The Problem of Universal Values," in Robert F. Spencer, ed., *Method and Perspective in Anthropology* (Minneapolis: University of Minnesota Press, 1954), pp. 145–168.

   Universality of values that are of special interest to the welfare field is focused upon in *An Intercultural Exploration: Universals and Differences in Social Work Values, Functions, and Practice* (New York: Council on Social Work Education, 1967). An earlier effort along similar lines is my "The Common Core of Social Work in Different Countries," *The Social Welfare Forum, 1951*, Proceedings of the National Conference of Social Work (New York: Columbia University Press, 1951), pp. 19–36. A more detailed analysis of the breadth of interest in a narrower range of values appears in my "The Universal Struggle for a Dignified Way of Life," *International Social Work*, II (October 1959), 4–16. See also Helen McCrae, "Concepts in Social Work: Differential Applications in International Settings," in Dickson, ed., *op. cit.*, pp. 84–97, and Cora Kasius, "Are Social Work Principles Emerging Internationally?" *Social Casework*, XXXIV (January 1953), 23–29.

   Sources relevant to the extent to which the society's values are held by different social classes within the United States may be found in Note 21, Chapter I. An exceedingly helpful guide to thinking about different value systems is Florence R. Kluckhohn and Fred L. Strodtbeck, *Variations in*

Value Orientations (Evanston, Ill.: Row, Peterson, 1961). An application of this book's thesis may be found in Leonard Schneiderman, "Value Orientation Preferences of Chronic Relief Recipients," *Social Work,* 9 (July 1964), 13–18. See also Professor Kluckhohn's "Dominant and Variant Cultural Value Orientations," *The Social Welfare Forum, 1951* (New York: Columbia University Press, 1951), pp. 97–113. The interest of the social work profession in restudying some of its positions on value differences is reported in *Values in Social Work: A Re-Examination* (New York: National Association of Social Workers, 1967).

4. Henry Steele Commager, "Our Declaration Is Still a Rallying Cry," *The New York Times Magazine,* July 2, 1961, p. 5.

5. Dean Rusk, during television interview, *CBS Reports: An Hour with the Secretary of State,* November 28, 1962. Another view of common denominators in value orientations that, on the surface, appear quite dissimilar is given in William Draper Lewis and John R. Ellingston, "Essential Human Rights," *The Annals,* 243 (January 1946), Introduction, viii–ix.

6. Stuart Gerry Brown, *Memo for Overseas Americans* (Syracuse: Syracuse University Press, 1960), p. 27.

7. Hajime Nakamura, *The Ways of Thinking of Eastern Peoples* (Japan: Japanese Commission for UNESCO, 1960), pp. 1, 634. Also available in revised edition, Philip P. Wiener, ed. (Honolulu East-West Center Press, 1964).

8. Suzanne Keller, *The American Lower Class Family* (Albany: New York State Division for Youth, 1965), pp. 17–18, 26–27. For an extended bibliography on subcultures see pp. 78–87.

9. Nathan E. Cohen, "The Ideology of Citizen Self-Help Organizations among the Poor" (paper presented at Neighborhood Action Conference held in Cleveland, Ohio, March 15–17, 1967, under auspices of National Association of Social Workers), p. 13. (Processed.) Joseph P. Lyford makes exactly the same point in *The Airtight Cage: A Study of New York's West Side* (New York: Harper & Row, 1966) and in "In My Neighborhood an Adult Is a Dead Child," *Center Diary: 13* (Santa Barbara: Center for the Study of Democratic Institutions, July-August 1966), p. 7.

10. Paul Bullock, "Economically Disadvantaged Populations" (paper presented at School of Social Welfare, University of California, Los Angeles, April 10, 1967). See also his *Fighting Poverty: The View from Watts* (Los Angeles: Institute of Industrial Relations, University of California, 1967), and Kenneth B. Clark, *Dark Ghetto: Dilemmas of Social Power* (New York: Harper & Row, 1965), pp. 12–19.

11. *Annual Report, 1966* (New York: National Urban League, 1967), pp. 2–3.

12. Linton, *op. cit.,* p. 166.

13. Margaret James, *Social Problems and Policy during the Puritan Revolution, 1640–1660* (London: Routledge, 1930), p. 344.

14. *Los Angeles Times,* October 4, 1960.

15. Eric Deakins, *A Faith to Fight For* (London: Gollancz, 1964), p. 11.

16. Linton, *op. cit.,* p. 166.

17. See "The Client Views the Caseworker: Part Two," *The Welfarer,* XIX (March 1967), 12.

18. Martin Wolins, *Welfare Problems and Services in Berkeley, California*

(Berkeley: Berkeley Council of Social Welfare and School of Social Welfare, University of California, 1954), pp. 3, 4.

19. Ilys Booker, "Project in Menfi, An Experiment in Social Development," *Social Service Quarterly*, XXXV (Spring 1962), 150.

20. Melvin Rader, *Ethics and Society* (New York: Holt, Rinehart and Winston, 1950), pp. 165–166.

21. Kenneth W. Kindelsperger, "Goals and Value Guides," in Roland L. Warren, ed., *Community Development and Social Work Practice* (New York: National Association of Social Workers, 1962), p. 20.

22. Howard S. Becker, *The Outsiders: Studies in the Sociology of Deviance* (New York: Free Press, 1963), p. 30. Group and peer influences affecting neophytes' use of marijuana are described in Chapter IV, pp. 59–78.

23. Quoted by Richard Cox in "Nyerere Seeks a Middle Way," *The New York Times Magazine,* December 3, 1961, p. 29.

24. Charles E. Silberman, *Crisis in Black and White* (New York: Random House, 1964), p. 316. See also Alan Keith-Lucas, "Self-Determination and the Changing Role of the Social Worker," and comment by Morton Teicher, *Values in Social Work: A Re-Examination, op. cit.,* pp. 84–97, 105–106. See also G. F. Lewis, "Implications of the Sociological Concept of Security for Social Work Practice," *Social Casework,* 46 (December 1965), 621–625.

25. Robert Coles, "The Poor Don't Want to Be Middle-Class," *The New York Times Magazine,* December 19, 1965, pp. 7, 54–58.

26. See Bentley R. Gilbert, "Winston Churchill versus the Webbs: The Origins of British Unemployment Insurance," *The American Historical Review,* LXXI (April 1965), 846–862.

27. See Robert H. Bremner, " 'An Iron Scepter Twined with Roses': The Octavia Hill System of Housing Management," *Social Service Review,* XXIX (June 1965), 222–231. For two particularly interesting accounts by persons outside the welfare field concerning the manipulativeness of charity organization societies, see David Owen, *English Philanthropy: 1660–1960* (Cambridge: Harvard University Press, 1964) and Melvin Richter, *The Politics of Conscience: T. H. Green and His Age* (London: Weidenfeld and Nicolson, 1964).

28. Graham Taylor, *Pioneering on Social Frontiers* (Chicago: University of Chicago Press, 1930), p. 29.

29. Samuel Mencher, "Perspectives in Recent Welfare Legislation, Fore and Aft," *Social Work,* 8 (July 1963), 63. Another writer to see the dangers envisaged by Professor Mencher is Mary E. Davis, who discusses "go to school or get off relief." See "The Misfit—The Involuntary Nonproducer," *Public Welfare,* XXIII (October 1965), 251–258, 294.

The ever-present temptation to use welfare services as means for "imposing" values is evident in Joel F. Handler and Margaret K. Rosenheim, "Privacy in Welfare: Public Assistance and Juvenile Justice," *Law and Contemporary Problems,* XXXI (Spring 1966), 412. The authors conclude their paper with regret for what they call "imposing value choices on the dependent poor and our own notions of what is good for them." A nationally famous New York court case on this issue is Wilkie v. O'Connor, 261 App. Div. 373, 25 NYS 2d 617. This decision includes the often quoted phrase (p. 619), "One would admire his independence if he were not so dependent."

In describing the Chicago program for "rehabilitating" assistance recipients, Raymond M. Hilliard, who was then director of the welfare department, once said, "We have very seldom had to use compulsion." See "New Techniques in the Rehabilitation of Welfare Dependents," in Margaret S. Gordon, ed., *Poverty in America* (San Francisco: Chandler, 1965), p. 274. However, Mr. Hilliard sometimes spoke in terms of more duress, as reported by Silberman, *op. cit.*, pp. 313–314.

30. Robert F. Peck, Robert J. Havighurst, Ruth Cooper, Jesse Lilienthal, and Douglas More, *The Psychology of Character Development* (New York: Wiley, 1964), p. 192.

31. Kurt Lewin, *Resolving Social Conflicts* (New York: Harper & Row, 1948), pp. 64, 65.

32. Paul R. Abrecht, *The Churches and Rapid Social Change* (Garden City, N.Y.: Doubleday, 1961), p. 86. For a more recent impression, see "Some Hindus Assert Missions Use Food in Mass Conversion," *The New York Times*, September 10, 1967.

33. Seneca, *On Benefits* (*De Beneficii*), Aubrey Stewart, tr. (London: Bell, 1900), p. 25.

34. Lewin, *op. cit.*, p. 59.

35. Peck, *et al., op. cit.*, p. 192.

36. Werner Boehm, *The Social Casework Method in Social Work Education* (New York: Council on Social Work Education, 1959), p. 48.

37. Henry Maas, "Social Casework," in Walter A. Friedlander, ed., *Concepts and Methods of Social Work* (Englewood Cliffs, N.J.: Prentice-Hall, 1958), p. 22.

Additional sources that treat the relationship of values to social welfare services include: Arthur Blum, "Values and Aspirations as a Focus for Treatment," *Social Work Practice, 1963* (New York: Columbia University Press, 1963), pp. 31–43; Louise A. Brown and Margaret E. Harford, "Effecting Value Change in Race Relations through Group Service Agencies," *Social Work Practice, 1965* (New York: Columbia University Press, 1965), pp. 139–149; Irving Weisman and Jacob Chwast, "Control and Values in Social Work Treatment," *Social Casework*, XLI (November 1960), 451–456.

38. T. R. Batten, *Training for Community Development* (London: Oxford University Press, 1962), pp. 3, 4.

39. Harold Wilson, *The War on World Poverty* (London: Gollancz, 1953), p. 40.

40. Warren C. Haggstrom, "Psychological Implications of the Community Development Process" (paper presented at School of Social Welfare, University of California, Los Angeles, April 1967), p. 32. (Processed.)

41. Quoted by Sidney Hook in review of *Justices Black and Frankfurter*, *The New York Times Book Review*, July 23, 1961, p. 6.

42. Speech in Parliament, November 4, 1952.

43. Seaman Knapp, quoted in *The University of California Extension Service: A Special Report* (Davis: Department of Agronomy, University of California, 1965), p. 1.

44. M. A. M. Dickie, "Rural Community Development in the Crofting Counties of Scotland," *Social Service Quarterly*, XXXV (Spring 1962), 162–163.

45. Eugen Pusic, ed., *Urban and Rural Community Development*, Proceedings of the XIth International Conference of Social Work (Brazil: Brazilian Committee of the International Conference of Social Work, n.d., *ca.* 1962), p. 216. An illuminating report of how Filipinos gradually came to eschew "disease, illiteracy, and poverty" after experiencing "health, literacy, and economic well-being" is available in Lawrence A. Fuchs, *"Those Peculiar Americans": The Peace Corps and the American Character* (New York: Meredith, 1967), pp. 67, 163, *i.a.*

46. David Caplovitz, *The Poor Pay More: Consumer Practices of Low-Income Families* (New York: Free Press, 1963), p. 188.

47. Gordon W. Allport, *The Nature of Prejudice* (Cambridge: Addison-Wesley, 1954), p. 509.

48. Hadley Cantril, *The Politics of Despair* (New York: Collier Books, 1962), p. 42.

49. Catherine S. Chilman, "Social Work Practice with Very Poor Families: Some Implications Suggested by Available Research," *Welfare in Review*, 4 (January 1966), 15.

50. Pansy Schmidt, *Democracy's Scrap-Heap: Rehabilitating Long-Stay Mental Hospital Patients*, Supplement #46 to *Canada's Mental Health* (May-June 1965).

51. Kenneth B. Clark, "Delusions of the White Liberal," *The New York Times Magazine*, April 25, 1965, p. 135.

52. Frank H. Knight, *Freedom and Reform* (New York: Harper & Row, 1947), p. 234.

53. Dorothy Lee, "Culture and the Experience of Value," in Abraham H. Maslow, ed., *New Knowledge in Human Values* (New York: Harper & Row, 1959), p. 165. See also Julien B. Rotter, Melvin Seeman, and Shepard Liverant, "Internal versus External Control of Reinforcements: A Major Variable in Behavior Theory," in Dorothy Willner, ed., *Decisions, Values and Groups* (New York: Macmillan, 1962), pp. 473–516.

54. Quoted in the *Los Angeles Times*, January 29, 1963.

55. Kaspar Naegele, "Conflicts within Society," in T. E. H. Reid, ed., *Values in Conflict* (Toronto: University of Toronto Press, 1963), p. 39.

III
SELF-HELP

Self-help, as discussed here, not only envisages self-care and self-support, but merges with intrafamilial cooperation as well as with mutual aid. It may be expressed through marketlike transactions or through social utilities. Thus, it is not the individual effort of a Robinson Crusoe but that of men in societies. In large areas of the world, as in Asia and Africa, where emphasis is upon social groupings and where individualism is frowned upon as unsocially aggressive and as callous disregard of one's obligations to his group, self-help might be better described as "selveshelp." This fuses, obviously, into what we have previously discussed as intrafamilial cooperation and mutual aid.

In at least the Western world, self-help is usually thought of in terms of paid employment. In the case of a seriously injured or paralyzed person, however, it may not involve work as such, but may be directed to, and exhausted by, quite modest objectives—for example, buttoning his own shirt or feeding himself.

Essential ingredients of self-aid, at its best, include aspiration, self-respect, self-confidence, and self-motivation, but we do not have space to discuss these, except as they are subsumed in the broader concept.

Individual effort as a means of achieving the good things of this world is probably so self-evident a value as to need little elaboration. This is not to suggest that people might not like to enjoy the good things of life without bestirring themselves. Doubtless more men than would like to admit it have secretly envied the movie queen who in luxurious languor could command, "Peel me a grape!" But, the world being what it is, there is exceedingly wide acceptance of the good inherent in individual effort. In the United States such aphorisms as "Let every man stand on his own two feet," "Paddle your own canoe," "Pull yourself up by your bootstraps," and the more recent "But mother, I'd rather do it myself" underline the point.

In song and in story, in fable and in biography, in comedy and in tragedy, self-help and help to one's kin have been glorified, and in many languages. This has been especially true when the effort has been against great odds—as by the twelve-year-old in Ralph Moody's *Man of the Family,* who continued to run his dead father's ranch and to support his family—or as by an indomitable but ever cheerful mother who scrounges along but holds her family together, as in Kathryn Forbes' *Mama's Bank Account* (on the stage: *I Remember Mama*). It is almost as if the whole world were dedicated, as was the autobiography of the one-time poor boy Horace Greeley "To . . . boys, who, born in poverty, cradled in obscurity, and early called from school to rugged labor, are seeking to convert obstacle into opportunity, and wrest achievement from difficulty." [1]

RELIGIOUS SANCTIONS

Individual effort is regarded as so noble that it has been cloaked with divine sanction. "God helps those," the saying goes, "who help themselves," or as the Spanish would say, "*A Dios rogando y con el mazo dando.*"

Supranatural support of self-help, it will be remembered (though not by chauvinists who think that the God of the Protestant ethic was the first to bless private enterprise), was anticipated by Aesop some 2,500 years ago. Aesop, however, gave no indication that his gods helped men to parlay achievement into further advantages as suggested by the Christian doctrine of "to him that hath shall be given." This, by the way, was one of Andrew Carnegie's two favorite texts.

In Catholic teaching the importance of individual effort is the cornerstone in the concept of "subsidiarity." In reference to this, Pope John XXIII reaffirmed the principle that "One should not withdraw from individuals and commit to the community what they can accomplish by their own enterprise and industry." [2] But no body of religious teaching that I know stresses the importance of self-help more than do Jewish teachings. After his study of "the great cultural traditions" throughout the world and in historical perspective, Ralph Turner reports: "[The Jews] placed a high value on labor and disliked providing charity for those able to work. 'Earn your wage' was their advice to the laborer." [3]

However, the Judeo-Christian tradition is not the only one that stresses self-help. For example, when the king of Thailand appeared before the United States Congress in 1960, he expressed gratitude for American aid, but added, "We intend one day to do without it." He then declared, "American assistance is to enable the Thai to achieve their objectives through their efforts. I need hardly say that this concept has our complete endorsement. Indeed, there is a precept of the Buddha which says: 'Thou art thine own refuge.' " [4]

In an international seminar on the intercultural dimensions of social work, a Pakistani social work educator quoted the Quran as saying, "Allah does not change the conditions of those who do not change themselves." [5]

SELF-HELP AROUND THE WORLD

The praises of self-help are sung in so many quarters—from school-boys' textbooks to declarations of high national and international policy—that it is difficult to choose among them. Interestingly, Aristotle, in striking a "golden mean" between humility on the one hand and, on the other, vanity, settled upon self-reliance, independence, standing on one's own feet, and repaying with interest any benefit received from another.

For all the lip service to self-help in highly developed countries, one must turn to other areas to see what it really means. There is the backwoodsman in Guatemala, making furniture, piling on his back a burden that would make a horse groan, trundling it over steep mountain trails to the not so nearby market town—and then, if it rains and customers are few, trundling it home again. There is the woman in India who, for every household need for water, must walk a mile to get it and then carry it back—a weight so heavy that even her insensate carrying pole protests. There are the coolies in the Far East who pull a boat against a rushing torrent and inch along with their bodies bent almost horizontal. Westerners who see such sights frankly wonder whether they could "take it" even for a day, to say nothing of taking it as a way of life. Yet choices are few in underdeveloped areas, and though the rewards, other than sheer survival, are virtually nil, they are better than the obvious alternative.

To outsiders, unrewarding, grueling effort—coupled with, and in part caused by, lack of materials, tools, or skills—may seem to represent failure "to progress" and deplorable apathy and fatalism. However, as we have already suggested, aspiration is as much a social as an individual product. Let him who is similarly without resources cast the first stone. To call upon *descamisados* to "roll up their shirt-sleeves" is a cruel mockery.

Small wonder that in the least advantaged areas of the world one hears most about self-help. They already know what it is, and there is little, if any, other kind. For example, when the Planning Commission of India launched its giant Community Projects program—whose lofty motto was "Destination Man"—it was a mammoth program of help to self-help. Its three tenets of faith were

"Muscles can do it," "Muscles can be trained to do it," and "Conditions can be created to do it." Toward its destination, in the words of the commission, "The road is to be built by the people themselves, to be travelled by the people themselves." [6]

One might paraphrase as follows an appeal made many years ago: "Peasants of the world unite. You have nothing to use but yourselves."

Emphasis placed by India upon self-help can be matched in country after country—from Mexico, where men are trying to pull themselves up by their guarache straps, to those many countries in which men do not have even guaraches. Under these circumstances, it is little wonder that in promotion of Community Development and other international programs all over the world, the United Nations and its specialized agencies iterate again and again the importance of help to self-help. One example is a plea made by the director of the United Nations Food and Agriculture Organization. On behalf of the 3 to 5 million hungry persons in the world, he appealed to both small and large nations (but especially to those in which millions were worried about getting fat and were spending huge sums on reducing aids and diets) to "help the developing countries help themselves. We are not asking for charity," he insisted, "but asking people to help . . . countries to help themselves." [7]

But it is not only the most disadvantaged areas of the world that stress self-help. Rapidly developing, forward-moving Israel is a case in point. Do-it-yourself is almost a national motto, "being served" disdained. Not long ago even the wife of the then Foreign Minister bragged to dinner guests that she herself had done the shopping and had cooked the meal. After the brief Israeli-Arab war in 1967, commanders of the victorious Israeli forces seemed almost as proud to say that "We did it ourselves" (in other words, without outside intervention as their adversaries had charged) as to say that they had indeed done it. They seemed to find satisfaction also in the fact that, upon mobilization, many men had "hitch-hiked" to their battle positions.

When Harold Wilson became Prime Minister and moved into No. 10 Downing Street, his wife dismissed the previous household staff in a do-it-yourself campaign of her own. Whether this was a bow to self-help, as such, or an "example" for the nation was not reported. Nevertheless, in broader terms, the chairman of Britain's Labour Party declared at about the same time, "To give an honest day's work is not only the satisfaction of our manhood, it is our duty to the nation; to cheat and lie about that day's work is treachery." [8]

Somewhat earlier a Fabian group in Britain had written, "Political measures cannot make people perfect, but they can give them the means to improve themselves." [9] As already indicated, less now seems to be said in Sweden than formerly about the Welfare State there. The new emphasis is upon the extent to which social policies are "help for self-help." Similarly, Norway's Social Care Act of 1965 has been described as emphasizing encouragement of self-support. Tribute paid in Japan to the do-it-yourself motif is described by Jean Stoetzel in *Without the Chrysanthemum and the Sword.* More recently, Professor Mamoru Iga of San Fernando State College, California, has stressed values placed in Japan upon "competition," "achievement," and "success." [10]

Lest it be forgotten that value seen in self-help is one that transcends East-West differences in socioeconomic philosophy, it may be useful to recall the emphasis put upon individual effort—for example, in Yugoslavia and Czechoslovakia. In both countries, the guiding principle is not the communist doctrine, as they define it, of "to each according to his need," but what they call the socialist principle of "to each according to his work." One surprising effect of this close tie between one's own efforts and the rewards available to him is that (at least in Yugoslavia) even such institutions as hospitals and post offices are run like any business enterprise, and not, as in the United States, as nonprofit corporations or as general government services.

Striking evidence of the breadth of support for Community Development and its self-help component is provided in an impressive collection of letters imaginatively solicited from heads of state and other officials by Glen Leet, president of the International Society for Community Development. Among replies published by the society are those from the prime ministers of Canada, India, Ireland, Northern Ireland, Korea, the Sudan, and Thailand, the presidents of Chile, the Dominican Republic, Honduras, and the United States, and King Faisal of Saudi Arabia.[11]

In view of the indicators from all over the world that individual effort and self-help have long been widely regarded as valued highways to achievement of both personal and national goals, it is not surprising that the concept should have been formally recognized in intergovernmental circles.

Although the United Nations Universal Declaration of Human Rights, like the United States Constitution, does not mention specifically the importance of self-help, it does—as does our Constitution —place great emphasis upon maintaining, as rights, conditions under which individuals may be better able to look after themselves. The declaration says:

Everyone, as a member of society, has the right to *realization* [emphasis added] . . . of the economic, social and cultural rights indispensable for his dignity and free development of his personality. . . . Everyone has the right to work.

The world situation, the variety and depth of human needs around the globe, and international relations being what they are, it is natural that, especially since World War II, self-help values have been so widely emphasized in international circles. But this emphasis is by no means new. Earlier programs of Red Cross Societies, the Near East Foundation, the Hoover-directed programs in Belgium and Russia after World War I, the American Friends Service Committee, among others, stressed help for self-help. More recently, UNRRA, the Marshall Plan, the Colombo Plan, the Truman Plan, the Alliance for Progress, Food for Peace, CARE, Save the Children Federation, WHO, FAO, UNICEF, and a great many others have taken special pride in their help to self-help.

The theme recurs again and again in interpretations of the various foreign-aid programs of the United States. For example, a report of the Agency for International Development (AID) declares, "The concept of 'self-help' is central to all AID programs." The report then cites many individual projects in which the principle was embodied.[12]

Whether or not United States foreign-aid programs today meet the high hopes expressed for them by David Lilienthal in 1960, his vision of them is noteworthy. "An American foreign-aid program," he wrote, "should be rooted in the most basic of our ideals and sentiments, and reflect the most admired of our talents—our sensitivity to the aspirations of others and our faith in what others can do to help themselves if given a fair chance." [13]

In passing, it is interesting to contemplate whether experience with international aid may not have had something to do with the recent sudden resurgence of interest in promoting self-help—as through the War on Poverty—within the United States. If so, it will not have been the first lesson learned abroad for subsequent domestic consumption.

SELF-HELP IN THE UNITED STATES

Again, the plethora of maxims, sermons, novels, and the like extolling self-help within the United States necessitates an almost arbitrary selection of examples. However, contrapuntal evidence from various quarters makes it difficult to assess accurately what American emphases upon self-help really mean. Nevertheless, it is probably not too much to say that red-blooded Americans would have found their blood running faster upon reading in the 1947 report of President Truman's eminent Committee on Civil Rights: "The central theme in our American heritage is the importance of the individual person. . . . The only aristocracy that is consistent with the free way of life is an aristocracy of talent and achievement." [14]

Chauvinistic Americans taking a possessive pride in an "aristocracy of achievement" would probably be startled (though gaining a clearer perspective) to know that in almost identical terms—700 years earlier and thousands of miles away—in the Florence of the Medici—it was said, "The real noble is the child of his own achievements." [15]

Official policy

Among numberless high-policy statements in favor of self-support we limit ourselves to only a few samples relating to recent major policy issues. In 1964, when the United States went to war on poverty, President Johnson declared, "We are not trying to give people more relief—we want to give people more opportunity. That is what the people want. They want education and training. They want a job and a wage which will let them provide for their family." In another context he urged, "Let us deny to no one the chance to develop and use his native talents to the full." [16]

Somewhat more specifically, the Council of Economic Advisers recalled that "conquest of poverty" could be relatively easy if the American people taxed themselves for the $11 billion (only 2 percent of the GNP, "certainly not an intolerable burden") necessary to "bring all poor families up to the . . . income level we have taken to be the minimum for a decent life." "But," contended the council, "Americans want to *earn* the American standard of living by their own efforts and contributions [emphasis added]." [17] If a plebiscite had been conducted to determine what "Americans want," this was not reported. The council's view was undoubtedly correct, however, as President Franklin D. Roosevelt and Harry L. Hopkins believed —and as millions of PWA and WPA workers proved—during the Great Depression. At that time, when unemployment rolls were several times higher than at present, a prime concern was to provide jobs, not just training for jobs, as under much of the War on Poverty.* In retrospect, however, the degree to which the later wartime employment boom virtually eliminated unemployment suggests that the Depression work programs may have been more effective than was appreciated at the time in preparing (or keeping alive the work skills of) workers for the later upsurge in employment.

When, in 1935, President Roosevelt announced his proposal to launch a gigantic work program, he declared:

I am not willing that the vitality of our people be further sapped by the giving of cash, market baskets, of a few hours of weekly work cutting grass, raking leaves or picking up papers in the public parks. We must preserve not only the bodies of the unemployed from destitution but also their self-respect, their self-reliance.

About the time the new work program was providing jobs for some 3 million workers, the President reaffirmed his position:

A dole would be more economical than work relief. That is true. But . . . in this business of relief we are dealing with properly self-respecting Americans to whom a mere dole outrages every instinct of individual independence.

Most Americans want to give something for what they get. That something, in this case honest work, is the saving barrier between them and moral disintegration. We propose to build that barrier high.[18]

But probably the most succinct of all Depression declarations extolling work was that in *The WPA Worker's Handbook*, which, in response to a question as to why work was important, said simply, "It keeps us from going nuts."

More than twenty years later, this prescription was confirmed when Nancy Morse and Robert S. Weiss of the University of Michigan asked a sample of employed men why they thought they would continue to work even if they had "enough money to live on comfortably without working." The second most frequent response was that

* The U.S. Senate Committee on Labor and Public Welfare in 1967 wrote into its version of the Poverty Bill a multibillion dollar crash employment program, which was opposed by the administration, however, and, at this writing, seems likely to be rejected.

without work they thought they would "feel lost, go crazy." The only response given more frequently was that work kept the men "occupied (interested)." This study clearly underlines men's interest in work because no fewer than 80 percent of the respondents indicated that they would continue working even if they could live "comfortably" without working.[19]

In retrospect, as at the time, it is amazing how right were those who held the views of President Roosevelt, Harry Hopkins, and others and how wrong were those who opposed the work programs. The latter thought that "reliefers" and "relief bums" (as they called them) would never turn a hand to help themselves and cynically contended that if men and women were out of jobs it was simply because "some folks won't work." On the contrary, the evidence— from high places and low—was almost unanimously that men preferred work over idleness and relief. However, it is not implausible to deduce that this emphasis upon self-help and that those persons Caroline Bird terms "the poor the New Deal forgot" may have contributed to the numbers of disadvantaged persons who, in the 1960's, were not sharing in the general prosperity.[20]

More recent experience with public assistance and the War on Poverty also suggests that, when at all possible, economically dependent persons (as shown in Chapter VII) greatly prefer self-support to public aid. Widespread evidence further reveals that jobless men and women prefer jobs to mere "work-training and experience programs" that might or might not lead to employment. Thus, evidence clearly suggests that President Johnson and his Council of Economic Advisers were indeed correct in saying that disadvantaged American people wanted not relief but opportunities and work. What is clear in welfare experience is that far fewer assistance recipients are "work-shy" than are "low-pay-shy" or "substandard-work-shy"—or shy away from downright exploitation, as in the case of "stoop-labor," which was paid 50 cents to 75 cents an hour in agricultural work.

Soon after the machines that were mobilized for the War on Poverty had begun to roll, R. Sargent Shriver, its commanding general, declared, "The war on poverty is not a struggle simply to support people, to make them dependent on the generosity of others. It is a struggle to give people a chance." [21]

In this same vein a United States senate committee reported:

No one will question that every man is entitled to the opportunity to provide for himself and his family. That is a fundamental right. . . .

And . . . society is going . . . to provide an opportunity for a man to sustain himself, or is going to sustain man. . . . Society may as well make every effort to do the job constructively, because no society can be strong in which its members are encouraged or forced to adopt the position and the place of those seeking charity.

Anyone reading this who is familiar with the War on Poverty and other problems of the latter 1960's might well assume that the senate committee was reporting on contemporary issues. Whimsically, though, the quotation is from a report on "Causes and Relief of Unemployment"—issued *in* 1929.[22] Thus, emphases in official policies upon self-help in the late 1960's reflected traditions of some years' standing. However, the opportunity that "no one will question that every man is entitled to" was still not a reality.

When speaking of work programs, it is easy to think almost exclusively of able-bodied unemployed men and women. Yet a great many other people are involved. At issue too is work for youths (as fostered by Youth Employment Programs); work for handicapped persons (highlighted through "Hire the Handicapped Week"); work for prisoners, whether in prison, or work-leave, or after release; work for patients in mental hospitals and after their release; work for older persons, even after the economic sun in their lives has set. For example, the President's Council on Aging in 1963 made an eloquent plea for nationwide measures to continue to utilize in service—paid or volunteer—the skills and experience of older persons. The council held:

Employment [is for many] a principal source of income to provide the necessities of life. For others, it provides the therapy of usefulness, belonging, and well-being. To many older people, employment is the badge of status in the family and the community and the center from which social contacts radiate. To some, it is one of these things and to others it may be all of them.[23]

The extent to which self-help is stressed in social welfare policy in the United States is discussed in some detail later. However, mention should be made here of the degree to which social insurance is widely accepted as virtually a do-it-yourself program. This can be illustrated in many ways, but we choose for our purposes the following explanation by Robert M. Ball, federal Commissioner of Social Security in 1965:

The genius of the social insurance approach is that the protection is earned by work and contributions. Social insurance is based on the concept that security for the individual should, to the extent possible, grow out of his own work. . . .

Basing eligibility on a demonstration of work and providing variable benefits related to the level of a worker's earnings fit in with the general system of economic incentives. . . . Because of its adherence to a conservative value system, social insurance has the stability that comes from widespread appeal and acceptance.[24]

This reference to work-related benefits, when compared with what was said earlier about Yugoslavia's and Czechoslovakia's current policies of "to each according to his work," may constitute further support for our assumption about the universality of at least some of our key values and the means to their attainment. This support, moreover, is well-grounded in history. For, as Wilhelm Hondrich reminds us in connection with Germany, where social insurance was born, "Bismarck's leitmotif . . . combined . . . the social obligation of the state and . . . the self-help of the individual." [25]

That American views of social insurance transcend party lines is evident not only in the language of President Roosevelt, under whom it was inaugurated on a large scale in the United States, but also in that of President Dwight D. Eisenhower. When he presented a check to the 10 millionth recipient of a social security benefit, the widow of an insured worker, he observed, "This money is not charity. In his daily work, out of his regular wages, your husband earned the monthly checks which will be coming to you. . . . You can accept them proudly." [26]

Arthur J. Altmeyer, "Mr. Social Security" himself, tells us fascinatingly by how slender a margin and against what opposing forces this connection between social security benefits and one's own work was largely, but not completely, maintained over the years.[27]

At about the time the War on Poverty was being launched, the self-help theme—with variations—appeared also in the protracted discussion concerning the reduction of the federal income tax. This reduction had been proposed by Presidents Eisenhower and Kennedy before it was finally effected under President Johnson. On this matter, former (Republican) President Eisenhower had written, "We need a complete overhaul of our tax structure to restore incentive." [28] In the same month (Democratic) President Kennedy declared, upon proposing both tax reforms (which were not made) and reduced taxes (which were later effected under his successor), "This . . . reduction in tax liabilities . . . will encourage the initiative and risk-taking on which our free system depends. . . . A massive increase in federal spending could also create jobs and growth—but, in today's setting, private consumers, employers and investors should be given full opportunity first." [29]

References by leaders of opposing political parties to the need for considerable financial inducement—amounting to some $12 billion for those lucky enough to be paying income taxes—as an "incentive" and to "encourage the initiative" of America's industrial giants fell with invigorating freshness upon the ears of welfare personnel. These workers had frustratingly toiled for generations within a climate of public opinion that held that deprivation, want, and despair (and, therefore, low relief and public assistance payments) were the only true incentives to spur men onward (see Chapter VI). Only time could tell whether the new moral would be applied also to the least privileged elements of the population, who were too poor to pay income taxes and so were in no position to have their initiative spurred by liberal tax reductions; and only time could tell whether what was considered good for the industrial goose would be considered good also for the disadvantaged gander.

But it did not take much of a cynic to note that the well-to-do (at least well-enough-to-do to be paying income taxes) were to be allowed reductions that totaled far more than what had been appropriated for the War on Poverty. Nor did it take too much cynicism to note that what the well-to-do were being allowed to retain was cold cash. By contrast, those on whose behalf the War on Poverty was being waged were allowed no similar windfall, but were offered, in large part, only a chance to struggle for job training, school completion, and the like. These advantages, even after all their struggles, still might not lead to any Expected Land—to say nothing of the Promised Land of America's true potential.

Anyone with any doubt about whose advantage was being served by United States policies of the day would have found it instructive to see a hypothetical tax case, presented by Bernard D. Nossiter, in which the tax saving under the tax reduction program could have been about $238,000, although the original net income, after taxes, might have been only about $143,000.[30]

Further traces of inimical class overtones in United States policies appear in provisions for the promotion of "self-care" (and "strengthening family life") written into federal public assistance legislation under President Eisenhower and strengthened under President Kennedy. These were clearly not related to "self-care" (and "strengthened families") as such, but to reduction of public dependency. For all the fanfare about self-care, there was nothing in the highly touted policy that would touch a wealthy dowager who was waited on hand and foot around the clock. Provisions for "strengthening family life" were similarly aimed at reducing dependency, but in no wise touched economically "independent" families that in other respects might have been coming apart at the seams.

Thus it is easy to exaggerate what United States policies really mean for certain purportedly valued ends. For the very terms in which they are couched and the mechanisms through which they are implemented rouse deep suspicions that they do not really mean what they say. Rather, they have a strong social-class aroma and clearly suggest a duality of standards of self-care and strong families—one for the poor but, for the rich, quite another—or none. More about this in Chapter VI.

Although self-help may today be preached by the advantaged to the disadvantaged rather than for the preachers themselves, the self-help gospel—in its heyday—may have been propagated in large part by newly rich industrialists bent upon winning status and privilege previously monopolized by aristocratic elites born to wealth and privilege.[31] However, at least one elite in the United States, the Protestant establishment, may have contributed to its own decline by failing to share its privileges more widely and more quickly.[32]

Eye-Level Views

An instance widely publicized by *Look* magazine 1962, but one that welfare workers see thousands and thousands of times, was that of a "miner" who did not work in the mines but cut weeds for the state at $1 an hour. "I know it's made work," the man is quoted as saying, "but at least it's work that needs to be done. No one is giving me something for nothing. All we've really got is our dignity." [33] More recently, Arthur R. Simon presented a number of poignant vignettes of some of his parishioners in New York's Lower East Side. Among these is an elderly couple, the Hemingsons, barely eking out an existence with their Social Security checks. When medical bills came along, however, they could not pay their utility bills. The gas and electricity were therefore shut off. Mrs. Hemingson said, "I used to sneak downstairs and heat soup in the basement. My son wanted to pay, but I wouldn't let him. . . . 'We want to take care of this ourselves,' I told him." [34]

Independence, *si*. Light and heat, *no*.

To social welfare workers all over the land, counterparts of the "miner" and the Hemingsons are familiar figures. Declarations of independence—sometimes ringing, sometimes faintly but determinedly uttered—are familiar sounds in welfare offices.

Among many who have heard these declarations is Professor Frances Lomas Feldman of the University of Southern California, who studied the Watts area of Los Angeles soon after the racial violence in 1965. There she saw Jim Thompson, a forty-three-year-old Negro who was the father of four children and had himself been brought up in a "relief family." Of him, Mrs. Feldman reports:

Jim Thompson had been on a Community Work and Training assignment in a park department for two days, performing his manual labor tasks with such ferocious energy that the supervisor urged him to slow down to avoid collapsing from sheer physical exhaustion. "No," Mr. Thompson replied, "This is my first chance in five years at a steady job; I can't stand to muff it." [35]

Space precludes more examples of this kind, but we will note further expressions of interest in self-support from two especially significant groups: handicapped persons, whom society seems most willing to support in idleness—and racially disadvantaged persons, to whom society seems least willing to accord opportunity for self-help.

Speaking on behalf of blind persons, the *Outlook for the Blind* had this to say about "sheltered" employment that is specifically accommodated to the capacities of disadvantaged persons:

The right to work was established about two decades ago. . . . The handicapped or ill person who is removed from or denied this right has, in addition to economic loss, added to it the loss of his social function in society. Psychologically the loss in ego satisfaction, in self-image, in interpersonal relations is great indeed. [36]

Far more than "sheltered" employment has repeatedly been demanded by blind persons. Professor Jacobus ten Broek, constitutional lawyer and University of California professor, who was himself blind and was president of the National Federation of the Blind, has made such repeated demands. In an appeal to a congressional committee he said:

The blind hold the view that, given an opportunity, they are able to achieve complete integration into society on a basis of equality. This involves . . . hastening the time when the mass of the blind of employable age will be working with their sighted fellows in the professions, trades, regular occupations, and common callings of the community . . .

. . . The blind are no longer greeted by society with open hostility and frantic avoidance, but with compassion and sympathy. . . . Good intentions are not enough. . . . Tolerance is a far cry from brotherhood, and protection and trusteeship are not the synonyms of equality and freedom.[37]

But about as vigorous a plea as one ever hears for opportunities to be self-sustaining is that of Henry Viscardi, the severely disabled (but to whom the word "handicapped" is anathema) head of Abilities, Inc., a business enterprise run by disabled persons. His staunch defense of—and demand for—opportunities for disabled persons is forcefully put in *Give Us the Tools,* which is perhaps the most eloquent plea in the English language for opportunity for self-help. After a sharp jab at all well-meaning sympathizers who "smother them in a soft blanket of charity, and turn away in embarrassed shock from the crippled man who wants a job," Viscardi declares:

They do not know they are killing with kindness.

. . . Abilities [Inc.] exists . . . to prove that the disabled can help themselves if people . . . will only give them a chance.

. . . One of the executives . . . wears two steel hooks in place of hands. . . .

A foreman in the packaging department was born without arms or legs. . . . Another employee . . . can neither sit nor stand. He reclines at his desk at a 45° angle in a special sling of his own devising. . . .

Still another man lies on a litter, flat on his back and does a day's work every day. . . .

. . . Having lost the chance to work, and having found it again, [Abilities people] know what it is worth. They have a fierce pride in their hard-earned skills, a fierce determination not to be dependent and helpless ever again.[38]

Self-help, anybody?

On behalf of "older Americans" who had already run the course the economy had laid out for them, the President's Council on Aging deplored "the gap between how the Older American lives and the democratic goal of an independent life." The council then went on to say, "Many Older Americans do not get the care they need because they are too proud to accept charity or other outside financial help. And they do not want to be a burden on their families."

"To most Older Americans," the council states elsewhere, "a

high degree of independence is almost as valuable as life itself. It is their touchstone for self-respect and dignity. It is the measure they use to decide their importance to others. And it is their source of strength for helping those around them.

"The Older American asks not for the gift of independence but the . . . opportunity to be independent." [39]

But the war for opportunities for self-help that was attracting wider public notice in the United States in the 1960's was that being waged by and on behalf of Negroes. In this, federal and state enactments and the accompanying surge of interest in civil rights were again not intended to hand to disadvantaged groups anything on a silver platter. The cry, rather, was for opportunity—to tear down barriers to voting, to employment, to places of public accommodation—to throw open schoolhouse doors and other doors to opportunity. The call was not "to the barricades," but "tear down the barricades" that block the way to opportunity. More room for individual effort was being asked. The Nobel Prize winner and civil rights leader, Martin Luther King, Jr., put it this way:

The struggle for rights is, at bottom, a struggle for opportunities. In asking for something special, the Negro is not seeking charity. He does not want to languish on welfare rolls. . . . With equal opportunity must come the practical, realistic aid which will equip him to seize it. Giving a pair of shoes to a man who has not learned to walk is a cruel jest.[40]

In the more placid climate of a university and in the cooler days before the civil rights movement had picked up momentum, Seymour M. Lipset and Reinhard Bendix, in a discussion of social mobility not only in the United States but also in other industrial societies, wrote, "The phrase [equality of opportunity] has had a strong appeal for the American people. . . . The legacies of American social and political theory have given this goal a value that is accepted throughout society."

"The overall pattern of social mobility," they had said earlier, "appears to be much the same in the industrial societies of various Western cultures." [41]

But one of the world's most unique pleas for a chance to work was the "strike in reverse" organized in Italy by the controversial Danilo Dolci. Taking seriously "the right to work" asserted in the constitution of Italy, a group of unemployed men simply turned up with their own tools and began to repair some streets that were in particularly bad shape. The leaders of the men were arrested, however, but only after the men had eloquently made their plea for work.[42]

Within the context of self-help New York City must be credited with what is surely a "first" of its kind. In a paid advertisement of the sort in which other cities brag about their low taxes and other advantages likely to attract business and industry, the New York advertisement presented the case stories of several disadvantaged youths and then described the local services available to them. It pointed out that the city's program took "two approaches: help and self-help." The advertisement then continued, "These stories were made to happen by us, the people of New York City, either through our city government, through the agencies we support, or the unions and businesses we run." [43]

What New York City was responding to; what Negroes were demanding; what the Viscardis, ten Broeks, and the "strikers in reverse" were pleading for; what the unemployed "miner" found; what President Johnson and other officials saw—millions of Americans were demanding. Unemployed persons, school dropouts, and others mired in "pockets of poverty" were asking for chances to help themselves—as social welfare personnel in all quarters of the country could testify from firsthand experience. Such modest gains as were being made in response to the demands would, in contrast with what remained to be done, hardly have warmed the heart of that ardent champion of social justice, Henry Demarest Lloyd. In the dark days of 1894, he closed his widely read *Wealth against Commonwealth* with these words:

Democracy is not a lie. There live in the body of the commonality the unexhausted virtue and the ever-refreshened strength which can rise equal to any problems of progress. In the hope of tapping some reserve of their powers of self-help this story is told to the people.[44]

For, nearly three-quarters of a century later, vast reserves of "powers of self-help" still remained untapped. Moreover, the previously mentioned social class connotations surrounding emphases upon self-help suggested something unworthy of genuine democracy. These class connotations seemed to imply that self-help was not advocated because of belief in the intrinsic merit of self-help per se, but as a device for reducing the claims for support that might otherwise have been made upon their more advantaged fellows by those unable (or failing) to help themselves.

Furthermore, in both domestic and international terms, self-help was sometimes viewed as a way of getting done in some areas what, in more privileged areas, was being done in quite different ways. Why, people were asking, should self-help be invoked to sweep the streets and collect rubbish in slum areas while the Sanitation Department did it elsewhere?

Even Julia Henderson, Director of the United Nations Bureau of Social Affairs, was concerned by 1966 that self-help was being relied upon in various countries to build roads, bridges, post offices, and other facilities that in more privileged areas within the same countries were being built as normal functions of government. In Chapter IV further dimensions of these problems are explored.

The View from the Social Welfare Front

In disputes over what are appropriate emphases upon self-help and what are not, the social welfare front is (as in other controversies too) caught in the cross fire. Being constantly on the firing line, welfare personnel are in close touch with disadvantaged and distressed individuals, groups, and communities that are continually battling against various woes and adversities. From the opposite side the welfare front is raked by the guns of the give-'em-too-much-and-you-spoil-'em brigade and by those of the money-down-a-rat-hole battalion. Hovering above all, the critics' air force pours almost indiscriminately upon helpers and helpees alike its barrage of contempt: "do-gooders," "no gooders," "bleeding hearts," "chiselers," "meddlers," "moochers."

Behind the welfare front, however, there are strong allies. Decent and humane taxpayers who, though not liking high taxes any better than the next man, like them better than what would remain undone without them. "Dedicated" voluntary contributors give money and time; "broad-visioned" public officials and legislators constantly strike balances between what needs to be done and what can be done.

Underlying all other problems is another to which we shall return later: the penchant of potential benefactors for bestowing their beneficence, not upon the helpless, but upon those able and likely to help themselves. Andrew Carnegie gave classical expression to this interest when, in explaining his delight in establishing libraries throughout the United States, he wrote, "The fundamental advantage of a library is that it gives nothing for nothing. Youths must acquire knowledge themselves." [45] This proclivity for placing one's gifts—and, in the case of welfare agencies, their energies—at the disposal of those who evidence more rather than less capacity for self-help has serious repercussions upon those who are most disadvantaged.

These phenomena, clearly seen in help given (or not given) to individuals, are also visible in help to nations. American aid to other countries, including India and Latin American countries, has often been delayed pending greater evidence that they were indeed taking steps to "help themselves." During economically dark days for Britain in 1964, Harold Wilson appeared on television to warn his people of sacrifices that would be required to stabilize the British pound. In this appeal he declared:

The international financial agencies and our friends abroad . . . have a right to expect that as a matter of urgency we shall take measures to ensure that we do stand on our own feet.

. . . The world does not owe us a living. We have done, it is true, a lot for the world in the past . . . but we cannot live either on memories or the hope of gratitude.[46]

Speaking for the underdeveloped areas of the world, Chief S. O. Adebo of Nigeria has declared, "The new nations recognize their responsibility to do as much as lies in their power to help themselves; that is the fundamental condition of getting help elsewhere." [47]

Any doubt the world may have had about the position of the United States on this score was surely dissolved in 1967 when continued American aid for the Alliance for Progress—and continued aid to India, even when it was confronted with stark starvation— was clearly made contingent upon more evidence that the countries concerned would do more to help themselves.

In still more general terms, it is probably not too much to say that self-help is often a condition for receiving not only help but also even empathy and sympathy from others. Abject, supine acquiescence to one's fate wins little such response. It is those who either win or "go down swinging" that bring crowds to their feet. Whether so intended or not, several books (such as *They Fought Back: The Story of the Jewish Resistance in Nazi Europe*, edited by Yuri Suhl), which showed the heroic lengths to which Jews had gone in thwarting and sabotaging German attempts to exterminate them, aroused public sympathy. This sympathy had been previously withheld in the belief that the victims had gone like sheep to their slaughter and had even collaborated in their own extinction.

In the 1960's Negro ghettos throughout the United States probably recognized this same tendency on the part of the public and were reacting to it. "If Charlie thinks we will take this lying down," they seemed to be saying, "we'll show him." Not inconceivably, public recognition that ghettos are no longer willing to be the doormats of more privileged communities may operate as effectively as anything in winning outside sympathies and effective help. At least some Negro leaders expected this result.

Roy Reed, *The New York Times* reporter based in Atlanta, has observed that "Many whites have deceived themselves into believing that . . . the Southern Negro . . . is docile, unaggressive and martially inferior" and suggests that "Part of the Negroes' task . . . is to convince the nation . . . that he is competitive, that he has will and backbone." Then, in describing the participation of "the Deacons" in a civil rights demonstration in the South, he quotes one of their leaders as saying of whites, "They finally found out that we really are men, and that we could do what we said, and that we meant what we said." [48]

One might think that welfare personnel, caught in the melange of forces confronting them, would become quite immobilized. However, in the matter of individual effort and self-help with which we are concerned, there is remarkable unanimity of opinion even among otherwise warring belligerents. Disadvantaged persons clamor for chances to support themselves. Their bitterest critics demand the same—but often with an extra fillip: *"Make* 'em." Consequently, it is not surprising that welfare personnel from their particular vantage point, seeing clearly the values of the larger society and knowing intimately the aspirations of those most excluded from enjoyment of those values, should take strong stands on the side of individual effort and self-help and, understandably, on the side also of genuine opportunities through which such effort can be effective. Unfortunately, the need for these opportunities is not always seen with equal clarity by others, who insist that poor and disadvantaged persons should do more to help themselves. Nor is there always agreement upon circumstances that affect the extent to which self-help be regarded as a preeminently important value.

Speaking on behalf of personnel in public welfare agencies, the American Public Welfare Association in 1964 declared itself in favor of "the important role of public welfare in . . . encouraging self-responsibility." Among legislative proposals made by the association were the following:

Federal financial aid . . . for preventive, protective, and rehabilitative services to all who require them, irrespective of financial need. . . .

Families receiving aid to families with dependent children should be allowed greater incentives for employment. . . . Work opportunities . . . should be available to persons for whom jobs cannot be found.[49]

Social work, which is the one profession most characteristically and widely identified with social welfare services, has long regarded as a central purpose the helping of individuals, groups, and communities to help themselves. In fact, a veteran social worker, Samuel C. Kohs, defines social work as "the art-science of helping people help themselves." [50] This emphasis is inherited from preprofessional days antedating even those of the Charity Organization Society in both England and the United States when much was done not only to help people to help themselves but to *make* them do so.

By 1915, however, an American social work leader could say that social work's "real purpose" was not only to help people to help themselves "but to help them achieve a freedom for themselves which can only be achieved through working for the freedom of others." [51]

When the National Association of Social Workers in 1958 reformulated its definition of social work practice, this objective continued to be reflected. One purpose, according to the association, is "to assist individuals and groups to identify and resolve or minimize problems arising out of disequilibrium between themselves and their environment . . . [and] to seek out, identify, and strengthen the maximum [sic] potential in individuals, groups, and communities." [52]

When this association in 1963 formulated its *Goals of Social Policy*—goals for society as a whole, and by no means those for social work alone—it declared:

Democratic society . . . must . . . be so ordered that its common resources are devoted to assuring to each of [its] members (a) opportunity for full growth and development; (b) the means for meeting economic needs in terms of the standards its productivity makes possible; (c) provisions of mutual aid for meeting these needs in which social interdependence is a basic factor; (d) a share in advancing and benefiting from the cumulative human heritage of knowledge, culture, and social organization; and (e) full participation in democratic social relationships. To achieve these objectives each member of society has an obligation to respect the dignity and rights of other members, to maintain himself and his dependents by his own resources to the extent that his capacity and circumstances permit, and to contribute his fair share to the common welfare, both financially and otherwise.[53]

This quotation and that harking back to 1915 emphasize a dimension of encouragement of self-help that is not often expressed but nonetheless characterizes many welfare services and is of special relevance to a topic that will be discussed later: help that not only aids individuals to help themselves, but also helps people to help themselves *and one another*—as is implicit in the reference earlier to mutual aid. This additional dimension is often much more explicit in community development programs in underdeveloped areas.

Emphases upon fostering self-help appear again and again in descriptions of specific social work methods, such as social casework, group work, and community organization. Referring to social casework, for example, Professor Helen Perlman of the University of Chicago says, "The aim of casework is to restore or reinforce or refashion the social functioning of individuals and families who are having trouble in their person-to-person or person-to-circumstance encounters." The various techniques employed, Mrs. Perlman explains, are designed, among other things, to "offer enhancement of the client's own powers and abilities to cope with his problems." [54]

Social work has not only been among society's defenders of the value of self-help, but has also produced some significant insights into why it is valuable. Memorable among these is a statement written some years ago by Grace Marcus, then of the Baltimore Department of Public Welfare and one of the nation's leading social workers:

In our culture that which entices the individual up the steep ascent to adult development is the reward of independence. . . .
. . . Self-dependence becomes a condition of self-preservation against the fear of helplessness always potential in having to rely on others. In a democratic society . . . a life in which the attainment of this functioning is not possible to the individual is not a good life for him or anybody else. . . .
On . . . self-dependence is built . . . [one's] self-respect, his title to acceptance . . . his very right to . . . pursue a life he can call his own.
. . . His right to be responsible to himself alone for his management of himself, his affairs and his relationships, is predicated on his ability to live his own life without having to ask for anything for which he cannot make some sort of return. [55]

Just as the branches of the social work profession stand united in favor of fostering individual effort and self-help, so do the various fields of practice, such as family service, probation, and institutional work. However, on this score none is more vocal than the social settlement and community center field.[56] In this context it is noteworthy that a brochure published by the Family Service Association of America in 1956 to recruit young persons to social work bore the title *Their Career: Helping People to Help Themselves*. A 1959 report of the Illinois Commission on Public Aid and Assistance carried the subtitle *Helping People to Help Themselves*. A great many services take as their motto "Not help, but a chance." Important implications of welfare services' stress upon fostering self-help are discussed in Chapter V.

Lest current emphases upon help for self-help be thought a recent discovery of the scintillating atomic age or only an outgrowth of the Protestant ethic, we might recall that nearly 800 years ago the great Maimonides (Rabbi Moses ben Maimon) of Córdoba, Spain, gave his famous dictum:

The highest degree [of charity], than which there is nothing higher, is to take hold of a Jew who has been crushed and to give him a gift or a loan, or to enter into partnership with him, or to find work for him, and thus to put him on his feet so that he will not be dependent on his fellowmen.[57]

In world terms of today it should not be surprising, in view of what has already been said about the value placed upon self-help throughout the world, that social welfare and broader social services include among their major objectives the fostering of exactly this kind of effort. As would be expected, therefore, when an eminent group of experts was convened under the auspices of the United Nations to consider the role of social services in modern societies, it declared that the objective of these services is in part "to enable individuals, groups and communities to meet their needs and solve their problems . . . and by cooperative action to improve economic and social conditions.[58]

In international circles nongovernmental groups also constantly emphasize self-help. The International Conference of Social Work (renamed in 1966 the International Council on Social Welfare) has repeatedly stressed this theme. In its seventh session, in Toronto in 1954, the entire program was developed around "Self-Help in Social Welfare." In preparation for this conference, national committees in many countries (including the United States) submitted reports on the relevance of self-help to their social welfare services. A more recent statement may be found in the report of the

Pre-Conference Working Party, presented to the XIIIth International Conference of Social Work held in Washington, D.C., in 1966. This gave first place, among the objectives of welfare services, "to help people to help themselves." [59]

In this discussion of the Welfare-Eye-View of self-help, it may be noted that although individual effort was often stressed, this tended to be in a context of available opportunities, of a society in which it can be effective, of responsibilities not to oneself alone but to others, and of others to oneself. Unfortunately for the encouragement of effective self-help, there is far more agreement upon it as an isolated mechanism than upon the context required to permit it to function constructively. These issues are further pursued in Chapter IV.

VALUE CONFLICTS REGARDING SELF-HELP

Unhappily for observers who like their values in neat, unchanging categories, values widely seen in self-help are, like other values, highly conditioned by a wide variety of factors.

The Question of Degrees

Self-help, like other values, poses difficulties for those who cannot see, or refuse to see, that "too much" of even "a good thing" may no longer be "good."

When, former Attorney General and United States Senator, Robert F. Kennedy wrote *The Pursuit of Justice,* he opened one chapter with the following quotation, " 'The American system of ours, call it Americanism, call it what you like, gives each and every one of us a great opportunity if we only seize it with both hands and make the most of it.' "

Of this Kennedy then says: "While the philosophy expressed in the above quotation may be spotless, its author was Al Capone." Capone was, of course, the notorious gangster of the 1930's. Kennedy then adds, "And in the thirty-five years since it was uttered, too many 'independent businessmen' have sought literally to 'make the most of it.' " [60]

The chapter in which this appears is entitled "Eradicating Free Enterprise in Organized Crime." Among the free enterprisers whose activities Kennedy particularly attacks are more recent criminal gangs, violators of civil rights laws, and the executives of the electrical industry who had been sent to jail for price fixing.

Even societies that value individual effort highly also place limits upon that to which a man may help himself (opium, medicines supplied only by prescription, other people's property, the affections of other men's wives). Limits are also sometimes placed upon how much—even of a good thing—a man may help himself to: for example, how much land he can own without having to share with others; how much income he may retain without being taxed; how much of an inheritance he may keep; how much of a monopoly he can control without unduly limiting opportunities of others or restricting reasonable access to such necessities as water or electricity.

On the other hand, societies tend to define circumstances under which an individual cannot be expected to help himself. In addition, societies often provide gratuitous help to such persons when, under the circumstances in question, they do not supply their own requirements.

SELF-HELP: BUT NOT FOR ONESELF ALONE: The concept of individual effort and self-help, but not only for oneself, is so widely recognized and supported by law, religion, ethics, citizenship, and human nature that elaboration is unnecessary. It is interesting to recall, though, that even in President Johnson's fervent plea for the War on Poverty to develop opportunities for people to help themselves, he quickly added that the second "prong" of the nation's effort should be "to assure all citizens of decent living standards regardless of economic reverses or the vicissitudes of human life and health." He also emphasized that the United States was seeking a "free and growing economy" that, among other things, *eliminates* with the compassion and foresight of which a free and abundant economy is capable, *avoidable suffering and insecurity* from the lives of our people." [61] [Italics in original.] President Roosevelt put the issue even more strongly in his second inaugural address (1937) when he contended, "The test of our progress is not whether we add more to the abundance of those who have much; it is whether we provide enough for those who have too little."

These sentiments are not the monopoly of any one political party. This is suggested by the fact that when Governor Nelson A. Rockefeller in 1964 appointed a Citizens Committee on Relief Costs, he asked them to study "all possible means of helping welfare recipients to become self-sufficient and of halting the rising spiral costs of relief." However, he immediately added, "The elements of moral responsibility and community compassion for those who, through no fault of their own, are unable to provide for themselves and their families, are and must remain the basis for all welfare programs. About that there must be no question." [62]

Nor are these sentiments peculiar to the United States. For, in the very appeal, mentioned earlier, in which Britain's prime minister called for sacrifices to improve the country's stringent economic position, he added:

But, if things are going to be tough, we have, as a national family, to show that we care, that we care for the old, and the sick, and those in greatest need. . . .

. . . If we are going to get the homes we need, the schools and hospitals, the factories, then less essential building, however profitable, will have to yield place to the more important national programme.

Nor did the prime minister forget the disadvantaged persons in other countries, for in this same appeal he declared, "To maintain the value of the pound lies at the heart of all . . . we intend to do to help weaker and poorer nations overseas." Some two years earlier he had said, "In this shrinking world, while political isolationism invites danger, and economic isolation invites bankruptcy, moral isolation invites contempt." [63]

It is noteworthy that the word "compassion" appears repeatedly in the language of Prime Minister Wilson as it does in that of President Johnson.

The Universal Declaration of Human Rights, though stressing largely the *rights* of individual persons, includes this notable paragraph about duties: "Everyone has duties to the community in which alone the free and full development of his personality is possible." [64]

But, about as succinct a statement of the issue as one ever encounters is that by Professor E. J. Urwick, long associated with the London School of Economics and the University of Toronto: "For the good members of society . . . 'I want' must wait upon 'You need.'" He points out further, though, that "The satisfaction derived . . . from the majority of our activities is enhanced . . . by . . . sharing it with someone else. It would hardly be an exaggeration to call this the essential principle of community." [65]

This is of course a commonly observed phenomenon, as evidenced by the adult's interest in having a spouse and children with whom to share the products of his toil and by the spinster's satisfaction in sharing even meager resources with a cat or a canary. The crucial question (discussed in Chapter VIII) is how far beyond one's own children, cats, and canaries Urwick's "principle of community" extends.

Even Ayn Rand, contrary to some interpretations of her views, leaves room in her "Objectivist" ethics for responsibilities to others. However, her approach is that of a trader and, although she has harsh words for those who would rob, plunder, and kill others, she has almost equally sharp language for "altruism" and "self-sacrifice" as usually interpreted. In *The Virtues of Selfishness* she contends:

Human good . . . cannot be achieved by the sacrifice of anyone to anyone. . . . There is no conflict of interests among men who do not desire the unearned, who do not make sacrifices nor accept them, who deal with one another as *traders*, giving value for value." [66] [Italics in original.]

What such a "trader" might think a lonely old lady might have to trade for a friendly visit, or what a needy blind man might have to trade for being helped across a street, is not clarified. Presumably, "sacrifices" made by others in either instance would be unjustifiable by Miss Rand's standards. However, it just might be possible that the "stock in trade" of persons who are aided can make the help given to them more like a "trade" than like "something for nothing."

The Stoic Seneca would probably have rejected Ayn Rand's view. In his classic essay *On Benefits*, he says that "the property" of according benefits is "to think nothing of any repayment." He observes further that if one hopes for profit then he has not accorded a benefit. He continues:

To take thought, not where your benefit will be best bestowed, but where it may be most profitably placed at interest . . . is not bestowal of benefits, but usury. . . .

. . . A benefit has in view the advantage of him upon whom we bestow it, not our own. . . . "I will give this order that I may get a return for it" is the language of a broker.[67]

But if Seneca, self-acclaimed Stoic though he was (although he may have been exposed to some early Christian teachings), would have taken a dim view of "trading" on kindnesses of one to another, serious followers of Christian and Jewish views would take a still dimmer view. The Christian injunction to "sell all that thou hast and give to the poor," or to "go the second mile," to give one's cloak also to him who asks for one's coat, does not smack much of trading —in *this* life, at least (whatever may be involved in terms of a *future* life or eternity).

When, in 1966, the Reverend John C. Bennett, President of Union Theological Seminary, addressed the fiftieth anniversary convocation of no less a body than the National Industrial Conference Board, he praised the profit motive for what it had helped to accomplish, but said that there was a tendency to overexercise it. "This self-serving and often family-serving motive . . . needs both to be tamed and to be used." [68]

Traditional Jewish views extolling anonymity in both giving and receiving (and declared by Maimonides to have ranked next to the highest among his famous eight degrees of charity) obviously left little scope for "trading."

In an article on altruism, Rabbi Emil G. Hirsch of Chicago describes it as a reaction against "exaggerated egoism." But overemphasis upon altruism, he said, "evoked the counter-revolution culminating in the apotheosis of the selfish . . . 'overman' of Nietzsche's doctrine." He then continued, with respect to the Jewish faith:

This fatal antithesis between self and others is avoided in the ethics of Judaism. . . . Morality is summed up in service. . . . But he who should efface himself would commit as grievous a breach of the covenant as he who should crush another. . . . What is ours is ours only as a means to enlarge the common life.[69]

Raising to an international level concepts like these, Robert Endicott Osgood says, with particular reference to America's foreign relations,

A balanced account of the real conditions under which the nation may hope to achieve a sound readjustment to its international environment calls for the specific recognition of the interdependence of national self-interest with ideal ends transcending self-interest.

. . . In its broadest aspect [this] interdependence . . . is simply a reflection of the fact that man has a moral sense as well as an ego and that both parts demand satisfaction. Consequently, nations act with the greatest consistency and stability when their actions are based upon a balance of egoism and idealism.[70]

How this balance appears in some foreign aid programs is discussed in Chapter VII.

Despite the prevalence of views to the contrary, there are nevertheless still strong-minded individualists of the devil-take-the-hindmost school who see no reason not to "look out for Number One" exclusively. Whether they actually practice what they preach or whether their preachments reflect only declared values, we cannot say. Nevertheless, this stance is repeatedly taken by ultraconservatives who, in justification of it, frequently—and understandably —cite as their authority that favorite of present-day conservatives William Graham Sumner. For it was he who wrote those words still widely quoted in ultraconservative journals, "The product of all history and all philosophy up to this time is summed up in the doctrine that [man] should be left free to do the utmost for himself that he can, and should be guaranteed the exclusive enjoyment of all that he does." Apart from reflecting a possibly incomplete grasp of "all history and all philosophy," this single sentence somewhat exaggerates Sumner's general position, however, because he elsewhere (as conservative journals usually forget to recall) leaves the door open to one man's helping another. What Sumner was really opposed to —so he said—was A's asking B for money to help C. Since this is the basic formula underlying the current social welfare structures, he obviously would not like them. But in somewhat more positive (though perhaps not overly generous) terms, Sumner also maintained:

The only help which is generally expedient, even within the limits of the private and personal relations of two persons to each other, is that which consists in helping a man to help himself. This always consists in opening the chances. . . . The aid which helps a man to help himself is not in the least akin to the aid which is given in charity.[71]

Thus, although Sumner, if one wants to follow him, may be read as condemning certain kinds of giving and helping, he was by no means the total misanthrope his latter-day followers try to make him appear. And current disciples who are quick to quote Sumner's opposition to certain kinds of "help" are singularly silent about "opening . . . chances." Moreover, Sumner (as we shall soon see) was at least consistent—as some of his current followers are not— in his application of his general "hands-off" policy.

Another idol of conservatives is, of course, Captain John Smith, whose alleged "work or starve" order at Jamestown is also frequently quoted: "Every one that gathereth not every day as much [of those fruits the earth doth yeeld] as I doe, the next daie, shall be set beyond the river, and for ever bee banished from the fort: and live there or starve." However, it is often overlooked that this stern order, issued under dire circumstances in 1609, was preceded by phrases seldom quoted, "You shall not only gather for your selves but for those who are sicke.

". . . The sick shal not starve, but equally share of all our la-bours." [72]

In retrospect it is interesting to conjecture whether this robust individualist—had he lived in our day—would have included be-sides "the sicke" others whom he thought there was some responsi-bility to support. Whatever might have been his decision, modern societies have given their own answers. As a result, with respect to individual effort, quite different expectations apply not only to the "sicke" but also to those who are mentally or physically handi-capped (who probably never even made it to Jamestown), to chil-dren and young persons, to persons deprived of requisite education and training, to widows who are needed at home for the care of young children, to aged persons, and even to potential workers for whom there are no jobs (a situation probably not encountered at Jamestown).

Other quotations often cited by the every-tub-on-its-own-bottom school are the famous ones of Ralph Waldo Emerson about "alms to sots" and "I hate thee, thou foolish philanthropist." However, pur-veyors of these words overlook others in the same essay, namely, "There is a class of persons to whom by all spiritual affinity I am bought and sold; for them I will go to prison if need be." [73] Just who these people were is not clear, but if Emerson really meant these words, too, he certainly cannot be included among those who aver that man should not serve the interests of others.

It is also noteworthy that, despite his alleged hatred of the "foolish philanthropist," Emerson nevertheless admits giving to phi-lanthropy—then hating himself for doing so. Whether the "real" Emerson was the one who did the giving or the one who alleged the hatred we will perhaps never know.

But what is most amazing is how advocates of harsh attitudes toward others have drawn upon the Bible for their inspiration, and how highly selective they have been of their texts. John Calvin was by no means the last to make a guiding principle of Saint Paul's injunction "If a man will not work, neither shall he eat," but at the same time to overlook the same writer's eloquent plea for love (or charity) in a letter to the Corinthians, and his injunction (Ephe-sians, 12:28) "to give to him that needeth."

"In the sweat of thy face shalt thou eat bread" is another favor-ite text often taken out of context. For, within a span of only thirty-nine chapters in Genesis one is carried swiftly from this stern in-junction to what was perhaps the world's first foreign-aid program —the giving of Egyptian grain to a band of Canaanites. Even the indirection in the handling of the money in this transaction, which started out as a purchase but ended up as a gift, has a modern ring.

It is also illuminating to review the context from which conservatives lift from the Book of Proverbs another of their favorite injunctions, "Go to the ant, thou sluggard; consider her ways and be wise."* Taken alone, this passage seems to serve the purposes of misanthropes who, however, never heed also the advice in the next several chapters about having pity on the poor, having mercy on the needy, giving and withholding not, having a "bountiful eye," giving bread to the poor, and so on. In fact, one authority on Proverbs says that in it "charity is exalted as one of the chief social virtues." [74]

This by no means exhausts the sources of inspiration for those who advocate "every tub on its own bottom," "tend to your own knitting," or as said in China, "Sweep the snow from your own door and don't worry about that on your neighbor's roof." However, even the most robust of individualists opened the door to relativities: Sumner and Emerson to undefined persons they would be willing to help and Captain Smith to the "sicke." Seneca, too, in stressing the "duty" of according "benefits" to others, introduced relativity when he employed such terms as "the most deserving"—or the person to whom a benefit would represent an "advantage." Thus, the central issue is not an open-and-shut question, but one of relativity: How much farther should doors that are left ajar be opened? Or should they be pulled shut?

Happily—at least for those taking the broad view of man's responsibility to man—social history has followed the course advocated by those who sensed that one's personal responsibility is more than to oneself alone. Moreover, societies often exempt certain groups from the usual expectation that "every man must stand on his own two feet" and underwrite the requirements of those whose efforts to "do it themselves" would be "too hurtful" to either themselves or others.

Although sociologist Robin M. Williams, Jr., in his list of values comprising the "major value-orientations in America," placed at the top "achievement, success, activity, and work," he quickly followed these with "moral orientation," "humanitarian mores," "equal-

---

* It would be a good joke if sometime some "sluggard" took seriously the advice so often thrown at him. For, if he did go to the ant, considered her ways, returned to his advice-giver, and reported the degree of cooperation, social organization, social control, regimentation, and discipline observed, these findings just might be enough to launch some of these advisers upon an effort to have ants declared subversive and un-American, and the sluggard branded a "fellow traveler."

ity," "freedom," and "democracy." [75] Thus, even societies that normally value it tend to ask, "What price self-help?" If the price is not right, they are likely to reevaluate their appraisal of such effort. And, in their reckoning of the price of self-help, societies are likely to think of what is "too hurtful" to either the individual or to others. What is regarded as "too costly" or "too hurtful" is of course debatable, and, obviously, involves exactly the kinds of relativities and calculuses to which we have already called attention. Equally obvious is the fact that the extremes of the continuum are interrelated: What is "too hurtful" to the individuals concerned may also be "hurtful" to others, and vice versa.

Some of the limits at either end of the spectrum may be legal prohibitions that, if transgressed, involve sanctions: as, for example, child labor laws (prohibiting as "too hurtful" to children "self-help" that might be expressed in factory employment at age eight) or laws forbidding the sale of narcotics (a sometimes highly lucrative field for a self-helper) as likely to be "too hurtful" to others.

Before leaving this question of balance between self-interest and responsibility for others, it should be noted that whereas the central problem in highly individualistic societies is often that individuals are not sufficiently sensitive to their responsibilities to others, the crux of the matter in other societies is that loyalty to one's group thwarts individual initiative and enterprise. This latter problem is apparent in some of the "cooperative" communities described by Margaret Mead and her colleagues in *Cooperation and Competition Among Primitive Peoples*. The problem extends beyond "primitive" groups, however, and may be seen in Japan, Africa, Asia, and Indian tribes in the United States. Whether Miss Mead's communities and other "cooperative" groups are to be valued for the degree of human solidarity they reflect or are to be disvalued for thwarting what more individualistic societies would see as "progress"—and whether the erosion of ingroup loyalties in Japan, the Philippine Islands, and elsewhere in favor of greater individualism and mobility represents progress or retrogression—are issues that may be settled only in terms of value orientations.

SELF-HELP: BUT NOT "TOO HURTFUL" TO THE INDIVIDUAL: Individual effort, even where it is highly valued, may not be required or may be proscribed as "too hurtful" to an individual in such instances as a truck driver who has a heart ailment and might drop dead if he continued his employment; a paraplegic who is unable to work; a young girl who can earn money but only through prostitution; a man who is receiving unemployment benefits, but is not re-

quired to take a job materially below his usual classification; a salesman who might jeopardize his life by driving too fast even in the
interest of seeing more customers; a man attempting suicide whose
self-destruction may be forcibly prevented; a youngster who wants
to drop out of school, thus jeopardizing his future, in order to help
support his family; a widow who is wearing herself to a frazzle because she is working to support herself and her six children, but
lacks energy to rear and discipline the youngsters properly, and so
on. In many of these instances public assistance, homemaker service, foster care, and other services would be available to make it unnecessary for individuals to help themselves at "too great" a cost—
even if they *could*, if they had to, do what was to be done.

"Too hurtful" may also be interpreted as having to do ordinary
things in extraordinary ways. In areas where clothes are generally
purchased ready-made, people would not be expected to make their
own. In urban areas, persons would not be expected to go every day
to a plot in the country where they could grow their own food. Opinions would differ, however, about doing such chores in a city as
one's own washing, particularly with an old-fashioned washboard,
which would not normally be done personally but at a laundromat
or by someone paid to do the job.

Although I have stressed the term "hurtful," nations do not necessarily conceive their broad social services in this way alone. In
Sweden, for example, the purpose of their family allowance program is to permit a particular type of worker with a family to enjoy
substantially the same level of living as other workers without children.[76] Thus, social policy may go beyond the "too hurtful" to questions of equity. But this is another story.

Nations stand ready to assist other nations long before they are
actually starving or, for that matter, before they have been drained
of every last resource through their own efforts to help themselves.
In this latter respect United States foreign aid is quite different from
public assistance within the country because (as we shall see in
Chapter VI) applicants for public aid are required to divest themselves of virtually every asset before qualifying for assistance.

Economist and former Ambassador to India, John Kenneth
Galbraith, in 1964 supported the United States foreign-aid program
on grounds that it "justifies itself fully in its promise of development
for other countries without *unbearable hardship* or violent (and perhaps also hopeless) revolution." [77] [Emphasis added.]

Just when any person or nation has reached the point where
the situation is "unbearable" and justifies help from others is suscep-

tible of different interpretations. However, there is one interesting phenomenon that is observable throughout the world, as also in past history: to more privileged and advantaged individuals or groups the situation of disadvantaged persons often seems more "unbearable" than it does to the disadvantaged persons themselves. The latter (for reasons advanced in Chapters I and II) do not always know what they are missing or that things might be better. The more advantaged, on the other hand, see clearly what others must forego and so are willing to help them attain it. This calculus of generosity explains why privileged groups often "give" to unprivileged ones (individuals or nations) what the latter do not "demand" for themselves—a point touched on in Chapter II.

Criteria by which societies judge whether a particular degree of individual enterprise is "too hurtful" are of course subject to change over time. As resources become more plentiful or as societies become more sensitive and humane, they may no longer be willing to stand by unconcernedly or even to tolerate what might previously have been accepted more or less as a matter of course. This was the reason, in the nineteenth century, for the vast improvement in conditions affecting, among others, child workers in cotton mills and "climbing boys," who cleaned chimneys. In fact, this phenomenon helps to explain what is widely deplored as an apparent deterioration of "good, old-fashioned rugged individualism," whose advocates bemoan the fact that "men aren't willing to work as hard" or "to make sacrifices for the sake of the future" the way they used to.

If men today are less bold and venturesome than in the past, it would be difficult to say whether this is due to a "weakening of the moral fiber" or to changing standards in a society as to what is "too hurtful" and therefore to be alleviated—or perhaps prohibited.

Questions about how far one should be allowed to go in helping himself without help from others resulted, late in the nineteenth century, in one of the most interesting whimsicalities in American social history. More interestingly still, this whimsicality resulted from the work of none other than Horatio Alger himself. Those who associate Alger only with the poor-boy-can-become-president-of-the-railroad tradition overlook a quite different influence he exercised in his day. For, having limned his "Pluck and Luck" stories against the background of scrounging, striving, self-sacrificing newsboys and "street Arabs" (as Charles Loring Brace called them), Alger drew attention to suffering and exploitation that the community was unwilling to condone or tolerate. It all seemed "too hurtful." Consequently, public support for "Newsboys' Homes," for additional activities of Brace and others and for restrictions upon the exploitation of boy-labor increased.[78] In fact, Alger himself spent much time in Newsboys' Homes and there picked up material for his stories. Although these did indeed popularize and glorify the self-help theme, they also alerted public opinion to the desperate lengths to which many city youngsters had to go in order to earn what little they received. This in turn led both to ameliorative measures and to moves to curb exploitation considered "too hurtful" to the children.

SELF-HELP: BUT NOT "TOO HURTFUL" TO OTHERS: Further limits placed upon individual effort as likely to be "too hurtful" to others include: stealing; murder; selling narcotics, poisons, or adulterated goods; trafficking in human beings; discriminating against others on the basis of race, creed, or color; employing underage children; paying too-low wages; "saving" money by not installing safety devices in one's factory; too-fast driving, likely to injure others; operating an unsafe automobile; and so on. Almost any of these activities might give quite good scope for self-help and prove quite profitable.

What is or is not regarded as "too hurtful" to the victim of an act is, of course, relative to the humane sensitivity of the perpetrator. The more avaricious a man, the more, probably, he makes others endure. But, although demands upon others may be heavy, there seem to be limits beyond which even the most demanding of men do not go. For example, Nubar Gulbenkian, son of the wealthy oil magnate Calouste Gulbenkian, tells not very amusingly about his grandfather, who had his servants beat another (whose job it was to bring coffee several times each hour) because when the grandfather once called for coffee, this servant had been found asleep. Unfortunately, the fellow servants did too good a job of it and the coffee server died. This was said to have led to a common Gulbenkian family saying, "I told you to beat him, not kill him." Such a slogan may not commend itself to all men as a reminder of how far one can properly go without hurting others "too much." Nevertheless, it does exemplify the fact that men do set for themselves limits—however far out, or close in, they may be.

Men become so accustomed to the view that "one man's meat is another man's poison" that they often lose sight of the possibility of a wider sense of social identification that leads a man to eschew action likely to be "too hurtful" to others. When Franklin D. Roosevelt first ran for the Presidency, he declared in his famous Commonwealth Club speech in San Francisco, "Individual liberty and individual happiness mean nothing unless both are ordered in the sense that one man's meat is not another man's poison." [80] This issue of man's identification of his own interests with those of others will reappear in Chapter VIII.

Notwithstanding the value that is typically placed upon helping oneself and at least one's immediate family, societies (as we have seen) tend not only to limit, but also to make unnecessary, actions that would be "too hurtful" to either oneself or others. Examples of ways in which societies underwrite the requirements of persons who, if left to "do it themselves," might hurt others too much, include the following: (1) a community's acceptance of responsibility for a mentally retarded child if the child's own parents cannot give him the necessary assistance, (2) complete support of a typhoid-carrier (even if he is wholly capable of working) on condition that he restrict his activities and not expose others in accordance with the principle that communities, since ancient times, have supported lepers who were isolated to protect their fellows, (3) help for a harassed mother by a homemaker if her children would otherwise not receive proper care, (4) public assistance for a mother so that she can care for her children, who would suffer neglect if she worked, (5) aid for a pregnant woman so that she can quit a type of work that might endanger her child, (6) free medical care for a father so that he need not "take food out of the mouths of his children" in order to pay his doctor bills.

It is exceedingly difficult to define the terms upon which individuals may be exempted from the usual standards of self-help and to prescribe the terms upon which they are entitled to assistance lest either they or others be hurt "too much." However, application of the resulting definitions and prescriptions to particular cases—a task that often falls to social welfare services—is even more difficult. Thus welfare agencies are again caught "in the middle," making decisions that some elements of a community might agree are proper to avoid "too much" hurt, while other elements might disagree.

The relativities in the various concepts presented here are depicted diagrammatically in Chart 2 on page 138.

What is regarded as "poison" or "too hurtful" to others is easily thought of only as overt harm imposed upon them. However, there is also the dimension of deprivation—withholding from them "goods" (dignity, equality of treatment, rights, privileges, power to direct their own affairs, and so on)—which is also hurtful. If one man's sense of dignity is supported by denigrating others, or if his status is preserved by impugning another's or by unfair actions to "keep him in his place," or if his power is enhanced by undue control

Chart 2. Range of Self-Help Commonly Regarded as "Good" (i.e., as Not "Too Hurtful" to Either the Individual Concerned or to Others) and Role of Outside Help in Averting Such Hurt

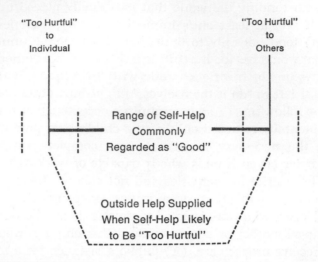

over others, all these others have been hurt. Thus, the issue may be stated, not in terms of meat and poison alone, but in terms of somewhat less "meat"—less dignity, status, and power—for some and somewhat more "meat" for others. Whether giving up a few morsels of previously enjoyed meat would be "too hurtful" to those yielding (or having to yield) them to others is a question on which opinions will differ. Similarly, judgments will vary as to whether continuing meatless (or on only short rations) would or would not be "too hurtful" to those thus denied. Advocates of "power for the poor," "black power," and the like are saying clearly that lack of an effective voice in, and a hand in directing, matters directly affecting them is "too hurtful" to be quietly borne. These issues will reappear in Chapters IV and VII.

:: Notes
and
References

1. Horace Greeley, as quoted by Clarence Clough Buel in *The Encyclopedia Americana* (New York, Chicago, Washington, D.C.: Americana Corporation, 1957), Vol. XIII, 419n.
2. His Holiness Pope John XXIII, *Mater et Magistra*, Encyclical Letter on Christianity and Social Progress, May 15, 1961 (Washington, D.C.: National Catholic Welfare Conference, 1961), p. 17.
3. Ralph Turner, *The Great Cultural Traditions; The Foundations of Civilization, The Classical Empires*, (New York: McGraw-Hill, 1941), Vol. II, 727.
4. Quoted in "Thailand: Land of the Free," advertising supplement to *The New York Times*, February 28, 1965, p. 3.
5. Rifat Rashid, "Social Work Practice in West Pakistan," *An Intercultural Exploration: Universals and Differences in Social Work Values, Functions, and Practice* (New York: Council on Social Work Education, 1967), p. 143.
6. *Road to the Welfare State* (New Delhi: Government of India, Planning Commission, n.d.), p. 41.
7. Dr. B. R. Sen, as quoted in *The New York Times*, June 23, 1963.
8. Roy Gunter, as quoted in *The New York Times*, January 24, 1965.
9. *The Future of Public Ownership* (London: Fabian Society, 1963), p. 2.
10. See Jean Stoetzel, *Without the Chrysanthemum and the Sword: A Study of the Attitudes of Youth in Post-War Japan* (New York: Columbia University Press, 1955). Also see Mamoru Iga, "Relation of Suicide Attempt and Social Structure in Kamakura, Japan," *International Journal of Social Psychiatry*, XII (1966), 229–231. See also *Japanese National Character* (Tokyo: Shiseido, 1961). For examples of persons from another area not noted for its devotion to the Protestant ethic, but who are "fiercely independent," take care of themselves and their own, see William McPhillips, "Cuban Refugees Here Fiercely Independent," *Los Angeles Times*, August 20, 1967.
11. *Messages on Community Development from Heads of State to International Society for Community Development* (New York: Community Development Foundation, n.d., *ca.* 1967). (Processed.)
12. *AID in Brief* (Washington, D.C.: U.S. Department of State, Agency for International Development, *ca.* 1963), pp. 4, 6.
13. David E. Lilienthal, "A New Credo for Foreign Aid," *The New York Times Magazine*, June 26, 1960, p. 28.
14. *To Secure These Rights*, President's Committee on Civil Rights (New York: Simon and Schuster, 1947), p. 4.

15. Quoted by J. Lucas-Dubreton in *Daily Life in Florence—In the Time of the Medici* (London: G. Allen, 1960), p. 17.

16. Lyndon B. Johnson, *My Hope for America* (New York: Random House, 1964), pp. 44–45, and *Economic Report of the President* (Washington, D.C.: Government Printing Office, 1964), p. 15.

17. *Report, 1964* (Washington, D.C.: Council of Economic Advisers, Government Printing Office, 1964), p. 77.

18. Franklin D. Roosevelt, as quoted in *The New York Times*, January 5, 1935 and November 30, 1935, respectively. That the view that unemployed workers preferred work to the "dole" is correct, see Note 10, Chapter VIII.

19. Nancy C. Morse and Robert S. Weiss, "The Function and Meaning of Work and the Job," *American Sociological Review*, 20 (April 1955), 192.

20. Caroline Bird, *The Invisible Scar* (New York: McKay, 1966), particularly pp. 320–322.

21. R. Sargent Shriver, as quoted in *The New York Times*, March 17, 1964.

22. "Report of Senate Committee on Causes and Relief of Unemployment," quoted in *Monthly Labor Review*, 28 (May 1929), 69, and in 88 (October 1965), 1203.

23. *The Older American* (Washington, D.C.: President's Council on Aging, Government Printing Office, 1963), pp. 19–20.

24. Robert M. Ball, "Is Poverty Necessary?" *Social Security Bulletin*, 28 (August 1965), 19.

25. Wilhelm Hondrich, *The Conception of Social Welfare in German History* (Dinslaken: Verlagsgesellschaft für Gegenwartskunde, 1965), p. 9.

26. Dwight David Eisenhower, as quoted by *The New York Times*, June 7, 1957.

27. Arthur J. Altmeyer, *The Formative Years of Social Security: A Chronicle of Social Security Legislation and Administration* (Madison: University of Wisconsin Press, 1966).

28. Dwight David Eisenhower, "Danger from Within," *Saturday Evening Post*, January 26, 1963, p. 18.

29. John F. Kennedy, as quoted in the *Los Angeles Times*, January 15, 1963.

30. Bernard D. Nossiter, *The Mythmakers: An Essay on Power and Wealth* (Boston: Houghton Mifflin, 1964), p. 36. See also Jerome R. Hellerstein, *Taxes, Loopholes and Morals* (New York: McGraw-Hill, 1963), and Gabriel Kolko, *Wealth and Power in America: An Analysis of Social Class and Income Distribution* (New York: Praeger, 1962), especially Chapter 2, "Taxation and Inequality," pp. 30–45.

31. See, for example, Irvin G. Wyllie, *The Self-Made Man in America: The Myth of Rags to Riches* (New Brunswick: Rutgers University Press, 1954).

32. See E. Digby Baltzell, *The Protestant Establishment: Aristocracy and Caste in America* (New York: Random House, 1964). Other useful sources on the self-help theme include John Tebbel, *From Rags to Riches: Horatio Alger, Jr., and the American Dream* (New York: Macmillan, 1963), and Moses Rischin, ed., *The American Gospel of Success* (Chicago: Quadrangle Books, 1965).

33. Quoted by Thomas B. Morgan in "Portrait of the Under-Developed Country," *Look* Magazine, December 4, 1962, p. 27.

34. Arthur R. Simon, *Faces of Poverty* (St. Louis: Concordia, 1966), pp. 52–53.
35. Frances Lomas Feldman, *Public Welfare: Dependency, Despair—and Opportunity* (Los Angeles: Governor's Commission on the Watts Riot, 1965), p. 29. (Mimeographed.) Also under slightly modified title in *Riots in the City: An Addendum to the McCone Commission Report* (Los Angeles: Los Angeles Area Chapter, National Association of Social Workers, 1967).
36. *Outlook for the Blind,* as quoted by James F. Garrett in "Sheltered Work Shops—Whither Goest Thou?" in Joseph Stubbins, ed., *New Horizons for Work Shops for the Handicapped* (Los Angeles: Los Angeles State College, 1960), p. 6.
37. Jacobus ten Broek, in *Education and Assistance to the Blind* (Washington, D.C.: Government Printing Office, 1959), pp. 66–67.
38. Henry Viscardi, Jr., *Give Us the Tools* (New York: Eriksson-Taplinger, 1959), pp. 2, 3.
39. *The Older American, op. cit.*
40. Martin Luther King, Jr., "Why We Can't Wait," *Life,* May 15, 1964, p. 98.
41. Seymour Martin Lipset and Reinhard Bendix, *Social Mobility in Industrial Society* (Berkeley and Los Angeles: University of California Press, 1959), pp. 81–82, 13.
42. James McNeish, *Fire Under the Ashes: The Life of Danilo Dolci* (London: Hodder and Stoughton, 1965), especially pp. 107–108.
43. Paul R. Screvane, "A Door Opens—to Hope," in advertising supplement "New York, N.Y.: The City Takes a Giant Step," *New York Times Magazine,* November 29, 1964.
44. Henry Demarest Lloyd, *Wealth Against Commonwealth* (New York: Harper & Row, 1894), pp. 535–536. Also available in Spectrum Books (Englewood Cliffs, N.J.: Prentice-Hall, 1963).
45. John C. Van Dyke, ed., *Autobiography of Andrew Carnegie* (Boston: Houghton Mifflin, 1920), p. 46.
46. Harold Wilson, *Purpose and Power: Selected Speeches of Harold Wilson* (Boston: Houghton Mifflin, 1966), pp. 6–8.
47. S. O. Adebo, in *On the Developed and the Developing* (Santa Barbara, Cal.: Center for the Study of Democratic Institutions, 1965), p. 10.
48. Roy Reed, "The Deacons, Too, Ride by Night," *The New York Times Magazine,* August 15, 1965, pp. 20, 11.
49. *Federal Legislative Objectives, 1965* (Chicago: American Public Welfare Association, 1965), pp. 1–3.
50. Samuel C. Kohs, *The Roots of Social Work* (New York: Association Press, 1966), p. 21.
51. John Lovejoy Elliott, "After Twenty Years in New York Tenement Houses," in Lorene M. Pacey, ed., *Readings in the Development of Settlement Work* (New York: Association Press, 1950), p. 117.
52. "Working Definition of Social Work Practice," *Social Work,* Vol. 3, No. 2 (April 1958), and in Appendix, *Encyclopedia of Social Work* (New York: National Association of Social Workers, 1965), p. 1028; see also pp. 680–683. And see Alfred H. Katz, "Application of Self-Help Concepts in Current Social Welfare," *Social Work,* 10 (July 1965), 68–74.

53. *Goals of Public Social Policy, 1963* (New York: National Association of Social Workers, 1963), p. 9.
54. Helen Harris Perlman, "Social Casework," *Encyclopedia of Social Work* (New York: National Association of Social Workers, 1965), p. 705.
55. Grace Marcus, "The Psychological Problem in Providing Assistance as a Public Service," *American Journal of Orthopsychiatry,* XVII (July 1947), 435–436.
56. See *i.a.,* Arthur Hillman in *Neighborhood Centers Today: Action Programs for a Rapidly Changing World* (New York: National Federation of Settlements and Neighborhood Centers, 1960), p. vi. See also *Annual Report, 1957–1958* (New York: National Federation of Settlements and Neighborhood Centers, 1958), pp. 4–5.
57. Rabbi Moses ben Maimon (Maimonides), "The Eight Degrees of Charity," in Jacob R. Marcus, *The Jew in the Medieval World* (Cincinnati: Sinai Press, 1938), pp. 364, 365.
58. *The Aims and Means of Social Service* (New York: United Nations, Department of Economic and Social Affairs, 1959), Annex II, p. 41.
59. Pre-Conference Working Party, "Report," *International Social Work,* IX (October 1966), 17.
60. Robert F. Kennedy, in Theodore J. Lowi, ed., *The Pursuit of Justice* (New York: Harper & Row, 1964), p. 41.
61. Johnson, *Economic Report of the President, 1964, op. cit.,* pp. 15, 18.
62. Nelson A. Rockefeller, as quoted in *Report . . . on Welfare Costs* (Albany: New York State Citizens Committee on Welfare Costs, 1965), p. 4.
63. Wilson, *op. cit.,* pp. 8, 9.
64. United Nations, *Universal Declaration of Human Rights,* Article 29, Paragraph 1. Easily accessible in *Americana Encyclopedia.*
65. E. J. Urwick, *The Values of Life* (Toronto: University of Toronto Press, 1948), pp. 112, 6.
66. Ayn Rand, *The Virtues of Selfishness: A New Concept of Egoism* (New York: New American Library of World Literature, 1964), p. 31.
67. Seneca, *On Benefits,* Aubrey Stewart, tr. (London: Bell, 1900), pp. 48, 88, 94, 97.
68. John C. Bennett, as quoted by Ernest Schonberger, *Los Angeles Times,* September 24, 1966.
69. Emil G. Hirsch, "Altruism," *The Jewish Encyclopedia* (New York: Funk & Wagnalls, 1916), Vol. I, p. 476.
70. Robert Endicott Osgood, *Ideals and Self-Interest in America's Foreign Relations: The Great Transformation of the Twentieth Century* (Chicago: University of Chicago Press, 1953), pp. 10, 17. For another analysis of United States foreign policy in ethical terms, see Ernest W. Lefever, *Ethics and United States Foreign Policy* (Cleveland: World Publishing, 1957).
71. William Graham Sumner, *What Social Classes Owe Each Other* (New York: Harper & Row, 1883), pp. 34–35, 165.
72. Edward Arber, ed., *Travels and Works of Captain John Smith* (Edinburgh: John Grant, 1910), Part I, pp. 156–177.
73. Ralph Waldo Emerson, "Self Reliance," in Brooks Atkinson, ed., *The Complete Essays and Other Writings of Ralph Waldo Emerson* (New York: Random House, 1940), p. 149.

74. Earle B. Cross, "Proverbs," in Frederick Carl Eiselen, *et al.*, eds., *The Abingdon Bible Commentary* (New York, Cincinnati, and Chicago: Abingdon Press, 1929), p. 611.

75. Robin M. Williams, Jr., *American Society: A Sociological Interpretation* (New York: Knopf, 1951), pp. 396, 398, 409, 417, 432.

Some effects of what Williams calls "humanitarian mores" in the United States are usefully traced in books such as Richard Hofstadter's *Social Darwinism in American Thought*, rev. ed. (Boston: Beacon Press, 1958); Sidney Fine's *Laissez Faire and the General-Welfare State: A Study of Conflict in American Thought, 1865–1901* (Ann Arbor: University of Michigan Press, 1964); and two books by Harry K. Girvetz, *From Wealth to Welfare: The Evolution of Liberalism* (Stanford, Cal.: Stanford University Press, 1950) and his revision of this book under the title *The Evolution of Liberalism* (New York: Collier Books, 1963).

In terms of developments in England, there is of course A. V. Dicey's classic, *The Relation Between Law and Public Opinion in England During the 19th Century*, 2nd ed. (London: Macmillan, 1962; first printing, 1914). A useful but hardly comparable updating of Britain's situation may be found in Morris Ginsberg, ed., *Law and Public Opinion in England in the 20th Century* (Berkeley and Los Angeles: University of California Press, 1959). This book contains contributions by G. D. H. Cole, Richard M. Titmuss, Brian Abel-Smith, Morris Ginsberg, and others.

76. See George R. Nelson, ed., *Freedom and Welfare: Social Patterns in the Northern Countries of Europe* (sponsored by the Ministries of Social Affairs of Denmark, Finland, Iceland, Norway, Sweden, 1953), p. 236. See also Alva Myrdal, *Nation and Family* (London: Kegan Paul, Trench, Trubner, 1945), especially pp. 146–153.

77. John Kenneth Galbraith, letter to *The New York Times*, January 12, 1964.

78. For an interesting discussion that illuminates this point, see Ralph D. Gardner, *Horatio Alger or The American Hero Era* (Mendota, Ill.: Wayside Press, 1964).

79. As reported in *Pantaraxia: The Autobiography of Nubar Gulbenkian* (London: Hutchinson, 1965), p. 9.

80. Franklin D. Roosevelt, "New Conditions Impose New Requirements on Government," *The Public Papers and Addresses of Franklin D. Roosevelt* (New York: Random House, 1938), Vol. I, p. 755.

IV
PROBLEMS
in
IDENTIFYING
and
EVALUATING
SELF-HELP

Men sing paeans for self-help the world over, but two recurring discordant notes warrant special attention: first, dissatisfaction with the criteria typically employed in identifying and appraising self-help, and second, disagreement over weighting the many complex and interrelated contributory factors even when criteria are agreed upon. These disharmonies are not created by songs that are against self-help. For, in terms of the world's declared values (whatever its operational values may be), there is—as we have seen—striking unanimity with respect to self-help. If there is a substantial "peel-me-a-grape" school anywhere, it has not openly declared itself. But even a school of this kind would seem to recognize the values of the larger society. For autobiographies, biographies, and tombstone inscriptions almost never identify as such even known, card-carrying "peel-me-a-grapers."

Apart from discrepancies between declared and operational values, further difficulties spring from the virtual impossibility—within complex societies—of identifying when and to what extent the widely valued self-help is being exercised. One result is that societies find it exceedingly difficult to accord their praise and favors for self-help justly, and justly to censure and penalize those properly seen as the "moochers," "spongers," "foot-draggers," and other "men on their backs."

DIFFICULTY OF ESTABLISHING CRITERIA

In an earlier and simpler day, when men knew each other more intimately and were familiar with more facets of their lives (they were not merely one's chief clerk or the driver of the 7:27 bus)—and when they knew more about the resources they had and did not have, and more about the vicissitudes that confronted them—rewards for self-help and penalties for lack of it could perhaps be meted out with some degree of justice. However, in complex and interdependent societies such judgments become almost impossible. In consequence, two simple (also *too* simple) criteria emerge: first, success (particularly material success) as itself validating effort and therefore worthy of praise and rewards; second, dependency (upon public assistance, for example) as evidencing or strongly suggesting the want of self-help and therefore deserving public disapproval—if not censure and penalties. These criteria are obviously opposite sides of the same coin. This simplistic approach was summarized by Irvin G. Wyllie in his historical study, *The Self-Made Man in America:* "Success required no explanations and failure permitted no excuses." [1]

Although pretense is widely made of honoring those who valiantly struggle but do not actually make the grade ("It matters not whether you win or lose, but how you play the game"), the real honors are reserved for those who succeed ("Winning is not the most important thing, it is the *only* thing"). Who, for example, recalls who placed second in all those years that the Yankees won the pennant? Notwithstanding the high value placed upon success, there is also a faint refrain—intended to be comforting—that "It is better to have loved and lost than never to have loved at all." This, however, tends to be balm for moments of defeat and despair. It is seldom heard when prizes are handed out (there are no prizes for "most-loved losers") and does not gainsay strong preference for loving and *not* losing. "Always a bridesmaid and never a bride" may get one near the altar but not to it.

No one familiar with American culture is surprised to learn that when sociologist Robin M. Williams, Jr., set out to describe the "Major Value-Orientations in America," he placed at the top of his list "Achievement," "Success," "Activity," and "Work." Of these he writes:

First, American culture is marked by a central stress upon personal achievement. . . .
    . . . Money comes to be valued not only for itself and for the goods it will buy, but as symbolic evidence of success and, thereby, of personal worth.[2]

Max Lerner in *America as a Civilization* gives short shrift to many of the traditional statements about values that, as he puts it, represent "What Americans believe they believe" (what we have called declared values). When Lerner turns to "What animates [Americans] and what their main energy drives actually are" (operational values, in our terminology), he declares:

In an idyllic vein American social historians look back to an earlier society in which the operative life goals were related to the Puritan virtues of work, pride in craftsmanship, thrift, achievement, and the fulfillment of the vocation and tasks to which one was called. . . . By the turn of the twentieth century a new pattern of life purposes emerged. Its components were success, prestige, money, *power,* and *security.* This is loosely termed the "success system," and . . . at its core is the cult of what William James called scornfully "the Bitch Goddess, success."

For the ordinary American the test of an idea is in the end product of action, and the proof that something is valid lies in its being effective.[3]

In accord with this view, an "ordinary" American's "proof" of the validity of something would, obviously, hinge on the criteria used for judging its effectiveness.

Lerner's view interestingly parallels a much earlier one published by Thorstein Veblen in 1919. Moreover, Veblen correctly foresaw that if then visible trends continued into the future, the tendency to evaluate activities in terms of their "industrial importance" would become more pronounced.

In passing let us note that what is or is not "effective" in Lerner's language and of "industrial importance," in Veblen's terminology, is as much a function of social response to, and support of, an idea or act as it is a function of the idea or act itself.

To the extent that Lerner's and Veblen's assessments are correct, one may say that the United States has modified Robert Burns' famous line to read, "A man's a man for a' that—money." Moreover, it might not be wholly incorrect to spell this major objective $uccess. Observers from abroad have been quick to notice that when the United States sought to call official attention to "higher" aspects of life, it was upon its coins that "In God we trust" was stamped.

Among others who have deplored the use of "success" as the single standard of excellence is Alfred North Whitehead, who once said:

The mischief of elevating the type that has aptitude for economic advancement is that it denies the superior forms of aptitude which exist in quite humble people. Who shall say that to live kindly and graciously and meet one's problems bravely from day to day is not a great art, or that those who can do it are not great artists? [4]

Further problems posed by the multidimensionality of values are alluded to in a later section.

DIFFERENCES IN ABILITIES AND RESOURCES

But success is often a composite resulting from many factors. To evaluate correctly any single factor (such as individual effort) is therefore uncommonly difficult. This is unfortunate, because there can be many a slip between the cup of self-help and the lip of success.

If success is accepted as Lerner's "proof" of the effectiveness of something that is thereby certified as "valid," and if this is the sole (or even primary) criterion for judging individual effort, we are embarked upon a circular and self-validating process: success itself constituting evidence of having exerted sufficient effort. On the other hand, it prejudges, as not having exercised sufficient effort, those who are "unsuccessful."

It is perhaps regrettable that in only the lower schools have attempts been made to evaluate effort as distinguished from outcome. There a youngster may get A for effort but D in the course. Or, he may get A in the course but D for effort. This at least enables him to get some credit for trying, even though he may not have what it takes to "succeed." Conversely, one who is "succeeding" but is capable of even higher attainment is encouraged to exert still greater effort.

In higher schools, as in later life, grades tend to be only for the course, never for effort, notwithstanding the fact that effort per se is something a society claims to value. This is really quite sad because all the honors and encouragement go only to winners, however easily they have won their victories, while truly heroic effort that somehow just does not turn out quite right goes unhonored. The Kennedy family is by no means alone in holding the view frequently attributed to it: "Second-best is still a loser."

Not even awards to the "most improved player" (sometimes given in the sports field) would get at the root of the matter. Such recognition would still give no basis for judging effort: who *did the most* with what he had, whether what he had was most, much, little, or least.

One reason why success is problematic as a basis for evaluating human behavior is that individuals (and nations) differ widely —not only in ability but in the resources available to them. It is a commonplace that making bricks without straw is difficult. But it is still more difficult to make them without straw, know-how—or mud.

It takes unusual perception and sensitivity to see in the arduous but (by Western standards) unrewarding work of many peoples of the world something worthy of admiration. William and Paul Paddock have this perception and sensitivity. One as an agronomist and the other as a Foreign Service Officer have worked in many parts of the world. They have written:

The typical American . . . is a firm believer in action, at least when it comes to other people's affairs. . . .

Observers have . . . noted that Americans . . . are not really very hard workers, after all, compared to such as the Chinese and Indian peasants, who labor from dawn to dusk, hungry, weakened by parasites, and with no decent place to live at night.[5]

Elsewhere the Paddocks pay high tribute to the wisdom and imaginativeness with which workers such as Ifugao farmers use their resources—although these are pitifully few.

After Ben H. Bagdikian had surveyed poverty throughout the United States, he wrote of poor persons, "They are not, most of them, without spirit and hope. Yet they are not confronted with the normal handholds with which the non-poor pull themselves to self-sufficiency." [6] In Sweden, this phenomenon is recognized in the saying "When it rains oatmeal, the poor man has no spoon to catch it with." Of the relevance of this point in the United States, Dr. Robert C. Weaver, who was later appointed as the first Secretary of the federal Department of Housing and Urban Development, wrote, with respect to "our attempts to motivate those of low status in our cities": "We have seemed to strike a false note by suggesting that personal effort alone will bring reward." [7]

The disadvantaged person's lack of Bagdikian's "handholds" was well illustrated by R. Sargent Shriver in testimony before a House committee:

Those of you who have visited . . . Job Corps installations . . . have seen the illiterate youngsters learning to read . . . seen some boys who have never been to a doctor—medical or dental. Over half of the people in the Job Corps have never been seen by a medical doctor. They are getting attention for the first time in their lives. In the first month at an average Job Corps installation enrollees put on 15 pounds, indicating that they have been suffering from undernourishment ever since they have been children.[8]

In assessing individual versus social responsibility for the kinds of disadvantages enumerated by Shriver, one must inevitably ask why —if these were a matter of public responsibility in 1964—they were not also a responsibility in 1954, when these youngsters were in grammar school—or in 1934, when their parents were probably suffering from the same deficiencies.

Professors S. M. Miller and Martin Rein, after reviewing a wide range of literature on the various effects of social class status in the United States, conclude:

To be born in different positions within society molds the ability to handle access to institutions and the development of levels of aspiration and achievement motivation. In this sense . . . equality of opportunity can never be fully present in a society with great social divides in it.[9]

American society has long been much more willing to apply uniform standards in judging success than to provide uniform opportunities for attaining it. Says Irvin G. Wyllie, "American opportunities have been magnificent, but they have never equaled the aspirations of the whole people; success has been for the few, not the many." [10]

In a simple rural community, where a man has access to the soil, it is one thing to say to him contemptuously—as one might to a wild hog when there are plenty of acorns around—"Root, hog, or die." Only a cruel man would put a hog in a shed with a cement floor, pen him in, and then tell him to root or die. Yet human beings separated from natural sources of supply by urbanization and industrialization (which they had little part in fashioning) are often expected to "root," as well they might, if they had some place to root, something to root with, and something to root for.

It was exactly upon this separation of man from his natural habitat by complex institutions that A. Delafield Smith, who long served as legal counsel to the Social Security Board, based his thesis that society should underwrite man's "right to life." He said:

All life . . . requires the support of its environment. It is neither self-supporting nor self-reliant.

. . . Most of man's vaunted independence and boasted self-reliance emanates from his justified confidence in the laws of nature. . . .

. . . Age-long existence in dependence upon such a law-constrained environment has bred into us humans a sturdy sense of independence, and of worth . . . , which dependency upon other human beings, unsupported by legal right and prerogative, has deeply wounded.[11]

Touching testimony in support of this position is presented by a perspicacious American Indian youth, Clyde Warrior, in a statement prepared for (but not presented to) a conference on the War on Poverty:

The indignity of Indian life, and I would presume the indignity of life among the poor generally in the United States, is the powerlessness of those who are "out of it," but who are yet coerced and manipulated by the very system which excludes them. . . .

"Hand outs" do not erode character. The lack of power over one's destiny erodes character.

In the old days the Ponca people lived on the buffalo and we went out and hunted it. We believe that God gave the buffalo as a gift to us. That alone did not erode our character, but no one went out and found the buffalo for us. . . . In those days we were not "out of the system." We were the system. . . . White businessmen and bureaucrats did not make the Ponca decisions.[12]

If one agrees that men may indeed be "wounded" by lack of a "law-constrained environment" or that character can be "eroded" by lack of power to control one's own destiny, the problem of justly evaluating individual effort obviously becomes complex. It becomes even more difficult if there is validity in the discussion in Chapter I about the social component in aspiration and its relation to achievement.

Imbalances in resources (including power) that are available to different individuals, social classes, and nations highlight the difficulty of closing gaps between "haves" and "have-nots" (whether they are individuals or nations). When it is recalled that dominant groups in any society tend to control the ways the laws are written, how they are enforced, how they are administered, how justice is accorded, how financial institutions and industries are organized and operate, it is evident that they get virtually the whole society to work for them.

Imbalance in the manner social forces work for different social classes can be illustrated in many ways. But none is more revealing than the contrast between the difficulties slum-dwellers encounter in actions against slumlords guilty of building and code violations and, on the other hand, the ease with which merchants can garnishee the wages of (or repossess goods supplied to) slum-dwellers who have overstepped their financial capabilities. It is for good reason that England's social historian George Macaulay Trevelyan speaks of the privileged classes as the "enjoying classes." Or, as someone has put it, "What we have now is socialism for the rich, and free enterprise for the poor." While serving as Attorney General, Robert F. Kennedy went even farther, saying, "For the poor man, the law is always taking something away."

Nor is it accidental that the "enjoyers" have worked to perpetuate their enjoyments. Irvin G. Wyllie reports that "In resisting programs for the common man [reform programs that 'attempted to redress grievances by reforming society, not by reforming individuals'], conservatives helped to advertise the fact that in the twenti-

eth century the success argument was much more useful as an instrument of social control than as an instrument of social progress." [13]

Similarly, nations that dominate international trade, credit,
and the money market have tremendous advantages even when less
developed nations expand their productivity.

Thus, when disadvantaged groups or countries are given special help by the advantaged, this help is typically much too small to
make up for the many advantages that keep improving even further
the already privileged position of the advantaged. Typically,
proffered help consists of "sending a boy to do a man's work" (as
noted in Chapter I). This has the whimsical effect or the tragic or
"just-what-the-doctor-ordered" effect highlighted by Professor Gunnar Myrdal:

Not only social security policies but almost all other policies—agricultural policies, taxation policies, housing policies, minimum-wage legislation, and so forth—have followed the perverse tendency to aid the not-
so-poor, while leaving a bottom layer of very poor unaided. The War on
Poverty will therefore have to be fought on many fronts and will in the
end have to imply not only an enlargement but a redirection of all
economic and social policies.[14]

What is even more ironic is that "boys" sent to do "men's" work
are often paid by other boys (economically speaking)—rather than
by men. For example, when Professor Oscar Ornati and his colleagues at the New School for Social Research, under the aegis of
the Twentieth Century Fund, studied poverty in the United States,
they found that "a larger proportion of the total anti-poverty tax burden [which was interpreted quite broadly and included even some
of the costs of social insurance and elementary education] is carried
by those earning under $4,000 than by any other income class." [15]

Unfortunately for the world, the United States has no corner on
these phenomena. For England, this has been well documented by
Richard M. Titmuss, Tony Lynes, Brian Abel-Smith, and others. Titmuss, for example, charges, "Many pension schemes . . . tend to
redistribute claims on resources from lower-paid to higher-paid employees." He also contends that even the "universalist Health Service
and educational system have benefitted the higher income groups
more than the poor." [16]

Because of phenomena of this genre and despite the American
War on Poverty, the National Urban League could say in 1966, "Certainly major gains have been made, yet the median income of white

and Negro families has been drawing further apart." To correct this imbalance, but even more, to begin to overtake centuries of deprivation and exploitation of Negroes, Whitney M. Young, Jr., was advocating a gigantic compensatory program. Of the necessity for this, Young contends:

The "discrimination gap" caused by more than three centuries of abuse, humiliation, segregation, and bias has burdened the Negro with a handicap that will not automatically slip from his shoulders as discriminatory laws and practices are abandoned.

. . . Equal opportunity, if it is to be more than a hollow mockery, must also mean the opportunity to be equal; to be given a fair chance to achieve equality.

. . . The scales of justice have been heavily weighted against the Negro for over three hundred years and will not suddenly . . . balance themselves by applying equal weights.[17]

From an international viewpoint, too, the gap between the "have" and "have-not" nations actually widened (although there were some absolute gains, to be sure) between 1947 and 1960, despite mammoth foreign aid programs of the United States, the Colombo Plan of the British Commonwealth, the United Nations, and others.

It is almost as if dominant groups agree to measures to help disadvantaged ones only upon the condition that their own privileges, prestige, and power are not substantially curtailed, if not indeed actually enhanced. It is unfortunate that the reaction of white groups to gains made by Negroes in the United States in the 1960's was termed "white backlash" because this obscures the more universal phenomenon of reaction on the part of any group (white or black, white- or blue-collar, landowner or industrialist, aristocrat or *nouveau riche*—or whatever) whenever the buffer zone protecting its privilege, prestige, or power is encroached upon—to say nothing of infiltrated—by new arrivals.

This phenomenon may explain the great social gains made in time of war. Certainly, as Professors T. H. Marshall and R. M. Titmuss have often said, World War II contributed greatly to Britain's adoption of Welfare State measures. Other countries, too—notably France and Australia—found that the social solidarity fostered by war served to improve their social legislation. When any group's privilege, prestige, and power seems likely to be utterly wiped out by an external foe, concessions to domestic groups—which the privileged might continue to resist in peacetime—seem small indeed, as contrasted with a possibly greater loss to an enemy.

But, short of similarly compelling reasons for action, anything like what Professor Myrdal called "a redirection of all social and economic policies" is exceedingly difficult to achieve. Of this, the Archbishop of Recife (Brazil), to whom the International Conference of Social Work gave its highest award in 1962, has said, "When we do social work, the extreme right says we are good. But when we promote development, we are called communists." [18] This, obviously perhaps, helps to explain why welfare services are so often "boys" sent to do the work of "men." Societies, apparently, simply do not want man-sized welfare jobs done lest existing buffer zones of privilege be threatened.

Although Whitney Young and others have proposed massive programs to compensate for imbalances born of centuries of deprivation and exploitation of Negroes, the National Committee of Negro Churchmen—meeting dramatically in Boston Common, by the statue of Crispus Attucks, Negro hero of the Revolutionary War —asks only that Negroes be treated no less well than their white fellows, a quite radical proposition, at that, considering existing realities. In the committee's words:

The revitalization of the *real* American Revolution will require not so much a *special* effort . . . as a *fair* concern for the welfare of non-white Americans, as measured by the concern . . . manifested for white Americans.

No real and sustained effort to put an economic foundation under non-white Americans has ever been made that compares with the subsidies provided largely white suburban users of super-highways, or the subsidies given to our nation's farmers, largely white.[19]

DIFFERENCES IN INHERITANCE

When, to problems posed by unequal current abilities, resources, and opportunities (which of course are affected by inheritance), are added further difficulties involved in inherited capacity or wealth, the calculus for appraising achievement becomes still more difficult. In his review of criticisms of various economic theories, John Kenneth Galbraith has said:

The inheritance of wealth was a special source of discomfort. Perhaps one could justify riches as the reward for the skill, diligence, foresight and cunning of the original creator. None of this justified its highly fortuitous devolution on the individual who happened to be the son.[20]

The familiar religious theme could still be true if it were amended to read, "To him that hath a father that hath, shall be given."

Alfred North Whitehead's answer to this problem was a simple one, "I would have inheritance taxes high enough so that a family of lazy aristocrats wouldn't survive." Even Andrew Carnegie advocated inheritance taxes sufficiently stiff to prevent passing one's money on to heirs.*

But it is Professor Charles Frankel who puts the issue in terms especially relevant to our discussion:

[The] notion that income should normally reflect work . . . is not used to justify the abolition of inheritance taxes or to reduce the incomes of the idle rich. . . . It is used only to place drastic limits on the help extended to the poor. The concept of "welfare" . . . is thus connected with a moral code that places special value not so much on work as on the work of the poor.[21]

One of the more popular programs established in conjunction with the War on Poverty in the 1960's was the grossly misnamed "Head Start" program. This was aimed at helping children in culturally and otherwise deprived homes to be more nearly ready to enter school. Without such a program, it was often said, a child in his first year of school would already be one year behind. "Head Start?" Perhaps so, but only in relation to what the children concerned would otherwise have experienced—not in relation to society as a whole. In this sense the program might better have been termed "Bring Up the Rear." The kind of head-start program that really helps was invented generations ago by the Rothschilds, the Vanderbilts, the Astors, the Rockefellers, *et al.*

But even persons with quite modest starts in life would find it hard to reply to an observation that was specifically directed by a disadvantaged mother to "those welfare ladies" (but could pertinently be related to 100 million others). Robert Coles quotes her:

---

* Behind this conviction was a strange mixture of belief that unearned money would only hurt the receiver, that the money should be returned to the community from which it had been derived, and that, in accord with the Biblical text, the "rich man" had to divest himself of his wealth if he wanted to enter the kingdom of heaven.

"Well, I'll tell you, they sure don't know what it's about, and they can't
. . . not if they come knocking on my door every week. . . . Do they
have any idea of what us is about? And let them start at zero the way we
do, and see how many big numbers they can become themselves." [22]

Yet sons with running head starts on the road to success tend to
set the standards of achievement by which are measured—inimically, of course—the apparently lesser accomplishments of others
who, without even a good start, might actually have run harder. Let
him whose father was also poor cast the first stone.

DEPENDENCY: OBVIOUS AND UNOBVIOUS

In order to clarify facts as they exist, we should perhaps forget the
concept of the "independent man" and think of him rather as unobviously dependent, thus distinguishing him from the obviously dependent man so familiar to welfare agencies. Both are dependent,
though degrees of obviousness differ.

Despite the difficulties in differentiating among different degrees of dependency, American society is quick to judge and to accord low status to those whose dependence is obvious. In his article
"The Sociology of Poverty," Lewis A. Coser of Brandeis University
contends:

To receive assistance means to be stigmatized and to be removed from
the ordinary run of men. It is a status degradation. . . . Once a person
is assigned to the status of the poor his role is changed, just as the career
of the mental patient is changed by the very fact that he is defined as a
mental patient.[23]

One ironic aspect of the stigma of obvious dependency is that
there is no leeway—as there is even in the case of murder—for
different degrees of culpability. To be obviously dependent is to be
treated with undifferentiated disdain, even though penalties for
"murder" differ in cases of premeditated murder, first degree, involuntary manslaughter, justifiable homicide, and the like. However
unpremeditated, involuntary, or justifiable one's poverty, it is treated
as any other is treated. This underscores the pertinence of the previously cited quotation "Failure permits no excuses."

Although we later discuss (Chapter VI) particular characteristics of justice meted out to poor persons, it is relevant to speculate
here about why it is that criminal procedures are often so much

more refined and equitable than those pertaining to law-abiding poor persons. Does this reflect the optimism of the larger society in which majority members see no likelihood that they may some day be "poor" but recognize that they may indeed be charged with crime or even *falsely accused*—and therefore need to be sure that procedures that may be applied to them are fair and just? Or is it, as Caroline Bird suggests, because of the majority "notion that a man gets what he deserves" and the view of the nonpoor that "If the poor are not poor through their own inadequacies, then I cannot rise through my own merit"? [24]

However elusive may be the explanation of the superiority of treatment often accorded to lawbreakers (or accused persons) as contrasted with that accorded to those who are only poor, the difference is cold reality.

Just how mixed, though, are American attitudes toward self-help, individual effort, and success is well illustrated by W. Lloyd Warner's Index of Social Class, in which, by the criteria he and his associates developed, the highest status was accorded not to those who earned their living by the sweat of their brows—as traditional declarations of values might lead one to suppose—but to those living on inherited wealth.[25]

Similarly, the widely used Index of Social Position more recently developed by Professors August B. Hollingshead and Fredrick C. Redlich attributes a higher position, even within their highest Class I, to inherited wealth than to "made money." [26]

The irony of these ratings is heightened still further if Bernard Berelson and Gary A. Steiner are correct in their observation (presented in their analysis of social stratification) that

Those on top . . . tend not only to rationalize the justice of the system [under which they reached the top] but sometimes try to solidify it as something natural or inherent (thus attempting to shift the basis from achievement to ascription).[27]

To the extent that this is true, it suggests that preferred position, supposedly won by achievement, need not be sustained or justified by continuing further achievement but by *ascription*. "I won the pennant five years ago, so don't bother me," this seems to say. "Just know I'm still the champ." This, to persons trying honestly to preserve and foster values seen in individual effort and enterprise, must surely seem to be the final irony—irony that is now come full circle.

MULTIDIMENSIONALITY OF VALUES

Still another element complicating the calculus is the degree to which chicanery, deceit, dishonesty, unfair practices, sacrifice of other values (health, family life, etc.), and even infractions of law or of moral justice may contribute to lauded "success." Acclaim for prestigious corporations seems undiminished even when they are fined or their officers are sent to prison for infractions of the law. Such prestige seems unimpaired also even when "sharp practices" like those in the early days of Standard Oil that affront the public conscience, but are not at the moment actually illegal, come to light. Indeed, the suspicion that many gains are "ill-gotten" leads cynics to modify the popular question "If you're so smart, why aren't you rich?" They turn it into "If you're so honest, why *are* you rich?" It is this kind of thinking that adds significance to the view that "Success needs no excuses."

Ralph Linton's observation on this point is noteworthy: "One of the least desirable features of our own system is that which accords high status to the man of wealth, *no matter how acquired* [emphasis added]." [28]

The pervasiveness of issues like these was revealed in Malta in 1964 when, to relieve unemployment there, plans were made to transfer Maltese girls to Sweden for employment, mostly as housemaids. However, when the girls' parents heard what wages were paid to housemaids in Sweden, they refused to allow their daughters to leave. What seemed to be such high wages surely could not, they thought, be earned respectably. [29]

The sins of the fathers may be visited upon their children even "unto the third and fourth generation," but the riches of the fathers are, too. However, the wide tendency to take material goods as the sole criterion of success means that inheriting generations tend, on balance, to come out as net winners. Chicanery and even illegal activities that may be involved in building up inheritances are likely not only to be overlooked or forgotten but also to be vindicated by the very existence of the bequests.

Little is heard these days about "tainted" money. Yet if one goes back to, say, Jane Addams' day, he will find much made of it. For example, Miss Addams even refused an offer to build a much desired home for working girls because she regarded the proffered money as "tainted"—wrung from the "sweated" labor of the very kinds of girls for whom the home was intended. She also made many enemies, of course, by her attacks upon the so-called philanthropies of George Pullman.[30] Opinion in that day was also sharply divided over the propriety of acceptance by religious groups of gifts proffered by John D. Rockefeller, Sr. Whether we hear less of these matters today because business practices are more sensitively adapted to ethical standards or because the conscience of possible recipients has become less sensitive is a matter we leave to the moralists.

In his scholarly dissertation, *The Self-Made Man in America*, Irvin G. Wyllie devotes a chapter, "The Way of the Just," to the moral principles historically advocated in America as important to success. But, in another chapter, "The Seat of the Scoffers," he reviews critiques of the morality of those who attained success. In this he quotes a governor of New Hampshire as observing that among the successful there was "a greater proportion of the disciples of . . . the lawless, than of . . . the philanthropist."[31] Surely, anything like a Fair-Trade-with-the-Indians Act would have put a crimp in John Jacob Astor's *modus operandi* and spread more widely the gains from the furs collected.

More recently, after Goronwy Rees' study of six of the world's richest men (one of whom had employed "slave labor" and been convicted as a "war criminal," and another of whom had been forced to pay enormous fines for transgressing laws), he painted into his composite portrait of "Mr. Millions" "a kind of ruthlessness and egotism that you do not find in men who place a lower value on their activities." Rees then remarks that although "the annals of the poor are open for everyone to read," as we shall see in some detail in Chapter VI, "the rich prefer not to keep records, unless suitably edited for public consumption or the scrutiny of the income-tax inspector." But, in two noted exceptions to this reticence of rich persons to reveal themselves, Rees reports "We seem to smell the real odor of great wealth and the lives it supports, so strongly compounded of savagery and sophistication." In fact, he conjectures that the charm "most people" seem to see in conspicuous wealth is, in part, that it is "somehow tainted with a flavor of wickedness."[32]

Adulation accorded even by disadvantaged persons to those who "succeed," however "ill-gotten" their gains may be, has been explained on the grounds that, to the poor man, law is always an enemy, and always the winner over him in any test of strength. Therefore he relishes the sight of anyone, whether outlaw, illegal profiteer, barely-within-the-law exploiter, or anyone else who can flaunt the law.

Confusion over values seen in "success" presents serious problems for those who believe that there are also other important dimensions to life: congenial marital relations, constructive family life (which several of Rees' multimillionaires were spectacularly *un*successful in achieving), aesthetic enjoyment, equity, and justice, to name but a few. Unfortunately, however, as one of the world's noblest successful men, George Cadbury, once observed, "Success is not a test of fine character." [33] Unfortunately, too, "failure" by conventional standards seems to indicate a defect of "character"; and poverty is almost universally interpreted as lack of material means, but seldom as poverty of family life, poverty of friendships, poverty of cultural appreciation, and the like.

Apart from questions of morality, equality, and justice in making money is the further question of these values in retaining it. For example, tax consultant, lawyer, and professor Jerome Hellerstein in 1963 reported in *Taxes, Loopholes and Morals* that "We have known for years that there are large discrepancies between the amounts of dividends paid by corporations and interest paid by savings banks and the amounts that show up on income-tax returns." He then cites a U. S. Treasury study of 1959 incomes. "This," he continues, "estimated that individual taxpayers failed to report in that one year some $940 million in taxable dividends and $2.8 billion of taxable interest, with a consequent revenue loss of $850 million." [34]

From statistics like these it takes little imagination—so long as apparent material success remains a prime criterion for judgment —to imagine even little men (from whose pockets that deficit might have been made up) deferentially "oh-ing" and "ah-ing" at the power and prestige reflected in status symbols that were purchased at their expense out of those 850 million illegally withheld dollars. One can readily imagine the withholders mutually admiring one another's yachts and ermine stoles, thus contributing to perpetuation of the "success system."

The degree to which illegal activities (e.g., disregard for minimum wage laws, price fixing, influence purchasing) contribute to the "success" of otherwise possibly respectable lawbreakers complicates still further any attempt to appraise success fairly.[35]

Here, in touching upon the multidimensionality of values, we have concentrated largely upon success at the expense of law observance. We might have shown that values of other dimensions too

—family life, aesthetic appreciation, health, leisure, longevity, and altruism, among others—may also be sacrificed for "success." These sacrifices in and of themselves are deplorable enough, but are even more so because of the standards they set for rising generations. For, young people exposed to quite different value systems have proved quite responsive to them. For example, American Peace Corps volunteers in the Philippines, according to Professor Lawrence H. Fuchs, who first directed the program there, became much enamored with Filipinos' devotion to their ingroups. On the basis of his experience Professor Fuchs writes:

Americans may become less self-reliant as they feel the beauty of belonging in relationships, even when it means counting on others and being depended on by them. They may . . . even see certain consequences of the cult of self-sufficiency as barbaric and unhuman.

. . . Many young Amricans . . . no longer want independence geared toward either production or consumption. . . . Now they speak of independence to fulfill or actualize themselves, but that often is seen as coming—at least in part—through intimate, caring relationships.[36]

This carries us back, obviously, to Chapter III, in which we discussed individual effort, but not for oneself alone. It is a point we shall come to again in Chapter VIII.

LUCK AND CATASTROPHE

Added to other complexities involved in evaluations of effort and of success are two further elements: luck and catastrophe. One has only to scan the history of fortunes that have been made to see how often sheer fortuity has played a major part. An exhausted silver mine had been painstakingly surveyed and tunneled by prospectors who never had the luck to strike the silver there. They finally abandoned the project. Not long afterward, however, a youngster returning home from school stumbled over a piece of ore. This encouraged his father to resume the exploration. This led to the discovery of fabulously rich veins of ore that ran within thirty-six inches of the tunnels that had been previously abandoned. By what calculus should the earlier effort go unrewarded and the latter be rewarded handsomely?

A similar stroke of luck reportedly led to a mining fortune in Idaho when a prospector ran across rich ore only because his pursuit of a runaway donkey had led him to it.[37] Just as sportsmen are wont to say, "I'd rather be lucky than good," it may not be too much to say that the most important partner in any enterprise is Dame Fortune—or a runaway donkey who knows just where to stop. One thing that makes it hard to identify the extent to which luck does indeed play a part in men's "success" is their penchant, in retrospect, to rationalize their good fortune as proof of their own "foresight" or "dogged determination." Fortune may be indistinguishable from fortuitousness.

On this Herman P. Miller of the U. S. Bureau of the Census writes, "Luck is hardly ever mentioned by millionaires or the men who write about them. This no doubt reflects a bias on their part. Luck may not be as important in making a million dollars as many poor people think, but it is probably more important than many rich men would have us believe.[38]

Berelson and Steiner, in surveying social science literature, found that "The upper class usually tends to think it is on top because of ability and energy, but the lower class tends to think the ranking is also due to connections and plain luck." [39]

The "bias" noted by Miller has been spoken of by Professor Kenneth E. Boulding as a "self-congratulation," which transposes a commonplace into "There, but for the justice of the universe, rather than the grace of God, go I." [40]

Yet luck, in and of itself, is not the main problem. Random luck, alone, may be seen as "the way the ball bounces," the "way the cookie crumbles," or as "God's will." In fact, even in primitive societies the random chance, as in the drawing of lots (much as highly organized societies, in time of war, draw draft numbers at random), is accepted as a form of elemental justice. Problems arise, though, when the dice seem loaded—always coming up in favor of previous winners. "First hired *and* last fired," which is just the opposite of what Negroes see as their fate. An even greater problem arises when luck in combination with other operating forces becomes "stacked luck"—as one lucky strike including being born into an advantaged family is parlayed into another and then another. It is as though one could buy a lottery ticket only if he had won with a previous drawing.

It is surprising that the Horatio Alger tradition has been so largely perpetuated in terms that are not true even to the tradition itself. Alger's stories have been held up as a testimonial to hard work, even though luck repeatedly played a leading role in them. For example, Ragged Dick and Paul the Peddler "just happened" to be in the right place at the right time. Compasses and chronometers to indicate the right place and the right time are scarce, however.

Even the economist Frank H. Knight has recognized the importance of luck as a factor. "The conventional classification of productive factors recognizes three classes, land, labor and capital . . ." he writes. Then he adds, "From an ethical point of view it would be more significant to analyze income into three sources of free choice or effort, inheritance, and luck. And the greatest of these is luck!" [41] If what one inherits is also seen as largely a matter of luck, Professor Knight's three sources may be reduced to two.

At the opposite pole from good fortune is adversity and, at worst, catastrophe. Amazingly, many successful persons who witness adversity in the lives of others realize how lucky they themselves are to avert it. "There, but for the grace of God, go I." Yet a human derelict, struck down by adversity, may not be regarded at all as being the victim of a catastrophe that "by God's grace" just happened to strike him rather than someone else. He is more likely to be considered the victim of his own lack of individual effort or assiduity. In retrospect, it is noteworthy that when Harry Hopkins during the Great Depression sent Lorena Hickok (and Martha Gellhorn) throughout the country to serve as his eyes and ears and to report back to him on what joblessness and despair were doing to men, women, youths, children, and families, he told Miss Hickok to remember, every time she talked with an unemployed person, "There, but for the grace of God, go I." [42] Others in the welfare field have kept this truism constantly in mind.

When adversity strikes others, a man senses that he alone may not be responsible for avoiding the same adversity himself. This thought contrasts strongly with his sense of accomplishment when he succeeds. When there is trouble, men readily admit to each other that "No man is an island, the bell tolls for thee." Yet when a man succeeds, he is likely to forget this interdependence with the universe and to think that he *is* an island. When the bell does not toll, but peals in victory, it is easy for one to think it peals for him alone. Because of this men speak of being "honest enough to be grateful." It was this phenomenon perhaps that made newsworthy the story of a highly religious pitcher in professional baseball. When, after losing several games, he finally won one, his first uttered words were "Thank you, Lord." [43] More commonly, men individualize their successes. However, they generally universalize their own failures, but individualize the failures of others. When men win, they like to credit their own prowess; when they lose, they "wuz robbed." But, when others lose, it is because they "blew it."

INTERDEPENDENCE WITHIN SOCIETIES

Difficulties in justly meting out rewards for self-help and penalties for its lack are considerably heightened as societies become more and more interdependent. As this occurs, it is hard to tell whether someone is "standing on his own two feet," on someone else's toes, or on someone else's shoulders. Drawing a fine line between independence and dependence becomes difficult if not impossible. When is someone failing? When is someone else failing him? Even a tub "standing on its own bottom" may be filled with someone else's molasses.

In an appraisal of contemporary American society, Henry Steele Commager concludes, "It would be misleading to insist that Americans [in the twentieth century] were less self reliant than formerly, but certainly society as a whole was more interdependent." [44] This interdependence was observed as long ago as 1909 by Louis F. Post, whose book *Social Service* dealt, not with what this title today denotes, but with business transactions. These he saw as involving even in his day a sufficient degree of interdependence to justify the title. [45]

Complex, interrelated, and interdependent societies pose two problems (discussed below) pertinent to handing out social awards and penalties and produce so many incommensurabilities that it becomes almost impossible to make judgments fairly and justly. In fact, if an observation once made by Leonard E. Read, president of the Foundation for Economic Education, is even one-billionth correct, the task is utterly impossible. "An individual's creativities [as in making a jet plane or a lead pencil] are meaningless," he contends, "except as they unite or configurate or coalesce with trillions upon trillions of creativities flowing through the minds of other individuals since the advent of human consciousness." [46]

One need not agree with the arithmetic in order to appreciate the concept.

Societies' Overlooked Contributions to Success

Somewhat earlier we noted that in less complex societies it was perhaps easier than it is today to accord favors justly for effort and attainment. While this seems plausible, it would be difficult to say

just when and where this might have been true. For, in his classic
On Benefits, Seneca as far back as the first century complained:

Those men . . . who take care to let as few persons as possible know
of the benefits which they have received . . . [and who] fear to receive
them in public, [do so] in order that their success may be attributed
rather to their own talents than to the help of others.[47]

It takes a strong public figure indeed to acknowledge that a
speech—however much he might have improved it by his delivery—
had been written by someone else. Similarly, it takes a strong man to
acknowledge help received from others—whether in winning an
election, conquering "the bottle," or in other respects. Therefore,
men commonly avoid those upon whose help they had once relied.
Otherwise, others may too clearly perceive that they did not "make
the grade" by their own efforts. What men thus deliberately hide,
other men, obviously, have even greater than usual difficulty in appraising.

Interdependence is so widely recognized today, however, that
the question is often raised as to whether any man in an interdependent society can properly be called "independent." President
Franklin D. Roosevelt thought not. And Lester B. Pearson, once
Canada's Minister of External Affairs and later Prime Minister, apparently agreed because, in a conference on self-help, in 1954, he
quoted Roosevelt to this effect.[48]

This view had been anticipated somewhat earlier by England's
Richard H. Tawney, who in 1926 contended:

Few tricks of the unsophisticated intellect are more curious than the
naive psychology of the business man, who ascribes his achievements
to his own unaided efforts, in bland unconsciousness of a social order
without whose continuous support and vigilant protection he would be as
a lamb bleating in the desert.[49]

More recently, a passionately humane Harvard-educated lawyer has suggested in even broader terms:

Each time a prosperous American peels a banana, let him remember
the peon who picked it; whenever a housewife uses a pan, let her recall that the copper from which it was made was probably mined by
slaves; the next time a middle-class citizen pays an insurance premium,
let him intercede for the people of the ghettos [in whose "homes," Stringfellow had said earlier, much insurance money is invested to pay interest
on premiums paid].

[The] interdependence of rich and poor is something Americans are tempted to overlook . . . but [the hardships of] . . . the vast multitudes of men on the face of the earth [who] are consigned to poverty for their whole lives . . . in great measure make possible the comfort of those who are not poor. . . . Their deprivation purchases the abundance most Americans take for granted.[50]

In German, all this is put simply: *Ein Mensch ist kein mensch.* Or, as someone has said, the term "self-made man" is self-contradictory. Although interdependence is all-pervading, it is perhaps nowhere more apparent at this writing than in the enjoyment of fruits and vegetables bought at prices that, profits being what they are, mean gross deprivation among agricultural workers, especially migrant workers. To read *They Harvest Despair* by Dale Wright or *The Ground Is Our Table* by Steve Allen may reduce one's relish in a piece of crisp celery or of fresh fruit, just as John Steinbeck's *Grapes of Wrath,* in its day, aroused guilt over what agricultural products "took out of the hides" of workers who produced them.

Virtually numberless "successful"—but sensitive—men have acknowledged their dependence upon others. For one, New York merchant Bernard Gimbel early recognized that his store could not prosper unless New York City did, too. He therefore supported a wide variety of civic enterprises. Similarly, some of the nation's greatest achievers—including John D. Rockefeller, Sr., and Andrew Carnegie—at least retrospectively acknowledged their debt to others for their "success" and directed their philanthropies to areas—including countries abroad—that had contributed to their wealth.

However, over 100 years ago, before interdependence had reached anything like its extent today, Ralph Waldo Emerson was already observing, "It is said that the world is in a state of bankruptcy, that the world owes the world more than it can pay." [51] The debt has subsequently increased and runs to much more than money. For example, at the 1965 Annual Convention of the National Association for the Advancement of Colored People, Malvin R. Goode, United Nations correspondent of the American Broadcasting Company, excoriated those Negroes who took for themselves undue credit for their advancement. He declared:

This albatross-type forgets that without an NAACP, without some of the fifty key Supreme Court decisions at a cost of $35,000 per decision, without the picket lines, yes, in many instances without the jailings . . . without the loss of Medgar Evers [and others] . . . he did it "all on his own." [52]

A leading Dutch social worker, Jan de Jongh, once shrewdly observed that self-help is only a "relative thing." He presented as an example of self-help a man who beat up a brigand who had attacked him. But De Jongh then pointed out that the man may have been able to do this

because he was strong, well-fed by his parents, well-trained at school, mentally well-adjusted to the possibility of sudden attacks, etc. . . . Our man was able to help himself only because society had given him the chance to grow and develop his physical and mental possibilities. . . . He was able to help himself thanks to the help he had previously got.[53]

Even Robinson Crusoe, a patron saint of the do-it-yourself cult, could thank his society for the training and skills as a sailor that helped him to live outside that society, and for the tools and supplies salvaged from his ship that gave him—even in his isolation—a few of the accoutrements of civilization.

Interdependence, however, even when perceived, is more frequently acknowledged by words than by action. When race riots break out, bystanders not uncommonly are guilt-stricken, beat their breasts, and admit that in some way it is their responsibility. Still, they seldom ask to share the jail cells of the persons falsely arrested or dig into their own pockets to pay fines or raise bail.

In New York City many years ago, Fiorello H. La Guardia, when sitting as a magistrate, is said to have felt obliged one day to fine a man although he seemed more sinned against than sinning. Then, in his own inimitable manner, La Guardia directed that a hat be passed around the courtroom for contributions toward the fine, because of society's complicity in the man's offense. Broader recognition of this complicity is reflected in provisions (as in New Zealand, California, and Illinois) for compensation to victims of crimes of violence and in the U.S.S.R. by police compensation for articles stolen from foreign visitors. In his article "No One Is Independent," T. W. Kent writes, "In twentieth-century society . . . 'independence' in a material sense is largely an illusion. . . . The retired millionaire is, in fact, just as 'dependent' on society as the old man who lives on his old-age pension." [54]

From Britain, Barbara Wootton rails at those who decry the poor who "get something for nothing" but do not similarly criticize the rich when they do the same thing.[55]

To discuss issues of this kind is difficult because of lack of clarity in the terms that are usually employed. For instance, "unearned income" is never really unearned but, rather, comes to persons who appear not to put out commensurately. "Socially produced income" would appear to be a more accurate term. Similarly, "unobvious dependency," as already suggested, may be a more realistic concept than "independence." Philosopher Charles Frankel writes of this:

Many [unemployed] men collect . . . insurance. . . . They are enjoying in a small way the same position as that of men of independent means—a phrase we choose to use to describe a man who is dependent on an elaborate system of law and public protection so that he can enjoy resources that have been bestowed on him through no doing of his own.[56]

Time and again throughout history, socially and economically privileged individuals and groups have felt obliged to make open declarations of their dependence upon others. As this is being written, the large growers of agricultural products in the United States are claiming that they would be "ruined" if they had to pay to seasonal workers the nation's minimum hourly wage instead of the 89 cents, or the 49 cents, they were paying a significant number of workers.

More dramatic perhaps were the 1830's in England, when child labor laws were first being seriously proposed. The then new industrialists resisted them, saying they were likely to destroy their industries. Employers thus openly declared their dependence upon children. Statesmen were startled to learn that Britain's vaunted industrialization was not being built upon the wits, energy, and capital of the new entrepreneurs, as had been widely supposed, but—as one of their number put it—"on the backs of little children." Even today English workers, noting measures often taken to redress adverse balances in international trade, claim that "the British £ rests on the back of the workingman."

When we referred earlier to William Graham Sumner, we noted that he was more consistent in his favor of "hands-off" policies than some of his alleged latter-day followers. Sumner at least opposed—as many of his current disciples do not—"help" to the privileged as much as to the underprivileged. He denounced such things as the tariff as much as organized charity. He took care to point out, for example, that the cost of tariffs—for the protection of industries —ultimately had to be borne by the likes of the seamstress who, because of the tariff, paid a higher price for needles and thread.

Even while World War II was still raging, President Roosevelt railed, "A noisy minority maintains an uproar of demands for special favors. . . . They have come to look upon the war primarily as a chance to make profits for themselves at the expense of their neighbors—profits in money or in terms of political preferment."

Thus he still saw in war what he had seen even before his election to the Presidency. He said, "The same man who tells you that he does not want to see the Government interfere in business . . . is the first to go to Washington and ask the Government for a prohibitory tariff on his product. . . . He will go with equal speed to the . . . Government and ask for a loan." [57]

Seeking special favors from government for industry is an old American custom, in fact one of the oldest. William Hill has traced "The First Stages of the Tariff Policy of the United States," and shown how the then newly established federal government extended its "fostering aid" to the manufacture of various products (beer, candles, paper, glass, anchors, etc.) that the several states had previously "protected." This study led Hill to the conclusion that "To secure these objects was a chief end sought in adopting the Constitution. It was natural that almost the first act of the new Congress should be a measure for the protection and encouragement of American industries." [58]

Whatever the extent to which federal power was established "to secure these objects," subsequent events clearly show that throughout history various groups have sought and secured special privileges. In early days road-building was considered an advantage to drayers and coachmen. Boatmen therefore countered with pleas for building canals. Then came the time when vast stretches of land were given to the railroads and when "grazing rights" were given to cattlemen to allow their herds to graze on public lands. It is noteworthy that each of the public amenities—roads, canals, and so on —now taken for granted, was attacked by critics as "socialistic."

At the moment social critics like to flay the policy that gives large payments to landowners for allowing their land to lie fallow— something the ancient Hebrews found to be good practice, even when there were no government grants to reward them. One critic of current agricultural policy, economist Theodore W. Schultz, contends, "By any meaningful welfare test, helping least those who need help most is absurd." [59]

Another form of government support and one that has recently been criticized in Europe is the vast sums given in the United States for industrial research and development. This subsidy, European countries are saying, creates "unfair competition" in that industries in other countries do not enjoy a similar boon. More recently, the problem of the "brain drain" has attracted international attention, including that of the United Nations. Questions are being raised as to whether the United States ought not to provide some kind of "compensation" to countries who have paid for the education and technical training of engineers, physicians, and others who are helping to advance America's already highly developed economy, while their own countries desperately need them. There are also "brain drains" within countries—from areas of less to those of greater opportunity.[60]

Looking over his shoulder at history, Everett Dean Martin, in 1935, wrote "business, big and little . . . while professing a creed of 'rugged individualism,' set the public the example of dependence on government and did much to teach the masses to believe that the government owed each of its citizens a good living." [61]

Thus, the fat is now in the fire—and has been for a long time.[62] This is true not only in the United States but in other major countries, too, as Andrew Shonfield makes clear in *Modern Capitalism*.[63] From the point of view of Great Britain, what T. H. Marshall calls "the ways in which members of the business world expect to receive manna from heaven" is described by Douglas Jay in *Socialism in the New Society*.[64]

In the United States advantaged groups look upon government supports for them as a matter of course but view government action on behalf of disadvantaged groups as unwarranted interventionism. It is phenomena like these that give point to the earlier observation about "socialism for the rich" but "private enterprise for the poor." Just how confused thinking along these lines can be is evidenced by University of Chicago Vice-President Lowell T. Coggeshall—with a twinkle in his eye, no doubt—when he quoted a proposal for a foundation grant: "The University recognizes the necessity of making this grant self-supporting at the expiration of the proposed grant. To this end, it will make a determined drive to secure funds from government sources." [65]

Thoroughgoing conservatives (such as economist Milton Friedman of the University of Chicago) do lament one kind of governmental intervention as much as another. Licensing of valuable TV channels and taxicab or other valued franchises is criticized as much as public assistance to needy persons. Less consistent followers, however, often seize upon this opposition to public relief, probably because such an attack—against the weakest elements of the population—gives greatest promise of success; but they are strangely silent on other texts in the conservatives' gospel. A sporting proposition to genuine conservatives would be to agree—*after*

TV channel licenses and taxicab licenses have been abolished and after other supports for advantaged groups have been rescinded (so that real opportunities are opened up and "equalized")—*then* to take up the lesser problem of public relief. But until more comprehensive adjustments are made, the question remains how governmental help to both advantaged and disadvantaged groups can be fairly viewed—and valued—and equitably distributed.

As matters stand at the moment, one has only to contemplate the extent of the dependence of even the greatest modern corporations and businessmen upon the educational, transportation, communication, financial, legislative, law-enforcement, and other systems that have been created by the larger society (and financed by taxpayers, consumers, investors, and so on) without which corporations could hardly function.

To appreciate the importance of the various societally provided systems supporting any given enterprise, one has only to look at the situation in underdeveloped countries where these services are not available. Consequently, for want of what is called, in modern parlance, an adequate "infrastructure," industries cannot be established. But, if an industry is founded, it may well have to set up its own training program, build its own roads and telephone lines, lay railway tracks to its door, and perhaps build its own wharf. In a more highly organized society these functions are performed for an industry by the larger society—and generally paid for by taxpayers, consumers, and investors, and not by the industry itself. Yet when, because of these socially created resources, a particular enterpriser succeeds, the lion's share of the credit goes to his enterprise with little recognition for the society that created the preconditions that made his success possible. Without public investments in streets, highways, and traffic controls, one wonders how far the automobile industry could have gone on its own.

Contributions made through social expenditures not only to business but to the improvement of life for citizens generally have nowhere been more cogently analyzed than by a Britisher, William A. Robson, in his now old but woefully neglected *The Relation of Wealth to Welfare*.[66]

The relevance of social support to business and industry is clearly revealed in a full-page advertisement placed in *The Wall Street Journal* by the State of Ohio in 1965. In an effort to attract new enterprises (and to invite existing ones to expand) the advertisement triumphantly announced "Lowest State and Local Taxes of any comparable industrial state" (but failed to say who *did* pay the state's bills); "Lowest transportation costs . . . Ohio's $2.5 billion program for new highways insures an unsurpassed system" (but did not mention who paid for these); "Excellent educational facilities" (supported by whom?); "Low utility rates"; "Superb recreational facilities"; and then, somewhat less prominently, mentioned even the pending improvements, expansion, and modernization of Ohio's mental hygiene and correctional facilities.[67]

A research foundation established to woo new industries to North Carolina also indicates that industries that contemplated locating in a new area were preeminently interested in the availability of a variety of community-provided advantages.[68]

Thus, it is evident that industrial development is fostered not only by governmental action—actions of entire societies affect it. Moreover, looking at the issue negatively, there is the degree to which entire societies—not just the industries directly concerned— must "pick up the tab" for air and water pollution, urban blight, hillsides defaced by strip mining, mountains denuded of trees, and so on, which Titmuss refers to as the "cost of disservices."

Theodore W. Schultz, in his article "Investment in Man: An Economist's View," tackles the question of why the economic growth of the United States is "three times as large as the rate of increase of labor and capital." His hypothesis is that the answer lies "in the large and rapid accumulation of human wealth [such as that contributed by education] that is being excluded from our conventional measures of 'manhours worked' and of tangible capital." [69] Education, obviously, represents a societal contribution.

From an international viewpoint, businessmen have taken pride in aggrandizing their initiative and enterprise by recalling that "Trade follows the flag." They seldom stress the point that for trade "to follow," "the flag" must go on ahead—and stay there. At whose financial cost? At the cost of whose lives?

Columbia University sociologist William J. Goode suggests a more subtle dimension of interdependence when he points out that the family, around the world, has prepared generation after generation of workers for industry and has absorbed many of the shocks, insecurities, and other social costs that have been inevitable byproducts of the very industrialization that has produced phenomenal material gains.[70]

In stressing the facts of interdependence and the relationship between socially provided resources and private enterprises, the point is not, of course, to belittle private enterprise. Rather, it is to keep in perspective both the roles of individual effort in complex societies and the facts of interdependence. Private enterprises, in turn, of course make reciprocal contributions to their nurturing societies. In his critique of United States farm policy, Leon Keyserling, in answering the question "Who is subsidizing whom?" clearly illustrates the interdependence we have been stressing and illustrates, too, the virtual incommensurability of the contributions of various members of a society to the whole.[71]

In fact, as one contemplates the glorification (at least retroactively) of frontiersmen, pioneers, "the Westbound immigrants," and the "forty-niners" in American history, it is easy to forget the extent to which their heroic efforts were socially supported. There were, for instance, army actions through which land was acquired; troops and "lawmen" through whom frontiers were stabilized; government-paid explorers, trailblazers, and guides; government-maintained posts for supplies; government-given land for settlements, and land patents and legal processes to protect them; government-built trails and roads; omnipresent cavalrymen to swoop out of nowhere to protect wagon trains and settlements from marauders. All these represented—even in those days—a socially provided infrastructure that supported the intrepid souls who carried on despite smashed wagons and dashed hopes, agonizing deaths in childbirth, bodies wracked by fever, and shallow graves that claimed loved ones. Monuments to "The Pioneer Spirit," "The Frontier Mother," and the like are all to the good. However, such monuments are incomplete without at least a by-line—as in commercial advertising today—such as "with the help of the American people" or "through the courtesy of the United States government."

At least one explorer, Sir Francis E. Younghusband (who was the father of Britain's great social worker Dame Eileen Younghusband), has acknowledged his dependence upon resources other than his own. On a hazardous journey to Tibet he admitted, "If I get into a tight place, I have the government behind me, which would use all of its resources to see me through." [72] If one prefers seafarers to landlubbers, it is noteworthy that economic historian Douglass C. North, in tracing America's economic development, mentions several times how much both American and British shipping interests benefited from the navies that cleared the seas of pirates and thereby reduced the expenses of self-defense.[73]

On the question of unobvious but nonetheless real dependency within interdependent societies, two sociologists have kept their sights unusually clear and singularly unobscured by conventional standards for assessing personal achievement. James Marrs, who entitled his study *The Man on Your Back,* tenaciously pursues his subject wherever he is to be found—and on whosoever's back. This pursuit leads him not only to beggars, relief recipients, unemployed workers, and the like, but also to monopolists, persons living on unearned income, ladies living in "glorified ease," as well as to economic and political exploiters of sundry other kinds. All these find themselves discussed—along with criminals, habitual beggars, and the helplessly defective—as "social parasites." [74]

The other sociologist, Harlan Gilmore, in *The Beggar* follows beggary wherever it is to be found. He writes, "The beggars from industry and high finance had already made government charity respectable before the unemployed got a hand in the national dole." [75]

These views were by no means novel. William A. Bailward had written in 1920:

The first step in pauperism . . . is an insidious thing. . . . The danger is common to rich and poor. . . . The pauper is not so much a poor person as a poor creature. There are paupers among the rich as well as among the poor.[76]

Looking at the issue more positively, Professors James Mac-Gregor Burns and Jack Walter Peltason, in a widely used text on government, objectively include in their chapter on "Government as Promoter," sections on Helping Businessmen (through the Patent Office, Weather Bureau, aids to transportation, loans, and so on), Aiding Farmers (through cheap land sales, loans, soil conservation programs, etc.), and—in the same matter-of-fact manner, with no inimical overtones whatsoever—Social Welfare.[77] If more observers had this perspective, many of the problems with which this book is concerned would be quickly abated.

In sum, the complexities and incommensurabilities of life make it almost impossible to determine with any real justice when an individual or enterprise "fully earns" what is taken from society or "fully pays" his or its way. In fact, Professor Frankel believes that to attempt to say what "any individual really deserves . . . would be a form of madness." [78] In interdependent societies there is both give and take. To emphasize the "give" and overlook the "take" is unrealistic and unfair, and vice versa. Folk wisdom readily responds to the view that "to know all is to forgive all." It is less often recognized that to know all is to praise less what might on the surface look like individual effort but is in reality more of a social product.

One may not wish for the return of the days of Solon (who, in the sixth century B.C., gave to the Areopagus the power to inquire from what sources each man obtained the necessities of life and to punish those who did not work).[79] Nor may one wish for a state of affairs in which, as described by Professor T. H. Marshall, "Sudden outbursts of conspicuous consumption, indicative of sudden increases of income or property would be regarded, not with envious admiration, but with deep suspicion." [80] But one might well wish for more equitable and just measures by which modern, interdependent societies could accord their favors and rewards for individual effort and mete out their censure and penalties for lack of it.

Hidden Similarities in Societies' Support of the "Successful" and the "Unsuccessful"

In the preceding discussion of the way a society as a whole obfuscates its contribution to the success of those who are regarded as "succeeding," attention was limited to broad institutional factors —such as the socially provided inducements offered by a state to industry. We now wish to present a more particular but frequently overlooked aspect of the sources of social support given to specific individuals. For our purpose we will take two retired men: first, one who, by current standards, is "obviously" dependent, because he is "needy" and is supported by old-age assistance provided from tax funds; and second, a retired executive of a large corporation. The first gets, say, $1,000 a year in tax money; the second, $40,000 from his former corporation. Notwithstanding apparent differences in the situations of these men (and in those of their many counterparts throughout the land), they have one important element in common: Both are receiving social support.

This is obvious, of course, in the case of the man who receives assistance provided by government out of tax funds. But the most generous private pension paid to a corporation executive (or all such pensions taken together—or, for that matter, all corporation salaries) may also be viewed as social support. For, ultimately, consumers pay these costs. If the retired executive had been with an auto company, his pension comes out of prices that purchasers pay for their cars. Consumers who did not want that particular make of car had the option, of course, of contributing to the pension of a rival auto manufacturer. Or, if they decided not to contribute (through the purchase of a car) to the pension of any auto magnate, they could have elected to ride the bus and contribute (through fares) to the pension of the head of the bus line. Or, if the consumers chose to walk rather than ride, they could contribute to the pension of a shoe manufacturer. If they chose to sit, rather than walk, they could help to brighten the golden years of a maker of rocking chairs.

In highly organized economies purchasers of many types of goods have little choice as to how much they will contribute to the support of the producers and distributors of those goods. Up against obstacles such as giant corporations, price leaders, price agreements, and price fixing, consumers may find themselves not concurring in the prices they must pay. Yet, they have little power to affect price structures, corporation salaries, bonuses, incentive allowances, stock options, or pensions. The historically cited twin certainties in life should really have been triplets: death, taxes—and prices. Pricing practices being what they are, "to take one's trade elsewhere" often means only to pay the same price elsewhere. Ironically, the poorer a man is and the more he needs to "shop around," the fewer are his opportunities to do so.

Thus we are brought back not to "dependence" and "independence," but rather to degrees of obviousness of the dependence upon a supporting society. But, it may be argued, when a consumer pays for a benefit for a corporation executive, he gets "something for his money"—a car, perhaps, or a bus ride, or shoes, or a rocking chair. So also does the taxpayer (or voluntary contributor) get something for his money for the help given to more obvious dependents—as we shall see in Chapter IX. This benefit may not be so specific, direct, tangible, or obvious as a new power mower or a Weimaraner puppy, but this is more a question of obviousness or one of perception than one of "something" as opposed to "nothing" for one's money. All this, obviously, heightens the problem of incommensurabilities involved in a society's accord of favors and censure, which it seems so ready to bestow without consideration to the unobvious, imponderable, and unmeasurable intricacies involved.

The "Grand Old Man" of the British Labour Party, George Lansbury, once declared, "I never could see any difference between . . . the pension of a widowed queen and outdoor relief for the wife or mother of a worker." [81] In fact, in 1834, Richard Cadbury in Parliament managed to get a spokesman for the government to concede that the "Pension List" was, in essence, a "Charity List." Although one might belittle these observations either as more appropriate to an earlier day, or as partisan propaganda, one must still confront the observation of erudite, tough-minded Professor Titmuss, who only recently wrote, with respect to Great Britain:

As at present organised, the cost to the Treasury (*the whole community*) of private pension schemes *substantially exceeds the Treasury contribution to social security pensions for the whole population.* The pensions *of the rich are more heavily subsidised by the community than the pensions of the poor* [all emphases added].[82]

In his pamphlet *The Irresponsible Society*, Titmuss describes in greater detail these perhaps surprising phenomena resulting from the miscellany of broad fiscal, industrial, and other policies not usually envisaged as part of what is commonly interpreted as Britain's "Welfare Statism."

If the present scene appears to be complicated, what lies ahead may be even more so. For if certain men are correct—economists such as Robert Theobald, observers such as W. H. Ferry (his essay "Caught on the Horn of Plenty" was a real eyeopener), others at the Center for the Study of Democratic Institutions, and still others who signed a memorandum addressed to President Johnson in 1964—at least the United States may, in the foreseeable future, need to consider the idea of breaking completely the historic tie between work (as hitherto defined) and support.[83]

With reference to Britain, Professor Morris Ginsberg has written:

While it may be that inequality of distribution was an important factor of industrial progress in the earlier stages of capitalism [when social prestige lay with the landed aristocracy and the "new industrialists" lacked the social rewards subsequently accorded to them], it does not follow that it is equally important in a stage of high technological development and large-scale organization. At such a stage egalitarian redistribution may be not only compatible with, but a condition of, further progress.[84]

Whatever the future may hold, the interrelatedness of life and the resultant imponderables that make it difficult for a society justly to mete out its favors and censure constitute a challenge even today. In view of many things—the degree to which even individual aspiration is socially conditioned (Chapter I), the degree to which societies have proscribed individual effort that is "too hurtful" to either the individual or others (Chapter III), the degree to which social factors enter into personal achievement, the lack of means for recognizing the efforts of persons who (though unsupported by any of the aids often required for "success") are not only "really trying" but whose struggle may be downright heroic—in view of all these, perhaps society should take a fresh look at the equity with which it distributes its prizes and penalties.

If an intricately interrelated society really wanted to "do justice" (to say nothing of "love mercy"), it could make at least a start in this direction. It could do so by describing more often in their true dimensions the accomplishments of those who are regarded as "successes"—without more praise than is due to individual effort or less than is due to social support. Or, it might find new ways of honoring achievements other than those in the economic realm. Or, if material success and avoidance of obvious dependency are, indeed, to be the controlling criteria for bestowal or withholding of social favor, it might be more honest to say so and to make fewer pretensions about the merit of individual effort as such and to be even less squeamish than now about how the vaunted success is achieved. But, whether or not these things are done, the very least a society can do, in recognition of the incommensurabilities inherent in interdependence, is to avoid treating as commensurable and to refrain from punishing obviously dependent persons whose efforts do not happen to be crowned by material success.

Among other things this would require abandonment of the current predominant criterion of "success" and abolition of dual standards of social support and dual standards of justice—one standard for the unobviously dependent and another for the obviously dependent, as if obvious dependency were virtually the worst crime in the book.

1. Irvin G. Wyllie, *The Self-Made Man in America: The Myth of Rags to Riches* (New Brunswick, N.J.: Rutgers University Press, 1954), p. 151.
2. Robin M. Williams, Jr., *American Society: A Sociological Interpretation* (New York: Knopf, 1951), pp. 390, 393, 395, 396.
3. Max Lerner, *America as a Civilization: Life and Thought in the United States Today* (New York: Simon and Schuster, 1957), pp. 689, 690. For related views of Thorstein Veblen, see "Some Neglected Points on the Theory of Socialism," *The Place of Science in Modern Civilization and Other Essays* (New York: Viking, 1932), pp. 387–408.
4. Quoted by Lucien Price in *Dialogues of Alfred North Whitehead* (Boston: Little, Brown, 1954), p. 252.
5. William and Paul Paddock, *Hungry Nations* (Boston: Little, Brown, 1964), p. 11.
6. Ben H. Bagdikian, *In the Midst of Plenty: The Poor in America* (Boston: Beacon Press, 1964), p. 6.
7. Robert C. Weaver, "Major Factors in Urban Planning," in Leonard J. Duhl, ed., *The Urban Condition: People and Policy in the Metropolis* (New York: Basic Books, 1963), p. 110.
8. *Examination of the War on Poverty* (Washington, D.C.: Government Printing Office, 1965), p. 20.
9. S. M. Miller and Martin Rein, "Poverty, Inequality, and Policy," in Howard S. Becker, ed., *Social Problems: A Modern Approach* (New York: Wiley, 1966), p. 476.
10. Wyllie, *op. cit.*, p. 174.
11. A. Delafield Smith, *The Right to Life* (Chapel Hill: University of North Carolina Press, 1955), pp. 10–11, 13, 17. See also Charles A. Reich, "The New Property," *Yale Law Journal*, 73 (April 1964), especially 785–786.
12. Clyde Warrior, "Poverty, Community, and Power," *New University Thought* (Summer 1965), pp. 7, 8, 9.
13. Wyllie, *op. cit.*, p. 161.
14. Gunnar Myrdal, in Ben B. Seligman, ed., *Poverty as a Public Issue* (New York: Free Press, 1965), p. viii. This same volume includes some very perceptive comments by Elinor Graham on the power struggle inherent in the War on Poverty; see "The Politics of Poverty," pp. 231–250. Another view, of about the same scope as Professor Myrdal's, may be found in Kenneth E. Boulding, "The Wisdom of Man and the Wisdom of God," *Human Values on the Spaceship Earth* (New York: Council Press for the

National Council of Churches, 1966), p. 6. Relevant also is Peter H. Rossi and Robert A. Dentler, *The Politics of Urban Renewal: The Chicago Findings* (New York: Free Press, 1962).

15. Oscar Ornati, *Poverty Amid Affluence: A Report on a Research Project Carried Out at the New School for Social Research* (New York: Twentieth Century Fund, 1966), p. 113. See also Gary T. Marx, *Protest and Prejudice: A Study of Belief in the Black Community* (New York: Harper & Row, 1967).

16. Richard M. Titmuss, "The Role of Redistribution in Social Policy," *op. cit.*, pp. 17, 19, 20. Further sources relevant to Britain include Tony Lynes, "Poverty in the Welfare State," *Aspect*, No. 7 (August 1963); Peter Townsend, "The Meaning of Poverty," *British Journal of Sociology*, Vol. XIII, No. 3 (1962); Titmuss' own *Essays on 'The Welfare State'* (New Haven: Yale University Press, 1959), especially pp. 34–55; Titmuss' "The Welfare State: Images and Realities," *Social Service Review*, XXXVII (March 1963), 1–11, and his *Income Distribution and Social Change* (London: G. Allen, 1962).

   See also T. H. Marshall, *Social Policy* (London: Hutchinson University Library, 1965), especially pp. 90–98. Relevant also is David C. Marsh, *The Future of the Welfare State* (Baltimore: Penguin Books, 1964), particularly pp. 118–140.

17. Whitney M. Young, Jr., *To Be Equal* (New York: McGraw-Hill, 1964), pp. 22, 23, 25. See also *A "Freedom Budget" for All Americans* (New York: A. Philip Randolph Institute, 1966).

18. Dom Helder Camara, as quoted by Thomas B. Morgan in *Among the Anti-Americans* (New York: Holt, Rinehart and Winston, 1967), p. 20. For an analysis of factors operative in the United States to "keep the poor in their place" and giving plausibility to our concept of buffer zones protecting the privileges, prestige, power, and profit of advantaged groups, see Paul Jacobs, "Keeping the Poor Poor," in Leonard H. Goodman, ed., *Economic Progress and Social Welfare* (New York: Columbia University Press, 1966), pp. 158–184; Leonard J. Duhl, M.D., "Are We Mentally Prepared for the Elimination of Poverty?" *The Social Welfare Forum, 1961* (New York: Columbia University Press, 1961), pp. 100–113; and Adam Walinsky, "Keeping the Poor in Their Place," *New Republic*, 151 (July 4, 1964), 15–18.

19. The National Committee of Negro Churchmen, "Listen, America, Listen!" *The Interchurch News*, IX (August-September 1967), 2.

20. John Kenneth Galbraith, *The Affluent Society* (Boston: Houghton Mifflin, 1958), p. 39.

21. Charles Frankel, "The Moral Framework of the Idea of Welfare," in John S. Morgan, ed., *Welfare and Wisdom* (Toronto: University of Toronto Press, 1966), p. 151.

22. Robert Coles, "The Poor Don't Want to Be Middle-Class," *The New York Times Magazine*, December 19, 1965, p. 55.

23. Lewis A. Coser, "The Sociology of Poverty: To the Memory of Georg Simmel," *Social Problems*, 13 (1965), 144.

24. Caroline Bird, *The Invisible Scar* (New York: David McKay, 1966), p. 321.

25. W. Lloyd Warner, Marchia Meeker, and Kenneth Eells, *Social Class in America* (Chicago: Social Research Associates, 1949), p. 142.

26. August B. Hollingshead and Frederick C. Redlich, *Social Class and Mental Illness: A Community Study* (New York: Wiley, 1958), p. 71.

27. Bernard Berelson and Gary A. Steiner, *Human Behavior: An Inventory of Scientific Findings* (New York: Harcourt, Brace & World, 1964), p. 461.

28. Ralph Linton, "The Problem of Universal Values," in Robert F. Spencer, ed., *Method and Perspective in Anthropology* (Minneapolis: The University of Minnesota Press, 1954), p. 160. See also Reich, *op. cit.*, especially p. 786.

29. *LO*, The Swedish Confederation of Trade Unions, Stockholm, Series III, No. 11 (December 1964), pp. 49–50.

30. See Jane Addams, "The Jane Club" and "A Modern Lear" in Emily Cooper Johnson, ed., *Jane Addams: A Centennial Reader* (New York: Macmillan, 1960), pp. 29–31 and 31–35, respectively.

31. Irvin G. Wyllie, *op. cit.*, p. 136. Historical perspective on the relation of unscrupulous practices to "success" may be found in Gustavus Myers, *History of the Great American Fortunes* (New York: Random House, 1936); in Mathew Josephson, *The Robber Barons: The Great American Capitalists, 1861–1901* (New York: Harcourt, Brace & World, 1962); and in Stewart H. Holbrook, *The Age of the Moguls* (Garden City, N.Y.: Doubleday, 1953). Noteworthy also are the biographies of some of the nation's most "successful" men. See, for example, Allan Nevins, *John D. Rockefeller* (New York: Scribner, 1959); this is a one-volume abridgment by William Greenleaf of Nevins' two-volume *Study in Power—John D. Rockefeller, Industrialist and Philanthropist* (New York: Scribner, 1953). See also Lawrence Stessin, " 'I Spy' Becomes Big Business," *The New York Times Magazine*, November 28, 1965, pp. 105–108.

32. Goronwy Rees, *The Multimillionaires* (New York: Macmillan, 1961), pp. 108, 102, 103.

33. A. G. Gardiner, *Life of George Cadbury* (London: Cassell, 1923), p. 116.

34. Jerome B. Hellerstein, *Taxes, Loopholes and Morals* (New York: McGraw-Hill, 1963), p. 220.

35. See Bernard D. Nossiter, "Of Consciences and Kings," *The Mythmakers* (Boston: Houghton Mifflin, 1964), pp. 77–105; Walter Goodman, *All Honorable Men: Corruption and Compromise in American Life* (Boston: Little, Brown, 1963); *Identical Bidding in Public Procurement* (Washington, D.C.: Government Printing Office, 1964); Lee Metcalf and Vic Reinemer, *Overcharge* (New York: David McKay, 1967); Philip M. Stern, *The Great Treasury Raid* (New York: Random House, 1962, and Signet Books, 1965).

36. Lawrence H. Fuchs, *"Those Peculiar Americans": The Peace Corps and the American Character* (New York: Meredith Press, 1967), p. 214.

37. As reported in *The New York Times*, May 26, 1963. Among more recent stories to the same effect is another *Times* story, "Businessmen Attribute Their Success to a Rat," November 20, 1966.

38. Herman P. Miller, "Millionaires Are a Dime a Dozen," *The New York Times Magazine*, November 28, 1965, p. 130. A notable exception to Miller's generalization may be found in Rees, *op. cit.*, p. 3.

39. Berelson and Steiner, *op. cit.,* pp. 461, 462. Ralph D. Gardner's *Horatio Alger or The American Hero Era* (Mendota, Ill.: Wayside Press, 1964) is relevant in this context, as is John Tebbel's *From Rags to Riches: Horatio Alger, Jr., and the American Dream* (New York: Macmillan, 1963). See also Moses Rischin, ed., *The American Gospel of Success* (Chicago: Quadrangle Books, 1965). This book suggests additional useful sources. See also F. X. Sutton, *et al., The American Business Creed* (Cambridge: Harvard University Press, 1956), especially p. 26.

40. Kenneth E. Boulding, in Frank G. Dickinson, ed., *Philanthropy and Public Policy* (New York: National Bureau of Economic Research, 1962), p. 61.

41. Frank H. Knight, *Freedom and Reform: Essays in Economics and Social Philosophy* (New York: Harper & Row, 1947), p. 10. See also pp. 151, 382–383. Wyllie, *op. cit.,* and Rees, *op. cit.,* also discuss luck as a contributing factor to success.

42. As reported in "Forgotten Men," television program, American Broadcasting Company, February 12, 1965. Read Miss Gellhorn's first-hand impressions in *The Trouble I've Seen* (New York: Morrow, 1936).

43. As quoted in *Newsweek,* August 2, 1965, p. 62.

44. Henry Steele Commager, *The American Mind: An Interpretation of American Thought and Character Since the 1880's* (New Haven: Yale University Press, 1950), p. 421.

45. Louis F. Post, *Social Service* (New York: Wessels, 1909).

46. Leonard E. Read, *Deeper Than You Think* (Irvington-On-Hudson: Foundation for Economic Education, 1967), p. 120.

47. Seneca, *On Benefits,* Aubrey Stewart, tr. (London: Bell, 1900), pp. 41, 43.

48. Franklin D. Roosevelt, as quoted by Lester B. Pearson in "The World We Live In," *Self-Help in Social Welfare* (Bombay: International Conference of Social Work, 1954), p. 8. On this same point, see Bertrand de Jouvenel in T. E. H. Reid, ed., *Values in Conflict* (Toronto: University of Toronto Press, 1963), pp. 22–24.

49. Richard H. Tawney, *Religion and the Rise of Capitalism* (West Drayton, Middlesex, England: Penguin, 1948), p. 264.

50. William Stringfellow, *Dissenter in a Great Society: A Christian View of America in Crisis* (New York: Holt, Rinehart and Winston, 1966), pp. 42–43.

51. Ralph Waldo Emerson, "Gifts," in Brooks Atkinson, ed., *The Complete Essays and Other Writings of Ralph Waldo Emerson* (New York: Random House, 1940), p. 402.

52. As reported by Gloster B. Current in *The Crisis* (August-September 1965), p. 441.

53. J. F. de Jongh, "Self-Help in Modern Society," *Self-Help in Social Welfare, op. cit.,* p. 49.

54. T. W. Kent, "No One Is Independent," *Canada's Health and Welfare* (February 1961), p. 213.

55. Barbara Wootton, assisted by Vera G. Seal and Rosalind Chambers, *Social Science and Social Pathology* (London: G. Allen, 1959), p. 271.

56. Charles Frankel, *The Democratic Prospect* (New York: Harper & Row, 1962), p. 130.

57. Franklin D. Roosevelt, Address on the State of the Union, January 11,

1944, *The New York Times*, January 12, 1944. See also Commonwealth Club speech, *The New York Times*, September 24, 1932.

58. William Hill, "The First Stages of the Tariff Policy of the United States," *Publications of the American Economic Association*, III (November 1893), 131.

59. Theodore W. Schultz, "Our Welfare State and the Welfare of Farm People," *Social Service Review*, XXXVIII (June 1964), 128. For another critique of farm policy, see Leon H. Keyserling, *Agriculture and the Public Interest: Toward a New Farm Program* (Washington, D.C.: Conference on Economic Progress, 1965).

60. An interesting discussion of both domestic and international "brain drains" is that by United States Senator Walter F. Mondale, "How Poor Nations Give to the Rich," *Saturday Review*, March 11, 1967, pp. 24–26.

61. Everett Dean Martin, *Farewell to Revolution* (New York: Norton, 1935), p. 42.

62. For an extended enumeration of governmental aids to a wide variety of private enterprises, see *Subsidy and Subsidy-Effect Programs of the U. S. Government, Materials Prepared for the Joint Economic Committee*, Congress of the U.S. (Washington, D.C.: Government Printing Office, 1965); H. L. Nieburg, *In the Name of Science*, in which he analyzes "The Contract State" (Chicago: Quadrangle Books, 1966); Anatol Murad, *Private Credit and Public Debt* (Washington, D.C.: Public Affairs Press, 1954). Another particular aspect of the general problem of governmental aid is discussed in Wesley Calef, *Private Grazing and Public Lands* (Chicago: University of Chicago Press, 1960).

   A particularly useful book in the present context is Douglass C. North, *Growth and Welfare in the American Past: A New Economic History* (Englewood Cliffs, N.J.: Prentice-Hall, 1966), especially pp. 98–107. *Encyclopedia of U. S. Government Benefits* (Union City, N.J.: Wm. H. Wise, 1967) was widely advertised as showing "how to obtain a fast cash return for the 21% of your salary withheld each week for taxes." The advertisement was headed: "See what the government owes you." A more staid report covering the same ground is *Catalog of Federal Programs for Individual and Community Development* (Washington, D.C.: Government Printing Office, 1965).

63. Andrew Shonfield, *Modern Capitalism: The Changing Balance of Public and Private Power* (London: Oxford University Press, 1965). This book provides an international perspective on the question of social support to business and industry in the United States, West Germany, Britain, France, and other major countries.

64. Douglas Jay, "The Windfall State," *Socialism in the New Society* (London: Longmans, Green, 1962).

65. Lowell T. Coggeshall, *Progress and the Paradox on the Medical Scene* (Chicago: Graduate School of Business, University of Chicago, 1966), p. 16.

66. William A. Robson, *The Relation of Wealth to Welfare* (New York: Macmillan, 1925).

67. *The Wall Street Journal*, May 12, 1965.

68. J. W. Davis, "New Breed of Communities Springing Up in Battle to Attract Industry," *Los Angeles Times*, July 4, 1965.

69. Theodore W. Schultz, "Investment in Man: An Economist's View," *Social Service Review*, XXXIII (June 1959), 115, 116.

70. William J. Goode, *The Family* (Englewood Cliffs, N.J.: Prentice-Hall, 1964).

71. Keyserling, *op. cit.*, pp. 118–119.

72. Sir Francis Younghusband, as quoted by Leslie D. Weatherhead, in *That Immortal Sea* (New York: Abingdon Press, 1953), p. 65.

73. Douglass C. North, *op. cit.*, pp. 17, 37, 53, *i.a.*

74. James W. Marrs, *The Man on Your Back* (Norman: University of Oklahoma Press, 1958).

75. Harlan W. Gilmore, *The Beggar* (Chapel Hill: University of North Carolina Press, 1940), p. 229.

76. William A. Bailward, *The Slippery Slope and Other Papers on Social Subjects* (London: John Murray, 1920), p. 186.

77. James MacGregor Burns and Jack Walter Peltason, "Government as Promoter," *Government by the People: The Dynamics of American National Government* (New York: Prentice-Hall, 1952), pp. 695–730.

78. Frankel, "The Idea of Welfare," *op. cit.*, p. 178.

79. This practice of Solon is discussed by Charles S. Loch in *Three Thousand Years of Social Service*, a reprint of *Charity and Social Life* (London: Macmillan, 1910; and London: Charity Organisation Society, 1938), p. 26.

80. T. H. Marshall, "The Affluent Society in Perspective," *Sociology at the Crossroads and Other Essays* (London: Heinemann Educational Books, 1963), p. 317.

81. George Lansbury, quoted by Karl de Schweinitz in *England's Road to Social Security* (Philadelphia: University of Pennsylvania Press, 1943), p. 182.

82. Richard M. Titmuss, "The Role of Redistribution in Social Policy," *Social Security Bulletin*, 28 (June 1965), 17. See also his *The Irresponsible Society* (London: Fabian Society, 1960).

83. *The Triple Revolution: An Appraisal of the Major Crises and Proposals for Action* (Washington, D.C.: Ad Hoc Committee on the Triple Revolution, 1964), pp. 16, 17. (Processed.)

84. Morris Ginsberg, *Law and Opinion in England in the 20th Century* (Berkeley and Los Angeles: University of California Press, 1959), p. 16.

V
VALUE
CONFLICTS
in
WELFARE
SERVICES:
IMPACTS
UPON
POLICY
and
PRACTICE

S ocial welfare services are both children of, and contributors to, the cultures within which they develop. As such, they understandably reflect values dominant in those cultures, although as contributors they may foster values not yet accorded general public favor. In Chapter III we noted the degree to which the social welfare field shares the values that are widely placed upon self-help. Therefore it should not be too surprising—although it often comes as quite a shock to unsophisticated observers—that welfare services tend to view the help they give as less than a wholly satisfactory means to the continuing enjoyment of the values served. Assuming that the welfare field sees value in its own services, the field's own disvaluing of gratuitous help for any longer than "necessary"—a period which is itself susceptible of varied interpretations—generates conflicts among values.

WELFARE POLICIES AND PRACTICES REFLECTING AMBIVALENCE ABOUT HELP

What was widely believed to be the relationship of social welfare services to the rest of society and some of its values was expressed by Norman V. Lourie, Deputy Secretary of the Pennsylvania Department of Public Welfare and former president of the National Association of Social Workers:

American social work goal norms are complementary to and supportive of a free-enterprise economy.

The conviction that society must provide for those who cannot care for themselves has corollaries: (1) Dependent and maladjusted persons should be helped to help themselves. (2) Remedial steps should be taken to eradicate the basic causes of distress. (3) Efforts with individuals should promote the more effective approaches of the free-enterprise economy.[1]

Social workers were far from unanimous, however, about how seriously self-help was indeed fostered and about the degree to which those served were enabled to be self-directing rather than controlled by the serving agencies. No one has been more vocal on these counts than Bertram Beck, Executive Director of Mobilization for Youth in New York City, who has charged:

Although it is a favorite slogan of social work to say that "we help people to help themselves," there is a great gap between the reality and the myth. . . . When we discuss "helping people to help themselves," we conveniently turn our back on the social control aspects of social work. . . . Although we stress freedom of choice for the clientele . . . social work engages in no helping process which lacks . . . a value judgment that the social worker brings to the helping task. . . .

    . . . By failing to face certain facts of life within social work and by clinging to a concept that we merely help people to help themselves—that somehow they define the way and we do not—we have obscured our real role and lessened our ability to confront the problem of what our function within society should be.[2]

If social workers, who are typically employees of organizations, did give intended beneficiaries too much leeway in making choices, some of these might run counter to what contributors and taxpayers expect from their gifts and taxes, a point touched upon again in Chapter VII. Should this occur too often, resources for the employing agencies might dry up—or the social workers be fired.

Preference for Promising Clients

One indication that the welfare field views help ambivalently is its tendency to regard as the most promising "clients" those individuals and groups that have a robust sense of independence. For, such clients are already on the road to resuming or establishing patterns of life by which they can live—as almost any welfare agency hopes—without unduly protracted reliance upon welfare-type help. In fact, preferences for "promising" clients often work against the interests of the "neediest" and most disadvantaged persons and groups. This is especially true of private agencies that deliberately limit their intake to the more promising clients and are thus able to make the best possible showing—or, as they are more likely to put it, are able to utilize to the best advantage their typically limited resources. However, even public agencies, when they cannot meet all needs, have been known to serve first not those with the greatest need, but those with the most promise. This has been true, for instance, in the Manpower Training, in Head Start, and in other programs under the War on Poverty. It cannot be said to what degree these predilections reflect the preferences of welfare services themselves and to what degree they are a response to public attitudes and expectations or to a desire to create for themselves the best possible public image. It is noteworthy, however, that a report on the Academic Assembly on Social Work held in Canada in conjunction with Expo '67 quotes an unnamed participant as saying,

What occupies most social workers is the problem of upgrading their status rather than the needs of their clients. Instead of being concerned with maximum benefits for those in poverty, the concern is with rehabilitation, because if one can become known as a "rehabilitator" there is a powerful uplifting, not so much of the clients, but of one's own professional status. But most people are not on the welfare rolls because they need rehabilitation. . . . Guidance and counseling cannot begin to overcome the economic inequities which led them to the welfare rolls in the first place." [3]

The penchant of social workers and welfare leaders for emphasis upon their own "success" and upon helping others to help themselves is, as already noted, a two-edged sword for it often results in denying help to those who are most disadvantaged and least able to help themselves. Among others who have deplored this tendency is the Most Reverend Edward E. Swanstrom, head of Catholic Relief Services, who complains:

If a needy person is to work or learn to contribute to the development of his community, his chances of doing so are minimal if his or his family's stomachs remain empty. . . .

During the past several years, as opportunities to mount self-help and socio-economic development projects have increased, I have become alarmed at the tendency among international social workers to downgrade the importance of . . . relief supplies, such as food, clothing and medicines. . . .

To feed, clothe and help cure the poor of the world is fundamental to efforts that will make them economically self-sufficient. [4]

This problem is not, however, limited to the social welfare field itself. For example, when the Rosenberg Foundation in 1964 contributed to establishment of a "private school for dropouts and pushouts," it explained as follows its reason for so doing: "In our success-oriented society, many institutions don't like to take probable failures. It doesn't look good on the records." [5] Or, as one educator put it, "Everybody loves the top 30 percent." Not even the church has escaped this success-orientation and its corollary effects according to Arthur R. Simon, a churchman who deplores the church's commitment to what he terms "success theology," one result of which is that churches "are much more interested in successful ventures than in suffering, more wrapped up in buildings than in people." [6]

Although welfare personnel like to couch in flowery language their devotion to self-help ("It's the American Way," and so on), it is not unlikely that even in highly developed countries, no less than in underdeveloped ones that frankly admit as much, this emphasis results as much from the need to stretch always inadequate resources as from dedication to self-help as an end in itself.

It is not known whether the attitudes of welfare services toward self-help and independence are the result of their own direct experience with inimical effects of helping and being helped, or whether they are, rather, reflections of the values of cultures in which "giving" is irksome and helping is viewed inimically. Each probably reinforces the other. It is not improbable, though, that emphasis upon self-help reflects more the reluctance of the "providers" of the services to supply them than the reluctance of the services to deliver them. Reluctance to help, whatever its source, is easily translated into policies and practices that not only help others to get along without them, but also make acceptance of help distasteful, if not hurtful.

Some of the same factors operating here may explain what has been criticized as welfare agencies' "dissociation from the poor." [7] These welfare agencies are primarily in the private sector. In the public sector, the problem is probably less one of "disengagement" as such than of primitive practices in dealing with poor persons (discussed in Chapter VI).

However these phenomena are explained, there are many indicators that welfare services themselves view their gratuitous help quite inimically or accommodate themselves to the hostility of others.

These days few would agree, probably, with Robert Burns' lines:

Affliction's sons are brothers in distress;
A brother to relieve—how exquisite the bliss!

Although neglect of the most disadvantaged in favor of those who show more promise of improvement is a grave problem, one should also note the quite different problem of providing only for seriously disadvantaged persons services urgently needed by less disadvantaged ones. Youngsters may get into trouble at school because they cannot keep up with their classes, then in juvenile halls (or other detention facilities) they may get the first individualized creative teaching they have ever known—only to be sent back to their unresponsive schoolrooms when their detention is ended. Or, a youth who would otherwise be placed on probation is sent to a correctional institution because only there can he get a psychological, social, and physical "work-up." Or, a youth in a correctional institution may choose to forego parole because the only chance he sees for completing his high school work is in the institution. Or, where a judge has the option of sentencing a man on different counts, the man may be sent to prison (on a felony charge) because the jail to which he would otherwise be sent (for a misdemeanor) has no provision for needed medical care. This phenomenon may be defined as forcing those who are less disadvantaged into the role of greater disadvantage so they can be given services they need.

A contrapuntal variation on this theme explains much social progress. Advantaged groups, seeing special services provided for underprivileged persons, often demand that these be made available to them too. It was thus that free public education, first given only to "pauper children," was transformed into free education for all. In this way, too, free medical care was gradually extended from Poor Law medicine to free treatment that reaches well into the "comfortable" classes (as in New York, where Medicaid—under Title XIX of the Social Security Act—is available for a family of four even if its net income is $6,000 a year). In Sweden, in 1967, the Confederation of Trade Unions was asking that training and relocation services available only to unemployed workers be extended to employed workers as well.[8] Thus, services originally provided for only a fringe of disadvantaged persons have a way of being woven into the larger social fabric. This phenomenon, by the way, helps to explain how "welfare measures" so often wind up favoring the advantaged as much as, if not more than, the disadvantaged, thus maintaining the privilege-prestige-power buffer zone discussed earlier.

Confidentiality

The penchant of welfare agencies to treat as "confidential" all transactions with beneficiaries reflects an inimical view of the need to be helped and of being helped. If this were not the case, one would expect a family service agency, for instance, not to cloak in secrecy but to divulge as a mark of honor the news that a particular family had applied to it for help—or, having been helped, was now functioning happily. However, resort to family service—or any other welfare service—is seldom thought to characterize "the Family of Distinction" in the sense that drinking a particular mineral water, smoking a certain brand of cigar, or using some other prestigious product is alleged to mark "the Man of Distinction."

Customary confidentiality is far more than a by-product of the Protestant ethic. This is clearly evidenced by the universal regard for it. Probably no country in the world gives more respect to this concept than does France to *le secret professionel.* Moreover, protection of the sensibilities of persons who are being helped has deep roots in ancient Jewish teachings and practices; anonymity for those receiving alms has long been respected.

Disguising the Nature of Help

A third indicator that welfare agencies are often inimical to gratuitous help is the lengths to which they go to disguise it. Disguises, it should be noted, are important not only with respect to the agencies concerned but also with respect to making proffered help more acceptable and palatable to beneficiaries who (as we shall see in Chapter VII) often disdain gratuitous help.

Among the disguises that make help look like not-help are "costumes" borrowed from the prestigious marketplace. A case in point is the age-old practice of giving help in the form of "loans"—a practice honored in ancient Jewish history, borrowed by many other cultural groups (and embraced by Savonarola in Florence), and perpetuated today (in international terms) through foreign aid in the form of "loans" that neither the lender nor the borrower really expects ever to be repaid.

Another cloak more recently borrowed from the marketplace to disguise the nature of help is the practice of rendering welfare services on a part-pay or fee-paying basis. Even when fees are clearly only token ones, they are patently an attempt to give the respectability of the marketplace to gratuitous help.

Another frequently borrowed disguise is one from the august field of jurisprudence. As already mentioned, various welfare agencies insist that their services are "not charity, but justice." When the Family Service Association of America issued a pamphlet designed to overcome people's natural reluctance to accept help with their family problems, it entitled the brochure *The Rights of the Individual Family in a Mass Society.* Then, to underline one's right to help in different types of situations, the theme is repeated time and again.

Or, a welfare service may be cloaked in the guise of a social utility. An interesting attempt of this kind was made in Great Britain in 1960 when the Conservative Party was in power and when Parliament was disturbed about the number of needy persons who refused to apply for aid. As a result, the National Assistance Board attempted to picture public assistance in the guise—not of the help that it in fact represented—but of a social utility. In the words of a report of the board:

The National Assistance Board are a part of the country's social services. Acceptance of the help which the Board can give should no more be regarded as involving any stigma than does acceptance of other social services paid for from public funds, such as family allowances and education.[9]

Although it may have been laudable to attempt to include public assistance in the august family of social utilities—available to all qualifying for them but without any test of need—it was unlikely that, as long as the hated means test and other demeaning aspects of obvious dependency were retained, the real nature of the help extended could be effectively camouflaged. In fact, a large part of the assistance that caused this concern was transformed in 1966 into new Social Security benefits quite like social utilities.

In later chapters we shall discuss further types of obfuscation of the degree of help in welfare services and, more importantly, ways in which gratuitous help is often transformed into other means of aiding individuals and groups to attain desired ends. However, we should take note here of one particular form of obfuscation of help, namely, "work relief," or as it is sometimes put, "work-for-relief." During the Great Depression in the United States no group was more vocal than social workers in advocating work relief in preference to "direct relief," but it was equally true that no group was more insistent about the preferability of *real* work (including that on genuine public works projects) to "work relief." In this connection it is noteworthy that although the 1967 Delegate Assembly of the National Association of Social Workers approved a strong endorsement of guaranteed incomes for all persons having less than a stipulated amount, the Assembly placed even higher priority on the expansion of employment opportunities that, presumably, would materially reduce needs for help.[10]

The view taken of work relief by the welfare field differs markedly from that of the man in the street. The latter wants assisted persons to "work for it," even if this means relatively useless "made work" (inimically termed "leaf-raking") and however unconstructive or even demeaning it might be. The welfare field, generally speaking, would not similarly value work for work's sake alone. From its vantage point this smacks too much of the oakum picking, rag picking, and treadmill of the long-gone workhouses and almshouses. But work done in return for aid would find favor among welfare workers if it does not displace wage-workers; is directed to a useful end; allows workers to feel productive and maintain a sense of dignity; is not looked upon as a source of exploitation; and represents not punishment for having to accept help, but a genuine return to the community for what one received, thus obfuscating the fact that one had been "helped."

Although obfuscations of gratuitous help may be highly useful, there is, anomalously, inherent in them a danger not only to welfare personnel and the public but to intended beneficiaries as well. The various disguises may be so effective that they may be mistaken for the real thing. Too successful an obscuration may lead all concerned to forget that, in avoidance of temporary embarrassment, they may be settling for less than more highly valued means. Underneath cloaks masking help that is really being given may also be hidden the circumstances that cause the continuing and real needs for help. In other words, social well-being may perhaps be better served by recognizing need and help for what they are, and by developing as quickly as possible means superior even to obfuscated help to make value attainment possible. There is another ironic aspect of devices intended to camouflage help; interpretations and expedients intended to be appealing to benefactors may be appalling to beneficiaries, while some that are acceptable to beneficiaries may be anathema to benefactors. However, considering the nature of community power structures and the typical weakness of those served by welfare agencies, it is hardly to be expected that forms of help not approved by the larger community could be long sustained.

Emphasis Upon Rehabilitation

A fourth indicator that help, as such, is viewed inimically in welfare policy is the emphasis repeatedly placed upon rehabilitation. By this, typically, is meant helping an individual to live by his own efforts or helping a family to get along on its own without further outside help. In 1962 the editor of the *Catholic Charities Re-*

view deplored federal-state public assistance to unemployed heads of families and advocated in its place greater emphasis upon services available under the Manpower Training Act. He wrote:

When one recalled the social work concepts of family strengths and the role played in creating them by the "image" given by the individual parent, it seemed to be poor casework to directly reduce the image of the father to that of an ineffectual male, unable to provide for his family.

. . . Far from beating him down with the weight of adverse public opinion, the devices made available through the Manpower Training Act will raise up his self-esteem and his goals for himself and for his family.[11]

Somewhat earlier the director of the California State Department of Social Welfare maintained that welfare is simply a way in which society tries to deal humanely and constructively with hardships that result from the failures of the more formal and established social mechanisms. He said:

Welfare constitutes nothing more than a sidetrack on the main line of social and economic developments which affect the lives of people.

. . . As long as the cars are on the sidetrack it doesn't matter much how we dress them up in terms of service and activities; we are not established by the community to maintain a museum or a showcase.

. . . It's up to us to apply the additional motive power that will shove our cars faster down the line and back on to the main stream.[12]

Earlier we cited several social work and social welfare authorities who favor self-help, family cooperation, and mutual aid. We noted also the broad societal objectives espoused in the United States by the National Association of Social Workers. The association says of these objectives and social work's concern about them:

A free society fulfills these obligations to its members through a wide range of social institutions, including the family, voluntary association [including "mutual association"], economic enterprise, and government.

. . . Social work is the [sic] profession which concerns itself with facilitating and strengthening of basic social relationships between individuals, groups, and social institutions.[13]

The New York State Department of Social Welfare in 1960 issued a report entitled *To Prevent and to Restore,* which described two projects designed to show "the rehabilitation potential of public social services in New York State." Raymond W. Houston, at that time Commissioner of Welfare, commended the report to all who want to know what personal satisfaction and professional fulfillment public welfare can offer and to all who want to know what public social service expenditures can mean in terms of restored human values. . . . Those who feel that nothing can be done for the so-called hard-core cases on the public welfare rolls will be surprised by the impressive achievements recorded.

The Commissioner then added the sobering note, "On the other hand, those who believe that every individual must respond to the imposing skills of the modern social caseworker will be equally surprised by the unexpected failures encountered." [14]

In Pennsylvania, where, it will be recalled, Norman V. Lourie was Deputy Secretary of the State Department of Public Welfare, a widely publicized "Project Independence" was launched to help former recipients of assistance to become wage earners. In fact, during the 1960's the emphasis shifted markedly from older work-for-relief programs to work-for-training, a trend given great impetus by the Economic Opportunity Act in 1964.[15]

In expectation of fostering—and better to symbolize—greater emphasis upon rehabilitation, the federal Department of Health, Education, and Welfare was extensively reorganized in 1967. The previously existing Welfare Administration was abolished and in its place was established the Rehabilitation Services Administration. Moreover, many of the new key posts were filled by persons from the former Vocational Rehabilitation Administration.

One straw that showed which way the rehabilitation winds were blowing in the public welfare field was the theme—"Farewell to Alms"—for a regional meeting of the American Public Welfare Association in 1967.

As in the case of work relief, values that welfare personnel see in training programs differ somewhat from those of the overall society. To the latter, compulsory training as a price to be paid for receiving assistance from the community had almost a Pauline flavor of "he that will not be trained, neither let him eat." This emphasis, which was strongly opposed by welfare, labor, civic, and other organizations, found wide support in Congress in 1967 and legislation ultimately enacted was designed to firmly—even sternly—reenforce it. In testimony presented to a Senate Committee by Walter P. Reuther, President of the International Union of Automobile (and other) Workers, on a bill already passed by the House, he said, "It seems inconceivable that anyone seriously could entertain the idea of 'starving' people off of assistance and into self-sufficiency. Regrettably, we have had enough experience with that inhuman approach to know it only increases the misery of those whose best efforts leave them economically dependent." [16]

Welfare personnel, knowing at first hand the enormous effort exerted by some of those who most need training, keep wondering whether, after all their sacrifice, there would be jobs for them. Of course, these jobs were not within the power of the welfare establishment to provide. In fact, there are indications that welfare personnel have more success in persuading and helping public assistance recipients to enter training programs than they—or anyone else—have in persuading employers to provide jobs. As George K. Wyman, Commissioner of Welfare in New York State, put it in 1965, "It would be pointless, wasteful, and cruel to try to prepare [financially needy] families for an economy into which they cannot be integrated because it can offer them no opportunities to become productive, self-supporting, and responsible citizens." [17]

Thus we see again conflicts in values. On the one hand there are those that view training and rehabilitation almost as ends in themselves. On the other hand, the welfare field, willing and ready to facilitate training and rehabilitation, was asking "to what end?" Unfortunately for the welfare field, the only end that would not be "pointless, wasteful, and cruel" could be effected not by itself but only by the larger society.*

Or, welfare leaders might see training and rehabilitation programs as serving useful purposes even though they only advanced the amount of self-care or raised the quality of life of an individual or family, whether or not a return to wage earning was effected. Whereas critics say they want "tax-eaters transformed into taxpayers," welfare personnel believe that individuals, even while still on assistance rolls, may be helped to play more constructive and useful social roles.

Exactly these kinds of conflicts among values may account for the hardened attitude in Congress and the reorganization of the Department of Health, Education, and Welfare. Although it is too early for studied assessment, it is also possible that too much was expected of earlier legislation (such as that enacted in 1962 and 1964), which was expected to produce—and was possibly oversold by its proponents as promising—greater reductions in assistance rolls than were in fact effected.

---

* Widespread disaffection in Congress with the role welfare agencies were playing in getting people "off relief" was reflected, in 1967, in strong pressure to take out of the hands of welfare agencies, and giving to the Department of Labor, more of the responsibility for work programs.

In world terms, a group of experts, meeting under the aegis of the United Nations to define *The Aims and Means of Social Service,* has declared that social service

. . . endeavours to provide a social climate in which the individual can satisfy his needs as a human being and fulfill his functions as a member of his group and community. . . .

. . . The provision of social service programmes should not only take into account the material needs of the individual, but should also enable him fully to develop his spiritual and cultural life so that he may participate usefully in the life of his community.[18]

Prevention, Early Diagnosis, and Treatment

Further indicators that typical welfare-agency help is not viewed even by the agencies as an optimal way of life are found in their emphasis upon "prevention" and upon "early identification and treatment."

Prevention is, of course, a relative concept because almost any "curative" treatment may be seen as preventing a worse situation. Even amputation of a gangrenous leg may be seen as preventive—in that it may prevent death.

On the other hand, prevention may sometimes have a some-what frightening aspect, in that effective preventatives may be worse than what they prevent. In this connection, I often think of the title of the book written over fifty years ago by S. Bennett: *Old Age—Its Cause and Prevention.*[19] Premature death or, as among primitive peoples, the abandonment of the aging—leaving them to cope alone with wild beasts—may be considered preventives of old age. But one approaching his golden years may be excused, perhaps, if he favors arriving at the sunset of life rather than departing in late afternoon.

I had a visitor several years ago from a Middle Eastern country, who marveled at the attention given in the United States to unmarried mothers and their "illegitimate" children. These, he insisted, were not an important problem in his country. When I remonstrated by saying surely unmarried girls must become pregnant or married women become pregnant by men other than their husbands, he replied, "Oh, certainly—but we kill them."

Thus prevention of a problem may not in and of itself be the prime desideratum. We shall not, therefore, be concerned here with inhumane prevention, but only with that which entails no disvalues that outweigh those of the ills to be prevented. In this sense prevention has long been stressed—as in Jewish tradition and, more broadly, by outstanding social thinkers such as Plato, Juan Luis Vives, Saint Vincent de Paul, and leaders of the Charity Organization Societies in both Britain and the United States. In fact, the statements that were cited by the United Nations group of experts and the California Director of Social Welfare were both preceded and followed by emphases upon the importance of prevention.

Among others in the social welfare field who have stressed this is the New York Community Service Society, which is among the most prestigious and forward-looking social welfare agencies, not only in the United States but in the world. After an extended study of its optimal role, this society's annual report for 1959–1960 declared:

A shift in emphasis should be made to a "more direct assault on the causes that lie behind our serious welfare problems." Thus, increasing efforts must be made to prevent social damage because to mend it is extremely costly in monetary and in human terms. . . . The study . . . made it clear that the Society's future Family Services program should concentrate on reaching people *before* they become so damaged that curative action is virtually impossible.[20]

The American Public Welfare Association in 1966 included in its statement of "Federal Legislative Objectives" the following:

The present scope of public welfare programs is a reflection of the gaps in the social and economic fabric of the nation. It is essential to the well-being and security of the nation that increased emphasis be placed upon all measures to prevent poverty, especially in families whose income is inadequate for the needs of children, including the elimination of racial and religious discrimination and the development of full and unrestricted opportunity for employment at a suitable wage, and for adequate housing, education, social insurance, and medical care.[21]

Looking back to 1894, it is noteworthy that Professor Amos G. Warner, in his classic *American Charities,* had strongly emphasized the importance of prevention. "He who takes an interest in trying to cure poverty in a single case," he wrote, "will soon come to find that nothing in politics or industry is foreign to him." It is interesting, in retrospect, to compare with the preventive measures advocated by the American Public Welfare Association in 1966 those enumerated by Professor Warner in 1894: crèches, kindergartens, cooking schools, laundries for the education of mothers, stamp deposit funds, and fuel funds through which summer savings could secure winter delivery of coal at summer prices.

Professor Warner also reports, "An active charity organization society loses many of its friendly visitors from the fact that through their interest in cases they come to have an interest in institutions, and pass from the work of caring for the one to the work of reforming the other." [22] This same writer gave currency to the term "philanthropology," a topic discussed at the International Congress of Charities, Correction, and Philanthropy, which was held in Chicago in 1893.

But, though it has been a favored theme throughout social history, prevention has proved to be an elusive goal. Historian Robert H. Bremner has said, "Prevention is not only one of the oldest principles of social welfare, but it is also one of the most difficult to apply." [23] Among welfare workers there always seems to be agreement that, in order to get at any human problem properly, a beginning should have been made "in the cradle." Here the consensus usually ends, however, because of the difficulty of agreeing upon whose cradle—the child's? his mother's? his grandmother's? whose? Nevertheless, the search goes on. And the broader the scope of preventive measures, the more prevention merges with social change and social reform.

Many discussants of "prevention" have contrasted this with "cure." However, when United States Commissioner of Welfare Dr. Ellen Winston addressed the International Conference of Social Work in 1966, she said with respect to social casework, group work, and the staffing of special services and facilities:

I include *prevention* of individual and social problems as an important therapeutic function. For, in the vast majority of cases, social pathology can be avoided—or minimized—by early recognition of the signs and symptoms.[24]

The wide range of the above-mentioned preventive services may, it is true, include some that would be offered in the form of gratuitous help by social welfare agencies. To advocate them, therefore, says nothing one way or the other about welfare leaders' preference of means. However, it is clear that many preventive services would be rendered by institutions outside the welfare field and on a different basis from those within the field. Moreover, prevention assumes that, if successful, individuals will be able to fulfill their requirements without gratuitous help from *any* quarter. Although such success might change the nature of problems brought to welfare agencies, social history clearly suggests that as old problems are avoided, new ones quickly arise.

Social Change, Social Action, and Social Reform

Social welfare leaders are virtually unanimous (in word, if not in deed) in their support of broad social action and social reform that might reduce the need for even preventive services. One of the most intriguing explanations of the source of interest in social reform is the one offered many years ago by George Herbert Mead of the University of Chicago. He wrote:

The bare impulse to help is on the same level with that of the dogs that licked the sores of Lazarus' body. The identification of ourselves with Lazarus puts in motion those immediate defensive reactions which give rise not only to efforts of amelioration but also of value and plans for social reform.[25]

Whatever the genesis of this interest, the welfare field has long declaimed its concern (honored more in the breach, possibly, than on the ramparts) for broad social action that, presumably, would reduce the number of problems that are given to welfare agencies or would at least change the nature of these problems. Throughout social history there have been examples of superseding "ambulance service" with "building fences at the top of the precipice." Notable examples include emphases upon industrial safety and workmen's compensation so as to save husbands' lives and thus reduce the need to support widows and orphans. Somewhat earlier, philanthropies to release debtors from jail were superseded by legal reforms that forbade imprisonment for debt. In retrospect it is surprising how long this "relief" function persisted before enlightened men thought of abolishing the cause of the need.

The whole point of issuing its *Goals of Public Social Policy*, published from time to time by the National Association of Social Workers, is to underscore the responsibility of social workers and welfare agencies for social action and social change. Of this the association declares:

Basic to all social work functioning is the concept of an accepted but developing standard of mutual obligation between individuals and their social organization. . . .

Social workers have an obligation with respect not only to such functions of society as lie within their own area of competence . . . but also to those social measures and policies that will prevent the needs with which they deal.[26]

To further its broad social goals the Association in 1965 issued a *Social Action Guide* for its members, chapters, and state councils across the nation. Justification for this emphasis was found in what Sanford L. Solender said in 1957:

Social work's preoccupation with the whole person and the total environment results in a breadth of social concern which is uncommon among the professions. Social work long ago discovered that its services to individuals, groups, and communities are inextricably related to the strengths and ills of the environment.[27]

What may well be American social work's "finest hour" in terms of social action came in 1912 when recommendations of a committee of the National Conference on Charities and Correction were embodied almost lock, stock, and barrel in Theodore Roosevelt's Progressive Party platform. An analysis of the committee's proposals that were incorporated, and those that were not, into the "Bull Moose" platform has been made by Professor Irving Weissman. Of greater practical significance, however, was how social work rallied its forces during the Great Depression in support of federal aid for the then utterly inadequate local and state relief programs.[28]

Undoubtedly one of social work's proudest moments in more recent years occurred during the famous Honolulu Conference when President Lyndon B. Johnson and Asian leaders discussed the fundamental social changes that needed to be made in Southeast Asia if stability was to be restored. First came the tribute by the President to General William C. Westmoreland, who, he said, had "the mind of a military man and the heart of a social worker." Then *Time* magazine reported that the President had sat down "to discuss the nuts and bolts of reform, just like a social worker in Chicago." [29]

However, pride did not swell every social worker's breast. The social ferment of the 1960's greatly heightened the disaffection of the many welfare leaders who had been thinking for years that welfare interests should be taking more of an activist role. For one, Professor Alfred Kadushin of the University of Wisconsin, speaking particularly of social casework, but with an underlying broader meaning, told a group of social work educators:

The real social deprivations which so many clients face—poor housing, structural unemployment, discrimination, marginal assistance budgets, limited income, low educational attainment, limited marketable skills, etc.—stem from situations over which neither the worker nor the client has any individual control. Solutions must be sought beyond the worker-client relationship. . . . Clinical intervention focused on the individual family subsystem and the "immediate environment" of the client cannot solve problems which, because they reflect inequities in wider institutional arrangements, require intervention at the institutional level of the social structure.[30]

Another observer, Alfred J. Kahn of Columbia University, declared to a national meeting of professional social workers, "The issue becomes one of whether the profession makes its basic contribution by retaining its clinical-therapeutic-rehabilitative core . . . or whether it seeks to reconstruct itself to become one of the primary disciplines of a social planning state." [31]

Ever since 1929 the welfare field had been contemplating its dual role, described in that year by Porter Lee, then head of the New York School of Social Work. His analysis of social work in terms of both "cause" and "function" underscored the profession's responsibility both for bold social action and for skilled technical performance.[32] The bulk of the profession (for reasons that many writers have analyzed) has undoubtedly clustered around the "function" pole on Lee's continuum, but hardly deserved the description in *A Dictionary of Social Reform*, which held:

The social worker of the 1930's was "socially conscious"; following the war, he tended to become "professional" in ways which removed him from the root questions of social disorder. . . . Social work had ceased to be a reform, and had become a function of the *status quo*.[33]

Still, in 1967, Margaret K. Rosenheim, a lawyer and a member of the faculty of the School of Social Service Administration at the University of Chicago, could write, "The noninvolvement [in social policy] of the membership [of the National Association of Social Workers] can be called conspicuous abstention of the theoried class." [34] Some years before, Marion Sanders had also needled the field with her article "Social Work: A Profession Chasing Its Tail." [35]

Whether or not these judgments were too harsh need not concern us here because in the 1950's and 1960's new winds were blowing, and, with the concurrent development of the War on Poverty

and agitation for the extension of civil rights, more and more welfare workers were gathering around Lee's "cause" pole. What might
be considered the bellwether of this new activism was the imagina-
tive and bold Mobilization for Youth (MFY) program in New York
City, under the sponsorship of the Columbia University School of
Social Work. Two workers identified with this program urged in
1965:

The idea advanced by MFY is that the social worker should fulfill his
professional function and agency responsibility by seeking a solution to
social problems through institutional change rather than by focusing on
individual problems and social functioning.[36]

To this banner more and more welfare workers are flocking
daily. Increasingly, interest previously limited to social casualties
has been shifting to causalities. But our point here is not to appraise
the social action role of social workers and others in the welfare
field, but to underscore the point that even those who do not rally to
the social action banner give at least lip service to the desirability of
social change that would reduce the kinds of problems requiring
help from welfare agencies.

A remarkable recrudescence of what Professor Warner, more
than seventy years before, had described as disaffection with mere
treatment and greater interest in social action could be seen in the
United States in the 1966 Annual Meeting of the National Social
Welfare Assembly. This meeting was devoted to consideration of a
committee report on "The Future Role and Program" of the Assembly. Of the proposed reorganization, the chairman of the Study Committee, Bernard L. Gladieux, reported, "We anticipate . . . that the
organization will find its major thrust and principal contribution in
the field of social policy, affecting the social environment and institutional structure of the country."

Strongly supporting this proposal, Sanford L. Solender, another
member of the Study Committee, spoke of "the growing concern of
. . . Assembly agencies with larger social questions and with their
responsibility . . . for having a significant impact on the shaping
of policies and programs designed to cope with the very basic social
problems that we face and that remain so seriously unsolved." [37]

In 1967 the Canadian Welfare Council was engaged in formu-
lating a "Comprehensive Statement on Social Welfare for Canada"
to "serve policy makers and citizens . . . over at least the next dec-
ade." This effort followed by ten years the Council's *Social Security*

for Canada, which had made many recommendations subsequently put into effect.

From India, Dr. M. S. Gore, director of the Tata Institute of Social Sciences, reports what observers in more advantaged countries may regard as somewhat more basic problems than they customarily encounter:

The psychological and domestic problems of individuals lose their significance when the vast majority is clamouring for the solution of its physical problems of food, shelter, and clothing. The social worker's job in India primarily calls for the fostering of attitudes, institutions, and processes in the community that would lead to greater production and a more equitable distribution of the means of life and subsistence.[38]

The United Nations group of experts who were mentioned earlier, in defining "the aims and means of social service," declared that the objective is

to enable individuals, groups and communities to meet their needs and solve their problems of adjustment to a changing pattern of society, and by cooperative action to improve economic and social conditions.

. . . Most activities designed to help human beings begin by being curative in nature . . . but it is important to stress . . . preventive action, which should operate on both the individual and his environment. . . . The aim of all such services is to raise the real standard of living of the community.[39]

World attention has been drawn by the International Conference of Social Work to the importance of broad social action to social well-being. In 1964, the conference, meeting in Athens, had for its theme "Social Progress Through Social Planning" and, in 1966 in Washington, D.C., the theme "Urban Development—Its Implications for Social Welfare." In this context it is noteworthy that the Conference in 1966 changed its name to International Council on Social Welfare in the hope that this would more accurately denote the more activist role it expected to play in world welfare circles.

Almost simultaneously the United Nations Social Commission, after its reappraisal of existing social welfare programs, recommended to the Social and Economic Council that the commission be rechristened Commission on Social Development. This was because the Social Commission had not attacked "with sufficient vigor such major problems of development as social reform, the role of the State in planning . . . and the social aspects of industrialization."

Looking to the future, "the ultimate objective of United Nations social activities, as well as of national development programmes" was
envisaged as no less than "the well-being and dignity of man." [40]

Interest in broad social action obviously puts social work and
welfare services in yet another "middle." Insofar as welfare services
are expected to preserve the status quo, to "keep in their places" poor
and otherwise disadvantaged persons, and to protect that buffer
zone safeguarding the privileges, prestige, and power of advantaged
groups, any change in any of these dimensions is understandably
disturbing to entrenched groups who might see themselves as the
"providers" of the services in question. In helping to strengthen the
hands of those whom welfare agencies seek to serve, they inevitably
appear to bite the hand that feeds them. This, of course, is another
factor making theirs a hazardous occupation.

Transformation of Services into Preferred Forms

The final indicator to be noted that gratuitous help tends to be
viewed inimically is the universal tendency to transform what were
once seen as "helping" functions into services less readily classifiable
as such.

Here, reference is to genuine transformation—not disguises of
the sort already discussed. In historical perspective, there were the
"charity schools" and free public education for "pauper children,"
which, in both Europe and the United States, were transformed into
social utilities. In Great Britain free public provision for medical
care, previously a Poor Law service, has also been transformed into
a social utility. Other cases in point are the various systems of public
or private relief that were transformed into social insurance programs (workmen's compensation, invalidity insurance, unemployment insurance, old age pensions, and the like), which were deliberately imbued with marketlike characteristics. These characteristics
were intended, in large part, to rid them of the antagonizing attributes of gratuitous help. Some countries have gone so far as to make
old-age pensions and family allowances "universal" so that they are
more like social utilities than social insurance—to say nothing of
gratuitous help. Professor Ralph E. Pumphrey has traced these kinds
of transformations, which he characterizes as shifts from "compassion . . . to alleviate present pain" to action designed to minimize the need for "compassionate" responses.[41]

Among recent actions along these lines in the social welfare
field are the proposals for virtually abolishing public assistance as it

is now organized and substituting for it some form of "guaranteed" income, shorn of denigrating means tests.[42] Noteworthy, too, is the widespread preference for extensive programs of public works as contrasted with "doles" or even work-relief.

Observers who exhibit a clear disdain for gratuitous help sometimes underscore this in quite subtle ways. For example, President Lyndon B. Johnson, in his State of the Union Message in 1964 declared, with respect to the War on Poverty,

Our chief weapons in a more pin-pointed attack will be better schools, better health, better homes, better training and better job opportunities to help more Americans—especially young Americans—escape from squalor and misery and unemployment rolls where other citizens help to carry them.[43]

What is significant here is the implication that schools, homes, health services, training, and jobs do not also "help to carry" the individuals served. But the President's declaration emphasizes the point that certain carriers are greatly preferred over others, that unobvious is preferred over obvious dependency.

Viewed historically, the "welfare establishment" of any day has not always lent its support to transforming welfare services into forms commanding wider social acceptance. One striking evidence of this was the opposition to social insurance by Charity Organization Society leaders in both England and the United States. More recently, spokesmen for the welfare field have been virtually unanimous in their preference for insurance over assistance.

Efforts to make a welfare service *appear* to be something else are notable in this context. "Not charity—but a chance." "This is no charity—only justice."

POSSIBLE INTERPRETATIONS OF ROLES OF SOCIAL WELFARE SERVICES

The foregoing analysis, including views of social welfare leaders regarding the social roles of their own services, suggests two interrelated interpretations of these roles.

In Chapter II, it will be recalled, we presented an interpretation of social welfare services in terms of helping individuals, families, groups, communities, and nations to achieve a level of value attainment that could not be effected in other, more desirable ways.

Insofar as the analysis in the present chapter is valid, we can now see that centrally important ways in which welfare services facilitate value attainment are through fostering self-care and self-help and through contributing to social change that will better enable individuals (families, groups, communities, and nations) to secure for themselves the "good" things they require. Thus one may say that a prime purpose of welfare services is to foster self-care and self-help so that it can be better effected through intrafamilial cooperation and mutual aid and through marketlike (and marketplace) transactions, and social utilities. To the extent that this is true, these means and mechanisms may be thought of as "more usual" than, or "preferable to," the gratuitous help of welfare agencies.

In Chart 3 we have presented the concept of normative self-care and self-help as being effected through marketlike transactions, intrafamilial cooperation, mutual aid, and social utilities. Insofar as an individual, group, community, or nation—for whatever reason—is unable by its own efforts to avoid what is regarded (by any group, community, or nation) as "too great" a deviation from normative expectations (or can fulfill these expectations only upon "too hurtful" terms, as discussed in Chapter III), welfare service may help correct this deviance (symbolized in Chart 3 by black sectors) so that self-care and self-help may be acceptably effected through mechanisms that are preferred to gratuitous help.

This concept can be related also to the functioning of usually preferred social institutions (economic, health, educational, familial and associational, and religious), which Martin Wolins has called the more "orthodox" ones.[44] When these fail to serve individuals (groups, communities, or nations) in the usually expected ways by which at least the key values (discussed in Chapter II) are attained, welfare institutions may be called upon to help correct the deficiency. Thus, as economic institutions fail to provide jobs (including jobs for, say, handicapped workers), adequate wages, or uninterrupted income, a welfare service may provide work-relief, sheltered employment, cash assistance, or rehabilitative service that would enable men to secure real jobs. If familial and associational institutions fail to meet the requirements of an individual or a family, then family service, child welfare, protective, or youth service may help to correct the deficiency. If a child has no parents, a welfare service may place a child in a foster home or an institution or arrange for his adoption. If an adolescent does not enjoy normal group associations, a group work service may aid him in developing intragroup relationships.

Similarly, educational institutions may fail to serve a particular child effectively because, for example, the child has no shoes and

Chart 3. Role of Social Welfare Services in Fostering
Self-Care and Self-Help

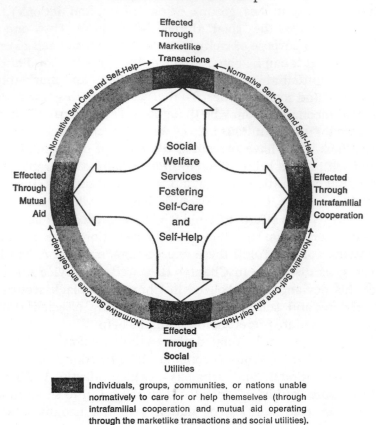

Individuals, groups, communities, or nations unable normatively to care for or help themselves (through intrafamilial cooperation and mutual aid operating through the marketlike transactions and social utilities).

cannot get to school. Or the child's mother may be ill and he may have to stay home to care for her. A welfare service might supply the shoes or provide visiting nurse or homemaker service so that the child can continue to be served by his educational institution.

Or a mother may not be able to enter a hospital because her children would be left without care. A welfare service might temporarily place the children in foster homes or might provide homemaker service so that the health institution could serve the requirements of the mother. Within a hospital a patient's recovery may be impeded or his return home delayed because of some social problem. This might well become the concern of a social welfare institution, thus helping the health institution to fulfill its role more effectively.

A religious institution may be ineffectively serving someone, but a welfare agency (as alert to spiritual as to dental or psychiatric needs) may be instrumental in helping him to reestablish communication with his church. Or a welfare agency may supply special foods for religious observances or furnish a confirmation dress or communion suit (things public assistance agencies are often criticized for *not* supplying), so that a child can participate in an activity of a religious institution that otherwise might not make it possible for him to do so.

Thus social welfare institutions might be viewed as "compensatory" institutions; they attempt to make up for some of the failures of other institutions that are usually expected to supply a variety of the "good" things of life. The failures may be due either to the institution or to the inability of a person, group, or others to take advantage of what the institution offers. Another observer, and a highly competent one, Miss Elizabeth Wickenden, takes a somewhat similar position in *Social Welfare in a Changing World.*[45]

Concepts presented herein are depicted diagrammatically in Chart 4. In this we have violated the usual custom of including, as a separate category, "governmental" institutions. However, since we are here looking at institutions from a functional point of view, it is obvious that government is represented in all of the functional fields shown. This is because some of the institutions performing economic, educational, health, familial, or religious functions are governmental institutions. If it seems strange that governmental participation in religious and in familial and associational institutions has been assumed, it should be recalled that government-paid chaplains serve with the armed forces, in prisons, and elsewhere in governmental facilities and that children's or old people's homes may be government homes. Also, public agencies provide foster-home care for children, aged persons, ex-patients of mental hospitals, and so on.

It is true that in looking at institutions from a functional viewpoint, we might have employed a category such as "Governing Institutions." However, not even these would be exclusively governmental (in the usual sense of the word), because a great deal of "governing" is done by nongovernmental instrumentalities. A man who loses his seat on the stock exchange because he violated its rules is as much deprived of his mode of making a living as one whose license to operate a TV station is revoked by government. An athlete who is fined $50 under professional baseball, football, or basketball "law" is as much deprived of $50 as a man who is fined in court. A

Chart 4. Role of Social Welfare Institutions in Relation to
Other Institutions Supplying Requirements for Living

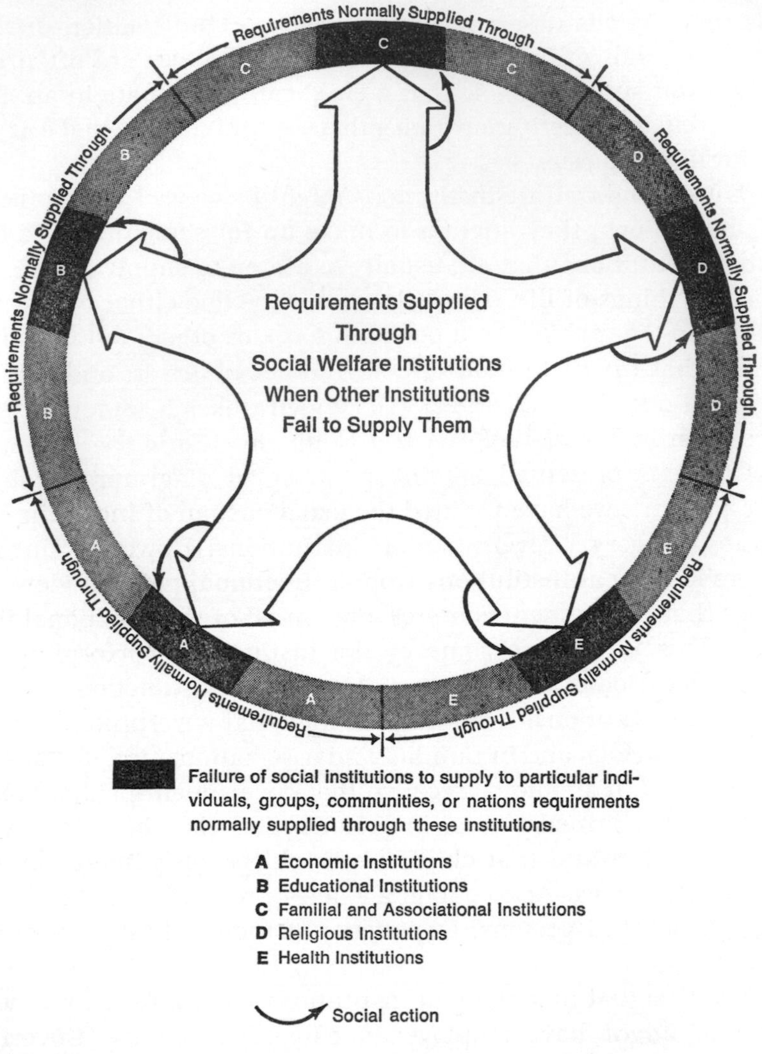

Requirements Supplied
Through
Social Welfare Institutions
When Other Institutions
Fail to Supply Them

Failure of social institutions to supply to particular individuals, groups, communities, or nations requirements normally supplied through these institutions.

A Economic Institutions
B Educational Institutions
C Familial and Associational Institutions
D Religious Institutions
E Health Institutions

Social action

man killed by a criminal gang (pursuant to gang "rules") for "squealing" is just as dead as though he were legally executed in an electric chair.

Moreover, governance—whether governmental or private—is seldom "pure governance," but is more likely to pertain to some economic, health, familial, educational, or other function that we have adopted as the basis for classifying institutions. For our purposes, therefore, we have excluded from consideration institutions whose only function is governance or whose governing functions apply to activities other than those enumerated.

In Chart 4 we attempt to represent also the interest of the welfare field in social change, social action, and social reform directed toward institutional change, so that the various institutions will perform their expected roles better and leave fewer individuals and groups "inadequately" served. Even slight institutional changes can make big differences. Relatively modest modification of a school program may permit a blind or deaf child to be served by a regular school and so avoid the necessity of sending him off to a special school. A relatively small change in hiring practices may enable older or handicapped workers, ex-patients of mental hospitals, former prisoners, or adolescents with police arrest records to get jobs and so avoid the necessity of turning to compensatory welfare services.

Or social action within the social welfare field may be directed toward much broader social change or institutional reform—as was recently the case in its support of Medicare and of "guaranteed annual incomes."

This interpretation of the role of welfare services may not commend itself to observers who prefer to classify as welfare services such things as social insurance (which, in its classical form, we have treated as a marketlike institution) or generalized services (such as universal pensions, Canada's and Britain's family allowances, or Norway's and Sweden's national health services), which we have treated as social utilities. Observers preferring broader interpretations might consider the presentation here as a way of viewing gratuitously offered services as falling within their more encompassing schemes. Our own preference is to classify as welfare services only those that are gratuitously offered and to distinguish these from services that are in the nature of marketlike transactions, social utilities, or mutual aid.

The compensatory view presented here assumes that welfare services have value and are "good" under certain circumstances, but that a higher "good" is realized when personal capacity is enhanced or institutional changes are effected so that living requirements can be attained through means that are more usual and more highly valued than gratuitous help.

VARIABLES AFFECTING VIEWS OF HELP

Until now, gratuitous help has been treated in undifferentiated terms—as though any gratuitous help is like any other. This is far from the case, however, and represents a gross oversimplification of the issues. For, in reality, help is viewed quite differently in relation to a wide range of variables. These, moreover, may be assessed quite differently by helpers and by helpees. Complicating appraisals still further is the fact that different helpees (or helpers) may themselves view the same help quite differently. This poses knotty problems for social policy, which must deal with broad generalities.

We do not have space to analyze the variables and the differences in their appraisal by the various types of persons concerned. We limit ourselves, therefore, to mere mention of some that are operative.

First: *Who* is the helper? What is his relationship to the helpee? How does he regard the helpee (as a *person*? as an object? as "dirt"?)? *How* does he help (imperiously? empathically? condescendingly? ostentatiously? modestly? anonymously?)?

Second: Who and what kind of person is the helpee ("pauperized" and "overdependent"? weak, but not pauperized? strong? vain or proud, like the "shamefaced poor" in Spain who got others to beg for them or like Aristotle's "highminded man" who was "ready to confer benefits but ashamed to receive them")?

Third: What is the nature of the help given? How does it compare with what *could* be given or with what is expected?

Other variables include the circumstances under which help is required. Help given or received in times of disaster or catastrophe is viewed quite differently from help accorded in "normal" times. Similarly, when needs are general (as when unemployment is widespread), help given or received is considered quite different from that given for highly idiosyncratic needs. Help that is required because of "no fault of one's own" is assessed very differently from help that is needed because of "one's own stupid mistake" (like running out of gas on a highway and having to "thumb" a ride to the next town). The degree to which help is needed because one is the victim of injustice is another important variable. So is the possibility of reciprocating favors (discussed in Chapter VIII). Although many other variables could also be noted (as are a few in Chapter VII), we mention only one more here: differences in attitudes toward need for basic essentials as contrasted with the need for more sophisticated "goods."

But before proceeding it should be noted that welfare agencies are always being caught in the middle inasmuch as helpers, helpees, and others place different valuations upon the variables we have noted. The agencies will be called upon to deliver what looks good to some elements but abominable to others. Worse still, in addition to different valuations placed upon help under various circumstances, welfare agencies must often mediate differences over facts. For example, families wiped out by flood or drought might attribute their plight to catastrophe whereas others might say they were stupid to live there in the first place. "Anyone should have known that dam wasn't safe." Or, "After those long dry spells, anyone in his right mind would have given up on that land." Or a man may attribute his woes to the injustices perpetrated against him ("Okay—you don't give me a chance to get a job, so just go ahead and support me"), whereas other observers would not see injustice as the root problem. From an international viewpoint, a nation may well say it would prefer trade to aid, but if powers dominating world trade do not control prices, amend tariffs, and so on, then they "owe" aid to those thus denied the opportunity to trade.

Special Problems Posed by Need for Basic Support

When self-help is highly valued, great emphasis is placed upon self-support and upon a man's ability to be "a good provider for his family." If a man cannot afford a car for every member of his family or cannot give all his children a university education, this is one thing. But if he cannot keep his family fed, clothed, and housed— and if he cannot see his children through elementary (if not high) school, this is quite another thing and is likely to be viewed inimically. Moreover, cultures being as powerful as they are, even men who cannot support themselves and their families tend to feel ashamed and guilty when they must turn to others for help. For others even to think or imply that one cannot provide needed essentials can arouse strong emotions. For example, a bride and groom would hardly view with equanimity a wedding present of paper towels, detergent, and insect spray even if their dollar value equaled that of one more—and possibly unneeded—silver candlestick.

On the other hand, help in the form of, say, a scholarship to attend college or a Guggenheim fellowship to permit study abroad (and to be spent there, possibly, for meat, potatoes, and rent) is unlikely to be considered demeaning. Looking at this issue from the standpoint of "givers," it is instructive to contrast the much higher standards of "need" for scholarships (as reflected in the *Financial Aid Manual* issued from time to time by the College Scholarship Service, Princeton, New Jersey) with the far more niggardly standards for basic support discussed in Chapter VI.

Societies emphasizing self-help seem particularly resentful when they are called upon for basic support of individuals who are unable to feed, clothe, and house themselves. This phenomenon has made relief and public assistance controversial issues over the centuries and has invited inhumane practices in the treatment of needy persons even by otherwise humane societies. And the phenomenon probably accounts for the fact that over the world and throughout history responsibility for the basic support of needy persons has gravitated into the hands of government. Recognizing the strains involved, societies seem unwilling to trust their own generosity and voluntary contributions, and so they legally bind themselves to contribute to the basic support of those requiring it. An interesting phenomenon in this context is the millions of dollars that are available for concert halls, art museums, college buildings, and endowments that would never go to "those who are starving."

These various responses on the part of both helpers and helpees are by no means automatic but are affected by the kinds of variables we have discussed. Yet, resentment of having to provide, or to be provided with, basic requirements *under more or less normal circumstances* is wholly understandable in light of the fact that societies, to protect their more cherished values, develop a wide range of sanctions that are not only highly efficient but may be frighteningly so (Chapter I). For societies recognize that preservation of their values depends upon appropriate regard for them. Self-help and self-support, for example, cannot continue to be respected where "everybody" sponges, mooches, and exploits others. (This problem of preserving values as values is discussed further in Chapter IX.)

In practice, however, societies reveal an ambivalence that poses perplexing policy choices. For, although they might strongly prefer that persons live by their own efforts instead of upon obvious social support, they would rather provide such support than allow people "to starve in the streets."

Punitive attitudes toward social support of obviously dependent persons have deep historical roots. Even as early as the time the biblical book of Proverbs was written—and long before the Protestant ethic appeared—a writer observed, "The poor is hated even of his own neighbor; But the rich hath many friends." It is probably fortunate that poverty-stricken persons have always been known as "God's poor." There were few others to claim them as their own.

Whether punitive attitudes toward obvious dependency spring from the consummate value attached to self-help and from resentment that some people fail to "get the word" about this—or whether self-help has come to be extolled in order to reduce dependency upon those able to offer support—is something we may never know.

However, in the present day one need not be too much of a cynic to wonder whether a modern society's tremendous stress upon self-help is really meant for those who preach it or only for those who might otherwise become "dependent" upon them. This suspicion is fed by the degree to which, short of obvious dependency, many are willing to "live by their wits," to "take advantage of others," and to live lives of leisure in financial "independence"—all of which square badly with such precepts as "Paddle your own canoe" and "Stand on your own two feet." The "man on your back" is usually visualized only as a beggar or relief recipient rather than in broader terms as defined by James W. Marrs or Harlan W. Gilmore. "Boondoggling," similarly, tends to be regarded as what is done (or not done) by typically underpaid and possibly undernourished work-relief recipients, but it is seldom regarded as the light work that supernumeraries do in executive suites for high salaries—salaries paid by consumers as work-relief wages are paid by taxpayers.[46] Whether or not this is regarded as an exaggerated view, it is clear that appeals for self-help often do not extol its merits per se but limn them against a background of disdain for obvious dependency.

In discussing the paeans in support of self-help cited in Chapter III, it will be recalled that the merits of this virtue were repeatedly contrasted with the disvalue seen in "dependency." For example, President Johnson's appeal, quoted earlier, was coupled with "[Poverty] means a lonely battle to maintain pride and self-respect in a family that you cannot provide for. . . . We are not trying to give people more relief—we want to give people more opportunity. That is what the people want." [47] R. Sargent Shriver was earlier reported as saying, somewhat more specifically, "The war on poverty is not a struggle simply to support people, to make them dependent on the generosity of others." [48] Similarly, the Council of Economic Advisers, which eschewed the simple redistribution of income as a means of wiping out poverty, had said, "Americans want to *earn* the American standard of living by their own efforts and contributions." [49] The council could undoubtedly have added, with equal truth, that other Americans, too, wanted those poor persons "to *earn*" for themselves their means of livelihood.

These views transcend party lines. This is clear from the following statement by a prominent spokesman for the Republican party, former Congressman Walter Judd:

We conservatives believe in supplying floors below which no citizens are allowed [*sic*] to fall in hunger or need, but we don't believe it is good to provide people beds on which to rest for the remainder of their lives. And we don't believe that normal Americans—unencouraged by government—want such a bed.* 50

That American society tends to disparage "dependency" is apparent in the way it confers social status. Although it was a long time ago (1949) by the social welfare calendar that W. Lloyd Warner and his associates developed their Index of Social Class and although one might question some of the criteria that went into its construction, the Index was undoubtedly correct in assigning the two lowest rungs of the status ladder to those whose income was derived from private and public relief. Warner's actual description of the source of income of his lowest class is "Public relief and non-respectable income." 51 These bedfellows have long had welfare personnel squirming, but they are grateful that the terminology was not "public relief and other nonrespectable income."

The Index of Social Position developed more recently by Yale Professor August B. Hollingshead is somewhat less explicit on this point than Professor Warner. Nevertheless, it is clear from discussions of Hollingshead's lowest Class V ("the bottom stratum of the class structure") that at least others in this class believe themselves to rank higher than relief recipients. As August B. Hollingshead and Fredrick C. Redlich report, there was, for example, the

second-generation Polish woman who . . . proceeded to tell the interviewer: "I'm working class, no more than that." A few sentences later she pointed out that she was much better off than her brother "Steven," who is not able to pay his bills and is on relief periodically. By both working, she and her husband are able to pay their bills and stay off relief. According to her value system, this definitely places them in the working class. By implication, people who do not pay their bills and go on relief are either lower class or, as she phrased it, "in the relief class." 52

---

* If Dr. Judd really meant what he said about "floors below which no citizens are *allowed* to fall" [emphasis added], he is going much farther than liberals who see these floors as levels below which people *need* not fall, but who do not suggest compulsory acceptance of benefits, which he seems to imply.

In this connection it is worth noting that when Norman V. Lourie was President of the National Association of Social Workers, he observed that one important respect in which the values of social workers differ from those of overall society is in the attitude toward persons in need. Unlike the society, social workers do not regard them as necessarily "inferior." [53]

With respect to at least the American culture, it is probably not inferring too much to conclude that from both a domestic and an international viewpoint, self-help is often extolled as a device for reducing the need for help that would otherwise be required from others. In fact, anthropologist Thomas Gladwin has observed that the term "worthy poor"—which, with its counterpart, "the deserving poor," has appeared and reappeared in various guises throughout human history—is now interpreted in the United States as meaning that the "undeserving" are those who do little to help themselves.[54]

Whether this is because self-help is viewed as an intrinsic "good," as a device for reducing claims upon others, or as a means of stretching always inadequate welfare dollars, welfare services place great stress upon it. Moreover, when it is not more sophisticated "goods" but basic support that must be provided for obviously dependent persons—in the United States or any place else where individual responsibility is stressed—basic support is typically accompanied by denigrating and even punitive practices. These are discussed in the next chapter.

But if (as suggested in Chapter IV) interdependence within societies makes fair appraisals of individual effort and worthiness virtually impossible, humane men will question denigration and punishment that are accorded as though fault and blame were, indeed, commensurable. Granting that societies may properly employ strong-armed sanctions—exercised through welfare services or otherwise—to reenforce their more cherished values, men must constantly be alert to the possibility that the historical circumstances under which the sanctions were developed may now be so changed that the sanctions can no longer be regarded as fair or just and that changed circumstances warrant new approaches more in keeping with current realities (a possibility discussed in Chapter X).

:: Notes
and
References

1. Norman V. Lourie, "Poverty," in Nathan E. Cohen, ed., *Social Work and Social Problems* (New York: National Association of Social Workers, 1964), p. 16.
2. Bertram M. Beck, "Social Work and Social Revolution," *Ninth Annual Social Work Day* (Buffalo: School of Social Welfare and Alumni Association, State University of New York, 1966), pp. 2–3.
3. *Social Work—Challenge and Change*, Highlights of Montreal's 3rd Academic Assembly on Social Work, *Canada's Mental Health* (September-December 1967), Supplement No. 55, pp. 15–16.
4. The Most Reverend Edward W. Swanstrom, *Quarterly Information Bulletin,* Catholic Relief Services, USCC, Summer Edition, 1967, p. 36.
5. *Annual Report, 1965* (San Francisco: Rosenberg Foundation, n.d., ca. 1966), p. 22. The problem posed in relation to mental health centers is touched upon in M. Brewster Smith and Nicholas Hobbs, *The Community and the Mental Health Center* (Washington, D.C.: American Psychological Association, 1966), p. 14.
6. Arthur R. Simon, *Faces of Poverty* (St. Louis: Concordia Publishing House, 1966), p. 112. For a Catholic view on this, with particular reference to Latin America, see Ivan Illich, "The Seamy Side of Charity," *America,* 116 (January 21, 1967), 88–91.
7. Richard A. Cloward and Irwin Epstein, "Private Social Welfare's Disengagement from the Poor . . . ," *Proceedings of Social Work Day Conference* (Buffalo, N.Y.: University of Buffalo, 1965).
8. *LO,* Series III, No. 7 (August 1967).
9. *Help for Those in Need* (London: The National Assistance Board, 1960), p. 4.
10. See *NASW News,* 12 (May 1967), 8. Work-relief programs of more recent times, but before federal legislation authorizing work-experience programs, are described in *Work Relief—a Current Look* (Washington, D.C.: Social Security Administration, Bureau of Family Services, 1962), Public Assistance Report No. 52. An extreme example of work-relief practice is presented by Betty Mandell in "The Crime of Poverty," *Social Work,* 11 (January 1966), 11–15. See also Sar A. Levitan, *Work Relief: Social Welfare Style* (Kalamazoo, Mich.: W. E. Upjohn Institute, 1966). (Mimeographed.) For a Canadian view of this issue, see *Work for Relief* (Ottawa: Canadian Welfare Council, 1963).

An extended discussion of the federal WPA program during the Depression is available in Donald S. Howard, *The WPA and Federal Relief*

Policy (New York: Russell Sage Foundation, 1943). Attitudes of a wide range of interests toward work as distinguished from "the dole" appear on pp. 805–835.

11. "On Target," Editor's Notes, *Catholic Charities Review*, April 1962, p. 1. See also Fedele F. Fauri, "The Long-Term Unemployed and the 1962 Public Welfare Amendments," *Public Welfare*, XXII (July 1964), 179–181, 221. Also see Ellen Winston, "The Shape of Welfare Programs to Come," *Public Welfare Projected* (Chicago: American Public Welfare Association, 1966), pp. 16–24.

   Although federal legislation in 1962 and 1965 greatly enlarged state opportunities for rehabilitative and restorative service, these depended for effectuation upon state action. On this, see Fred H. Steininger, "Implementation of the 1962 Public Welfare Amendments: Current Progress—Future Prospects," *Welfare in Review*, 2 (October 1964), 1–6; also see Eleanor V. Swenson, "Provisions for Social Services: Characteristics of State Public Assistance Plans," *Welfare in Review*, 4 (June-July 1966), 14–18; Juanita L. Cogan, *Employability Planning in Public Welfare Agencies* (Washington, D.C.: Welfare Administration, Department of Health, Education, and Welfare, 1967). (Mimeographed.) And see the substantially less optimistic *Antipoverty Work and Training Efforts: Goals and Reality* by Sar Levitan (Ann Arbor: Institute of Labor and Industrial Relations, University of Michigan, 1967).

12. J. M. Wedemeyer, *Railroads and Back Scratching* (Sacramento: California Department of Social Welfare, 1961), pp. 3, 5. (Mimeographed.)

13. *Goals of Public Social Policy* (New York: National Association of Social Workers, 1963), p. 10.

14. Raymond W. Houston, *To Prevent and To Restore: A Report on the Rehabilitation Potential of Public Social Services in New York State* (Albany: New York State Department of Social Welfare, 1960), Foreword, p. 3. A report from Chicago may be found in Raymond M. Hilliard, "New Techniques in the Rehabilitation of Welfare Recipients," in Margaret S. Gordon, ed., *Poverty in America* (San Francisco: Chandler, 1965), pp. 267–277.

15. E. J. Finegan, "Project Independence," *Employment Service Review*, 1 (1964), 31, 33. See also Norman V. Lourie, "Are We Learning How to Help Recipients Become Self-Supporting?" *Public Welfare*, XX (July 1962), 170–174. See also Robert D. Rippeto, "Training Public Welfare Clients for Employment," *Public Welfare*, XXV (April 1967), 122–128. The gradual shift from "work-relief" to "work-experience" programs is discussed by Helen E. Martz and Earl E. Huyck in "From Work Relief to Rehabilitation Through Work and Training," *New Directions in Health, Education and Welfare* (Washington, D.C.: Government Printing Office, 1963), pp. 250–257.

16. Walter P. Reuther, *Statement Before the Committee on Finance of the U. S. Senate Concerning "The Social Security Amendments of 1967" H.R. 12080* (Detroit: International Union, United Automobile (and other) Workers of America, 1967), p. IV–5.

17. George K. Wyman, *98th Annual Report on Social Welfare in New York* (Albany: State Department of Social Welfare, 1965), Introduction, p. xiii.

For a discussion of the often limited work skills of assistance recipients and of difficulties encountered in determining employability, see Denton J. Brooks, Jr., *et al.*, *A Study to Determine the Employment Potentials of Mothers Receiving Aid to Dependent Children Assistance* (Chicago: Cook County Department of Public Aid, 1964). (Mimeographed.) See also Richard A. Cloward and R. Ontell, "Our Illusions about Training," *American Child*, 47 (1965), 6–10, and M. Elaine Burgess, "Some Implications of Social Change for Dependency Among Lower-Class Families," *American Journal of Orthopsychiatry*, 34 (1964), 895–906.

18. *The Aims and Means of Social Service* (New York: United Nations, Group of Experts, Department of Economic and Social Affairs, 1959), Annex II, pp. 41–44.

19. S. Bennett, *Old Age—Its Cause and Prevention* (New York: Physical Culture, 1912).

20. *Annual Report: 1959–1960* (New York: New York Community Service Society, 1960), pp. 6, 12. A subsequent account of this agency's work in Harlem is reported in *The New York Times*, May 7, 1967.

21. *Federal Legislative Objectives—1966* (Chicago: American Public Welfare Association, 1965), p. 5.

22. Amos G. Warner, *American Charities* (New York: Crowell, 1894), pp. 391, 397. See also Charles R. Henderson, *Modern Methods of Charity: An Account of the Systems of Relief . . . in the Principal Countries Having Modern Methods* (New York: Macmillan, 1904), pp. 506–511. How far upstream preventive measures extend is apparent in the discussion of the prevention of poverty in Oscar Ornati, *Poverty Amid Affluence* (New York: Twentieth Century Fund, 1966).

23. Robert H. Bremner, "The Rediscovery of Pauperism," *Current Issues in Social Work Seen in Historical Perspective* (New York: Council on Social Work Education, 1962), p. 18. Also relevant in this same brochure is Rudolf T. Danstedt, "Political Action *vs.* Individualized Treatment in Social Welfare Work," pp. 45–50.

24. Ellen Winston, "Urban Development—Implications for Training Social Work Personnel," in *Urban Development: Its Implications for Social Welfare*, Proceedings of the XIIIth International Conference of Social Work (New York: Columbia University Press, 1967), p. 287.

Further significant discussions of prevention include Bertram Beck, "Can Social Work Prevent Social Problems?" *The Social Welfare Forum* (New York: Columbia University Press, 1960), pp. 180–193; Milton Wittman, "Preventive Social Work: A Goal for Practice and Education," *Social Work*, 6 (January 1961), 19–28; and Wittman's "The Social Worker in Preventive Services," *The Social Welfare Forum* (New York: Columbia University Press, 1962), pp. 136–147.

25. George Herbert Mead, "Philanthropy from the Point of View of Ethics," in Ellsworth Faris, Ferris Laune, and Arthur J. Todd, eds., *Intelligent Philanthropy* (Chicago: University of Chicago Press, 1930), p. 140.

26. *Goals of Public Social Policy* (New York: The National Association of Social Workers, 1963), p. 11. Policy statements adopted in 1967 by the Delegate Assembly of this association are reported in *NASW News*, 12 (May 1967), 1, 8 ff. See also Daniel Thursz, "Social Action as a Professional Re-

sponsibility," *Social Work,* 11 (July 1966), 12–21; David R. Hunter, "Canute, Sand Crab, or Leonardo," *Public Welfare Projected, op. cit.,* pp. 199–206; A. R. McCabe, "Social Policy Issues and the Family Agency: An Action-Oriented Program," *Social Casework,* XLVI (October 1965), 483–489; and *The Past Is Prelude: Fifty Years of Social Action in the YWCA* (New York: National Board of the Young Women's Christian Association of the U.S.A., 1963).

27. Sanford L. Solender, as quoted in *Social Action Guide* (New York: National Association of Social Workers, 1965), pp. 5–6. The quotation is from the author's "Definition of Social Action," *Social Work Year Book* (New York: National Association of Social Workers, 1957), pp. 517–524. Also relevant are Elizabeth Wickenden, "Social Action," in Harry L. Lurie, ed., *Encyclopedia of Social Work* (New York: National Association of Social Workers, 1965), pp. 697–703; Donald S. Howard, "Social Work and Social Reform," in Cora Kasius, ed., *New Directions in Social Work* (New York: Harper & Row, 1954), pp. 159–175; Donald S. Howard, "New Horizons for Social Work," *The Compass,* November 1947, pp. 9–13, 28; Benjamin E. Youngdahl, *Social Action and Social Work* (New York: Association Press, 1966); L. K. Northwood and William Key, eds., *Social Welfare and Urban Planning* (New York: National Association of Social Workers, 1966); *Social Work and Social Planning* (report of a workshop) (New York: National Association of Social Workers, 1964); Karl de Schweinitz, "Social Values and Social Action," *Education for Social Work: 1956, Proceedings of Annual Program Meeting* (New York: Council on Social Work Education, 1956), pp. 55–68. A view from Canada is available in Adrian J. Marriage, "Social Work and Social Reform: Opportunities and Obstacles," in William G. Dixon, ed., *Social Welfare and the Preservation of Human Values* (Vancouver: Dent, 1957), pp. 215–233.

   Also see Clarke A. Chambers, "An Historical Perspective on Political Action *vs.* Individualized Treatment," *Current Issues in Social Work Seen in Historical Perspective* (New York: Council on Social Work Education, 1962), pp. 51–64, and his extensive reference notes, pp. 76–80; see also his *Seedtime of Reform: American Social Service and Social Action, 1918–1933* (Minneapolis: University of Minnesota Press, 1963). Also, A. Davis, "Settlement Workers in Politics, 1890–1914," *Review of Politics,* 26 (1964), 505–517.

28. Irving Weissman, "Standards of Living and Labor in National Party Policy," *The Social Welfare Forum,* 1963 (New York: Columbia University Press, 1963), pp. 206–223. The National Conference Committee's proposals reflected in the "Bull Moose" platform may be found in Owen R. Lovejoy, "Standards of Living and Labor: Report of the Committee," *Proceedings of the National Conference of Charities & Correction, 1912* (Fort Wayne, Ind.: Fort Wayne Printing, 1912), pp. 376–394. See also Joanna C. Colcord, "Social Work and the First Federal Relief Programs," *Proceedings of the National Conference of Social Work* (New York: Columbia University Press, 1943), pp. 382–394.

29. *Time,* February 18, 1966, p. 21.

30. Alfred Kadushin, "Two Problems of the Graduate Program," *Journal of Social Work Education,* 1 (Spring 1965), 42.

31. Alfred J. Kahn, "The Social Context of Social Work," *Social Work*, 10 (October 1965), 149. Further critiques of the role of social work in social action appear in Herbert Bisno, "How Social Will Social Work Be?" *Social Work* (April 1956), 12–18; Wilbur J. Cohen, "What Every Social Worker Should Know About Political Action," *Social Work*, 11 (July 1966), 3–11; Charles I. Schottland, "Social Work Issues in the Political Arena," *Social Work Forum, 1953* (New York: Columbia University Press, 1953), pp. 18–33; Harry A. Wasserman, "Social Work in the 'Best of All Possible Worlds,'" *Social Work*, 6 (July 1961), 111–115; Edgar May, "The Disjointed Trio: Poverty, Politics, and Power," *The Social Welfare Forum, 1963* (New York: Columbia University Press, 1963), pp. 47–61; David R. Hunter, *Who's Got the Action? Welfare Planning in the City* (New York: Ford Foundation, 1963). (Mimeographed.)

32. Porter Lee, "Social Work as Cause and Function," *Social Work as Cause and Function and Other Papers* (New York: Columbia University Press, 1937), pp. 3–24. Also available in *Proceedings of the National Conference of Social Work, 1929* (Chicago: University of Chicago Press, 1930), pp. 3–20. For comment on this theme by a preeminent authority on social casework, see Charlotte Towle, "Social Work: Cause and Function," *Social Casework*, XLII (October 1961), 385–397.

33. Louis Filler, "Social Work," *A Dictionary of American Social Reform* (New York: Philosophical Library, 1963), p. 711.

34. Margaret K. Rosenheim, "Social Insecurity: An Essay Review," *Social Service Review*, 41 (June 1967), 193.

35. Marion K. Sanders, "Social Work: A Profession Chasing Its Tail," *Harper's Magazine*, 214 (March 1957), 56–62.

36. Frances P. Purcell and Harry Specht, "The House on Sixth Street," *Social Work*, 10 (October 1965), 75. See also Charles E. Silberman, *Crisis in Black and White* (New York: Random House, 1964), especially pp. 311–312.

37. Elma Phillipson Cole, ed., *The Future Role and Program of the National Social Welfare Assembly* (New York: National Social Welfare Assembly, 1967), pp. 6, 9.

38. M. S. Gore, "Philosophy of Social Work," *Social Work and Social Work Education* (New York: Asia Publishing, 1965), p. 66. See also "Social Work and the Social Context," pp. 7–24.

39. *The Aims and Means of Social Service, op. cit.*

40. *Report on the Seventeenth Session of the Commission* (New York: United Nations, Social Commission, 1966), pp. 7, 8.

41. Ralph E. Pumphrey, "Compassion and Protection: Dual Motivations in Social Welfare," *Social Service Review*, XXXIII (March 1959), 21–29.

42. See, for example, Alan D. Wade, "The Guaranteed Minimum Income: Social Work's Challenge and Opportunity," *Social Work*, 12 (January 1967), 94–101.

43. Lyndon B. Johnson, *Public Papers of the Presidents of the United States* (Washington, D.C.: Government Printing Office, 1965), p. 114.

44. Martin Wolins, *Welfare Problems and Services in Berkeley, California* (Berkeley: Berkeley Council of Social Welfare and School of Social Welfare, University of California, 1954), pp. 10–11.

45. Elizabeth Wickenden, *Social Welfare in a Changing World: The Place of Social Welfare in the Process of Development* (Washington, D.C.: Government Printing Office, 1965). Consonant with this view are those presented in Eugen Pusic, *Reappraisal of the United Nations Social Service Programme* (United Nations Document, E/CN.5/AC.12/L.3/Add.1); the Secretary General's *Reappraisal of the United Nations Social Service Programme* (E/CN.5/AC.12/L.3) (New York and Geneva: United Nations, 1965), and *Report on the Seventeenth Session of the Social Commission* (E/CN.5/405) (New York and Geneva: United Nations, 1966).

    A somewhat narrower view, but relating to philanthropy, not to social welfare services as such ("philanthropy may be said to be a result of the imperfections of the market place") appears in Frank G. Dickinson, "Highlights of the Conference," *Philanthropy and Public Policy* (New York: National Bureau of Economic Research, 1962), p. 121.

46. One observer who sees "boondoggling" among the bourgeoisie is William Stringfellow, *Dissenter in a Great Society: A Christian View of America in Crisis* (New York: Holt, Rinehart and Winston, 1966), p. 8.

47. Lyndon B. Johnson, *My Hope for America* (New York: Random House, 1964), pp. 40, 44.

48. R. Sargent Shriver, as quoted in *The New York Times*, March 17, 1964.

49. *Report, 1964* (Washington, D.C.: Council of Economic Advisers, Government Printing Office, 1964), p. 15.

50. Walter H. Judd, "Our Greatest Source of Strength," *The Reader's Digest*, November 1964, p. 67.

51. W. Lloyd Warner *et al.*, *Social Class in America* (Chicago: Social Research Associates, 1949), p. 142.

52. August B. Hollingshead and Fredrick C. Redlich, *Social Class and Mental Illness: A Community Study* (New York: Wiley, 1958), p. 115.

53. Lourie, "Poverty," *op. cit.*, p. 16. This writer's entire discussion of "values" (pp. 10–16) is worthy of note.

54. Thomas Gladwin, "The Anthropologist's View of Poverty," *The Social Welfare Forum, 1961* (New York: Columbia University Press, 1961), p. 76.

VI

VALUE
CONFLICTS
in
PROVIDING
BASIC
SUPPORT:
PUBLIC
ASSISTANCE
in the
UNITED
STATES

In taking public assistance in the United States as the basis for analyzing a society's ambivalence about providing for the basic requirements of individuals and families, we should note that this basis has been selected with pain and not with delight. Public assistance, in my opinion, represents an inestimably valuable product of a democratic society—and I would like to think that my professional activities and writings over thirty years would so prove.

In writing about a program for which I have high regard, I have sometimes felt as a poet might who wanted to write about a tree, but instead wrote about saving it from the smog and blight that were threatening to kill it. A smog of public ambivalence *does* surround public assistance programs, and in these programs there *are* indications of blight that seriously jeopardize their potentialities. These threats to publc assistance will now engage our attention.

To concentrate upon public assistance in the United States is by no means to imply that this is the only field in which ambivalence about basic support contributes to denigration of, and to punitive attitudes toward, disadvantaged groups. Nor is it suggested that the same phenomena do not also exist in other countries. In fact, I can say that no other country with which I am familiar has successfully avoided many of the conflicts analyzed here.

Although social workers and other social welfare personnel actually carry out the policies to be discussed here, they do not make these policies. Policies are prescribed by local, state, and federal legislative bodies, often over the vigorous protests of welfare personnel.

Public assistance has been selected as the prototype for our discussion because public attitudes toward dependency tend, as we have seen, to be more marked in the matter of basic support that is provided by other people, and such basic support is what public assistance essentially provides.

Another reason that public assistance makes a useful case example is that social ambivalence concerning it springs largely from differences of opinion about how self-care and self-support can best be encouraged. At issue, too, are numerous value conflicts: how much surveillance of recipients in exchange for how much of their dignity and privacy; how much self-determination for how much social concern about how they spend their money; how much economy of public funds for how much loss of family life; how much law enforcement for how many civil and constitutional rights.

To discuss details of public assistance administration in the United States is somewhat hazardous because of the diversity of policies and practices among the several states and even among local jurisdictions within a single state. Therefore many practices will be identified here with specific times and places. To write of public assistance at the present moment is particularly hazardous because of the current ferment and agitation for change. Much of this is due to the fervor of Neighborhood Legal Services, as is readily apparent in the *Welfare Law Bulletin,* a most useful periodical that keeps abreast of developments in public assistance.[1] Few writers, probably, like to see their work quickly dated or rendered inaccurate by changed circumstances. Nevertheless, in my opinion, the more quickly some of the things described in this chapter become "dated," the better.

ISSUES REFLECTING AMBIVALENCE

Means Tests

Of the ignominy inherent in applying and qualifying for public assistance, through what many have called "the mean means test," the Deputy Commissioner of Welfare in New York State wrote in 1962:

Those who've been forced to seek aid have no illusions that welfare offers the easy life. Critics should experience the humbling and humiliating process—starting with the personal admission that they cannot cope alone, and continuing through the interviews, the investigations, the search for responsible relatives, the surveillance of their homes, their habits, their budgeting.[2]

This follows the classical tradition, of course.* But observers are questioning increasingly whether this denigrating process is indeed an appropriate or effective starting point for fostering incentive for self-care, self-help, and self-support. Although some successful applicants are so relieved to have, at last, some visible means of support that they welcome "their workers" with open arms, experienced

* When novelist-newspaperman Konrad Bercovici wrote *Crimes of Charity* (New York: Knopf, 1917), he described practices by which private agencies of the day determined eligibility for their services. These he refers to repeatedly as "the Inquisition" in a blistering chapter entitled "The Test."

welfare people report that often when newly approved "cases" are assigned to them, it takes as many as two or three visits before the hostility engendered in the application process can be allayed.

One whimsical aspect of the insistence of public welfare officials to "see all" and to "judge all" (as if "all," as pointed out in Chapter IV, were not virtually immeasurable) is the unwillingness of many to "tell all." Despite the fact that public policy is quite clear as to who does and who does not qualify for public aid or other available services (notably those related to family planning), many workers will not tell an applicant more than he specifically asks about what he might be eligible to receive. It is as though the Bill of Rights and other parts of the Constitution were to be put under lock and key and no one told about his rights "unless he asked." [3] It is little wonder that the federal Advisory Council on Public Welfare in 1966 recommended "a positive program for informing recipients and applicants of their rights to assistance and services through public welfare, utilizing all appropriate means of communication." [4]

The importance of such publicity is well illustrated by a recent case. A probationer told his probation officer that he was going "to skip"—thus risking not only revocation of probation but possible incarceration— because he had no job and if he left home his family would qualify for assistance. The probation officer believed that the man could be given aid and telephoned the welfare worker who had talked earlier with the probationer. The welfare worker said that the man was certainly eligible for aid, but that the probationer "hadn't asked about that."

Of the means test and its effect on welfare recipients, students in the University of Michigan School of Social Work (who were involved in a project directed by Professor Wilbur J. Cohen, who later became Secretary of the federal Department of Health, Education, and Welfare) report:

Eligibility requirements are stiff and procedures are designed to make the experience very uncomfortable. . . .

After an individual has accepted the disgrace of applying for welfare, the procedures designed to spur him back to independence often have an opposite effect. Instead of feeling moved to constructive action, the students find that many clients accept the treatment passively and feel relieved of responsibility since they are paying a penalty for their dependency and are expected to act like children. More clients who unsuccessfully fight for their pride eventually give up and sink into passive resentment.[5]

Other observers also believe that the humiliation imposed upon applicants for assistance may retard rather than hasten their resumption of more nearly normal social roles.[6] To those who share such views it can come as no surprise that the federal Advisory Council on Public Welfare in 1966 excoriated means tests that were then being applied. The council said, "The methods for determining and redetermining eligibility for assistance . . . are, in most states, confusing, onerous, and demeaning . . . and incompatible with the concept of assistance as a legal right." [7]

Paul Jacobs' description of the process of applying for assistance—which he went through in order to get a first-hand view—reveals discrepancies, between cold realities and rhetorical statements of purpose, that might be amusing if they were not true and tragic in their consequences.[8]

While many assistance agencies euphemistically denote as "Intake" their offices where needy persons first apply for aid, the practices often pursued suggest that a more realistic sign would be "Keep Out!"

The rising tide of criticism of means tests in various parts of the United States has led to experiments in which affidavits filed by the applicants themselves are being substituted for the onerous and meticulous investigations by welfare personnel. These affidavits are then subjected to only spot checks, like those given to income tax returns by the Internal Revenue Service. Relaxation of means tests was also promulgated by the federal Welfare Administration and was strongly urged by the Advisory Council on Public Welfare.

However, even the less burdensome "affidavit" system for establishing eligibility for public assistance is not, as widely heralded, an abandonment of means tests as such. It is only a blunting of the meaner aspects of such tests. Nevertheless, enthusiasm for such departures from the means test was considerably dampened by the Senate Appropriations Committee. In 1966 it took a slap at the proposal of the Welfare Administration when it wrote into a committee report, "To insure maximum utilization of Federal funds for the people for whom they were authorized, the committee strongly urges the department . . . to direct the states, that thorough checks, including inspections of the premises . . . are required." [9]

In light of the increased discomfort over the humiliating means tests, it is not surprising that when Congress, in 1965, enacted a provision for greatly expanded medical care for persons who could not afford it, numerous limitations were placed upon the means tests that states could impose. That these limitations should have applied to medical care and not to basic support is relevant to the point about differences in attitudes—of both "providers" and "recipients." After all, "anyone can fall ill," but to lack life's basic essentials is viewed quite differently.

In passing it should be noted that the main problem with means tests is not with the tests as such but with what they must reveal. They are in fact tests less of means than of revelations that one has no means. We have been discussing welfare means tests. There are, of course, many other kinds. One may be asked to pass them to get a bank loan, membership in an exclusive club, or even a place on a prestigious welfare agency board. But these tests are designed to reveal strength. In the welfare field, means tests are designed to reveal weakness. As such, they are western counterparts of India's well-meaning provisions for "reserved places" in universities and stipulated civil service positions that can be secured, however, only by members of the formerly "untouchable" caste who are willing to come forward and admit the "untouchability" of their forebears.

Liquidation of Assets

Another problem born of America's distaste for obvious dependency is the level of penury to which one must sink before being able to qualify for public aid. In this situation appear the diametrically opposed philosophies, as discussed in Chapter IV, with respect to how initiative and enterprise can best be spurred. In the world of business, deprivation is seldom considered a proper incentive to greater effort. Yet in the world of the disadvantaged, deprivation is still relied upon for this purpose.

Before permitting poor persons to qualify for public aid, some states may no longer "grind the faces of the poor," but even these clearly make mincemeat of their assets. Before qualifying for public aid, families are typically required to strip themselves of all but an exceedingly few assets and even to tear out their telephones and to lose household equipment on which payments can no longer be met. All this, obviously, deprives them of exactly the kind of "hand-holds" (to use Ben H. Bagdikian's term) that, after a short economic setback, may be most useful in recapturing their capacity for self-support. This has been described by one state administrator as "the serious and crippling consequences of the divestiture of property . . . that . . . literally [force applicants] deeper into poverty." [10]

One whimsical aspect of public aid is that it tends to be given more generously to older and blind persons (who are seldom ex- pected to become self-supporting again) and more restrictively to unemployed persons and their families (who are almost invariably expected to become self-supporting as quickly as possible).

An important element in this problem was revealed by a survey that showed that in 1964 half the families receiving Aid to Families with Dependent Children left the rolls within eighteen months after receiving their first assistance payments. Moreover, the 50,000 un- employed fathers heading families that were given Aid to Families with Dependent Children received such help for only nine months. Yet, to qualify for even short-term aid, families are first reduced to the same dead level of indigency.

Still more ironic is the fact that persons not quite eligible (or not yet proved to be eligible) for federally aided public assistance may have to turn temporarily to state or locally financed General Assistance. To secure this for even a transitional period, they may have to surrender resources and assets that, had they been found eligible for federal-state aid in the first place, they would have been allowed to retain. In 1966 one of the nation's largest counties took a giant step out of the eighteenth century when it adopted the policy that liens on real property and assignments of insurance policies would no longer be required in the case of General Assistance appli- cants—but only if the application was for food and not cash, and only if food orders were limited to two weeks.

The complexities involved in qualifying for public assistance make one wonder why more has not been written on the fine art of applying for it. For it is indeed a fine art. An applicant (or, if one prefers, a suppliant) must avoid both the Scylla of appearing "too needy" and the Charybdis of appearing not needy enough. From all over the country, public assistance workers have reported that if an applicant appears "too needy," workers or their supervisors may re- gard the situation as "too pat" and deny or delay aid on grounds that things could not really be as bad as depicted or the application would have been made sooner.

On the other hand, an applicant may seem "not needy enough"; this may lead to the suspicion that he may still have resources he can continue to exploit before public assistance is "really needed." One highly competent observer, Frances Lomas Feldman, after close study of public aid in the now world-infamous Watts section of Los Angeles, which was wrecked by racial violence in 1965, de- scribed this aspect of the problem under the apt heading "A Sign of Drowning":

A "rule of thumb" . . . operates on a theory that the first time a person asks for emergency assistance, it can be assumed that he has some resources upon which he can call for the handling of the emergency: relatives, neighbors, credit, etc. If he returns in a few days or in a week, it can be presumed that he was successful in using such resources and that these could be "tapped" for another week. If he returns the third time and still believes himself to be in need of emergency assistance, a grocery order may be issued." [11]

How fine an art it is to qualify for public aid is evident in the fact that if one times his application so that it follows "too soon" after disposing of some long-treasured resource, he may be disqualified for having disposed of it "in order to" qualify for aid. If, on the other hand, he hangs on to a resource that is presumably available to meet his immediate requirements, he may be turned down on grounds of "excess resources—not in need." Thus, applicants must not only search their own souls as to when to apply for aid, but must virtually read the minds of intake workers (and their supervisors) as to "when" is too soon—and "when" is too late.

The tortuous process of qualifying for aid (especially when more than one agency is involved and an applicant is bounced from the pillar in one to the post in another) can exact a tragic toll. This is clear in Arthur Simon's poignant story of protracted delay in authorizing a glass replacement for a man who had lost an eye. By the time all authorizations were in order, the eye socket had shrunk so much that only a baby-size glass eye could be inserted. This gave the man a grotesque appearance that, understandably, seriously affected his ability to relate to other human beings.[12] In this case, "when" would seem to have been pretty late.

Some day a society that really believes in self-support will apply to disadvantaged persons the psychology that seems to work among the advantaged; it will grant social support to families on the basis of "incomelessness" and not require them to descend into the slough of "assetlessness" before aid is made available. With the aid of computers to calculate the probabilities, such a society might establish a time limit. This might be six months or a year, within which time a family would be helped to catch its economic breath and could then go on with its assets not materially reduced. What is ironic now is that to receive assistance for even a short period a family may have to forfeit—and never be able to recoup—small assets painstakingly accumulated over many years.

On this score the contrast between social insurance and public assistance policy is marked—as if a nation were talking out of both sides of its mouth. For social security has long been justified (in part) on grounds that future beneficiaries, with their basic security thus underwritten, would have greater incentive to add to this security in other ways. The nation requires, however, that public assistance give lip service to incentives and self-help but demand liquidation of exactly the kind of assets that might stimulate and facilitate a return to self-support.

Winston Churchill sensed the reality of this issue many years ago and in a speech on unemployment in 1908 declared: "If terror be an incentive to thrift, surely the penalties of the system we have abandoned ought to have stimulated thrift as much as anything could have been stimulated in this world. . . . It is a great mistake to suppose that thrift is caused only by fear; it springs from hope as well as from fear; where there is no hope, be sure there will be no thrift." [13]

Levels of Benefits

The ancient belief that the best way to stimulate a man's enterprise is to make life on public aid as hard as possible is probably nowhere more evident than in the levels of assistance that are granted. This belief has deep historical roots in Poor Law history, not only in the United States and England, but throughout the world. In fact, upon contemplating the history of this world-wide tendency, I can recall only one major departure from it. This single exception was the program initiated by Benjamin Thompson of Massachusetts, who, as the fabulous Count Rumford, established in Munich a workhouse with the primary objective of helping needy people to be "comfortable and happy." Most others, if not all, who have engaged in these enterprises appear to have been guided by the theory that the less comfort and happiness to be found in public aid the better.

During the 1830's, in both England and the United States, the "treat-'em-rough" philosophy gained tremendous momentum. Britain's social historian G. M. Trevelyan reports that the Poor Law commissioners, operating under the stringent Poor Law of 1834, "felt obliged to lower the standard of happiness of the workhouse." [14] Not even when Thomas Bernard, William Wilberforce, and others, somewhat later on, offered to finance the experiment, were the Marylebone workhouse authorities willing to try Count Rumford's idea of making workhouses happier places. In consequence, the would-be reformers organized the significantly named Society for Bettering the Condition and Increasing the Comforts of the Poor. Among the other rare few who sought to brighten the lot of disadvantaged persons was Robert Dingley, who wanted not a House of Correction but a "happy Asylum" for prostitutes; however, in order not to overdo things, it was for "penitential prostitutes" only. [15]

One mother who is familiar with "welfare" aid in the United States was quoted in 1967 by no less an authority than the federal Welfare Administration as saying, "Webster has the most inaccurate definition of 'Welfare' in existence. . . . My dictionary defines welfare as being 'Prosperity and Happiness'. . . . Anyone who has ever received public assistance knows that it certainly isn't prosperity. . . . and I do not think in all my years on welfare that I met anyone who was happy in their situation." [16]

This effect of public assistance programs (or, for that matter, of any welfare program—public or private) will be deplored especially by those who agree with Michael Graham that "gaiety"—one of the needs that he analyzes in *Human Needs*—is a fundamental one.[17]

Public assistance in the United States is not designed to allow much "prosperity" or "happiness." This is evident in the fact that public assistance grants in 1961 to families with dependent children, *when added to their other income,* averaged 11.6 percent below what the state agencies themselves thought the families needed. For families with unmet needs this meant, on the average, a monthly deficit of $39.86—*an amount roughly equivalent to the nation's average payment for one member of an AFDC family for an entire month.* These deficiencies varied widely, of course, from state to state and from region to region. Only in the Middle Atlantic states (New York, New Jersey, and Pennsylvania) were the full needs of families—as measured by state standards—reported as fully met through assistance and other income. At the opposite extreme was the East South Central region (Kentucky, Tennessee, Alabama, and Mississippi) where AFDC grants *and other available income* still left families 39.3 percent short of what the state agencies themselves thought was required. In these states, no fewer than 96.8 percent of the aided families had unmet needs. This averaged no less than $55.28 per family per month. This deficit represented about what, on the average, would be made available for one person for a month and a half.[18]

This means in effect that the most affluent nation in the history of the world does not support, out of its own pocket, its most disadvantaged people. It means, instead, depriving those it does help of a part of what they are officially declared to need in order to provide something for others who are also in need. From one viewpoint this might be thought of as a forced "share-the-wealth" program. From another viewpoint it might be thought of as sharing the destitution.

For nearly two millennia men have scorned giving a "stone" when another asks for a "loaf." The travesty of states giving less in public assistance than even what they themselves regard as necessities presents an even sorrier spectacle. It is as if they *offered* a "loaf," but then gave only a "stone."

In 1964, estimates of the adequacy of public assistance grants were based on the assumption that a "conservative, minimum standard of living" for families of various sizes would require three times the cost of food for such families under even the economy food plan (which is the lowest-cost plan developed by the U. S. Department of Agriculture). On the basis of this assumption, "the amount of unmet need among all AFDC families, even with public assistance, approximates the staggering sum of $700 million annually—about $700 per family." [19] This was about the time, it will be recalled, that income-tax payers received their windfall of some 12 billion dollars; and so there were lowered income taxes for some, lowered food intake for others.

Although New York was included in the region meeting in full, in 1961, the requirements of families *as measured by prevailing state standards,* no other state has been more vociferous in condemning these low standards. This is evident in the 1964 Annual Report of the New York State Department of Social Welfare. Moreover, detailed studies such as *Life at the Bottom* by Violet Weingarten, made for the Citizens Committee for Children of New York, and Mrs. Alice McCabe's study of "Forty Forgotten Families," made under the aegis of the prestigious Community Service Society, show in flesh-and-blood terms the human toll taken by even New York's assistance standards.[20] Even Philip Sokol, who was Deputy Commissioner and legal counsel to the New York City Department of Welfare in 1965, contended that "It may be argued *that states which do not provide sufficient funds to adequately feed a needy family may be guilty of deprivation of life without due process.*[21]

The plight of those who must depend upon public assistance in New York is mirrored across the continent. In California the State Department of Social Welfare in 1966 admitted that "most of the public assistance money being spent . . . goes to feed and clothe adults and children at less than the minimum requirements for decent living." [22]

In the same year the State Board of Social Welfare reported that a "typical payment" for a mother with two children left only about 93 cents per person per day for everything but medical care and rent. Moreover, according to the board:

Much of the housing is disgraceful. Many of California's poor are forced to live in houses unfit for anything but cockroaches. Plumbing is run down, toilets are clogged and stinking. Sinks fail to discharge fetid water. . . . Windows are out. Single unshaded bulbs hang from solitary bare wired outlets. . . . And the rents they pay . . . to slumlords are often up to 50% higher than for the same living space in other areas.

The board's self-styled "horrifying footnote" on food recalled that "in the health studies done on children in the Headstart programs in California, it was found that 62% suffered from malnutrition. *Shocking* is not the adjective to be applied here. *Criminal* is." [23]

When Professor Robert T. Lansdale of the University of Maryland in 1965 reviewed twenty-three studies made in sixteen states by a number of different bodies including several consulting firms, he found that public assistance grants to families with dependent children "were reported inadequate in amount (sometimes grossly so) in urban communities in 12 states." These ranged from New Hampshire to Texas and from Delaware to California. [24]

Two years later the federal Welfare Administration itself reported that "much" of the estimated $1.1 billion in public assistance money that went for housing in 1966 was spent for "clearly substandard housing." [25] The cruel irony is that if the federal and state governments put "much" of any $1.1 billion into *decent* public housing, this would have raised charges of socialism and of undue threats to private enterprise. But the pouring of large amounts of public funds into, literally, ratholes, leaky drains, holes in roofs, walls, and ceilings goes virtually unnoticed.

When, in 1961, Congress took a giant step and made it possible for states to use federal funds to aid families in which the problem was not necessarily the absence or disability of one of the parents, the nation heaved a sigh of relief. It would no longer be necessary—as was long the case—for fathers just to walk away from their families so that their children could eat and have a roof over their heads. But whatever rejoicing there was proved to be short-lived. States were exceedingly slow to take advantage of the new federal provision, and by January 1967—more than five years after the legislation was enacted—only twenty-two states (and not one among the southeastern states) were aiding families suffering from unemployment. Moreover, fixed maximum limits that even some of these states placed upon assistance payments meant that although an unemployed father's presence in the home no longer disqualified his family for aid, the extra amounts allowable for him might be only 50 to 65 cents a day—hardly much of a "welcome home." [26] Thus, an unemployed father who might previously have "absented" himself from the home would, upon return, literally be taking "food out of the mouths" of his wife and children. And this, it should be recalled, is under a program whose purpose had only recently been declared to be to "strengthen family life."

While he was Welfare Commissioner for New York City and before assuming the deanship of Fordham University's School of Social Work, James R. Dumpson observed, "We prattle about strengthening family life, yet we continue to humiliate parents in the process of attempting to help them, embarrass children of these families by our regulations, and destroy their respect for their parents." [27] If ever public policy reflected conflicts among values, surely this is one of the most glaring examples.

We have concentrated here upon allowances for families because these tend to be the most inadequate. This does not mean, however, that payments to the more favored aged or blind recipients are much more nearly adequate. Late in 1960, for example, Old Age Assistance payments fell short of state standards by an average of $3.90 per recipient. In Missouri and Alabama the average deficiency ran to over $11 a month per recipient.[28] However, absolute dollar amounts in these contexts are misleading. Even the seemingly modest average monthly deficit of $3.90—the amount a more privileged person might pay for a single meal in a restaurant—comes to a typical allowance for food for *four days*.

Inadequate though they are—even by the states' own standards —assistance payments must sometimes be shared with a technically ineligible, though needy, family member who is not included in the computation of a grant: for example, a wife who is not yet 65 and is therefore ineligible for Old Age Assistance—an adolescent who does not qualify for aid because he is not in school or is already "too old."

As if these problems were not already grievous enough, the Social Security Amendments of 1967 open the door to possibilities that stagger the imagination. When we spoke in an earlier chapter of our presumably mythical Tantalusia we had no idea of how soon so hypothetical a land might become a grim reality. For, the 1967 amendments exclude from assistance payments "appropriate" family members who, without "good cause," refuse employment or training. Needless perhaps to say, both "appropriate" and "good cause" are interpreted by administrative personnel in welfare departments and employment offices (or both), but decisions may, fortunately, be challenged through appeal. The new legislation also requires that states must exclude from family budget computations the requirements of any "appropriate" person who, without "good cause," refuses a work or training assignment and must provide, but only in the form of protective or vendor payments or foster care, for any dependent child of such a person. Thus, the amendments suggest the possibility that third parties ("interested in or concerned with the welfare" of the children concerned) may intervene and feed, say, a brood of needy children, but withhold food from a no less needy mother. Or, if the mother is to eat, she must consume food calculated as necessary for the children alone.

Not infrequently, serious crises arise when an assistance check is lost in the mails—or stolen from one's mailbox. Assistance agencies usually make up such losses, but this often takes time. In some places a check is not even regarded as "lost" until at least seven days after it was due to arrive—one-half or one-fourth of the time one was expecting to live on it. In a day of automation, errors in mailing can result from wholly mechanical failures—"nothing personal, you understand; the machine just skipped," as one welfare worker put it. However, such errors take time and effort to rectify.

Apart from the amounts of public assistance payments, there is also the issue of the climate surrounding these payments. Under prevailing circumstances, it is perhaps inevitable that recipients report, as did one quoted by Violet Weingarten in *Life at the Bottom*, "You have to beg and whine, and it makes you feel—well, terrible." [29] Whimsically, public relief and assistance laws enacted in the United States in the twentieth century have included provisions intended to prohibit aided persons from "begging." These apply, of course, to "begging in the streets." But indefiniteness of assistance standards, lack of complete information about what one is entitled to receive, reluctance of workers to meet "special needs" even as authorized, and the low levels of the standards themselves—all these factors were still contributing at mid-century to the perpetuation of begging: begging within public assistance offices, though no longer in public.

After public hearings in different parts of the country, the Advisory Council on Public Welfare reported in 1966:

. . . Questions about the harmful effects of the low assistance payments are raised by most of those who testified at the regional meetings. . . . Many graphically described payments providing for less than minimum subsistence in such terms as "shockingly inadequate," "utterly indecent," "inhuman," "demoralizing existence grants," "tragically sub-minimum," "miring people into a poverty from which there is no escape," and "unrealistic in relation to current costs." [30]

Notwithstanding prevailing assistance standards, and despite recommendations from both the Advisory Council and the Administration that states be required to make assistance payments in conformity with at least their own standards of need, the Social Security Amendments of 1967 include no such provision. One small liberalization was however enacted to permit federal matching of the costs of minor house repairs (not exceeding $500) for homeowners receiving assistance. The amendments also specify that by July 1, 1969, the amounts used by states to determine needs must be adjusted to reflect changes in living costs since such amounts were established.

One aspect of public assistance policy that is most bitterly condemned from coast to coast is the general refusal of agencies to make any provision for gifts or celebrations. This is always distressing when children's birthdays roll around—but especially at Christmas time. In *In the Midst of Plenty: The Poor in America*, Bagdikian poignantly describes what a needy mother called "those awful months." These are the months in which Easter and Christmas fall and schools open.[31] Welfare personnel also share this distress and particularly deplore the necessity to require a mother who earns a little money on the side to devote it to the "basic needs" of the family; she cannot use even her own earnings for gifts. One welfare worker tells bitterly of being in a recipient's home on Christmas Eve when the small boy came in, beaming, and triumphantly carrying a small Christmas tree he had been given. The mother's face went blank. She then explained sadly that there was to be no Christmas for them. Finally, after a painful pause, the daughter's face brightened. "I know where there are some old newspapers," she said. "We can get them, crumple them up, and put *them* under the tree."

Unfortunately, there is little definite knowledge of the effect that assistance standards, or the climate within which public assistance is granted, have upon individual enterprise and upon incentives to help oneself. Does deprivation drive men to exercise their own initiative? Or, to fight adversity, does man need a foothold in security? Those who believe that some security is necessary feel that insufficient money for food may reduce energy for self-help, that inadequate allowances for rent (so inadequate almost everywhere that they must be supplemented by food money) pin people down in low-rent slum areas (and in deteriorated and dilapidated, if not actually condemned, housing). Moreover, such inadequate allowances seriously reduce mobility, lower morale, result in overcrowding: Too many people in too small an area can easily thwart self-help, make homework for school children a mockery, disturb rest and sleep. Inadequate allowances for shoes and clothing can keep children out of school, keep a whole family from church or other community groups, undermine one's spirit, and lead people to think that they are so unbecomingly dressed that no one would ever give them jobs even if jobs were available.

Among the many who believe that too-low assistance standards are self-defeating and thwart their major purpose is Andrew R. N. Truelson, Assistant Director of the federal Bureau of Family Services, who puts the case this way:

If a program of assistance is only a subsistence program, the individual will just subsist. . . . His energies will allow him to survive, but he will have little surplus. Initiative, "self-go," drive, all require some surplus energy. . . . When a person lives at this marginal level for long periods of time, with nothing to look forward to or hope for, there will develop a sense of hopelessness—"What's the use?" "Why try?" [32]

Apart from the level of living (bread, milk, jeans, and roof) permitted by current assistance standards, there is also the issue of the effect that inadequate grants have upon services to help resolve problems of family members, to encourage self-support, and "to strengthen family life." One national child-welfare expert, Elizabeth Glover, has written, "It is sheer folly—if not hypocrisy—to talk about relief clients, children and adults, being able to use casework service, psychiatric service, and better educational resources while they are going hungry." [33] At about the same time another qualified observer stated the issue sharply in the title of a paper: "The Primary Factor in Good Services—Adequate Assistance Grants." [34]

In view of the denigrating treatment handed obviously dependent persons, it is not surprising that Joan Gordon found that welfare agencies foster among "their low-status clients a certain aggressiveness, toughness, and manipulativeness if their needs are to be met. These are qualities that hardly make for close interpersonal relations." [35] Although she does not go on to say so, "close interpersonal relations" are likely to be exactly what is needed to evoke and encourage self-confidence, initiative, and enterprise.

However inadequate the programs serving disadvantaged persons, the plight of the unknown numbers of others not served by these programs—or even by the federal Food Stamp program—is even less enviable. The American people were shocked in 1967 by revelations made by a United States Senate committee (under the chairmanship of Joseph S. Clark of Pennsylvania) concerning the extent of hunger and malnutrition. The public controversy centered around conditions in Mississippi, but it soon became apparent that the problem had much larger dimensions. Wide publicity was accorded to the newly discovered problem by Robert Sherrill's article, "It Isn't True That Nobody Starves in America," published in *The New York Times Magazine*.[36]

At this writing, remedial legislation seems limited to liberalization of the Food Stamp plan but with no other federal assistance to needy persons or requirement that states establish federal-state assistance programs which states have the option to adopt—or eschew. However, a 1967 amendment to the Social Security Act opened the door to federal financial participation in a state program of "emergency relief" to certain needy families with children, but for not more than thirty days in any twelve-month period. Although the law explicitly declares that this assistance can be provided for the families of migrant workers, the context in which the provision was enacted suggests primarily situations in which families are catapulted into need by fire, eviction, or other crises, not by ongoing, chronic circumstances.

Treatment of Those Attempting Self-Help

Probably no aspect of public assistance policy highlights the divergent views of man and his motivations as effectively as the policies concerning rewards and safeguards for those who do exert themselves to contribute to their own support. When they pick up an odd job now and then, the ways in which public assistance agencies over the country treat this extra income are quite varied. However, a general tendency (except in the case of blind persons, who are usually treated most liberally) is to deduct from a subsequent assistance grant virtually all of the earnings, except for job costs actually incurred (carfare, lunch money, and so on). In the case of young persons, policies tend to be somewhat more liberal, allowing them to keep for themselves a bit of pocket money if they are able to find jobs.

Dr. Ellen Winston, United States Commissioner of Welfare, reported in 1964 that the nationwide review of the AFDC program made a short time before "confirmed our belief in the importance of building more incentives into public welfare programs." [37] Four years earlier, the federal Advisory Council on Public Assistance had reported, "Too often poverty is perpetuated and people's efforts to maintain a constructive family life and to move toward self-support are thwarted." [38]

The first real break through the barrier that prevented public assistance recipients from materially improving their existence through their own work came with an amendment to the Social Security Act in 1962. Also in 1962, states were authorized to establish community work and training projects. But by March 1966 only ten states had taken advantage of the possibilities offered, and these were providing work and training experience for members of only 20,545 families. Despite the work performed, some families were for a time given no more than they would have received in direct assistance. Later, however, families were permitted to receive as reward for their participation in the work and training program the full amount of their "requirements," as measured by state standards, even though these were not being fully met through assistance payments alone. Thus one's work appeared to be less like an incentive payment than like "bailing out" a state that was failing to provide what it claimed every family "required."

Another important break in the barrier against real rewards for self-help came when the Economic Opportunities Act in 1964 required that, if youths in families receiving public assistance were employed in the Job Corps, they were to be allowed to keep for their own use the first $85 per month and half of all earnings over this amount. Although this marked an important forward step, it resulted in a weird sort of discrimination against the youngster who had developed his own jobs (delivering papers or cutting grass) or was working for a private employer.

Continuing concern, over the country, about the lack of appropriate incentives in public assistance programs led Congress in 1965 to enact provisions giving states more leeway in disregarding earnings in the computation of assistance payments. These exemptions were, as usual, more liberal for aged persons, blind persons, and the disabled. Youths, too, were to be allowed—the states being willing— somewhat greater opportunity to benefit from their own work. Adult men and women, however, were accorded few similar advantages.[39]

Still more recently, in 1966, amendments to the federal Elementary and Secondary Education Act and the Manpower Development and Training Act required public assistance agencies to disregard stipulated amounts received under programs covered by these acts.[40]

However, most of these possible liberalizations and stimuli to incentive were often dependent for their implementation upon state action. In consequence, it is noteworthy that of the fifty-four jurisdictions affected (the fifty states, the District of Columbia, Puerto Rico, the Virgin Islands, and Guam), by April 1966 only twenty-six had taken advantage of the provision to permit the earnings of youths to be conserved for their future needs, and only eighteen jurisdictions had acted to permit aged persons to benefit from the exemptions of earned income that were permissible under federal law.

Even the federal provision to permit recipients of Old Age Assistance—a provision that is relatively liberal by public assistance standards, but that only a few states have implemented—contrasts strangely with similar provisions concerning receipt of Old Age Insurance. Under public assistance provisions, an aged person can at best have exempted only the first $20 of earned income, half of the next $60 per month, and $5 (increased to $7.50 in 1967) in income from other sources. Under the social insurance program, however, a retired man can earn up to $1500 a year with no reduction in benefit. Beyond this he can keep half of his additional earnings if these do not exceed $2700 a year.* As a result, he can have earnings —*over and above his Social Security benefit*—up to more than double the average Old Age Assistance payments in 1966.

Beyond the differences in allowed exemptions under the two programs for aged persons, there is another striking difference. Under the Old Age Assistance program, apart from the possible $5 exemption, it is only *earnings* that are *exempted*. Other income, such as rent, profits, gifts, or bequests would not be disregarded. By contrast, under the social insurance program it is only *earned in-*

---

* The Social Security Amendments of 1967 increased the $1500 to $1680 and the $2700 to $2880, thus heightening discrepancies between insurance and assistance.

come that is *limited*. One may have a private pension of $40,000 a year, stock dividends, rents, honoraria, and so forth, without losing one penny of his insurance benefit.

Further anachronisms that deprive assistance recipients of genuine benefit from such work as they can find may be seen in allowances made by states for expenses—such as those for travel, lunch money, and work uniforms—involved in employment. These allowances which often amount to only $25 a month are widely regarded as insufficient and, therefore, as eroding the value of any incentive pay that may be permitted. Prior to the Social Security Amendments of 1967, the combination of low exemptions and inadequate provision for work expenses may have left a worker with a net gain—if any—of only 10 to 20 cents per hour worked.

In this context it is a striking fact that when Governor Nelson A. Rockefeller appointed to a State Committee on Relief Costs a number of leading New York businessmen (the president of the Marine Midland Corporation, the vice president of the Pepsi-Cola Company, and the president of Macy's in New York, among others), they reported, in part:

One of the most important methods of motivating toward self-improvement and eventual self-support is to provide some means of allowing ADC and Home Relief recipients the opportunity to get a "taste of the carrot" being held before them.

The basic problem is that a welfare recipient can make strenuous efforts to obtain work, become employed, and end with less income than he received from welfare payments.[41]

The American Public Welfare Association's *Goals for Federal Legislation* in 1966 proposed that "greater incentives" be accorded to public assistance recipients to stimulate self-help efforts.[42] Other organizations were doing the same. What may prove to be a major breakthrough along these lines is a plan for which New York City's highly innovative Commissioner of Welfare, Mitchell Ginsberg, won federal approval in 1967. This will permit assistance recipients to earn $85 a month without suffering any reduction in benefit. Even if earnings exceed this amount, public assistance benefits are reduced by only 70 percent of the excess. One striking aspect of this innovation is the pride New York's Mayor John Lindsay has publicly shown in it.[43]

In contrast with the wisdom of the business and welfare worlds, public assistance policy preponderantly continues strictly applied means tests. Of these the President-appointed National

Commission on Technology, Automation, and Economic Progress has said:

> This has the absurd consequence that additional earnings are taxed 100 percent. Unless the family can earn enough to dispense with public assistance entirely, it loses a dollar of welfare payments for every dollar it is able to earn. It would be hard to imagine a system less consistent with our society's high valuation of work and self-help.[44]

From many quarters one hears also of various conflicts in policy that catch assistance recipients in a cross fire: Recipients may be placed under pressure to report regularly to public employment offices (often many miles away). Yet these recipients may be "bumped" from their work projects if they miss "too much" work. The same result has been reported in the case of men who take time off to pick up their monthly assistance checks (or surplus commodities)—also possibly many miles away. Various other devices that seem calculated more to humiliate people than to help them find jobs include the requirements that one remain at the employment office *all day,* or that, to remain eligible for assistance, one periodically submit written statements from a specified number of employers (perhaps weekly, perhaps monthly). These statements are to the effect that the individual had applied for a job but that no job existed. Some case records are said to be "loaded" with hundreds of these futilely collected statements. Expenses incurred in *seeking* work are seldom, if ever, provided for. Yet, various observers have pointed out that the expenses of looking for work can be greater than the expenses incurred while working.

There are additional obstacles to self-support. For example, free medical care is given to families who receive assistance, but it is denied to those who leave assistance rolls and take a job. Also, to abandon public assistance for employment may be to sacrifice urgently needed and highly desirable work-training.

Jurisdictions that take liens on property and assignments of insurance policies also impose barriers to acceptance of jobs. For, as long as people continue to receive aid, they are virtually certain that no action will be taken on the liens or assignments. But if they begin to earn wages, who can say what will happen—or when?

One commonplace misconception concerns the values that families who receive public assistance are expected to find in work —even though it does not give them opportunities to raise their level of living. The misconception is that these families should feel some pride in saving government money that they would otherwise receive in assistance. But, to expect these or any other persons to work without material gain for themselves is like expecting a man to work but to be paid in the coin of what, for him at least, is a foreign realm.

One particularly weird quirk in public assistance policy would seem ludicrous if its effects were not so serious: In many places persons whose earnings fall below what they might receive in public assistance may not receive supplemental aid if they work *full time* —but may receive supplemental assistance if they work only part time. The longer one works for wages that fall below public assistance standards, the less some agencies do to encourage his enterprise.

The injustice of these various policies has led some to conclude that as long as public assistance standards and policies remain what they are, a child's collecting "old bottles and papers" or an able-bodied man's picking up "a day's casual work" inevitably leads to a certain amount of unintentional chiseling or marginal "fraud." In fact, it is not unusual for welfare workers to admit—usually guiltily —that they sometimes "look the other way" or tell recipients to "say nothing about it" when they do earn a little on the side.[45] Although recipients are the ones who are usually accused of "chiseling," a not uncommon view is that agencies that do not give what they themselves think is essential should also be regarded as "chiselers."

To existing anomalies, Congress in 1967 added a prohibition on the use of federal funds to aid needy families of unemployed fathers in any month in which a father receives (or is qualified to receive) unemployment compensation. Previously the states were free either to do this or to supplement unemployment benefits—a provision the Senate wanted to retain, but on which it receded in favor of the House position. When it is recalled that unemployment compensation is only a fraction of one's wages and that even full wages of many of those who must resort, every now and then, to public assistance are often lower than even assistance standards, the hardships likely to be imposed by this new limitation are readily apparent.

Even persons who voluntarily leave assistance rolls for employment are likely to find that public policy only poorly encourages their interest in helping themselves. Although some agencies allow almost automatic reinstatement after temporary employment, the re-application process often takes so long that temporary earnings are more than wiped out before aid again becomes available.

Considering the power of the profit motive in American society and the obeisance typically paid to it as the mainspring of our economic system, it is remarkable that it has not been put to work among those who most need an incentive. If a $100,000 corporation executive requires another $100,000 as a "bonus incentive," is it too fantastic to think that families receiving public assistance should be allowed at least some significant improvement in their level of living if they manage to pick up a little money on the side? The double standard now in effect leads one to wonder which group indeed represents the "real America." Are public assistance recipients thought to be such superior human beings that they do not need material rewards? Conversely, are business and professional men who must seemingly be motivated by such lures as high salaries and bonuses to be regarded as lesser men?

To release among public assistance recipients the stupendous power of the profit motive, which has built up our tremendous American economy, would, in my opinion, do more than any other known device to tear down within them the obstacles to greater effort and self-help. Failure of public assistance policy to unleash this force that is so characteristic of our society seems to me to be, perhaps, not un-American, but surely non-American.

It is too early to assess, in these terms, the previously mentioned "incentives" built into assistance programs for needy families late in 1967—the exemption of $30 a month and one-third of any excess within, of course, a state's standard of total need. It has been a long time since workers in the United States thought of "a-dollar-a-day" as much of an "American standard."

Denial of Aid as a Means of Encouraging Self-Help

Added to all other devices reflecting punitive attitudes toward obvious dependency is the rigorous practice of refusing or discontinuing grants when administrative officials feel that certain individuals (or categories of persons) "should" be able to find work—whether or not jobs actually exist; and, if jobs do exist, whether or not they find them; and, if they find them, whether or not they are hired; and, if they are hired, whether or not they are paid enough to feed their families.

Pressures against aiding men or women who "ought" to be able to find work explain why, by 1966, only twenty-one states had taken advantage of the federal funds available for aid to families in which a parent is unemployed. Not even federal assistance laws cover unemployed men or women (other than those who are aged, blind, or disabled) unless there are dependent children. Thus, other unemployed persons, if in need, must look to state and local General Assistance. Yet, in 1965, in seventeen states, families that included employable adults were not eligible even for this aid.

Even where General Assistance is not categorically denied to employable persons, such aid may be granted upon only very limited terms. In one county, for example, if the rate of unemployment was over 7.5 percent, General Assistance was available to a person for only sixty days. If unemployment fell below 5.5 percent, this aid was extended for only fifteen days.

When seasonal workers are needed in agriculture, public assistance benefits to potential workers may be terminated to "encourage" them to take jobs. In some states this practice, applied even to women, has strong racial overtones, as only Negro women are thus "encouraged." In 1966, Georgia's practice in this regard was challenged as unconstitutional.[46]

In some instances, even under federal-state programs, allowances for children have been automatically discontinued when summer began so as to "encourage" them to find summer employment. In at least one state this practice was applied even to children of only fourteen years of age, although the legal age for obtaining work permits was sixteen.

If, after receiving such strong "encouragement," former recipients can prove that they were unable to find work, they may be reinstated on the assistance rolls—but only after a time lag (which varies from jurisdiction to jurisdiction).

Observers have reported that in some states Aid to Families with Dependent Children has been reduced by amounts that agencies think the mothers might earn if they worked. Even under programs that do not categorically deny aid to employable but unemployed workers, it is not uncommon to refuse assistance if they leave a job *for the purpose of receiving aid*. Obviously, such a purpose is not easily proved—or easily refuted.

How successful or unsuccessful (even if constitutional) these types of encouragement to incentive have been—or what have been their social costs—unfortunately is not known. However, the effectiveness of almost diametrically opposite approaches has been demonstrated. For example, University of California Professor Kermit T. Wiltse and Justine Fixel, who conducted a one-year experiment in the San Francisco Welfare Department, have reported, "We never introduced the subject of employment. Recipients are anxious to 'get off relief' provided they can make a realistic plan that nets them financial benefit and a sense of personal achievement. As they were helped to think more positively about themselves and their situation, and to tackle the things that concerned them most . . . they were soon thinking positively about how they could gear themselves to move toward self-support." [47]

In defending the new pressures developed by Congress in 1967 to force assistance recipients to accept employment or training, Senator Long spoke of the undesirability, for children, of the example of a "mother who could refuse with impunity a good [*sic*] job. . . ." (*Congressional Record*, Vol. 113, No. 204, December 13, 1967, p. S 18609.) Many who agree with Senator Long about the importance of a "good" job will regret that there is no word in the 1967 amendments to suggest that assistance will be terminated only when "appropriate" persons "without good cause" turn down "good" jobs. The amendments speak often of the peril of turning down a "bona fide offer of employment" (as in P.L. 90–248, Section 204) but there can be "bona fide" offers of "bad"—low-paying, exploitative, strikebreaking—jobs.

One might well wish that Congress in 1967 had done less brandishing of the stick and more cultivation of the carrot of masses of "good" jobs to which assistance recipients would have been attracted by their interest in being in the "mainstream." In fact, estimates prepared by the Department of Labor which was given responsibility for developing the new "work incentive" program suggest that far more persons are to be drawn (forced?) into it than the department thinks will find full-time jobs. These projections indicate that by 1972 some 757,000 persons will have been trained but, after training, only 238,000 will have secured full-time job placements. (*Congressional Record*, Vol. 113, No. 202, December 11, 1967, p. H 1670.) Thus, even prospectively the Department of Labor seems to sense the harsh realities which (as mentioned in Chapter V) welfare agencies have long encountered.

Contrary to popular belief that assistance rolls consist of chronic freeloaders who never again stir to support themselves, their spouses, and their children, the body of assistance recipients changes constantly and rapidly. We have already noted the relatively short time that certain categories of persons require aid until they find—or find again—that they can "make it on their own." For example, during the last six months of 1965, "employment or increased earnings" of a person in the home of an assistance recipient resulted in the closing (in thirty-one states) of nearly 61,000 cases that had been receiving Aid to Families with Dependent

Children, over 19,000 cases that had been receiving Old Age Assistance, and nearly 800 cases that had been receiving Aid to the Blind. For the same reason (in thirty states) nearly 10,000 cases receiving anachronistically named Aid to the Permanently and Totally Disabled were closed; and in thirteen states approximately 18,000 General Assistance cases were closed. Unfortunately, it is not known whether these persons "left" assistance rolls or were pushed or driven off. Nor is it known whether they were better off or worse off, whether the earnings or "increased income" was really enough for their subsistence needs. That earnings were below assistance standards in many instances would be a safe conclusion. In fact, many former recipients are on record as saying that their earnings were less than they had previously been receiving in aid, but that they were nevertheless delighted to be "off relief." In the case of those who do "leave" the rolls, it is not known whether this is because of, or in spite of, the kinds of policies and practices that prevail. Opinions will differ.

Vagaries of current public assistance policies in the United States are nowhere more apparent than in the striking number of persons (and not only employable persons) who are refused further aid even though they are officially acknowledged as still in need. The reasons for this are technical, disqualifying factors that have nothing to do with increased ability to "go it on their own." Data for the latter half of 1965, for example, show the number of cases that were closed under various programs because they no longer met eligibility requirements *other than* need. These included, in thirty-one states, nearly 2,900 cases that had been receiving Aid to Families with Dependent Children, approximately 6,000 cases that had been receiving Old Age Assistance, and nearly 450 cases that had been receiving Aid to the Blind.[48]

Numerous studies, large and small, made in various parts of the country, clearly reveal that individuals and families have been disqualified for continued aid while still in economic need. A nationwide study of some 6,000 families that had previously been receiving Aid to Dependent Children showed that "approximately one-third of the cases were closed while still in need." This meant that, even in this relatively small sample, no fewer than 1,851 families with an average of 3.4 persons per family—or the equivalent of a small town of nearly 6,300 persons—mostly women and children, were in economic need but were disqualified on other grounds for receipt of aid.[49]

Perhaps it is only because pressure is remorselessly kept on assistance recipients to "leave the rolls" that one is struck by a provision in Britain's Ministry of Social Security Act of 1966 (Chapter 20, Schedule 2) that entitles a recipient of "supplementary allowance" to receive a small increase in benefit if he has been receiving one "for a continuous period of not less than two years." In all the world, this provision recognizing "seniority rights," as organized labor has long demanded in employment, is the only such provision in welfare legislation I can recall.

The Double Standard with Reference to Assistance Recipients

When the term "duality" or "dualism" is used here, it will always connote inimical dualism. There is, of course, nothing wrong with treating persons in different circumstances in different ways. "Let the medicament fit the case"—if one may paraphrase. Although quite proper differences in treatment might accurately be denoted as dualism—or even "quadruplism"—there is little quarrel with these, as such. Horses and houses, babies and bandits, maidens and madmen may all be treated differently from one another, and quite properly so. Differences in treatment, as such, are not at issue. The issue is differences in treatment that are unwarranted or unfair in relationship to the differences in people's circumstances. This is what we shall refer to as inimical dualism.

Among the commonest complaints of assistance recipients are that they are treated as "second-class citizens"; that their treatment is by "second-rate standards"; that workers, though not actually "breaking into" their homes, "just open the door and walk in without asking"—or, "without first seeking permission, they walk straight into the bathroom"; or, "without asking, they look in drawers and open closet doors." Even where there is not actually illegal "invasion of privacy" (which does crop up somewhere in the country every so often), there is frequent abrogation of plain "good manners" that quickly but by no means painlessly shows recipients that they are not to be treated like other human beings in conventional interpersonal relationships.

From his parish in New York City's lower East Side, Arthur Simon makes the significant observation that although poor persons may be "better off . . . than the poor of a generation ago . . . their improved position is largely superficial. They may have some modern appliances . . . and more toys for their children, but they do not have as much hope or as much dignity." [50]

When to lack of dignity is added the personal impugnment inherent in many public assistance policies and practices, recipients are placed in gravely sore straits. As a result, when they began in the late 1960's to find their own voice through newly organized Welfare Rights Organizations, their first pleas were not (as one might think) for larger grants; what they wanted most of all was to be treated with more respect and to be accorded greater dignity; in short, they wanted to be treated more like fellow human beings. An eloquent plea along these lines was made by one of the representatives of the Clients' Advisory Group working with one of New York City's Welfare Centers. This representative stated:

It is most important that the welfare worker treat me with courtesy, as a human being and as an individual—with individual needs. . . . Let him not invade my privacy more than necessary nor make derogatory or belittling remarks—above all—not resorting to abuse or threats like "I'll cut you off. . . ."

. . . The friendly caseworker . . . is the one we are glad to see. Even if he is unable to get very much for us of material substance, his kindness and interest are to be valued beyond measure. Under such warmth, a client *feels* better—feels he is recognized as a human being, and this is as important as food to a lonely person.[51]

When the Ohio Citizens Council for Health and Welfare in 1966 gave public assistance recipients a chance to "speak their piece," a mother of seven, who was once a Chairman of the State-wide Committee for Adequate Welfare, declared, "I just want to say that . . . [we] welfare mothers . . . are human beings and the thing is, at that welfare office we are just not treated as human beings. . . . It may take a very long time—but still [the Welfare Department] should realize that we *are* human."

Like others throughout the country, another mother (of five children) complained of the derogation involved when workers failed to read "the record" and kept asking anew for personal information given many times before.[52]

In scores and scores of face-to-face encounters with, and written communications from, social welfare personnel from all parts of the country, one theme appears most frequently: Recipients want, even more than money, respectful treatment; not special respect, but respect as fellow humans. "Our money was gone before we came here; now you're taking away what dignity we had left." "Maybe you have to ask the questions you do, but do you have to ask them the *way* you do?" One could write a book: *What Price Help?*

Although many public assistance workers would fill the bill as respectful and helpful in their relationships with recipients, many do not. One hears frequently of welfare workers who share so fully prevailing attitudes toward obvious dependence that they "hate their clients." [53] But, even workers who want to be kindly and helpful often find that the nature of policies, pressures from administrators, and practical demands of the job make it tough to "buck the system."

The fundamental dilemmas that confront a welfare worker were incisively presented by John M. Wedemeyer when he was Director of the California Department of Social Welfare. He said:

His position is virtually untenable. He is under orders to spy as well as to counsel, to expose as well as reassure, to enforce technical denials of eligibility in the face of stark and appalling need, and to maintain his sanity and sense of dedication in an atmosphere that is often hostile, suspicious, mocking and resentful.[54]

In circumstances like these, it is little wonder that recipients of assistance feel more "pushed around" than "helped forward."

Among many sobering findings reported to the governor by the California State Social Welfare Board after it had talked directly with several hundred persons—including "welfare recipients"—few were more sobering than the "wave after wave of complaints about indignities," the "bad relations" with caseworkers, and the "alienation from the helping agency and inadequate financial support for family needs." [55]

Similar attitudes were mirrored three thousand miles away by Mrs. McCabe's "forty forgotten families." [56]

Focusing not on a state but specifically on directors of welfare agencies, Professor Russell Smith of California's State College at Sacramento observes that they are often responsible to local governing bodies, are "not expected to administer welfare humanely," but are required to have "the ability to say 'no' to the needy, keep out the occasional 'soft' welfare worker . . . and [have] a businesslike approach to running the department." [57]

With the whole nation within her purview, and looking specifically at programs of Aid to Families with Dependent Children (previously known as Aid to Dependent Children), Dr. Winifred Bell reports in an admirable study, "Administrative reviews support the claim that where restrictive policies exist, constructive relationships between welfare workers and poor families are very unlikely." Her study of practices that encouraged mothers to give up their children (to aunts, grandmothers, and so on) led her to conclude, "*No worker whose primary function is eligibility determination for financial assistance should be permitted to approach parents about possible placement of their children.*" [58] [Emphasis in original.] Other observers go even farther and urge separation of service functions from the giving of financial assistance.* [59]

These recommendations, born of recognition of the widespread disdain for obvious dependency, take on deeper significance in the light of observations made by Arthur Mandelbaum, Chief Social Worker of the Menninger Foundation. He believes that if the "supports" required to help people to

feel strengthened, sustained, and then . . . to grow toward maturity and increased self-reliance . . . are given meanly, grudgingly, sparingly, with sullen resentfulness, with hidden insidious conviction . . . then our help will only intensify aggression; and dependency needs become twisted, infantilized, stunted, perverted.[60]

The relevance of decent treatment to the goals of public assistance has been underscored by Professor Lloyd Setleis of the University of Pennsylvania. He maintains that restrictive practices mean for clients "fear, hatred, and distrust," which hamper self-betterment and rehabilitation.[61]

Richard Elman, after a long, broad look at public assistance, reported in the aptly titled *The Poorhouse State*, "There is no other group in America whose rights have been so often impugned and trampled upon as the citizenry of our Poorhouse State." [62]

Paul Jacobs, never one to pull a punch, was described as follows in a publication issued by professional social workers whose organization he had addressed: "He sees social work in public welfare as a potato grater on the already raw skins of the poor with whom they work. According to him welfare is not living up to its nature as a nonabrasive institution." [63]

One veteran social worker long associated with public assistance in the United States has observed that there is a common expectation that "individuals and families in receipt of public aid should maintain *higher* moral standards than is true for the self-supporting population." [64] [Emphasis added.] A widely publicized aspect of this dualism has been the popular uproar in various parts of the country (most notably in Louisiana and Florida) about the

* In the 1967 reorganization of the federal Department of Health, Education, and Welfare, administrative responsibility for "rehabilitation services" was separated from that for money payments.

"suitability" of the homes of families receiving public aid. However, standards by which homes were judged to be "suitable" were not applied to homes in general but only to those of assistance recipients.* Even in relation to social insurance, no consideration whatsoever is given to living arrangements, which, under public assistance, may be heavily penalized.

Similarly, alleged public concern about illegitimacy tends to be directed at families receiving public assistance, in which families only 20 percent of the country's illegitimate children are to be found. This strongly suggests that what disturbs the public is not really illegitimacy, as such, but the public support of illegitimates, a suggestion that is strongly reinforced in the Social Security Amendments of 1967. If one were to focus, rather, upon the 80 percent of illegitimate children who were not on assistance rolls, he might consider measures to reduce illegitimacy among elites who serve as the "taste-makers," and models for less privileged groups.

Only against the backdrop of the widely prevailing attitudes toward and within public assistance agencies can one fully appreciate the significance of a 1966 ruling of the federal Welfare Administration. This ruling prescribes that state policies and practices for the determination of eligibility for assistance after July 1, 1967, not only must conform to all legal and constitutional protections, but also must not result in "practices that violate the individual's privacy or personal dignity, or harass him." Continuing this thought, the ruling says:

States must especially guard against violations in such areas as entering a home by force, or without permission, or under false pretenses, making home visits outside of working hours, and particularly making such visits during sleeping hours; and searching in the home, for example, in rooms, closets, drawers, or papers, to seek clues to possible deception.[65]

If all of these provisions seem to be little more than ordinary "good manners" that one would not think of violating in normal human relationships, their inclusion in a federal directive only underscores the fact that obviously dependent persons are treated differently. Moreover, it was this directive to which the Senate Finance Committee was reacting when it warned that public assistance agencies must keep informed about the "true living conditions" of assistance recipients in order to make sure that public funds were being properly spent. There was nothing in the committee report,

* In 1967 a federal court ruled Alabama's "substitute father" provision unconstitutional (*Los Angeles Times*, November 10, 1967).

however, to suggest that since members of the Senate are also supported by the public purse, some agency should be concerned with "true living conditions" in their homes. In the twentieth century we do not "badge the beggars," as people once did, but we still do badger the poor.

Inasmuch as providing money to persons who would otherwise lack the means for subsistence is the heart of a public assistance program (money being, in fact, not only the most important thing that most families need but in many cases the only thing), public interest in how recipients spend their money goes right to the core of the matter. However, except in cases such as bribery or investments involving "conflict of interests," similar concern is not manifested in how government employees—also supported at public expense—spend their money or in how artists, professional men, or businessmen—supported by patrons, clients, customers, or consumers—spend theirs.

Of the importance of spending one's money as one chooses, Professor Leonard Schneiderman of Ohio State University has this to say:

How we spend our money . . . is as unique to each of us as a fingerprint. . . . When a client is told . . . that certain expenditures can be taken into account and others not . . . there is immediately an intense and appropriate feeling that his way of life is being controlled and manipulated.[66]

Ever since the Great Depression, but more particularly since the passage of the Social Security Act in 1935, the "money payment principle" has been of central importance. Having money in hand greatly reduces distinctions between "haves" and "have nots" in ways that food orders and issued clothing cannot. Money in hand helps to reduce the "cap-in-hand" mentality. Consequently, those who seek to heighten inimical dualism in the treatment of obviously and unobviously dependent persons often make the money payment principle their first point of attack.

In the face of these pressures, the money payment principle has been preserved in many parts of the country only through strong federal laws and administrative regulations. Federal law recently gave the states a little leeway, but only upon defined terms and within strict limits.

The congressional stance on this issue changed materially with the enactment of the Social Security Amendments of 1967. These, as already noted, require in some instances and encourage in others erosion of the money payment principle. (See P.L. 90–248, Secs. 204 [b] and 207.) When a spokesman for the National Association of Social Workers testified before a senate committee on this issue, he declared, "You cannot ever expect persons to become independent if you treat them as incompetent children." (*Washington Memorandum,* No. 90–1–10, September 8, 1967, p. 8.)

What some states and localities would do under pressure from the "beggars-can't-be-choosers" school, if it were not for the long-sustained counter pressures from federal law and administration, is clearly apparent in state and local General Assistance programs that are administered without benefit of federal participation.[67]

Although the grosser abridgments of the rights of assistance recipients to spend their money at their own discretion have been curbed substantially in federal-state assistance programs, numerous subtle ways of restricting recipients still remain. Here are some examples. However dilapidated and worn an assistance family's bed or sofa may be, the family may not be free to replace it—even from money that is earned or given to it—unless their public assistance worker agrees. Unless the worker concurs, money given a mother by a brother to avert repossession of, say, a washing machine may have to be diverted to other necessities upon pain of having the next assistance check reduced by the amount of the gift. Children's earnings set aside under recently liberalized federal law for "the future interest of the child" may be drawn upon (in jurisdictions that permit the conservation of such earnings) only as the assistance worker permits; and bankbooks must be submitted periodically for inspection. A family left a small bequest that enables it to "live on its own" for at least a while may find their exuberance over newly found "independence" somewhat cooled by the discovery that if the resources are, in the opinion of the assistance worker, spent "too rapidly," the family can be accused of "having disposed of property in order to qualify for assistance," thus making itself ineligible for further aid once the nest egg is gone.

In their report on welfare services in the state of Washington, Greenleigh Associates give a particularly poignant example of what can happen:

Mrs. V, like many aged persons, was anxious to make advance arrangements for her own burial since she knew that death was not far off. She cashed in her life insurance policy for $200, received $168 from a daughter, and for the total cost of $368 made a written contract with a funeral parlor. When this came to the Department's attention the entire sum was considered a new resource. The Department suspended her grant for two months and noted in the record that at the time of her reapplication a monthly deduction would be required until the $168 was repaid.[68]

Whether or not Mrs. V, during the months her assistance was suspended, was supposed to have lived in the funeral parlor is not reported.

Observers who believe that encroachments upon, and harassment of, public assistance recipients are deplorable enough, in and of themselves, should contemplate how these are augmented by encroachments and harassment by related "serving" instrumentalities. The penchant of administrative organizations for "coordinating" their activities with each other means that what public assistance officials do about particular recipients is coordinated with what public housing, family service, and other welfare agencies also may be doing. Thus there is a sort of geometric progression of encroachment and harassment when an individual or family is served by various organizations bent on coordinating their services. It is as if an employed man had to deal with his employer *and* his banker *and* his minister *and* his grocer and liquor dealer every time he wanted to make a decision.

Persons who are incensed over the degree of self-direction one forfeits upon accepting public assistance may see a glimmer of hope if they make some comparisons with the not too distant past, when even employed men were closely regulated. Their employers told them what they could wear, what they could and could not drink and smoke, how often a week they could go "courting," and even that they should attend church. If they did not obey any of these injunctions, they were in danger of losing their "positions." Now that this kind of close supervision of the private lives of employed persons has been relaxed, perhaps the greater degree of freedom generally accorded to the unobviously dependent may soon be extended to the obviously dependent also.

In addition to the problems already discussed, there are still other evidences of dualism in the "contributions" from relatives who are required by law to support needy kinfolk. These problems go further even than the "beggars-can't-be-choosers" theme and, to put the matter in similarly abrasive terms, might be recast as "even the relatives of beggars can't be choosers." For example, an adult son, who is himself "financially independent," but whose aged father applies for or receives assistance, may find his affairs closely scrutinized in order to determine what he can contribute to his father's support. Need one say that the final decision as to what the son "can afford" is not left to him alone? The true character of this dualism is evident when we recall that to require adult children to maintain aged parents who receive public assistance runs counter to society's usual tendency to have parents help their children. Public assistance policy attempts to enforce the opposite.[69] Moreover, even needy elderly persons eschew public aid because it would mean demands upon their children to whom they do not want to be "a burden."

One particularly galling evidence of dualism is evidenced by jurisdictions that make a great show of respect for courts and court "orders for support" (as in the case of a deserting father ordered to contribute stipulated amounts to support his wife and children), yet urge welfare personnel to secure "voluntary" contributions over and above what the court ordered.

Further evidence of dualism may be found in "residence laws." A person or family is typically not eligible for public assistance until he (or it) has resided in a particular area for a specified period of time. This requirement contrasts strangely with the situations of those who require, not aid, but other services, such as police and fire protection, or (which is more to the point, in terms of cost), education. A newcomer can march his eleven children to school—at substantial cost to taxpayers—and have no questions asked about residence—except his address.

Whether residence restrictions will in the future continue to plague disadvantaged persons—as they have in the past—seems highly unlikely at this writing. Already courts in Connecticut and Delaware have declared state residence for welfare aid to be unconstitutional.[70]

Although our discussion of dualism has been in connection with public assistance programs, these take their coloring from society. Assistance agencies would not be nearly so heavily burdened if society's more thoroughgoing dualism did not preclude normal schooling, training, employment, and other opportunities to persons who, denied these, must turn to public assistance. No one has better stated the reciprocal responsibilities of welfare and other social institutions than George K. Wyman, Commissioner of the New York State Department of Social Welfare:

To attack the . . . public welfare problem . . . we must consider what practical efforts can be made *by the community* to integrate adult welfare recipients into the economy through changes *in the economy*.[71] [Emphasis added.]

Thus, again, a conflict of values emerges. There are interests in society that like, and benefit from, dualism. And inimical dualism affecting needy persons cannot be expected to be rooted out of welfare institutions as long as it slips into them from the society at large. Nor can we expect burdens thrown upon welfare services to diminish until inimical dualism in the overall society abates.

Dualism in Law and Justice

Further indications of public antipathy toward obviously dependent persons appear in the inimical dualism inherent in law that is applicable (or applied) to them and in the justice that is given or denied them. We are not referring to problems of "justice and the poor," or the kind of dualism that Professor Jacobus ten Broek of the University of California, Berkeley, has excoriated in a penetrating analysis of family law in California.[72]

Important though these broader issues are, we are concerned here more specifically with dualism in the treatment of obvious dependents and others served by welfare agencies—a theme that ran throughout a national conference of lawyers, teachers of law, and others. This conference was held in 1965 on "The Law of the Poor"; it came about largely as a result of Professor ten Broek's inspiration and leadership.[73]

A 1963 report of a committee of the United States Attorney General declared, "One of the prime objectives of the civilized administration of justice is to render the poverty of the litigant an irrelevancy." [74] Far from being "an irrelevancy" to laws, poverty—or, more specifically, receipt of public assistance—is the raison d'être of the inherent dualism.

The dualism in standards of behavior expected of—and treatment accorded to—assistance recipients has (to the extent of its legality) its basis in law. Dualism in law is evident in differential requirements concerning contributions to the support of others by a stepfather, by "a man in the house," by one "assuming the role of spouse," or by one who, apart from law specifically applicable to public assistance, would have no similar responsibilities for support. Of this anomaly, as it appears in California law, Professor ten Broek has observed that a state that does not "recognize common-law husbands . . . [has] created . . . common-law stepfathers." [75] On the other hand, there are jurisdictions in which common-law marriages are recognized, but when public assistance is accepted, these become "illegal unions."

In passing, we may note that dualism inherent in differential responsibilities for the support of others can, paradoxically, result in a bizarre reverse dualism, placing real fathers at a disadvantage. For a real father—even in the few jurisdictions that give able-bodied men assistance—will often find all assistance to his family cut off the moment he gets a *full-time* job, regardless of the amount of his earnings. On the other hand, a man who merely "assumes the role of spouse"—who is not the blood father of any of the children and is not married to their mother—may continue to hold even full-time employment without jeopardizing continuation of the assistance to the family as long as he pays at least his share of the family's expenses. I sometimes wish I were a Lewis Carroll and thus capable of doing justice to so preposterous a contradiction.

Another aspect of inimical dualism appears in the abrogation, vis-à-vis public assistance applicants or recipients, of the historic right of husbands and wives to refuse to testify against one another, even in cases of heinous crime. But this is not so in cases involving obvious dependency. For to qualify for public aid, a wife, for example, may be required in some jurisdictions not only to *file and sign the complaint* that her husband has deserted her or is failing to support her, but may also have to *testify against him*. Thus, a historic privilege is abrogated for obvious dependency that need not be forfeited even in a case of murder.

Beyond laws are law-enforcement practices that weigh especially heavily upon public assistance recipients, who are often harassed by welfare officials or law-enforcement officers—or by both acting in concert. That some of these harassments have later been restricted by higher courts or administrative bodies underscores the inimical dualism that at least these authorities saw in them.[76] As this is written, the "substitute parent" rules in Arkansas and Georgia (under which needy families in these as in other states are denied assistance when they are alleged to include a "substitute" father) are being attacked in the courts as unconstitutional.[77]

Nationwide interest (with help from a national TV report "in depth") was recently focused upon Newburgh, New York. There, restrictive sanctions were invoked against families and unemployed men, but were finally thwarted by court action.[78] This kind of harassment can break out at almost any time, anywhere. Few sections of the country have escaped—Florida, Mississippi, South Carolina,

New Jersey, Illinois, Michigan—yes, and California—to name but a few of the settings for some of the more notable recent episodes. A notorious California case involved the arrest of a woman who was receiving "welfare aid" for herself and her illegitimate daughter. A municipal court judge made sterilization a condition of her probation. Upon appeal, the superior court held that the lower court had no authority to order sterilization upon any grounds and, moreover, that even a higher court could not order sterilization in the circumstances of this case.[79]

All over the United States in the 1960's there was a rash of "midnight raids" in which law-enforcement officers, welfare officers, or both would burst into the homes of assistance recipients (often without search warrants) in order to discover, if possible, "something"—such as a "man in the house"—that might disqualify the family for assistance. In 1963 Professor Charles A. Reich of the Yale Law School set forth in the *Yale Law Journal* a persuasive argument that challenged the constitutionality of such raids.[80] National organizations and others then took up the cause, and the flurry of raids was somewhat abated and their nature somewhat modified. In some jurisdictions the raids could no longer be at midnight but only, for example, before 10 P.M. or after 7 A.M.—or, in more liberal areas, before "sundown" or after "sunup."

On this highly sensitive issue the board of directors of the National Association of Social Workers (NASW) in 1964 issued, on behalf of its 40,000 members, a public statement declaring, in part:

The National Association of Social Workers is deeply concerned about the way in which "midnight raids" may . . . make it difficult for the social worker to aid his clients to improved social functioning. . . .
. . . When [the public welfare agency] uses "midnight raid" techniques, it . . . shifts the emphasis of the relationship from a mutual effort to an effort by the agency to catch the client through surprise visits. . . . These visits constitute an invasion of privacy contrary to the social worker's Code of Ethics.[81]

This association's assumption about the constitutionality of midnight raids was borne out by the California Supreme Court, which, in 1967, ruled them unconstitutional and ordered reinstatement of an employee who had been fired for refusing to participate in one.[82]

Persistent *cherchez-l'homme* practices of assistance agencies are born of the conviction that if there is a man in the picture somewhere, the woman *must* be receiving money from him. This marks a striking reversal of the "crime never pays" doctrine, as it assumes that "sin" always does.

Societies can hardly have things both ways—at least not simultaneously. They cannot expect welfare agencies, on the one hand, to build up self-confidence and to encourage a spirit of enterprise and, on the other, to denigrate and to undermine still further the security of those whom it purports to help toward independence. Nor can they expect to reduce possible cheating and dishonesty or to foster respect for law through means of instruction that are themselves dishonest and illegal.

In cases where there is at best only a suspicion (however falsely based) that an assistance recipient is ineligible for further aid, he is often, perhaps usually, treated in exactly the opposite way that a suspected criminal would be treated. The suspected criminal would be tried first and then, if found guilty, sentenced and either fined or sent to prison. The suspected public assistance recipient, however, may be immediately "cut off assistance"—even before all the facts are in. This is finding him guilty before he is proved guilty, and it is worse than fining him because it means depriving a family of its *entire livelihood*. The aggrieved party may be told "You can, of course, appeal." This takes time, however, and for children can mean a long, long wait for supper.

One "welfare" case that has received wide attention is that of six men who were employed on work-relief projects in upstate New York. On one bitterly cold morning, when the snow was knee-deep and when the regular employees with whom these assistance recipients normally worked on roadways had been transferred to indoor work, these men also asked for similar transfers. Their request was interpreted as "refusal to work" (which it was not); they were indicted and found guilty of interfering with welfare administration. Not surprisingly, a higher court reversed this ruling.[83] Unfortunately, however, "pending appeals" are not known for nutritional value. Nor do they offer much protection against cold.

Much has been made—and emphatically—throughout history of "equality before the law" and "equal protection of the laws." Less is heard, unfortunately, about "equal enforcement" of laws. Yet, within welfare departments, "investigators" (commonly miscalled "social workers") drawn from all walks of life (including previous police service) keep public assistance recipients under close surveillance. In addition, district attorneys deploy significant proportions of their investigators to keep an eye on "welfare cases." [84]

To the already heavy hand of the law laid on obviously dependent persons still further weight was added by the Social Security Amendments of 1967 which required states to be explicit about their arrangements with law enforcement officers and courts for referring cases of child neglect, illegitimacy, nonsupport, and the like. The amendments also extended access to the usually sacrosanct files of the Social Security Administration and Internal Revenue Service to facilitate tracking down putative fathers and those charged with failure to support wives or children and even prescribed federal reimbursement for local law enforcement officers engaged in these chases. Were it not for the concentration of law enforcement resources directed at obviously dependent persons, perhaps the currently abhorred "violence in the streets" might be more effectively curbed by releasing investigatory personnel for searches other than those for poor "runaway pappys" and other than under the beds of women who receive public aid.

Further questions of equal and fair enforcement of law are raised by the mixed nature of the services rendered by public assistance agencies, by the "case records" they maintain, and by the access that law enforcement officers have to records. Because of their "service" function, these agencies elicit much highly personal information, which, if it discloses some actionable offense— whether deliberately or inadvertently divulged by assistance recipients—must often be reported to law enforcement officers.[85] The usual "You can feel free to tell me everything. This is between you and me" should sometimes be "Between you and me—and the district attorney."

Conflicts among values are obvious here: How much "due process," equity, and justice for how much "punishment" for obvious dependency and how much possible saving of public funds?

Just after the historic Supreme Court decision in the Gideon case establishing an "indigent's" right to counsel in criminal proceedings, the then Attorney General of the United States, Robert F. Kennedy, declared, "We have secured the acquittal of an indigent person—but only to abandon him to eviction notices, wage attachments, repossession of goods and termination of welfare benefits." [86]

For the nation as a whole, probably the one device best calculated to assure (as far as possible) protection of the rights of applicants for, and recipients of, public assistance has been the provisions for "fair hearings." But even if persons are fully informed about procedures for "fair hearings," this avails little unless they are also fully informed (as they often are not) about what they may appeal *for* and about the reasons for denial or discontinuance of aid, and unless they are assured that if they appeal (which many are downright *afraid* to do), this will not jeopardize their later status as applicants or recipients. Even more fundamental, however, is the pervasive problem that assistance recipients are so much the children of their (highly efficient? frightening?) culture that they see themselves only as suppliants and not really entitled to what their society says they should have. Moreover, formal appeal procedures apply only to a relatively narrow range of welfare services, which include, of course, the federal-state public assistance programs, but ironically exclude virtually all General Assistance programs and also exclude, I believe it safe to say, *all* private agency services.

Incidentally, since our preoccupation here is with value, it is noteworthy that even the miscarriages between congressional intent and the actual delivery of benefits must be viewed as a conflict in values: How much nondelivery of service for how much "states' rights," how much "local control?" What price "diversity," what price "lack of national uniformity?"

When the then Attorney General, Nicholas de B. Katzenbach, addressed the 1964 Conference on the Extension of Legal Services to the Poor, he declared:

There are large numbers whose public assistance is reduced or revoked—who have no concept of their rights of appeal.

. . . For a poor person to hold rights in theory satisfies only the theory. We have to . . . help the poor assert those rights. Unknown, unasserted rights are no rights at all.

Then to make his point clearer still, the Attorney General cited the case of "a woman with seven children who was supported by welfare. Fire destroyed the roof of her house but she lacked money either to repair it or to move. The response of the welfare agency was to cut off her welfare payments. She was living, they said, in unsuitable housing." [87]

Much is being done these days to meet the "legal needs of the poor." But much less is heard of "meeting the needs of the poor—legally." However, the surge of interest that lawyers were showing in welfare issues, largely through the neighborhood legal service programs under the War on Poverty, was markedly changing the face of the welfare world.[88] For observers interested in justice for even obviously dependent persons, the various issues of *Welfare Law Bulletin* were about as heartening as anything for decades. Moreover, the U. S. Commission on Civil Rights and its state advisory bodies were devoting increasing attention to welfare matters.[89]

As a result, welfare agencies, which for years had remained unchallenged with respect to their well-meant decisions as to what in their judgment was someone's "real need" or "in the best interests" of a child, were being brought to the bar of community opinion and legality. Good intent and even sincere—by their lights—desire to help were no longer enough. Civil rights and due process were stressed as important, too. Increasingly it was being recognized that, as Professor Charles A. Reich in 1964 had written in "The New Property"—a paper that can be thought of as a shot heard 'round the welfare world—government cannot "buy up" constitutional rights.[90]

Extending to disadvantaged persons the elements of justice discussed here is a far cry from undesirable paternalism and unwarranted "coddling." Rather, it is the application—indeed an almost disgracefully belated application—to disadvantaged persons of benefits long enjoyed by the advantaged. On this, in referring to the part lawyers might play in the War on Poverty, Professor Abram Chayes declared:

In this program there is a built-in promise that . . . the poor man, by learning about his rights under law and by acting to vindicate them, can gain self respect, a sense of personal worth . . . and is not just an object to be manipulated by the system. It is the lack of these, and not the lack of money, that shackle him to poverty.[91]

Some may think that if it is recognized that poor persons have more rights than at present, they will lose "self-reliance." On the other hand (as suggested in Chapter IV), advantaged groups for a long, long time have had the legal system (other systems, too) working in their favor. Consequently, even a substantial increase in the legal power of poor persons may be viewed as a belated equalizer (or, at least, a disparity-reducer), which at last gives to them some of the advantages the nonpoor have long enjoyed. Privileged groups were not ready for such an equalization of legal power. How much so was evidenced by the consternation expressed when, in 1967, a civil rights group in Washington, D.C., embarked upon a campaign to encourage poor persons overwhelmed by consumer debt to apply for bankruptcy. What had long been thought to be "good" for businessmen overwhelmed by financial difficulties was clearly regarded as much "too good" for disadvantaged persons.[92]

Almost as if it were intended as a comment on this point, the preparatory report for the 1965 Conference on Law and Poverty states, "Lawyers must educate the poor to . . . assert their basic legal rights against landlords, sellers, even the police, to seek legal help when they need it, to trust the courts, to utilize the full potential of the law for *self-help*." [93] [Emphasis added.]

CONCLUSION

One day some complex but humane society will recognize the incommensurabilities inherent in interdependence and will acknowledge the degree to which even individual aspiration and achievement are socially conditioned. This society will then abandon practices that treat as commensurable the "fault" of obvious dependency and will discontinue as calculable the odium, censure, and denigration now visited upon this fault.

This society will recognize, more honestly than have others, the capacity of its culture to get down to the last man "the word" about self-help and will do a turnabout. It will open up more opportunities to attain the values of the culture; it will not unjustifiably punish those who *seemingly* fail to appreciate these values, because it will understand that to some these values are more unattainable than unappreciated.

The relevance of this concept for basic support in contemporary society is suggested by Professor Reich, who has written:

If the individual is to survive in a collective society, he must have protection against its ruthless pressures. There must be sanctuaries or enclaves where no majority can reach. . . . Just as the Homestead Act was a deliberate effort to foster individual values at an earlier time, so we must try to build an economic basis for liberty today—a Homestead Act for rootless twentieth century man. We must create a new property.[94]

This, of course, was the same concept that A. Delafield Smith was vigorously propounding, as in his *Right to Life*, long before the widespread renascence of interest in the rights of poor persons.[95]

In ancient times the Hebrew people had their "Cities of Refuge," and others had their "places of asylum" to which even those who had committed major crimes could repair for protection. If one could make his way to a "City of Refuge" or a "place of asylum," he could escape the wrath of an angry mob and death on the spot from stoning or by the sword.

Is it too fantastic to think that some day some perceptive and humane society will establish a refuge for those who do not find it possible to support themselves? a refuge, not from aroused vigilantes, but from gnawing and destructive insecurity, from public scorn and denigration? a refuge or asylum of assured security? Those given such asylum would not, as in the old days, have broken established law, but instead would be those who—because of some failing of society, perhaps, or because of some shortcoming of their own —had failed only to "make the grade" in usually expected ways. This protection would symbolize a society's rejection as commensurable the social disfavor and penalties that are now accorded for action (and inaction), the true blame for which, in complex societies, is virtually immeasurable.

Even in his day, Seneca saw that

. . . Good and bad men share alike in all the . . . privileges which a man receives, because he is a citizen, not because he is a good man. . . . Cities are founded for good and bad alike; works of genius reach, by publication, even unworthy men; medicine points out the means of health to the wicked. . . . Even a thief receives justice; even murderers enjoy the blessings of peace; . . . assassins . . . are defended against the common enemy by the city wall; the laws protect even those who have sinned most deeply against them.[96]

Is it too much to expect that, as city walls once provided protection for the "good and bad alike," the productivity of our hypothetical, humane society might some day—with no more inimicality than a city wall—provide at least basic support for its obviously dependent members as it does for those who are unobviously dependent?

1. *Welfare Law Bulletin* (New York: Project on Social Welfare Law, New York University School of Law).

2. Antonio A. Sorieri, "A View from the Inside," *Viewpoint* (Winter 1962), p. 5. See also *Report to the Moreland Commission on Welfare Findings of the Study of the Public Assistance Program and Operation of the State of New York* (Albany: Moreland Commission, 1962), p. 78. On the historical development of means tests in current public assistance programs, see Jack R. Parsons, "The Origins of the Income and Resources Amendment to the Social Security Act," *Social Service Review*, XXXVI (March 1962), pp. 51–61. For a now dated but still perceptive analysis, see "The Means Test," in Hilary M. Leyendecker, *Problems and Policy in Public Assistance* (New York: Harper & Row, 1955), pp. 193–214. A British analysis may be found in Arthur J. Willcocks, "The Means Test," *Sociological Review*, 5 (December 1957), 265–286.

3. Joan Gordon, *The Poor of Harlem* (New York: Office of the Mayor, Interdepartmental Service Center, 1965); "An Anxious Mother Writes," *The Welfarer*, August 1965, p. 2; Hugh McIsaac and Harold Wilkinson, "Clients Talk About Their Caseworkers," *Public Welfare*, XXIII (July 1965), 147–164; Marvin E. Larson, "Equal Justice for Public Welfare Recipients," *Equal Justice* (Chicago: American Public Welfare Association, 1965), p. 3; *Restructuring Public Welfare Administration to Meet the Needs of People in an Urban Society* (Washington, D.C.: Welfare Administration, Department of Health, Education, and Welfare, 1966), pp. 10, 11; Thomas R. Brooks, "The Caseworker and the Client," *The New York Times Magazine*, January 29, 1967, p. 27.

4. *"Having the Power, We Have the Duty"* (Washington, D.C.: Department of Health, Education, and Welfare, 1966), p. 68.

5. Catherine M. Watson, "Future Directions in Research," in Wilbur J. Cohen and Sidney E. Bernard, eds., *The Prevention and Reduction of Dependency* (Ann Arbor: Washtenaw County Department of Social Welfare, 1961), Appendix D, p. 88.

6. For two appraisals of means tests from a legal viewpoint, see Joel F. Handler and Margaret K. Rosenheim, "Privacy in Welfare: Public Assistance and Juvenile Justice," *Law and Contemporary Problems*, XXXI (Spring 1966), 377–412, especially "The Means Test and Its Implementation," 381–385; and Daniel R. Mandelker, "The Need Test in General Assistance," *Virginia Law Review*, 41 (1955), 893. For additional views see Jules H. Berman, "The Means Test: Welfare Provisions of the 1965

Social Security Amendments," *Social Service Review*, XL (June 1966), 169; Advisory Council on Social Security, "Report . . . : The Status of the Social Security Program and Recommendations for Its Improvement," *Social Security Bulletin*, 28 (March 1965), 4–5; Robert C. Stone and Frederic T. Schlamp, "Characteristics Associated with Receipt or Non-receipt of Financial Aid from Welfare Agencies," *Welfare in Review*, 3 (July 1965), 1–11; Walter C. Bentrup's two articles: "The Profession and the Means Test," *Social Work*, 9 (April 1964), 10–17, and "What's Wrong with the Means Test?" *Public Welfare*, XXIII (October 1965), 235–242; George Hoshino, "Can the Means Test Be Simplified?" *Social Work*, 10 (July 1965), 98–103. A significant discussion of the subject is Jacobus ten Broek and Floyd W. Matson, "Social Insecurity: The Means Test," *Hope Deferred: Public Welfare and the Blind* (Berkeley and Los Angeles: University of California Press, 1959), pp. 131–157.

For a recent British criticism of means tests, see Douglas Jay, *Socialism in the New Society* (London: Longmans, Green, 1962), especially p. 226.

7. *"Having the Power, We Have the Duty," op. cit.,* p. xii. The Council's positive recommendations on means tests are on pp. xii–xiii.

8. Paul Jacobs, "Getting on Welfare," *Harper's Magazine,* October 1967, pp. 74–75; this article is taken from Jacobs' *Prologue to Riots* (New York: Random House, 1967).

9. As reported in *Washington Memorandum,* National Association of Social Workers, September 28, 1966, p. 2.

10. John M. Wedemeyer, speech at *Recognition Dinner for Graduating MSW's,* (Sacramento: California State Department of Social Welfare, 1966), p. 3. (Mimeographed.)

11. Frances Lomas Feldman, *Public Welfare: Dependency, Despair—and Opportunity* (Los Angeles: The [California] Governor's Commission on the Watts Riot, 1965), p. 56. (Mimeographed.) This report has been published under a slightly modified title in *Riots in the City: An Addendum to the McCone Commission Report* (Los Angeles: National Association of Social Workers, Los Angeles Area Chapter, 1967).

12. Arthur R. Simon, *Faces of Poverty* (St. Louis, Mo.: Concordia, 1966), pp. 15–16.

13. Winston Spencer Churchill, *Liberalism and the Social Problem* (London: Hodder and Stoughton, 1909), pp. 208–210.

14. G. M. Trevelyan, *English Social History: A Survey of Six Centuries, Chaucer to Queen Victoria* (London: Longmans, Green, 1944), p. 538.

15. David Owen, *English Philanthropy: 1660–1960* (Cambridge: Harvard University Press, 1964), pp. 106, 58.

16. As quoted by Juanita L. Cogan, ed., *Employability Planning in Public Welfare* (Washington, D.C.: Welfare Administration, Department of Health, Education, and Welfare, 1967), p. 84. (Mimeographed.)

17. Michael Graham, *Human Needs* (London: Crescent Press, 1961).

18. Data taken from Gerald Kahn and Ellen J. Perkins, "Families Receiving AFDC: What Do They Have to Live On?" *Welfare in Review,* 2 (October 1964), 10.

For an analysis of ADC in Detroit, see Charles Lebeaux, "Life on A.D.C.: Budgets of Despair," *New University Thought,* 3 (Winter 1963), 26–35;

reprinted in Louis A. Ferman, Joyce L. Kornbluh, and Alan Haber, eds., *Poverty in America: A Book of Readings* (Ann Arbor: University of Michigan Press, 1965), pp. 401–411. See also Lenore A. Epstein, "Some Effects of Low Income on Children and Their Families," *Social Security Bulletin,* 24 (February 1961), 12–17; Mollie Orshansky, "Children of the Poor," *Social Security Bulletin,* 26 (July 1963), 3–31; Catherine S. Chilman, "Child-Rearing and Family Relationship Patterns of the Very Poor," *Welfare in Review,* 3 (January 1965), 9–19; E. Elizabeth Glover, "Hunger Won't Wait," *Child Welfare,* XLIII (April 1964), 1; "Evaluation of Standards and Allowances in the ADC Program in Cook County," *Addenda to Facts, Fallacies and Future: A Study of the Aid to Dependent Children Program of Cook County, Illinois* (New York: Greenleigh Associates, 1960), pp. 111–119.

Illuminating data on the circumstances in which various types of assistance recipients live are provided periodically by the federal Bureau of Family Services (Welfare Administration, Department of Health, Education, and Welfare) on "Characteristics of Recipients."

Vivid pictures of life on public assistance allowances are given in Ben H. Bagdikian, *In the Midst of Plenty: The Poor in America* (Boston: Beacon Press, 1964); Edgar May, *The Wasted Americans: Cost of Our Welfare Dilemma* (New York: Harper & Row, 1964); Simon, *op. cit.;* Richard M. Elman, *The Poorhouse State: The American Way of Life on Public Assistance* (New York: Random House, 1966).

19. Kahn and Perkins, *op. cit.,* p. 9. Further discussion of levels of assistance payments may be found in Ellen J. Perkins, "Unmet Need in Public Assistance," *Social Security Bulletin,* 23 (April 1960), 3–11; Lenore A. Epstein, "Unmet Need in a Land of Abundance," *Social Security Bulletin,* 26 (May 1963), 3–11; Hilda Siff, "Feeding a Family on a Public Assistance Budget," *Welfare in Review,* 3 (May 1965), 8–11; Alice B. Spalding, "Eating Low on the Hog," *Harper's Magazine,* CCXXX (March 1965), 139–147; Gladys O. White, *State Methods for Determining Need in the Aid to Dependent Children Program* (Washington, D.C.: Department of Health, Education, and Welfare, 1961), Public Assistance Report No. 43; *Monthly Cost Standards for Basic Needs Used by States for Specified Types of Old Age Assistance Cases and Families Receiving AFDC* (Washington, D.C.: Bureau of Family Services, Department of Health, Education, and Welfare, 1965); Ellen J. Perkins, "How Much Is Enough Today?" *Biennial Papers* (Chicago: American Public Welfare Association, 1963), pp. 20–25; and Duncan M. MacIntyre, *Public Assistance: Too Much or Too Little?* (Ithaca: New York State School of Industrial and Labor Relations, Cornell University, 1964), Bulletin 53–1. A broad but detailed picture of public assistance in the state of Washington is available in *Public Welfare: Poverty—Prevention or Perpetuation* (New York: Greenleigh Associates, 1964). A picture based upon observations in Chicago appears in Eugene H. Kelley, "Cold, Hungry and Despairing," *Agenda,* 2 (September 1966), 23–27.

Pennsylvania has one of the most forthright departments (if not *the* most forthright) responsible for public assistance. This department publishes annually *Public Assistance Allowances Compared with the Cost of*

Living at a Minimum Standard of Health and Decency (Harrisburg: Commonwealth of Pennsylvania Department of Public Welfare).

In this context, two books by Alvin L. Schorr are important: *Slums and Social Insecurity* (Washington, D.C.: Government Printing Office, 1963) and *Poor Kids* (New York: Basic Books, 1966).

20. See Alice R. McCabe, "Forty Forgotten Families," *Public Welfare*, XXIV (April 1966), 167.

21. Philip Sokol, "Due Process of Law," *Equal Justice* (Chicago: American Public Welfare Association, 1965), p. 10.

22. *Welfare Information Package* (Sacramento: California State Department of Social Welfare, 1966), p. 8. (Mimeographed.)

23. *Second Annual Report* (Sacramento: California State Social Welfare Board, 1966), p. 11. A critique of assistance standards in nearby Washington is available in *Public Welfare: Poverty—Prevention or Perpetuation, op. cit.*, especially pp. 25 ff. and 71 ff.

Additional references on assistance standards include Jane De Melto, "The Crisis of the Tenth of the Month," *Public Welfare*, 21 (October 1963), 179 ff; and Sherman Barr, "Budgeting and the Poor: A View from the Bottom," *Public Welfare*, 23 (October 1965), 246 ff.

24. Robert T. Lansdale, *Inadequacies of Statewide Programs of Public Assistance in Urban Areas* (Baltimore: School of Social Work, University of Maryland, 1965), p. 22. See also *The Public Welfare Crisis in the Nation's Capital* (Washington, D.C.: The Washington Center for Metropolitan Studies, 1963); *Children in Need: . . . in Cleveland and Cuyahoga County, Ohio* (Washington, D.C.: United States Commission on Civil Rights, 1966); *Public Assistance in the South* (Atlanta: Southern Regional Council, 1966). (Mimeographed.)

25. *Cities in Crisis: The Challenge of Change* (Washington, D.C.: Government Printing Office, 1967), pp. 9, 11. See also J. Nordstrom, "ADC Housing: Costs, Conditions, Consequences," *Smith College Studies in Social Work*, 35 (1965), 125–154.

26. Computed from *State Maximums and Other Methods of Limiting Money Payments to Recipients of the Special Types of Public Assistance* (Washington, D.C.: Division of Program Statistics and Analysis, Bureau of Family Services, Welfare Administration, Department of Health, Education, and Welfare, 1965).

27. James R. Dumpson, "Our Welfare System—Radical Surgery Needed," *Public Welfare*, XXIII (October 1965), 231.

28. Data derived from Gladys O. White, "Meeting Financial Needs under Old-Age Assistance," *Welfare in Review*, 1 (December 1963), 5.

29. Violet Weingarten, *Life at the Bottom* (New York: Citizens' Committee for Children of New York, ca. 1966), unpaginated. On this same point see Gordon, *op. cit.*, pp. 73–74. Brooks, *op. cit.*, also comments on this point as on the previous one of lost checks (p. 71).

30. *"Having the Power, We Have the Duty," op. cit.*, p. 18.

31. Bagdikian, *op. cit.*, pp. 4–5.

32. Andrew R. N. Truelson, *The Economic Opportunity Act and Public Welfare* (Washington, D.C.: U.S. Department of Health, Education, and Welfare, ca. 1965), p. 3.

33. Glover, *op. cit.*, p. 1. See also E. Elizabeth Glover and Joseph H. Reid, "Unmet and Future Needs," *The Annals*, 355 (1964), 9–19; and Chilman, "Social Work Practice with Very Poor Families . . . ," *op. cit.*, p. 21.

34. James H. Reilly, "The Primary Factor in Good Services—Adequate Assistance Grants," *Public Welfare*, 22 (October 1964), 242–245 ff.

35. Gordon, *op. cit.*, p. 127.

36. Robert Sherrill, "It Isn't True That Nobody Starves in America," *The New York Times Magazine*, June 4, 1967, pp. 22–23, 101–108. See also Nan Robertson, "Hunger in U.S.," *The New York Times*, July 16, 1967.

37. Ellen Winston, "Implications of the AFDC Review," *Social Work Practice, 1964* (New York: Columbia University Press, 1964), p. 39.

38. *Report* (Washington, D.C.: Advisory Council on Public Assistance, U.S. Department of Health, Education, and Welfare, 1960), pp. 18–19.

39. These possible liberalizations of state policies are described in Wilbur J. Cohen and Robert M. Ball, "Social Security Amendments of 1965: Summary and Legislative History," *Social Security Bulletin*, 28 (September 1965), 3–21, particularly p. 20.

40. See *Handbook Transmittal Letter No. 106* (Washington, D.C.: Welfare Administration, Department of Health, Education, and Welfare, January 24, 1967).

41. New York State Citizens' Committee on Welfare Costs, *Report* (Albany: New York State Citizens' Committee on Welfare Costs, 1965), pp. 49–50. See also Hugh A. Storrow, M.D., "Money as a Motivator," *Public Welfare*, 20 (October 1962), 199–204, 233; Jane M. Hoey, "The Lack of Money: Its Cost in Human Values," *Social Casework*, XXXVIII (October 1957), 406–412; and Helen Harris Perlman, "Are We Creating Dependency?" *Social Service Review*, XXXIV (September 1960), 323–333.

42. American Public Welfare Association, *Federal Legislative Objectives—1966, op. cit.*, p. 3.

43. A report on the New York experiment is available in *Welfare Law Bulletin*, No. 9 (July 1967), pp. 15–16. An expression of Mayor John V. Lindsay's pride may be found in *The New York Times Book Review*, July 30, 1967, p. 25.

44. *Technology and the American Economy*, 1 (Washington, D.C.: National Commission on Technology, Automation, and Economic Progress, 1966), 39.

45. See, for example, Joseph P. Lyford, *The Airtight Cage: A Study of New York's West Side* (New York: Harper and Row, 1966), p. 269; Simon, *op. cit.*, p. 31; and "The Client Views the Caseworker: Part Two," *The Welfarer*, XIX (March 1967), p. 7.

46. See *Welfare Law Bulletin*, October 1966, p. 3.

47. Justine Fixel and Kermit T. Wiltse, "A Study of the Administration of the ADC Program," *ADC: Problem and Promise* (Chicago: American Public Welfare Association, *ca.* 1960), p. 34.

48. Data derived from Tables 6–10 in *Reasons for Opening and Closing Public Assistance Cases* (Washington, D.C.: Division of Program Statistics and Analysis, Bureau of Family Services, Welfare Administration, Department of Health, Education, and Welfare, August, 1966).

49. Data derived from M. Elaine Burgess and Daniel O. Price, *An American*

Dependency Challenge (Chicago: American Public Welfare Association, 1963), Table XXXVIII, p. 281. For another study of how needy families try to make do when assistance is terminated, see *The Ineligibles: A Study of Fifty Families Terminated or Ineligible for Public Assistance* (Washington, D.C.: Bureau of Social Science Research, 1963).

50. Simon, *op. cit.*, p. 64.

51. As quoted in "The Client Views the Caseworker: Part Two," *op. cit.*, 6–7.

52. As quoted in *The Poor Speak* (Columbus: Ohio Citizens' Council for Health and Welfare, 1966), pp. 19, 14. (Mimeographed.) See also McIsaac and Wilkinson, *op. cit; Facts, Fallacies and the Future, op. cit.*, p. 64; and sources in note 3 above.

53. An interesting but admittedly somewhat speculative analysis of hostility toward disadvantaged persons is by psychoanalyst and University of California (Berkeley) Law School Professor Bernard L. Diamond, "The Children of Leviathan: Psychoanalytic Speculations Concerning Welfare Law and Punitive Sanctions," *California Law Review*, 54 (May 1966), 357–369. See also Peter M. Blau, "Orientation Toward Clients in a Public Welfare Agency," *Administrative Science Quarterly*, 5 (December 1960), 356, 358–359.

54. As quoted in *Second Annual Report*, 1966, *op. cit.*, p. 45.

55. *Ibid.*, pp. 15, 21. A detailed analysis of the San Francisco Public Welfare Department and client attitudes toward it in 1960 is available in Fixel and Wiltse, *op. cit.* See particularly p. 29.

56. McCabe, *op. cit.*, pp. 167–169, 170. Similar findings with respect to a Midwest agency are presented in Cohen and Bernard, eds., *The Prevention and Reduction of Dependency, op. cit.* See especially p. 94.

57. Russell E. Smith, "In Defense of Public Welfare," *Social Work*, 11 (October 1966), 92. For a similar view of administrative pressures in Southern states, see William J. Page, Jr., "Three Dimensions of Expectations of Social Welfare Programs," *Public Welfare*, XXV (April 1967), 117–121. An older but incisive and still relevant source is Alan Keith-Lucas, *Decisions About People in Need: Administrative Responsiveness in Public Assistance* (Chapel Hill: University of North Carolina Press, 1957).

58. Winifred Bell, *Aid to Dependent Children* (New York: Columbia University Press, 1965), pp. 180, 83, 197.

59. See, for example, Alfred J. Kahn, "Social Services in Relation to Income Security: Introductory Notes," *Social Service Review*, XXIX (December 1965), 381–389. Also see Mitchell Ginsberg, Welfare Commissioner of New York City, *The Welfarer* (July-September 1966), p. 6; Elizabeth Wickenden and Winifred Bell, *Public Welfare: Time for a Change* (New York: New York School of Social Work, Columbia University, 1961), pp. 81–92; Davis McEntire and Joanne Haworth, "The Two Functions of Public Welfare: Income Maintenance and Social Services," *Social Work*, 12 (January 1967), 22–31.

60. Arthur Mandelbaum, "Dependency in Human Development," *Public Welfare Projected* (Chicago: American Public Welfare Association, 1966), p. 10.

61. Lloyd Setleis, "Civil Rights and the Rehabilitation of AFDC Clients,"

Social Work, 9 (April 1964), 6. An outstanding contribution with this same emphasis is made by Fixel and Wiltse, *op. cit.,* pp. 23–40.

62. Elman, *op. cit.,* pp. 5, 10. See also pp. 281, 297. See also Lyford, *op. cit.,* Chapter 12, "Money and Sympathy."

63. As reported in *NASW* (*Los Angeles Chapter*) *Record,* November 1966, p. 1.

64. Peter Kasius, "ADC: A Reassessment of Its Dimensions," *ADC: Problem and Promise* (Chicago: American Public Welfare Association, n.d., ca. 1960), p. 15. See also Ellen Winston, "Implications of the AFDC Eligibility Review," *Welfare in Review,* 2 (July 1964), 1–7; *AFDC: Fact vs. Fiction,* Biennial Papers (Chicago: American Public Welfare Association, 1963), especially pp. 26–34; Alvin L. Schorr, "Problems in the ADC Program," *Social Work,* 5 (April 1960), 3–15; and Wickenden and Bell, *op. cit.,* pp. 28–29. The most extensive study yet made of Aid to Dependent Children and one that treats many topics touched in this chapter is in Burgess and Price, *op. cit.*

65. "Methods for Determination of Eligibility," *Handbook of Public Assistance* (Washington, D.C.: Welfare Administration, Department of Health, Education, and Welfare, March 18, 1966), Part IV, Sections 2220, 2230. See also *"Having the Power, We Have the Duty," op. cit.,* pp. 16, 74.

66. Leonard Schneiderman, "The Practical and Cultural Significance of Money," *Public Welfare,* XXIII (July 1965), 201. See also Jane M. Hoey, "The Significance of the Money Payment in Public Assistance," *Social Security Bulletin,* 7 (September 1944), 1–3. The author was long director of the federal Bureau of Public Assistance and an ardent advocate and implementer not only of money payments but also of "unrestricted" money payments.

A classic in its day but now dated (except among administrators of General Assistance) is Joanna C. Colcord's *Cash Relief* (New York: Russell Sage Foundation, 1936). Other useful sources are Wickenden and Bell, *op. cit.,* pp. 36, 78–79; Frances Lomas Feldman, *The Family in a Money World* (New York: Family Service Association of America, 1957), especially pp. 86–96; and William Kaufman, "Some Emotional Uses of Money," *Pastoral Psychology,* 16 (1965), 43–56. A more general but useful discussion that puts the cash payment principle in a broader context is "Negotiated Exchange," in Harry C. Bredemeier and Jackson Toby, *Social Problems in America* (New York: Wiley, 1960).

67. See *Characteristics of General Assistance in the United States,* Public Assistance Report No. 39 (Washington, D.C.: Bureau of Public Assistance, Social Security Administration, Department of Health, Education, and Welfare, 1959), especially p. 13. A relatively old (but, unfortunately, still a probably quite accurate) description of General Assistance in various localities may be found in Felix M. Gentile and Donald S. Howard, *General Assistance—With Special Reference to Practice in 47 Localities of the United States* (New York: American Association of Social Workers, 1949).

68. *Public Welfare: Poverty, Prevention or Perpetuation, op. cit.,* p. 80.

69. See, for example, Charles O'Reilly and Margaret Pembroke, *Older People*

in a Chicago Community (Chicago: Loyola University, 1956), p. 25; Otto M. Reid, "Aging Americans," *Welfare in Review*, 4 (May 1966), 5; James N. Morgan, *et al.*, "Voluntarism and Philanthropy," *Income and Welfare in the United States* (New York: McGraw-Hill, 1962), pp. 257–287; and Winifred Bell, "Relatives' Responsibility: A Problem in Social Policy," *Social Work*, 12 (January 1967), 32–39.

Broader aspects of the problem of relatives' responsibilities are discussed in Alvin L. Schorr, *Filial Responsibility in the Modern American Family* (Washington, D.C.: Department of Health, Education, and Welfare, 1960); Jacob T. Zukerman, "Legal Provisions Which Cause Family Stress," *Equal Justice* (Chicago: American Public Welfare Association, 1965), pp. 13–21; and Zukerman's "Role of the Public Agency with the Deserted Family," *Public Welfare*, XV (July 1957), 101–106, 120–124. Philip Sokol's "Who Pays—and Who Cares," *The Welfarer*, XVI (March 1964), is an incisive analysis of relatives' responsibilities and, although no longer wholly relevant to New York State because of changes in the law in 1966, still has relevance for other states.

70. See Thompson v. Shapiro, Civ. No. 11821 (D. Conn., June 19, 1967), and Green v. Department of Public Welfare, Civ. No. 3349 (D. Del., June 28, 1967).

71. George K. Wyman, *98th Annual Report on Social Welfare in New York* (Albany: State Department of Social Welfare, 1965), pp. xii, xiii.

72. Jacobus ten Broek, *California's Dual System of Family Law: Its Origin, Development, and Present Status* (Berkeley: Department of Political Science, University of California, n.d., *ca.* 1965). Quotations in text are from p. 258 (Part I), p. 283 (Part III), and ff. For a somewhat different view of duality in family law, see Thomas P. Lewis and Robert J. Levy, "Family Law and Welfare Policies: The Case for 'Dual Systems,'" *California Law Review*, 4 (May 1966), 748–780; and Walter O. Weyrauch, "Dual Systems of Family Law: A Comment," *California Law Review*, 54 (May 1966), 781–791.

73. Papers presented and discussed at this conference are available in *California Law Review*, Vol. 54, No. 2 (May 1966). These papers were subsequently reprinted: Jacobus ten Broek and editors of the *California Law Review*, *The Law of the Poor* (San Francisco: Chandler, 1966).

74. Robert F. Kennedy, in Theodore J. Lowi, ed., *The Pursuit of Justice* (New York: Harper and Row, 1964), p. 6. See also Chapter 10, "The Injustice of Inequality." Another useful source on the same theme is *Poverty and the Administration of Federal Criminal Justice*, Report of the Attorney General's Committee on Poverty and the Administration of Federal Criminal Justice (Washington, D.C.: Government Printing Office, 1964). A history of federal procedures in cases involving "indigents" is available in John P. Comer, *The Forging of the Federal Indigent Code* (San Antonio, Texas: Principia Press of Trinity University, 1966).

75. Jacobus ten Broek, "The Impact of Welfare Law on Family Law," *California Law Review*, 42 (July 1954), 483.

76. See, for example, Bell, *op. cit.*

77. The *Welfare Law Bulletin* is an excellent and readily accessible source in which to follow court actions in welfare issues.

78. A blow-by-blow description of the "Battle of Newburgh" and its outcome may be found in Joseph P. Ritz, *The Despised Poor: Newburgh's War on Welfare* (Boston: Beacon Press, 1966). For the New York State Supreme Court decision that enjoined Newburgh and prevented the plan from going into effect, see State Board v. Newburgh, 28 M 2d 539 (1961). See also Samuel Mencher, "Newburgh: The Recurrent Crises of Public Assistance," *Social Work,* 7 (January 1962), 3–11; and Bertram Beck, "After Newburgh, What?—The Role of Welfare," *Commonweal,* Vol. 77, No. 7 (November 9, 1962).

79. See *Memorandum of Decision, No. 76757,* Hon. C. Douglas Smith, Judge, The Superior Court of the State of California in and for the County of Santa Barbara, June 8, 1966.

80. Charles A. Reich, "Midnight Welfare Searches and the Social Security Act," *Yale Law Journal,* 72 (June 1963), 1347–1360.

81. *"Midnight Raids": A Statement from the Social Work Profession on the Right of Public Assistance Recipients to Privacy* (New York: National Association of Social Workers, *ca.* 1964).

82. See Parrish v. Civil Service Commission of the County of Alameda, 35 U.S.L.W. 2583 (Cal. Sup. Ct., March 27, 1967).

83. See People v. La Fountain, 21 AD 2d 719 (1964). This whole situation is discussed in some detail by Betty Mandel, "The Crime of Poverty," *Social Work,* 11 (January 1966), 11–15.

84. See, for example, *Report for 1961–62 and 1962–63* (Los Angeles: District Attorney's Office, 1963), p. 9. (Mimeographed.) For a discussion of the elaborate arrangements for pursuit and prosecutions of "deserting fathers," see Maurine McKeany, *The Absent Father and Public Policy in the Program of Aid to Dependent Children* (Berkeley: University of California, 1960), Vol. 1 in Publications in Social Welfare; and William J. Brockelbank, *Inter-State Enforcement of Family Support: The Runaway Pappy Act* (New York: Bobbs-Merrill, 1960). (This, incidentally, is the first book I have ever seen dedicated to "The Destitute Families of America."—D.S.H.) See also Irving F. Reichert, Jr., "A Report on Relationships Between Welfare and Law Enforcement Agencies in California, 1962," *Consultants' Reports* (Sacramento: California Welfare Study Commission, 1962), Part 11, pp. 253–345. How apparently "general" law may weigh with special force on needy persons is discussed in Margaret K. Rosenheim, "Vagrancy Concepts in Welfare Law," *California Law Review,* 54 (May 1966), 511–566. See also Handler and Rosenheim, *op. cit.,* 376 ff., especially 386–392, and Jacobus ten Broek, *The Law of Crimes and the Law of Welfare* (Address before Region 2, California Social Welfare Workers Organization, February 7, 1961). More recently Professor ten Broek has written of welfare as a system of control in "The Disabled and the Law of Welfare," *California Law Review,* 54 (May 1966), 830–832.

85. For a broader treatment of confidentiality, see "The Social Worker-Client Relationship and Privileged Communications," *Washington University Law Quarterly,* No. 3 (June 1965), pp. 362–395.

86. Robert F. Kennedy (address on Law Day, University of Chicago Law School), quoted by Patricia M. Wald, *Law and Poverty: 1965* (Washington, D.C.: National Conference on Law and Poverty, 1965), pp. 3, 2.

87. Nicholas de B. Katzenbach as reported by Jeanette Stats, ed., *The Extension of Legal Services to the Poor, op. cit.*, pp. 11, 12, 13. In addition to papers presented at this conference that have already been cited, another that is particularly relevant is one by Edward V. Sparer, "The New Public Law: The Relation of Indigents to State Administration," pp. 23–40. See also E. S. and J. C. Cahn, "The War on Poverty: A Civilian Perspective," *Yale Law Journal*, 73 (1964), 1317–1352; and Jane Handler, *Neighborhood Legal Services—New Dimensions in the Law* (Washington, D.C.: Office of Juvenile Delinquency and Youth Development, Welfare Administration, Department of Health, Education, and Welfare, 1966), pp. 37, 67–68.

88. See, for example, William T. Downs, "Providing the Social Worker with Legal Understanding: Specific Need," *The Extension of Legal Services to the Poor, op. cit.*, pp. 140–147; Setleis, *op. cit.*, pp. 3–9; Elizabeth and Karl de Schweinitz, "The Place of Authority in the Protective Function of the Public Welfare Agency," *Child Welfare*, XLIII (June 1964), 286–291, 315; Kimberley B. Cheney, "Safeguarding Legal Rights in Providing Protective Services," *Children*, 13 (May-June 1966), 87–92; Zona Fairbanks Hostetler, "Poverty and the Law," in Ben B. Seligman, ed., *Poverty as a Public Issue* (New York: Free Press, 1965), pp. 177–230; Floyd W. Matson, "Social Welfare and Personal Liberty: The Problem of Casework," *Social Research*, 22 (Autumn 1955), 253–274; Charles A. Reich, "Individual Rights and Social Welfare: The Emerging Legal Issues," *Yale Law Journal*, 74 (June 1965), 1245–1257; Daniel R. Mandelker, "Judicial Review in General Assistance," *Journal of Public Law*, 6 (Spring 1957), 100–122; Handler and Rosenheim, *op. cit.*, 377–412, especially pp. 392–394 on "Expanded Treatment Services" and pp. 410–412 on "Treatment, Privacy, and Public Policy"; and Jacobus ten Broek, "The 1956 Amendments to the Social Security Act: After the New Look—the First Thought," *Journal of Public Law*, 6 (Spring 1957), 123–162.

Papers presented at the Conference on the Law of the Poor and published in the *California Law Review*, 54 (May 1966) that are particularly relevant to our present subject include: Albert M. Bendich, "Privacy, Poverty, and the Constitution" (407–442); Robert M. O'Neil, "Unconstitutional Conditions: Welfare Benefits with Strings Attached" (443–478); Joel F. Handler, "Controlling Official Behavior in Welfare Administration" (479–510); Bernard Evans Harvith, "The Constitutionality of Residence Tests for General and Categorical Assistance Programs" (567–641); and Jacobus ten Broek and Floyd W. Matson, "The Disabled and the Law of Welfare" (809–840), which really covers more ground than the title implies. These papers are also available in *The Law of the Poor, op. cit.* (note 73 above).

Further useful sources include Smith, *op. cit.*, pp. 90–97, and Harry W. Jones, "The Rule of Law and the Welfare State," *Columbia Law Review*, 58 (February 1958), 143–156.

89. *Children in Need: A Study of a Federally Assisted Program of Aid to Needy Families with Children in Cleveland and Cuyahoga County* (Washington, D.C.: United States Commission on Civil Rights, 1966).

90. Charles A. Reich, "The New Property," *Yale Law Journal*, 73 (April 1964), 779.
91. Abram Chayes, *Law and Poverty: 1965, op. cit.*, Foreword, pp. v, vi.
92. As reported in *The New York Times*, July 9, 1967. Wald, *op. cit.*, pp. 3, 4.
93. Patricia Wald, ed., *Law and Poverty: 1965, op. cit.*, p. 4.
94. Reich, "The New Property," *op. cit.*, p. 787.
95. Smith, *The Right to Life, op. cit.* See also Neva L. Itzin, "The Right to Life, Subsistence, and the Social Services," *Social Work*, 3 (October 1958), 3–11.
96. Seneca, *On Benefits, op. cit.*, pp. 110–111. An interesting source relevant to this topic is J. Charles Cox, *The Sanctuaries and Sanctuary Seekers of Mediaeval England* (London: G. Allen, 1911).

VII
VALUE CONFLICTS
in
RECEIVING
HELP

The cultural coin that symbolizes the merits of self-help circulates widely indeed. It is little wonder that, as suggested in Chapter III, even (perhaps *especially*?) the poorest peasant clearly senses the message on its face: "In Self-Help We Trust." This carries the cultural message that self-help is "good." On the reverse, then, is read: "In Dependence We Blush." This inference, within a culture stressing self-help as a cardinal virtue, appears inescapable.

Moreover, if one somehow fails to "get the message" from his general culture, there are always those sober reminders from high places (some are mentioned in Chapter V). Furthermore, if one cannot quite make the grade on his own and turns to a welfare agency, he is likely to find this, too, as we have seen, reinforcing the self-help doctrine. Finally, if one must turn to an assistance agency, the cultural message is likely to be still more strongly reinforced—in possibly quite stern and abrasive terms, as already shown.

CONFLICTS ABOUT BASIC SUPPORT

In the United States

That the cultural message has gotten through "loud and clear" —whether from the general culture or as subsequently reinforced— is plain; sometimes, depending upon one's values, painfully plain. About as terse testimony as any on this point are statements made to Mrs. Alice McCabe by mothers receiving public assistance:

> I feel like an alley cat.
> The sooner I get off, the better.
> I can't stand it—I feel worried all the time.[1]

Welfare workers from coast to coast can cite a great many similar reactions. One welfare worker, for example, said of a man and a woman, both aged fifty-eight, the man unable to find work after an operation for a brain tumor, "They felt humiliated and embarrassed." Similarly, Professor Scott Briar of the School of Social Welfare at the University of California, Berkeley, found in a study made in 1965 that a sample group of unemployed men and their wives felt embarrassment, guilt, and resentment over having to request public aid.[2] Since the respondents had encountered the welfare system only a short time before, it would be instructive to know whether reinforcement of the self-help doctrine by punitive practices is really essential to "getting the word" to men in general.

A group of students in the School of Social Work of Michigan State University concluded, after making a study of public assistance, "The average person in our community views 'going on relief' as a disgrace too great to be borne, short of the most extreme need. . . . Since there is such widespread scorn for people on relief, it can hardly be a casually sought help, at least not the first time." [3]

A further suggestion from Michigan of how societal values (efficiently? frighteningly?) filter down even to seriously disadvantaged groups is offered by Charles Lebeaux and his associates in Detroit. After making inquiries in the "inner city" about public assistance, these reporters say of the responses, "The over-all tone is a kind of super-rugged individualism: 'Make 'em work for what they get; . . . if they won't do for themselves, let them starve.'" Their report particularly cites one old woman who, "although her only source of income was the $50 or $60 a month she got from two roomers, and her house taxes were two years in arrears . . . wanted no help, only more employment in the community so that she could have more roomers." [4]

That these were not merely provincial Middle West views is suggested by Justine Fixel and Kermit Wiltse, who, in their study of public assistance in San Francisco, "did not encounter a single client who did not have a real desire to be self-supporting and off assistance, although some were unable without help to see any alternative." [5]

From New York, the long-established Community Service Society reports that in 1964 more than half of the families served by its Family Service Centers were "poor." The society reports further:

Of the older people served . . . nearly 43% . . . were living at or below the Department of Welfare budget level. . . . In spite of their economic straits, less than 40% of these persons sought public assistance.
. . . Our caseworkers see these older people clinging to the feeling of self-respect that being self-sufficient gives them.[6]

Before one rejoices over the efficiency of either the broader culture or public assistance policies designed to reenforce it, he should see, as in Arthur Simon's *Faces of Poverty*, the tremendous personal sacrifices often laid on the altar of "independence." [7]

How values involved here become grossly distorted is strikingly illustrated by Joseph Lyford who, in *The Airtight Cage*, tells of a young woman who had been incarcerated repeatedly on charges of both prostitution and use of narcotics. Despite her sordid life, however, she still took pride in two things: her body (which she had painstakingly protected from obvious disfigurement from hypodermic needles) and the fact that she had never been "on welfare." [8] Another interesting example of relativities is presented in Roul Tunley's report of a young woman who, after a prenatal examination at a maternity clinic, was told to follow a diet that she could not afford. When asked why she had not mentioned her financial straits earlier, she replied that she never discussed such "business" affairs with "a stranger." [9] Apparently the pelvis can be more subject to examination than the purse.

Just before his election to the Vice-Presidency Hubert H. Humphrey wrote, "I have spent most of my life in public service and my experience is that most people on relief are desperately trying to get off the rolls. The stigma of 'being on relief' keeps many of those eligible from applying for assistance." A study made in Westchester County, New York—one of the wealthiest counties in the nation—revealed, as reported by *The New York Times* in 1964, that only about 20 percent of the families living in "abject poverty" were receiving public aid.[10]

That many poor persons do not apply for aid must come as a surprise to those who think that families flock into welfare offices at the first sign of deprivation. Yet James N. Morgan, *et al.*, in *Income and Welfare in the United States*, report:

Despite the . . . assistance . . . and social insurance programs operating in this country, nearly half of the families whose incomes are inadequate received no transfer aid during 1959. Only 23 per cent of all poor families received public assistance.[11]

More recently an official federal report (1966) maintained that throughout the United States there were as many who qualified for, but were not receiving, public assistance as were then receiving it. The number *qualifying for* but not receiving aid was of course smaller than the number who were officially defined as "poor" but not being aided. Assistance standards, generally, fell far below standards of "poverty."

Lest it be assumed that only adults including older persons share the social disdain for obvious dependency, it is noteworthy that Reese Cleghorn, associate editor of *The Atlanta Journal*, writes as follows concerning the younger generation in a corner of Appalachia: "Although it is estimated that hundreds of pupils could qualify for . . . free [school] lunches, hardly any of them accept the free meal tickets." He then tells of a widow's daughter who did accept the free lunches but who cleaned the tables in the lunchroom "in payment for her lunch, although she is not required to do so." The girl's mother is then quoted as asking, "Could you make your boys say they wanted to eat free?" [12]

When medical care for needy persons became available (under Title XIX of the Social Security Act), eligibility requirements were somewhat less onerous than those for financial assistance. As a result, many, many persons applying for the new medical care were found to be eligible for assistance, but, even upon being offered financial aid, refused to accept it. In one county, where the policy was to issue a check when an applicant for medical care was found to be eligible also for financial aid, one elderly lady still refused the check and endorsed it back to the state.

Incidentally, this willingness to accept medical care ("anybody can get sick") is at least one datum in support of our hypothesis that basic support is more embarrassing than other requirements. In California in 1966, the new medical-aid program revealed that only about half of those eligible for financial aid were receiving it.

Offers of employment also reveal reluctance to apply for assistance unless one can "work for it." When work experience and training projects were developed, but restricted to persons who had been receiving assistance, needy persons who could previously have qualified for aid came forward so they could "get a job." Work programs during the Great Depression revealed the same phenomenon.

With his nationwide purview the Assistant Director of the federal Bureau of Family Services said in 1965 that response to the work projects "disputes the myth that today's needy unemployed adults prefer to remain idle and receive assistance, rather than work." To disprove the myth he then quoted a letter received from a man who had written, "I have a job now—at last. My children know this, and are proud of me. I want them to be proud of me every day." [13]

In New York, Betty Mandell remarks especially about the enthusiasm of men for work-relief even though there were no workmen's compensation, grievance procedures, sick leave, or Social Security benefits. In fact, she said, these projects represented "little more than forced labor." Notwithstanding these unpromising circumstances, she reports, "Most of the men employed . . . would rather do this kind of work than nothing. However, they would much prefer not to be welfare recipients at all but to work on regular jobs or train for them so that they can be self-sustaining members of society." [14]

When Welfare Rights organizations began to spring up all over the country in the late 1960's, their first demands were often for more work programs and against reduction of these programs. Even in Minnesota, where assistance benefits were then said to be the highest in the nation, the demands were for work.

But the culture that teaches about work also teaches that there are different kinds of work. Camouflages of help are sometimes too thin for their purpose. For example, a carpenter quoted by Robert Coles tells of wanting a real job; he did not want to "rake leaves" or have to get "on his belly" to get relief.

Reluctance to be—or seem to be—obviously dependent is manifested also in dogged determination to "pay one's own way"—or, at least part of it. This was evidenced by assistance-receiving mothers who were working and insisted upon contributing to the cost of day care for their children even though they were not required to do so. They did not want to "receive something for nothing." They wanted to feel that *they* were "taking care of their children" even though some of the payments averaged only about 4 cents per hour of child care. These mothers clearly "had the word," and in this instance without reinforcement from the welfare agency concerned, for it was willing to forego payment.

What was said in another context in Chapter VI about turnover rates in public assistance rolls is also relevant here, because the common conception is that the typical recipient remains on and on as if the culture—and welfare policies—were not edging him off and off. Correlations between levels of assistance rolls and seasonal variations in employment are instructive in this regard. In fact, General Assistance rolls are more closely correlated with unemployment than is unemployment compensation.[15] The culture's call to work is clearly louder than calls to "come and get it" at the welfare office.

There is, however, one startling fact in data about turnover in assistance rolls. Morgan, Wilbur J. Cohen, and their associates estimated in 1962 that no fewer than one-tenth of all Americans had been "on welfare" at some time in their lives. This was true, incidentally, of at least one gentleman of national prominence, who at this writing is governor of one of the states. The American people probably have never directly faced the fact that every tenth American—

including boys who have fought, are fighting (as this is written), or will fight for freedom, dignity, and other values abroad—is sooner or later subjected to the kinds of policies described in Chapter VI.

It seems almost unbelievable that, in a culture that claims to value so highly certain "goods," the Office of Economic Opportunity would be reporting to a committee of the United States Senate that for able-bodied but unemployed fathers receiving public assistance "pride and self-respect become luxuries which can no longer be afforded." If this is the case even with families that have the level of living underwritten by assistance (which is available to unemployed men in only a few jurisdictions), one must wonder what happens to "pride and self-respect" in areas where public policy does not even recognize men and their families as deserving food, shelter, and clothing.

Then, midway between needy persons who get nothing and those who receive assistance is that army who receive "surplus commodities only." In June 1966, for example, no fewer than 1.7 million "needy" families, which were not receiving assistance, did receive surplus foods.[16] These are provided in kind, typically require one to stand in line in public view and to carry large parcels of foodstuffs through the streets in ways often considered "stigmatizing."

The smog of public opinion about obvious dependency not only surrounds recipients in the streets but seeps into their homes.

Catherine S. Chilman found in her study of very poor families that "Negative public attitudes toward mothers who are dependent on AFDC tend to transfer to the mothers and their children, with an associated sense of failure, strong self-disparagement and hopelessness." [17] If societies stood as staunchly *for* children and families as they stand against obvious dependency, the "strengthening of family life" might be more a matter of fact and less a matter of only declared policy.

In countless autobiographies and biographies one can see how painful, even in retrospect and after the persons involved had attained success, had been earlier periods of "dependency." For instance, there is the case of Jack Dempsey, one-time heavyweight boxing champion of the world (to choose one illustration—not quite at random, but because we want to refer later to the kind of help he received). Of his earlier days he recalls:

We were never hungry. Mormons are never hungry. They keep close check on one another through the visits of Mormon "teachers." A "teacher" . . . drops in, casually, and asks how things are going. Polite and easy without prying.

. . . If he has seen or sensed a bare cupboard, it's filled before nightfall. Without comment. . . .

The Dempseys ate many a meal by grace of this silent, almost-but-not-quite-painless charity. And they ate and stayed warm that way in many a town long after Manassa was behind us.[18]

If even such help by closely knit coreligionists—given "casually," promptly, "polite and easy without prying," and "without comment"—seemed like "not-quite-painless" charity, one wonders how Dempsey and his family might have reacted if they had had to depend for survival upon less humanely administered assistance, characterized by formalism, delay, constant prying, and ceaseless cajoling.

Dick Gregory paints a more poignant picture of "the shame" of being on relief. Even his autobiography does not explain how, out of a childhood of such painful humiliation, an entertainer emerged. The humiliation, however, comes through clearly. There was, for instance, that day in grammar school when all the children were asked to report what their fathers planned to give to the Community Chest. Although Daddy had deserted the family, young Dick was prepared to report a fictitious amount and then to present it himself —out of his shoeshine money. However, when the roll was called, Gregory's name was passed over. He relates that when the teacher's attention was called to the apparent oversight, she responded:

"We are collecting this money for you and your kind, Richard Gregory. If your Daddy can give fifteen dollars you have no business being on relief. . . . And furthermore . . . we know you don't have a Daddy. . . ."

. . . I walked out of school that day, and for a long time I didn't go back very often. There was shame there.

Now there was shame everywhere. . . . There was shame in going to the Worthy Boys Annual Christmas dinner for you and your kind, because everybody knew what a worthy boy was. . . . There was shame in wearing the brown and orange and white mackinaw the welfare gave to 3,000 boys. Why'd it have to be the same for everybody so when you walked down the street the people could see you were on relief? . . . There was shame in running out to meet the relief truck. I hated that truck, full of food for you and your kind.

Just after his mother's funeral, Gregory recalls, "I . . . looked up at the sky and said: 'I'm sorry, Momma, sorry I was embarrassed because we were on relief, sorry I was ashamed of you because you weren't dressed the way other kids' mothers were dressed.' " [19]

Some may say, "Fine! The culture and relief policies certainly did a good job on those Gregorys." Others may think that instead of young Gregory's apology to his dead mother, society owed *them* some apologies. If Gregory seems to some Americans to be more hostile than humorous, perhaps experiences of the kind he describes may be responsible.

Walter Dawkins, who also grew up in a family on relief, is now serving in the War on Poverty. Ralph Matthews, Jr., reports that Dawkins recalled "that many of his neighbors lived from welfare check to welfare check but seethed with a quiet rage all the while because 'nobody wants welfare, not really, it's like being a zombie.'" [20]

The seriously disabled but fiercely independent Henry Viscardi, founder of Abilities, Inc., has already been quoted as passionately calling for self-help opportunities for disabled workers. It follows therefore that he should have disdain for the other side of the self-help coin:

We'd dispense . . . with charity drives and professional hand holders. We'd run a real shop. . . . No paternalism, no charity drives, no subsidies. Workers would be employees, not pets. Our backers would be investors, not donors. . . .
    . . . All we ask is the right to struggle.[21]

Some may think that Viscardi and his associates epitomize the best of American independence. Others may think they are pathologically resistive to help. However, a study, "Adjustment to Visible Injuries," reveals that what was most frustrating to other injured persons, too, was the need for help.[22]

An interesting light was thrown upon the reluctance to be helped following an analysis of this phenomenon in a class for social work students. One student, who had almost disbelieved the class discussion, later dropped by to say, "I see now what you mean." She had just visited a public assistance family while she was doing some research. But even before hearing what she was there for, the lady of the house barked through the partially opened door, "I don't want any of your help." The outcome of this encounter will be reported later when we come to the point that the remainder of the dialogue illuminates.

The pervasiveness, among even "lowest income" groups, of certain views about self-help and dependency is strikingly illustrated by a 1965 Gallup Poll. Representatives of this income group constituted approximately one-fourth of the entire sample. When asked if "all men on relief who are physically able to work" should be required to accept "any job offered which pays the going wage," 84 percent of the national sample favored the proposal, as did 85 percent of those in the lowest income group. Similarly, when asked if able-bodied male relief recipients should be required to work for their assistance, 82 percent of the entire sample and 79 percent of the lowest income group agreed.[23]

This recital of attitudes of disadvantaged persons toward being helped is not intended, of course, to imply that nobody wants anybody's "charity." The point, rather, is to challenge the assumption that has underlain welfare and public assistance policy for centuries, namely, that everybody wants anybody's charity and that policies and procedures must therefore be restrictive so as to curb this presumably universal tendency to "sponge." The realities of life seem to me to point in a quite different direction.

In the preceding discussion most of the examples cited were deliberately chosen to illustrate widely prevailing attitudes toward help for basic support. These, as already intimated, are probably more pronounced than attitudes toward help for less basic requirements. The people in these examples were, by definition, "poor" and often are thought to have their own subculture, in which "something for nothing" is a painless, if not an actually enjoyable, "way of life." The evidence, I believe, suggests just the opposite. Like other cultures, as we shall soon see, the American culture has done its work far "better" than many critics imply. Ironically, some of the very groups that press for illiberal and even punitive public assistance policies "in order to preserve our culture" are the very ones who least trust that culture. However, the coin carrying the messages "In Self-Help We Trust" and "In Dependence We Blush" does indeed circulate widely—even among groups whose opportunities (as suggested in Chapter IV) often make that coin, for all practical purposes, more specious than specie.

So far we have treated largely as a combined influence the power of a culture as it is reenforced by public assistance policies. This leaves unanswered the important question of whether a culture alone—not reenforced by punitive public assistance policies—could by itself do the job of communicating to even disadvantaged persons the importance a society attaches to self-help and self-support. This question, unfortunately, cannot be answered. However, several observations may be made about it.

First, it is clear that cultural values placed upon self-help are shared by many disadvantaged persons, both in the United States and elsewhere, who have had no direct experience with punitive assistance policies. This does not preclude, however, direct experience with even more punitive "hard facts of life" where there are no public assistance measures. Nor does it preclude hearsay evidence or general knowledge of what happens to others who *do* seek public aid. That considerable number of persons (in the United States, Britain, France, and elsewhere) who are unwilling to turn to others for basic support are undoubtedly deterred, at least in part, by their knowledge of how they would be treated, much as "fear of the house" in early nineteenth-century England deterred even persons in dire need from seeking help.

But, if one is concerned about self-help that (as suggested in Chapter III) is "too hurtful" to the individuals concerned, he will ask whether too high a price is being paid by men, women, and children who scrounge along on less than the society would be willing to give them. He will also ask whether tuition costs in the school of public aid are not "too high"—and "too hurtful" not only to those subjected to this schooling, but also to those kept out of the school because they are unwilling to accept, in Arthur Simon's phrase, "the onus with the bonus." Societies can hardly have things both ways—at least not simultaneously. They cannot establish floors below which they believe no one should need to fall and then make access to them so onerous that many who should take advantage of them will refuse to do so. Thus, throughout history, social support provided by societies has, ironically, gone only to those who swallowed their pride (if, indeed, they had any), while those who remained "too proud" to accept support on demeaning terms went unsung and unfed.

Perceptive souls, sensing that disadvantaged persons often share societal values but are unable to live by them, will insist, not on punishing further those who require basic support, but on opening up wide opportunities for genuine participation in the society. Perceptive men will also recognize their society's complicity in individual performance; they will acknowledge the incommensurabilities of fault and blame in interdependent societies and will therefore be unwilling to supply only upon punitive terms the basic support of people whose efforts to help themselves just do not happen to pan out as normally expected. However, those who do require basic support will not, as now, be considered so superior to others (such as corporation executives) that they do not need the stimulation of the profit motive.

To cite one more alternative to treating punitively only the obviously dependent, there is the possibility of similarly treating elites —the pace-setters and the "taste-makers" who are indolent, who are moochers or spongers, or who "succeed" only by abrogating legal and moral standards or by flaunting other social values. There is the possibility of applying to them some of the social disfavor now accorded only to the obviously dependent person.

From a historical viewpoint we can say with certainty that despite centuries of burdensome and inequitable practices, these practices have not been spectacularly successful. Perhaps the late twentieth century is "the time," and the affluent United States the place, for "a change." This would be marked by recognition of how effectively the culture has "gotten the word" about self-help all the way down to those who are most disadvantaged—and by recognition of the inequity of adding the insult of onerous assistance practices to the injury already inflicted by the broader culture. Later we shall consider ways in which the "hurt of being helped" may be assuaged —or, if one prefers, ways in which the screws of humiliation may be tightened. Even as things now stand, I cannot forget the aptness, for today, of what Tolstoy wrote in "What Shall We Do Then?": "I am sitting on a man's neck, choking him and demanding that he carry me, and, without getting off him, I assure myself and others that I am sorry for him and want to alleviate his condition by all possible means except by getting off his neck." [24]

In Other Cultures

Pride in self-support and shame in obvious dependency are by no means a monopoly of the United States and products only of the Protestant ethic. A broad viewpoint will indicate this. Before turning to it, however, it is worth noting that an eminent Catholic layman, intimately associated with efforts to help disadvantaged groups in the United States, has frequently quoted (even to congressional committees) Saint Francis as saying, "Before you go out and help the poor, you must first beg their pardon." Another phenomenon that casts doubt on the alleged potency of the Protestant ethic is the degree to which Japanese-Americans in the United States share the "do-it-yourself" and "provide-for-your-own" traditions. William Peterson, for example, has written in *The New York Times* of the achievements of Japanese-Americans in the United States: "Even in a country whose patron saint is the Horatio Alger hero, there is no parallel to this success story." [25]

In the long history of emphases in Jewish tradition upon anonymity in both giving and receiving, the "Cell of Silence" and the almsbox in the temple are only a few of the practices to alleviate the shame of the poor. [26]

In a contemporary world review of rugged independence it is noteworthy to recall what Manuel, eldest of *The Children of Sanchez*, said after crossing clandestinely from Mexico into the United States in search of work:

We were tired and hungry, but we went to look for a job in one of the bakeries. There was no work. . . . The maestro took out three pesos to give us. "Take this, boys. Drink a cup of coffee to my health." I felt humiliated, as though we were beggars or something.

"Look, maestro," I said, "we came to ask for work, not charity. I thank you from the heart, but we don't want a handout." I guess he caught on and saw the sadness we felt, because he said we could work it off the next day.[27]

When Norte Americanos contemplate the grueling daily grind of Manuel and of Lewis' other real-life characters—the constant struggle for food, the heartbreaking misadventures, the exploitation even by friends and relatives, the casual and intermittent nature of the only jobs available—they might well ask themselves whether they, in similar circumstances, could "take it." Lest Manuel be considered unique, it is noteworthy that Glen Leet, Executive Director of the Community Development Foundation, which has instituted remarkable self-help projects in Mexico, reports:

. . . Repeated drought and unemployment in some areas . . . have created conditions of distress. . . . Yet the inherent pride and independent spirit of the Mexican people make them reluctant to accept outside assistance. . . . But . . . when they found that the help given would be but a small percentage when compared with the value of their own contribution of volunteer labor and materials, their attitude changed to one of friendly cooperation.[28]

Here we may again quote from the *Child of the Dark*. It will be recalled that the writer, who lived in São Paulo, had to scrounge for bits of food and even the scraps of paper on which she wrote her memorable diary. One passage reads:

[Other mothers] . . . are supported by charity organizations.

My kids are not kept alive by the church's bread. I take on all kinds of work to keep them. And those women have to beg or even steal.[29]

In Pakistan, one might go with I. W. Moomaw to a cooperative sponsored by a welfare agency where they emphasized that the goods produced must be well-made because "Our work must sell because of its quality—not as charity." Or, one might follow Moomaw on to Korea and overhear the Korean pastor who told him that he did not "approve of giving charity except in emergencies. In the long run, the people may become embittered by charity alone." [30] In India one might meet, as did Norman Cousins, a young Indian whom he wanted to help but who refused assistance, even in the form of a loan.[31] Or one might see in New Delhi the motto of the Fellowship of the Physically Handicapped: "Not charity—but a chance."

In Vietnam, one might encounter the same reaction as that sensed by the French reporter, Max Clos, in 1964. Says Clos, "A certain anti-American feeling is developing among the Vietnamese. . . . Advice and suggestions, whether they come from friends or foes, are regarded as an intolerable insult to their national honor." [32]

In China I saw almost the same reaction. When the war ended and it was possible to bring in personnel to augment the small staff that had gone in "over the hump," a high Chinese official said to me, "Now that more workers are coming in and will be going out into the provinces, please tell them that the Chinese people are different and do not like outsiders to tell them how to meet their problems." In reply I said as politely as I could, "No. I will not tell them that. I will tell them, though, that Chinese, like any other people, do not like outsiders to tell them how to meet their problems." It is my impression that after the early days of flag-waving and flower-throwing, the presence of even liberating troops is soon quickly resented, as reminders perhaps that a country had been unable itself to resist invasion and could not without help drive out the invader.

In Sicily, Danilo Dolci, who had gone there from mainland Italy, found that his proffered help was at first rejected because, although he was also an Italian, he was regarded as an outsider.[33]

In Japan one might hear one of the nation's leading social workers, Professor Aiji Takeuchi, say, as he has in the past:

Many Japanese will say, "I don't want any of your charity." Family members requesting public assistance to which they are entitled as a legal right may be forced out of the household by other "responsible" family members as disgracing the family even though they may not be able to provide the needed help.[34]

To Americans, British attitudes toward "being helped" would seem to be quite familiar. In London during the V-bomb days of

World War II, when I was working with England's marvelously organized and humanely administered V-bomb relief services, I first sensed the depth of English passion for independence. What is more remarkable is that the discovery was in conjunction with a V-bomb "incident"—a catastrophe in the area struck—and notwithstanding the fact that catastrophes have a way of mitigating, as almost nothing else does, the hurt of being helped.

Near the devastated area one bombed-out family after another applied for the services that were available. Then a little old lady came to the desk. Not only were her clothing and hair badly disheveled, but she was covered from head to toe with plaster dust from her destroyed home. After arranging for a number of services, the Assistance Board officer gave her one of those miracle-working 5-pound notes that were handed out on the spot and obviously worked wonders in raising morale by giving resourceless people something with which to fight adversity. The officer then handed her the required chit to sign in acknowledgment of the payment. The little lady looked at the chit with a wary eye and, with pencil uncertainly poised in midair, asked, "This ain't *chirity*, is it?"

The tone—although one could not of course be sure—suggested that if it were "chirity," she wanted none of it. But, in the marvelous spirit of those London services, the officer replied sympathetically and with dignity, "*No, ma'am*. This ain't chirity." He then explained how all Londoners were in the same boat and even pointed out that in the previous week an internationally known person had been bombed out and had received emergency relief services. Convinced that no "chirity" was involved, the little lady signed and, with 5-pound note in hand and other services arranged for, walked out to begin to reconstruct her shattered world.

That our little old bombed-out lady was not the last of her breed in England is suggested by a study made by the Birmingham Council of Churches. When asked about National Assistance, a number of people, including some in relatively poor circumstances, said that they had never had any help from anywhere, or that they had always managed and would not apply if they could help it. According to a report:

One [housewife] . . . needed to be told that to apply for a supplementary pension would not be asking for "charity." In the same household, the husband, aged 75, was deaf; he had never had a deaf aid and did not know he could get one through the National Health Service. Twenty years ago, he had broken his dentures and after he had tried to mend them himself, they were pronounced beyond repair. He could not afford to replace them and had no teeth ever since. The family had no idea that dentures also could be provided.[35]

Even the National Assistance Board itself (and Parliament, too), deplored the reluctance of even needy persons to apply for assistance and in 1960 observed:

Although it is over ten years since the National Assistance Board were entrusted with the task of helping all those in need, old prejudices sometimes die hard. Some elderly people, particularly, with memories of the days of the Poor Law, may still regard applying for a supplement to their pensions as "asking for charity" and in some way hurting their self-respect.[36]

The Board then attempted, as already noted, to interpret this assistance as what we have termed a social utility. Even these moves failed of the purpose, however, and in 1966 Parliament launched a program of virtually universal Social Security benefits to replace much of the aid that had been previously supplied by the National Assistance Board. In newspaper advertisements describing the new benefits and eligibility requirements, the new Minister of Social Security added a typically British flourish, "Do please" (emphasis as in the original), after the request to apply.

In this connection, it is significant that when Sir William Beveridge was redesigning Britain's social security system during World War II, the form he decided upon for family allowances was chosen deliberately—because he feared that if they took the form of assistance and looked more like "help," they would be refused by some of the very families for whom they were intended. Similarly, the National Health Service was deliberately designed to make clear its total divorcement from "Poor Law medicine."

In France, an American observer studying that country's social security program reports, "Unmet need is not negligible. . . . French families are proud and do not like to ask for supplementary allowances (even though assistance is a right)." [37]

A German spokesman in 1961 told an audience of social welfare workers that, according to an old German proverb, "Asking costs more than buying."

Again, in citing from around the world these examples of individuals and groups that—often amidst great deprivation—have eschewed even available "help" or have struggled to pull themselves up by their *guarache* straps, *geta* cords, or leg-braces, I am not pretending that these illustrations "prove" more than that man's indomitable spirit frequently finds expression in almost unbelievable determination to live without "help." No less important than the wide-ranging suggestions of man's indomitability is the breadth of the recognition accorded to this spirit as "a good thing." Consequently, if welfare services are to avoid breaking down this high spirit—where it exists—and are to respond to the broader appreciation of it as a valuable human trait, these services must be developed with these values in mind. And certainly they must avoid, wherever possible, damaging or destroying that spirit.

So widely diffused is resistance to "being helped" that it is no exaggeration to say that in many, many circumstances it *hurts* to be helped. We have already made some observations on the unanswerable question of whether this sense of hurt results from general cultural emphases upon self-support or from reenforcement by societies of these influences by inflicting hurt upon those they purport to help. Both the cultural emphases and "hurtful" practices in giving may, in turn, stem from a pervasive lack of genuine generosity and from a prevailing reluctance, among men generally, gratuitously to help others (except those in their own families, mutual aid groups, and so on) without exacting at least a drop of blood, if not, in fact, "a pound of flesh." In any event, there are other aspects of help—and hurt. In certain circumstances, for example, it may actually help to be hurt. But we are here concerned with "the hurt of being helped."

Another observer who would agree with this view is the veteran social work leader Bertha Capen Reynolds, who included in a book she wrote a chapter entitled, "Must It Hurt to Be Helped?" [38] One might ask appositely, "Must help be made to hurt?" Other observers have gone even farther than to link help and hurt. For one, Dora Peyser, writing from experience in both Germany and Australia, speaks of "the deep-lying fear of being helped." [39] This view, seasoned with a little anger perhaps, might well have appealed to Ralph Waldo Emerson for, in his essay on "Gifts," he contended, "It is not the office of a man to receive gifts. How dare you give them? We wish to be self-sustained. We do not quite forgive a giver." [40] That this was not only an exaggerated view of a nineteenth-century New Englander, swathed in the Protestant ethic, is indicated even today in many quarters—Brazil, Egypt, and Japan, among others.[41]

The "hurt of being helped," as we shall be speaking of it, is in terms of the embarrassment, humiliation, shame, or denigration that is felt, whether deliberately imposed or not. Nowhere will we mean by "hurt" any other kind of damage done to, or suffered by, one who is helped. The "hurts" are also relative to the sorts of variables noted in Chapter V.

In this discussion we have been a great deal concerned with the hurt of being helped in relation to what we have termed basic support. We have done so deliberately because, as pointed out earlier, there are many indications that help of this kind presents rather special problems. This does not mean, however, that other kinds of help are not also embarrassing, humiliating, and hurtful.

OTHER PERSPECTIVES ON THE CONFLICTS

In the course of explaining to a social welfare audience the phenomenon that at least one-third of those who applied to casework agencies in the United States never returned after the first interview, research anthropologist David Landy declared in part: ". . . Major value orientations of American culture militate against the use of help of others in the struggle to fulfill emotional or material needs." [42]

It was exactly this reticence to seek help that led the Family Service Association of America to issue the pamphlet *The Rights of the Individual Family in a Mass Society*. It is shot through with reassurances that not only is it all right to secure help, but families have a right to it.

Although in our discussion of basic support we had occasion to report indications that it was often somewhat easier to accept medical care than bread and butter, it is noteworthy that in their survey of mental health, Gerald Gurin and his associates estimated that, although one in every four persons in the group that was studied needed help, only one in seven sought it.[43] The President's Council on Aging declared in 1963 (before Medicare was enacted) that aged persons did not get the care they needed because "they are too proud to accept charity or other outside financial help." [44] A bold physician reflected this same view when, in support of the then pending Medicare bill, he contended, "If [patients] can't pay, they're worried and lose self-respect, whether they show it or not. Nobody has the right to take away a person's dignity, not even his doctor." [45]

Before Medicare was instituted, physicians often overlooked the central point at issue, which was that although persons were getting (through clinics or donated service) the care they needed, they often deplored the terms upon which it was available. "Free choice of physician," so loudly espoused by organized medicine, becomes a mockery when the care must be free.

When Martin Wolins made his study in Berkeley, he found that 40 percent of the clients using service designed to help in cases of marital conflict felt ashamed or hesitant before using it. He also discovered that every client receiving assistance because of economic deprivation had been reluctant to apply for it; that 40 percent of the clients interviewed at a part-pay clinic reported that, prior to their first contact with it, they had been ashamed or hesitant to use it. In generalizing upon his findings and what he terms "barriers to service," Wolins writes, "Many persons in the community and even among the agency clientele still consider the use of welfare services as socially unacceptable, degrading and humiliating, though the actual use of services tends to reduce and even eliminate these attitudes." [46]

In Detroit, the study by Charles Lebeaux and Eleanor Wolf concluded that, because of the reticence of disadvantaged persons to take advantage of available services, "It is clear that the helping agencies of the city need to devise new ways of making contact with these people." [47]

Welfare agencies, knowing that their services are not used as widely as they "should be," often assume that this is because potential users do not know they are available. But the larger problem may be that they do not like the terms upon which services are available. We will present some observations on this point in later chapters.

Charlotte Towle placed these issues in broad perspective: "It may always hold that people, by and large, will be ambivalent about social work because they cannot identify with the group it traditionally has served and will continue to serve. Because of the ego threat implied, they cannot envisage themselves as needing such help." [48]

The Amish religious sect gives a novel twist to receiving help. One was not permitted to receive a favor (including even a buggy ride to church) from anyone who had been "shunned" or excommunicated. However, others could do favors for the banned person. [49] Part of the "punishment," apparently, was not only to be denied the opportunity to help, but also to suffer the "hurt" of being helped. It is quite likely that early perceptions of the "unblessedness" of receiving contributed to recognition that "It is more blessed to give than to receive."

Throughout this discussion of the hurt of being helped, the help we have had in mind is gratuitous help, which we defined earlier as excluding intrafamilial cooperation and mutual aid. We are not unmindful that even within our context there may be—and, within families and close ingroups, undoubtedly is—what Professor Henry A. Murray of Harvard included among his "Variables of Personality" and termed "Succorance" ("the tendency to cry, plead, or ask for nourishment, love, protection, or aid"). "The Succorant Need," Murray continues, "is always a sub-need, inasmuch as it is evoked in the service of some other drive: . . . Food . . . Water . . . Affiliation, and so forth." [50]

But even to grant "a need to be helped" is by no means to concede that there may not be strong preferences for, and equally strong antipathies to, help of certain kinds, under particular circumstances, and for different ends.

Whether help hurts, how much, and under what circumstances, are relative matters, of course.

Richard Cobden, in the nineteenth century, was in many ways a bold man, but never more so than when trying to make his help, as he said, "that masculine sort of charity which would inculcate . . . the love of independence, the privilege of self-respect, the disdain of being patronized, the desire to accumulate, and the ambition to rise." [51] Such agenda—challenging though they are—would probably have wide acceptance even today. However, some observers will believe that items among Cobden's agenda, such as "love of independence," will be best fostered by aggravating the hurt of dependence. Others will believe the end will be best served by assuaging that hurt so that the energy and spirit required "to rise" are not damaged but strengthened. Opinions will differ also on how best to realize Cobden's other objectives. Similarly, there are different views about what it is about help that hurts. Unfortunately, definitive knowledge of these points is in short supply. Consequently their exploration must necessarily be somewhat speculative.

DIFFICULTIES IN DIAGNOSING THE HURT OF BEING HELPED

Throughout history, sensitive souls have discerned that it hurts to be helped. This is strongly suggested by age-old rules governing constructive giving and help. The Christian religion, for example, has enjoined giving cheerfully, secretly, and generously—giving more than is asked. To be sure, these injunctions are said to find favor in heaven, but it is plausible that they reflected recognition that certain kinds of help are less embarrassing to accept and are more pleasant on earth, as well as pleasing in heaven. Anonymity in both giving and receiving and other attributes of helping that Maimonides codified in his famous "Eight Degrees of Charity" had deep roots in Jewish history and tradition. When one reflects upon these principles and recognizes that they are plausible means, even today, for alleviating the embarrassment, if not the hurt, of being helped, it is not unreasonable to surmise that these hurts were encountered in other days, too. In view of the tremendous significance attributed by all religions and by philosophers, moralists, and the like to the importance and merit of giving, it is surprising that so little attention has been accorded to its reciprocal: receiving.

Nearly 2,000 years ago, Seneca, in his essay *On Benefits,* said about as much about both giving *and* receiving as anyone has said since: "Among the numerous faults of those who pass their lives recklessly and without due reflexion . . . I should say that there is hardly any one so hurtful to society as this, that we neither know how to bestow or how to receive a benefit." [52] And society is still hurting because we still do not know.

What is amazing about the neglect of the psychology of receiving (perhaps we might call it the art of graceful receiving) is that the problem of giving and accepting favors was known to affect human relationships at least 500 years before even Seneca's day. Aristotle, for one, saw friendships as being thus affected, and observed, "Benefactors are thought to be better friends to those they have helped than the latter are to their benefactors." [53]

Without knowing it, perhaps, worldly-wise advisers borrow from Aristotle when they say, "To win a friend, don't do him a favor; get him to do you one." For example, Senator Claiborne Pell of Rhode Island has said, "The way to make a friend is to let him do you a favor. We are deluding ourselves when we think we make friends by giving aid." Then, in a rather novel way, Senator Pell translates this view into a suggestion on a point that we discuss later. In his words, "It is almost to our advantage to mask the fact we are giving aid, and to do it through the multilateral agencies." [54]

Despite the plethora of age-old folk wisdom and maxims about giving and helping, these acts have long been disturbers of human relations. Henry David Thoreau is on record as saying that if he knew that a man was on his way to help him, he would run for his life. Although this statement may seem far-fetched, Thoreau's general idea reappeared in these lines from "My Fair Lady":

> *The Lord above made man to help his neighbor,*
> *No matter where—on land or sea or foam.*

> *But, with a little bit of luck,*
> *When he comes around you won't be home.*[55]

Henry Ford is often quoted as having said, "Give the average man something and you make an enemy out of him." Mark Twain put the issue more cynically, "If you pick up a starving dog and make him prosperous, he will not bite you. This is the principal difference between a dog and a man." [56]

Similar views still prevail and are often expressed in relation to both domestic and foreign aid. Richard Carter, for example, quotes national officials of the American Red Cross as agreeing, "The easiest way to antagonize somebody is to give him something." [57] When even the epochal Marshall Plan (later judged to have been a great success) was being launched, the then Secretary of State, George C. Marshall, told a committee of the Senate, "You always get into trouble when you give." [58]

Some Americans who are sensitive on this point may find some solace in the fact that foreign-aid programs of the U.S.S.R. have had similar effects, as shown by Victor Lasky in *The Ugly Russian*. The problem is one the human race has apparently long encountered. Historian Henry Breasted quotes King Amenemhet of ancient Egypt as complaining: "He who ate my food made insurrection; he to whom I gave my hand aroused fear therein." [59] Although many are quick to generalize about "making enemies when you give," not much is heard about a point we shall discuss later: making enemies by *not* helping others when one can.

Anyone who doubts the extent of problems in interpersonal relationships—problems that are caused by the abrasiveness of some giving that makes receiving painful or that are caused by the ungraciousness of some receiving that makes giving disappointing— might find it instructive to follow newspaper columns that give answers to letters about personal problems. These used to be thought of as "advice for the lovelorn" but are often "advice for the giftlorn." It was problems of this kind that led a Los Angeles minister to take as a sermon topic: "Forgive Us Our Christmases as We Forgive Those Who Christmas Against Us."

Although giving and receiving, helping and being helped, can indeed disturb human relations, little is definitively known about what it is about help that is often hurtful and what circumstances aggravate or assuage the hurt. However, we noted in Chapter V a number of variables that seem to be operative. We have few guides to diagnosis, unfortunately, and fewer X-rays to confirm what hypotheses we have. As a result, prescriptions to ease the hurts are difficult to write. Consequently, in exploring possibly relevant factors, we must deal largely with conjecture. Behind this conjecture, however, stand many observable phenomena. Even these are susceptible of quite different interpretations, which suggests that we have not yet discovered the circumstances under which a given interpretation is correct.

Among the many uncertainties with which we will be concerned, at least one point seems clear: When there is hurt in being helped, it is highly relative—relative to who is helped, who is the helper, the nature of the help, the circumstances giving rise to the need for help, and many other factors. What might be balm under some circumstances might be a bomb under others. Conversely, what might in one instance be a deadly potion might be a welcome poultice in another.

Among the few observers who have analyzed in any depth these phenomena in the welfare field is Dora Peyser, whom we have quoted on the "deep-lying fear of being helped." Her concept of help includes the help that family members give one another, mutual aid, and other types that we have here excluded from our own definition of gratuitous help, with which we have been mostly concerned. Nevertheless, even with her broader view, Dr. Peyser declares:

To be dependent on help is for the normal person a humiliation, a trauma to the ego. "It hurts their pride," as is often said. On the other hand, to be able to give raises the helper's self-esteem and enhances his social reputation. . . .

. . . Every help-relationship has by itself the tendency of creating a from-above-downwards position [which, she recalls, was what Aristotle saw it to be]. The helper is above the receiver.

It is exactly this "being pressed into the unwanted, inferior position of the recipient . . . ," says Dr. Peyser, "that is responsible for the "deep-lying fear of being helped." One of her major concerns, therefore, is the ways—symbolized, for example, by some religious groups through the washing of feet—by which "the from-above-downwards pressure of the helping relationship" can be upset.[60] Our own interest in correcting what we see as the imbalance in giver-receiver relationships is discussed in Chapters VIII, IX, and X.

Before further analyzing the hurt of being helped, I cannot forbear mention of what—to both the individuals concerned and to at least some members of their societies—must be the hurt of having a social system within which one does not even ask for help because he thinks it utterly unlikely to be forthcoming. For example, some American listeners were probably startled by a radio newscast in 1965 about a child in the Midwest. The child, who was suffering from polio, was being kept alive at home in an iron lung. Because his family could not meet the electric bill, the electricity was shut off. The mother then kept the boy alive by using the emergency handpump, but after a number of hours of pumping, fell asleep. When she awoke, the boy was dead. When friends, deeply hurt that such a tragedy had occurred, asked why she had not told the utility company of her plight, she replied that it had never occurred to her that they would restore the power. The company quickly said that if they had known the circumstances, the power would of course never have been interrupted.

The culture shrieking, "Help yourself," "Stand on your own two feet," "Do your own pumping," had obviously done its job, perhaps overdone it. While the hurt of being helped may be born of such a culture, it produces also other hurts—to individuals and to communities—when the do-it-yourself theme is overplayed.

Probably the greatest single difficulty in attempting to diagnose any hurt of being helped is to distinguish it from the hurt of *needing* help. How does one distinguish between, say, the "pinch of poverty" and whatever "hurt" may be felt when that poverty is relieved? Is the hurt in the disease or the remedy? With his eye upon "the Hungry World," I. W. Moomaw often speaks of "the shame of hunger." If food were given to appease this hunger, how would one ever isolate any "shame" that is felt in "being helped" from that already felt about the hunger?

Nearly 2,000 years ago, Seneca put his finger on this problem when he wrote, "Think what torture it must have been for me, even if I receive your help, to have stood in need of it." [61] Exactly this "torture" of standing in need of help has led humane individuals throughout history to work for improved social conditions, so that people could meet their own requirements in ways that are more widely approved than "help" has been.

Uncertainty About the True Nature of "Gifts" and "Help"

One reason that being helped is so differentially viewed and therefore gives rise to value conflicts is that helping and giving, for all the nobility of their birth in religion and high principle, have been very careless over the ages about the company they have kept.

"Gifts" and "help" have, from time to time, merged almost impercep-
tibly with purchases, bribery, and manipulation. Consequently, unless there is absolute clarity in the minds of *both* the "giver" and the
"receiver" (the helper and the helpee) about the real nature of any
particular "gift" (or help), this is likely to be variously interpreted.

"GIFTS" AS A MEDIUM OF EXCHANGE: In primitive societies especially, "exchange of gifts" is indistinguishable from business
transactions. In fact, social scientists frequently refer to these ex-
changes as "silent trade." Yet this phenomenon is found not only
among primitive peoples. This may be seen in our discussion earlier
about value propagation by purchase.

John H. Patterson, who instituted a gigantic industrial welfare
program in his National Cash Register plant, was forthright enough
to say of his concern for the welfare of his employees, "It pays."

It was on exactly this point that George M. Pullman went
wrong, because he sought to portray as "industrial welfare" and as
philanthropy what his "hands" bitterly condemned as "industrial
hellfare" and as "philanthropy at four per cent." In retrospect, it is
not surprising that the town of Pullman was the scene of one of
America's bitterest labor strikes. For all his "good intentions," Pullman failed to distinguish between "business" and "philanthropy."

After the demise of the paternalistic and manipulative industrial welfare programs of the nineteenth and early twentieth centuries, there was a resurgence of industry-centered welfare programs in the United States during and after World War II. These,
however, tended to be not unilateral devices susceptive to manipulation of employees, but joint industry-union programs governed by
contracts between labor and management.

But Pullman and Patterson were by no means the first or the
last to attempt to "buy" pacification. Indeed, even today, industrial
welfare programs (and social workers associated with them) in
Latin America are widely believed to be, in reality, instruments to
thwart the unionization of workers. Some years ago this seemed so
great a problem in France that social workers in industry were given
protection from discharge unless both management and workers
agreed. Moreover, attempting to "buy" pacification is an old human
custom. In many parts of the world—ancient Athens, China, and
India, among others—states have sought to "buy up" the support of
dissidents by the distribution of gifts—a purpose hardly alien to
modern foreign aid programs. In older times, interestingly, such
gifts went not to the "middle masses" but to smaller segments of the
population—the very rich and the very poor—with the view, per-

haps, that the rich were a source of needed support and the poor a possible threat.[62]

These considerations raise the perplexing problem of the degree to which modern social welfare services should be viewed as "buying" perpetuation of the status quo. One need not go to the lengths of an Adolf Hitler or an Eva Perón, who deliberately used welfare services to promote their nefarious systems of social control, to recognize that welfare services, when they bandage the wounds inflicted by any social order, may be diverting attention from needed changes in it. Naturally, vested interests may like to see an established order further entrenched by gift-giving, whereas advocates of social change may view such gifts more skeptically. On these grounds Communists in various places have opposed "welfare" measures lest these delay "the revolution." When is a "gift" a gift? And when is it the price of a "purchase"?

Closely related to "gifts" that are more like purchase prices than true beneficence are other types of "giving" that also smack of marketlike transactions. Apart from giving that is intended to enhance the privilege, prestige, and power of the givers is that calculated to increase their profits. Cases in point are "gifts" whose cost is more than offset for the "giver" by tax savings and the "philanthropies" of corporations that are clearly in their own self-interest. Richard Eells, who has served as director of Public Policy Research for the General Electric Company, has urged that such contributions be thought of not as philanthropy but as "prudential investment." [63] But it is in the foreign aid programs of America and other countries that self-serving ends are most apparent—apparent because of public discussion. Even the broadly humane Paul G. Hoffman, who has been Managing Director of the United Nations Special Fund and been identified with foreign aid programs of the United States, has said, "The moral and political reasons for assisting underdeveloped nations are compelling enough by themselves. But there are solid business reasons as well." [64] Other Americans, and leaders in other countries too, have stressed the economic advantage of their foreign aid programs.[65]

These claims that "trade follows the gift," as once it followed "the flag," give rise abroad to all kinds of questions. "Why not frankly call the *Alianza para el Progreso* the *Alianza para el Esso* (Esso meaning, of course, Standard Oil)?" Or, as a Greek social worker recently asked, "Why call it 'foreign aid'? Why not *call* it 'aid to American business'?"

If foreign aid were forthrightly acknowledged to be trade promotion—like distribution of soap samples from door to door—and if the recipients were not expected to act as if they had received a gift (to say nothing of showing gratitude)—many problems surrounding foreign aid would be dissolved. What plays the mischief with these programs is that they are interpreted at home as preempting future markets abroad, but are expected to be seen abroad as "gifts."

To countries that clamor for "trade not aid," and ask not for "help" but for stabilization of the prices of their raw materials, for flexibility in currency exchange, and for lower tariff barriers, continued "aid" that further entrenches the already dominant trade position of the prosperous nations understandably appears as a hindrance to their own economic expansion. Also, to the extent that they see existing trade arrangements as "unjust," any aid they may be given is seen less as a "gift" than as inadequate compensation for the "injustices" perpetrated against them. When I asked not long ago in South America about the reaction to a particular "gift" from the United States, the response was, "So you give us a school. When are you going to pay us for the rest of the oil you took?" More recently, the Archbishop of Recife, Dom Helder Camara, who received the René Sand Award of the International Conference of Social Work in 1962, said:

For internal use, capitalism in the United States is twenty-first century capitalism. But for foreign use, it is nineteenth century capitalism. The position of the Soviet Union is the same—very selfish. You both take with the left hand what you give with the right. . . .

. . . Justice would be to give each person not only aid . . . but to pay adequately for his products.[66]

When he was with the Economic Cooperation Administration, Asher Brynes, former consultant to Paul Hoffman, entitled his book on American foreign aid *We Give to Conquer*. One can well understand why he chose this title.

In moral terms, expectations of returns from one's gifts would appear to be beyond question. "Give, and it shall be given unto you; good measure, pressed down . . . running over." (Luke 11:38.) But it is another matter when—for individuals or nations—"giving" displaces equity, when Micah's ordering of "justice" and "mercy" is reversed and "mercy" precludes "justice," or when narrow self-interest works against the interests of others. A recipient can hardly be expected to view as a "gift" something given primarily to enhance the privileges, prestige, power and—like soap samples that are distributed from door to door—the profits of the "giver" at the expense of similar advantages for the receiver. "Enlightened" self-interest that takes into account the interests of others, too, presents fewer problems. Thus, effects of self-interested giving are governed by how narrowly—or broadly—a giver sees his "enlightened" self-interest extending. On this point, to quote Paul Hoffman again because of his wide experience in both national and international aid programs:

The basic principle of foreign aid—to new and old nations alike—is that such aid has no chance for lasting success unless its *purpose* is one which the countries themselves can wholeheartedly share—namely, to strengthen each of them so that it will be genuinely independent. . . . A program with any narrower goal would be bad politics, bad psychology and bad morals, and would fail even if it were good economics.[67]

In passing, it may not be inappropriate to question whether such a shared purpose, shared by givers and receivers, may not be equally relevant to domestic assistance (welfare) programs. But, questions of one's "purpose" hinge upon who and what one thinks himself to be—a question that will be pursued in Chapter VIII.

"GIFTS" AS BRIBES: A "gift" may be a bribe. Uncertainty on this score has driven otherwise estimable men out of public service —even men within the White House. Vicuna coats, deep-freezes— are they gifts or bribes? The calculus here is a difficult one and is heightened by the importance of avoiding even "the appearance of evil," as sages have long recognized.[68]

Willy Brandt, who was long mayor of Berlin, tells in his biography how, when he was eight years old, he secured two loaves of bread from one of the directors of the factory in which his grandfather worked; the employees, however, were then on strike. Willy was ordered to take the bread back because, the grandfather said, "A striker accepts no gifts from his employer. We will not let ourselves be bribed by our enemy." [69]

One must still question whether welfare services even today— though possibly not intentionally designed to do so—may not be absorbing the shock of social injustice so that their intended beneficiaries are invited to "settle for them" rather than to seek the more fundamental justice to which they might rightfully be entitled.

GIFTS AS TOOLS OF MANIPULATION: Bribery, in turn, merges into manipulation. This is likely to be somewhat more open-ended, however. A bribe is likely to be aimed at securing a specific and defined end. Manipulation, on the other hand, may be effected by creating a more diffuse sense of obligation, not necessarily to be "cashed in" for a predesignated response, but to be drawn upon "as needed."

The expectation that giving may entail obligations is widely recognized: "Who pays the piper, calls the tune." "Whose bread I eat, his song I sing." This is widely assumed whether the "pay" and "bread" are viewed as "purchase prices," "bribes," or "gifts." But difficulties arise when one does not know what tune he may be called upon to sing or play—or when. "America"? the "Marseillaise"? civil rights songs? anti-civil rights songs? Some other song?

That a giver should attempt through his "gifts" to control others is not as surprising as it sometimes seems—not if one recalls the phenomenon of attempts of employers to control employees even when they presumably give full value in return for their wages.

Problems encountered in getting one's way through gifts are closely related, obviously, to what has already been said (Chapter II) about value propagation through coercion. And the more basic the gift, the more difficult it is to refuse it, and the greater, therefore, the duress and the more acute these problems become.

Whether many who have manipulated others through "help" have ever savored the worldly wisdom of Henry Taylor is uncertain. Nevertheless, many have employed his methods. Writing in 1836 on how to get ahead in politics, Taylor spelled out how not only giving but the pace of giving could be made to serve one's political interests.[70] Taylor's views are strangely reminiscent of those expressed a couple of centuries earlier by the Spanish moralist and novelist Baltasar Gracian, who advised in 1653: "Create dependents. . . . He who knows, desires more that men shall need him than thank him." [71]

In more recent times a Pennsylvania political boss is quoted as saying, "Take care of your people and your people will take care of you." [72] In fact, it may be that the clarity and singularity of purpose behind relief and other help given by political organizations (such as New York's Tammany Hall, which is said to have been built upon it) were responsible for their apparent popularity.

One social work leader likes to tell about a young delinquent who once turned on him and demanded, "Say, what's your racket?" The social worker replied, "Just keep your nose clean. Keep out of trouble." The *quo* to follow the *quid* was clear, the bargain made, and the "help" accepted.

The question "What's your racket?" appears to withstand sea change. In 1961 a student in India asked about United States aid,

"You Americans, what do you care? Why should you help us? What tricks have you up your sleeve?" [73]

Frederick G. Friedmann, in describing broad-scale development projects in Italy, comments:

Although the peasants of Southern Italy do not always understand the plans and motives of those who . . . have taken up their cause, they do seem to realize that, in general, human solidarity is not the outstanding motive. This helps to strengthen the peasants' traditional attitude of suspicion toward would-be benefactors.[74]

George Kimble explains an East African proverb as "a comment on the widespread 'dash' system in which every favor has its price." [75]

Yet, as poignant a story of extortion as one can read is that told by William and Charlotte Wiser in *Behind Mud Walls*. Even the smallest favors asked by Indian villagers of postmen, petty officials, and others were subject to exorbitant charges.[76] But societies tend to react against this kind of exploitation and manipulation. As a result, laws, civil service regulations, and a variety of ethical codes are developed to bring it under control.

As long as gifts and help came from highly individualized sources (such as a community's wealthiest citizen or its single industry), it was to be expected that recipients of this bounty would be beholden to their benefactor. When entire communities began to look after their own, the more individualized control was broken. We once spoke of "vest pocket" welfare agencies, meaning those that were so dependent upon one or a few benefactors that they were completely under their control. With the "spreading of the control," by transferring welfare services to government (in which all would have a vote), or by organizing Community Chests in which voices other than those of the few biggest donors could be heard, the possibility of manipulation of beneficiaries by single benefactors was reduced. With so many wills to be served, the danger of having to submit to any single will was minimized. "Lady Bountiful" had to share with ladies less bountiful her previously unchallenged authority. Incidentally, the central problem posed by Lady Bountiful in her day was not her bounty but the fact that she was really not a lady. Her condescension toward those she purported to help squared badly with the behavior expected of ladies.

Even broadly based programs that dilute the control that any one individual may have over the disposition of his gift do not, however, wholly escape the likelihood that they may be used manipulatively. In Chapter VI we saw this difficulty as reflected in public assistance programs in the United States.

In terms of the world at large, many nations clearly prefer multilateral to unilateral aid programs. In the latter, it can hardly be expected that a receiving nation will not become beholden to the "giver." In a discussion of this problem, Chief S. O. Adebo of Nigeria once declared,

Aid designed to promote the exports of the donor is bad aid. Aid that is intended directly or indirectly to bribe the recipient into being a satellite or fellow-traveler is bad aid. Aid that is given with an air of condescension is also bad aid.

. . . There is no doubt that, given the choice, recipient countries prefer international channels of aid to bilateral.[77]

In multilateral programs, the possibility of forced submission to the will of any one nation is reduced. David Owen of the United Nations Secretariat makes much of this point and goes further, saying, "Aid from the United Nations must be known to have no strings whatever attached—not even United Nations strings." [78] Professor Gunnar Myrdal, in *Beyond the Welfare State*, has underlined on the same grounds the advantages of multilateral as distinguished from unilateral aid.[79]

Among critics of unilateral aid programs of the United States is Asher Brynes. In *We Give to Conquer*, he contends, "All unilateral foreign aid to poorer nations, and this is the only kind ever given by Soviet Russia, is essentially imperialistic. It seeks to create, maintain, and defend spheres of influence and thus under the guise of philanthropy it carries on the old statecraft in a new way." United States aid to the Dominican Republic in 1965 constituted, according to Brynes, "A striking example of the difficulties of control by handout." In passing, it is noteworthy that this critic proposes (as do other observers) that administrative responsibility for aid be separated from that for control (which Brynes calls "diplomatic bribery"). The reasons for this are, of course, similar to those advanced (see Chapter VI) for separating assistance and "service" functions under public assistance programs.[80]

Another observer, Professor Morton A. Kaplan, Chairman of the University of Chicago Committee on International Relations, who decries use of aid for purposes of manipulation, argues the case thus:

Attempts to condition aid on foreign-policy support confuse the purpose of the aid, injure the national pride of the aided nations, and eventually undercut the purposes of the aid either by identifying local regimes with the United States in ways that alienate them from their bases of local support, or by driving such regimes into anti-American positions.[81]

Gifts with strings attached are probably as old as any gifts. To what was perhaps the first recorded gift—the fruits of the Garden of Eden, given to Adam and Eve—a historic and ultimately fateful string was affixed: "But of the fruit of the tree which is in the midst of the garden . . . ye shall not eat."

Strings attached to gifts may be perfectly obvious, or they may be invisible—at least to the recipient. Or there may be "ex post facto" strings; not even the givers may be aware of them at the moment of giving, but they may be brought into the open if "gifts" do not effect what they are supposed to. "Don't burn down any more of our embassies if you want more aid" (although the matter of embassy-burning had not come up at the time a gift was made). Or— a church that may not be clearly aware of its reasons for establishing a service center in a slum area may lose interest and close it if the community fails to found a church or at least a Sunday school.

Criticism of charity, philanthropy, and welfare services as "something for nothing" perhaps reflects interest in possible manipulation—getting not only "something" for one's gift, but getting explicitly what one wants in return for it. On a very elemental level, one can see this mechanism in the panhandler's request for money "for a cup of coffee." A highly suspicious person, not begrudging the coffee, might refuse to give any money but be willing to lead the panhandler to a lunch counter, order and pay for the coffee, and depart. Close supervision of one's gifts may reflect a fear of "being suckered" by those one succors.* It takes a broad man to help another unconditionally, without strings, even ex post facto strings, which hold back future gifts because one disapproves of the use made of a past gift. This phenomenon explains the common saying that "beggars can't be choosers." It is not so much that "beggars" lack capacity to choose as that "givers"—determined to get from their gifts exactly what they want from them—insist upon doing all the choosing and preempt the choices. When this occurs, it under-

---

* Although we have been concentrating here upon manipulation by givers, we recognize that receivers (and beggars, notoriously) manipulate those from whom they want contributions. Historically, perhaps the most dramatic example of this problem was the reaction of Frenchmen to the *cours des miracles* in fourteenth-century Paris. This was a section of the city to which apparently blind, disabled, or otherwise handicapped beggars would return every night after begging in other quarters of the city. Upon their return they miraculously recovered from their "disabilities."

lines of course the "powerlessness of the poor" about which much is being said these days and to which we will return later.

Dangers of (and possibilities for) manipulation through "gifts" are heightened by the sense of obligation that many feel when they have been helped by others. Many years ago Professor Henry Sidgwick identified what he termed the "impatience of obligation" sensed by one who had been done a substantial favor. Jane Addams spoke of "that irksome sense of obligation" one feels when a substantial benefit is conferred.

Thus, what cultures teach about reciprocation—"returning the favor"—plays directly into the hands of any who want to exploit the resulting sense of obligation. The strength of this force is not to be lightly dismissed. Inherent in it is a grave danger or, depending upon one's values, a great opportunity. As Professor Briar, Mrs. Mc-Cabe, and others have shown, assistance recipients are often so thoroughly attuned to their culture that they accept as a matter of course the close surveillance and control that they assume to be proper concomitants of "being aided." To some observers this forfeiting of self-direction seems more deplorable than the behavior that might result if such controls were not exercised. Other observers will say, "Good. We're lucky they don't put up more of a fight and resist being 'kept in line.' "

In later chapters we shall discuss channels into which the sense of obligation to reciprocate favors may be constructively directed. In the meantime it is sufficient to point out that welfare agencies not uncommonly find themselves caught in still another "middle": between beneficiaries who feel a sense of obligation and supporters of the agencies, who, having contributed, may want to see their gifts effect an end beyond the ends that the agencies ostensibly serve.

In passing we might note that the ancients' recognition of the importance of the anonymity of *receivers* may have been inspired in part by recognition that this anonymity reduced opportunities for manipulation. Yet, contrary to common supposition, anonymity in giving does not necessarily preclude control, as any parent can testify. "Better not pout, better not cry, Santa Claus is comin' to town."

Those who oppose use of welfare services to manipulate beneficiaries may well regret the passing of the day when givers expected that they would be rewarded "in heaven" for their benefactions. Those who want their reward in the here and now often cannot resist using their gifts as devices to get what they want through manipulation.

In the private sector, the problem of possible manipulation may be encountered in sectarian agencies. These and their respective constituencies may see welfare services not only as ends in themselves, but also as means for proselytizing or for hanging on to wavering adherents who, however, may not want to be hung on to.

In the public sector, one of the most notable fights against manipulation of beneficiaries was waged by Harry L. Hopkins during the Great Depression. This fight eventuated in the "unrestricted money payment" discussed in Chapter VI. Critics of this principle seem less concerned with the democratic principles at stake than with interest in manipulating public assistance payments to secure conformity with particular behavior and buying patterns.

The inescapable corollary of manipulation by givers is, of course, that receivers are treated as "objects"—or, as Dr. Bernard L. Diamond calls them, "non-persons" [82]—controlled by givers' strings. And, it might be added, by the strings of givers who, in theory, espouse "self-help," "self-determination," and the like. Giver-power similarly underscores receiver-powerlessness, incapacity to resist manipulation, particularly if a wolf is at the door or duress is otherwise present. Inability to be "one's own man" is in large measure responsible for current outcries about the "powerlessness of the poor," which will be discussed in Chapter VIII. Moreover, suspicion that "givers" are employing welfare measures to serve their own interests leads even persons who could benefit from them to avoid them.

To reinforce protections against manipulation, A. Delafield Smith has persistently advocated recognizing, as a defined right, the claim of needy persons upon society for support. He said:

There is only one proved method of avoiding the growth of the sense of dependency in company with any increased reliance upon proffered services. That method is to make him who is dependent the legal master of that on which he depends. The will retains its natural prerogatives when its needs are met through the exercise of a legal right.

. . . Law should teach us that it is the fact of having a legal right to what we need rather than the fact of having produced it or secured it by our own efforts, that furnishes the primary condition for preserving human dignity and independence.[83]

If a culture reflects disdain for "something for nothing," it is not improbable that to be bought, bribed, or manipulated in return for some benefit may, in such a culture, actually make acceptance of that benefit "less-hurtful" than if it were purely gratuitous. One may question, though, whether there are not more constructive ways of lifting from welfare services the onus of appearing to be "something for nothing."

Added to all other complexities of problems noted here is the one that persons who sense no hurt in being bought, bribed, or manipulated present a greater social problem than those who do feel thus hurt.

As we have said before, a society cannot easily or justly have things both ways—not simultaneously, at any rate. It can hardly expect intended beneficiaries of welfare services to embrace in their daily lives such values as self-respect, self-direction, and independence, if, at the same time, it employs its welfare services to keep beneficiaries hopping to tunes called by the alleged providers of these services. Guaranteeing to people a *right* to at least their basic requirements—whatever the policy with respect to more sophisticated values—could remove the element of duress, which makes manipulation particularly suspect. Such manipulation—when people's basic requirements are at stake—smacks of trafficking in flesh and blood. Humane and sensitive spirits therefore welcome the prospect of assured social support of needy persons—as a right— wholly dissociated from attempts to use welfare services as a means of control. On the other hand, those who want to exploit the sense of obligation that is quite naturally absorbed from a culture by recipients of gifts will find in their "gifts" ready instruments for buying, bribery, and manipulation. The ancient Athenians, Chinese, Indians, and Romans used "gifts" in this way, as Hitler and Perón did in recent times, as the Mafia and many political bosses do today.

:: Notes
and
References

1. Alice R. McCabe, "Forty Forgotten Families," *Public Welfare*, XXIV (April 1966), 168. Among numerous sources, see Juanita L. Cogan, *Employability Planning in Public Welfare Agencies* (Washington, D.C.: Welfare Administration, Department of Health, Education, and Welfare, 1967), especially Appendix, pp. 37–153.

2. Scott Briar, "Welfare from Below: Recipients' Views of the Public Welfare System," *California Law Review*, 54 (May 1966), 375. Also available in Jacobus ten Broek and the editors of *California Law Review*, under the title *The Law of the Poor* (San Francisco: Chandler, 1966).

3. Wilbur J. Cohen and Sydney E. Bernard, eds., *The Prevention and Reduction of Dependency* (Ann Arbor: Washtenaw County Department of Social Welfare, 1961), p. 88.

4. Charles Lebeaux and Eleanor Wolf, *Studies in Change and Renewal in an Urban Community, "515": A Study of a Low-Income Negro Area* (Detroit: Wayne State University, 1965), Vol. I, Part 11, pp. 81, 78.

5. Justine Fixel and Kermit Wiltse, "A Study of the Administration of the ADC Program," *ADC: Problem and Promise* (Chicago: American Public Welfare Association, ca. 1960), p. 34.

6. *Annual Report, 1963–1964* (New York: Community Service Society of New York, 1965), pp. 9, 11, 18, 12.

7. Arthur R. Simon, *Faces of Poverty* (St. Louis: Concordia, 1966).

8. Joseph P. Lyford, *The Airtight Cage: A Study of New York's West Side* (New York: Harper & Row, 1966), pp. 66–67.

9. Roul Tunley, *The American Health Scandal* (New York: Harper & Row, 1966), pp. 60–61.

10. See Hubert H. Humphrey, *War on Poverty* (New York: McGraw-Hill, 1964), p. 107, and *The New York Times*, October 29, 1964.

11. James N. Morgan, Martin H. David, Wilbur J. Cohen, and Harvey E. Brazer, *Income and Welfare in the United States* (New York: McGraw-Hill, 1962), p. 217.

12. Reese Cleghorn, "Appalachia—Poverty, Beauty and Poverty," *The New York Times Magazine*, April 25, 1965, p. 126. See also Cogan, *op. cit.*, which, like many other sources, reflects the pride of children when a father (or a mother) goes to work and the family goes "off relief."

13. As quoted by Andrew R. N. Truelson, *The Economic Opportunity Act and Public Welfare* (Washington, D.C.: U. S. Department of Health, Education, and Welfare, ca. 1965), p. 8. See also "Why Do They Call Us Reliefers?" *Public Aid in Illinois* (September 1965), pp. 7, 8, and *The Poor Speak*

(Columbus: Ohio Council for Health and Welfare, 1966), p. 4. (Mimeographed.)

14. Betty Mandell, "The Crime of Poverty," *Social Work,* 11 (January 1966), 15.

15. See, for example, C. T. Brehm, "The Demand for General Assistance Payments," *American Economic Review,* 54 (1964), 1002–1018. See also John M. Lynch, "Effect of Seasonal Variation in Employment Opportunities on Unemployed-Parent-Segment of Aid to Families with Dependent Children," *Welfare in Review,* 2 (May 1964), 10–14.

16. Data derived from *Health, Education, and Welfare Indicators* (September 1966), p. S-25.

17. Catherine S. Chilman, *Growing Up Poor* (Washington, D.C.: Government Printing Office, 1966), p. 7.

18. Jack Dempsey, *Dempsey, By the Man Himself,* as told to Bob Considine and Bill Slocum (New York: Simon and Schuster, 1960), pp. 16–17.

19. Dick Gregory, with Robert Lipsyte, *Nigger: An Autobiography* (New York: Dutton, 1964), pp. 45–46, 97, 103.

20. As reported by Ralph Matthews, Jr., " 'Nobody Wants Welfare!' A Profile of Newark's Blazer Training Program," *Communities in Action,* 1 (May 1966), 15.

21. Henry Viscardi, Jr., *Give Us the Tools* (New York: Eriksson-Taplinger, 1959), pp. 1–2, 14–15, 266, 178–179.

22. Gloria Landieu, Eugenia Hanfman, and Tamara Dembo, "Studies in Adjustment to Visible Injuries: Evaluation of Help by the Injured," *Journal of Abnormal and Social Psychology,* 42 (1947), 169–192. With respect to the need for another kind of help, see Delwin M. Anderson and Frank Kiesler, M.D., "Helping Toward Help: The Intake Interview," *Social Casework,* XXV (February 1954), 72–76; and with respect to maternity clinics, see Roul Tunley, "America's Unhealthy Children: An Emerging Scandal," *Harper's Magazine,* May 1966, especially p. 42. See also Jona Michael Rosenfeld, "Strangeness Between Helper and Client: A Possible Explanation of Non-Use of Available Professional Help," *Social Service Review,* XXXVIII (March 1964), 17–25; and Elvira Hughes Brigg, "The Application Problem: A Study of Why People Fail to Keep First Appointments," *Social Work,* 10 (April 1965), 71–78.

"Resistance" to use of welfare services has long been recognized as a problem and is widely discussed. See, for example, Alice Overton, "Serving Families Who Don't Want Help," *Social Casework,* XXXIV (July 1953), 304–309; Grace Dickstein, Priscilla H. Young, and Herman Levin, "Helping Applicants Become Clients," *Child Welfare,* XL (December 1961), 1–6, 15; Arthur Leader, "The Problem of Resistance in Social Work," *Social Work,* 3 (April 1958), 19–23; Ruth Michaels, "Giving Help to Resisting Patients," *Social Work,* 1 (October 1956), 76–83; Sidney Love and Herta Mayer, "Going Along with Defenses in Resistive Families," *Social Casework,* XL (February 1959), 69–74; George Levinger, "Continuance in Casework and Other Helping Relationships," *Social Work,* 5 (July 1960), 40–51.

23. George Gallup, "Public Backs Tighter Relief Rules," reported in the *Los Angeles Times,* January 24, 1965. See also Lebeaux and Wolf, *op. cit.*

24. Leo Tolstoy, "What Shall We Do Then?" *The Complete Works of Count Tolstoy* (Boston: Dana Estes, 1904), Vol. XVII, pp. 96–97.
25. See William Peterson, *The New York Times*, January 9, 1966. See also Mamoru Iga, "Relation of Suicide Attempt and Social Structure in Kamakura, Japan," *International Journal of Social Psychiatry*, 12 (1966), 221–232.
26. See, for example, Louis Mann, "Altruism," *The Universal Jewish Encyclopedia* (New York: Universal Jewish Encyclopedia, 1939), Vol. I, p. 214.
27. Oscar Lewis, *The Children of Sanchez: Autobiography of a Mexican Family* (New York: Knopf and Random House, 1961), p. 327.
28. Glen Leet, "Partnership Across the Border," *World Reporter* (Norwalk, Conn.: Community Development Foundation, Fall 1963), pp. 1, 2.
29. Carolina Maria de Jesus, *Child of the Dark*, David St. Clair, tr. (New York: Dutton, 1962), pp. 24, 49, 50.
30. I. W. Moomaw, *Crusade Against Hunger: The Dramatic Story of the World-Wide Antipoverty Crusade of the Churches* (New York: Harper & Row, 1966), p. 137.
31. Norman Cousins, "Incident in India," *The Saturday Review*, July 2, 1955, p. 39.
32. Max Clos, "5,000 Vietnamese Students Study—in Paris," *The New York Times Magazine*, December 6, 1964, p. 132.
33. As reported by James McNeish, *Fire Under the Ashes: The Life of Danilo Dolci* (London: Hodder and Stoughton, 1965). Similar suggestions of difficulty that "outsiders" encounter in their efforts to help others may be found in Velma Adams, *The Peace Corps in Action* (Chicago: Follett Publishing, 1964); in I. W. Moomaw, *The Challenge of Hunger: A Program for More Effective Foreign Aid* (New York: Frederick A. Praeger, 1966); D. Spencer Hatch (one of the earliest proponents of what has since been popularized as Community Development) and Geoffrey Cumberlege, the classic *Toward Freedom from Want: From India to Mexico* (London: Oxford University Press, 1949).
34. See also Thomas B. Morgan, *Among the Anti-Americans* (New York: Holt, Rinehart and Winston, 1967), p. 69.
35. *Responsibility in the Welfare State?* (Birmingham, England: The Birmingham Council of Christian Churches, 1961), pp. 33, 42, 28. See also Audrey Harvey, *Casualties of the Welfare State* (London: Fabian Society, 1962), p. 8. Another brochure that is relevant in the present context is Howard Glennerster, *National Assistance: Service or Charity?* (London: Fabian Society, 1962). See also Maurice Bruce, *The Coming of the Welfare State* (London: Batsford, 1961).
36. *Help for Those in Need* (London: National Assistance Board, 1960), p. 4.
37. Alvin L. Schorr, *Social Security and Social Services in France* (Washington, D.C.: Social Security Administration, U. S. Department of Health, Education, and Welfare, 1965), p. 28.
38. Bertha Capen Reynolds, *Social Work and Social Living: Explorations in Philosophy and Practice* (New York: Citadel, 1951), pp. 13–34.
39. Dora Peyser, *The Strong and the Weak: A Sociological Study* (Sydney, Australia: Currawong, 1951), p. 8.

40. Ralph Waldo Emerson, *The Complete Essays and Other Writings* (New York: Random House, 1940), p. 403.
41. See, for example, Morgan, *op. cit.*, pp. 12, 19, 21, 111, *i.a.*, and Lawrence H. Fuchs *"Those Peculiar Americans": The Peace Corps and the American Character* (New York: Meredith, 1967), pp. 127, 158–159, *i.a.*
42. David Landy, "Problems of the Person Seeking Help in Our Culture," *The Social Welfare Forum*, The National Conference on Social Welfare, 1960 (New York: Columbia University Press, 1960), p. 129.
43. Jack R. Ewalt, M.D., and director of the study, in "Staff Review," *Americans View Their Mental Health* by Gerald Gurin, Joseph Veroff, and Sheila Feld (New York: Basic Books, 1960), p. xx.
44. *The Older American* (Washington, D.C.: The President's Council on Aging, 1963), p. 12.
45. As reported in *Los Angeles Times*, June 20, 1965.
46. Martin Wolins, *Social Welfare Problems and Services in Berkeley, California* (Berkeley: Berkeley Council of Social Service and School of Social Welfare, University of California, 1954), p. 4.
47. Lebeaux and Wolf, *op. cit.*, Vol. II, p. 58.
48. Charlotte Towle, "Implications of Contemporary Human and Social Values for Student Selection," *Education for Social Work* (New York: Council on Social Work Education, 1959), p. 30.
49. John A. Hostetler, *Amish Society* (Baltimore: Johns Hopkins Press, 1963), pp. 64–65.
50. Henry A. Murray, *Explorations in Personality* (New York: Oxford University Press, 1938), pp. 181, 182.
51. Richard Cobden, as quoted by William A. Bailward in *The Slippery Slope and Other Papers on Social Subjects* (London: John Murray, 1920), p. 99.
52. Seneca, *On Benefits*, Aubrey Stewart, tr. (London: George Bell, 1900), p. 1.
53. Aristotle, "Nichomachean Ethics," Book IX, Ch. 7, *On Man and the Universe* (New York: J. Black, 1943), pp. 216–217. For examples of how some of these conceptions have been tested, see Pitirim Sorokin, *Forms and Techniques of Altruistic and Spiritual Growth* (Boston: Beacon Press, 1954).
54. Claiborne Pell, *On the Developed and the Developing* (Santa Barbara, California: Center for the Study of Democratic Institutions, 1965), p. 21.
55. Frederick Loewe, *My Fair Lady: A Musical Play . . . Based on Pygmalion by Bernard Shaw* (New York: New American Library, 1958), p. 30.
56. As quoted by Edward Wagenknecht, *The New York Times Magazine*, May 17, 1959.
57. Richard Carter, *The Gentle Legions* (New York: Doubleday, 1961), p. 49.
58. George C. Marshall, testimony in hearings before Committee on Foreign Relations, U. S. Senate, 80th Congress, 2nd Session, on *Assistance to European Recovery Program*, 1948, p. 35.
59. James Henry Breasted, *The Dawn of Conscience* (New York: Scribner, 1933), p. 206.
60. Peyser, *op. cit.*, pp. 8, 62, 9.
61. Seneca, *op. cit.*, p. 181.
62. See, for example, Will Durant, *Our Oriental Heritage* (New York: Simon

and Schuster, 1954), p. 698; Stanley A. Wolpert, *Tilak and Gokhale: Revolution and Reform in the Making of Modern India* (Berkeley and Los Angeles: University of California Press, 1962), p. 93; Wilbur R. Jacobs, *Wilderness Politics and Indian Gifts* (Stanford, Cal.: Stanford University Press, 1950).

63. Richard Eells, "Corporation Giving: Theory and Policy," *California Management Review* (Fall 1958), pp. 40–42. See also Eells' *Corporation Giving in a Free Society* (New York: Harper & Row, 1956). Another useful analysis is Covington Hardee's "Philanthropy and the Business Corporation, Existing Guidelines—Future Policy," in Frank G. Dickinson, ed., *Philanthropy and Public Policy* (New York: National Bureau of Economic Research, 1962), pp. 103–110. A brief discussion of the same issue from Britain's viewpoint may be found in David Owen, *English Philanthropy: 1660–1960* (Cambridge: Harvard University Press, 1964), pp. 539–541.

64. Paul G. Hoffman, "Bread Upon the Waters: The Problems and Promises of Development," *1962 Britannica Book of the Year* (Chicago: Encyclopaedia Britannica, 1962), p. 8.

65. Noteworthy, among others, are Leon H. Keyserling, *Agriculture and the Public Interest* (Washington, D.C.: Conference on Economic Progress, 1965), pp. 104–105; and George S. McGovern, *War Against Want: America's Food for Peace Program* (New York: Walker, 1964), in which he advocates adding, to the more usual farm products given in foreign aid, dairy products and meat so that markets for eggs and hamburger will be encouraged. That this issue is not a peculiarly American one is evident in Hugh Wilson, *The War on World Poverty* (London: Gollancz, 1953) and in *Technical Co-operation: A Progress Report* (London: Her Majesty's Stationery Office, 1962).

66. Dom Helder Camara, as quoted by Thomas B. Morgan, *op. cit.*, p. 19.

67. Paul G. Hoffman, "Blueprint for Foreign Aid," *The New York Times Magazine*, February 17, 1957, p. 38. An exceptionally valuable analysis of United States foreign policy from the viewpoint of self-interest as related to concern for others is Robert Endicott Osgood, *Ideals and Self-Interest in America's Foreign Relations* (Chicago: University of Chicago Press, 1953).

68. How one eminent political figure solved this problem is described by Paul H. Douglas, "Ethical Problems in Politics," Stuart E. Rosenberg, ed., *A Humane Society* (Toronto: University of Toronto Press, 1962), pp. 104–107. An illuminating discussion of the danger of confusing "gifts" with something quite different may be found in Walter Goodman, *All Honorable Men: Corruption and Compromise in American Life* (Boston: Little, Brown, 1963). An example of how this problem appears in the U.S.S.R. is given by Irving R. Levine, *Main Street, U.S.S.R.* (Garden City, N.Y.: Doubleday, 1959), p. 60.

69. Willy Brandt, *My Road to Berlin,* as told to Leo Lania (New York: Doubleday, 1960), p. 32. A strikingly similar—but much earlier—incident is described in J. Lucas-Dubreton, *Daily Life in Florence in the Time of the Medici* (London: G. Allen, 1960), p. 175.

70. Henry Taylor, *The Statesman* (New York: New American Library of World Literature, 1958), pp. 39, 74, 118.

71. Baltasar Gracian, *A Truthtelling Manual and the Art of Worldly Wisdom*, 2d ed., Martin Fisher, tr. (Springfield, Ill.: Charles C. Thomas, c. 1943), pp. 19, 179, 236.

72. Ralph G. Martin, *The Bosses* (New York: Putnam, 1964), p. 17.

73. Quoted by Paul Grimes, "Shadow of Catastrophe over Calcutta," *The New York Times Magazine*, December 12, 1961, p. 120.

74. Frederick G. Friedmann, *The Hoe and the Book, An Italian Experiment in Community Development* (Ithaca: Cornell University Press, 1960), p. 147.

75. George H. T. Kimble, "Words of the Wise—from Africa," *The New York Times Magazine*, January 28, 1962, p. 51.

76. William and Charlotte Wiser, *Behind Mud Walls: 1930–1960* (Berkeley and Los Angeles: University of California Press, 1963).

77. Chief S. O. Adebo, *On the Developed and the Developing* (Santa Barbara, Cal.: Center for the Study of Democratic Institutions, 1965), pp. 10, 13.

78. David Owen, as quoted by Andrew Shonfield in *The Attack on World Poverty* (New York: Random House, 1960), p. 240.

79. Gunnar Myrdal, *Beyond the Welfare State: Economic Planning and Its International Implications* (New Haven: Yale University Press, 1960), pp. 219, 238–239, 254.

80. Asher Brynes, *We Give to Conquer: A New Look at the United States Foreign Aid Program* (New York: Norton, 1966), p. 20. Suggestions on reorganizing aid programs may be found on pp. 202–205.

81. Morton A. Kaplan, ed., *The Revolution in World Politics* (New York: Wiley, 1962), pp. 436, 437.

82. Bernard L. Diamond, M.D., "Children of Leviathan . . . ," *California Law Review*, 54 (May 1966), 357–369.

83. A. Delafield Smith, *The Right to Life* (Chapel Hill: The University of North Carolina Press, 1955), pp. 3, 7. See also Alanson W. Willcox, "Patterns of Social Security Legislation," *Journal of Public Law*, 6 (Spring 1957), especially 9–10.

VIII
RECIPROCATION
and
MUTUALISM

One exceedingly important element in assuaging both the hurt of being helped and the hurt of helping is reciprocation. To be able to "return the favor" can often go far to alleviate the embarrassment of having been "favored" by another. It often hurts more to be helped if the helpee is never allowed to be a helper, too.

Within limits, reciprocation can also relieve the hurt of helping. When helpers see clearly that helpees "do something" in return for help received (such as work on county roads in return for public assistance), they seem less reluctant to provide help. Conversely, help that looks like "something for nothing" seems to be the kind that is most reluctantly given.

However, the complex nature of the helping process and the reluctance of helpers to be helped in return (as would be necessary to accommodate genuine reciprocation) make it appear that it is much easier for some persons to be their brothers' keepers than to play the part of brother. Even Aristotle's "high-minded man" had difficulty on this score.

Reciprocation, when complete—with a full exchange of tit for tat—and when practiced on a continuing basis, merges with marketlike transactions or mutual aid, which, it will be recalled (Chapter II) are excluded from our definition of gratuitous help.

Help of the sort provided through mutual aid has a wide appeal among humane persons and groups. There is often a romantic flavor and nostalgia about it. Cornhusking bees and the barn raisings of the early agricultural communities in the United States are often romanticized, as are the small-town volunteer fire departments (when the men and boys fought the fires, the women served coffee and doughnuts, and the whole community joined in the periodic firemen's ball), and other mutual aid activities. In Britain, Sir William Beveridge lamented the passing of the old Friendly Societies and was quite bitter that they were never permitted to play the role he envisaged for them in the Welfare State structure that he had recommended.

Intriguing as is mutual aid as a mechanism for supplying life's essentials, lack of space prevents further discussion—except to note that it appears to be succumbing all over the world to the forces of social change. As young couples can afford to pay baby-sitters or to hire movers and as communities can afford to employ paid firemen, they tend to stop providing services on a mutual aid basis and to "hire" them. Even the warm fellowship of "club night," which Beveridge thought of as the heart of the Friendly Societies, tended to dissolve as workingmen's homes became more attractive as places to spend leisure hours. Perhaps the demands of close personal relationships and the commitments necessarily involved in true mutual aid are today just too much to sustain, apart from an exceptionally high idealism, as in the case of the Israeli kibbutzim. Nevertheless, even in the absence of real mutual aid, it is important to see in human relations such lesser degrees of mutualism as may realistically be envisaged and often appear in reciprocation.

RELIGIOUS SANCTIONS

In religious circles, mutual aid has long had a special sort of sanction. The Essenes, who antedated the Christian era, appear to have been a closely knit mutual aid group. So were the early Christians who held "all things in common." Saint Paul's "Bear ye one another's burdens" reflects the very essence of mutual aid. In fact, many of the Judeo-Christian teachings about "giving" are often overlooked (such as the Talmudic teachings about "help for the helper and mercy for the merciful" and the promise of long life for welldoers— even in a time and a country of high death rates.) In our own day, at least the concept of "help for the helper" is so often "rediscovered" in practice that it is easy to forget that wise men long ago put their finger on it. As a result, poverty workers think they invented it when they discover that school failures or dropouts enlisted to tutor other disadvantaged youngsters themselves show great improvement. Similarly, health educators think they have discovered "help for the helper" when a prime benefit of using parents to provide health education for their children turns out to be improved health practices on the part of the parents.

"Casting one's bread upon the waters," for instance, was not enjoined as a self-sacrificing act of profligacy, but as one that would be repaid "manyfold." Even the famous injunction to give "in secret" did not imply that this would go unrewarded, but that it would be rewarded "in secret." The commandment "Give and they will give to you" suggests more than tit for tat, for the promise of return is in "good measure, pressed down and running over": Here is reciprocation *with interest.*

In retrospect, it is perhaps regrettable that the concept of the Lord as a great Supra-Natural Bank toting up good deeds and calculating interest rates should diminish in importance because, as "givers" cease to look forward to God-given profit on their "good deeds," they may be more inclined to seek, more immediately, their own self-interest or to serve their own ends through manipulation of others.

Mutuality in giving is far more widely stressed than is generally realized, not only in Judeo-Christian doctrine, but also in the Confucian, Mohammedan, and Buddhist religions.* Alms to the poor, for example, are viewed in different religions as winning for the giver merit that will supposedly count in his favor in a future life (or when he is reincarnated).

RECIPROCATION IN EVERYDAY EXPERIENCE

Everyday experiences illustrate just how fundamental is the need sensed by "normal" people to reciprocate for favors.

Take, for instance, a situation in which a total stranger does one a favor—gives him "a lift" along a highway because his car has run out of gas, or pays his fare on a bus because he has lost his wallet. On such occasions colloquies invoking reciprocation are not at all unusual. In the former case, at least, they would probably be preceded by an offer to pay for the ride so as to bury in a marketlike transaction the embarrassment of having needed it. Short of direct payment, an ego-saving offer of reciprocation may present only a remote possibility of fulfillment, but it assuages the embarrassment of being helped. To the stranger who was his benefactor, the beneficiary may say, "I hope I can do as much for you sometime." Or the beneficiary may say, more realistically, "I'll probably never see you again, but I'll give a lift to the next guy I see who needs one." The benefactor, in turn, may respond, "Someone gave me a lift [or paid my bus fare] last week, so I'm glad to do the same for you. Next time maybe you'll be the one to help somebody."

Thus, reciprocation may be either direct (returning or hoping to return a favor directly to one's benefactor) or indirect. Indirect reciprocation may be in either of two dimensions: first, in having

---

* Among Buddhists, almsgiving has a rather unique element of mutuality because of the practice of men in many walks of life to leave temporarily their various pursuits and to don saffron robes for periods of spiritual "refreshment." During these periods they go out with their begging bowls and look to others for alms just as others had previously asked alms of them.

the benefactor rewarded by triangulation, not by the beneficiary himself but by someone else, as by the Heavenly Father's rewarding in secret what one has secretly done for another; and second, not in "returning a favor" directly to one's benefactor but in "passing on" a favor. Benjamin Franklin gave an impetus to the latter when, upon lending some money to another, he asked only that the borrower "repay" it by making a loan to another with the stipulation that he, in turn, "repay" that loan by lending to still another, until at last "some knave," doubtless, would fail to reciprocate similarly and the magic chain would be broken.

It takes a man of some breadth, a voluntary agency of some idealism, and a nation of some vision to regard, as reciprocation, a benefit passed along to someone else. Nevertheless, in highly interdependent societies within an interdependent world, it may be exactly such breadth, idealism, and vision that need to be developed.

In passing, it should be recalled that one reason strong men may find it less difficult to accept help is the probability that they may be able to pay it back.

Scratching another's back may give the scratcher a noble sense of service. But unless the scratchee can reciprocate by being a scratcher himself once in a while, he may well weary of being constantly scratched by another. The validity of this observation may be seen in many relationships. There is the "friend" who always insists that you come to his house, but who never comes to yours; there is the rich "friend" who always picks up the tab for meals, but never lets you pay (or, possibly, never even lets you say where or what you would like to eat). Relationships upon such bases have a tendency, sooner or later, to pall. A person imbued with the spirit of Saint Paul might well say, "Take ye one another out to lunch."

RECIPROCATION IN BROADER EXPERIENCE

Upon reflection, it is a little surprising that the world's leading religions, which have done so much to stress man's duties to man, have stressed so preponderantly the concept of service and emphasized so little the merit of being served, or even of accepting reciprocal favors after having served. One notable exception to this observation is the manifesto adopted in 1963 by the Third World Congress of the Anglican Church. This declared, in part:

Mission is not only a giving to others, it is equally a sharing and receiving. . . .

. . . To use the words "older" or "younger" or "sending" or "receiving" with respect to churches is unreal and untrue in the world and in our communion. Mission is not the kindness of the lucky to the unlucky; it is mutual. . . . The form of the church must reflect that.

The manifesto then recommended that "every church of the Anglican Communion, without exception . . . seek the way to receive as well as to give, asking expectantly what other churches and cultures may bring to its life and eager to share its tasks and problems with others." [1] Similarly perceptive and noble sentiments, unfortunately, are rare indeed—even in religious circles.

However, the Council of Churches in Birmingham, England, has also demonstrated remarkable perspicacity in this respect. Because many newcomers were arriving in its community and were known to be lonely and to feel isolated, the council embarked upon a communitywide program of friendly visitation. The visitors were unprepared, however, for the necessity of accepting, in return, visits in their own homes when the families they had intended to serve wanted to reciprocate by visiting them. It is a tribute to the vision of the council that it quickly modified instructions to the church visitors to prepare them not only for the visits they would pay, but also for the return visits they would be expected to receive.[2]

In complex societies, and especially when welfare services are highly institutionalized, direct reciprocation of the kind observed in Birmingham is not often possible. But indirect reciprocation—that accomplished by triangulation—appears to be a widely acceptable alternative. Soon after a discussion of this possibility in a class of social work students, one of them saw a concrete example. This was the student, mentioned earlier, who had reported radiantly, with respect to the hurt of being helped, *"Now* I see what you mean." You will recall that during a research project she had called upon a family that was receiving public assistance and that the lady of the house—who was already being helped by the local welfare department—barred the door, exclaiming, "I don't want any of your help." Here is the rest of the story. With difficulty, the student was finally able to say, "Oh, but I'm not here to help you. I want you to help *me.*" With surprise, the lady responded, "Oh, come right in. I'll be glad to help *you.*" She threw open the door and gave the student cordial cooperation. Apparently it was indeed more blessed to give than to receive.

It is this mechanism that, as earlier chapters have repeatedly stressed, leads men and women to prefer to "work for what they get";

leads mothers to prefer to pay even four cents an hour for child-care although not required to do so; and leads a youngster to volunteer to help with the serving of school lunches rather than get "something for nothing." It is this mechanism that was operating in one of the witnesses at the meeting under the aegis of the Ohio Citizens' Council for Health and Welfare; the witness offered to fix the clothes of other women in return for "so many pounds of hamburger or a chicken or whatever I need for my table—then I don't feel I am asking anyone for anything." [3]

The same mechanism perhaps explains the alleged popularity of help received from political bosses and such organizations as Tammany Hall. "You help me, and I'll vote for you." [4] Reciprocation can also be seen in gifts and bequests left to hospitals and other institutions from which donors had received treatment or care.

From a quite different quarter—Mexico City—anthropologist Oscar Lewis reports a strikingly similar response from those interviewed in conjunction with his classic studies, *Five Families* and *The Children of Sanchez*. "They . . . often told me," writes Lewis, "that if their stories would help human beings anywhere, they would feel a sense of accomplishment." [5]

In quite similar terms, Guido Rosa tells of a young man in North Africa who, upon encountering some undefined "disaster," returned to his village. There, "the man of wealth" of the village helped the young man to make a fresh start. "And I resolved," the young man said, "that as soon as my feet once again feel solid ground under them, I shall not forget my obligation. It is only by helping each other so, that the world can move." [6]

To witness what, in all the world, is perhaps the fiercest determination to reciprocate, one would have to go to the Far East. There, the sense of obligation to return favors is so highly developed that, to Westerners at least, it appears almost pathological. In Japan, for example, the tradition we mentioned and *giri* or *on* imposes a heavy burden indeed upon one who has received a favor.[7] The fact is that helping another in Japan and China, and perhaps elsewhere, often places the person who is helped under so heavy a sense of obligation that this provides an excuse for not helping him at all.

"In the Philippines," according to Velma Adams in *The Peace Corps in Action*, "the idea of 'I'll scratch your back and you scratch mine' is 'If I scratch your back, then you *must* scratch mine in return.' " [8]

Generalizing broadly, Dora Peyser in *The Strong and the Weak* writes:

Analysing . . . the formal character of help, we find that there is a strong *urge to reciprocity* . . . Social relations between persons are by nature bilateral. In the help-relationship it usually takes the form of gratitude . . . words, . . . a prayer, . . . some service, or . . . a return gift.[9]

The "need to reciprocate" is by no means universal. But the "moochers" and "spongers" who seem willing to receive without ever giving may be thought of as overly dependent, ungrateful, ill-mannered—or as not recognizing their "plain duty." When encountered by welfare agencies, they may be given special service designed to arouse their sense of responsibility to society in acknowledgment that society is meeting its responsibilities to them. However, the complexities of modern societies and their highly organized welfare services seriously complicate the age-old practice of "returning the favor" and necessitate greater emphasis upon indirect, rather than upon direct, reciprocation. In fact, efforts of beneficiaries of welfare services to reciprocate directly (for example, a woman knits a sweater for "her social worker" or a man makes an ashtray for his) raise for welfare agencies many perplexing problems we do not have space to discuss.

Considering the prevalence of the urge to reciprocate, it is regrettable that there is so little deliberate planning to channel this urge. Such planning would result in the conservation of human energy and would increase the social good. An even greater loss, perhaps, is that this urge takes unproductive directions when more productive ones are not available. For example, some public assistance recipients seem almost convinced that they are doing their welfare workers a favor by accepting assistance, since the workers might not otherwise have jobs. But the most notable example that has come to my attention (and one that drew praise in Parliament) was a practice of Assistance Board officers in Britain. They made a big show of what a hard job it was to prepare reports on the applications of those requesting aid and then would plead with the applicants to help them in the preparation of the required forms.

RECIPROCATION IN SOCIAL WELFARE SERVICES

Social welfare policy has always given importance to work programs and "work relief." The general public often interprets these as reciprocation: paying back, through work, what one has received from the community. Welfare personnel well know that able-bodied men and women often, and perhaps usually, actually prefer "to work for what they get" as did the workers cited earlier. Certainly, during the Great Depression there were indications (as shown in my *The WPA and Federal Relief Policy*) that virtually all unemployed workers greatly preferred work relief to direct relief.[10] For many this was true even when work-relief wages were lower than the direct-relief grants. Although work relief has subsequently shrunk to negligible proportions, there are still strong indicators that this is preferred to direct aid.* To what has already been reported on this score can be added what Lee E. Dirks reported in *The National Observer*: A poverty-stricken wife brightened when she recalled, "At least my husband is working for what we have—he works for the state to get his relief check. It's good. He comes home tired, like other men do. He plays with the kids; he doesn't growl at them like he used to." [11]

However, although the general public and even the employees themselves may regard work relief as reciprocation for social assistance, many welfare personnel would not so regard it, but would look upon it instead as self-help—the best opportunity available to an unemployed man or woman to support himself or herself—and comparable to self-support through a job in, say, an automobile factory or a cafeteria, or through government's "gift" of a lucrative franchise.

Recognizing the prevailing desire to reciprocate for benefits received, welfare agencies often go to considerable lengths to help beneficiaries see themselves as reciprocating indirectly: through serving their own families and by being "good citizens." These attempts must be recognized in the wider society, too, however—and not just by welfare personnel—if they are to assuage the hurt of being helped.

In the United States in the 1960's there were many bold innovations to give public assistance recipients really significant opportunities for service—service not only to members of their own families, but also to peers and to their communities. This really represented a resurgence—after thirty years—of widespread effort during the Great Depression to help people to help themselves *and one another*. These activities had included cooperative raising of vegetables, harvesting vegetables and fruits, on the farms of others, stringing electric wires from houses with electricity to those where it had been cut off for nonpayment of bills, cobblers' fixing the shoes of tailors and tailors' repairing the pants of cobblers. And so on and

* When Congress, in 1967, was considering amendments to the Economic Opportunity (War on Poverty) Act, there was widespread support for a multibillion dollar work program.

so on. Also, the great emphasis upon work relief and emergency public works provided unemployed workers with opportunities to return benefits to society for benefits received. Why so much of this Depression experience was forgotten for nearly thirty years is still somewhat uncertain.

The 1960's saw renewed recognition of the importance of people's doing something for others in return for what was being done for them. The Chicago public assistance agency has a noteworthy record in this regard. For example, mothers who are receiving public aid and who have, say, special sewing skills are encouraged to help other mothers to make curtains or dresses, while those with special competence in cooking or housekeeping help others less skilled in these tasks. It has come as a surprise, even to optimistically hopeful welfare officials, how pleased these assistance recipients are to have opportunities to be useful to others outside their own family circles.

Even before becoming Vice-President, Hubert H. Humphrey was suggesting that public assistance recipients be engaged as babysitters, playground supervisors, teachers of arts and crafts, and so forth. "Most people who have no job," he observed, "want something to do. Even if unpaid, constructive enterprise always gives people dignity." [12] Experience in the welfare field certainly corroborates this view and even suggests that many people would actually rather be helpful to others than to be helped themselves and that even a greater number of persons would welcome opportunities to reciprocate favors. This concept is central to Mormon relief and welfare programs that immediately involve any person who is helped in giving help to others.

That these phenomena are not characteristic of the United States alone is suggested by Lady Mary Morris' review, in 1961, of a survey of users' reactions to the extensive social services in Britain (education, health services, family allowances, and others). Lady Morris writes:

The impression left by this book is not of a supine population waiting for bounties to be poured into its lap, but of responsible mothers anxious to do their best for their families, prepared to pay (through taxes and contributions) for the benefits they enjoy, and prepared too to help themselves and one another, for it was to families and friends that eighty-six per cent of the sample turned for help in time of trouble.[13]

One of the most publicized welfare projects involving reciprocation was the "cow project" of the American Friends Service Committee in Austria after World War I. There was a milk shortage in the cities, so the Service Committee imported cows from Switzerland and The Netherlands and placed them with farmers who agreed, as John Forbes recalls, "to provide milk to Friends Centers in the cities as token payment, thus insuring both delivery and the farmers' self-respect." [14]

More recently there have been "pig programs"—and rabbit, duck, chicken, and other programs—developed under the Food for Peace, Peace Corps, and other projects. The central idea is substantially the same in all: Any individual who is started out with a few animals or fowl commits himself to share with others the broods, flocks, and so on as they are produced. The Community Development Foundation places tremendous emphasis upon reciprocation by triangulation, and practically every child or adult who receives help almost anywhere in the world is expected, in turn, to assume responsibility for someone else.

In Taiwan, according to Dan Q. R. Mulock Houwer (Secretary General of the International Union for Child Welfare), a school health program "in which children help children, has cured 1 million out of the 2 million school children of trachoma." [15] In Morocco I have myself seen youths, in the afternoon, teaching eager adults basic reading skills that the "teachers" had themselves learned only that morning. "Each one teach one" is a motto in many countries.

The importance of reciprocation goes far beyond the possible assuagement of embarrassment or hurt one might feel upon being helped, and far beyond reciprocal services that might be rendered to others. This broader need is identified by Brandeis University sociologist Lewis A. Coser in "The Sociology of Poverty." In this he traces the development of assistance-giving from an earlier day (in which it was more informally organized) to the present, when this function is highly institutionalized. Such *reciprocal* flow of affect and emotion" as existed in more informally organized settings, Professor Coser contends, is now precluded by higher degrees of institutionalization and professionalization. He then concludes that "Poverty . . . can never be eliminated unless the poor are enabled to give as well as take. . . . Poverty can be solved only through the abolition of unilateral relationship of dependence." [16]

As Charles E. Silberman puts it in Crisis in Black and White, "The politics of human life do not permit of equality or freedom when one person is constantly in the position of magnanimous donor and the other in the position of perennial recipient. . . . Accepting help . . . is a submission—one that erodes the dignity and destroys the spirit." [17] In this connection it is noteworthy that when mothers whom Alice McCabe describes in "Forty Forgotten Families" were asked what they wanted most from the Welfare Department, they did not say higher grants but "more courtesy and respect," more understanding, and "someone to talk with." Three thousand miles away, and a few years later, the president of a Welfare Rights Organization said much the same thing at a conference on Alternatives to Poverty. In this conference such nationally eminent authorities as economists Milton Friedman and Leon H. Keyserling were charging each other with failure to "ask the right question." When it came the turn of the Welfare Rights spokesman to respond—a woman who had reared a brood of children on public assistance grants that ranged from $217 to $257 a month—she replied that *none* of the eminent speakers had asked the "right question." This, she declared, was "how to give assistance and let people retain self-respect and dignity."

An intriguing perspective on the failure of welfare agencies to see as whole persons those whom they seek to serve has been supplied by Britain's Dame Eileen Younghusband. She once gave a Canadian audience one explanation for the "excessive proneness" of England's "problem families" to buy on credit (to enter into what Britishers call "hire-purchase" agreements) from door-to-door salesmen (tally men). According to this interpretation, "From the whole army of people who call upon . . . problem families, with counsels, ministrations, offers of help, . . . the tally man is the only one who wants something from them. He, in other words, is the only visitor whose very presence makes for a sense of self-enhancement." [18]

If welfare personnel had the perspicacity to see in those they serve some of the same promise and potential (desire to be like others and have what others have) that profit-conscious salesmen see in them, perhaps everybody from the beneficiaries to the society —with the possible exception of the tally men—would be better off.

Until society can learn to see as human beings with something to give and can learn to receive from, as well as give to, those who are disadvantaged, society may well be the loser. After an extended study of poor persons, Harvard University research psychiatrist Robert Coles reports:

Money and work are what the poor people I know demand and need, but I am not so sure that some of the qualities they already have are not in turn needed by the rest of us—the unmasking humor, the caustic distrust of fake morality, hypocritical authority, and dishonest piety.

Coles believes also that if these people were to break out of their poverty and could live more comfortably, they would draw upon "their distinctive past experiences, and in so doing make us all pricelessly, truly richer." [19] Another observer with the sensitivity to see that there is something to learn from poor persons is Dr. Leonard J. Duhl of the National Institute of Mental Health.[20] Frank Riessman, too, has spoken of advantages gained from working with disadvantaged persons in that this work has made "aloof professionals into . . . concerned citizens." [21]

In his study of societies in tropical Africa, Guy Hunter of the Institute of Race Relations in London goes even further. He suggests that the West has much to learn in tropical Africa in terms of intrafamilial and other interpersonal relationships. Professor Lawrence H. Fuchs writes at length about what Peace Corps volunteers found in the Philippines and wanted to incorporate into their own lives.[22]

But, if the "haves" are to learn from the "have nots" and if the helpers are to learn from the helped, wholly new concepts of, and channels for, reciprocity will need to be developed. If this is to be done, though, there are vast problems posed by highly organized and complex societies that must be overcome.

Today it is commonplace to acknowledge difficulties presented by separation of people in suburbia from those in "inner cities," by the remoteness of Appalachia and the Mississippi delta from Newport and Grosse Point, and by the exclusion of "The Other America" from the life of *the* America. These are not new problems, however. Even in the heyday of Athens there was concern because that monument to civilization was in fact "two cities"—one of the rich and one of the poor. Some 2,000 years later, Disraeli was concerned about "The Two Nations" within England. At about the same time, the adjective that William Booth put into the title of his book on the disadvantaged classes—*In Darkest England*—was one commonly applied to distant Africa. Within the United States, at approximately the same time, Jacob Riis gave to his influential book the title *How the Other Half Lives*. Thus, separation within societies, of the advantaged from the disadvantaged, is no new phenomenon. Nor is concern about the separation.

But this ever-old, ever-new concern has nowhere been more emphatically deplored than by Joseph P. Lyford, one-time University of California faculty member and one-time staff member of the

Center for the Study of Democratic Institutions. With respect to what might be termed "The 'Other' West-Siders," Lyford wrote after several years given to a study of New York's West Side, "If they could speak, I doubt that we could hear them, anyway. By some great bit of psychological magic we have surrounded ourselves with a transparent material that admits no sound or even a breath of air from the world in which they live." Somewhat earlier he had spoken of the "autoanesthesia" of turning "one's eyes away from the object or the act of cruelty itself." [23]

Such "anesthesia" or even the sheer fact of social distance that impairs one's view is the more deplorable in light of the common human trait to respond more quickly and generously to clearly perceived need than to respond to what is more impersonal and less clearly seen by others. This phenomenon occurs over and over again. For example, a child is trapped in a well or is lost on a mountainside or at sea. Help is rushed to the scene from many and often distant quarters. Hourly radio broadcasts report progress to an anxiously waiting nation. But, although a nation's eyes and ears may easily be riveted to some highly specific need, continuing deaths from preventable causes (including needless household accidents) and chronic deprivations make hardly a ripple in public consciousness. A dramatic story in a popular magazine of a youngster in a foreign land can elicit more help than the child can use, but the slum—or *barrio* or *favela*—that is responsible for the child's plight commands no similar response.

Gulfs between the "haves" and the "have-nots," between the "advantaged" and the "disadvantaged," between potential helpers and those needing help present difficult obstacles indeed not only to possibilities for help, but for reciprocation also.

Concerning one aspect of the broader problem, anthropologist Ralph Linton has observed,

Where . . . there are frequent face-to-face contacts between members, the potential antisocial consequences of extreme extensions of individual ownership . . . are neutralized by social pressures. The wealthy man finds it more rewarding to be admired and praised for his generosity than to continue hoarding, subjected to the disfavor of the group and to the spectacle of individual suffering from want with whom he inevitably feels a considerable identification. Only the absentee landlord or slaveholder and the modern corporation manager are immune to these social pressures, and it is under them that the potential evils of private ownership have found fullest expression.[24]

This view, in part, is strongly reminiscent of Reinhold Niebuhr's earlier contention that "Power is never quite so unjust, and its rule is never quite so vexatious, when relations between ruler and ruled are personal as when they are hidden behind the impersonal transactions of a moneyed civilization." [25]

In the early 1960's, the New York State Charities Aid Association became convinced that apathy toward, and criticism of, public welfare programs was due, in part at least, to lack of direct knowledge about them. Accordingly, under the direction of Pulitzer Prize-winning newspaperman Edgar May (who later wrote *The Wasted Americans*), the Association embarked upon a bold project to permit community leaders to see at first hand the homes and lives of assistance recipients. Among those engaging in this "come and see" program were seventeen corporation executives, thirteen newspaper editors, thirteen county officials, six members of the state legislature. Of the results from this "look see" project, the Association reported, "This demonstration has proved its value in helping to lift the fog of public suspicion about welfare. . . .

". . . If public welfare is ever to find its proper place on the list of community priorities, it first must show its difficulties to persons who draw up that list." [26]

If these views are correct, the main problem with today's much maligned absentee landlords (and slumlords) may be not so much their property holdings as their absenteeism. In some respects it may well be—as consolers of separated lovers have long maintained —that "absence makes the heart grow fonder." In other respects it seems equally true that absence lets the heart grow harder. If slumlords themselves had to deal with stopped-up drains or had to rush a rat-bitten child to a hospital, their attitudes toward such abuses might change. Similarly, more personal relationships between helpers and helpees, givers and receivers, might also mitigate the often criticized abrasive quality of some giving and helping and might open more doors to widely desired opportunities for reciprocation.

RECIPROCATION IN INTERNATIONAL AID PROGRAMS

"Being helped" is widely viewed inimically even by nations, and this induces their leaders urgently to plead for "trade, not aid." Trade, obviously, is reciprocal but aid is not. But the more developed nations are understandably interested in continuing to help themselves and to further their own self-interest. Thus we again see an example of conflicts among values and of self-help that may be "too hurtful" to others.

Worse still, from the viewpoint of disadvantaged nations—nations that are denied opportunities for trade and must accept aid—is the tendency of this aid-giving to be a one-way street that does not permit reciprocity or reflect genuine mutuality. To be sure, the governments of receiving nations may be expected to reciprocate (or, as it is sometimes put, "to show their gratitude") by supporting a giver's foreign policy, or by remaining unaligned, or by actually participating in mutual defense programs. These expectations, of course, represent reciprocity of sorts, but may not represent true mutualism and may approach what we have already described (Chapters II and VII) as manipulation or as purchasing devotion to particular values. Also, a nation may regard the urgency of its need as duress, leaving it little scope for decision and consent that are truly mutual.

In addition to the frequently voiced feeling of "being used," there is often the complaint that, while the United States appears willing "to help" other peoples, the American people are not really interested in them as human beings, are not really interested in their art, architecture, dances, languages, or ways of life. Americans, they charge, seem far more willing to export than to import good will.

The Peace Corps appears to have made significant inroads into these impressions. But Peace Corpsmen, upon returning to the United States, have had an opportunity to see at home exactly the kinds of sentiments that are widely criticized in aided nations. Some of these returnees have reported that, while abroad, they tried sincerely to understand and really to appreciate the people among whom they served. However, they have found upon their return that fellow Americans—even if they recognize the name of the country in which a Peace Corpsman has served—are not much concerned about what he learned there. Many Americans apparently believe they have a way of life that they want other nations to learn about, but do not themselves think there is anything further to learn from others. In short, Americans seem to be much more willing to "give it" than to "take it." *

When Thomas B. Morgan went around the world probing for explanations of anti-American feelings, he repeatedly encountered

* How little Americans know about the art, literature, and other aspects of life in other countries—even those Americans who are sufficiently interested in these countries to visit them—is tellingly portrayed by Harlan Cleveland, Gerard J. Mangone, and John Clarke Adams in *The Overseas Americans* (New York: McGraw-Hill, 1960).

resentment of what seemed a lack of understanding of peoples in other countries. As one of his informants put it, "More important than your money is your comprehension." [27] These reactions recall ancient Jewish emphasis not only upon helping needy persons, but also upon "considering" them ("Blessed is he that considereth the poor." Psalms 41:1).

All this, from time to time, has smacked of disinterest and disdain, if not actual contempt, for the peoples of other nations. They have felt, as a consequence, a sense of personal impugnment, an offense to their dignity. Among others, William Benton, a former United States Senator from Connecticut and Assistant Secretary of State, has diagnosed this problem and offered the following prescription:

One answer is clear above all others. Our best hope for improving relations with the Latin Americans—and for countering the challenge of Castro and communism—lies in becoming warm friends with them once again.

The problem is psychological as well as economic—as friendship usually is. We must seek friendship sincerely out of the genuine liking and admiration the people of Latin America deserve from us.

This was written against the background of a trip that Senator Benton had made with Adlai E. Stevenson to twelve countries in Latin America. Among criticisms the senator encountered were some that are reminiscent of what we reported earlier in connection with self-interest. Other criticisms go further:

Americans support dictators when it seems good for business. . . . The U.S. wants Latin America safe for business, not safe for democracy.

. . . The business man or traveler from the United States tends to be overcordial and not genuinely polite. He does not mix. His ineptitude for foreign languages is incredible, and consequently he is unacquainted with many of the cultural achievements of the southern part of the hemisphere.[28]

This grim picture raises the inescapable question: Can the intended "helper" in the North turn "friend"—in time?

"Buying" with gifts either personal loyalty or political power is of course familiar. Distribution of "favors," emoluments, and privileges has caulked many a leaky ship of state. However, to cement friendships, there must be true reciprocity. They cannot long survive on one-way giving. In a letter to the editor of *The New York Times Magazine*, B. K. Nehru, while serving as India's Commissioner for Economic Affairs, asked, "Is it impossible that foreign aid should be given in the form not of fatherly, but of 'brotherly' assistance?" [29]

Among American social workers, who believe that "brotherly" assistance is not only not impossible but essential—if international aid programs are to succeed—is Professor Herbert Aptekar of Brandeis University, who has seen service in India and other countries abroad. Writing about mutuality in the education of personnel for international service, Professor Aptekar declares:

We Americans like to think of ourselves as generous givers, and indeed we are. But we are sometimes naive givers. . . . We do not think of ourselves as receiving too. Especially on the international scene, we give little thought to *mutuality* in the help-giving, help-taking process. . . . Many countries on the help-taking side . . . know they have something to give us in return for our giving, and they are pained when they see that we do not know it. In many ways they show that they want to help us, too, but we seldom let them do so.[30]

After a lifetime of work in underdeveloped areas, I. W. Moomaw reports, "We would be in error if we thought of the world situation only as the poor clamoring for bread. . . . Above all is their passionate desire to be recognized, to achieve human dignity in the community of free nations." [31]

But it should not be too surprising, perhaps, that nations—vis-à-vis other nations—have difficulties in these respects because even individual Christians whose doctrines should have helped them to do better have been criticized for not exporting true brotherhood along with the tenets of their faith. Arnold J. Toynbee, for example, has said, "Christianity . . . has had an aggressive missionary spirit that has aroused opposition." [32] More recently, in 1966, American participants in the Church and Society Conference sponsored by the World Council of Churches were badly shaken by recognition that participants from the developing nations "feel strongly that their views are not really taken into account and that they resent this neglect." [33]

Lest these difficulties seem to be afflictions of only Protestantism, it is noteworthy that Monsignor Ivan Illich, who was director of the Center of Inter-cultural Documentation in Cuernavaca, Mexico, and who had for six years been preparing Catholic missioners for work in Latin America, has written in the Jesuit publication, *America*, criticizing the "massive, indiscriminate importation of clergy" into Latin America from other countries. Of this, Monsignor Illich says,

The people soon see that the Church *is* distant, alienated from them—an imported, specialized operation, financed from abroad, which speaks with a holy, because foreign, accent.

. . . We want to build community, relying on techniques, and are blind to the latent desire for unity that is striving to express itself among men.[34]

More broadly, but also with particular reference to Latin America, Frank Tannenbaum has written:

American business and American policy have been guilty of obtuseness and insensitivity. No amount of good will, back-slapping, or offers of material aid are adequate substitutes for understanding and being sensitive to the values that give meaning and direction to life itself.[35]

Whatever the view from abroad of American foreign-aid programs, of the degree of true mutualism reflected in them, and, more particularly, of reciprocation, the extent to which this last point is stressed by the U.S. Agency for International Development (AID) is noteworthy. In a report made in 1963, AID observes that the United States, in 1948, was "the free world's only important source of aid." But, continues the report:

By 1963, 17 free world countries other than the United States (many of them former recipients of United States economic aid) were contributing $2.5 billion annually through their own bilateral aid programs. International agencies . . . were providing another $1.2 billion.[36]

Happily, many American statesmen have seen in clear perspective the need for greater mutualism in foreign aid programs. Paul G. Hoffman, who has observed that "no nation is so rich it cannot profit from the development of other countries," also observed that "no nation is so poor it has nothing with which to assist other countries." [37]

Interestingly, when the National Social Welfare Assembly submitted to the United Nations in 1966 its "Comments and Recommendations" on the "Reappraisal of the United Nations Social Service Programme," it declared, in part:

The Assembly . . . concurs wholeheartedly that all countries can benefit from cooperation in this field. With the present focus in the U.S. on our unsolved social problems, we urge our representatives to stress our desire and, indeed, our need to study the experiences of others and to state explicitly our recognition that we have much to learn from them.[38]

However, "giving" nations may be too filled with false pride to recognize that so-called "have-not" nations do, indeed, have something to contribute to enrichment of life in the "have" nations. Former Secretary of State Christian Herter sought to stress exactly this point when he spoke on the subject of "What Foreign Countries Can Do for Us." He said:

Both here and abroad there is a misconception that foreign aid is strictly a one-way street—away from the United States. . . .

The truth is that the so-called underdeveloped countries have been making real contributions to the everyday lives of the American people.

He then elaborated a number of tangible returns and proposed a "Point V Program" (obviously so named to suggest an advance beyond the generally successful United States Point IV Program of the Truman era). Of his proposition Herter said:

Under this program, the United States would not give things away. We would not show people how to do things. Instead, we would say to less advanced countries, "What can we learn from you?" And, "Please . . . teach *us* how to do things."

Not only would we make direct gains from such a program, but the whole picture that these developing countries have of the United States would change. No longer would they regard us as a smug, rich nation that has everything and thinks it knows everything.[39]

Considering the difficulty we have mentioned that advantaged groups in a society have in learning from the disadvantaged, it is hardly surprising that advantaged nations have difficulty in learning from other nations.

Only time can tell whether a nation that prides itself upon being a world's helper can evolve into a true reciprocator (and, in Talmudic terms, be willing to accept "help for the helper")—and whether it can transform itself from its brother-nation's keeper into a genuine brother-nation. True devotees of mutualism—whether they be "givers" or "receivers"—do not insist that a receiver necessarily reciprocate vis-à-vis a giver directly, but see the sense of mutuality served if a receiver in turn gives to someone else. Exactly this kind of reciprocity by triangulation was highly gratifying to spokesmen for American nongovernmental agencies that gave relief to Germany (the erstwhile enemy) after World War II. In fact, this is the theme that runs through the report of these programs written by Eileen Eagan and Elizabeth Clark Reiss under the title *Transfigured Night*. This report, Miss Eagan says, ". . . documents for the first time the essential link between the fraternal help brought to Germans and the later outpouring of help from Germans to some of the neediest people in the world." [40] This story of the "transfiguration" of help from former "enemies" into help to others eloquently describes the more mundane term "reciprocation by triangulation."

What we have said about the indirect reciprocation of individual favors applies also to nations. It takes a nation or society of considerable spirit and humanity to recognize a favor done to another as a benefit to itself. This is an issue to which we shall soon turn.

FORMS AND PERCEPTIONS OF RECIPROCATION

In our discussions of catastrophe, generality of need, "no fault of one's own," self-interest of "givers," and injustice, we suggested that these concepts involve high degrees of relativity. What and when, indeed, is a "catastrophe"? When, and when not, is one "at fault"? When, and when not, has "justice" been fulfilled?

In the matter of reciprocation, too, the issue is far from an open-and-shut question. For what one sees as a reciprocal contribution is relative to the breadth of his social vision and to the scope of his sense of mutualism. It is one thing if one expects direct reciprocation (as, for example, a storekeeper who expects to get back in trade approximately what he contributes to a Community Chest or pays in taxes for public assistance). But if one makes his contributions for welfare services for the good of a society, to whose general good beneficiaries of welfare services also contribute, then reciprocation becomes something quite different.

Reciprocal relations between men and institutions assume widely different forms, and some are much more readily perceived than others. Compare, for instance, the rewards to one who contributes to the support of a welfare service with his rewards from the support of his own family. (And who *does not* contribute to a welfare service, if not as a voluntary contributor, then as a taxpayer, or as a consumer who indirectly pays the cost of employee benefits and of corporation contributions to charitable causes?) The reward for contributing to a welfare service is very different from the kiss a man gets from his wife upon returning home, from his pride in his ten-year-old child's good report card, or from the smile of an infant when he chucks its chin.

The coin of the welfare realm is quite different from that in families, mutual aid groups, and the marketplace. Because of this, and because men do not often get back, in exchange for their contributions to welfare services, the kinds of returns they are accustomed to receive from other institutions with which they are probably more familiar, it is not surprising that they so often speak of their welfare contributions as "something for nothing."

This concept may be interpreted from two quite different perspectives: first, from that of a contributor who may feel he gets "nothing" (of the more usual kinds of rewards) for the "something" he gives; second, from that of the beneficiary who *gets* "something for nothing." This term, "something for nothing," commonly means a gratuitously conferred benefit that has not been "earned" in the marketplace or in a mutual aid group or has not been received from a member of one's family. In this sense something for nothing is, rather, "something" for *no thing,* such as work, mutual aid, or family help by which most men's requirements are usually fulfilled. A more general discussion of "something for nothing" will be deferred to the next chapter. However, one aspect of the problem will be presented here before we move too far from the discussion of reciprocation.

From Whom "Something"? For Whom "Nothing"?

The extent to which a gift or help is likely to be considered something for nothing depends in large part upon who the giver is, who the recipient is, and the directness of the relationship between them. In person-to-person or nation-to-nation giving, a donor is in a position to make of his gift what he will (a purchase price, bribe, or tool of manipulation, as discussed in Chapter VII), and can make sure that he gets from it whatever "something" he wants in return. But, if one gets for his "gift" exactly what he wants from it, a discriminating observer might choose to regard this not as a gift but as a transaction smacking of the marketplace.

When a donor group is a cohesive ingroup such as an extended family, a labor union, a fraternal order, a closely knit religious denomination, or a religious community (as, for instance, the Mormons or Amish in the United States or the Parsees in India), the degree of consensus within it may be so high that it is shared by helpees and helpers alike. Thus, a tightly knit group encounters little difficulty in getting what it wants from a beneficiary.

However, as donor groups become more disparate and hetero-
geneous, the more varied and diverse the expectations of their members are likely to be. In consequence, donees may be confronted not
only by a variety of expectations, but also by actual conflicts among
them. Thus the possibility is necessarily reduced of responding in
such a way as to permit any given donor to feel that he got what he
wanted for his money. At the international level it is exactly this
disparateness of expectations that leads nations to prefer multilateral to unilateral aid. For, the more varied the responses expected
from an aided nation, the more difficult it is to comply with any of
them. Similarly, individuals who benefit from contributions from a
wide variety of contributors or taxpayers can hardly be beholden to
any of them. The larger the number who pay the fiddler, the greater
the variety of tunes that will be called, and the greater the difficulty
of satisfying requests.

In complex societies in which welfare services are highly institutionalized, and in which their support is widely dispersed—where
voluntary contributions to United Funds and Community Chests are
solicited from entire communities and where taxpayers of entire
counties, states, and nations support governmental welfare services
—older concepts of getting exactly what one expects from one's gifts
become obsolete. The scope of present-day welfare services is so
vast, the sources of their support so extensive, and their ramifica-
tions so broad that they are much more properly regarded as products of entire societies than as products of individuals or of highly
particularized groups. Even munificent gifts of individual philan-
thropists must be viewed as social rather than personal gifts, for
they tend to be derived from profits on what consumers paid for
goods or services and, where tax policy permits, tend to avoid taxes
that other taxpayers must then make up for. In this sense, social
welfare services are indeed *social* in nature, products of entire societies.

Given the social nature of these services, it follows that individuals who look for "something" in return for what they contribute
voluntarily or through taxes must look for this return in social
rather than in individual terms. If a supporter of a welfare service
does not see himself as an integral part of the social group that supplies it and benefits from it, he may well think that his welfare
dollar went "for nothing." Direct reciprocation is virtually impossible to effectuate in complex societies. However, if those who contribute to the support of services can consider themselves intimately

related to the entire social group that is really the provider of these services, then the two kinds of indirect reciprocation we have discussed become relevant.

If to a highly individualistic giver in a complex society the phrase "something for nothing" really means "something for nothing *for me*," he may well be correct. However, a more humanely sensitive giver, feeling himself an integral part of a complex society providing welfare services, would not be likely to think of these as "something for nothing" as long as the supplying society does indeed get something for the something it gives. This raises again the question posed in Chapter VII about how self-centered or how "enlightened" one's self-interest is. The narrower the social interests of an individual, the more likely it is that he will think his welfare dollar (or pound or rupee or peso) is something for nothing. But the broader an individual's interests—and the greater his grasp of the possibilities of reciprocation by triangulation—the more he will be likely to see his contribution as "something for something." Thus, one key to our problem is how broadly a man views his social identification. And a man's evaluation of a welfare service may be as much a measure of his dimensions as a man as it is an appraisal of the service.

Man's Sense of Community: A Crucial Measure

Values that men place upon today's welfare services depend largely, as we have suggested, upon their views of themselves as human beings. What, to a narrow-minded man, may appear as nothing for something may appear to a broadly humane man as something really important as a return upon the something invested. We are necessarily concerned, therefore, with how men view their various communities of interest. This is equally important whether we think of men primarily as suppliers of welfare services or as consumers. These considerations are related, obviously, to what has been said in Chapter III about self-help, but not for oneself alone, and what has been said in Chapter VII about degrees of enlightened self-interest.

Consideration of man's sense of community brings us face to face with issues that have plagued philosophers, religionists, moralists, and statesmen for centuries: that of man's view of himself not only as a unique human being but also as a card-carrying, voting, and active member of the human race. To this problem there are two dimensions: the lateral one in which man sees his identification and interrelatedness with other human beings of his own day, and the longitudinal one in which he sees himself as part of the continuity of the race—the heir of generations that have preceded him and the legator to posterity. Looking backward, man sees that he now enjoys far more than he has created. Looking forward, he must be concerned that what he does today will permit his grandchildren and great-grandchildren to make the choices they will want to make in their day.

Phrases such as "the brotherhood of man" and "the family of nations" may be heavy with tradition, but for average men they have little substantiality. Even some who are willing to pray for those in the "uttermost parts" of the earth often seem strangely unwilling to identify more actively with those parts. Intercession, apparently, comes much more easily than does a sense of interrelatedness.

"The basic moral issue of our times," wrote philosophy professor Melvin Rader in 1950, "is whether we believe in the widest possible community of human beings." He had said earlier:

The reasonable way to avoid selfishness is not to crush or harass the self, but to expand it until the good of oneself and others coincide. . . . To eliminate the conflict between self-interest and social interest . . . [requires] changing both the self and society: by making society more cooperative, and the individual more altruistic and far-ranging in his interests.[41]

In England, Professor Morris Ginsberg wrote in 1965, "The development of morality consists . . . in the widening of human sympathies." [42] A fellow countryman of his, Professor L. T. Hobhouse, had written many years earlier, "In ethical truth, there is only one ultimate community, which is the human race." [43]

Early in the twentieth century Max Scheler, German philosopher-sociologist, stated as an ethical axiom, "Consideration for the conditions which favour the propagation of the human race, the organic development of peoples and the maintenance of their vital welfare . . . shall take *absolute precedence* over all concern for the maximal accumulation of wealth and material goods. The reversal of this scale of values is the product of *ill-feeling towards the weak and helpless* and betrays a corrupted morality.[44]

Professor T. V. Smith of the University of Chicago wrote in *The Democratic Way of Life,*

Perennially there arise in the dreams of men these three goals: liberty, equality, fraternity. And the brightest of these is fraternity. . . . Families have grown into clans, clans expanded into tribes, and tribes have grown into nations. The human touch tends to grow from more to more. The intrinsic good of intimate kindliness . . . furnishes a goal in terms of which to conceive an ideal community where all would not only have friends, but be friends. . . . Fraternity is the great spiritual objective of the democratic way of life; liberty is the indispensable means to a meaningful brotherhood; and equality is but a reminder that if liberty is good for the few, it is also good for all. Thus is fraternity ennobled through liberty, and liberty generalized through equality.[45]

New dimensions added to these issues by modern technological developments have been stressed by Nobel prize-winning biologist Hermann J. Muller. In his words:

Now that advances in science, along with technological achievements in communication, transportation, and industry are drawing all peoples closer together into an increasingly interconnected *de facto* world-wide community . . . the pressure of feeling is everywhere strong to extend to all men the fellowship earlier reserved for others of the same nationality. . . .

Only in recent times, however, has it been practicable for men to extend their fellowship to all humanity.[46]

What is whimsical, though, is that the very winds of change that are blowing up social tensions all over the world and are blowing down some social solidarities may, of their very force, be driving men to new patterns of social cohesiveness. This possibility suggests that one might not only agree with Professor Muller that technical achievement at last makes it "practicable for men to extend their fellowship to all humanity," but might also conclude that it may be utterly impractical to fail to do so.

Dr. Brock Chisholm, former Director General of the World Health Organization, thought that the hurricane force of the winds of change in the 1960's were blowing into obsolescence the old concept of "my country right or wrong." "This has been our standard system," Dr. Chisholm told an American audience in 1962, and then added:

. . . The system worked as long as a group was defensible, which meant until about 15 years ago when, quite suddenly, it became apparent that no . . . people could be assured of security against attack from outside. . . .

Our whole system of survival in groups . . . had quite suddenly become obsolete, because the survival group had quite suddenly become the human race itself.[47]

Although the magnitude and extent of the forces of change that were in motion in the 1960's were unprecedented, it is noteworthy that even when Graham Wallas wrote the *Great Society*—by which he meant, of course, not a national society like the one being popularized today, but a world society—he did so because he saw the complex developments that even in the nineteenth century were heightening interdependence of men, communities, and nations. Even in the fifth century before Christ the Chinese philosopher Mo-Ti, whom Dagobert Runes calls "an apostle of human brotherhood," set down criteria for what he too was calling (in translation, at any rate) the "Great Society." [48]

Historically, men have looked to religion to help bring about world unity, because major religions emphasize the brotherhood of man. Even religions that are comparatively unknown in the Western Hemisphere stress this concept. One of the most moving experiences I ever had was to hear a Buddhist monk in a monastery in far western China say, during World War II, "There is no white man, no yellow man, only man. There are no nations, only men."

How effective religions will yet prove themselves to be in effectuating the concept of universal brotherhood is, of course, subject to debate. Still, men widely hope for the best from them.

In 1965 theologian Reinhold Niebuhr stated the well-known Christian view on this issue in these terms, ". . . The unique freedom which distinguishes men from brutes was and is truly the basis of a common humanity and of a potential sense of kinship with all men. . . . The true self needs other selves in order to be itself." [49]

Not only philosophers and religionists speak of man's need for "community." President Johnson has several times referred to man's "hunger for community."

Social scientists, too, have written much about the importance of man's sense of community. Robert A. Nisbet of the University of California, in *The Quest for Community*, contends that this is so earnest a quest that, if more normal community relationships are not developed, man will rather go to war or accept a dictatorship that does give him a sense of community than continue to feel unaligned with some purpose outside himself.[50]

Earlier, in 1948, Robert S. Lynd had written, "No large society can long exist which is careless of [the] element of community in feeling and purpose. The tactics of a Hitler are profoundly right in so far as they recognize and seek to serve the need of human beings for the constant dramatization of the feeling of common purpose." [51]

In 1966 Whitney M. Young, Jr., addressed the International Conference of Social Work on the subject "Developing a Sense of Community in Today's Urban Areas: Overcoming Apathy, Anxiety, and Alienation." He said, in part, "There is something positive in all cultures and perhaps the greatest sense of community comes in the recognition by the individual that he has something to offer and a positive contribution to make. Perhaps it is a question of dignity." [52]

To appreciate fully the importance of a sense of community, one will do well to look at situations in which it is weak or nonexistent. When Edward C. Banfield, in 1958, wrote *The Moral Basis of a Backward Society*, he explained:

This book is about a single village in southern Italy the extreme poverty and backwardness of which is to be explained largely (but not entirely) by the inability of the villagers to act together for their common good or, indeed, for any end transcending the immediate, material interest of the nuclear family. This inability to concert activity beyond the immediate family arises from an ethos—that of "amoral familism." [53]

Americans who smugly think that such social isolation might characterize some "backward" society but not one so advanced as their own would doubtless be shocked by the picture that Lyford paints in *The Airtight Cage*.

When Robert J. Havighurst of the University of Chicago, Robert F. Peck, and others studied "'character development'" in "Prairie City," they identified a number of "character-types." Among them was one they called "Rational-Altruistic." Persons of this type were described as follows:

The Rational-Altruistic person feels, and is, both well-loved and loving, warmly and spontaneously so. Being accurate in his perceptions and realistic in his judgment, he is able to express his liking for others in ways that effectively advance their well-being.

Upon conclusion of this study, Robert F. Peck, in a section entitled "Toward a Scientific Basis for Ethics," writes:

If man is by nature a social being, as seems an inescapable fact, then he cannot stand to be rejected or continually frustrated by other people. . . . It is an observable fact that friendly, considerate treatment by others is essential to the genuine happiness of every human being.

From this study, Peck concludes—and religionists have long sensed this—". . . the most practical rule for real personal happiness is the golden rule." [54]

Though traveling by a quite different route, that anthropologist extraordinary, Ashley Montague, reaches the same conclusion. In *On Being Human* he wrote:

Co-operative behavior clearly has great survival value. . . . The dominant principle which informs all behavior that is biologically healthy is love. Without love there can be no healthy social behavior, co-operation, or security. To love thy neighbor as thyself is not simply good text material for Sunday morning sermons but perfectly sound biology.[55]

Another anthropologist who has come to similar conclusions is Weston La Barre, as is clear in *The Human Animal*.[56] Moreover, biologists themselves are increasingly regarding man as part of nature, which is much more cooperative and less "red in tooth and claw" than some observers in the past have suggested.[57]

With respect to the constant broadening of what a man views as his ingroup, University of California philosopher Hugh Miller observed:

The progress of primitive man was advanced by the continued extension of domestic response to the group. . . . As the family became stronger, and endured longer, it deepened its influence upon individual development, and so more effectively socialized [the term is used, of course, in its sociopsychological, not its political sense—D.S.H.] the group, which then still better protected the family, and so on. This *repercussion between domestic and social habit* was, and still is, the *dynamo* of *human progress*. The true society is a large quasi-domestic group, in which domestic affection is brought to each and all.[58]

In this light, it is not too much to say that a significant index of a man's character is how far his bonds of brotherhood can be stretched, how many others he can see as equal to himself, how far out he believes his ingroup reaches. Subscription to a policy of "You scratch my back and I'll scratch yours" demands little social imagination—or civilization. Mice and monkeys do that. However, both social imagination and civilization are required for men to retain their identity with, their sense of mutualism with, and their feeling of responsibility toward members of widely dispersed groups.

In fact, historian Ralph Turner, in his classic history, *The Great Cultural Traditions*, has interpreted cultural progress throughout the ages as the ever-broadening expansion of what men consider their ingroups:

The subversion of the individual's interest to his in-group's interest . . . has always been the fundamental factor giving substance to altruism. . . . The redefinition of the in-group interest has been always—and is today—a significant aspect of cultural growth; indeed, moral growth may be said to occur almost entirely in terms of such redefinition.[59]

Men: Brothers or Coexisters?

Some will see the optimal relationship of man to his fellow men as one of brotherhood, but others will see it as mere coexistence, living and letting live (which is much less demanding). Some will seek to be helpful, but without reciprocity; others will see giving and helping as necessarily involving receiving and "help for the helper." However, increasing knowledge of men's social needs and their ever greater interdependence—to say nothing of shrinking the world through instant communication and near-instant travel—emphasize the reality that one's community can no longer be regarded as coterminous with his neighborhood, or his world with his nation. Whether men see themselves as brothers or only as coexisters, they will differ also on how far they visualize the reach of their community of interest beyond their immediate groups.

A society's great debates in any day seem often to be directed to "the previous question" rather than to the most urgent questions currently "before the house." Within the United States, for example, preoccupation with such niceties as whether a local health department should be administered by a city or by a county may preclude needed discussion as to whom Americans, Nigerians, Pakistanis, Indonesians, Mainland Chinese, or Russians should include in their ingroups—and how they would go about doing so. Within countries, decisions must be made as to how much different geographical areas or social classes owe one another. By contrast with a debate on issues of this magnitude, it seems like small talk indeed to debate whether topless bathing suits should be regulated by county ordinance or state law or whether the federal government should bear 75 percent or only 50 percent of the cost of any given program.

Although welfare services may not, to employ Professor Miller's terminology, necessarily be much of a "dynamo of human progress," there is reason to think that they can at least foster what he termed the "repercussion between domestic and social habit," and that they can help to serve what Turner referred to as the "redefinition of in-group interest." These possibilities are the theme of Chapter IX.

:: Notes
and
References

1. As reported in *The New York Times*, August 18, 1963. See also *New Delhi Speaks, The Message of the Third Assembly of the World Council of Churches* (London: SCM Press, 1962), p. 52.
2. *Responsibility in the Welfare State?* (Birmingham, England: Council of Christian Churches, 1961).
3. *The Poor Speak* (Columbus: Ohio Citizens' Council for Health and Welfare, 1966), p. 10. (Mimeographed.)
4. See, for example, Eveline Burns, "Inventory and Challenge in Services to People," *Inventory and Challenge* (New York: National Social Welfare Assembly, 1965), p. 6. (Mimeographed.)
5. Oscar Lewis, *The Children of Sanchez* (New York: Random House, 1961), p. xxi.
6. Guido Rosa, *North Africa Speaks* (New York: John Day, 1946), pp. 19, 20. See also William and Paul Paddock, *Hungry Nations* (Boston: Little, Brown, 1964), pp. 141–142, and John Forbes, *The Quaker Star Under Seven Flags: 1917–1927* (Philadelphia: University of Pennsylvania Press, 1962).
7. See, for example, Jean Stoetzel, *Without the Chrysanthemum and the Sword: A Study of the Attitudes of Youth in Post-War Japan* (New York: Columbia University Press, 1955). An excerpt from this publication is available in the author's chapter "Personal Relations" in Bernard S. Silberman, ed., *Japanese Character and Culture: A Book of Selected Readings* (Tucson: University of Arizona Press, 1962), pp. 260–274. In this same volume, see also the excerpt, "Debtor to the Ages and the World" (pp. 289–354) by Ruth F. Benedict from her *Chrysanthemum and the Sword* (Boston: Houghton Mifflin, 1946).
8. Velma Adams, *The Peace Corps in Action* (Chicago: Follett, 1964), pp. 171–172. See also Lawrence H. Fuchs, *"Those Peculiar Americans": The Peace Corps and the American Character* (New York: Meredith Press, 1967), and Frank J. Lynch, S.J., ed., *Four Readings on Philippine Values* (Quezon City: Manila University Press, 1962).
9. Dora Peyser, *The Strong and the Weak* (Sydney, Australia: Currawong, 1951), p. 9.
10. Donald S. Howard, *The WPA and Federal Relief Policy* (New York: Russell Sage Foundation, 1943), especially pp. 811–826. See also two excellent and (in their day) very bold books by E. Wight Bakke that well illustrate the same phenomenon: *Citizens Without Work* (New Haven:

Yale University Press, 1940) and *The Unemployed Worker* (New Haven: Yale University Press, 1940). See also Grace Adams, *Workers on Relief* (New Haven: Yale University Press, 1939), and a fictionalized but still realistic novel of "salvation by work," Jerome Ellison's *The Dam* (New York: Random House, 1941).

11. *The National Observer*, January 27, 1964.
12. Hubert H. Humphrey, *War on Poverty* (New York: McGraw-Hill, 1964), p. 116. An up-to-date and useful analysis of the role of work today may be found in Aaron Levenstein, *Why People Work: Changing Incentives in a Troubled World* (New York: Collier Books, 1964). There is an extensive bibliography, pp. 298–313.
13. Mary Morris, in review of PEP, *Family Needs and the Social Services* (London: G. Allen), in *Social Service Quarterly*, XXXIV (Spring 1961), 32.
14. Forbes, *op. cit.*, p. 77.
15. Dan Q. R. Mulock Houwer, "A Look at the Needs of Children Around the World," *Selected Addresses: [U.S.] Children's Bureau's Fiftieth Anniversary Celebration, 1962* (Washington, D.C.: Government Printing Office, 1963), p. 16.
16. Lewis A. Coser, "The Sociology of Poverty: To the Memory of Georg Simmel," *Social Problems*, 13 (1965), 147. An incisive discussion of donor-donee relationships may be found in Alvin W. Gouldner, "The Norm of Reciprocity: A Preliminary Statement," *American Sociological Review*, 25 (April 1960), 161–178.
17. Charles E. Silberman, *Crisis in Black and White* (New York: Random House, 1964), p. 316.
18. Eileen Younghusband, "The Indivisibility of Social Welfare," in William G. Dixon, ed., *Social Welfare and the Preservation of Human Values* (Vancouver: Dent, 1957), p. 59.
19. Robert Coles, "The Poor Don't Want to Be Middle-Class," *The New York Times Magazine*, December 19, 1965, p. 58.
20. See Leonard J. Duhl, "Planning and Poverty," *The Urban Condition: People and Policy in the Metropolis* (New York: Basic Books, 1963), p. 304.
21. Frank Riessman, "The Revolution in Social Work: The New Nonprofessional," *Trans-action*, 2 (November-December 1964), 12–17. See also Robert Reiff and Frank Riessman, *The Indigenous Nonprofessional: A Strategy of Change in Community Action and Community Mental Health Programs* (Lexington, Mass.: Community Mental Health Journal Monograph, 1965), with an extended bibliography on pp. 30–32.
22. Fuchs, *op. cit.*
23. Joseph P. Lyford, *The Airtight Cage: A Study of New York's West Side* (New York: Harper & Row, 1966), pp. 348, 346. See also William Stringfellow, *Dissenter in a Great Society: A Christian View of America in Crisis* (New York: Holt, Rinehart and Winston, 1966), especially p. 25.
24. Ralph Linton, "The Problem of Universal Values," in Robert F. Spencer, ed., *Method and Perspective in Anthropology* (Minneapolis: University of Minnesota Press, 1954), p. 164.
25. Reinhold Niebuhr, *The Contribution of Religion to Social Work* (New York: Columbia University Press, 1932), p. 84.

26. *Is It Safe? Is It Wise? Is It Right?* (New York: State Charities Aid Association, *ca.* 1963), not paginated. Quotation is from inside back cover. See also Edgar May, "The Disjointed Trio: Poverty, Politics, and Power," *The Social Welfare Forum, 1963* (New York: Columbia University Press, 1963), pp. 47–61.

27. Thomas B. Morgan, *Among the Anti-Americans* (New York: Holt, Rinehart and Winston, 1967), p. 28. See also pp. 143–144, *i.a.*

28. William Benton, "The Communist Threat at Our Back Door," *The New York Times Magazine,* July 17, 1960, pp. 44, 10. See also John Plank, "Our Good Neighbors Should Come First," *The New York Times Magazine*, June 6, 1965, pp. 31, 98–100.

29. B. K. Nehru in "Letters to the Editor," *The New York Times Magazine,* May 7, 1961, p. 12.

30. Herbert Aptekar, "The Preparation of Americans for Social Work Abroad," *Social Work Education Reporter,* XIII (June 1965), 19.

31. I. W. Moomaw, *The Challenge of Hunger: A Program for More Effective Foreign Aid* (New York: Praeger, 1966), pp. 86, 36, 43.

32. Arnold J. Toynbee, *On Coexistence* (Santa Barbara, Cal.: Center for the Study of Democratic Institutions, 1965), p. 33. Lawrence H. Fuchs interestingly contrasts the attitudes of Peace Corps volunteers in the Philippines with those of "missionaries of previous times," *op. cit.,* p. 172. For a less restrained comment on this point, see Dagobert D. Runes, *Despotism: A Pictorial History of Tyranny* (New York: Philosophical Library, 1963), p. 124. In his encyclical, *Populorum Progressio,* Paragraph 12, even Pope Paul VI speaks of the "human" and therefore "not perfect" work of missionaries. This may be found in various editions, including *On the Development of Peoples* (Washington, D.C.: United States Catholic Conference, 1967). In this edition, Paragraph 12 appears on p. 12.

33. As reported by Arthur J. Moore, Jr., in *The Interchurch News,* VIII (August-September 1966), 6.

34. Ivan Illich, "The Seamy Side of Charity," *America,* 116 (January 21, 1965), 89.

35. Frank Tannenbaum, *Ten Keys to Latin America* (New York: Knopf, 1963), p. 131.

36. *The Foreign Assistance Program: Annual Report to the Congress for the Fiscal Year 1963* (Washington, D.C.: U. S. Agency for International Development, Government Printing Office, 1964), p. 3.

37. Paul G. Hoffman, *The Significance of World Conditions to the Well-Being of People in America* (New York: National Social Welfare Assembly, 1960). (Mimeographed.)

38. *Social Welfare and the United Nations Social Commission* (New York: National Social Welfare Assembly, 1965), p. 2 of fifth statement.

39. Christian A. Herter, with Donald Robinson, "What Foreign Countries Can Do for Us," *This Week Magazine,* July 15, 1962, pp. 4, 5. For suggestions of what the world might learn from African tribes, see Anthony Sampson, "From Veld to City: The Bantu Drama," *The New York Times Magazine,* May 22, 1960, p. 28.

40. Eileen Egan and Elizabeth Clark Reiss, *Transfigured Night: The CRALOG Experience* (Philadelphia: Livingston Publishing Co., 1964), pp. x, 161–

162. For a German view of this matter, see Wilhelm Hondrich, *The Conception of Social Welfare in German History* (Dinslaken: Verlagsgesellschaft für Gegenwartskunde, 1965), pp. 22–23. A similar response, by Norway, is reported by I. W. Moomaw, *op. cit.*, p. 121.

41. Melvin Rader, *Ethics and Society* (New York: Henry Holt, 1950), p. 223. A similar view is expressed by E. J. Urwick, *The Values of Life* (Toronto: University of Toronto Press, 1948), p. 3.

42. Morris Ginsberg, *On Justice in Society* (Baltimore: Penguin Books, 1965), p. 56.

43. L. T. Hobhouse, *Morals in Evolution: A Study in Comparative Ethics* (London: Chapman and Hall, 1951), p. 235.

44. Max Scheler, *The Nature of Sympathy,* Peter Heath, tr. (London: Routledge and Kegan Paul, 1912), pp. 107–108.

45. T. V. Smith, with Eduard C. Lindeman, *The Democratic Way of Life: An American Interpretation* (New York: New American Library, 1951), pp. 19–20, 21, 64. See also "Liberty, Equality, and Fraternity," in Barrows Dunham, *Man Against Myth* (Boston: Little, Brown, 1948), pp. 309–316.

46. Hermann J. Muller, *Therefore Choose Life* (Santa Barbara, Cal.: Center for the Study of Democratic Institutions, 1965), p. 31.

47. Brock Chisholm, "Children 2012," *Selected Addresses,* [U.S.] *Children's Bureau's Fiftieth Anniversary Celebration, 1962* (Washington, D.C.: Government Printing Office, 1963), pp. 6–7. See also *On The Developed and the Developing* (Santa Barbara, Cal.: Center for the Study of Democratic Institutions, 1965), pp. 18–19 and Richard Lichtman, *Toward Community* (Santa Barbara, Cal.: Center for the Study of Democratic Institutions, 1966). See President Lyndon B. Johnson's address to the American Legion in 1966, as reported in *The New York Times,* August 31, 1966.

48. Mo-Ti, "On Standard Patterns," in Dagobert Runes, ed., *Treasury of Philosophy* (New York: Philosophical Library, 1955), p. 850.

49. Reinhold Niebuhr, *Man's Nature and His Communities* (New York: Scribner, 1965), pp. 74, 93, 118.

50. Robert A. Nisbet, *The Quest for Community: A Study in the Ethics of Order and Freedom* (New York: Oxford University Press, 1953), p. 41.

51. Robert S. Lynd, *Knowledge for What?* (Princeton: Princeton University Press, 1948), p. 85.

52. Whitney M. Young, Jr., "Developing a Sense of Community in Today's Urban Areas," in *Urban Development: Its Implications for Social Welfare,* Proceedings of the XIIIth International Conference of Social Work (New York: Columbia University Press, 1967), p. 63.

53. Edward C. Banfield, *The Moral Basis of a Backward Society* (Glencoe: Free Press, 1958), pp. 10, 39–40.

Two highly relevant and significant books are by Robert Cooley Angell, *Free Society and Moral Crisis* (Ann Arbor: University of Michigan Press, 1958), and his earlier and somewhat more limited in scope *The Integration of American Society: A Study of Groups and Institutions* (New York: McGraw-Hill, 1941).

Relevant also in the present context is the extensive literature on anomie. See, for example, two papers with deceptively modest titles by

Melvin Seeman, "Alienation and Social Learning in a Reformatory," *The American Journal of Sociology*, LXIX (November 1963), 270–284, and "Alienation and Learning in a Hospital Setting," *American Sociological Review*, 27 (December 1962), 772–782. See also Dorothy L. Meier and Wendell Bell, "Anomia and Differential Access to the Achievement of Life Goals," *American Sociological Review*, 24 (April 1959), 189–202.

54. Robert F. Peck, with Robert J. Havighurst and Ruth Cooper, Jesse Lilienthal, and Douglas More, *The Psychology of Character Development* (New York: Wiley, 1964), pp. 171–172, 200, 201.

Another paper that is interesting in this context is "The Golden Rule in the Light of New Insight," presented in India by Harvard Professor Erik H. Erikson, who said he was speaking "primarily as a clinician," in *Insight and Responsibility: Lectures on the Ethical Implications of Psychoanalytic Insight* (New York: Norton, 1964), pp. 219–243.

55. Ashley Montague, *On Being Human* (New York: Henry Schuman, 1950), p. 100. For a more extended analysis of this theme, see his *The Direction of Human Development: Biological and Social Bases* (New York: Harper & Row, 1955), especially pp. 288–298.

56. Weston La Barre, *The Human Animal* (Chicago: University of Chicago Press, 1954), especially pp. 303–334.

57. Noteworthy among biologists who have written on this theme are W. C. Allee, *Cooperation Among Animals* (New York: Henry Schuman, 1951) and Theodosius Dobzhansky, *The Biological Basis of Human Freedom* (New York: Columbia University Press, 1956).

58. Hugh Miller, *The Community of Man* (New York: Macmillan, 1949), pp. 68, 67.

59. Ralph Turner, *The Great Cultural Traditions: The Foundations of Civilization, The Ancient Cities* (New York: McGraw-Hill, 1941), Vol. I, pp. 121–122.

IX
"SOMETHING
for
NOTHING"

T here's nothing so exciting as getting something for nothing." Thus wrote Daphne Athas in *Greece by Prejudice*.[1] Whether *nothing* else would be so exciting may be debatable. However, probably few would disagree that to find in the street $100,000 that one could keep legally *would* be exciting.

It would be nearly as exciting to come out a winner in a national lottery, a football pool, or the Irish Sweepstakes. Especially when tickets cost only a penny, a peso, or $2 or so, such winnings can be regarded (if not literally) as something for nothing. But what might at first appear to be something for nothing may, upon closer view, prove to be considerably less exciting.

"SOMETHING" FOR "NOTHING"?

For example, if a Sweepstakes winner, in a jurisdiction where traffic in Sweepstakes tickets is illegal, lands in jail, his excitement would understandably be somewhat subdued. Or if upon finding $100,000 in the street, one fails to attempt to locate its true owner and is therefore sent to prison, the something he thought he had for nothing would have cost him dearly after all. In fact, when Daphne Athas wrote as she did about "getting something for nothing," she was talking about relief supplies that were being distributed after a typhoon had struck a Greek island. Although the shoes, garments, and blankets that were distributed might have been "something" (and something important to survival), many would question whether these gifts were actually "for nothing" since the price paid for them was in a sense the devastation of the island.

In other words, appearances can be misleading. Although some things may seem to fall into one's lap "for nothing," closer inspection may reveal that they have been exceedingly costly.

WELFARE SERVICES—"SOMETHING" FOR "NOTHING"?

To the extent that considerations advanced in earlier chapters have validity, it follows that inability to attain for oneself and his family the key goods of life will be accompanied at best by embarrassment and shame and at worst by downright hurt. Thus, one could hardly regard as "for nothing" the welfare services required. Against the "something" that is received must be debited the cost. And if any individual does not realize that welfare services are not a wholly acceptable alternative to getting along on his own, news media and the policies of some welfare agencies will undoubtedly correct his perspective.

Apart from his own feelings in the matter, a beneficiary might find the cost of being served by a welfare agency increased by the scorn of relatives, neighbors, friends, associates—and the public.

Among the heaviest costs of public assistance are those borne by a man whom his wife and children regard as a failure because he is unable to be a "good provider." Not to go off to work every day as other men do, not to be the family's breadwinner, can (as welfare personnel well know) undermine his role and authority as head of the house—especially if, as some agencies insist, assistance checks are made out to his wife. To assume that such loss of face within his own household—and in his community—is "nothing" is to overlook elements that are exceedingly important in the relevant cost accounting. In consequence, superficial views of welfare services as being "something for nothing" must be corrected in order to take into consideration the costs, and possibly heavy costs, that are exacted by a society that places high values upon self-help and "making your own way." How real these costs are, even to the point of deterring acceptance of needed and available welfare services—and the relief expressed by beneficiaries, their spouses, and children when they can dispense with services they had accepted—has already been suggested.

FOR "SOMETHING"—"*NOTHING*"?

Benefits derived by societies from their social welfare services are both material and nonmaterial. They can be measured in part, but only in part, in economic and material terms, and in the values placed upon these. Like other social institutions, they must be appraised also in moral and philosophical terms. The dividends paid to a society are both positive and negative. Some of the "goods" are constructive benefits for society, while others are *avoidance* of problems that societies appear to deplore more than the cost of the welfare services that are designed to avert them.

The greater the imbalance between what a man thinks he contributes to welfare services and what he sees as redounding to his own benefit, the more likely he is to think of his contribution as money down the drain. Some cynics so define almost any expenditure for welfare. However, even the less cynical person will think in this way if he is endlessly called upon to contribute to a specific purpose, if the object of his gift is particularly remote, or if the behavior of beneficiaries is obnoxious to him—as it may be when public assistance recipients keep having illegitimate children or people who receive foreign aid burn down his country's embassies.

If one's money indeed went down the drain—or were "poured down a rathole"—his resentment would be not only understandable and excusable but commendable. However, even if a gift seems not to yield the expected results or is swallowed up in ratholes of virtually unlimited and unending needs, perhaps the problem is not so much the use to which the gift is put as it is the figure of speech used to describe it. Perhaps the gift should not be pictured as "money" fruitlessly expended in attempting to effect some particular purpose, but rather as rat poison to counter nefarious forces at work and to prevent further damage and deterioration that would further delay more positive solutions.

Few efforts have been made in welfare history, unfortunately, to see to it that contributions to welfare and other philanthropic causes appear to be anything other than "gifts." One notable exception, necessitated, it is true, by the illegality of the enterprise, was the "underground railroad" in the United States, which in the nineteenth century helped slaves to escape to freedom. Contributors to this cause were known as "stockholders," partly because the term was consonant with "railroading," but primarily to becloud their illegal activities. "Railroaders" took special glee in this ruse when even slave owners became "stockholders." It is regrettable that welfare agencies have found no similar substitute for "givers," "contributors," "supporters," and the like, which emphasize their "providing" role but obscure the very real benefits directly and indirectly redounding to them. Exactly these benefits were what we had in mind when, in Chapter II, we included in our definition of welfare services their role in helping others to enjoy key values not only because these are regarded as important to them, but also because such enjoyment is "essential also to the well-being both of those who offer the aid and of larger communities of which they are a part."

Societies attaining a relatively high level of social sophistication are probably so far removed from some of the stark realities of life that some of the social benefits gained from welfare services are easily overlooked. Among the reasons advanced in support of American foreign aid none is more stressed than its contribution to world security and to the security of the United States. Within the United States, state and federal welfare legislation is now increasingly justified on grounds that it serves "the general welfare"—a term that is so vague and variously interpreted that the realities behind it, which were quite clear in an earlier day, tend to become obfuscated.

This problem was clearly underlined in the Economic Report of the President in 1954, only eight years after passage of the Employment Act of 1946. "Because the flow of security to the individual has been built primarily on welfare considerations," declares the report, "its contribution to the economic progress of the United States has not been adequately appreciated." [2] This observation is remarkable in that it is related to unemployment compensation, which, though widely recognized as a "built-in stabilizer" of the economy, was still thought to have been insufficiently appreciated as such. If this is true of unemployment benefits, whose economic role has been analyzed time and again, it is far more true of welfare services, whose observable effects have hardly been identified, much less measured, in anything like the terms in which unemployment insurance has been studied.

However, if one goes back into the history of welfare services, to days in which the kinds of activities that today are blithely defended as promoting the "general welfare" were first established, one gains a quite different perspective. We shall consider this after we discuss certain other returns to society for its welfare dollars.

Self-Interest

Prominent among reasons why individuals, groups, and societies support welfare services is self-interest. One need not enter the lists in the historic fray about whether man is more individualistic or more altruistic in nature in order to recognize that self-interest is a prominent, if not the preeminent, factor. Certainly it is unnecessary to belabor the point—especially in the light of what we have observed about the relationship of giving to the clear self-interest of the giver, whether the giver is an individual or a nation—and also in the light of what we have observed about the use of "gifts" as purchase prices, bribes, and tools of manipulation; and what we have observed about the preference of some groups for injustice to others even at the price of having to throw them a welfare sop.

One particularly ironic twist to this phenomenon is that power blocs that determine the nature of a society's social welfare programs are likely to bend them to serve their own particular interests, even when these are in direct conflict with the interests of those ostensibly served by these programs. And when this happens it is of course a welfare agency that—knowingly or unknowingly—is the instrumentality of the power structure.

Broadened Enjoyment of Society's Values

One obvious gain from welfare services is the broader enjoyment of a society's key values: food, clothing, family life, and so forth. The "good" resulting from this would be what the society sees in these values.

Another dimension of this consideration is that values can be preserved only if they continue to be valued. If, as previously suggested, chastity is widely disregarded, it is likely to lose its position as a value, and if widespread cheating in college examinations is tolerated, this is an open invitation for more cheating. What "everybody does" is likely to become a new norm, however much it may previously have been disvalued. Or, as law enforcement officers say, "Law unenforced becomes unenforceable." Thus, preservation of values as values is dependent upon their continuing to be valued and not widely abrogated.

Although many of the key values served by welfare programs are so fundamental in nature that it is almost inconceivable that even widespread fasting, nudism, or moving into tents would ever lead to disvaluing food, clothing, and shelter, the same cannot be said of all values. For example, a sense of personal dignity and worth, aspiration, self-support, constructive family living, and basic group participation can easily atrophy if not actively supported, encouraged, and propagated. Against what seem insuperable odds, a sense of dignity and worth can wither into self-deprecation, aspiration can devolve into fatalism, family living can be wrecked, and anomie and alienation can displace social identification and social living. The more widely social disvalues prevail—whatever the reason—the more likely it will be difficult to sustain their opposites as values.

In this context, it is noteworthy that Professor Roy Lubove has uncovered the fact that "The New York Charity Organization Society [as long ago as 1887] warned that 'if we do not furnish the poor with elevating influences, they will rule us by degrading ones.' " [3] On this point Karl Mannheim has some trenchant observations. Of insecurity resulting from unemployment, for example, he says, "Even if the immediate needs of life are satisfied, by means of unemployment relief, the whole life-organization and the family hopes and expectations are annihilated. . . . The validity of established principles and values comes to be doubted."

When men's usual goals and activities are continually thwarted, they tend, Mannheim maintains, to substitute for them "symbolic" ones (swastika, hammer and sickle, and the like). "The utopian symbol makes people act . . . against the system of established relationships, and . . . they . . . seek to call in question the former definition of the situation, *devaluating* meaning and significance of the original level of aspirations." [4] [Emphasis added.]

The very gradualness of this process is in itself cause for concern. "Barbarous acts are rarely committed out of the blue," United States Senator Frank Church has observed. "Step by step, a society becomes accustomed to accept, with less and less moral outrage, and with greater and greater indifference to legitimacy, the successive blows." [5] According to John Toland, even Heinrich Himmler is said to have vomited upon first witnessing an execution. [6]

Possibly the most serious result of failure to accord respect to one's values, however, is that one may not only cease to respect them, but may actually come to discredit if not hate them. This seems possible even of supreme values, including people. At worst, this phenomenon suggests that if one is cruel to others, he gradually comes to think of them as somewhat less than human and so not deserving of humane treatment. When Alexander Donat, after his experiences in concentration camps during World War II, wrote of the cruel treatment that was meted out there, he observed, "The authorities hated their victims as a group because when you wrong people for no reason, sooner or later you must come to hate them." [7]

When slaves are known to be wrongfully enslaved, it is easy to salve one's conscience with the thought that the slaves are somehow something less than human. When cheap agricultural "stoop labor" is required, it is easy to convince oneself that Mexican laborers are peculiarly adapted to it because of physiological characteristics. If these things can happen to others whom one wrongs, there would appear to be danger in the possibility of similarly downgrading values inherent in those whom one neglects. Thus, if people are to continue to be looked upon as people, it is important to treat them as people.

Just as this can be true of end values, so it can apply to means for the attainment of ends. If mooching and sponging become widespread, self-support can deteriorate into living by exploitation or crumble into "overdependency," and the difficulties encountered in encouraging self-aid and individual effort are likely to be heightened.

In assuming, as they do, the encouragement of respect for particular values, whether of ends or of means, welfare agencies assume a grave responsibility. For it is possible that they may be fostering for particular groups certain values that, for these groups at least, may conceivably have lost their relevance. New situations may be teaching new duties while welfare agencies continue to emphasize outdated ones. Or, welfare agencies may be maneuvered into attempts to keep alive among disadvantaged groups "values" that the advantaged have already abandoned but think are still appropriate for others. Or, these agencies may be expected to perpetuate values—such as self-help—in contexts where resources usually construed to be essential to its realization may be lacking.

Social Morality

Morality, whether of individuals or societies, is costly. Men become so accustomed to think of the costliness of sin that it is easy to forget that virtue, too, may be expensive. What wine, women, and song can do to a bankroll is chronicled in biography, story, and fable. But morality also has its costs—in money, effort, and freedom, among others. To beg or steal bread may well require less effort than to earn it by the sweat of one's brow. To care for, nurture, and support an infant and to educate a child costs a great deal in terms of money, effort, and time. If a comparison in terms of "cost" is possible, it "costs" less to strangle it at birth or to abandon it at a church door.

Viewed historically, one can see the issue in the stark contrast between the ways in which problems presented by widowhood have been treated. In Jewish tradition the widow, along with "the orphan and the stranger within thy gates" was the subject of special solicitude. In the Indian tradition of suttee, they got rid of the widow. But—solicitude is costly.

Monogamous marriage has its costs not only in money but in other obligations and in reduced freedom for license. Many men in South American countries are unwilling to pay some of these costs, with the result that illegitimacy rates in some countries run to 50 percent or more of live births. These rates do not reflect wanton promiscuity so much as unions that remain relatively stable but are not legal marriages. In explanation of this phenomenon, it is said that many men believe that, if they married, their mates would become uppity and less susceptible of control than if the men are free to walk away from them and to owe them nothing.

Decency and humaneness in war can be costly. A wounded comrade may temporarily divert the attention of fellow soldiers from the fighting, and medical and hospital services can permanently divert into noncombatant roles manpower that might usefully be employed in combat.

Morality is costly among nations, too. To shoot prisoners on the spot would undoubtedly be "cheaper" than guarding, transporting, and supporting them, and possibly giving them expensive medical care. General William C. Westmoreland, when commander of United States forces in Vietnam, was reported to have "hit the ceiling" when he saw pictures of American troops burning down whole villages in the hope of uncovering members of the Viet Cong. He ordered, in the interest of "humanity," a reduction in this practice even though it might mean the loss of American lives to bullets of snipers hiding in peasant homes.

Morality, decency, humaneness can be costly—in money, perhaps, or in effort, freedom, or lives. Individuals or societies that place high value upon helpfulness, giving, and sharing cannot, of course, expect that these values can be realized without cost. When Paul G. Hoffman spoke as he did of the degree to which foreign aid served the self-interest of "giving" nations, he also said that this is not the only reason for them to give it. Another, he maintained, is that it is "good for the soul." [8] Soul-improvement, like that glow of satisfaction one feels upon doing what he believes is right, can be costly. How costly it can be, if it is sensed as being costly at all, depends, as suggested in the previous chapter, upon one's interpretation of himself. For example, Britain's Barbara Ward (Lady Jackson) contends that "expansion of opportunity sought for the sake of others ends by bringing well-being and expansion to oneself. . . . Our morals and our interests—seen in true perspective—do not pull apart. Only the narrowness of our own interests, whether personal or national, blinds us to this moral truth." [9]

Closely related to what we are speaking of as moral considerations is what Leonard E. Read, president of the Foundation for Economic Education, terms "psychic gain." "The reason why so many of us, when making a contribution . . . overrate our 'goodness'—is that we pay no heed to our psychic profit." [10] Sargent Shriver has said of the War on Poverty, "The ultimate dimension of this war is a spiritual dimension . . . the war . . . is a movement of conscience, a national act of expiation." [11] Somewhat similarly, the federal Advisory Council on Public Welfare said, in 1966, with respect to income maintenance programs, "For the Nation as a whole a floor under income constitutes a clear declaration of conscience." [12] These attitudes are met in Britain, too. When Lloyd George was pressing for the Pensions Bill in 1925, much was said about "conscience." More recently the National Assistance Board in Britain has been described as "trustees for the Public conscience." All of which recalls the position taken by Professor L. T. Hobhouse many years ago. "Society," Professor Hobhouse wrote, "has a soul to be saved, and its salvation is the justice, humanity and freedom realized in its inward and outward relations." [13]

Whether the level of social morality represented in welfare services is as high as it should be, and whether welfare services were cloaking in mercy what beneficiaries should be entitled to in terms of fuller justice, are issues on which opinions will differ.

Public Images

Almost as important as morality itself are the outward signs of being moral. This is what makes the issue of public images important—whether they are the images of individuals or of societies. When the founders of the United States were drafting the Declaration of Independence, they did it with one eye on public image ("a decent respect to the opinions of mankind").

The social usefulness of morality is not served, of course, by hypocrisy, in the sense of attempting to present an image different from reality. But neither is it served by hiding morality under a bushel. Some individuals, societies, and nations will think first of morality and will be content to let the images take care of themselves. Others will think first of the images they wish to project and then of the morality necessary to create them. In either case images are expensive, since the morality behind them is costly.

As to nations, the images they project have probably always been important. However, in a day of virtually instantaneous communication—when radios carry word of the world even into remote Bedouin tents or to isolated mountain villages in the Himalayas or the Andes—appearances have more significance than ever. This greater importance is heightened still more in a world embroiled in ideological conflict, in which antagonistic propaganda machines are on the qui vive, ready to grind out diatribes against any nation guilty of a miscue—or guilty even of inaction when action seems needed.

Depending upon when they left the United States, many American travelers have been consternated when abroad by the acidity and frequency of questions—from hosts, colleagues, taxi drivers, shop-keepers, and others—about violence in Little Rock, Birmingham, Watts; about "pockets of poverty" in Appalachia; or about irresponsible remarks made by public figures about foreign aid. It would be interesting to know how many millions of dollars' worth of work of the U. S. Information Administration abroad is offset by just one noxious incident at home. Transoceanic information services may be costly, but establishment and preservation of the reality that a nation might wish to have projected in its image is even more costly.

If, beyond the mere projection of an image, the American people wish to exemplify a way of life that they would like to see other peoples emulate, something Luther Gulick said is relevant, "We can hardly expect that our attachment to freedom will be contagious internationally unless we can demonstrate its values here at home." [14]

Many years ago, within the context of public relief policy, I presented under the heading "The 'National Interest' and Federal Responsibility for Relief" considerations relevant to this issue and still pertinent today.[15] One needs little imagination to envision some of the possibilities. For example, who would want to calculate, in international terms, the cost if just 1 percent of New York City's public assistance recipients were to be cut off from assistance and were to mill around the United Nations headquarters, begging from members of the General Assembly? Yet, rendering beggary unnecessary as a means of gaining a livelihood is costly. Many countries, though deploring beggary, cannot begin to afford to abolish it.

The effect upon the image of the United States would be incalculable if, instead of 1 percent of New York's assistance recipients, the millions of public assistance recipients in the United States were reduced to beggary and panhandling in every city and town in the country.

If we also visualize widespread stealing and looting (which present special problems because "stealing bread for one's children" is often widely condoned), the effect would be even more unfathomable. And, the impact upon the American people directly confronted by begging, hungry mothers, fathers, and children would be beyond reckoning. To live in a country whose image is not besmirched by beggary and whose citizens are not plagued by pilferage may yield a certain satisfaction. This does not come, however, as a free gift of the gods. It is costly, its price being paid partly in cash, partly in effort, partly in other values that must be foregone if social morality is to be actualized and its image projected.

We would not venture to guess whether social morality and public images are "worth" their cost. Much too complicated are the cost accounting involved and the calculus by which costs and credits must be weighed against each other. Our point is not to attempt to strike a balance. It is, first, to question the validity of the contention that it is "for nothing" that the "something" represented by welfare services is provided and, second, to suggest that in the calculus questions of morality and public images cannot be excluded.

Opinions will differ as to whether the reality projected as an image is as good as it should be. Some might argue that more opportunities and justice and less compensatory welfare service would represent a reality more worthy of projection. Whatever one's judgment of this, welfare services contribute to the image that *is* projected.

Social Order and Structures

Historically, the prime social purpose of welfare services (and of their forebears) has probably been the preservation, or restoration, of social order. This is revealed much more clearly today in newly emerging nations than in established societies. Appeals for support of foreign aid programs of the United States are liberally sprinkled with urgings to feed, clothe, and provide medical care for underdeveloped nations lest their continuing needs lead to social unrest or threaten world security and peace. John W. Gardner, when Secretary of the U. S. Department of Health, Education, and Welfare, said in 1967, "The combination of poverty and rising expectations that exists among half the world's population today is as volatile and threatening in its own way as the bomb. If bridges to peace are to be built among nations, the widening economic and social chasm that divides the world today is going to have to be narrowed." [16] It is the truth inherent in views of this kind that makes credible the names of programs such as "Food for Peace" and "Water for Peace."

A variation on this theme is the widespread belief that if underdeveloped nations are not helped to maintain at least a minimal level of well-being, they will rush to embrace communism. The fact that nations aided by others in the free world have not done this is widely accepted as prima facie evidence of the success of the free world's foreign aid programs.

In 1966 the governments of Vietnam and the United States stated their positions concerning pacification of Vietnam in the Declaration of Honolulu. The declaration stressed the importance of promoting the well-being of the Vietnamese people in order to win their support for the government and social order. Significantly, when George K. Tanham and his associates described Vietnamese and American economic and social pacification programs antedating the declaration, they entitled their account *War Without Guns*.[17] In Thailand, in 1966, the prime minister declared, "The people know the efforts of the Government in developing the rural areas in order to raise the living standards and this encourages the loyalty of the people and makes them into a strong unit to resist aggression and infiltration from external hostile forces." [18]

The same theme appeared in the Western Hemisphere; the whole point of the Alliance for Progress was to foster social and other reforms and so, hopefully, forestall antidemocratic tendencies, primarily Castroism. On the eve of the meeting of presidents of nations in the Organization of American States in 1967, President Eduardo Frei Montalva predicted that if Latin-American nations did not voluntarily revolutionize their lives, totalitarian revolutions would be forced upon them within ten years.[19]

What was here being said about preservation of national institutions had been said twenty years before about preservation of the United Nations. In his biography of Herbert H. Lehman, first Director-General of the United Nations Relief and Rehabilitation Administration (UNRRA), historian Allan Nevins reports, "One mode of keeping the United Nations together was to use the resources of the richer members to assist the prostrate." [20]

During World War II one also saw the structure-preserving value of health and welfare services offered by underground movements, such as those in France, Belgium, The Netherlands, and Yugoslavia. These services which, at the risk of torture and death, were offered to wounded fighters, to widows and children of slain fighters, and to fallen Allied airmen or escaping Allied prisoners were essential to the very preservation of resistance movements.

The idea that deprivation foments unrest has wide currency. Edwin Markham's "The Man with the Hoe" furthered the idea:

> *How will it be with kingdoms and with kings—*
> *With those who shaped him to the thing he is—*

> *When this dumb Terror shall rise to judge the world,*
> *After the silence of the centuries?*

In German tradition there is of course the specter of Hatto in the Rhineland legend of the Mouse Tower.

Even Saint Augustine seemed to give some lawbreaking a moral sanction when he held, "Necessity knows no law." More recently, President Franklin D. Roosevelt reaffirmed the view that "necessitous men are not free men" and then added, "People who are hungry and out of a job are the stuff of which dictatorships are made." [21] Still more recently, President Lyndon B. Johnson told the United States Chamber of Commerce:

What you have and what you hope to acquire is not secure when there are men that are idle . . . and when there are thousands that are out of school and millions that are out of work, and the aged are lying embittered in their homes.[22]

Not for nothing have relief and welfare services, over the years and over the world, been thought of as "riot insurance." Widespread belief that poverty, deprivation, and destitution are the seedbeds of insurrection and revolution foster this concept. On this point Philip Sokol, Deputy Commissioner and Legal Counsel of the Welfare Department in New York City has declared, "Welfare programs do not exist as a matter of choice. They were brought into being as a matter of sheer necessity and must be continued as the only alternative to chaos. If we accept this with the objectivity with which we accept the fact that we must spend money to put out fires, then we will be willing to finance the means needed to quench the fire of human need and distress." [23]

Although amidst the racial unrest in 1967, Whitney M. Young, Jr., of the National Urban League, attacked as "just riot insurance" the small appropriations for the War on Poverty, Sargent Shriver, the war's generalissimo, was taking pride in what it was doing to "cool" the unrest.[24]

In ordered times and stable communities where riot and revolution are not "in the air," welfare services are not appreciated for their order-preserving propensities and must be defended on more subtle terms. However, behind these subtleties the stark necessity of preserving order remains an operative—if undiscussed—factor. For example, although in the United States it may now be sufficient to justify welfare services on grounds that they serve the "general welfare," it would be indisputable that subsumed within this broad term (but no longer much discussed publicly) would be the importance of maintaining social order. But, one need not go back far into American history to find when terms far more specific than "general welfare" were employed. Take, for example, a 1932 decision of the Pennsylvania Supreme Court. A new unemployment relief act was being challenged, in part, on constitutional grounds because the state's constitution prescribed that "No appropriations, except for pensions or gratuities for military services, shall be made for charitable, educational or benevolent purposes, to any person or community." In upholding the constitutionality of the act in question, the court first restated two earlier decisions in which it had been held that "the obligation of the government to care for poor persons was not a charitable undertaking any more than the performance of any other public function is a charity." The court then declared:

The support of the poor . . . is and has always been a direct charge on the body politic for its own preservation and protection; and . . . as such, in the light of an expense, it stands exactly in the same position as the preservation of law and order.

. . . To hold that the State cannot or must not aid its poor would strip the State of a means of self preservation.

In a concurring opinion one justice declared:

An act manifestly dictated by enlightened self-interest is not an act of charity. Expenditures which are made as a matter of self-protection cannot be classed as benevolent. . . . An appropriation . . . to relieve . . . suffering [of unemployed workers and their families] is no more a "charitable" appropriation than an appropriation made to suppress an uprising, repel an invasion or to combat a pestilence.[25]

When an unemployment relief act in the state of Washington was challenged on constitutional grounds, the supreme court of that state, in 1933, touched on this same point about public order.[26]

Abolishing or reducing the necessity to beg has also been seen as contributing to public order. The long enduring connection between poor relief measures and the control of vagrancy has been ably documented by Professor Margaret K. Rosenheim of the University of Chicago.[27]

In the more enlightened present one hears less about such stark realities. Not much is said openly about the importance of welfare services for eliminating begging, preventing stealing, or suppressing riots. Yet only a foolish man would suggest that these grim specters do not lie in wait behind such euphemisms as "the general welfare." It takes little imagination to envision beggars swarming the streets, a massive outbreak of raids on food stores, and great social unrest— all of which would be triggered if the billions of dollars distributed annually to millions of families in the form of public assistance payments were suddenly discontinued. For "something"—"nothing"?

Writing about an earlier period, Clifford S. Griffin, in *Their Brothers' Keepers: Moral Stewardship in the United States, 1800– 1865*, depicts the work of various organizations such as the American Bible Society, Anti-Slavery, Temperance and other groups. In this he contends:

The leaders of the benevolent groups have personal reasons for wanting to control society. . . . The trustees believed that they would suffer if men playing lesser roles on the great American stage did not respect their economic and social obligations, and if American voters did not choose proper men as rulers. Religion and morality, as dispensed by the benevolent societies throughout the seemingly chaotic nation, became a means of establishing secular order.[28]

Over the years many private groups such as religious bodies and fraternal organizations have developed welfare services to attract and hold members and to help maintain the cohesiveness of the groups themselves. Most notable in this regard are the welfare services developed by Jewish communities not only within different countries but on a world scale. When Jews were forced into ghettos, were denied participation in the broader life of their communities, and were deprived of services available to others, they developed programs and institutions of their own as a means to achieve sheer survival. These sometimes had a quasi governmental character because the governments of the surrounding areas often turned over to the ghettos responsibility for their governance.

As external pressures upon Jewish groups were reduced and as Jews were permitted to participate in the wider life of their communities, the emphasis of their welfare services shifted from preserving the lives of Jews to preserving, among Jews, Jewish values and the cohesiveness of the Jewish community. This shift was described at the 1966 convention of the Jewish Welfare Board as a move from preoccupation with survival to "survival with quality." Of this, Sanford Solender, Executive Vice-President of the Board, declared, "Jewish knowledge and experience are central to affirmative Jewishness. . . . We have completed the phase of American Jewish experience emphasizing the integration of the Jew into the total

American community. Now we address ourselves to maintaining our integrity as a Jewish group." [29]

Social welfare services—whether governmental or private—are confronted with a grave responsibility. They may be enlisted to support and perpetuate beneficent orders that afford less than equity and justice for welfare agencies' intended beneficiaries. This danger has been clearly underlined by the degree to which welfare services have been employed in the service of inhumane orders—as Hitler, Eva Perón, the Mafia, Tammany Hall, and others have proved. In South Africa, *apartheid* is buttressed by the separatist and allegedly "welfare" provisions for Bantus. In fairness to South African welfare agencies it must be said that although, as a price of survival, they cannot openly flaunt national policy, many of them gently needle officially proclaimed discriminatory practices.[30] Even democratic societies are freer to throw fathers and mothers into jail—and keep them there—because welfare services are available to care for their children.

Here, again, as in the case of broad social action (Chapter V) welfare personnel are often called upon to live dangerously. When they engage in value propagation and, as Dame Eileen Younghusband put it, help beneficiaries "to come alive," all is unlikely to remain as placid as before. Such ruffling of the waters, though in the "best interests" of beneficiaries, understandably rouses public criticism. This was clearly apparent in Community Action programs fostered under the War on Poverty in the United States. Although Congressional intent to encourage the "maximum feasible participation" by poor persons was perfectly clear, local and state politicians —and, to some extent, even welfare establishments—became highly critical when their boats were rocked by Community Action programs, welfare rights organizations, and others.*

Economic Values

Unfortunately, the overall economic effects of welfare services are not known. In fact, economists have given little attention to welfare services generally. When a group of these erstwhile "dismal" but now often optimistic scientists was brought together to discuss

---

* Widespread congressional opposition to Community Action programs in 1967 led the House of Representatives to pass a bill giving local public officials greater control over them. Sophisticated observers, recognizing from the beginning what was likely to happen if these programs were taken seriously, were surprised by the fact that unsophisticated observers were surprised at what happened.

philanthropy and welfare issues, one finds almost amusing their attempts (as reflected in *Philanthropy and Public Policy*) to translate phenomena in the welfare field into familiar economic terms, such as prices, profit, input, output, and so on. More heartening is the recognition that as economists they had neglected this field for much too long.[31]

This latter-day neglect is but part of a more general neglect—that of overlooking the importance of human and social resources as distinguished from money and other material ingredients of economies. This oversight is being corrected within the United States by economists such as Professors John Kenneth Galbraith, Theodore W. Schultz, and Leon H. Keyserling, and, at the international level, by Professor Gunnar Myrdal, Barbara Ward, and Andrew Shonfield.

Even more disillusioning than economists' neglect of social welfare is the degree to which social welfare personnel have neglected—or sidestepped—economic considerations. One notable exception to this generalization is the field of rehabilitation, which takes delight in reporting how much it has helped to transform "tax eaters" into "tax payers."

"ECONOMICS" OF SOCIAL WELFARE SERVICES: At various intervals the federal Vocational Rehabilitation administration publishes pertinent statistics regarding its operations. It estimates that increased earnings attributed to rehabilitation net, in federal income taxes alone, from $1 to $7 for every dollar of the cost of rehabilitation.[32]

Few other services have gone so far. Various efforts have been made, however. For example, family planning services offered in Mecklenburg County, North Carolina, were estimated to have saved some quarter of a million dollars in public assistance funds over a four-year period. Each dollar spent was believed to have saved twenty-five.[33] With the inauguration and extension of Work Experience and Training programs for public assistance recipients, public assistance agencies like to report the numbers of workers who find employment upon completing these programs and like to estimate amounts thus saved in public assistance.[34] These data are not wholly convincing, however, because little is known about how long these often marginal workers hold their jobs before returning to assistance rolls. In broader perspective one must also wonder, at least when unemployment is high, who the unemployed workers were who did not get jobs that were filled by Work Experience "graduates." It is not impossible that social investment and interest in the latter led to placing some whose skills were actually inferior to those of unemployed workers in whom there was less social investment. Of this little is known. It is heartening, though, that serious cost-benefit analyses are being undertaken.[35]

Attention to the economics of welfare services has been largely in the relative cost of one type of service vis-à-vis another, not in terms of a broader economy. For example, a study of homemaker services rendered to more than 10,000 children, parents, and infirm and elderly persons at a cost of $2.7 million over a five-year period revealed that provision of this same care through other community resources would have cost "well in excess of $8 million." [36] Also, attention has been given to what welfare services have meant to a particular county or state because these services had brought in money from outside the area.[37] It is not known what these transfers of funds mean in terms of areas or states that might be termed the "paying" ones or in terms of low-income states that are often favored under federal grant-in-aid programs.

Other types of "economies" are frequently cited. For example: assisting persons (children, the disabled, aged, sick, mentally ill, or otherwise afflicted) in their own homes, thus saving higher institutional costs; providing probation or parole services to reduce expensive prison care; placing children in adoption and thus, although not exactly "saving" the cost of their care, shifting it to adoptive parents. The degree to which even these kinds of intrawelfare economies were *not* more widely effected was excoriated by New York's Judge Justine Wise Polier: "Only the mad hatter could explain this." [38] Responsibility cannot be laid at the doorstep of social welfare services alone, however, since social policy itself is more largely to blame.

One of the most disturbing aspects of the "economics" of welfare services is this: They are considered preponderantly in terms of expenditures rather than costs. Public assistance programs, for instance, are analyzed almost exclusively in terms of expenditures for public assistance rather than in terms of the costs—to individuals, families, and society—of the deprivation, anxiety, family disruption, lost opportunities for schooling, bad health, asocial attitudes, and the myriad other "prices" exacted of needy individuals and families. To save a public assistance dollar is not to reduce by a dollar the costs of "need." It only leaves the needy person instead of his community carrying the cost. How heavy a burden this can be is apparent in a number of publications already cited (particularly in

Chapter VI) and notably in Arthur R. Simon's *Faces of Poverty*. Also noteworthy in this regard is *The High Cost of Unhappy Living*, published by the Family Service Association of America.[39]

Or, if needy persons themselves are not to be saddled with the full cost of their own need, one must think of the costs to relatives, friends, neighbors, grocers, landlords, physicians, and others who shoulder parts of the cost if public assistance agencies fail to underwrite them. Not much is known about such redistribution of costs, but a study made in Clermont County in Ohio in 1963 shows what happens when public relief is discontinued to still needy persons.[40]

In short, costs of need are inescapable. The central question is "How shall the unavoidable costs be borne?" There will inevitably be costs; the issue therefore becomes "Costs—to whom?"

An important turn for the better seemed to be taking place in the late 1960's; more and more attention was being devoted to the "economics" of social welfare services as shown, for example, in several chapters in *Economic Progress and Social Welfare*, edited by Leonard H. Goodman.[41] But, the length of time it has taken to reach this turn in the road suggests itself what answer the welfare field has long given to the question Rufus C. Rorem put to the National Conference of Social Work in 1937: "Social Work Accounting —Tool or Torment?" [42]

Failure of welfare agencies to document more widely—and more rigorously—the observable economic effects of their services is the more unfortunate because the general social climate in which a business or industry operates is extensively believed to be an important factor in its success. This was noted in Chapter IV. Relevant here, too, is what was said there about the family's role in preparing persons for employment and in absorbing some of the shocks encountered in contemporary economic life.

For, as social welfare services contribute to family solidarity and to the general social climate, it seems to follow that they do, in fact, play economic roles. These go virtually unnoticed and unmeasured, however. Some things that are seldom recognized in this connection can be illustrated, if in a microcosmic way. For instance, a few years ago an aircraft factory in the Los Angeles region urgently needed someone with a highly specialized skill. This need was finally met by relocating a worker from a distant state. Although this arrangement permitted production to go on uninterruptedly, the worker suddenly reported that he intended to return to his home state—not because of any disaffection on his part, but because his wife was lonely in their new community. The factory referred the situation to a local welfare agency, which succeeded in sufficiently involving the wife in group and community activities to overcome the pressures to "go home." Thus the welfare agency saved a critically needed worker for the factory. Unfortunately, though, so far as I know such economic side-effects have not been paid much attention or ever "added up." This is the more regrettable because, as David Owen has reported, English philanthropy of even the seventeenth and eighteenth centuries can be regarded as "instruments of mercantilist policy" and as safeguarding "national power." He cites the role of foundling hospitals, medical charities, and the Royal Humane Society (which saved and resuscitated drowning persons) as protections against a decline in population; he cites the role of schemes for putting the poor to productive work and the role of foundling hospitals and charity schools in supplying manpower (not always with the consent of those sent) for England's all-important maritime interests.[43]

BROAD ECONOMIC EFFECTS: Notable exceptions to the general neglect of the economic aspects of welfare services are the studies made of them by scholars such as William Haber, Margaret S. Gordon, Robert G. Lampman, Eveline M. Burns, Leon Keyserling, and Ewan Clague. Even these, however, have been concerned with questions like "How much social welfare can an economy afford?" or with the economic effects of the redistribution of income through public assistance, social insurance, and related measures, rather than with the more subtle aspects of welfare services we have been discussing. For example, even in Margaret Gordon's monograph *The Economics of Welfare Policies*, whose title would seem comprehensive enough to include the gamut of effects referred to earlier, Dr. Gordon (who is Research Economist of the University of California, Berkeley) limits consideration to the federal Old-Age, Survivors, and Disability Insurance program, and to Unemployment Compensation. And this despite the fact that in her Introduction she says, "Welfare programs will be defined as social programs designed to transfer income, in cash, *in kind, or in the form of services,* to those whose capacity for self-support has been impaired, interrupted, or (in the case of children) has not yet reached maturity."[44] [Emphasis added.]

Notwithstanding the broader expectations raised by her title, Dr. Gordon excludes from her detailed analysis such transfers in kind as the distribution of surplus commodities—despite their importance to welfare programs, both domestic and foreign. Omitted, too, is consideration of the economic effects of welfare *services* (other than some money payments), of private programs, and even of some public programs such as public assistance and workmen's compensation.

But the welfare field cannot quarrel with economists for failure to appraise more broadly the economic effects of its services. The field itself has given them little help through, for example, clear delineation of welfare functions and the reporting of results in terms that are sufficiently objective to be measurable. For instance, almost nothing is known of the degree to which welfare services in fact strengthen incentive for self-support and self-improvement, sustain health and employability, and maintain in off-seasons a labor supply for seasonable employment. Nor is much known, unfortunately, about the degree to which (as critics constantly allege) welfare services only reinforce "disincentives" and foster malingering or unnecessary nonproductiveness. At best, though, generalizations about the broad overall economic effects of welfare services would be exceedingly difficult to come by, because of the widely disparate nature of their functions, the vast differences in the ways in which they are financed and in the sources of their support.

In the United States, long before the highly publicized War on Poverty, Area Redevelopment, Appalachia, and related programs of the early 1960's came into operation, welfare agencies had been working (albeit too gingerly, perhaps) at exactly the kinds of basic education, training and retraining, and health, medical, and rehabilitation services that were greatly expanded subsequently through the massive resources later made available under the new programs.

Also, there was no belittling what welfare and related services were doing to help sustain purchasing power and consumer demand generated by, say, public assistance, which in 1965 was being provided at a rate of nearly $6 billion a year. Unemployment compensation was being paid at a yearly rate of nearly $3 billion. In addition, Old Age, Survivors, and Disability Insurance (OASDI) payments under the Social Security Act were being made at a yearly rate of nearly $16 billion. When it is recalled that public assistance is given only to persons with few other resources and that unemployment compensation goes only to workers with no jobs, there can be little question about these beneficiaries' "propensity to consume" or about what is known as the "high velocity" of these income maintenance benefits. Spent as they are for food, clothing, medicines, and rent, these benefits help grocers, clothiers, pharmacists, and landlords. These people are helped thereby to pay their clerks, stockmen, and maintenance personnel and to pay for trucking of supplies from warehouses. These payments in turn help to pay the salaries of warehousemen, to pay for long-distance transportation, and help to sustain demand upon productive facilities. Unfortunately, however, we do not know to what extent these effects may be offset by contributions made to welfare—voluntarily or through taxes.

Tribute to the contribution that welfare services can make to economic expansion is interestingly, if sometimes soberingly, paid by economists such as Galbraith, Keyserling, Theobald, and Myrdal. In pleas for increased investment in the "public sector," these writers frequently urge expansion of employment opportunities in welfare and pseudowelfare activities, such as those of social service aides, playground attendants, readers for blind persons, friendly visitors to aged persons, day care of children, and the like. Repeated implications that significant parts of welfare jobs can be handled by minimally trained and possibly uneducated individuals often seem deprecatory to professionals. However, they are comforted by the apparent contributions of their services to economic growth.

One particularly interesting aspect of an economic purpose served by welfare programs is the support often given to public assistance in rural areas. Welfare programs are not usually popular among farmers, but they suddenly come into high favor when they are needed to keep in a given area seasonal workers who are not immediately needed, but who are likely to be needed in the future. In this respect—as in many others—welfare services are a double-edged sword and, just as they can be employed constructively, can also be employed viciously. For example, discriminatory practices can deliberately deny welfare services to certain groups so as to force out or even—as was widely charged and sometimes admitted in the South in the 1960's—"starve out" of the community "undesirable" persons. Restrictive relief practices can also "starve" persons into jobs paying only starvation wages and even into the roles of strikebreakers.

The overall economic effects of welfare and allied services naturally differ, from time to time, according to the general state of the economy. Moreover, the basic data for any generalized appraisal are woefully lacking. However, the role of these services as "built-in stabilizers" of an economy is worthy of note. Professor Eveline M. Burns, like many other economists, comments upon the widespread recognition of unemployment insurance as such a stabilizer, but then adds, "It is less frequently noted that OASDI and the public assistance programs also operate in the same way, for their beneficiary or caseloads also fluctuate inversely with levels of employment." [45] Of this, economics Professor Paul T. Therkildsen has written, "Most economists will agree that public assistance payments are important in a contracyclical fiscal policy, especially in the deflationary phase of the cycle." [46]

Thus, welfare services may be looked upon not only as "riot insurance" but also as recession and depression insurance, or, at the least, a degree of insurance against the worsening or deepening of a recession or depression.

Although there is much that economists have not yet documented about the economic effects of welfare services, there is one point that seems clear to the welfare field, but to which economists have not seemed to give much attention. It is indisputable, for instance, that the more income a person has, the more he will spend for luxuries, such as new cars or second cars, furs, entertainment, travel, savings, and investments. However, if persons capable of making such purchases were to see brothers and sisters, aged parents, or even uncles, aunts, or cousins—or for that matter, unrelated fellow citizens—in want, they would probably defer luxury purchases for themselves in favor of basic essentials for others. As between a second deep-freeze for oneself and the dire necessity of another, the latter might well take precedence. Thus, not only the market for bread and milk and housing, but also luxury markets and savings and investments are at least partially dependent upon welfare services.

ECONOMICS NOT ALL-CONTROLLING: Although it would be useful to have more knowledge than is yet available on the economics of welfare services *in toto*, the relative importance of economic as distinguished from moral, social, political, and other considerations must not be overemphasized. In historical retrospect it is somewhat frightening that not only economic facts but also unproved and undocumented economic theories figured so largely in the formulation of welfare policy. We have already noted (especially in Chapters IV and VI) that, even in the absence of evidence justifying the practice, economic theories applied to obviously dependent persons are the exact opposites of those applied to more privileged classes. But what were probably two of the most colossal miscarriages in social history were the application of classical (but unproved) economic theory to welfare policy in both England and the United States in the 1830's and 1860's.

Just as man has come to be more than "economic man," so have societies increasingly come to be more than "economic societies." While issues involving bread and butter, rice and fish, or beans and tortillas remain of consummate and often of controlling concern in both economically sophisticated and underdeveloped societies, men do not today feel that they supersede all other values. Home ownership for a couple may be considered clearly uneconomic, yet the couple may go ahead and buy a home anyway just to enjoy those intangible values inherent in "owning a home of your own." A big car may be entirely uneconomic for a family, yet as a status symbol that has no economic significance whatsoever, it may be well worth the cost. From a strictly economic viewpoint, what a man gives annually to his church might be better invested in securities or insurance for the future protection of his family.

Similarly, societies may recognize that a given expenditure for social welfare may detract somewhat from the economic growth that they could otherwise achieve. Still, a society may sacrifice some economic development in favor of greater social justice or of social morality and social order. In fact, even the discourses of economists dealing with the economics of welfare (and allied services) are shot through with references to the relationship of transfer payments to the "redistribution of income," to "regressive" as contrasted with "progressive" taxes, to the "equity" of particular fiscal and economic policies, and to "welfare." These concepts, obviously, involve questions of social philosophy, morality, justice, and value to which economists can of course contribute, but that are by no means their exclusive domain.

When Professor Richard M. Titmuss was invited to go to Israel in 1964 to consult on social policy there, he pointed out that welfare might be regarded as either inhibiting economic growth or fostering humanitarian values. What these views had in common, he added, was that "They are largely assertions and do not rest on any firm basis of fact." He then went on to say that these views might possibly conflict in the short run and that a nation might be tempted to wait until it is richer when it "can afford to be more generous to the less fortunate." But, he asks, ". . . can we be sure that in the processes of getting richer and of concentrating only on getting richer we shall not, as a society, lose the impetus to create a more equal and socially just society?" [47]

How an individual or a nation answers a question like this hinges on the degree to which they believe that values can maintain their positions as values if they are not put into practice.

From an international viewpoint Ernest W. Lefever has observed, "Economic factors impinge upon world politics in a thousand ways, and in some cases they may be the decisive factors, but they are not the *exclusive* or even the *primary* factors in international affairs." [48] William and Paul Paddock, who wrote *Hungry Nations*, would probably not agree with this (or answer, as Professor Titmuss probably would, the question he posed). For, the Paddocks believe that developing and "hungry" nations should eschew such frills as public health, lowered mortality, education, and so on and concentrate more of their efforts and resources upon food production. Proposals of this kind are so seldom advanced these days that few attempts have been made, in welfare literature, to reply to them. However, way back in 1925, one of the "grand old men" of social welfare, Homer Folks, felt compelled to respond to what Savel Zimand calls "the pseudo-scientific attacks on the validity of social service and public health work." [49]

Social Economy of Welfare Services

Once a society has made certain moral commitments and high policy decisions, it faces the problem of relative financial and social costs of honoring these commitments. For example, if a society takes a moral stand against infanticide, exposure of infants, the strangulation of defective children, the abandonment of unwanted children, abandonment of aged persons when they are no longer economically productive—and if it opposes putting unemployed workers into workhouses or prohibits the deportation ("transportation") of poor persons or the execution of misdemeanants—that society inescapably faces the question of what alternate treatment shall be accorded to such persons. A society may decide not only that it will not authorize strangling, exposure, execution, and the like, but also that it will prohibit its members as individuals from solving problems by these means. By thus imposing its standards of morality upon its members, a society almost inevitably finds itself saddled with at least part of the cost of that morality.

Given the fact that, although children—whether legitimate or illegitimate—are not to be destroyed, put in deep-freeze, or plowed under, but are deprived of a level of parental care that is conscionable to the society, the society finds itself committed either to their care or to contributing to the cost of their care by others. In this connection, a fact that is often overlooked is that the slightly more than 1 million families who were granted Aid to Families with Dependent Children (in April 1965) were rearing nearly 3,400,000 children—future citizens and possibly future soldiers. Thus, these families were rendering an inestimable service to the nation. For doing this they were being given an average of about $31 per month per recipient—roughly one dollar a day per person, not even the equivalent of one hour's pay under the federal minimum wage law. Worse still, the monthly average per person was only $11.83 in Alabama and $9.31 in Mississippi, although in six states the average exceeded $40. In comparison with even these high rates, foster care (outside of the children's own homes) that would be socially conscionable, but that still might not give the children the love they need, would undoubtedly have cost at least three times what their own relatives were being paid for their support and nurture. Socially acceptable institutional care would have cost perhaps ten times as much. Similarly, more than 2 million aged persons receiving Old Age Assistance were maintaining themselves on payments that averaged $80.81 per month. These amounts would not begin to pay for the foster home or institutional care that would be tolerated in modern societies.

Although societies are often very conscious of welfare costs, they do not often reflect upon the signal reciprocal services rendered to them by individuals who, notwithstanding the denigration and humiliation frequently heaped upon them, nevertheless accept assistance for their own support, care for themselves and nurture their children, do not revolt, do not beg in the streets, do not pull down the levels of living of neighbors, friends, or relatives upon whom they might otherwise call for support, and do not require from society foster home or institutional care that would be much more expensive than maintenance in their own homes. Societies should thank —not denigrate—all these who, often at terrible personal cost, thus serve them.

It took a perceptive and bold social worker to do what Dame Eileen Younghusband, dean of British social workers, did when she addressed a meeting on the subject of adoptions. After enumerating the many services rendered to society by unmarried mothers, under what are often distressingly difficult circumstances, she boldly closed her presentation with "All honor to them!" [50] Such sensitivity, especially in relation to unmarried motherhood, is rare indeed. But societies often overlook the many who contribute a good deal to them, but who are, typically, considered merely recipients of aid from others. Nevertheless, within the United States, several studies reflect "the strengths" of unmarried mothers and the contributions they make to the mothering of their children.[51]

Significant contributions made in similarly unlikely quarters have been reported by Dr. Harold M. Skeels of the National Institute of Mental Health after a follow-up of an experiment undertaken during the 1930's. In this experiment thirteen very young mentally retarded orphans (three of whom had IQ ratings of only around 40) were placed in an Iowa institution for older retarded children as "house guests" of these older retardates, who served as "loving aunts" for the very young ones. This degree of personal attention was thought to be responsible for the fact that, of the thirteen thus placed, eleven (including the three "imbeciles") attained normal intelligence and were placed in adoption. At the time of the follow-up study thirty years later, all thirteen of the "house guests were self-supporting, none was a ward of an institution, none was mentally retarded and, of the twenty-eight children born to the thirteen, none was mentally retarded." [52] For "something"—"*nothing?*"

I once had occasion in an open meeting to refer to this experiment and was startled by the look on the face of one of those present. After the meeting this person came to me and said, "You are *so* right. My sister has served as one of those 'aunts.' She *does* have a lot to give." Further suggestions of contributions from similar quarters may be found in *The Gifts They Bring: Our Debt to the Mentally Retarded*, by Pearl Buck and Gweneth Zarfoss.[53]

Additional examples of significant social contributions from unlikely sources have been reported from Foster Grandparent programs fostered in conjunction with the War on Poverty. Under these, assistance-receiving or other poor, elderly persons are engaged for perhaps twenty hours a week to offer love, help, and stimulation to a variety of unloved or incapacitated persons. In Illinois, for example, foster grandfathers and grandmothers, devoting perhaps two hours a day to individual children who are institutionalized because of mental retardation, have accomplished wonders that seemed beyond the capacity of the institution's staff. Six- and eight-year-old youngsters were being helped by "grandparents" to learn, for the first time, to talk, walk, go up stairs, or do something other than staring at the wall. That white children may have a Negro "grandfather" or "grandmother" seems to make no difference in their capacity to benefit from the love, solicitude, and help given.[54]

We have deliberately concentrated here upon social contributions from quite unexpected sources and to particularly disadvantaged beneficiaries. We leave to the imagination further potential "somethings" that beneficiaries of welfare services return to societies for the "something" given to them. But failure to see these contributions, as also those made to family life, health, education, and so on by welfare services, reflects the national tendency to disregard social accounting of all kinds. Perhaps because of tendencies discussed in Chapter IV, to appraise success predominantly in material terms, achievements of other kinds tend to be overlooked. This is underlined by preoccupation with the concept of the Gross National Product (GNP), which does not take into account the social wealth represented by family life, educational achievement, health and so on. It is little wonder that in the late 1960's this problem was increasingly recognized and more and more interest was displayed in "social accounting" and in a social counterpart of the President's Council of Economic Advisers. At this writing, happily, there is under way a study, sponsored by The Twentieth Century Fund and to be made by Professor Bertram Gross of Syracuse University, which is expected to provide "an overview of major changes in social structure and of the growth in services whose value is not adequately reflected in the federal calculations of Gross National Product." [55]

Safeguards for Individualism and Excellence

It may seem strange to pair "individualism" and "excellence." For individualism may not necessarily lead to excellence, and excellence may be achieved other than by individualism. In these respects these two terms may seem to have little in common. But for our purposes they have a great deal in common because it is widely believed that welfare services undermine both. It is often alleged that gratuitously given public assistance and other benefits weaken men's moral fiber and invite them to "live off others" rather than by their own effort. Or, once becoming accustomed to welfare's "bed of ease," men fail to pursue excellence in any direction except, perhaps, by devising ingenious rationales for remaining "on welfare." Having already discussed self-help and value propagation and the interest of welfare services in fostering them, we are not here concerned with individualism and excellence in relation to beneficiaries of these services, but in relation to society in general.

We have mentioned that, although societies may place a very high value upon self-help, they also set limits beyond which one's pursuit of his own interests is considered "too hurtful" to others. We have also noted that societies often make alternate provisions for supplying the basic requirements of those whose efforts at self-help would be "too hurtful" to either themselves or others. Beyond this, when the individual enterprising of some results in hurt to others, welfare services help to absorb the "hurtful" impact. Thus, welfare services permit individual enterprising to a degree that would not otherwise be tolerated. They represent, therefore, part of the price a society pays for individualism. If it were not for welfare services that absorb part of the shock of a capitalistic, industrial order, a society might well turn against that order or, at least, limit it more strictly if it was considered "too hurtful" to "too many" people. Professor Charles Frankel has put the issue in these terms: "The resources modern societies pour into welfare programmes are the tax they pay . . . for their commitment to the morality of individualism." [56]

Even in primitive societies one sees counterparts of welfare services (i.e., treating people in ways outside the customary patterns for the exchange of goods and services) as "taking up the slack" in what Margaret Mead and her associates call "competitive" societies. Miss Mead points out, for example, that the competitive Manus and Kwakiutl treat their old people better than do the cooperative, secure Bathonga. Speaking more broadly, Miss Mead observes, "The cooperative societies depend upon the existence of a well-defined, well-integrated social structure within which the individual can play a cooperative role. . . . Among the individualistic societies, *helpfulness* takes the place of cooperation." [57] [Emphasis added.]

In broad perspective, it seems reasonable to hypothesize that most men recognize a "welfare gap" that makes them uncomfortable when they are "too much" more comfortable than others. This perhaps explains in part the concepts of *noblesse oblige* and the propensity to give. Except for "callous," "conscienceless," "insensitive" princes, sheiks, tycoons, absentee landlords, and the like, who seem content to live in luxury in the face of stark poverty, men more generally oppose "too wide" a welfare gap between themselves and others.

One might modify significantly a common saying and still leave it a true statement of fact: "The more men have, the more they want—*for others*." If this is true and if the concept of the welfare gap has validity, it follows that the higher the welfare floor underneath a society as a whole, the freer individual men will feel to advance by their own effort. In this respect welfare services are a safeguard for individual effort.

To regard these services as a safeguard for excellence, too, is a matter of degree. For example, as more and more of "the advantaged" go on for not only higher education, but for higher and higher and then still higher education, social concern for those without elementary, then high school, and then college education is likely to mount. As private homes become better and better, as they are more and more efficiently heated, lighted, air-conditioned, and equipped, the less tolerant a society is likely to be of substandard, dark, damp, stuffy, walk-up, cold-water flats.

Thus, the kind of underpinning welfare services can provide for a society leaves men of conscience freer to pursue excellence in their own way, and without the undue guilt that the welfare gap might otherwise engender.

In 1952 the theoretical physicist Sir Charles Galton Darwin made a literary side trip into the realm of his grandfather (author of *Origin of Species*) and that of his godfather (eugenicist Sir Francis Galton). He entitled this effort *The Next Million Years*—the time span he believed necessary to develop a new human species. In this book he, as a Britisher, turned his guns on welfare measures and complained, "The policy of paying most [sic] attention to the inferior types is the most inefficient way possible of achieving the perfectibility of the human race." [58]

Observers tempted to respond "Hear! Hear!" may be somewhat sobered by the recognition, however, that Sir Charles' questions relate not only to those who are seriously disabled but also to those suffering from less dramatic imperfections. For example, those who wear spectacles may see themselves in unhappy company (along with half-wits, prisoners, problem children, and so on), for there is the thinly veiled suggestion that if persons with deficient eyesight were to forego eyeglasses, this would contribute to their earlier demise and therefore to the improvement of the eyesight of the race.

Many years ago Mary Richmond of the Russell Sage Foundation made the point that the availability of welfare services facilitated social innovation and experimentation. In her day, when child labor legislation and laws for the protection of working women were being hotly debated, she contended that the availability of welfare services helped to reassure those who feared that these measures "would do more harm than good."

Whether it would be "better" for a society if resources were not diverted to underwriting the requirements of the disadvantaged, but were devoted to higher and higher degrees of "excellence"—like the magnificent ancient cathedrals that stood in the midst of squalor, want, and disease—is a calculus I gladly leave to others. But I believe that *the social conscience of today* requires that the rear guard of the disadvantaged be brought up as the advance guard of the advantaged proceeds. Thus, welfare services that help to bring up the rear make it more probable that the van can advance. In this respect welfare services may be looked upon as safeguards for excellence.

CONCLUSION

What does a society get for the money and effort it invests in welfare services? Not all observers will agree upon what this is. Nor will there be agreement upon whether what it gets is worth the investment. In fact, by heading this chapter with a question (For "Something"—"*Nothing*"?), I sought to suggest only that dividends are indeed to be expected; I have scrupulously avoided any implication that a balance could be struck between social costs and social benefits. Still, societies all over the world appear to have given their own answers. For, although activities that were once known as welfare services have been transformed into other types of social institutions (such as social utilities) or may have been rendered less necessary by modifications in other institutions (economic, educational, health, and the like), welfare services have not been reduced in magnitude. In fact, they have actually been expanded to ever-widening ranges of values and to social groups not reached in the past.

If the considerations advanced in this chapter have validity, the input and output as related to welfare services may be seen, I believe, in terms analogous to the bomb shelters and modern buildings built in Chungking during World War II. As Chungking dug into its hillsides to make caves to protect its people from bombing, it quarried rock for the construction of new buildings. Similarly, welfare services can be viewed as a society's digging into its resources for the protection of its own social and political order, economic stability, and social economy, while at the same time it is erecting monuments to its key values, its social morality, its justice, and an excellence worthy—in the eyes of its own members and of the world—of the image it wishes to project.

:: Notes and References

1. Daphne Athas, *Greece by Prejudice* (Philadelphia and New York: Lippincott, 1962), p. 222.
2. *Economic Report of the President, 1954* (Washington, D.C.: Government Printing Office, 1954), pp. 96–98.
3. Roy Lubove, *The Professional Altruist: The Emergence of Social Work as a Career, 1880–1930* (Cambridge: Harvard University Press, 1965), p. 5.
4. Karl Mannheim, *Man and Society: In an Age of Reconstruction* (New York: Harcourt, Brace & World, 1940), pp. 128, 129, 133.
5. Frank Church, as reported in *The Interchurch News*, April 1966, p. 3.
6. John Toland, *The Last 100 Days* (New York: Random House, 1965), p. 160.
7. Alexander Donat, *The Holocaust Kingdom: A Memoir* (New York: Holt, Rinehart and Winston, 1963), p. 177.
8. Paul G. Hoffman, *The Significance of World Conditions for the Well-Being of People in America* (New York: National Social Welfare Assembly, 1960), p. 10. (Mimeographed.)
9. Barbara Ward, *The Rich Nations and the Poor Nations* (London: Hamilton, 1962), p. 150.
10. Leonard E. Read, *Deeper Than You Think* (Irvington-on-Hudson, N.Y.: The Foundation for Economic Education, 1967), pp. 111, 113, 116. Economist Kenneth E. Boulding makes an interesting comment on the return one gets from dropping "a dime in a blind man's cup" in Frank G. Dickson, ed., *Philanthropy and Public Policy* (New York: National Bureau of Economic Research, 1962), pp. 57–58.
11. R. Sargent Shriver, in testimony before the Subcommittee on the War on Poverty Program of the Committee on Education and Labor, House of Representatives, Eighty-ninth Congress, 1st Session, *Examination of the War on Poverty Program* (Washington, D.C.: Government Printing Office, 1965), p. 22.
12. *"Having the Power, We Have the Duty"* (Washington, D.C.: Advisory Council on Public Welfare, Government Printing Office, 1966), p. xvii.
13. L. T. Hobhouse, *Morals in Evolution: A Study in Comparative Ethics* (London: Chapman and Hall, 1951), p. 605.
14. Luther Gulick, *The Metropolitan Problem and American Ideas* (New York: Knopf, 1962), p. 8.
15. Donald S. Howard, *The WPA and Federal Relief Policy* (New York: Russell Sage Foundation, 1943), pp. 706–708.
16. John W. Gardner, "The Ten Commitments," *Saturday Review*, July 1,

1967, p. 39. See also Harrison Brown, "The Combustibility of Humans," *Saturday Review*, June 24, 1967, pp. 14–17, 66.

17. George K. Tanham, W. Robert Warne, Earl J. Young, and William A. Nighswonger, *War Without Guns: American Civilians in Rural Vietnam* (New York: Praeger, 1966).

18. His Excellency Thanom Kittikachorn, in *Statements of Heads of State on Community Development* (New York: International Society for Community Development, 1966), not paginated.

19. As reported in *The New York Times*, April 11, 1967.

20. Allan Nevins, *Herbert H. Lehman and His Era* (New York: Scribner, 1963), p. 247.

21. Franklin D. Roosevelt, address on the State of the Union, January 11, 1944, as reported in *Congressional Record*, Vol. 96, part 1, pp. 55–57.

22. Lyndon B. Johnson, as quoted by Hubert H. Humphrey, *War on Poverty* (New York: McGraw-Hill, 1964), p. 31.

23. Philip Sokol, "Providing for the Dependent," in R. M. MacIver, ed., *The Assault on Poverty: And Individual Responsibility* (New York: Harper & Row, 1965), pp. 18–19.

24. As reported in *The New York Times*, August 13, 1967.

25. Commonwealth of Pennsylvania *ex rel.* Schnader, Attorney General v. Liveright, Secretary of Welfare *et al.*, 308 Pennsylvania State Reports 35, 60–91 (1932).

26. State *ex rel.* Hamilton, Attorney General v. Martin *et al.*, 23 Pacific Reporter (2nd) 1; 173 Washington 249 (1933).

27. Particularly relevant in the present context are a number of the sources already cited in Chapter VI. See especially Margaret K. Rosenheim, "Vagrancy Concepts in Welfare Law," Jacobus ten Broek, *The Law of Crimes and the Law of Welfare*, and so on.

28. Clifford S. Griffin, *Their Brothers' Keepers: Moral Stewardship in the United States, 1800–1865* (New Brunswick, N.J.: Rutgers University Press, 1960), p. xii.

29. Sanford Solender, *JWB Circle*, June 1966, p. 15.

30. See, for example, Brunhilde Helm, *Social Work in a South African City* (Cape Town: Board of Sociological Research, 1962).

31. See, for example, Frank G. Dickinson, ed., *Philanthropy and Public Policy* (New York: National Bureau of Economic Research, 1962), pp. 111–112.

32. An extended analysis of the economics of rehabilitation is available in Ronald W. Conley, *The Economics of Vocational Rehabilitation* (Baltimore: Johns Hopkins Press, 1965). In Canada, too, estimates of economies effected by rehabilitation services have been made. See "Rehabilitation— Does It Pay?" *Canada's Health and Welfare*, March 1959, p. 4.

An illuminating discussion of many kinds of expenditures that are often regarded as wasted or as "money down a rathole" may be found in Anatol Murad, *Private Credit and Public Debt* (Washington, D.C.: Public Affairs Press, 1954).

33. See Jack Shepherd, "Birth Control and the Poor," *Look*, April 7, 1964, p. 63.

34. See, for example, Juanita L. Cogan, *Employability Planning in Public Welfare Agencies* (Washington, D.C.: U. S. Department of Health, Educa-

tion, and Welfare, 1967). (Processed.) See also Andrew R. N. Truelson, "Helping Needy People Get Jobs and Hold Them," *Welfare in Review,* 3 (November 1965), 14–19, and *Impact on Public Assistance Caseloads of: . . . Work and Training Programs and Programs Under Manpower Development and Training Act, January–March 1966* (Washington, D.C.: Welfare Administration, Department of Health, Education, and Welfare, 1966).

35. Especially noteworthy is Abraham S. Levine, "Cost-Benefit Analysis of the Work Experience Program," *Welfare in Review,* 4 (August-September 1966), 1–9.

36. Press Release, *HEW-P* 50 (Washington, D.C.: Children's Bureau, U. S. Department of Health, Education, and Welfare, March 26, 1967).

37. See, for example, Homer E. Detrich, *Dollars and Sense, 1963–1964* Annual Report (San Diego: Department of Public Welfare, San Diego County, California, 1964), p. 1.

38. Justine Wise Polier, "The Legal Needs of the Poor, Problems Involving Family and Child," paper presented at National Conference on Law and Poverty, Washington, D.C., June 1965, as reprinted in *Law and Poverty* (Sacramento: California State Department of Social Welfare, n.d., *ca.* 1965), Selective Reading Series, No. 6, p. 20.

39. *The High Cost of Unhappy Living* (New York: Family Service Association of America, 1964). (Pamphlet.) *Family Service Highlights,* November 1961, published by the same association, contended (p. 176) "Family Service Is a Bargain." Relevant in this context is Jane M. Hoey, "The Lack of Money: Its Cost in Human Values," *Social Casework,* 38 (October 1957), 406–412.

40. *Effect on Families and Individuals in a Rural Community Where Poor Relief Was Exhausted* (Cincinnati, Ohio: Community Health and Welfare Council, 1963).

41. See, for example, (1) Robert J. Lampman, "How Much Does the American System of Transfers Benefit the Poor?" (pp. 125–157), (2) Morris H. Hansen and Genevieve W. Carter, "Assessing Effectiveness of Methods for Meeting Social and Economic Problems" (pp. 92–124), and (3) Eleanor Bernert Sheldon and Wilbert E. Moore, "Toward the Measurement of Social Change: Implications for Progress" (pp. 185–212), in Leonard H. Goodman, ed., *Economic Progress and Social Welfare* (New York: Columbia University Press, 1966). Noteworthy in this context, though of much more limited scope, is Robert Elkin, "Cost Analysis," *Public Welfare Projected* (Chicago: American Public Welfare Association, 1966), pp. 69–78. Additional useful sources may be found on pp. 77, 78. An example of the problem of ascertaining what is "economical" *for whom* is supplied by Seth Low, "The Economics of Adoption," *Welfare in Review,* 4 (March 1966), 12–14. Difficulties in measuring "cost" in only economic terms (as in the case of "midnight raids") are described by Floyd Hunter, *The Big Rich and the Little Rich* (Garden City, N.Y.: Doubleday, 1965), p. 166.

Also significant: Professor Lampman's "Toward an Economics of Health, Education and Welfare" (pp. 45–53) and Burton A. Weisbrod's "Investing in Human Capital" (pp. 5–21) in *The Journal of Human Re-*

sources, Vol. 1, No. 1 (Summer 1966). See also Theodore W. Schultz, "Investing in Poor People: An Economist's View," *American Economic Review,* Papers and Proceedings, LV (May 1965), 510–520; *Investment in Poor People* (Washington, D.C.: U. S. Department of Labor, 1967). A now dated but still interesting essay is Jessica B. Peixotto's "Charitable Endeavor from the Economic Point of View," in Ellsworth Faris, Ferris Laune, and Arthur J. Todd, eds., *Intelligent Philanthropy* (Chicago: University of Chicago Press, 1930), pp. 182–224.

42. Rufus C. Rorem, "Social Work Accounting—Tool or Torment?" *National Conference of Social Work,* Proceedings (Chicago: University of Chicago Press, 1937), pp. 645–654.

43. David Owen, *English Philanthropy: 1660–1960* (Cambridge: Harvard University Press, 1964), pp. 14–15.

44. Margaret S. Gordon, *The Economics of Welfare Policies* (New York: Columbia University Press, 1963), p. 4. See also Otto Eckstein, ed., *Studies in the Economics of Income Maintenance* (Washington, D.C.: Brookings Institution, 1967); Ewan Clague, "Economic Myth and Fact in Social Work," in W. Wallace Weaver, ed., *Frontiers for Social Work* (Philadelphia: University of Pennsylvania Press, 1960), especially p. 41; and, for a more specialized approach, William Haber and Merrill G. Murray, *Unemployment Insurance in the American Economy* (Homewood, Ill.: Richard D. Irwin, 1966).

For an interesting attempt to appraise social security measures in another country, see Carl G. Uhr, *Sweden's Social Security Program: An Appraisal of Its Economic Impact in the Postwar Period* (Washington, D.C.: Government Printing Office, 1966). For international perspectives on this issue, see Senator George S. McGovern, *War Against Want: America's Food for Peace Program* (New York: Walker, 1964), p. 122. See also Barbara Ward, "Proof It Is *Not* 'Down the Drain,'" *The New York Times Magazine,* April 23, 1961, pp. 9, 106–108.

A similarly broad perspective, but in terms other than economics, has been presented by Peggy and Pierre Streit with respect to United States foreign aid in "No, It Is Not Money Down the Drain," *The New York Times Magazine,* August 28, 1960, pp. 12, 62–65.

Gunnar Myrdal explains in "The Swedish Way to Happiness," *The New York Times Magazine,* January 30, 1966, pp. 14–22, how "the welfare state can be so economically progressive." An even broader comparative perspective on the effects of social expenditures upon economic development may be found in Andrew Shonfield, *Modern Capitalism: The Changing Balance of Public and Private Power* (London: Oxford University Press, 1965).

45. Eveline M. Burns, *Social Security and Public Policy* (New York: McGraw-Hill, 1956), p. 222.

46. Paul T. Therkildsen, *Public Assistance and American Values* (Albuquerque: Division of Government Research, The University of New Mexico, 1964), p. 43. See also *"Having the Power, We Have the Duty,"* op. cit., p. xvii.

47. Richard M. Titmuss, *Major Goals in Today's Welfare State* (paper presented in consultation in Israel, August 1964), p. 19. (Processed.)

48. Ernest W. Lefever, *Ethics and United States Foreign Policy* (Cleveland: World Publishing, 1963), p. 114. See also Joseph Grunwald, "The Alliance for Progress," in Sigmund Diamond, ed., *Economic and Political Trends in Latin America*, XXVII (Proceedings of the Academy of Political Science, 1964), 89.

49. Homer Folks, "Jungle Rule or the Golden Rule," in Savel Zimand, ed., *Public Health and Welfare: The Citizens' Responsibility* (New York: Macmillan, 1958), pp. 243–257.

50. Eileen Younghusband, "Adoption and the Unmarried Mother," *Social Work and Social Change* (London: G. Allen, 1964), p. 61.

51. Noteworthy among numerous relevant sources are Mignon Sauber and Janice Paneth, "Unwed Mothers Who Keep Their Children: Research and Implications," *Social Work Practice, 1965* (New York: Columbia University Press, 1965), pp. 94–106; Renee Berg, "Utilizing the Strengths of Unwed Mothers in the AFDC Program," *Child Welfare*, XLIII (July 1964), 333–339; Philip Hovda, a review of three books in *Social Service Review*, 41 (March 1967), 102–104.

52. As reported in *The New York Times*, Sunday, November 6, 1966.

53. Pearl Buck and Gweneth Garfoss, *The Gifts They Bring: Our Debt to the Mentally Retarded* (New York: John Day, 1965).

54. "The Foster Grandparent Program," *Public Aid in Illinois*, 34 (September 1967), 2–8.

55. *Newsletter*, Twentieth Century Fund, 58 (Spring 1967), p. 1.

56. Charles Frankel, "The Moral Framework of the Idea of Welfare," in John S. Morgan, ed., *Welfare and Wisdom* (Toronto: University of Toronto Press, 1966), p. 152.

57. Margaret Mead, ed., *Cooperation and Competition Among Primitive Peoples*, rev. paperback ed. (Boston: Beacon Press, 1961), pp. 496, 482.

58. Charles Galton Darwin, *The Next Million Years* (Garden City, N.Y.: Doubleday, 1953), pp. 78, 94, 104, 84.

X
SOMETHING
for
ALL—
FROM
ALL

Even to have raised, in a work on social welfare, momentous questions about man's sense of his own identity, his sense of community, and his broad responsibilities to fellowmen (as we did in Chapter VIII) may appear somewhat presumptuous. However, as suggested many times, these considerations significantly affect men's views of and attitudes toward welfare services. Moreover, it is not implausible that welfare services themselves may have something significant to contribute to men's relationships with other men and with social institutions, and to the relationships of nations with each other.

CONTRIBUTIONS TO SENSE OF WORLD COMMUNITY

The basically fundamental nature of the key values served by social welfare services and the universality of the esteem accorded them may do better in opening up avenues to a broad sense of world community than can more sophisticated concerns. One could see this possibility in the early days of UNRRA and, in truth, even before its establishment, when high officials of various cooperating governments stressed the importance that UNRRA's success would be as a harbinger of wider possible international cooperation through the broader United Nations organization (then envisioned but not yet established). "If nations cannot work together for postwar relief and rehabilitation," these statesmen were saying in essence, "how can they be expected later to cooperate on matters about which there is less unanimity?" One can also see in *Transfigured Night* that the concern about the fundamental well-being of German children, women, and men after World War II led people of the United States —even while still thwarted by the Trading with the Enemy Act—to breach the walls of enmity thrown up around Germany by war.

The capacity of welfare interests to transcend sociopolitical differences is reflected in the fact that half of the first six biennial meetings of the International Conference of Social Work, after meetings in Paris (1950), Madras (1952), and Toronto (1954), were held in what were, for most national members of the Conference, cobelligerent Italy (1960), former enemy Germany (1956), and former enemy Japan (1958). Conversely, when Hitler began establishing his own brand of brutality and dehumanization, social welfare agencies and particularly their international connections were among the institutions and relationships first attacked.

Even great Christian churches with high-sounding theological concepts ("the Fatherhood of God," "the brotherhood of man," "Christ died for all men," and the like), upon which their views of the unity of mankind are based, have found that a central thrust toward this unity has been found in more mundane joint efforts to promote social well-being. These common interests frequently have overridden differences that separate Protestant sects from one another and that separate Protestants from Catholics.

The Message of the Third Assembly of the World Council of Churches declares, in part, "In no field has Christian cooperation been more massive and effective than in service to people in every kind of distress." [1] Even the peaceful Quakers, according to John Forbes in *The Quaker Star Under Seven Flags,* found a new sense of unity through their support of the American Friends Service Committee.[2]

From a Catholic viewpoint, Father Bernard Coughlin, S.J., now dean of the School of Social Work at St. Louis University, has written, "Ecumenicalism in social policy formation can be a gateway to religious ecumenicalism. For this reason religious leaders who are interested in the ecumenical movement look with favor and hope on the collaboration of the churches in social welfare and social action." [3]

Evidence of the validity of this view appears in the degree to which Catholics and Protestants stood shoulder-to-shoulder in civil rights marches and presented a united front before governmental agencies granting funds for church-oriented War on Poverty and more traditional welfare services.

Presenting the Catholic viewpoint more broadly, Pope Paul VI declared in his encyclical, *Ecclesiam Suam,* "[We] recognize and respect the moral and spiritual values of the various non-Christian religions, and we desire to join with them in promoting and defending common ideals of religious liberty, human brotherhood, good culture, social welfare and civil order." [4]

The degree to which relief and welfare programs have today taken on international dimensions (United States foreign aid, the British Commonwealth's Colombo Plan, United Nations services, and so on) is surprising when one remembers how recently this supranational concern was thought to be wholly beyond the realm of reason.

Before the United States entered World War II, I was engaged in writing *The WPA and Federal Relief Policy*.[5] Having reviewed the ever-broadening circle of responsibility for public relief—first with parishes, then with towns and townships, and then with counties, states, and later the federal government—I could not see how the forces at work could stop this expansion short of transcending national boundaries and so declared myself in my manuscript.

However, the thought of "foreign aid" was ridiculed in some quarters as "globaloney," and critics scoffed at the thought of "a pint of milk for every Hottentot." But, even thoroughly humane and world-minded persons raised so many questions and expressed so much skepticism that, before publication, I finally compromised to the extent of modifying the subtitle introducing this seemingly hallucinatory idea. The new subtitle was put in the form of a question: "And What of the Rest of the World?"[5] For the American people alone and within a very short time, this soon proved to be a $15 billion question. Other nations also responded generously—in fact, in relation to their resources, even more generously than the United States. Yet, even the current extent of international involvement may be hardly more than a hint of what lies ahead.

Looking to the future, it is noteworthy that through the work of the European Court on Human Rights, national jurisdiction over domestic matters—including social welfare and allied issues—is actually being superseded by supranational jurisdiction. A recent decision of the court involved a Belgian action that denied unemployment benefits to a Jewish claimant because he had not (as required in order to qualify for benefits) registered as unemployed every day for a week including Saturday, his Sabbath. The supranational court held that denial of benefit on this ground violated the claimant's "human rights"—and the benefit was paid.[6] This example of judging before an international bar how sovereign nations treat their own citizens equitably may become much more commonplace in the world of tomorrow.

CONTRIBUTIONS TO SENSE OF COMMUNITY WITHIN NATIONS

Apart from contributions made by welfare programs to men's sense of world community—contributions of a fundamental nature and reflecting universal values—experience suggests that these same considerations foster a sense of community among different social groups within nations. This may be accomplished, in any country, in either of two ways: the first might be termed a microcosmic approach and the second a macrocosmic approach.

The Microcosmic Approach

Throughout the world today there are two tendencies profoundly affecting social life and, more particularly, welfare services: first, the ever greater institutionalization of all sorts of governmental and private enterprises and, second, the widely deplored erosion of intimate face-to-face groups—the relaxation of family ties, the decline of neighborliness and geographically based community life, and the dissolution of true mutual aid groups. Despite these latter tendencies, one significant countertrend lies in the rapid development in many countries of what might be called problem-centered, mutual-assistance groups. These have been developed to give group members mutual support while they wrestle with a common problem (such as alcoholism or narcotic addiction); they have also been developed to seek more adequate social recognition of, and resources for dealing with, that problem.

In Great Britain, for example, there are the self-help groups established in New Towns, ex-prisoners' clubs, and the Psychiatric Rehabilitation Association clubs for ex-patients of mental hospitals. In the United States these problem-centered groups include Alcoholics Anonymous, Al-Anon (for relatives and friends of alcoholics), Synanon (for narcotics addicts), Parents without Partners (widowed or divorced spouses who give each other support and help one another with the care and rearing of children), Compulsive Gamblers Anonymous, Joint Weight Reducers, Parents of Retarded Children (who have exerted potent forces for better community facilities for mentally retarded children), and many others.[7]

Mutual assistance has also played a large part in home-building and community renewal programs in the United States, Puerto Rico, Venezuela, and many other countries.

In France and Latin America there are Family Associations within which families help one another, attempt to influence social policy with respect to family allowances and other services, and arrange for common purchase and use of household equipment and the like.

These kinds of mutual assistance groups are widely applauded in welfare circles. They represent a renascence of the good old-fashioned face-to-face relationships. Mutual assistance groups are also proving effective in difficult situations in which professional help often is unavailing. The power of peers is sometimes greater, apparently, than that of professionals.[8] Moreover, mutual assistance involves direct reciprocation that is lacking in highly institutionalized services but that often appears to make help more acceptable and palatable.

For those to whom current emphasis upon group activities has a novel ring, it may be of interest that in the nineteenth century Canon Barnett, of Toynbee Hall, and the "classes" characterizing the early Methodist movement in England, relied heavily upon group activity.

If mutual assistance, reciprocation, and sense of community are, as seems likely, valued not only for their own sake but also as devices for expanding the limits of what men see as their "ingroups," these values might be furthered through organization of still more types of problem-centered peer groups, additional kinds of "communities of common needs." Moreover, these groups might be helped to see interests in common with other groups organized around related problems or needs, thus enlarging the perspective and human horizons of all the groups. It was a great day for the attack on discrimination, for example, when Jewish groups in the United States turned their guns on practices discriminating against Negroes and no longer concentrated on anti-Semitism alone.

Still wider extension of the circle of Jewish concerns was recently urged by Rabbi Emil G. Hirsch. Since their very survival as a people is no longer threatened, he called upon his coreligionists to think no longer only of what is good for the Jew, but also of what is good for the world.[9]

Circles of mutuality and community might be broadened beyond problem-centered peer groups by organization of preproblem or probable-problem groups. Thus "Probable School Dropouts," or "Already Sliding-Outs," or "Parents of Probable Dropouts" might help to get running starts on some school problems and involve in mutual helpfulness persons not already overwhelmed by difficulty. The possibility that the concept of "communities of common needs" might be extended to include also "communities of common strengths" would also appear to merit the attention of those who see value in mutual assistance and in furthering men's sense of community.

This emphasis was picking up momentum in the later 1960's in the United States, as Community Action programs under the War on Poverty got under way, as Welfare Rights Organizations began to speak up for themselves, and as more and more was done to help "the poor" shed their sense of being immobilized and develop their power. In his widely heralded article "The Power of the Poor," Warren C. Haggstrom wrote, "When the poor do not live in actual deprivation, increases in money make relatively little impact on the dependency relationships in which they are entangled. The opportunity to participate in *interdependent* relationships, as a member of the majority society, requires an increase in *power*." [10]

It was exactly this sense of power that the above-mentioned services were being developed to enhance—and that the newly emerging neighborhood legal services (Chapter VI) were established to support. All, obviously, were directed toward overcoming the "powerlessness" and "nobodiness" that aggravate "the hurt of being helped."

By this time, thanks to Michael Harrington, Edgar May, Sargent Shriver, and others, poverty in America had been vividly depicted; and interest was shifting from what Dwight Macdonald had called the "invisible poor" to the inaudible poor. Moreover, efforts to help disadvantaged persons to find their voices and to realize their capabilities were also making it more possible for them to help themselves. Of this, Haggstrom has written:

Most central of all, rather than to provide opportunities for the "lower class," the poor must as a group be helped to secure opportunities for themselves. Only then will motivation be released that . . . will enable them to enter the majority society and make it as nurturant of them as it is at present of the more prosperous population. [11]

As this is done, disadvantaged groups can shuck off their "You-can't-fight-City-Hall" negativism and can join, though belatedly, those who "run City Hall."

Saul Alinsky, arch exponent of helping disadvantaged groups to develop "power" (whose *Reveille for Radicals*, published in 1946, is still useful), has made the same point but in terms less restrained than Haggstrom's. "I tell people," Patrick Anderson quotes Alinsky as saying, " 'The hell with charity—the only thing you get is what you're strong enough to get, so you'd better organize.' " [12]

One exceedingly important fact about power is that feelings of personal inadequacy often make it difficult to accept help even when it is needed. Of this phenomenon, Charles E. Silberman, in describing the Alinsky-inspired Woodlawn Organization in Chicago, observes, "[Its] greatest contribution . . . is its most subtle: it gives Woodlawn residents the sense of dignity that makes it possible for them to accept help."

Somewhat earlier Silberman had said, "Experience in every city in the nation demonstrates that any paternalistic program imposed from above will be resisted and resented as 'welfare colonialism.'" [13]

This is reminiscent of Haggstrom's diagnosis, "It is . . . not surprising that marginal people react with apathy to helping efforts which assume their inability and inferiority." [14]

Soon after Vice-President Hubert H. Humphrey proposed his "Domestic Marshall Plan" (proposed in Detroit following racial disturbances there in 1967), he told Robert B. Hemple, Jr., "We're dealing with people who are non-participating isolated members of society—who need to feel they have a place in the scheme of things." [15]

It was exactly this "place in the scheme of things" that the Haggstroms, Alinskys, Community Action programs, Welfare Rights Organizations, "maximum feasible participation," and so on were helping people to find. Although they would not claim that these activities would give everyone the place he should have in the "scheme of things," it was clear that they thought they could, at least, make inroads on the problem.

It was ironic, though, how quickly some critics changed their tunes. In one breath they would chastise as "no good loafers" those who needed help, but, when these "no accounts" succeeded in organizing cooperative food-buying programs and other devices for helping themselves (thus by-passing local stores and businesses), the critics turned on them and charged them with being "Communists —or something." To these critics, the previously invisible and inaudible poor suddenly became insufferable, once they began solving their own problems in their own ways, but in so doing encroached upon those buffer zones protecting the privileges, prestige, power, and profits of others.

Turning to Britain, it is important to note that, in looking to the future and what he called "the needs that remain in a social service state"—the very one he did much to design—Sir William Beveridge believed that the greatest future needs in Britain would be not for money, but for service.

Accordingly, he urged Friendly Societies to devote themselves to providing a wide range of services. Among his suggestions was one that could virtually revolutionize organized philanthropy:

The friendly society movement is a democratic movement of mutual aid. . . . But mutual aid, in the more equal society of the future must broaden into philanthropy, into the promotion of social advancement, not simply each for himself, but for the whole of society. . . . The friendly societies . . . might become leaders or active partners in every movement of social welfare or citizen service.[16]

Although Beveridge does not himself make the point clear, Professor T. H. Marshall, emeritus Professor of Sociology at the University of London—in commenting upon the above and upon other proposals made by Beveridge—observes:

This implies not merely that the Friendly Societies as we know them should extend their philanthropic services, but that the voluntary social services, through which help is rendered by the privileged to the underprivileged, should hand over to new associations built on the principle of mutual aid.[17]

While Beveridge's proposals, and Marshall's comments upon them, do not refer to mutual aid as more strictly defined in this book, what they both propose clearly involves a far greater degree of mutualism and reciprocity than do conventionally organized welfare services.

A veteran American social worker who, during World War II, helped to develop the United Seamen's Service, wrote of this union-oriented experience, "Clients (despite the history of the word) will feel themselves *belonging* to the community only when they take part in a real effort of the plain people to see that their social services are truly social and really serve." [18]

Even though a society might not go as far as Marshall suggests in his reinterpretation of Beveridge's views, great gains could still be made through proliferation of mutual assistance groups like those described. If this were done, it would obviously overcome many of the inimical aspects that we have discussed of helping and being helped. For example, help would be much more in the nature of mutual aid, would permit hurt-assuaging reciprocation, and would be shorn of hurtful elements of gratuitousness. Through their own efforts the groups could fight the particular injustices victimizing them and thus contribute to realization of fuller justice. The groups could conduct their affairs in the interest of their members and of the groups as a whole and thereby avoid subservience to the self-interest of outside "benefactors." Mutual assistance groups could thus kill two birds with one stone—or to put the issue more positively, could feed two birds with one handful of corn—fulfill requirements the groups were formed to supply *and* do this in a way that avoids many of the characteristically hurtful ways of being gratuitously helped by others.

The Macrocosmic Approach

An approach quite different from the microcosmic approach, to help broaden men's sense of social identity, would be to aid them to see the degree of mutualism, really inherent but not always apparent, in large social entities.

Realities of contemporary life suggest that even very large-scale social institutions can be developed in ways that effectively symbolize and express social solidarity and mutuality. Take, for example, government—democratic government in an open society in which all citizens are free to participate in political processes. We deliberately choose government as our example here because it (especially large government) has been a favorite whipping boy, characterized as an inevitably impersonal, distant, and unyielding bureaucracy.

"OF, BY, AND FOR THE PEOPLE." Yet, if one wanted to describe an intimate mutual-aid group, how much better could he do than to quote Abraham Lincoln's characterization of *government*—"of the people, by the people, and for the people"? But, the critics might say, that was just talk and the realities are something quite different. Are they? Even if they are, are they necessarily so?

One factor that affects the degree to which men can feel that what government does is in fact what citizens together are doing is the degree to which persons and groups become vocal and organized and make themselves heard when decisions concerning them are made. The importance—and novelty—of disadvantaged persons' doing just this is a central point in Gilbert Y. Steiner's *Social Insecurity: The Politics of Welfare,* which shows that although government usually consults those most directly affected before postal rates are raised, farm subsidies modified, or businesses regulated, and so on, intended beneficiaries of welfare services (notably public assistance) are virtually never consulted.[19] It is to help correct this historic imbalance that disadvantaged persons, too, are now being helped to raise their voices.

One cannot expect—in terms of power politics alone—that newly raised voices can soon be heard above the clamor of the experienced voices of well-financed and long-standing lobbyists who for many years have successfully persuaded government to use its power to further *their* interests. Nevertheless, increased participation in the give-and-take of legislative debate should contribute to some larger sense of government as a "we" group than has been possible under the historic system of taking only what others choose to grant.

Professor Marshall wrote about government in his country, "There are many ways in which citizens can be made to feel that the public services belong to them." He then enumerates the wide range of official positions in which citizens can serve as voluntary workers, elected councillors, members of special committees, hospital-management committees, school boards, and so on.[20] He might have mentioned also the roles of citizens who sit as judges in juvenile courts (a function which in the United States is professionalized) and citizens who participate in advisory boards and appeal boards connected with different social services.

Mutualism in government in Britain has been underscored by the Conservative Party, which, in 1949, issued the pamphlet *The Right Road for Britain*. This pamphlet declared:

The social services . . . are a cooperative system of mutual aid and self-help provided for the whole nation and designed to give all the basic minimum of security, of housing, of opportunity, of employment and of living standards below which our duty to one another forbids us to permit any one to fall.[21]

In France, the tradition of mutualism has had a somewhat different history from that in Britain. Even a very recent official report still related French welfare services to the spirit of the Revolution and—even in 1966—quoted the chairman of the Committee for Mendicity in 1790 as saying, "Care for the public welfare is not a compassionate virtue, it is a duty, it is justice. Wherever there is a class of men without subsistence, there is a violation of the rights of man; the social balance is upset." [22]

According to Wallace C. Peterson, the sense of social solidarity engendered by the resistance movement during World War II led to demands for "the kind of social revolution envisaged in the welfare state." [23]

Nor is the sense of mutualism inherent in governmental welfare services characteristic of only highly developed countries. In Thailand, for example, the prime minister in 1966 declared:

Community development plays a part in improving relationships between the people and the government. . . . The participation of the people . . . creates not only a sense of belonging . . . [but] also creates favorable attitudes towards the government. The people realize that the government cares about their welfare, they no longer hold the idea that they are isolated.[24]

Among others who, within the United States, have seen that government can properly be viewed as symbolizing a sense of mutuality is Professor Samuel Mencher. Even during a discussion of "The Future for Voluntaryism," he observes, "Only the State could provide the sense of mutual aid in those services where the condition of need and its satisfaction precluded any but equal treatment." [25]

This conception is often encountered in the social welfare field when persons who are reluctant to feel that they are "being helped" like to believe—rightly or wrongly—that their very citizenship, their rearing of children, and their payment of taxes have qualified them for the benefits received. One of my oldest professional memories is that of an aged lady my wife and I used to visit in a Colorado poorhouse. "I'm not receiving charity," she used to say, "I've paid taxes for thirty years and I've *bought* myself a place here."

Although Old Mary never knew it, she had on her side a great authority in the person of one of social welfare's greatest leaders, Homer Folks, of the New York State Charities Aid Association. In *Making Relief Respectable: A Radical Reconstruction of Our Conception of Public Relief*, written way back in 1934, he contended:

The idea that the recipient of public relief is getting something for nothing is directly contrary to fact. Public relief is something to which each recipient has contributed all his life, to which he still contributes, and to which he will continue to contribute indefinitely.

. . . Instead of something for nothing, public relief is a two-way business all the way, coming and going, everybody contributing roughly in proportion to his ability, and everybody receiving that particular form of public service or aid which at the moment he may require.[26]

Old Mary would have concurred heartily also with the California Supreme Court, which handed down a decision against requiring payment from a daughter's estate of the cost of her mother's care in a state mental hospital. The court declared:

In resolving the issue now before us, we need not blind ourselves to the social evolution which has been developing during the past half century; it has brought expanded recognition of the *parens patriae* principle . . . and other social responsibilities . . . and divers . . . public welfare programs to which all citizens are contributing through presumptively duly apportioned taxes.[27]

That Old Mary was far from alone in her view of her relationship to government is evidenced in *Income and Welfare in the United States*. Findings by this study of how a nationwide sample views support for older persons are mixed—as would be expected in view of the ambivalence of the American people about such support. Say the authors:

Those who believed that the primary responsibility belonged to the government spoke mostly of the responsibility in terms of the government's role and its obligations. Many people felt that "old folks have been paying taxes all of their lives, they should get some of it back." . . . The idea that old people should get some kind of payment in return for their taxes was the most prominent reason given by those who felt that the government should be responsible for older people.[28]

Like other opinions of the kind, these, because of the substantial ambivalence that exists and because of differences between declared and operational values, must be taken with a grain of salt. For example, 30 percent of the spending unit heads who responded to the question and who had not already retired thought relatives *should* have sole responsibility for the aged. Yet no less than 60 percent of those who responded in this way did not expect to care for their own aged parents themselves. Conversely, of the unit heads (23 percent of the total) who believed that *government* should have sole responsibility for aged persons, no less than 23 percent were *themselves* either caring already for their own aged parents or expected to "give them general financial help," "pay specific expenses," "house them," or "give them general care." [29]

Although "having paid taxes all my life" has here been stressed as one reason why government is thought to have responsibility for the support of older persons, other interpretations are also frequently encountered. Among these are "I've been a good citizen all my life"; "I've been a good mother (or father) to my children and have raised them to become good citizens"; "My boy's abroad with the Army, fighting (or was killed)." Critics who wish to make receipt of welfare services as onerous as possible and to have them appear to be "something for nothing," would of course belittle if not deny the relevance of these implications of mutualism. Such denial, within many countries, would be confronted, however, not only by widespread contrary views, but in several of them also by high court decisions.

In this connection we should note one small but exceedingly important aspect of Poor Law history that is often overlooked. One reason that the unprivileged "we" have had so hard a time overtaking the privileged "they" is that when the early precedent-setting Poor Laws were enacted in England—before being imported into the United States, lock, stock, and barrel—poor persons did not have the franchise. When it came to how "the poor" were to be treated, the privileged had things all their own way. Thus, with a head start of centuries, and with those already privileged continuing to vote themselves still more privileges, even after voting rights were extended to others, it was perhaps inevitable that belatedly franchised poor persons should for so long have seen government as "they."

With the growth of democracy and with the ever-growing sense of social solidarity—greatly heightened in England under the rain of bombs during World War II—the centuries-old imbalance in power was gradually reduced. The United States, however, does not seem very willing to import some of these corrections—the National Health Service and family allowances or the recent Social Security benefits that were inaugurated in 1966 to make deep inroads on public assistance. At least, the United States seems far less willing to import them than it did the unequal and discriminatory Poor Laws in the first place.

MUTUALISM IN SELECTED GOVERNMENTAL SERVICES: A number of strongly democratic countries have already established a variety of universally available health services, programs for the support of children, and support for aged persons. These countries include Canada, Great Britain (where great emphasis is laid upon "fair shares"), Sweden, Norway (where, as Dr. Karl Evang, "father" of the nation's Health Security program, likes to say, "We can't let one another down"), and West Germany. These services and programs, in the form of social utilities, reflect high degrees of mutualism.

Other cases in point in the United States and elsewhere include: public health services; emergency medical care; certain preventive health services; well-baby clinics (even in the United States where, however, age two—or thereabouts—is somehow regarded as a mystical age before which health services may be free but after which they become marketplace transactions or welfare services, or are unavailable); public recreation and cultural programs; and maintenance of parks, forests, recreation areas, and the like. All may be viewed in the light of "everybody pays, everybody benefits" mutualism.

To strengthen the ties between her citizens and social insurance schemes, France and other countries such as Denmark, Norway, and Sweden have given labor unions and other organizations

considerable responsibility for the administration of these programs. This has been done, in part, to strengthen "grass roots democracy" and to preserve workers' sense of direct identification with
social insurance—as something of their own, not something that
"others" provide for them.

To an international conference on "Self-Help in Social Welfare"
a French national committee reported:

The creation in France of Social Security, of Family Allowances and of
all Security and Mutual Aid Organizations, far from making the individual lose his sense of responsibility, had, in freeing families from
being concerned with the very great and considerable material worries,
made them the more available for tasks of general interest and for participation in collective action. A considerable number of users, family
delegates to the Boards of Directors of the Social Security and Family
Allowance Agencies and Farmers' Mutual Insurance Societies there become aware of general problems and of the solid ties which bind them
to other people.[30]

The antecedents of the Welfare State evolving in Great Britain
undoubtedly help people there to regard it as "theirs." For, as Professor Richard M. Titmuss recalls, "In the historical development of
social security measures in Britain the major impulse came from
the working-man's ethic of solidarity and mutual aid." Tracing
backward the development of this "ethic," Titmuss reports:

A great network of friendly societies, medical clubs, chapel societies,
brotherhoods, co-operatives, trade unions and savings clubs, schemes of
mutual insurance were developed. . . . They constituted microscopic
welfare states. . . .

. . . This great movement . . . expressed . . . the ordinary
man's revulsion from a class-conscious, discriminating charity and a
ruthless, discriminating poor law. The poor law was hated because it
spelt humiliation; it was an assault on the individual's sense of self-
respect in an age when "respectability"—the quality of meriting the respect of others—governed the *mores* of society.[31]

This was written with an eye on developments in Great Britain.
But it was exactly this same desire to strip governmental welfare
measures of connotations of "a class-conscious, discriminating charity" and of other "discriminating" and humiliating features (such as
the inequities in public assistance in the United States, as discussed
in Chapter VI) that led many countries to substitute social utilities,
which carried no inimical connotations of "help," gratuitously
proffered through their welfare services.

BASIC SUPPORT IN THE UNITED STATES: We have referred several times to the quite special problem presented in the United States by the need for basic support for persons who would otherwise lack the fundamental requirements for living. This problem is heightened both by the greater embarrassment of people who cannot meet their own basic needs and "provide for their own" and by the reluctance of societies to make provision for the basic rather than the more sophisticated requirements of others. We now turn to further consideration of these issues in light of views already presented in this chapter.

"SOCIAL INSURANCE" OR "SOCIAL SUPPORT"? The California Supreme Court decision holding that care given to a mother in a state mental hospital was in the nature of a public service, not something which could be charged against a daughter's estate, has already been mentioned.

Another program that is interesting in this same respect is the federal Old Age, Survivors, and Disability Insurance (OASDI) program. Official interpretations of this measure, such as that made by the Advisory Council on Social Security in 1965, repeatedly extol its superiority to public assistance, which, by contrast, is viewed quite inimically. Of OASDI, the council claims:

The fact that the program is contributory . . . protects the rights and dignity of the recipient and at the same time helps to guard the program against unwarranted liberalization.

. . . The covered worker can expect, because he has made social security contributions out of his earnings during his working lifetime, that social security benefits will be paid in the spirit of an earned right, without undue restrictions and in a manner which safeguards his freedom of action and his privacy.[32]

Here, as often, the distinguishing feature of social insurance is said to be the "contributions" made by those covered. However, this emphasis would disparage noncontributory insurance programs such as unemployment insurance and workmen's compensation (which covers industrial accidents) that in the United States are financed by employers. Is one seriously to say that a worker has less "right" to benefits under either of these programs merely because he made no contribution to them?

In this connection it is important to note that in the defense (1966) by Social Security Commissioner Robert M. Ball (quoted in Chapter III) he stressed not the contributions to social insurance but its relatedness to work, a linkage that characterizes unemployment insurance and workmen's compensation also. Whether one thinks of the contributory nature or work-relatedness of social insurance—both of which seek to surround such programs with the aura of marketlike transactions—it should be emphasized that "rights" can also be acquired in ways other than by purchase or through work. Even without specific contributions or work-relatedness, people are acknowledged to have rights to public education, police protection and service, justice, fire protection, public libraries, parks, and the like. These also respect freedom and dignity, but are not financed by payroll taxes or acquired through work. The basis for according rights is not some mystical entity whose peculiar nature derives from a special way a service is financed. Civil rights and other constitutional rights, for example, are by no means related to either work or payroll deductions.

Granting that public assistance, as historically and currently administered in the United States, may deserve the invidious position attributed to it in 1965 by the Advisory Council on Social Security (and others mentioned in earlier chapters), this is not the only conceivable position that the American people might accord it. It would be very possible, if the American people so chose, to strip current public assistance programs of virtually all of their obnoxious attributes. Or, if they wanted to go farther, "the negative income tax," currently being advocated even in conservative quarters, "guaranteed incomes," or "demogrants" (as suggested by Eveline M. Burns), might be adopted. Or, the total problem might be broken down into automatically paid universal pensions to aged persons and family allowances to families with children. Any of these choices would obviously place such a support program outside the realm of social welfare service as here defined.

Just as many observers seem to underrate income-maintenance possibilities other than social insurance, they seem to exaggerate the true merits of this device. For example, even the United States Supreme Court, in its decision in *Flemming v. Nestor*, declared:

It is hardly profitable to engage in conceptualizations regarding "earned rights" and "gratuities." . . . To engraft upon the social security system a concept of "accrued property rights" would deprive it of the flexibility and boldness in adjustment to ever-changing conditions which it demands.

Rather, the Court held, the social insurance program was one "enacted pursuant to Congress' power to 'spend money in aid of the general welfare.' " [33]

In line with this concept, even the council's own report repeatedly reveals that many benefits are greater than the amounts financed by the contributions made by the insured person and, if not self-employed, by those of his employer. The benefits that are referred to include those to low-paid workers, persons covered only a short time but receiving at least minimum benefits, workers with large families, and beneficiaries getting the advantage of new statutory benefits after their own contributions had ceased.

But the Medicare program enacted in 1965 marked an even further departure from the insurance principle, because persons who never had contributed to OASDI and others whose contributions were already completed could qualify for hospital benefits on the same basis as "contributors." Then, in 1966, many persons seventy-two years of age and over were made eligible for "insurance benefits" even though they had never contributed a nickel to the program.[34]

Even before many of the recent relaxations of the "insurance principle" had come into effect, economists who were brought together to discuss "philanthropy and public policy" were already objecting to the term "social insurance" and thought that it might better be called "philsurance."

Moreover, whether one is included in, or excluded from, social insurance programs has been a matter for legislatures to decide, not the individuals affected. Fair-minded men therefore often question whether it is just to "take out of the hides" of innocent victims—through inimical assistance policies—what is really attributable to the timidities of a Congress or of state legislatures that exclude or do not soon enough include many who could well have been covered earlier.

Any insurance, whether social or private, obviously assumes "spreading the risks" so that a few dollars for an airplane accident policy, for example, may yield a quite handsome return if the insured person is unlucky enough to be killed. However, the imbalances between social security contributions and benefits go beyond this kind of risk-spreading.

No less a body than the Advisory Council itself has strongly hinted that the OASDI program may be more "social" than "insurance." For, in support of its 1965 recommendation that self-employed physicians, who had been excluded at the request of organized medicine, be covered by the social security program on the same basis as other self-employed persons, the council declared, in terms reminiscent of the Supreme Court's language:

Social security . . . is an institution through which all Americans together promote economic security by financing, from the contributions
of all, a continuing income to families whose earnings are cut off by the
old age, death, or disablement of the worker. Physicians, like all other
Americans, benefit in general tax savings and in other ways from the
prevention of dependency through social security. Like other Americans,
they should share in its support.[35]

But probably the most striking developments in all the world
that reflect broader social support rather than "insurance" of the
classical type are the many retirement programs that are future-
oriented rather than past-oriented. These look forward to what the
society does, not backward to what the retired person did. In the
United States, for example, federal civil service and military retirement benefits now automatically go up when costs of living rise by
specified degrees. Similarly, labor unions every so often renegotiate
the retirement pension provisions of their retired members to reflect,
not specific past contributions by the members, but the current capacity of the employer.

By 1964 at least eleven countries (Belgium, Chile, Denmark,
Ecuador, Finland, France, Israel, Luxembourg, The Netherlands,
Sweden, Uruguay) had grafted on to their social insurance programs features that adjusted the pensions of retired persons in accordance with price increases or changes in current wage levels.
West Germany has subsequently joined the ranks of countries making adjustments in terms of changes in wage levels.

Thus, in modern societies productivity has become what the
city wall, which was mentioned in Chapter VI as protecting "the
good and bad alike," was to ancient cities. Since so many hands go
into the building of today's "walls," it is being increasingly questioned
whether *any* should be denied their protection. If there is validity in
what we said in Chapter IV about interdependence within complex
societies, about the degree of social support of even those individuals
who seem to be most "successful," and about the virtual immeasur-
ability of who contributes what to whom, the problem of who should
and should not be assured of basic support becomes complex indeed.

In that earlier discussion, it will be recalled that Professor Theodore W. Schultz has said that development of the human resources
of the United States, and particularly education, has probably contributed more to the nation's economic development than the increases in capital and man-hours worked.

Even the poorest widow and poorest family who pay rent—
which is sometimes 40 to 60 percent of all they have to live on—

contribute to the payment of property taxes, which are largely relied upon for the support of education. Even the poorest also pay sales and other taxes on consumers. If one further agrees with Professor William J. Goode (see Chapter IV) that the family in any industrialized country contributes to economic development—by preparing persons for, and absorbing the "shocks" of, industrial employment, he will realize that many, many hands have helped to build the "city wall." In addition, one must remember that poor families rear sons for the armed forces. Thus, to say that some should have respectable social support and others may be treated inimically is to judge as commensurable what is virtually incommensurable.

Recently a West German high court threw an interesting sidelight on this policy issue. The case involved an able-bodied man who, in accordance with the policy then prevailing, had been denied public assistance because he had refused to work. The court held that, although he might properly be denied the full level of benefit to which able-bodied men were normally eligible, he could not be denied—even though he had failed to comply with prevailing policy—basic subsistence.[36]

Imbalances between the benefits one receives and contributions one has made are by no means limited to social insurance programs. For example, a notice issued to shareholders of a major United States corporation discloses the pensions to be paid to a number of its officers upon retirement and shows the amounts contributed by these officers toward their pensions. The pensions ranged between approximately $43,000 and $49,000 annually. If it is assumed that these will be paid for an average of about fifteen years (the average life expectancy, at age sixty-five, for white males in the United States), the total contributions of these officers is only about 12 percent of the grand total of the pensions they would be expected to collect. This imbalance, made possible by consumers who have paid or who will pay the prices charged for the corporation's products, means that these pensioners will really be supported by consumers in much the same way that some social security beneficiaries are supported by other contributors to the system.

A hard look at social insurance—and the degree to which it is veering away from the very marketlike principles that have been invoked to give it special dignity in the past—suggest that it is rapidly moving in the direction of the broader types of social support that are discussed in this chapter and in Chapter IV. Critics who recognize the extent to which this has already occurred understandably wonder whether there is, indeed, anything in principle that would preclude going all the way in this direction and to assure at least basic support for all members of a society that can afford it.

Repeated insistence that rights must be "earned" through work or paid for with "money on the barrelhead" is utterly misleading. Rights can be freely *given*. A right can as readily accrue from a promise as from a purchase. Who must pay how much in cash—or work how long in "covered employment"—before he is accorded protection under the Fourteenth Amendment? Or the First, Second, or other amendments? Rights are what a society says they are; they are not necessarily acquired only through purchase for cash or earned through work.

BASIC SUPPORT: GRATUITY OR SOCIAL UTILITY? To suggest that basic support of all a nation's people might be assured through a social utility is now neither novel nor radical. In fact, it was a conservative economist, Professor Milton Friedman of the University of Chicago, who has popularized this concept through advocacy of what he calls a "reverse income tax." [37] Subsequently, others have urged "guaranteed incomes" in various forms, but without the strictures attending Professor Friedman's proposal.[38]

The proposal that a program of basic support might well take the form of a social utility does not imply that current social welfare services should all take this form—although some undoubtedly will, just as various welfare services have in the past. But, as noted several times already, men's inability to provide for themselves and their families the elemental necessities of life creates rather special problems that do not arise in the case of more sophisticated "goods." Consequently, societies may think of special arrangements for social support with respect to necessities. Justification for such arrangements is seen in the difficulties in equitably assessing either rewards for self-help or penalties for its alleged lack (Chapter IV); in the greater embarrassment and humiliation when a man cannot supply himself and "his own" the most basic requirements (Chapter VII); in the relativities involved in realistically identifying such factors as catastrophe, "no fault of one's own," and injustice (all of which lead men to want to help others who are victimized, but that are singularly difficult to identify accurately and to appraise justly).

A truly humane society, recognizing these relativities and aware of its own frailties and its tendency to treat harshly persons who lack basic support, just might be willing to commit itself to a program of general support of people who cannot work or for whom there are no jobs. This possibility is supported by the fact that men do not trust themselves to be as generous at all times as they are sometimes. Consequently, in their better moments, men frequently commit themselves to actions they do not trust themselves voluntarily to carry out without such commitment. Cases in point are the pledges men make to churches, educational institutions, United Funds, Community Chests, and the like. Thus, in moments of sober reflection, they commit themselves to obligations they do not otherwise trust themselves to fulfill. Or we might return to the example of marriage, through which men take on obligations and accord to others rights that they do not trust themselves to respect voluntarily without a formal "I do."

Many years ago the British philosopher, Professor T. H. Green, whose thought greatly influenced social policy in his day, wrote that "for the slavery to appetite [man] substitutes the freedom of subjection to a self-imposed law." [39] Although we are not concerned in this chapter with man's "appetite," there is reason to think that "subjection to a self-imposed law" can equally well free a man from "slavery" to punitiveness and inequity in the matter of basic support of others.

If some socially decent and just people sometime, somewhere, were to assure all of its fellows basic social support, when jobs—including public jobs—cannot be made available for all, it would be establishing what we mentioned in Chapter VI as a modern, economic counterpart of the old "Cities of Refuge" and "places of asylum."

Or, to change the analogy, such a society could be viewed as establishing a " 'Geneva Convention' for the Disadvantaged"—a domestic and economic counterpart of *the* Geneva Convention.

Through the Geneva Convention signatory nations commit themselves to treat prisoners of war decently and humanely. This means that soldiers—who only minutes before might have been killing another nation's soldiers or might have dropped a bomb upon one of its cities—would be accorded humane care upon capture or surrender. And even costly medical care would be provided to heal their wounds or save their lives. If nations can commit themselves to such solicitude for enemies who only moments before were bent upon the destruction of their own nationals and property, surely it is not too fantastic to think that a nation might properly commit itself to the humane care (including medical care) of its own people, who had never lifted a hand against it—and to do so despite the fact that, because they are not or cannot be self-supporting, they may not be living wholly in accord with its values.

However plausible this idea might seem, there is one barrier—

perhaps insuperable—to its realization. Disadvantaged persons do not possess one inestimable advantage that an enemy nation possesses to secure compliance with the Geneva Convention: They hold no hostages. By contrast, if a nation, in wartime, refuses or fails to give decent and humane treatment to enemy nationals, an enemy nation can exact reprisals through neglect, mistreatment, or even torture of the war prisoners who fall into its hands.

Disadvantaged persons cannot exact reprisals. For, the only bargaining point they have is their own millions of lives and the lives of more millions of children. The latter will be the nation's future citizens and, ironically, may be called upon to bear arms in defense of their country and its values. If so, they may come under the protection of the Geneva Convention, whether or not a domestic counterpart had ever given them a fair share in the life of their country or a fair chance to experience in their own lives the values they may be called upon to defend elsewhere.

In passing, we might note how many of the presumed hurts of being helped would be greatly assuaged by a "Geneva Convention" for the disadvantaged or, in less martial terms, by a program of basic support in the form of a social utility. Gratuitous help (which, as we have indicated repeatedly, seems to be especially hurtful) would be supplanted by justice. Powerlessness would be reduced, because all members of the society would be "voting members of the corporation." Feelings of inferiority and guilt over inability to provide for one's own would be offset by the societal recognition that such incapacity may not be an idiosyncratic aberration, but a social product of highly complex and interrelated factors—factors not always subject to individual control or accurate assessment by others. Ignominies, humiliations, and inimical dual standards of behavior and justice now inherent in public assistance practices would become irrelevant, as they now are in the use of public libraries or highways. Injustice would be compensated for, at least to the extent of assuring basic support. Mutualism would be firmly underlined because the entire enterprise would be an embodiment of the one-for-all and all-for-one spirit that it would indeed exemplify.

Thus, assurance of basic support in the form of a social utility would represent what Mrs. Alva Myrdal described a number of years ago (1945) as the third stage in the development of social policy in a democratic society. Of her three stages, she says:

The first ["a paternalistic conservative era, when curing the worst ills is enough"] was the period of curative social policy through private charity and public poor relief; the second ["a liberal era when safeguarding against inequalities through pooling of risks is enough"] was the period of social insurance broad in scope but yet merely symptomatic; and the third ["a social democratic era when preventing the ills is attempted"] may be called the period of protective and cooperative social policy.

At the time Mrs. Myrdal was writing, she was specifically concerned with children's or family allowances—provided as social utilities, in our terminology—and says of these, in the context of her third stage of policy:

Cooperation . . . may be the key word for this social policy . . . because it rests fundamentally on social solidarity, on pooling of resources for common aims, wider in their loyalty than just insurance of individual interest. If children shall continue to be born and if they shall be reared according to standards that our democratic culture can be proud of, the competitive and destructive society of yesterday must yield to a society of solidarity. A new era in social policy will then dawn, a century of child care and family security.[40]

A firm declaration of policy along these lines, but not limited to persons who happened to have children, would reassure the innumerable "Old Marys"—and, for that matter, the "young Marys" and the young and old Toms, Dicks, and Harrys—who have long *felt* that this should indeed be a government's responsibility to those who cannot otherwise support themselves or who are not otherwise given an opportunity to support themselves. Hitherto, however, these persons have lacked confirmation of their beliefs and have had only the comfort of their own reiterated self-assurance that they "had it coming to them," even though "it" often never came.

Government per se need not be viewed as some far-off "they-group" quite different from something that is genuinely "of," "by," and "for" people. Views of and attitudes toward government are affected as much by how a society chooses to define it as by the nature of government as government. Moreover, any definition is affected by circumstance, and views born in one day are not necessarily appropriate to another. Yet attitudes are slow to change, and it is easy for a people to carry along into a day of highly complex and interdependent social life concepts of government—or anything else, such as attitudes toward self-help—developed under quite different circumstances.

But, conceptions of government can change not only over protracted time spans but also overnight, given sufficiently dramatic changes in circumstance—such as the outbreak of war or the occurrence of a catastrophe. For example, when President Johnson in 1965 visited areas of the United States that had been stricken by tornados and floods, he said, "At an hour and time like this the federal government must not be something cold and far away, but a warm friend and a warm neighbor." [41] Why the federal government could not be a warm friend and neighbor at other hours and times was not explained, but it is a safe presumption that any such explanation would turn as much upon men's attitudes toward government as upon the warmth and friendliness of government itself. For, government is widely regarded (except, of course, by those intimates seeking lucrative defense contracts, TV licenses, or other privileges) as a "foul-weather" friend, and many men tend not to reach out to it—any more than to friends or God—when things are going well. Often they regard both government and friends, and even relatives, as they do God—only as an ever-present help in time of trouble. "Don't call me, I'll call you."

But if disaster does indeed have the power to alter men's attitudes toward government, and if enough of the American people fully sensed the toll of deprivation and poverty and recognized the elemental need of so many of their fellows for basic support *and dignity,* very possibly they would regard the current situation as enough of a national calamity to justify abandonment of history-bred concepts of governmental roles and to invoke government's "disaster" powers. This would be tantamount to declaring that all the nooks and crannies, slums and ghettos, rundown farms and abandoned mines where persons lack basic support are "disaster areas" warranting governmental assurance of such support.

If, on these or any other grounds, a people chooses to redefine the role of government as properly underwriting the support of all its members who do not have the opportunity—or ability—to support themselves, this certainly is within the realm of possibility. Moreover, it is something that some sensitive and humane society will some day surely do.

IF NOT GOVERNMENT—WHO? If government does not reflect the true mutualism inherent in an entire society and its welfare services, what institution can? No other has similar breadth; no other permits all members to vote, to participate in policy decisions and in the election of their representatives and officials, to pay their fair share (as determined by tax policy) of the cost; no other offers effective avenues for the appeal of decisions. Both the "providers" and the "consumers" (insofar as they represent different elements of a population) of governmental welfare services have these advantages in ways that contributors to, and intended beneficiaries of, nongovernmental welfare services do not. A beneficiary of such a service usually has no vote on policy or in the selection of a private agency's board of directors; and he may or may not have made a financial contribution to the service.

City or county officials, members of a state or national legislative body (such as Members of Parliament in Britain or congressmen in the United States) take it as a matter of course that intended beneficiaries of governmental welfare services—individually or collectively—will call upon them to protest one aspect or another of public policy or administration. By contrast, the bank president or the busy lawyer who is president of the board of a voluntary agency is not geared to hearing or handling such protests.

With respect to programs of basic support, there is virtually no disagreement in the welfare field over the necessity for government to assume this responsibility. However, the *only* argument sometimes cited in favor of government's assumption of this responsibility is that "only government can command the requisite resources." This is a telling and commanding reason, but it is by no means the only one, as conservatives often imply. The peculiar circumstances that obtain when it comes to providing the basic essentials of life require not only the financial resources of government, but the elements of justice and mutualism just described. These only government can supply.

True mutualism, as we suggested earlier, means not only being *in* a social group but being *of* it also. It means having a voice in its control and contributing to its support. It means, in short, being a card-carrying, voting, listened-to, supporting member. Government offers these privileges—attenuated because there are so many members, but in any case equally distributed among them all—with responsibility for support possibly differentiated in accordance with "ability to pay." Consequently, if true mutualism in welfare services cannot be effected in government, one wonders where, other than in closely knit mutual assistance groups, it can be found.

Through Voluntary Services

To have said so much here about the possibility of building into the macrocosm of government a true sense of mutuality is not to imply that mutualism cannot be fostered through nongovernmental welfare services. It can. Nongovernmental welfare agencies are admirably situated to reflect the mutualism inherent in the microcosmic approach discussed earlier. Here is almost unlimited scope for voluntary effort, although governmental action in this area will also continue to be needed. Voluntary services hold great promise for mutual assistance groups because they can take as their starting point religion-centered, church-centered, labor-union, ethnic, and other natural ingroups to which governmental agencies cannot so easily limit their services. If a society is indeed interested in genuine pluralism, here is a natural field for promoting it through voluntary effort. The shortest road to a monolithic society is not through government but through voluntary effort that does not remain distinguished from governmental activities.

Apart from voluntary agencies that will have opportunities to promote and serve mutual assistance groups, the more traditional kinds of private agencies will also continue to be needed. However, as these come to take more seriously some of their own professed tenets (such as their commitment to human dignity and to self-determination by their intended beneficiaries), one might hope that there will be some rethinking of the bases upon which their services are now offered.

It is an illuminating but sobering experience, in seminars and conferences with leaders of the private welfare sector, to ask them to enumerate the advantages they see in voluntary services as compared with those offered by government. Responses commonly include the usual textbook generalities: "local initiative," "grass-roots democracy," "freedom from outside controls," "freedom to make our own decisions and meet problems in our own ways." Then, when one asks whether these advantages are largely limited to the lay board members and staffs of the private agencies or are enjoyed as well by those they serve, the answer almost invariably is that beneficiaries do not effectively share these advantages.

The private sector often confuses even itself by its claims about the degree of mutualism it represents. These claims are based largely on the fact that so many people in a community contribute to the support of voluntary agencies. "Everybody gives, everybody benefits." This emphasis is undoubtedly inspired by the desire to make private services appear to be virtually as mutual as governmental services that are supported by taxes that "everybody" does indeed pay. However, this approach overlooks important considerations—other than the paying of taxes—that are applicable in the public sector. The financial base is not the only factor here, any more than in the case of government's responsibility for basic support programs. There are also the other significant elements that have been mentioned: opportunities to vote on issues, to elect representatives and officials, to be heard in public hearings, to appeal decisions, and so on. All these enhance the sense of mutualism, but have few counterparts in the private sector—at least for intended beneficiaries.

The Family Service Association of America has taken a step, though only a timid one, in the right direction by issuing the pamphlet *The Rights of the Individual Family in a Mass Society*. It is designed to help overcome the reluctance of families to seek help and does this by reiterating over and over again the phrase "the rights of the individual family in a mass society." What is lacking, unfortunately, is any of the above-mentioned steps that give substance to such concepts as "rights" and justice. Rhetoric, however commendable, is a poor substitute for reality.

Perhaps it was only because civil rights were so much in the air in the late 1960's that one began to hear, with respect to the private sector of the welfare field, language that had not been used much before. For example, various observers were charging that private agencies operated in a "colonial spirit" [42] or represented "welfare colonialism." [43]

It will be recalled that Beveridge and Marshall criticized British voluntary services (on grounds that they represented services provided by "the privileged for the unprivileged"), and proposed that control of them should be handed over to modern counterparts of the Friendly Societies. One need not go as far as this, perhaps, to recognize that greater degrees of mutualism can be built into voluntary services than has been done to date. Also, there are ways in which the gratuitousness of private agency services can be reduced and erstwhile "colonials" be given independence. Agencies might enter into contracts with labor unions or other groups (such as the employees of an industry who contribute to a United Fund), so that persons served in accordance with these agreements could feel more realistically that the needed services are "coming to them," and not that they are offered as only a gratuity. Or, instead of having "clients" come to an agency for service, the agency might delegate a particular staff member to work directly with, and under the direction of, a group of clients organized into a mutual assistance group. If self-determination is indeed a desideratum, why not think of ways in which intended beneficiaries have fuller opportunity to say what they want, by what means, and upon what terms, and not limit them to a narrow range of choices that any particular agency might offer?

Representation of clients and potential client groups on agency boards and on United Fund boards would also help to introduce into them a greater sense of mutualism. One exceeedingly hopeful sign, in this respect, is the support given by a division (Christian Life and Mission) of the National Council of Churches to the federal policy of "maximum feasible participation" of poor persons in Community Action programs under the War on Poverty. The policy was defended as

an embodiment of two fundamental principles which commend themselves to the Christian conscience, viz. a) recognition that every human being possesses inherent worth and dignity . . . ; and b) recognition that every person in a democratic society is entitled to participate effectively in the decisions which shape the policies and programs affecting his life.

Moreover, the Division then struck a refreshing note by commending to churches and church agencies the application of this principle to their own programs.[44]

Greater clarity in private agency policy and wider publicity for that policy would also be helpful. And, perhaps, as in government, there might even be an opportunity for public comment on proposed policies before they are adopted. Helpful, too, would be clear and publicized procedures for appeals from decisions of voluntary agency personnel affecting the interests of clients or applicants. Such appeals might be heard by panels nominated by a United Fund, Welfare Planning Council, or even by an agency's own board. In this connection it is interesting that the AFL-CIO Constitutional Convention in 1964 adopted a resolution in favor of having private agency services recognized as a *right* for those seeking to utilize them.[45] Little has been heard since of this resolution. Nevertheless, the advantages of obtaining private agency services less in the form of gratuities and more in the nature of private rights (such as one gains under "stock exchange law," "baseball law," labor union by-laws, and so on) are great. "Standing on one's rights," even when these are private rather than civil rights, represents much more dignity, mutuality, and reciprocity than does "standing cap in hand." In other words, "full justice" assumes not only that one has his "day in court," but also that he has it in the voting booth, too, and has easy access to the hearing room and to the chambers of aldermen who are beholden to him at least as an elector.

Those who fear that greater participation by disadvantaged persons in the management of welfare services might upset all the applecarts of existing establishments—if not actually open the sluice gates to revolution—would do well to recall points made earlier in this book. There is, for example, the power of cultures (efficient? frightening?), which means that disadvantaged persons are likely to see things in much the same light as more privileged persons do. There is also the point of the tendency of disadvantaged persons to have modest aspirations.

These phenomena were strikingly evidenced in an Eastern seaboard community of about 40,000 when priorities of social welfare needs as seen by "planners" were checked against those of "consumers." The greatest difference in the priorities of the two groups was in relation to "better leisure-time services and facilities"—hardly revolutionary objectives—which were favored by "less than half the planners but nearly three quarters of the consumers as an important or most important need."

The most striking aspect of this study is the greater emphasis that the planners gave to "community planning for minority groups," while the strong preference of the consumers ran to services of "universal character," not services only for persons with handicaps.[46] This preference, incidentally, may be an important datum concerning what has been said in this book about social utilities.

The central problem in opening up participation in the management of welfare services to disadvantaged persons is not that applecarts will be upset. In fact, disadvantaged persons may be so much the children of their cultures that they will think, as Joseph C. Lagey and Beverly Ayres found in their study of 136 Community Chests in North America, that there was "very little evidence of any attempt to question either the legitimacy or the validity of priority determination by the planners and policy makers of welfare services." [47]

Cultures are strong, and even disadvantaged persons absorb the message in the folk wisdom of not looking a gift horse in the mouth. "They're giving it to us, aren't they? Why should *we* try to tell them what to do with *their* money?" People who do not want to rock the boat welcome these attitudes. But others, more interested in dignity, self-determination, mutualism, and equity, will deplore them.

Those interested in dissolving the "we-they" dichotomy will, ironically, often confront the phenomenon that advantaged persons frequently want for those who are disadvantaged more than the latter seek for themselves. This carries us back to what was said in Chapter II about value propagation. Then, as greater degrees of mutualism are effected, more people will sense—vis-à-vis private welfare services—what Kurt Lewin used to call "belongingness."

It is this "belongingness" that we—along with Beveridge, Marshall, and many others—see as most important in mutualism, even if no dramatic shifts in welfare policies and practices immediately follow.

We are not suggesting that voluntary services should necessarily be "of, by, and for" disadvantaged persons. But we are questioning whether they may not for too long have been "of and by" the privileged, and "for" the unprivileged, and whether it may not be time to give disadvantaged persons more privileges of management and control that have long been limited to those more favorably situated. In a discussion of voluntary associations in *The Dimensions of Liberty*, Oscar and Mary Handlin had this to say:

. . . The voluntary association [business, labor, reform, and other groups] added to the liberty of the American by extending his power to act. At the cost of the strains involved in making decisions on matters that other men took for granted, he was able to make choices rather than face the brute alternatives of inaction or compulsion by the state. This was an important element in the pattern of freedom that developed in the United States.[48]

Greater mutualism in welfare services is advocated in order to obtain such additions to liberty—extensions of the power to act and opportunities to "make choices"—not only with respect to the state, which was what the Handlins were talking about, but also with respect to the benevolent intent of self-selected "benefactors." Mutualism, obviously, can help offset manipulation of receivers by givers and can curb the penchant of givers for using welfare services to further their own self-interest at the expense of broader social well-being. Greater degrees of mutualism, within countries, recall what is often said in international circles about the preference of newly independent nations for self-government to even "good" government by others and about the preference of nations for multilateral to bilateral aid, because the latter leaves them more susceptive to control by the givers.

During the days of UNRRA, when representatives of nations

that were to receive help sat down with representatives of nations that would be doing the helping, it was a thrilling sight to see them jointly work out the policies to be effectuated. Welfare personnel incline toward emphasizing the importance of self-determination by persons who are to receive help, but often this is actualized only in narrow terms (to take or leave one or another of a usually very narrow range of services offered, or of specific choices to be made). It is seldom seen—except in the case of social settlements and community centers—at the level of policy formulation. In this, the United Nations does much better.

Community Action programs under the War on Poverty are intended to bring representatives of the groups to be aided into policy-making. The degree to which these programs have proved controversial in community after community reveals how unready American communities are to give an effective voice to, and to share power with, the very persons and groups to be served. Instead of encouraging potential recipients to "look gift horses in the mouth," the givers seem determined to do all the looking themselves.

To infuse more mutualism into welfare services will undoubtedly entail what the Handlins termed "the cost of . . . strains." In fact, it may mean offering to disadvantaged persons what Bradford Smith (borrowing the term from De Tocqueville) discusses in *A Dangerous Freedom*—the freedom to associate with others voluntarily, whether to improve a community's schools, promote temperance, run an underground railroad, or whatever. Of the hazards implicit in this freedom, Smith concludes, "Ours is a dangerous freedom, but what freedom is not? Since we know that life without freedom would not be worth living, we must accept the danger too. . . . Danger is in the end a safer thing than safety." [49]

Greater mutualism in welfare services inevitably involves risk. It also pinpoints some value conflicts (and possible alternate choices) that a "welfare colonialism" would be glad to see swept under the rug: How much manipulation by and self-interest of givers versus how much dignity, worth, and self-determination of receivers? How much humane treatment versus how much blame, fault, unworthiness attributed to human actions as commensurable when, in complex and interdependent societies, these are virtually incommensurable? How much privilege, prestige, and power for some versus what cost of denying them to others?

Contemporary readers may find somewhat incredible how long helping agencies have gone their beneficent ways without really consulting those whom they sought to benefit. Yet a little historical perspective can show some gains that have already been made. Consider, for example, how far a cry is the present discussion of "participation of the poor" from the highly paternalistic attitude of only a few generations ago. In 1901, for example, even so enlightened a philanthropist as Andrew Carnegie maintained that "the man of wealth" should consider

all surplus revenues . . . as trust funds, which he is called upon to administer . . . in the manner which, in his judgment, is best calculated to produce the most beneficial results for the community . . . thus becoming the mere trustee for his poorer brethren, bringing to their service his superior wisdom, experience, and ability to administer, doing for them better than they would or could do for themselves.[50]

He nowhere suggests, of course, that intended beneficiaries should have a voice in electing such "trustees" or in shaping policies to guide them. Nor could he have dreamt that Neighborhood Legal Services would, by today, be calling before the bar of justice well-meaning "trustees."

And it was not too long ago that Lincoln Steffens had to explain, to the surprise of Judge Elbert H. Gary, president of United States Steel, why workers disliked the "welfare work" of which the judge was very proud (but which Steffens dubbed "hellfare work") and preferred to arrange their own lives rather than have their employers dictate where and how they should live, eat, and play as well as work.[51] Just as in the recent past employers have relinquished or been forced to relinquish controls over those whom they employ, perhaps the immediate future will see relinquishment, by intended benefactors, of unilateral control hitherto exercised over their benefactions and over their intended beneficiaries.

CONCLUSION

If, as suggested in Chapter VIII, the twentieth century demands the broadest possible sense of community, this can be fostered within the welfare field: through microcosmic approaches, under both governmental and nongovernmental auspices, to mutualism and the gradual broadening of mutualism in ever-expanding problem-centered mutual assistance groups; through macrocosmic approaches by which even the largest social institutions can be regarded and interpreted as possessing the mutualism actually inherent in them; and through voluntary services willing to take into partnership those they are designed to serve. To the extent these approaches succeed, not only can the hurt of gratuitous help be reduced, but the social advantages that statesmen, religionists, philosophers, and others see in broad mutualism can be better actualized, and new degrees of reciprocation and justice, both public and private, more fully realized.

The relevance of these considerations to the questions "From whom something? For whom nothing?" is, of course, that the validity of a concept like "something for nothing" depends upon who the provider of the "something" considers himself to be and who it is that allegedly gets "nothing." If these "who's" are interpreted in highly individual and personal terms, one arrives at one answer. If, however, one sees oneself as an integral part of a society, he arrives at quite another.

Societies that choose to do so can abandon punitive and denigrating attitudes toward obviously dependent persons, can build into their governmental welfare services more mutualism and "more perfect justice," and can effectuate higher degrees of mutualism and private justice through voluntary services. They may not offer, in the classical sense of the concept, "charity for all," but they can at least assure—to take liberties with Lincoln's historic phrase—malice toward fewer and justice toward more.

1. *New Delhi Speaks* (London: SCM Press, 1962), p. 10.
2. John Forbes, *The Quaker Star Under Seven Flags: 1917–1927* (Philadelphia: University of Pennsylvania Press, 1962), p. 193.
3. Bernard J. Coughlin, S.J., *Church and State in Social Welfare* (New York: Columbia University Press, 1965), p. 149.
4. His Holiness Pope Paul VI, *Ecclesiam Suam* (Glen Rock, N.J.: Paulist Press, 1964), Section 112, p. 64.
5. Donald S. Howard, "And What of the Rest of the World?" *The WPA and Federal Relief Policy* (New York: Russell Sage Foundation, 1943), pp. 838–839. See also pp. 706–709.
6. See A. H. Robertson, Head of Directorate of Human Rights, Council of Europe, "Regional Institutions," *Institutions for the Protection of Human Rights* (Paris: World Veterans Federation, 1965), pp. 48–49.

   A brief and readily available statement giving examples of how national and state (including New York State) courts have invoked provisions of the Universal Declaration of Human Rights may be found in *The Universal Declaration of Human Rights: A Standard of Achievement* (New York: Office of Public Information, United Nations, 1962).
7. See, for example, Alfred H. Katz, "Self-Help Groups," in Harry L. Lurie, ed., *Encyclopedia of Social Work* (New York: National Association of Social Workers, 1965), pp. 680–683. A somewhat dated but still relevant source is *The People Act*, a series of twenty-six CBS Radio Network programs showing American citizens uniting to solve their local problems (January–June, 1952). See also Marshall B. Clinard, *Slums and Community Development: Experiments in Self-Help* (New York: Free Press, 1966); *Alcoholics Anonymous* (New York: Alcoholics Anonymous Publications, 1965); M. B. Bailey, "Al-Anon Family Groups as an Aid to Wives of Alcoholics," *Social Work*, 10 (January 1965), 68–74; Max Gunther, "The Fraternity of Crippled Men: Ex-husbands Who Feel Injured by Alimony . . ." *The New York Times Magazine*, September 9, 1965; Lewis Yablonsky, *The Tunnel Back: The Story of Synanon* (New York: Macmillan, 1965); *The Self-Help Organization in the Mental Health Field: Recovery, Inc.* (Washington, D.C.: U. S. Joint Commission on Mental Illness, 1960); Elizabeth T. Harris, "Parents without Partners, Inc.: A Resource for Clients," *Social Work*, II (April 1966), 92–98; Bill Sands, *The Seventh Step* (New York: New American Library, 1967); and a major study by Alfred H. Katz, *Parents of the Handicapped* (Springfield, Ill.: Charles C. Thomas, 1961).

Also relevant is O. Hobart Mowrer, *The New Group Therapy* (Princeton: Van Nostrand, 1964), and Frank Riessman, "The 'Helper' Therapy Principle," *Social Work,* 10 (April 1965), 27–32. The American Conference of Therapeutic Self-Help Clubs publishes a periodical, *Action.*

Two interesting sources providing historical perspective are Bradford Smith, *A Dangerous Freedom* (New York: Dell, 1963), and Oscar and Mary Handlin, "Voluntary Associations," *The Dimensions of Liberty* (Cambridge: Harvard University Press, 1961), pp. 89–112.

Insight into the workings of Community Associations in Britain is available in *Working with Communities,* compiled and edited by Raymond T. Clarke (London: National Council of Social Service, 1963); this includes an extended bibliography (pp. 84–88), including publications of the National Federation of Community Associations. See also Richard and Hephzibah Menuhin Hauser, *The Fraternal Society: Toward Freedom from Paternalism* (New York: Random House, 1963).

8. See sources cited in preceding note, especially Lewis Yablonsky's *The Tunnel Back.* Other relevant sources include Arthur Pearl and Frank Riessman, *New Careers for the Poor: The Nonprofessional in Human Service* (New York: Free Press, 1965), and Frank Riessman, "The Revolution in Social Work: The New Non-Professional," *Trans-action,* 2 (November-December 1964), 12–17; Jona M. Rosenfeld, "Strangeness Between Helper and Client: A Possible Explanation of Non-Use of Available Professional Help," *Social Service Review,* XXVIII (March 1964), 17–25; Norman Fenton and Kermit Wiltse, eds.; *Group Methods in the Public Welfare Program* (Palo Alto, Cal.: Pacific Books, 1963); George Brager, "The Indigenous Worker: A New Approach to the Social Work Technician," *Social Work,* 10 (April 1965), 33–40.

Closely related to the services of peers to one another are the services of volunteers who may or may not be from essentially the same social class or area. There is an extensive literature on this subject, as related to the social welfare field. See, for example, Nathan E. Cohen, ed., *The Citizen Volunteer: His Responsibilities, Role, and Opportunity in Modern Society* (New York: Harper & Row, 1960); Rosemary Morrissey, *Strengthening Public Welfare Services Through the Use of Volunteers* (Chicago: American Public Welfare Association, 1961); Joseph F. Phelan, Jr., "The Volunteer as a Member of the Therapeutic Team," *Child Welfare,* 42 (May 1963), 226–229. There are many, many others.

In Britain, the Citizens' Advice Bureaux present rather special opportunities for volunteers. These opportunities are described in *Advising the Citizen* (London: National Council of Social Service, 1961), and in Margaret E. Brasnett, *The Story of Citizens' Advice Bureaux* (London: National Council of Social Service, 1964).

9. As reported by Mrs. Milton E. Kahn in *Progress Versus Poverty* (New York: Council of Jewish Federation and Welfare Funds, 1966), p. 2.

10. Warren C. Haggstrom, "The Power of the Poor," in Frank Riessman, Jerome Cohen, and Arthur Pearl, eds., *Mental Health of the Poor* (New York: Free Press, 1964), p. 219. Oscar Lewis, in *A Study of Slum Culture: Backgrounds for La Vida* (New York: Random House, 1968), suggests

(pp. 4–21) that mutual assistance groups may well prove effective in off-setting ill effects of slum cultures.

11. *Ibid.*, p. 220.

12. Saul Alinsky, as quoted by Patrick Anderson, "Making Trouble Is Alinsky's Business," in *The New York Times Magazine*, October 9, 1966, pp. 28–31, 82–104. See also Saul Alinsky, *Reveille for Radicals* (Chicago: University of Chicago Press, 1946), and Charles E. Silberman's *Crisis in Black and White* (New York: Random House, 1964), especially pp. 318–350, which describe Alinsky's activities in the Woodlawn area of Chicago. Another useful source is Bernard E. Loshbough, "Social Action Programs in Urban Renewal," in Margaret S. Gordon, ed., *Poverty in America* (San Francisco: Chandler, 1964), pp. 335–348.

13. Charles E. Silberman, *Crisis in Black and White* (New York: Random House, 1964), p. 348.

14. Warren C. Haggstrom, *Culturally Deprived Populations*, seminar paper (Los Angeles: School of Social Welfare, University of California, 1967). (Processed.)

15. Hubert H. Humphrey, as quoted by Robert B. Hemple, Jr., *The New York Times*, August 20, 1967. See also Harry Specht, *The Role of the Poor in the War on Poverty* (Walnut Creek, Cal.: Contra Costa Council of Community Services, 1965).

16. Sir William Beveridge, *Voluntary Action: A Report on Methods of Social Advance* (London: G. Allen, 1948), pp. 298–299, 300–301.

17. T. H. Marshall, *Sociology at the Crossroads and Other Essays* (London: Heinemann Educational Books, 1963), p. 331.

18. Bertha Capen Reynolds, *Social Work and Social Living* (New York: Citadel, 1951), p. 174. See also Chapter III, "Eligible or Belonging?" pp. 35–52. A related discussion pertaining not to labor unions but to racial groups is available under the somewhat surprising title "The Case Against Urban Desegregation," *Social Work*, 12 (January 1967), 12–21. The authors are Frances Fox Piven and Richard A. Cloward.

19. Gilbert Y. Steiner, *Social Insecurity: The Politics of Welfare* (Chicago: Rand McNally, 1966).

20. Marshall, *op. cit.*, pp. 227, 331–332. A somewhat more subdued but nevertheless positive view, related particularly to Britain's national hospital service, may be found in John Trevelyan, *Voluntary Service and the State* (London: George Barber, 1952). A considerably more negative view than that presented by either of the above is presented by Michael Graham, *Human Needs* (London: Crescent Press, 1951), especially pp. 14–15.

21. Quoted by Asa Briggs, "The Welfare State in Historical Perspective," *Archives Européennes de Sociologie*, 11 (1961), 227. See also the Dowager Marchioness of Reading, *Report on 25 Years Work, WVS, Civil Defence, 1938–1963* (London: Women's Voluntary Service for Civil Defence, n.d., *ca.* 1963), pp. iii–iv.

22. *Social Welfare in France*, prepared under the direction of Pierre Laroque (Paris: La Documentation Française, 1966), p. 131.

23. Wallace C. Peterson, *The Welfare State in France*, University of Nebraska Studies, New Series No. 21 (Lincoln: University of Nebraska, 1960),

p. 101. For a somewhat different slant on mutualism in relation to government in France, see Paul K. Padover, *French Institutions: Values and Politics* (Stanford, Cal.: Stanford University Press, 1954).

24. His Excellency Thanom Kittikachorn, in *Statements of Heads of State on Community Development* (New York: International Society for Community Development, 1966), not paginated.

25. Samuel Mencher, "The Future of Voluntaryism," in Alfred J. Kahn, ed., *Issues in American Social Work* (New York: Columbia University Press, 1959), p. 226.

26. Homer Folks, *Making Relief Respectable: A Radical Reconstruction of Our Conception of Public Relief*, Publication No. 212 (New York: State Charities Aid Association, 1934), pp. 10–11. This citation is available also in Savel Zimand, ed., *Public Health and Welfare: The Citizens' Responsibility* (New York: Macmillan, 1958), pp. 293, 294.

27. Department of Mental Hygiene v. Kirchner, 60 Cal. 2nd 716 at 722; 388 P. 2nd 720.

28. James N. Morgan, *et al.*, *Income and Welfare in the United States* (New York: McGraw-Hill, 1962), p. 277.

29. *Ibid.*, Table 18–23, p. 278.

30. As reported by Georges Desmottes, "Threats to Self-Help," *Self-Help in Social Welfare*, Proceedings (Bombay and New York: International Conference of Social Work, 1955), pp. 33–34.

31. Richard M. Titmuss, "The Limits of the Welfare State," *The Correspondent*, 31 (March-April 1964), 46.

32. Advisory Council on Social Security, "Report: The Status of the Social Security Program and Recommendations for Its Improvement," *Social Security Bulletin*, 28 (March 1965), 4–5.

33. Flemming v. Nestor, 363 U.S. 603 at 610, 609. See also Jacobus ten Broek and Richard B. Wilson, "Public Assistance and Social Insurance—A Normative Evaluation," *U.C.L.A. Law Review*, 1 (April 1954), 237–302.

34. See, for example, Wilbur J. Cohen and Robert M. Ball, "Social Security Amendments of 1965: Summary and Legislative History," *Social Security Bulletin*, 28 (September 1965), 3–21; Gerald Hutchinson and Terence Hawkes, "Benefit Increases Resulting from the Conversion of Monthly Rates Under the 1965 Amendments," *ibid.*, 29 (February 1966), 43–45; "Benefits Awarded Under 1965 Amendments, September-November 1965," *ibid.*, 29 (March 1966), 15–17; and "New OASDI Provisions" [under the Tax Adjustment Act of 1966], *ibid.*, 29 (May 1966), 1–2.

35. Advisory Council on Social Security, *op. cit.*, p. 35.

36. See *United Nations Yearbook on Human Rights for 1958* (New York: United Nations, 1960), p. 61.

37. See Milton Friedman, "The Alleviation of Poverty," *Capitalism and Freedom* (Chicago: University of Chicago Press, Phoenix Books, 1963), pp. 190–195.

38. See, for example, Michael D. Reagan, "Washington Should Pay Taxes to the Poor," *The New York Times Magazine*, February 29, 1966, pp. 24–25, 84–90, and this same author's "For a Guaranteed Income," *ibid.*, June 7, 1964, pp. 20, 120–121. The latter article is also available in Arthur B.

Shostak and William Gomberg, eds., *New Perspectives on Poverty* (Englewood Cliffs, N.J.: Prentice-Hall, 1965), pp. 134–141.

An overview of a number of proposals is available in Helen O. Nicol, "Guaranteed Income Maintenance: A Discussion of Negative Income Tax Plans," *Welfare in Review*, 4 (April 1966), 1–10; George H. Hildebrand, *Poverty, Income Maintenance and the Negative Income Tax* (Ithaca: New York State School of Industrial and Labor Relations, Cornell University, 1967); and Herman P. Miller, ed., *Poverty American Style* (Belmont, Cal.: Wadsworth Publishing, 1966), especially Chaps. 7 and 8.

The prestigious National Commission on Technology, Automation, and Economic Progress gave its support in 1966 to a "guaranteed . . . floor under family income"—*Technology and the American Economy* (Washington, D.C., 1966), Vol. 1, p. 110. However, the commission placed primary importance upon effectively maintaining "full employment" as a prior choice.

The most comprehensive discussion to date is Robert Theobald, ed., *The Guaranteed Income: Next Step in Economic Evolution?* (Garden City, N.Y.: Doubleday, 1966). In this, in "The Background to the Guaranteed-Income Concept," Theobald himself writes (p. 91), "I am convinced that if we desire to maintain freedom, a guaranteed income will necessarily have to be introduced." About as bold a series of proposals (including guaranteed incomes) as one ever sees may be found in A *"Freedom Budget" for All Americans: Budgeting Our Resources, 1966–1975, to Achieve "Freedom from Want"* (New York: A. Philip Randolph Institute, 1966).

39. Thomas H. Green, *Lectures on the Principles of Political Obligation* (London: Longmans, Green, 1927), p. 124.

40. Alva Myrdal, *Nation and Family: The Swedish Experiment in Democratic Family and Population Policy* (London: Kegan Paul, Trench, Trubner, 1945), pp. 151, 152.

41. Lyndon B. Johnson, as quoted in the *Los Angeles Times*, April 15, 1965.

42. See S. M. Miller, "The Public Responsibility of the Voluntary Agency" (paper presented at Ninth Annual AFL-CIO National Conference on Community Services, Syracuse University Youth Development Center, 1964), in Robert Schasre and Jo Wallach, eds., *Readings in Social Agencies and Social Change* (Los Angeles: Youth Studies Center, University of Southern California, 1966), Vol. III. (Processed.)

43. Richard A. Cloward, in testimony before Select Subcommittee on Poverty of the Committee on Labor and Public Welfare, U. S. Senate, eighty-ninth Congress, 1st session, *Expand the War on Poverty* (Washington, D.C.: Government Printing Office, 1965), p. 264. Extended discussion of "Welfare Colonialism" may be found in Silberman, *op. cit.*, pp. 308–355.

44. Division of Christian Life and Mission, The National Council of Churches, "A Resolution on Involvement of the Poor," *The Interchurch News*, November 1966, p. 5.

45. *Policy Resolutions Adopted November 1963 by the Fifth Constitutional Convention* (Washington, D.C.: American Federation of Labor and Congress of Industrial Organizations, 1964), pp. 130–131.

46. Ludwig L. Geismar and Bruce W. Lagay, "Planners' and Consumers' Priorities of Social Welfare Needs," *Social Work Practice, 1965, op. cit.,* pp. 89–90.
47. See Joseph C. Lagey and Beverly Ayres, *"Priority Determination Plans* (Vancouver: Community Chests and Councils of Greater Vancouver Area, 1960). (Mimeographed.)
48. Oscar and Mary Handlin, *The Dimensions of Liberty* (Cambridge: Harvard University Press, 1961), p. 109.
49. Bradford Smith, *A Dangerous Freedom* (New York: Dell, 1963), p. 365.
50. Andrew Carnegie, *The Gospel of Wealth and Other Timely Essays* (New York: Century, 1901), p. 15.
51. See Lincoln Steffens, *The Autobiography of Lincoln Steffens* (New York: Harcourt, Brace & World, 1931), p. 693. For a modern counterpart of Judge Gary's views, as related to large agricultural interests, see Steve Allen, *The Ground Is Our Table* (Garden City, N.Y.: Doubleday, 1966), pp. 106, 117.

Bibliography

GENERAL

This bibliography is a limited one inasmuch as the numerous citations and other relevant sources in the text provide a guide to more than a thousand publications. To repeat very many of them here would be needless duplication.

Because the references after each chapter are related to the specific points treated in the chapter, the works cited below are arranged in accord with the way the relevant literature is organized, rather than with the ideology of the text itself.

In the interest of brevity, only one place of publication is cited below for many works whose publishers operate in different cities and even different countries. No effort has been made to indicate publications available in paperback editions except when these were the editions that were consulted.

Serious students of particular welfare services will undoubtedly want to consult a wide range of annual and biennial reports, policy manuals, and administrative memoranda that, because of space limitations, are not cited below.

As is well known, standard encyclopedias (such as *Americana* and *Britannica* as well as others in foreign languages), yield a vast amount of reliable information on our subject matter. It may be less apparent, however, that a number of specialized encyclopedias (such as *The Catholic Encyclopedia, New Catholic Encyclopedia, The Encyclopaedia of the Social Sciences, The Jewish Encyclopedia, The Universal Jewish Encyclopedia,* and others—to say nothing of the *Encyclopedia of Social Work,* cited below) often supply particularly valuable information. Rewarding articles may be found under such headings as "Alms," "Altruism," "Charity," "Humanitarianism," "The Poor," "Poverty," "Philanthropy," "Justice."

VALUES

Nature of Values and Ways of Viewing Them

Ayer, Alfred Jules. *Language, Truth and Logic*. London: Gollancz, 1947.
Bronowski, J. *Science and Human Values*. New York: Messner, 1956.
Fletcher, Joseph. *Situation Ethics: The New Morality*. Philadelphia: Westminster Press, 1966.
Frankel, Charles. "The Moral Framework of the Idea of Welfare" and

"The Transformation of Welfare," in John S. Morgan (ed.), *Welfare and Wisdom*. Toronto: University of Toronto Press, 1966, pp. 147–164 and 165–184, respectively.

————. *The Case for Modern Man*. New York: Harper & Row, 1955.

————. *The Democratic Prospect*. New York: Harper & Row, 1962.

Graham, Michael. *Human Needs*. London: Crescent Press, 1951.

Green, Thomas H. *Lectures on the Principles of Political Obligation*. London: Longmans, Green, 1927.

Hobhouse, L. T. *Morals in Evolution: A Study in Comparative Ethics*. 3rd ed. London: Chapman and Hall, 1951.

————. *The Elements of Social Justice*. New York: Holt, Rinehart and Winston, 1922.

Hook, Sidney. *The Quest for Being, and Other Studies in Naturalism and Humanism*. New York: St. Martin's Press, 1961.

————. *Reason, Social Myths and Democracy*. New York: Humanities Press, 1950.

Kaplan, Abraham. *The Conduct of Inquiry: Methodology for Behavioral Science*. San Francisco: Chandler, 1964.

Maslow, Abraham H. (ed.). *New Knowledge in Human Values*. New York: Harper & Row, 1959.

Mering, Otto von. *A Grammar of Values*. Pittsburgh: University of Pittsburgh Press, 1961.

Naegele, Kaspar D. "Conflicts within Society," in T. E. H. Reid (ed.), *Values in Conflict*. Toronto: University of Toronto Press, 1963, pp. 28–41.

Perry, Ralph Barton. *Realms of Value: A Critique of Human Civilization*. Cambridge: Harvard University Press, 1954.

Towle, Charlotte. *Common Human Needs*. New York: National Association of Social Workers, 1953.

Williams, Robin M., Jr. *American Society: A Sociological Interpretation*. New York: Knopf, 1961.

Values and the Analysis of Social Institutions and Systems

Angell, Robert Cooley. *The Integration of American Society: A Study of Groups and Institutions*. New York: McGraw-Hill, 1941.

————. *Free Society and Moral Crisis*. Ann Arbor: University of Michigan Press, 1958.

Banfield, Edward C. *The Moral Basis of a Backward Society*. New York: Free Press, 1958.

Becker, Howard S. *Through Values to Social Interpretation*. Durham, N.C.: Duke University Press, 1950.

Berelson, Bernard, and Gary A. Steiner. *Human Behavior: An Inventory of Scientific Findings*. New York: Harcourt, Brace & World, 1964.

Blum, Arthur. "Values and Aspirations as a Focus for Treatment," *Social Work Practice, 1963*. New York: Columbia University Press, 1963, pp. 31–43.

Boehm, Werner. "The Role of Values in Social Work," *Jewish Social Service Quarterly*, XXVI (June 1950), 429–438.

Gordon, William E. "Knowledge and Value: Their Distinction and Relationship in Clarifying Social Work Practice," *Social Work*, 10 (July 1965), 32–39.

Hellenorand, Shirley C. "Client Value Orientations: Implications for Diagnosis and Treatment," *Social Casework*, XLII (April 1961), 163–169.

Kindelsperger, Kenneth W. "Goals and Value Guides," in Roland L. Warren (ed.), *Community Development and Social Work Practice*. New York: National Association of Social Workers, 1962, pp. 15–21.

Lynd, Robert S. *Knowledge for What?* Princeton, N. J.: Princeton University Press, 1948.

McCormick, Mary J. "The Role of Values in Social Functioning," *Social Casework*, XLII (February 1961), 70–78.

————. "The Role of Values in the Helping Process," *Social Casework*, XLII (January 1961), 3–9.

Merton, Robert K. *Social Theory and Structure: Toward the Codification of Theory and Research*. Rev. ed. New York: Free Press, 1957.

Myrdal, Gunnar. *An American Dilemma*. New York: Harper & Row, 1944. This study not only remains a classic analysis of a social problem, but was also one of the first to analyze a problem in light of value systems. See especially Appendix 1, "Note on Valuation and Beliefs," pp. 1027–1034, and Appendix 2, "A Methodological Note on Facts and Valuations in Social Science," pp. 1035–1070.

Therkildsen, Paul T. *Public Assistance and American Values*. Albuquerque: Division of Government Research, University of New Mexico, 1964.

Towle, Charlotte. "Implications of Contemporary Human and Social Values for Student Selection," *Education for Social Work*. New York: Council on Social Work Education, 1959, pp. 25–38.

Weisman, Irving, and Jacob Chwast. "Control and Values in Social Work Treatment," *Social Casework*, XLI (November 1960), 451–456.

Wessel, Rosa (ed.). *Journal of Social Work Process*, Vol. XVI (1967). Entire issue explores "the world of values and the world of action."

Universality of Values and Differences Among Them

UNIVERSALITY OF VALUES

American Law Institute Committee on Essential Human Rights. "Statement of Essential Human Rights," *The Annals*, 243 (January 1946), 18–26. See also C. Wilfred Jenks, "The Five Economic and Social Rights," *ibid.*, pp. 40–46.

Carlston, Kenneth S. *Law and Organization in World Society*. Urbana: University of Illinois Press, 1962.

Council on Social Work Education. *An Intercultural Exploration: Universals and Differences in Social Work Values, Functions, and Practice*. New York, 1967.

Fuchs, Lawrence H. *"Those Peculiar Americans": The Peace Corps and the American Character*. New York: Meredith Press, 1967.

Howard, Donald S. "The Common Core of Social Work in Different

Countries," *The Social Welfare Forum, 1951*. New York: Columbia University Press, 1951, pp. 19–36.

——. "The Universal Struggle for a Dignified Way of Life," *International Social Work*, II (October 1959), 4–16.

National Association of Social Workers. *Values in Social Work: A Re-Examination*. New York, 1967.

Parsons, Talcott, and Edward A. Shils (ed.). *Toward a General Theory of Action*. Cambridge: Harvard University Press, 1951. See especially Parsons and Shils, with James Olds, "Values, Motives, and Systems of Action," 47–223; Edward C. Tolman, "Value Standards, Patterns, Variables, Social Roles, Personality," pp. 343–354); Clyde Kluckhohn, "Values and Value-Orientations in the Theory of Action," pp. 388–433.

Stein, Herman D., and Richard A. Cloward (eds.). *Social Perspectives on Behavior: A Reader in Social Science for Social Work and Related Professions*. New York: Free Press, 1958. See, in particular, "The Impact of Values on Practice," pp. 263–344.

Kasius, Cora. "Are Social Work Principles Emerging Internationally?" *Social Casework*, XXXIV (January 1953), 23–29.

Lee, Dorothy. "Are Basic Needs Ultimate?" in Clyde Kluckhohn and Henry A. Murray (eds.), *Personality in Nature, Society, and Culture*. Rev. ed. New York: Knopf, 1953, pp. 335–341.

Linton, Ralph. "The Problem of Universal Values," in Robert F. Spencer (ed.), *Method and Perspective in Anthropology*. Minneapolis: University of Minnesota Press, 1954, pp. 145–168.

Nakamura, Hajime. *The Ways of Thinking of Eastern Peoples*. Japan: Japan-Commission for UNESCO, 1960. Also in a revised edition: Philip P. Wiener (ed.). Honolulu: East-West Center Press, 1964.

Robertson, A. H. "Regional Institutions," *Institutions for the Protection of Human Rights*. Paris: World Veterans Federation, 1965, pp. 41–51.

Sanders, Irvin T. (ed.). *Societies Around the World*. 2 vols. New York: Dryden Press, 1953.

Turner, Ralph. *The Great Cultural Traditions: The Foundations of Civilization*. 2 vols. New York: McGraw-Hill, 1941.

United Nations. *Yearbook on Human Rights*. New York: United Nations, published annually.

——, Office of Public Information. *The Universal Declaration of Human Rights: A Standard of Achievement*. New York: United Nations, 1962.

NATIONAL, CULTURAL, AND CLASS DIFFERENCES AMONG VALUES

Brown, Stuart Gerry. *Memo for Overseas Americans: The Many Meanings of American Civilization*. Syracuse, N.Y.: Syracuse University Press, 1960. Includes excellent bibliography.

Chilman, Catherine S. *Growing Up Poor*. Washington, D.C.: Government Printing Office, 1966. Cited references cover a wide range of sources.

Cloward, Richard A., and Lloyd E. Ohlin. *Delinquency and Opportunity.* New York: Free Press, 1960.

Coleman, Lee. "What is American? A Study of Alleged American Traits," *Social Forces,* XIX (May 1941), 492–499.

Coles, Robert. "The Poor Don't Want to Be Middle-Class," *The New York Times Magazine,* December 19, 1965, pp. 7, 54–58.

Du Bois, Cora. "The Dominant Value Profile of American Culture," *American Anthropologist,* 57 (December 1955), 1232 ff.

Gould, Rosalind. "Some Sociological Determinants of Goal Strivings," *Journal of Social Psychology,* 13 (May 1941), 461–473.

Hayden, Robert A. "Spanish-Americans of the Southwest: Life Style Patterns and Their Implications," *Welfare in Review,* 4 (April 1966), 14–25.

Hyman, Herbert H. "The Value Systems of Different Classes: A Social Psychological Contribution to the Analysis of Stratification," in Reinhard Bendix and Seymour M. Lipset (eds.), *Class, Status and Power.* New York: Free Press, 1966, pp. 488–499.

Inkeles, Alex. "Industrial Man: The Relation of Status to Experience, Perception, and Value," *The American Journal of Sociology,* LXVI (July 1960), 1–31.

Irelan, Lola M. (ed.). *Low-Income Life Styles.* Washington, D.C.: Government Printing Office, 1966.

Keller, Suzanne. *The American Lower Class Family: A Survey of Selected Facts and Their Implications.* Albany: New York State Division for Youth, 1965.

Kluckhohn, Clyde. "Values and Value-Orientations in the Theory of Action," in Talcott Parsons and Edward A. Shils (eds.), *Toward a General Theory of Action.* Cambridge: Harvard University Press, 1951, pp. 388–433.

Kluckhohn, Florence R. "Dominant and Variant Value Orientations," *The Social Welfare Forum, 1951.* New York: Columbia University Press, 1951, pp. 97–113.

———. "Variations in the Basic Values of Family Systems," in Norman W. Bell and Ezra F. Vogel (eds.), *A Modern Introduction to the Family.* New York: Free Press, 1960, pp. 304–315.

———, Fred L. Strodtbeck, *et al. Variations in Value Orientations.* Evanston, Ill.: Row, Peterson, 1961.

Lee, Dorothy. "Culture and the Experience of Value," in Abraham H. Maslow (ed.), *New Knowledge in Human Values.* New York: Harper & Row, 1959, pp. 165–177.

Lerner, Max. *America as a Civilization: Life and Thought in the United States Today.* New York: Simon and Schuster, 1957.

Lewis, Oscar. *The Children of Sanchez: Autobiography of a Mexican Family.* New York: Random House, 1961.

Manning, Seaton. "Cultural and Value Factors Affecting the Negro's Use of Agency Services," *Social Work,* 5 (October 1960), 3–13.

Meier, Dorothy L., and Wendell Bell. "Anomia and Differential Access to the Achievement of Life Goals," *American Sociological Review,* 24 (April 1959), 189–202.

Mizruchi, Ephraim H. *Success and Opportunity: Class Values and Anomie in American Life.* New York: Free Press, 1964.

Raab, Earl, and Hugh Folk. *The Pattern of Dependent Poverty in California.* Sacramento: California Social Welfare Study Commission, 1963. (Mimeographed.)

Rodman, Hyman. "The Lower-Class Value Stretch," *Social Forces,* 42 (December 1963), 205–215.

Schneiderman, Leonard. "Value Orientation Preferences of Chronic Relief Recipients," *Social Work,* 9 (July 1964), 13–18.

Silberman, Bernard S. (ed.). *Japanese Character and Culture: A Book of Readings.* Tucson: The University of Arizona Press, 1962.

Turner, Ralph H. *The Social Context of Ambition: A Study of High School Seniors in Los Angeles.* San Francisco: Chandler, 1964.

SOCIAL WELFARE AND RELATED SERVICES

What are regarded as "social welfare services" naturally differ from country to country. References cited below therefore do not relate only to those services treated in the text as "social welfare services."

Descriptions of Welfare Programs in Various Countries

The United Nations has embarked upon a highly significant and promising program of publishing a series of studies of the "organization and administration of social welfare programmes" in various countries. Those published to date (1967) cover Canada, Norway, Union of Soviet Socialist Republics, United Arab Republic, United Kingdom of Great Britain and Northern Ireland.

The United Nations also issues, from time to time, publications in three series that, directly or indirectly, throw light on the social welfare services of different countries:

International Survey of Programmes of Social Development (1955, 1959)
Report of the World Social Situation (1952, 1957, 1961, 1963, etc.)
Training for Social Work (1950, 1955, 1958, 1964)

Further highly relevant United Nations publications include:

Assistance to the Needy in Less-Developed Areas (1956)
The Development of National Social Service Programmes (1960)
Family, Child and Youth Welfare Services (1965)
Report on the Organization and Administration of Social Services (1962)

An invaluable source of information about materials published all over the world is the *Monthly List of Books Catalogued in the Library of the United Nations.*

Proceedings of the biennial meetings of the International Conference of Social Work (reconstituted in 1966 as the International Council on Social Welfare) often include materials on welfare programs in different countries. Reports submitted to a number of these conferences by national committees are a gold mine of information about welfare services in the reporting countries. Unfortunately, these reports are not widely available, but doubtless could at least be consulted through arrangements with the several national committees.

An important source of information about welfare services in various countries is the quarterly journal *International Social Work,* published jointly by the International Council on Social Welfare (Bombay and New York), the International Association of Schools of Social Work (New York), and the International Federation of Social Workers (Geneva and New York).

Comparative information about social security programs in different countries is issued from time to time by the Social Security Administration of the U.S. Department of Health, Education, and Welfare. At this writing, the latest issue is *Social Security Programs Throughout the World, 1967.* Washington, D.C.: Government Printing Office, 1967. This issue provides comparative information about programs in 120 countries, from Afghanistan to Zambia.

Two journals reflecting the ever-changing social security scene are *International Labour Review* (published by the ILO, Geneva), and the *Bulletin of the International Social Security Association* (also in Geneva).

A classic presenting in historical perspective a wide range of information about welfare services is Charles R. Henderson's *Modern Methods of Charity: An Account of the Systems of Relief . . . in the Principal Countries Having Modern Methods.* New York: Macmillan, 1904.

Works Published in Various Countries*

THE UNITED STATES

An indispensable source of information about the whole gamut of welfare and related services in the United States is Harry L. Lurie (ed.), *Encyclopedia of Social Work.* New York: National Association of Social Workers, 1965. This is officially designated "Volume 15" because it is successor to *Social Work Year Book,* which was usually published biennially (despite its title), first by the Russell Sage Foundation (1929–1949), then by the American Association of Social Workers (1951 and 1954), then by the present publisher (1957, 1960, and 1965). The various articles in the *Encyclopedia* are not only succinct and authoritative but are followed by valuable bibliographies.

Further useful descriptive publications include:

Ferguson, Elizabeth A. *Social Work: An Introduction.* Philadelphia: Lippincott, 1963.
Vasey, Wayne. *Government and Social Welfare: Roles of Federal, State, and Local Governments in Administering Welfare Services.* New York: Holt, Rinehart and Winston, 1958.

* Analyses and critiques of services are presented below under "Analyses and Critiques of Social Welfare Services and Their Roles in Society."

For historical perspective, a useful survey of services at the time may be found in

Warner, Amos G. *American Charities: A Study in Philanthropy and Economics.* New York: Crowell, 1894. Subsequent editions, with different authors and titles, were published by Crowell in 1908, 1922, and 1930.

Among numerous publications that give abstracts relevant to social welfare, that which is most highly and consistently relevant is *Abstracts for Social Workers,* published quarterly by the National Association of Social Workers, New York, and covering, at last count, some 200 journals published largely, but not exclusively, in the United States. Another series, more limited in scope, but exceedingly valuable in relation to its coverage, is *Poverty and Human Resources Abstracts,* published bimonthly by the Research Division of the Institute of Labor and Industrial Relations at the University of Michigan in Ann Arbor and at Wayne State University in Detroit.

Journals that are valuable for helping to keep abreast of welfare developments in the United States include:

Public Welfare. Chicago: American Public Welfare Association.

Social Security Bulletin. Washington, D.C.: Social Security Administration, U.S. Department of Health, Education, and Welfare.

Social Service Review. Chicago: School of Social Service Administration, University of Chicago.

Social Work. New York: National Association of Social Workers.

Welfare in Review. Washington, D.C.: Welfare Administration, U.S. Department of Health, Education, and Welfare.

Welfare Law Bulletin. New York: Project on Social Welfare Law, New York University School of Law.

Readers interested in what at least two components of the "Welfare Establishment" in the United States envisage, from time to time, as the changes most needed to improve welfare services and social policy should consult: American Public Welfare Association, *Federal Legislative Objectives,* issued annually in Chicago, and, in New York, the National Association of Social Workers, *Goals of Public Social Policy* (revised from time to time).

GREAT BRITAIN

A standard authoritative source on social services (including social security, health, and welfare services, education, etc.) is the brochure *Social Services in Britain,* updated from time to time (most recently, at this writing, in 1966) by British Information Services; the United States address in 845 Third Avenue, New York, N.Y. 10022.

The National Council of Social Service, 26 Bedford Square, London, W.C.1, also reissues from time to time:

Public Social Services: Handbook of Information (1966, *i.a.*)

Voluntary Social Services: Handbook of Information and Directory of Organisations (1964, *i.a.*)

Readers interested in a high degree of up-to-the-month detail about Britain's social services (and other programs) will find the National Council's *CANS* (Citizens Advice Notes Service) an invaluable if bulky and expensive tool. The council also publishes the highly useful *Social Service Quarterly*.

Further important descriptive materials are:

Hall, M. Penelope. *The Social Services of Modern Britain*. London: Routledge and Kegan Paul, 1964.

Parker, Julia. *Local Health and Welfare Services*. London: G. Allen, 1966.

FRANCE

The single most comprehensive and authoritative description in English of social welfare services in France is Pierre Laroque (ed.), *Social Welfare in France*. Paris: La Documentation Française, 1966. This is a translation and up-to-date version of *Les Institutions Sociales de la France,* 1963 ed. See also:

Laroque, Pierre, *et al. Succes et faiblesses de l'effort social français.* Paris: Librairie Armand Colin, 1961.

Peterson, Wallace C. *The Welfare State in France*. New Series, No. 21. Lincoln: University of Nebraska Studies, 1960.

Schorr, Alvin L. *Social Security and Social Services in France*. Washington, D.C.: Social Security Administration, U.S. Department of Health, Education, and Welfare, 1965.

Among journals issued in France, one likely to be of general interest to readers in other countries is *Informations Sociales,* published by L'Union Nationale des Caisses d'Allocations Familiales, 47 Chaussée d'Antin, Paris, IX.

SCANDINAVIA

The classic and still valuable (though now unfortunately somewhat dated) overview of welfare and related services throughout Scandinavian countries is *Freedom and Welfare: Social Patterns in the Northern Countries of Europe,* edited by George R. Nelson, and published in 1953 by the Ministries of Social Affairs of Denmark, Finland, Iceland, Norway, and Sweden. See also *Social Security in the Nordic Countries: Expenditure Incurred for and Extent of Certain Social Security Measures.* Oslo: Statistical Reports of the Nordic Countries, 1965.

The Ministries of Social Affairs in Denmark, Finland, Norway, and Sweden issue in English from time to time a variety of brochures on various aspects of their social welfare programs.

INDIA

The most comprehensive picture of welfare services is that presented in *Social Welfare in India*. New Delhi: Planning Commission of the Government of India, 1960. See also:

Gore, M. S. *Social Work and Social Work Education.* New York: Asia Publishing House, 1965.

Jacob, K. K. *Methods and Fields of Social Work in India.* London: Asia Publishing House, 1965.

Khinduka, S. K. (ed.). *Social Work in India.* Rajasthan, Jaipur, India: Sarvodaya Sahitya Samaj, 1962.

Wadia, A. R. (ed.). *History and Philosophy of Social Work in India.* Bombay: Allied Publishers Private, 1961.

The *Indian Journal of Social Work* (published by the Tata Institute of Social Sciences, Bombay), constantly reflects changes in India's welfare services, as do the successive *Proceedings* of the India Conference of Social Work.

Analyses and Critiques of Social Welfare Services
and Their Roles in Society

Abel-Smith, Brian, and Peter Townsend. *The Poor and the Poorest.* London: G. Bell, 1965.

Bruce, Maurice. *The Coming of the Welfare State.* London: Batsford, 1961.

Burns, Eveline M. *Social Security and Public Policy.* New York: McGraw-Hill, 1956.

————. "Social Security in Evolution: Toward What?" *Social Service Review*, XXXIX (June 1965), 129–140.

————. "Where Welfare Falls Short," *Public Interest*, 1 (Fall 1965), 82–95.

Farndale, James (ed.). *Trends in Social Welfare.* Long Island City, N.Y.: Pergamon Press, 1965. This is devoted to services in Britain and has been described as that nation's equivalent, in the United States, of *Encyclopedia of Social Work* (*op. cit.*).

Ginsberg, Morris (ed.). *Law and Public Opinion in England in the 20th Century.* Berkeley and Los Angeles: University of California Press, 1959.

Goodman, Leonard H. (ed). *Economic Progress and Social Welfare.* New York: Columbia University Press, 1966.

Hancock, Keith (ed.). *The National Income and Social Welfare.* Melbourne: F. W. Cheshire, for the Australian Council of Social Service, 1965.

Harris, Ralph, and Arthur Seldon. *Choice in Welfare, 1965.* London: Institute of Economic Affairs, 1966.

Hondrich, Wilhelm. *The Conception of Social Welfare in German History.* Dinslaken, Germany: Verlagsgesellschaft für Gegenwartskunde, 1965.

Howard, Donald S. *The WPA and Federal Relief Policy.* New York: Russell Sage Foundation, 1943.

Jefferys, Margot. *An Anatomy of Social Welfare Services.* London: Michael Joseph, 1965.

Kadushin, Alfred. "Two Problems of the Graduate Program," *Journal of Social Work Education,* 1 (Spring 1965), 33–46.

Kahn, Alfred J. "The Social Context of Social Work Practice," *Social Work,* 10 (October 1965), 145–155.

———— (ed.). *Issues in American Social Work.* New York: Columbia University Press, 1959.

Kasius, Cora (ed.). *New Directions in Social Work.* New York: Harper & Row, 1954.

King, Joan F. S. (ed.). *New Thinking and Changing Needs.* London: Association of Social Workers, 1964.

Klein, Philip. *From Philanthropy to Social Welfare.* San Francisco: Jossey-Bass, 1968.

Kohs, Samuel C. *The Roots of Social Work.* New York: Association Press, 1966.

Lee, Porter R. *Social Work as Cause and Function.* New York: Columbia University Press, 1937.

Lubove, Roy. *The Professional Altruist: The Emergence of Social Work as a Career, 1880–1930.* Cambridge: Harvard University Press, 1965.

Marsh, David C. *The Future of the Welfare State.* Baltimore: Penguin Books, 1964.

Marshall, T. H. *Social Policy.* London: Hutchinson University Library, 1965.

Myrdal, Alva. *Nation and Family: The Swedish Experiment in Democratic Family and Population Policy.* London: Kegan Paul, Trench, Trubner, 1945.

Myrdal, Gunnar. *Beyond the Welfare State: Economic Planning and Its International Implications.* New Haven: Yale University Press, 1960.

National Council of Social Service. *Welfare State and Welfare Society: A Guide to Studies for the Sixth British National Conference on Social Welfare.* London, 1967.

————. *Report of the Sixth Meeting of the British National Conference on Social Welfare.* London, forthcoming.

Page, William J., Jr. "Three Dimensions of Expectations of Social Welfare Programs," *Public Welfare,* XXV (April 1967), 117–121.

Peyser, Dora. *The Strong and the Weak.* Sydney, Australia: Currawong, 1951.

Pray, Kenneth L. M. *Social Work in a Revolutionary Age and Other Papers.* Philadelphia: University of Pennsylvania Press, 1949.

Rennison, G. A. *Man on His Own: Social Work and Industrial Society.* Melbourne, Australia: Melbourne University Press, 1962.

Reynolds, Bertha Capen. *Social Work and Social Living: Explorations in Philosophy and Practice.* New York: Citadel, 1951.

Schottland, Charles I. (ed.). *The Welfare State: Selected Essays.* New York: Harper & Row, 1967.

Steiner, Gilbert Y. *Social Insecurity: The Politics of Welfare.* Chicago: Rand McNally, 1966.

Titmuss, Richard M. *Commitment to Welfare.* London: G. Allen, forth-
coming.
————. *Essays on "The Welfare State".* New Haven: Yale University
Press, 1959.
————. "The Welfare State: Images and Realities," *Social Service Re-
view,* XXXVII (March 1963), 1–11.
————. "The Limits of the Welfare State," *The Correspondent,* 31
(March–April 1964), 45–52.
————. "The Role of Redistribution in Social Policy," *Social Security
Bulletin,* 28 (June 1965), 14–20.
United Nations, Group of Experts. *The Aims and Means of Social Serv-
ice.* New York: United Nations, 1959.
United Nations, Secretary General. *Reappraisal of the United Nations
Social Service Programme.* New York: United Nations, 1965.
United Nations, Social Commission. *Report of the Seventeenth Session.*
New York: United Nations, 1966.
Wickenden, Elizabeth. *Social Welfare in a Changing World: The Place
of Social Welfare in the Process of Development.* Washington, D.C.:
Government Printing Office, 1965.
Wilensky, Harold L., and Charles N. Lebeaux. *Industrial Society and
Social Welfare.* New York: Russell Sage Foundation, 1958.
Woodroofe, Kathleen. *From Charity to Social Work: In England and the
United States.* Toronto: University of Toronto Press, 1962.
Wootton, Barbara, *et al. Social Science and Social Pathology.* London:
G. Allen, 1959.

SELF-HELP, SOCIAL SUPPORT, SUCCESS, AND DEPENDENCY

Self-Help, Social Support, and Success

Calef, Wesley. *Private Grazing and Public Lands.* Chicago: University
of Chicago Press, 1960.
De Jongh, J. F. "Self-Help in Modern Society," *Self-Help in Social Wel-
fare.* Bombay, India: International Conference of Social Work,
1955, pp. 48–65.
Fine, Sidney. *Laissez Faire and the General-Welfare State: A Study of
Conflict in American Thought, 1865–1901.* Ann Arbor: University
of Michigan Press, 1964.
Gardner, Ralph D. *Horatio Alger or the American Hero Era.* Mendota,
Ill.: Wayside Press, 1964.
Gilmore, Harlan W. *The Beggar.* Chapel Hill: University of North Caro-
lina Press, 1940.
Girvetz, Harry K. *From Wealth to Welfare: The Evolution of Liberalism.*
Stanford, Calif.: Stanford University Press, 1950. This book was re-
vised under the title *The Evolution of Liberalism.* New York:
Collier Books, 1963.
Goodman, Walter. *All Honorable Men: Corruption and Compromise in
American Life.* Boston: Little, Brown, 1963.
Greenleaf, William. *John D. Rockefeller.* New York: Scribner, 1959.
This is an abridgment of Allan Nevins' two-volume *Study in*

Power: John D. Rockefeller, Industrialist and Philanthropist. New York: Scribner, 1953.

Hellerstein, Jerome R. *Taxes, Loopholes and Morals.* New York: McGraw-Hill, 1963.

Hofstadter, Richard. *Social Darwinism in American Thought.* Rev. ed. Boston: Beacon Press, 1958.

Holbrook, Stewart H. *The Age of the Moguls: The Story of the Robber Barons and the Great Tycoons.* Garden City, N.Y.: Doubleday, 1953.

International Conference of Social Work. *Self-Help in Social Welfare.* Bombay and New York, 1955.

Josephson, Matthew. *The Robber Barons: The Great American Capitalists, 1861–1901.* New York: Harcourt, Brace & World, 1962.

Katz, Alfred H. "Application of Self-Help Concepts in Current Social Welfare," *Social Work,* 10 (July 1965), 68–74.

Kent, T. W. "No One Is Independent," *Canada's Health and Welfare,* February 1961, pp. 2, 3.

Kolko, Gabriel. *Wealth and Power in America: An Analysis of Social Class and Income Distribution.* New York: Praeger, 1962.

Landieu, Gloria, Eugenia Hanfman, and Tamara Dembo. "Studies in Adjustment to Visible Injuries: Evaluation of Help by the Injured," *Journal of Abnormal and Social Psychology,* 42 (1947), 169–192.

Landy, David. "Problems of the Person Seeking Help in Our Culture," *The Social Welfare Forum, 1960.* New York: Columbia University Press, 1960, pp. 127–145.

Marrs, James W. *The Man on Your Back.* Norman: University of Oklahoma Press, 1958.

Murad, Anatol. *Private Credit and Public Debt.* Washington, D.C.: Public Affairs Press, 1954.

Myers, Gustavus. *History of the Great American Fortunes.* New York: Modern Library, 1936.

Nossiter, Bernard D. *The Mythmakers: An Essay on Power and Wealth.* Boston: Houghton Mifflin, 1964.

Perlman, Helen Harris. "Self-Determination: Reality or Illusion?" *Social Service Review,* XXXIX (December 1965), 410–421.

Reich, Charles A. "The New Property," *Yale Law Journal,* 73 (April 1964), 733–787.

Rischin, Moses (ed.). *The American Gospel of Success.* Chicago: Quadrangle Books, 1965.

Robson, William A. *The Relation of Wealth to Welfare.* New York: Macmillan, 1925.

Schultz, Theodore W. "Investment in Man: An Economist's View," *Social Service Review,* XXXIII (June 1959), 109–117.

Shonfield, Andrew. *Modern Capitalism: The Changing Balance of Public and Private Power.* London: Oxford University Press, 1965.

Stern, Philip M. *The Great Treasury Raid.* New York: Random House, 1962.

Sumner, William Graham. *What Social Classes Owe Each Other.* New York: Harper & Row, 1883. A new edition was published in Caldwell, Idaho: Caxton, 1952.

Tebbel, John. *From Rags to Riches: Horatio Alger, Jr., and the American Dream*. New York: Macmillan, 1963.
U.S. Congress. *Subsidy and Subsidy-Effect Programs of the U.S. Government* (materials prepared for the Joint Economic Committee). Washington, D.C.: Government Printing Office, 1965.
Viscardi, Henry, Jr. *Give Us the Tools*. New York: Eriksson-Toplinger, 1959.
Wyllie, Irvin G. *The Self-Made Man in America: The Myth of Rags to Riches*. New Brunswick, N.J.: Rutgers University Press, 1954.

Dependency and Social Support

Advisory Council on Public Welfare. *"Having the Power, We Have the Duty."* Report to the Secretary of Health, Education, and Welfare. Washington, D.C.: Government Printing Office, 1966.
American Public Welfare Association. *AFDC: Fact vs. Fiction*. Chicago, 1963.
———. *ADC: Problem and Promise*. Chicago, *ca.* 1960.
———. *Public Welfare Projected*. Chicago, 1966.
———. *Equal Justice*. Chicago, 1965.
Bagdikian, Ben H. *In the Midst of Plenty: The Poor in America*. Boston: Beacon Press, 1964.
Barr, Sherman. "Budgeting and the Poor: A View from the Bottom," *Public Welfare*, XXIII (October 1965), 246 ff.
Bell, Winifred. *Aid to Dependent Children*. New York: Columbia University Press, 1965.
Briar, Scott. "Welfare from Below: Recipients' Views of the Public Welfare System," *California Law Review*, 54 (May 1966), 370–385.
Burgess, M. Elaine, and Daniel O. Price. *An American Dependency Challenge*. Chicago: American Public Welfare Association, 1963.
California Law Review, 54 (May 1966), entire issue. This is a particularly important source, comprised largely of papers presented at a conference on "The Law of the Poor." These papers and a few others are available also in Jacobus ten Broek and the editors of the *California Law Review* (eds.), *The Law of the Poor*. San Francisco: Chandler, 1966.
Coser, Lewis A. "The Sociology of Poverty: To the Memory of Georg Simmel," *Social Problems*, 13 (1965), 140–148.
Elman, Richard M. *The Poorhouse State: The American Way of Life on Public Assistance*. New York: Pantheon Books, 1966.
Epstein, Lenore A. "Unmet Need in a Land of Abundance," *Social Security Bulletin*, 26 (May 1963), 3–11.
Glennerster, Howard. *National Assistance: Service or Charity?* London: Fabian Society, 1962.
Gordon, Joan. *The Poor of Harlem: Social Functioning in the Underclass*. New York: Interdepartmental Service Center, Office of the Mayor, 1965.
Greenleigh Associates. *Public Welfare: Poverty—Prevention or Perpetu-*

ation, A Study of the State Department of Public Assistance of the State of Washington. New York, 1964.

————. *Facts, Fallacies and Future: A Study of the Aid to Dependent Children Program of Cook County, Illinois.* 2 vols. New York, 1960.

Handler, Joel F., and Margaret K. Rosenheim. "Privacy in Welfare: Public Assistance and Juvenile Justice," *Law and Contemporary Problems,* XXXI (Spring 1966), 377–412.

Keith-Lucas, Alan. *Decisions about People in Need: A Study of Administrative Responsiveness in Public Assistance.* Chapel Hill: University of North Carolina Press, 1957.

Lebeaux, Charles. "Life on A.D.C.: Budgets of Despair," *New University Thought,* 3 (Winter 1963), 26–35. Reprinted in Louis A. Ferman, Joyce L. Kornbluh, and Alan Haber (eds.), *Poverty in America: A Book of Readings.* Ann Arbor: University of Michigan Press, 1965, pp. 401–411.

Lyford, Joseph P. *The Airtight Cage: A Study of New York's West Side.* New York: Harper & Row, 1966.

MacIntyre, Duncan M. *Public Assistance: Too Much or Too Little?* Ithaca: New York State School of Industrial and Labor Relations, Cornell University, 1964. Bulletin 53–1.

McCabe, Alice R. "Forty Forgotten Families," *Public Welfare,* XXIV (April 1966), 159–172.

McKeany, Maurine. *The Absent Father and Public Policy in the Program of Aid to Dependent Children.* Berkeley: University of California Press, 1960.

Mandelbaum, Arthur. "Dependency in Human Development," *Public Welfare Projected.* Chicago: American Public Welfare Association, 1966, pp. 1–15.

Marcus, Grace. "The Psychological Problem in Providing Assistance as a Public Service," *American Journal of Orthopsychiatry,* XVII (July 1947), 435–436.

May, Edgar. *The Wasted Americans: Cost of Our Welfare Dilemma.* New York: Harper & Row, 1964.

Perkins, Ellen J. "Unmet Need in Public Assistance," *Social Security Bulletin,* 23 (April 1960), 3–11.

————. "How Much Is Enough Today?" *Biennial Papers, American Public Welfare Association.* Chicago, 1963, pp. 20–25.

Reich, Charles A. "Individual Rights and Social Welfare: The Emerging Legal Issues," *Yale Law Journal,* 74 (June 1965), 1245–1257.

Reilly, James H. "The Primary Factor in Good Services—Adequate Assistance Grants," *Public Welfare,* 22 (October 1964), 242–246.

Ritz, Joseph P. *The Despised Poor: Newburgh's War on Welfare.* Boston: Beacon Press, 1966.

Rohrlich, George F. "Social Security: Freedom from Want without Want of Freedom," in Lyman Bryson, Louis Finkelstein, *et al.* (eds.), *Freedom and Authority in Our Time: Twelfth Symposium of the Conference on Science, Philosophy and Religion.* New York: Harper & Row, 1953, pp. 95–102.

Siff, Hilda. "Feeding a Family on a Public Assistance Budget," *Welfare in Review*, 3 (May 1965), 8–11.

Simon, Arthur. *Faces of Poverty*. St. Louis: Concordia, 1966.

Stats, Jeanette (ed.). *The Extension of Legal Services to the Poor*. Washington, D.C.: Government Printing Office, 1965.

ten Broek, Jacobus, and the editors of the *California Law Review* (eds.), *The Law of the Poor*. San Francisco: Chandler, 1966.

ten Broek, Jacobus, and Floyd W. Matson. *Hope Deferred: Public Welfare and the Blind*. Berkeley and Los Angeles: University of California Press, 1959.

ten Broek, Jacobus, and Richard B. Wilson, "Public Assistance and Social Insurance—A Normative Evaluation," *U.C.L.A. Law Review*, 1 (April 1954), 237–302.

U.S. Commission on Civil Rights. *Children in Need: A Study of a Federally Assisted Program of Aid to Needy Families with Children*. Washington, D.C., 1966.

Wald, Patricia M. *Law and Poverty: 1965*. Washington, D.C.: Attorney General of the United States and Office of Economic Opportunity, 1965.

Weingarten, Violet. *Life at the Bottom*. New York: Citizens' Committee for Children of New York, *ca.* 1966.

White, Gladys O. *State Methods for Determining Need in the Aid to Dependent Children Program*. Washington, D.C.: Department of Health, Education, and Welfare, 1961.

————. "Meeting Financial Needs Under Old-Age Assistance," *Welfare in Review*, 1 (December 1963), 1–6.

MUTUALISM AND SENSE OF COMMUNITY

Alinsky, Saul. *Reveille for Radicals*. Chicago: University of Chicago Press, 1946.

Allee, W. C. *Cooperation Among Animals: With Human Implications*. New York: Schuman, 1951.

Bailey, M. B. "Al-Anon Family Groups as an Aid to Wives of Alcoholics," *Social Work*, 10 (January 1965), 68–74.

Beveridge, Lord. *Voluntary Action: A Report on Methods of Social Advance*. London: G. Allen, 1948.

Bowen, E. R. *The Cooperative Road to Abundance: The Alternative to Monopolism and Communism*. New York: Schuman, 1953. This includes a useful and generous list of relevant references.

Clinard, Marshall B. *Slums and Community Development: Experiments in Self-Help*. New York: Free Press, 1966.

Dobzhansky, Theodosius. *The Biological Basis of Human Freedom*. New York: Columbia University Press, 1956.

Farrell, Gregory R. *A Climate of Change: The New Haven Story*. New Brunswick, N.J.: Urban Studies Center, Rutgers University, 1965.

Gouldner, Alvin W. "The Norm of Reciprocity: A Preliminary Statement," *American Sociological Review*, 25 (April 1960), 161–178.

Haggstrom, Warren C. "The Power of the Poor," in Frank Riessman,

Jerome Cohen, and Arthur Pearl (eds.), *Mental Health of the Poor.* New York: Free Press, 1964, 205–223.

Hatch, D. Spencer, and Geoffrey Cumberlege. *Toward Freedom from Want: From India to Mexico.* London: Oxford University Press, 1949.

Katz, Alfred H. *Parents of the Handicapped.* Springfield, Ill.: Charles C. Thomas, 1961.

——. "Self-Help Groups," in Harry L. Lurie (ed.), *Encyclopedia of Social Work.* New York: National Association of Social Workers, 1965, pp. 680–683.

Kropotkin, Peter. *Mutual Aid as a Factor in Evolution.* London: Heinemann, 1908.

Levy, Joseph H. "A Study of Parent Groups for Handicapped Children," *Exceptional Children,* 19 (October 1952), 19–29.

Lewin, Kurt, with Paul Grabbe. "Conduct, Knowledge, and Acceptance of New Values," in Gertrude Weiss Lewin (ed.), *Resolving Social Conflicts: Selected Papers on Group Dynamics.* New York: Harper & Row, 1948, pp. 56–58.

Lloyd, Henry Demarest. *Wealth Against Commonwealth.* New York: Harper & Row, 1894.

Montague, Ashley. *On Being Human.* New York: Schuman, 1950.

——. *The Direction of Human Development: Biological and Social Bases.* New York: Harper & Row, 1965.

Niebuhr, Reinhold. *Man's Nature and His Communities.* New York: Scribner, 1965.

Nisbet, Robert A. *The Quest for Community: A Study in the Ethics of Order and Freedom.* New York: Oxford University Press, 1953.

Paull, Joseph E. "Recipients Aroused: The Welfare Rights Movement," *Social Work,* 12 (April 1967), 101–106.

Peck, Robert F., with Robert J. Havighurst, Ruth Cooper, Jesse Lilienthal, and Douglas More. *The Psychology of Character Development.* New York: Wiley, 1964.

Piven, Frances F. "Participation of Residents in Neighborhood Community Action Programs," *Social Work,* 11 (January 1966), 73–80.

Purcell, Frances P., and Harry Specht. "The House on Sixth Street," *Social Work,* 10 (October 1965), 69–76.

Reiff, Robert, and Frank Riessman. *The Indigenous Nonprofessional: A Strategy of Change in Community Action and Community Mental Health Programs.* Monograph Series, No. 1. Lexington, Mass.: Community Mental Health Journal, 1965. Includes an extended bibliography.

Riessman, Frank. "The Revolution in Social Work: The New Nonprofessional," *Trans-Action,* 2 (November–December 1964), 12–17.

Shiffman, Bernard M. "Involvement of Low-Income People in Planned Community Change," *Social Work Practice, 1965.* New York: Columbia University Press, 1965, pp. 188–204.

Silberman, Charles E. *Crisis in Black and White.* New York: Random House, 1964.

U.S. Joint Commission on Mental Illness. *Self-Help Organization in the*

Mental Health Field: Recovery, Inc. Washington, D.C., 1960.
Yablonsky, Lewis. *The Tunnel Back: Synanon.* New York: Macmillan, 1965.
Young, Whitney M., Jr. "Developing a Sense of Community in Today's Urban Areas: Overcoming Apathy, Anxiety, and Alienation," *Urban Development: Its Implications for Social Welfare.* New York: Columbia University Press, 1967, pp. 54–66.

GUARANTEED INCOMES FOR ALL

Ad Hoc Committee on the Triple Revolution. *The Triple Revolution: An Appraisal of the Major Crises and Proposals for Action.* Washington, D.C., 1964. (Mimeographed.) This influential and widely cited report is readily available in Louis A. Ferman, Joyce L. Kornbluh, and Alan Haber (eds.), *Poverty in America: A Book of Readings.* Ann Arbor: University of Michigan Press, 1965, pp. 443–457.
Friedman, Milton. *Capitalism and Freedom.* Chicago: Phoenix Books, 1963. The proposal for a "negative income tax" is in Chapter XII, "The Alleviation of Poverty," pp. 190–195.
Green, Christopher. *Negative Taxes and the Poverty Problem.* Washington, D.C.: Brookings Institution, 1967.
———, Robert J. Lampman, George H. Hildebrand, and Earl R. Ralph. "A Symposium: Negative Income Tax Proposals," *Industrial Relations,* 6 (February 1967), 121–165.
Nicol, Helen O. "Guaranteed Income Maintenance: A Discussion of Negative Income Tax Plans," *Welfare in Review,* 4 (April 1966), 1–10.
Randolph, A. Philip, Institute. *A "Freedom Budget" for All Americans: Budgeting Our Resources, 1966–1975, to Achieve "Freedom from Want."*
Reagan, Michael D. "Washington Should Pay Taxes to the Poor," *The New York Times Magazine,* February 29, 1966, pp. 24–25, 84–90.
———. "For a Guaranteed Income," *ibid.,* June 7, 1964, pp. 20, 120–121. This article is also available in Arthur B. Shostak and William Gomberg (eds.). *New Perspectives on Poverty.* Englewood Cliffs, N.J.: Prentice-Hall, 1965, pp. 134–141.
Schorr, Alvin L. "Alternatives in Income Maintenance," *Social Work,* 11 (July 1966), 22–29.
Schwartz, Edward E. "A Way to End the Means Test," *Social Work,* 9 (July 1964), 3–12.
Smith, A. Delafield. *The Right to Life.* Chapel Hill: University of North Carolina Press, 1955.
Theobald, Robert (ed.). *The Guaranteed Income: Next Step in Economic Evolution?* Garden City, N.Y.: Doubleday, 1966.
University of Chicago, School of Social Service Administration, Ad Hoc Committee for Guaranteed Income. *GAIN* (Guaranteed Annual Income Newsletter), issued periodically.
Wade, Alan D. "The Guaranteed Minimum Income: Social Work's Challenge and Opportunity," *Social Work,* 12 (January 1967), 94–101.
Young, Whitney M., Jr., *To Be Equal.* New York: McGraw-Hill, 1964.

Appendix

Social Welfare Services Typical of Those Implementing Attainment of Specific Values

VALUES*	TYPICAL WELFARE SERVICES (ILLUSTRATIVE ONLY AND BY NO MEANS EXHAUSTIVE LISTING)
Essentials for Fundamental Human Functioning†	
Life and Health	Free and part-pay medical care; social welfare service in hospitals and clinics; rehabilitation services; public assistance for needed food; distribution of surplus foods, food stamps; protective service; foster home and institutional care; suicide prevention services.
Sense of Dignity, Worth and Purpose	Almost any service that acknowledges the importance of the individual and particularly those that take special steps to protect the sensibilities of persons served; confidentiality of transactions, administering services as "rights" or as not belittling beneficiaries; casework and counseling services designed to encourage purposeful recognition of worth and facilitation of role performance and achievement of status; avoidance of humiliating and denigrating practices in administering needed services.
Aspiration to Achieve	Counseling and case- or group-work services directed at "motivating" individuals; making available elemental necessities of life, thus giving persons strength enough to aspire; removal, or help in overcoming, social and structural barriers (racial discrimination, discrimination against older workers, handicapped workers, inexperienced workers, etc.), which, historically, have thwarted aspiration; education about and opportunity to experience and, hopefully, to want to achieve new values not previously regarded as attainable or even as desirable.

* Key values are those presented in Chapter II.
† Grouping of values is in accord with discussion in Chapter V.

Freedom to Make
Choices

Services are *offered* to intended beneficiaries, not imposed upon them; alternate courses of action (such as help to an unmarried mother to enable her to keep a child who otherwise would have to be relinquished) made possible by any service create for beneficiaries effective choice without which there can be no freedom.

Status and Role

Counseling and case- or group-work to help individuals recognize and preserve status and to assume their expected roles; help in attaining self-support in socially preferred as opposed to non-preferred ways; provision of resources to permit at least semblance of role-performance; public assistance to an unemployed worker who is thus enabled, in the eyes of his children, to appear still to be the family "breadwinner"; employment service to aid in finding status- and role-preserving employment; visiting nurse or homemaker service to help mothers to fill roles and to preclude necessity of breadwinners' losing work to care for sick relatives; provision of clothing to permit, without undue embarrassment, attendance at community meetings in which one has a status or role.

Food, Housing,
Clothing

Financial assistance for persons in their own homes; distribution of surplus commodities and "food stamps"; institutional care of infants, children, mentally retarded persons, aged persons, etc.; privately subsidized housing.

Education and
Training

Public assistance that helps families to manage without sending school-age children out to work or that is continued for an older child on condition he continue in school; provision of clothing to permit school attendance; social work service in schools to help reduce social problems interfering with education; visiting nurse or homemaker service to avoid necessity of keeping children at home to care for sick relatives; training or retraining unemployed or disabled persons or persons (such as widows in receipt of public assistance) who had not previously been in the labor market; financial support for families during training.

Employment

Employment service to help unemployed workers find jobs; compensatory employment such as workshops for the blind, Good-Will Industries, etc.; work-relief when unemployment becomes widespread; retraining for employment (as above); day-care of children to permit mothers to work; public assistance for maintenance of car needed when work is available or for clothing or tools required for work; visiting nurse or homemaker service to preclude losing paid employment.

Legal Protection

Legal aid and counsel to enable persons to pursue court action; moves to secure protection of neglected or abused children, deserted wives, etc.; guardianship proceedings for protection of children, senile, mentally ill, or other incapacitated persons; defense in criminal proceedings when not available under legal system.

Leisure and Its Use

Provision of household aids (washers, etc., through public assistance) and homemaker service to relieve parent(s) of undue burdens of family care; vacations and camp experiences for children, thus relieving pressures at home; holiday camps for mothers; day-care of children; recreational facilities and activities for children, youths, middle-aged adults and older persons.

Religion

Religious counsel, referral to ministers, priests, rabbis; provision of special foods or clothing required for religious observances or of money for contributions to churches; religious observances in welfare institutions.

*Essentials for
Constructive Family
Living*

Family Relationships

Marriage counseling; family counseling and service; public assistance for food, clothing, housing, etc., essential to family maintenance; homemaker service; adoptive homes for unwanted children; adoption service for childless couples; foster-homes for children in need of care (perhaps relieving pressures in children's own homes and thus permitting "more constructive relationships" for children remaining in own home); foster-home care for delinquent youths, mentally ill persons, aged persons, handicapped persons, etc., who do not need institutional care but whose own homes are not suitable; institutional (pseudofamily) care where needed; Big Brother and Big Sister service.

Home Management

Public assistance providing essential household and housekeeping equipment, supplies, and counsel; homemaker service.

Role (in family)
Status (in family)

See entries opposite Role and Status, above.

Group and Community
Participation

Social settlements; community center activities; group-work and recreational services; self-help programs; civic organizations for neighborhood improvement; community development projects.

Essentials for Basic
Social Participation

Opportunities for Social Living and Constructive Use of Leisure	Medical care, health and rehabilitation service to increase mobility; social centers; camping programs for children; holiday camps; recreation centers and playgrounds; informal adult-education; free trips (for children, inmates of institutions for delinquents, handicapped persons, mental hospital patients, etc.), to baseball games, museums, etc.
Opportunities for Religious Observance	Provision of transportation to church; provision of clothing, special needs (such as confirmation dress) or even money for church "collections" if necessary; counsel and encouragement to participate, if indicated; conduct of religious exercises in social welfare institutions.
Role, Status, Clothing, Employment	See entries opposite Role, Status, Clothing, and Employment above.
Means of Transportation	Public assistance provision of carfare (or perhaps even of car-maintenance) for attendance at specified social gatherings; volunteer transportation (e.g., Red Cross station wagons) to take children, aged or handicapped persons to football or baseball games; encouragement and assistance to participate in peer group activities such as Senior Citizen Clubs, etc.

Index

Abrecht, Paul R., 86
Adams, Velma, 331
Addams, Jane, 159–60, 315
Adebe, Chief S. O., 120, 313
Alinsky, Saul, 405
Allport, Gordon W., 5, 91
Altmeyer, Arthur J., 112
American Public Welfare Association, 121–2, 200, 246
anomie, 30
Aptekar, Herbert, 342
Aristotle, 303
aspiration:
    as a social product, 29, 37–53, 152
    encouragement of by welfare services, 50
    escalation of, 39, 41, 47–53
    frustration of, 27–30, 37–43
    relation to experience, 29, 37–52
    social class differences in, 29, 38, 151
aspirations, modesty of, 44–7, 428
Ayer, Alfred Jules, 10
Ayres, Beverly, 428

"backlashes," 154
Bagdikian, Ben H., 29, 150
Bailward, William A., 175
Baldwin, James, 27
Ball, Robert M., 111
Banfield, Edward C., 352
basic requirements, social support of, Chs. VI and VII, 414–24; see also dependency, obvious
basic support:
    disdain for, 215–19, Chs. VI and VII
    disdain for in the U.S., 284–94, 300–1
    disdain for in various countries, 294–9
Batten, T. R., 88
Beck, Bertram, 189
Becker, Howard S., 11, 81
being helped, "hurt" of, 299–301, 362–3, 407, 421

assuaged through reciprocation, 295, 301–17, 407; see also reciprocation; work relief
    variables affecting, 214–15
Bell, Winifred, 28, 255
Bendix, Reinhard, 117
Bennett, John C., 129
Benton, William, 341
Berelson, Bernard, 45, 48, 158, 163
Besner, Arthur, 27
Beveridge, William, 406–7
Bevin, Ernest, 48
Bird, Caroline, 110, 158
Boehm, Werner, 88
Booker, Ilys, 80
Boulding, Kenneth E., 163
Boy, Christian, 37
Brandt, Willy, 310
Breasted, James Henry, 304
Bremner, Robert H., 201
Briar, Scott, 284
Brinton, Crane, 46
Brown, Stuart Gerry, 65
Brynes, Asher, 309, 313
"buffer zone," 154–5, 192, 207, 406
Burns, Eveline M., 383
Burns, James MacGregor, 175

Cadbury, George, 161
calculus, process defined, 16
calculus of generosity, 135
calculus of "hurt," 133
Camara, Dom Helder, 155, 309
Cantril, Hadley, 45, 47, 91
Caplovitz, David, 91
Carlston, Kenneth S., 11
Carnegie, Andrew, 33, 48, 103, 119, 156, 431
Carter, Richard, 304
catastrophe:
    as assuagement of the "hurt" of being helped, 214, 423
    as contributor to sense of interdependence, 164, 423
    as element in appraisals of self-help, 164
charity, degrees of, 124, 129